PARENTING

An Ecological Perspective

Second Edition

MONOGRAPHS IN PARENTING
Marc H. Bornstein, Series Editor

Borkowski, Ramey, and Bristol-Powers • Parenting and the Child's World: Influences on Academic, Intellectual, and Social-Emotional Development

Bornstein and Bradley • Socioeconomic Status, Parenting, and Child Development

Kalil and DeLeire • Family Investments in Children's Potential: Resources and Behaviors that Promote Children's Success

Cowan, Cowan, Ablow, Johnson, and Measelle • The Family Context of Parenting in Children's Adaptation to Elementary School

Luster and Okagaki • Parenting: An Ecological Perspective, Second Edition

Bornstein and Cote • Acculturation and Parent–Child Relationships: Measurement and Development (In Preparation)

Bornstein • The Parent: Essential Readings (In Preparation)

Goldberg • Father Time: The Timing of Fatherhood in Men's Lives (In Preparation)

For more information on LEA titles, please contact Lawrence Erlbaum Associates, Publishers, at www.erlbaum.com.

PARENTING

An Ecological Perspective

Second Edition

Edited by

Tom Luster
Michigan State University

Lynn Okagaki
Purdue University

 LAWRENCE ERLBAUM ASSOCIATES, PUBLISHERS
2005   Mahwah, New Jersey   London

Lawrence Erlbaum Associates, Inc., Publishers
10 Industrial Avenue
Mahwah, New Jersey 07430
www.erlbaum.com

Cover design by Tomai Maridou

Library of Congress Cataloging-in-Publication Data

Parenting : an ecological perspective / edited by Tom Luster and Lynn Okagaki.—
    2nd ed.
        p.   cm. — (Monographs in parenting)
    Includes bibliographical references and index.
    ISBN 0-8058-4806-1 (alk. paper)
    ISBN 0-8058-4807-X (alk. paper)
    1. Parenting. 2. Social ecology. I. Luster, Tom. II. Okagaki, Lynn.
III. Monographs in parenting series.

HQ755.8.P379123   2005
649'.1—dc22   2004065021
                                                                      CIP

Books published by Lawrence Erlbaum Associates are printed on acid-free paper,
and their bindings are chosen for strength and durability.

Printed in the United States of America
10 9 8 7 6 5 4 3 2 1

For
Urie Bronfenbrenner

Contents

Series Foreword: Monographs in Parenting   ix
Marc H. Bornstein, Series Editor

Introduction   xi
Tom Luster and Lynn Okagaki

I   CHARACTERISTICS OF THE PARENTS

1   Parents' Social Cognitions and Their Parenting Behaviors   3
Lynn Okagaki and Gary E. Bingham

2   Developmental Origins of Parenting: Personality
and Relationship Factors   35
Joan Vondra, Helen Bittmann Sysko, and Jay Belsky

3   Adolescent Mothers and Their Children:
An Ecological Perspective   73
Tom Luster and Julie Laser Haddow

4   Fathers: Cultural and Ecological Perspectives   103
*Ross D. Parke, Jessica Dennis, Mary L. Flyr, Kristie L. Morris,
Melinda S. Leidy, and Thomas J. Schofield*

II CHARACTERISTICS OF THE CHILD

5 The Effects of Child Characteristics on Parenting   147
       Katherine Hildebrandt Karraker and Priscilla K. Coleman

6 Parenting Children with Developmental Disabilities   177
       Robert M. Hodapp and Tran M. Ly

III CONTEXTUAL INFLUENCES ON PARENTING

7 Parenting and the Marital Relationship   205
       Frank D. Fincham and Julie H. Hall

8 Parenting and Personal Social Networks   235
       Moncrieff Cochran and Susan K. Walker

9 The Long Arm of the Job Revisited: Parenting
       in Dual-Earner Families   275
       Ann C. Crouter and Susan M. McHale

10 Neighborhood and Community Influences on Parenting   297
        James Garbarino, Catherine P. Bradshaw,
        and Kathleen Kostelny

11 Socioeconomic Status, Ethnicity, and Parenting   319
        Birgit Leyendecker, Robin L. Harwood, Lisa Comparini,
        and Alev Yalçinkaya

12 Searches for What Works in Parenting Interventions   343
        Douglas R. Powell

IV PARENTAL BEHAVIOR AND CHILDREN'S DEVELOPMENT

13 Research on Parental Socialization of Child Outcomes:
        Current Controversies and Future Directions   377
        Lynn Okagaki and Tom Luster

About the Authors   403

Author Index   411

Subject Index   435

Series Foreword
Monographs in Parenting

Parenting is fundamental to the survival and success of the human race. Everyone who has ever lived has had parents, and most adults in the world become parents. Opinions about parenting abound, but surprisingly little solid scientific information or considered reflection exists about parenting. *Monographs in Parenting* intends to redress this imbalance. The chief aim of this series is to provide a forum for extended and integrated treatments of fundamental and challenging contemporary topics in parenting. Each volume treats a different perspective on parenting and is self-contained, yet the series as a whole endeavors to enhance and interrelate studies in parenting by bringing shared perspectives to bear on a variety of concerns prominent in parenting theory, research, and application. As a consequence of its structure and scope, *Monographs in Parenting* will appeal, individually or as a group, to scientists, professionals, and parents alike. Reflecting the nature and intent of this series, contributing authors are drawn from a broad spectrum of the humanities and sciences—anthropology to zoology—with representational emphasis placed on authorities actively contributing to the contemporary literature in parenting.

Parenting is a job whose primary object of attention and action is the child—children do not and cannot grow up as solitary individuals—but parenting is also a status in the life course with consequences for parents themselves. In this forum, parenting is defined by all of children's principal caregivers and their many modes of caregiving. *Monographs in Parenting* encompass these central themes in parenting.

WHO PARENTS?

Biological and adoptive mothers, fathers, single-parents, divorced and re-married parents can be children's principal caregivers, but when siblings, grandparents, and nonfamilial caregivers mind children their parenting is pertinent as well.

WHOM DO PARENTS PARENT?

Parents parent infants, toddlers, children in middle-childhood, and adolescents, but special populations of children include multiple births, preterm, ill, developmentally delayed or talented, and aggressive or withdrawn children.

THE SCOPE OF PARENTING

Parenting includes genetic endowment and direct effects of experience that manifest themselves through parents' beliefs and behaviors; parenting's indirect influences take place through parents' relationships with each other and their connections to community networks; the positive and negative effects of parenting are both topics of concern.

FACTORS THAT AFFECT PARENTING

Evolution and history; biology and ethology; family configuration; formal and informal support systems, community ties, and work; social, educational, legal, medical, and governmental institutions; economic class, designed and natural ecology, and culture—as well as children themselves—each helps to define parenting.

THE NATURE, STRUCTURE, AND MEANING OF PARENTING

Parenting is pleasures, privileges, and profits as well as frustrations, fears, and failures. Contemporary parenting studies are diversified, pluralistic, and specialized. This fragmented state needs counterforce in an arena that allows the extended in-depth exploration of cardinal topics in parenting. *Monographs in Parenting* vigorously pursues that goal.

—*Marc H. Bornstein*
Series Editor

Introduction

Tom Luster
Lynn Okagaki

Parenting: An Ecological Perspective was created to answer questions such as: Why do parents differ markedly in the ways in which they care for their children? What factors contribute to individual differences in parenting behavior? The framework used for addressing these questions is the ecological perspective developed by our mentor and friend, Urie Bronfenbrenner. Bronfenbrenner (1979, 2000) recognized that children's development is influenced by the interactions that they have over time with the people, objects, and symbols in their immediate environment; he referred to these as proximal processes. Of particular importance are the increasingly complex and reciprocal interactions that occur between children and their parents as children develop. Both the enduring and emotional nature of the relationship between a parent and a child make it a powerful force in the development of both parties. When asked about his views on what children need most to develop optimally, on various occasions Bronfenbrenner responded that what children need more than anything else is someone who is crazy about the child (Hamilton & Luster, 2003). Typically the people who have the strongest emotional attachment to the child are his or her parents.

Although parents typically share strong feelings of love and concern for their children, they differ in the ways they approach the task of caring for their children. Bronfenbrenner recognized that the proximal processes that occur in the home and other settings depend on characteristics of the child that reflect both genetic predispositions and the child's history of experiences up to that point in time. Proximal processes are also influenced by the unique characteristics of the parents and other individuals who interact with the child; characteristics of the parents, such as their personality, childrearing beliefs, educational background, and psychological well-being, affect parents' day-to-day interactions with their children and how the relationships with their children evolve. In addition to the characteristics of child and the parent, the interactions between the child and parent are influenced by the context in which the relationship is occurring. The context includes aspects of the immediate setting such as other relationships in the household, including the parent's relationship with a spouse or partner. The parent's relationships with other members of their social networks, including relatives and friends, are also important. Network members provide informational, instrumental (e.g., child care), and emotional support for parents; they can also be sources of stress and take time away from child care activities. Other contexts also influence parent–child interactions; these include the parents' work place and the neighborhood context. These other settings may influence parents' values and childrearing beliefs, their concerns for their children, and their perceptions of the opportunities available to their children. The transactions that occur in the home environment and other important setting are also influenced by socioeconomic status, ethnicity, and culture. In addition, parenting behavior is influenced by parent education and family support programs designed to enhance the quality of care that parents provide. Clearly, many factors play a role in the way parents care for their children.

Drawing on the work of Bronfenbrenner, Jay Belsky (1984) developed an influential model on the determinants of parenting. Belsky identified three main determinants of parental behavior: (a) the personality and personal resources of the parent; (b) characteristics of the child; and (c) contextual sources of stress and support. In addition, the developmental history of the parents, including all of their experiences prior to becoming a parent, was viewed as an important influence on the parents' personality and personal resources. The organization of this volume is based on Belsky's conceptual model. The first part of the book focuses on the characteristics of the parent. In the first chapter, Okagaki and Bingham summarize the research on parents' social cognitions—beliefs, attitudes, perceptions, attributions, and expectations. They review studies that have focused on why parents differ in their social cognitions and the relation between parents' ideas about children and caregiving and their behavior. This is followed by Vondra, Sysko, and Belsky's chapter on the personality and developmental history of the parent. This chapter examines the relation between the *Big Five* personality factors and parenting behavior. It also explores reasons for continuity and discontinuity between patterns of parenting across generations. Why do some people who experienced poor parenting as children manage to provide very supportive care for their children while others with similar backgrounds struggle in their parenting role? Chapter 3 focuses on adolescent mothers and their children. Although intuitively it seems reasonable that age and maturity are important influences on parental behavior, Luster and Haddow conclude that other factors are likely to be more important influences on how they parent than their age; these factors include who becomes an adolescent parent and the context in which adolescent mothers care for their children. A fourth characteristic of the parent that is likely to influence behavior is the parent's gender. To date, much of the research on parenting has focused on maternal behavior. However, in recent decades there has been growing interest in the parenting behavior of fathers. In Chapter 4, Parke, Dennis, Flyr, Morris, Leidy, and Schofield review this research on fathers.

The second part of the book examines characteristics of the children. Karraker and Coleman provide a comprehensive overview of research on how children and parents influence each other's behavior over time. How parents respond to their children is likely to depend on the children's age, temperament, gender, and other factors. Some children have special needs which require parents to adjust their practices to accommodate these needs. Hodapp and Ly summarize research on parents with special needs children in Chapter 6.

The third part of the book focuses on contextual influences on the parent–child relationships. In Chapter 7, Fincham and Hall focus on the marital relationship. This is followed by Cochran and Walker's review of research on social networks. Chapter 9 explores the world of work; Crouter and McHale discuss links between parents' experiences in the workplace and their behavior in the home. Garbarino, Bradshaw and Kostelny consider the many ways in which neighborhoods influence children directly and indirectly via their parents; risks and assets vary by neighborhood and parents adjust their parenting strategies based on their perceptions of their neighborhood characteristics. In Chapter 11, Leyendecker, Harwood, Comparini and Yalçınkaya consider the unique and combined influences of socioeconomic status and ethnicity. In many communities, programs have been designed to influence parenting behavior and ultimately the development of their children. Powell reviews the literature on these intervention programs in Chapter 12, noting both the effects of these programs and changes in the questions that have been addressed by evaluators of these programs.

The first edition of this book was published more than a decade ago. Since that time, there has been a plethora of research on parenting practices, and these new findings are incorporated into each of the chapters of the second edition of the book. In addition, new chapters were added to each of the three parts of the book. Part I was expanded to include a chapter on fathers. A chapter on special needs children was added to Part II. Part III includes new chapters on socioeconomic status and ethnicity, and parenting education programs. These additional chapters make the book a more comprehensive resource for scholars and students interested in why parents do what they do.

The final chapter differs from the earlier chapters in that it considers the extent to which parents influence the development of their children. During the past decade, several scholars have raised questions about much influence parents have on their children's development; they have also questioned the methods that have been used to examine parental influences on children's development. Parenting research has been criticized by researchers who employ behavioral genetics designs to study human development (Scarr, 1992; Rowe, 1994). These critics point out that studies of parents and their biological children make it difficult to disentangle the effects of nature and nurture. Another critic, Harris (1998), proposed that over the long run, peers have a more enduring effect on children's personality development than parents. In the final chapter, we discuss the concerns and the evidence of those who have been critical of socialization researchers. We also summarize some of the evidence and counter-arguments put forth by parenting researchers in response to these criticisms. The last chapter was written primarily for students who are not familiar with these debates. It is intended to help them understand why scholars have reached differing conclusions about the role that parents play in children's development.

Having been influenced by Bronfenbrenner's work, we recognize that children's development is influenced by myriad factors including genetic endowment, peers, and parents. Proximal processes that occur in the home are among the most important influences on children's development. For this reason we believe that it is essential to understand factors influencing experiences in the home. Which factors influence the way parents interact with their children, structure the home environment, and help their children understand the world beyond the home? This book summarizes the latest research on parenting, with each chapter providing a look at one important influence and the linkages among the various factors. An ecological perspective draws attention to the fact that the lives of parents and children are intertwined, and that understanding influences on parents is important for understanding the experiences of children.

REFERENCES

Belsky, J. (1984). The determinants of parenting: A process model. *Child Development, 55*, 83–96.

Bronfenbrenner, U. (1979). *The ecology of human development: Experiments by nature and design.* Cambridge, MA: Harvard University Press.

Bronfenbrenner, U. (2000). Ecological systems theory. In A. E. Kazdin (Ed.), *Encyclopedia of psychology* (Vol. 3, pp. 129–133). New York: Oxford University Press.

Hamilton, S., & Luster, T. (2003). Urie Bronfenbrenner. In J. R. Miller, R. M. Lerner, L. B. Schiamberg, & P. M. Anderson (Eds.), *The encyclopedia of human ecology* (pp. 84–89). Santa Barbara, CA: ABC-Clio.

Harris, J. R. (1998). *The nurture assumption: Why children turn out the way they do.* New York: The Free Press.

Luster, T., & Okagaki, L. (1993). *Parenting: An ecological perspective* (1st ed.). Mahwah, NJ: Lawrence Erlbaum Associates.

Scarr, S. (1992). Developmental theories for the 1990's: Development and individual differences. *Child Development, 63,* 1–19.

Rowe, D. (1994). *The limits of family influence: Genes, experiences, and behavior.* New York: Guilford Press.

I

CHARACTERISTICS OF THE PARENTS

1

Parents' Social Cognitions and Their Parenting Behaviors

Lynn Okagaki
Purdue University

Gary E. Bingham
Washington State University

INTRODUCTION

In this chapter we examine parents' social cognitions—beliefs, attitudes, perceptions, attributions, and expectations—from two perspectives. In the first section, we ask questions about the origins of parents' social cognitions. What influences the development of parents' social cognitions? How do they develop over time? We look at parental social cognition as a focus of study and consider the ways in which it emerges as a function of parents' social context. As others have argued (e.g., Goodnow & Collins, 1990; Sigel & McGillicuddy-De Lisi, 2002), the study of parents' social cognitions is important in and of itself. They constitute an important aspect of adult cognitive development. In the first edition of this book, Okagaki and Divecha (1993) reviewed research describing contextual factors thought to influence the development of parents' social cognitions following Bronfenbrenner's (1979) ecological approach to the study of human development. For this edition, we limit our discussion to macrosystemic influences on parents' social cognitions and consider the ways in which broad contextual factors may shape beliefs, attitudes, perceptions, attributions, and expectations relevant to childrearing and parent–child relationships. In the second section of this chapter, we review research on the relation between parents' social cognitions and their childrearing behaviors. Many have argued that parents' social cognitions influence their behaviors and, in turn, children's developmental outcomes (e.g., Goodnow, 2002; Holden & Buck, 2002). We consider the evidence that supports these claims. In the final section, we conclude with our perspectives on developments in research on parental social cognition that have the potential to move the field forward.

CONTEXTUAL INFLUENCES ON PARENTS' SOCIAL COGNITIONS

Before we examine contextual influences on parents' social cognitions, we want to define the types of social cognitions that have been the focus of studies on parenting. An important change in research on parents over the last decade is that the developmental researchers who have been interested in parents' social cognitions have drawn more heavily on research from social and cognitive psychology and become more sophisticated in their understanding of social cognition. In earlier studies, many researchers used the term *beliefs* interchangeably with other social cognitions, such as attitudes or attributions. This broad usage contributed to Goodnow and Collins' (1990) adoption of the term *parent cognitions* to highlight the distinctions among beliefs, attitudes, and attributions and to emphasize that they are interrelated phenomena.

To the extent possible, we separately consider parents' beliefs, attitudes, perceptions, attributions, and expectations in this chapter. Oftentimes, in the existing research, items included on a scale reflect a mixture of social cognitions (e.g., beliefs and attitudes), and it is not possible to consider them separately (Holden & Buck, 2002). Parental beliefs are ideas or knowledge that parents consider to be factual or true (McGillicuddy-De Lisi & Sigel, 1995; Sigel, 1985). Research on parental beliefs has encompassed parents' ideas about many aspects of parenting, such as childrearing strategies, child development, parent–child relationships, and children's sibling relationships. Attitudes build on beliefs by adding an evaluative dimension—a negative or positive valence—to ideas about the target entity or attitude object (Holden & Buck, 2002). For example, researchers have examined parents' attitudes toward the importance of child obedience and the use of corporal punishment (Danso, Hunsberger, & Pratt, 1997; Holden, Thompson, Zambarano, & Marshall, 1997; Jambunathan, Burts, & Pierce, 2000). Perceptions are a type of belief. They are ideas about the attributes, characteristics, and behaviors that an individual develops about a particular person or social group (Fiske & Taylor, 1991). In the parenting literature, most of the attention has focused on parents' perceptions of children's characteristics (e.g., temperament) and their perceptions of their own childrearing ability (i.e., parental self-efficacy). Attributions build on perceptions by assigning or inferring a cause or intention to the observed characteristics or actions of an individual (Bugental & Happaney, 2002). Research on parental attributions has primarily been conducted in the context of understanding child abuse. Finally, parental goals and expectations are the outcomes that parents hope to achieve when they interact with or socialize their child—the behaviors and traits they want their child to develop (Hastings & Grusec, 1998). Parents' goals include long-term goals that represent the type of person parents want their child to become, as well as the immediate goals that emerge in the context of daily interactions with the child (e.g., wanting the child to hurry up and get dressed so he does not miss the school bus; Dix, 1992).

Substantial research documents cultural and social class variation in parents' social cognitions (e.g., Bornstein et al., 1996; Harkness & Super, 1996; Harwood, Schoelmerich, & Schulze, 2000). Across these broad social contexts, differences have been reported in (a) parents' beliefs about childrearing (e.g., Okagaki & Frensch, 1998), (b) attitudes about parental control and discipline (e.g., Chen et al., 1998; Gershoff, Miller, & Holden, 1999; Gorman, 1998), (c) perceptions of their own efficacy as parents and of their children (e.g., Bornstein et al., 1998; Cote & Bornstein, 2003), (d) attributions (e.g., Hess, Chih-Mei, & McDevitt, 1987) and (e) expectations for children's behavior (e.g., Hao & Bornstead-Bruns, 1998; Harwood, 1992). In this section, we highlight a few examples of research on cultural and social class variation in parents' social cognitions particularly emphasizing studies that have attempted to link cultural differences in parenting to differences in general cultural values or have described parenting in non-Western cultures within a broader psychological context that is appropriate to that culture.

Parental Beliefs

A fundamental parental belief has to do with what it means to be a parent. What is the proper role of a parent? Cultural groups vary in the ways in which they understand the role and responsibilities of parents. Much of the research on cultural variation in parents' social cognitions focused on parents' informal or folk theories about parenting. For example, Chao (1994) has examined mothers' beliefs about childrearing and what it means to be a good parent. In a study of immigrant Chinese mothers and third-generation or higher European American mothers in the United States, Chao observed differences in the ways in which mothers defined their roles. For example, in contrast to European American mothers, Chinese immigrant mothers believed that young children should only be cared for by their mothers or by some other family member. Also in contrast to European American mothers, the Chinese immigrant mothers placed a strong emphasis on training and teaching children. Being a good mother meant that one started training the child as soon as the child was ready to learn. Chinese immigrant mothers expressed the belief that the primary way in which mothers express their love to their child is by helping the child succeed, especially in school. The ideas expressed by the Chinese immigrant mothers reflect what Chao (1994, 1996, 2000) described as the Chinese concept of training a child (*chiao shun*). Similar to the Western concept of parenting style, training is comprised of beliefs about parental demandingness and responsiveness to the child. The demandingness dimension of training emphasizes "a continuous monitoring and guidance of children" (Chao, 2000, p. 234). Unlike parenting style, however, the demandingness dimension in training a child does not include restricting or dominating the child. The responsiveness dimension of training emphasizes parental involvement and support, but does not include overt demonstrations of the parent's affection for the child (e.g., praising or hugging the child). Thus, the concept of training a child is similar to the Western understanding of parenting style, but distinct in important ways and reflects a Chinese conceptualization of parenting.

Another view of what it means to be a parent comes from Native American communities. Among many Native American nations, the role of the parent is defined in ways that are distinct from Western models of parenting. For example, in some Native American nations, caring and nurturing children is a shared responsibility that extends beyond the biological parents to members of the extended family and members of the community. Primary responsibility for the discipline of the child may be given to grandparents, aunts, or uncles (Machamer & Gruber, 1998). Tribal elders may have a formal role on matters regarding the care of the child (Joe & Malach, 1992). To be a parent does not mean that one has sole authority for making decisions about the child.

The majority of research on ethnic and cultural variation in parenting in the United States has relied on Western psychological traditions and has not situated parenting by specific ethnic groups within their own cultural traditions (e.g., Dornbusch, Ritter, Leiderman, Roberts, & Faleigh, 1987; Okagaki & Sternberg, 1991; Steinberg, Dornbusch, & Brown, 1992; Steinberg, Mounts, Lamborn, & Dornbusch, 1991). Chao's work (1994, 2000) on examining immigrant Chinese mothers' beliefs about parenting from the Chinese concept of training illustrates development in research on cultural variation in parenting—understanding parenting within the psychological context of the target culture, rather than using Western psychological theories as the framework. More research in this vein—connecting parents' social cognitions to broader cultural values within specific cultural contexts—is needed to increase our understanding of the role of culture in shaping parental cognitions.

Parental Attitudes

Many studies of cultural variation in parents' attitudes have compared parents from Western and Eastern Hemispheres (e.g., parents from the United States and China) in an attempt to examine differences associated with the broader cultural values of individualism and collectivism. For example, Chen and colleagues (1998) compared European Canadian mothers' and Chinese mothers' attitudes toward their child's responses to novel situations. In this instance, the attitudes of Canadian parents of European origin who traditionally hold a more individualistic orientation that values independence were compared with those of Chinese parents who traditionally value mutual interdependence.

In any group of infants or toddlers, variation in responses to novelty exists. Some children are relatively relaxed when confronted with an unfamiliar situation and show few indications of distress. Other children react to novel objects and situations with high anxiety and try to remain close to their mother or other primary caregiver. They do not readily explore novel objects or easily interact with unfamiliar people. These actions are indicators of behavioral inhibition. In this study (Chen et al., 1998), the researchers observed that Chinese mothers and European Canadian mothers had quite distinct attitudes toward behavioral inhibition. In Chinese families, mothers viewed behavioral inhibition in toddlers as a positive trait. Behavioral inhibition was positively associated with maternal acceptance of the child and maternal belief in encouraging children's achievement. In contrast, in Canadian families, behavioral inhibition was negatively associated with maternal acceptance and encouragement of children's achievement. Among Chinese families, children who displayed higher levels of behavioral inhibition had mothers who were less likely to believe that physical punishment is the best way to discipline the child and who were less likely to feel angry toward the child. However, maternal punishment orientation was positively correlated with behavioral inhibition in Canadian families (i.e., mothers whose children displayed higher levels of behavioral inhibition were more likely to believe that physical punishment was the best discipline strategy). In short, behavioral inhibition was associated with positive attitudes in Chinese mothers and negative attitudes in Canadian mothers. Although these attitudes toward behavioral inhibition are quite opposite from each other, each one is consistent with the broader values of its culture.

Within the context of identifying specific cultural influences on parenting, religion has been posited to be a source of attitudes and beliefs related to childrearing. To date, the majority of research on parental social cognitions and religion has focused on parents' attitudes and beliefs about discipline (e.g., Bartkowski & Ellison, 1995; Danso, Hunsberger, & Pratt, 1997). For example, Gershoff and colleagues (1999) examined parents' attitudes toward corporal punishment in mainline Protestant, conservative Protestant, and Roman Catholic parents as well as parents who identified themselves as unaffiliated with a religious group. Consistent with findings from other studies, conservative Protestant parents were more likely to believe that corporal punishment was an effective childrearing strategy and had more positive attitudes toward the use of corporal punishment. Ellison and colleagues have argued that belief in the utility of corporal punishment reflects specific religious beliefs held by conservative Protestants—beliefs in the sinfulness of human nature, in the need for punishing sins, and in the Bible as an infallible guide for parenting practices (Bartkowski & Ellison, 1995; Ellison & Sherkat, 1993).

As in research on the variation in parents' beliefs across cultural groups, research on the variation in parents' attitudes across groups needs to explicitly test hypothesized links between general beliefs and values and specific parenting attitudes. For example, researchers might explicitly measure collectivism and individualism as well as parents' attitudes toward behavioral inhibition to determine if observed differences in parents' attitudes toward behavioral inhibition are, in fact, related to differences in parents' attitudes about collectivism and individualism. Similarly researchers might explicitly measure parents' religious beliefs and assess the degree to which belief in specific religious tenets is associated with parents' attitudes toward specific disciplinary practices within religious groups as well as across groups. Such studies would move the field beyond mere speculations that it is these broader cultural beliefs and values that lead to differences in parental attitudes.

Parental Perceptions

Less research has examined cultural differences in parents' perceptions. However, like parents' beliefs and attitudes, parents' perceptions about their own parenting abilities (i.e., parenting efficacy) does appear to vary across cultural groups. Parents in some cultures express less confidence in their childrearing skills on average than do parents in other groups (Bornstein et al., 1996; Bornstein et al., 1998). For example, although Italian and Japanese mothers described themselves as being as willing, or more willing, to invest time and effort into their parenting than did mothers from the other nations, they expressed less confidence in their childrearing skills as compared to mothers in Argentina, Belgium, France, Israel, and the United States.

Not surprisingly, parents' perceptions of their parental efficacy also varies by childrearing strategy. Parents are more confident in their abilities to enact some childrearing skills relative to other childrearing strategies. For example, Perozynski and Kramer (1999) found that mothers of young children were more confident than fathers in their ability to use strategies that involved reasoning or talking to the child. In contrast, fathers reported greater confidence than mothers in their ability to use strategies that used directives (e.g., "Stop fighting!") or the threat of force.

Parental Attributions

Cultural values appear to be an important factor to consider when examining parents' attributions about children's positive and negative behaviors (Chiang, Barrett, & Nunez, 2000) and attributions about children's academic achievement (Hess et al., 1987). For example, several studies have documented that Asian parents (e.g., parents from Japan, Taiwan, and the People's Republic of China) and Asian American parents (e.g., U.S. or Canadian parents of Asian descent) as compared to European American parents attribute the effort the child directs toward school work to be a more important contributor to the child's academic success (e.g., Hess et al., 1987; Okagaki & Sternberg, 1991; Stevenson & Lee, 1990).

Cultural variation also exists in parents' attributions about successful parenting. In a study of mothers of 20-month-old children, mothers from Argentina, Belgium, Italy, Israel, Japan, and the United States identified causal factors contributing to successes and failures in seven parenting tasks. For example, mothers were asked if being able to successfully comfort their child when he or she cries was due to their parenting ability (e.g., "I am good at this"), effort (e.g., "I have tried hard"), mood (e.g., "I am in a good mood"), task difficulty (e.g., "This is easy to do"), or a child characteristic (e.g., "My child makes this easy to do"). The degree to which mothers attributed success to specific factors varied across nations. Japanese mothers, for example, were less likely than mothers from all other nations to attribute success to their own ability and more likely to indicate that, when they were successful, it was because of the child's behavior (Bornstein et al., 1998).

Parental Goals and Expectations

Much of the research on cultural variation in parents' social cognitions has addressed differences in parents' goals and expectations for their children. Similar to research on parents' attitudes discussed previously, research on parents' expectations has been framed within the context of broader cultural values (Bornstein et al., 1998; Goodnow, 1995; Papoušek & Papoušek, 1995). For example, as previously noted, many Western societies encourage independence, self-reliance, and individual achievement among their children (Spence, 1985; Triandis, 1995; Triandis, Bontempo, Villareal, Asai, & Lucca, 1988). In contrast, in many Asian and Latin American cultures, interdependence, cooperation, and collaboration are widely held values (Harrison, Wilson, Pine, Chan, & Buriel, 1990). Differences in these general cultural values or expectations for members of communities are associated with differences in the socialization goals and strategies which parents adopt for their children (Harwood, 1992; Ogbu, 1981). As LeVine (1988) observed, differences in parental goals and expectations arise, in part, because societies have different expectations for the adult members of their communities.

Harwood's (1992) comparison of Puerto Rican and European American mothers' goals and expectations for their young children illustrates cultural differences in expectations. As compared to Puerto Rican mothers from lower-class families, European American mothers from both lower- and middle-class families were more likely to focus on socialization goals that related to personal development (e.g., self-confidence, independence, development of talents and abilities) and self-control (e.g., restraining oneself from being greedy, aggressive or selfish). For the middle-class European American mothers, 35% of the responses emphasized some aspect of personal development. In contrast, the Puerto Rican mothers were more likely to talk about characteristics that focused on being respectful (e.g., be polite, obedient) and loving (e.g., be friendly, get along with others). Nearly 40% of the characteristics spontaneously mentioned by the Puerto Rican mothers were related to respectfulness. In contrast, less than 3% of the traits mentioned by the middle-class European American mothers fell into this category. Thus, mothers' long-term goals for their children differed across cultural groups, and these differences appear to reflect general cultural orientations toward individuals and relationships. Although Harwood did not measure general cultural values in her study, her data are consistent with the notion that general cultural values are translated by parents into specific socialization goals for their children.

Substantial attention in the parenting literature has also focused on variation in parents' developmental expectations that are associated with differences in social class or socioeconomic status (SES). Early research on the relation between social class and childrearing identified variation in parents' beliefs about the role of parents and in their expectations and goals for their children as a function of social class differences (e.g., Kohn, 1963, 1969, 1979; Kohn & Schooler, 1983; Miller, Schooler, Kohn, & Hiller, 1979). Kohn hypothesized that social class differences in paternal goals and expectations for children were related to differences in the requirements and expectations fathers needed to meet to succeed in their jobs (Kohn & Schooler, 1983).

Research by Crouter (1984) supports Kohn's hypothesis. Through extensive interviews Crouter found that parents who worked in more participative environments (e.g., where team meetings are used to discuss issues and to problem solve) emphasized the importance of cooperation among family members at home and even adopted some of the strategies used at work, such as team meetings, to achieve more collaboration and cooperation among their children. Research by Greenberger, O'Neil, and Nagel (1994) further supports these findings. In their study, parental work complexity (e.g., level of supervising or negotiating) and work challenge (e.g., variation and self-direction in work) predicted mothers' and fathers' reports of the importance of firm but flexible control in their parenting.

Other research on social class variation in parents' goals has found that higher-SES mothers generally give earlier age estimates for children's attainment of developmental milestones than lower-SES mothers (e.g., Mansbach & Greenbaum, 1999; von der Lippe, 1999). For example, in a study of Israeli parents of 6-month-old children, parents from middle- to high-SES backgrounds expected their infant to reach cognitive developmental milestones at earlier ages than did low-SES parents (Mansbach & Greenbaum, 1999). In a study of Filipino mothers of preschool-age children, mothers estimated the age at which their child would acquire cognitive, psychosocial, and perceptual–motor skills (Williams, Williams, Lopez, & Tayko, 2000). As compared to mothers with lower educational attainment, mothers with higher educational attainment had higher expectations for children's cognitive and psychosocial development (e.g., emotional maturity, independence).

Parents' developmental expectations have also been found to vary across cultural groups (e.g., Rose, Dalakas, & Kropp, 2002; Schulze, Harwood, & Schoelmerich, 2001). For example, middle-class European American and Puerto Rican mothers of 1-year-olds differed in expectations regarding the age at which infants were typically expected to drink from a cup and use utensils on their own (Schulze et al., 2001). These differences in maternal developmental expectations have been linked to differences in cultural values emphasizing individualistic or collectivistic orientations (Schulze, Harwood, Schoelmerich, & Leyendecker, 2002). However, despite the observed differences in developmental expectations across cultural groups, it should be noted that considerable variation in parents' expectations has been found to exist within cultural groups (Harwood, Handwerker, Schoelmerich, & Leyendecker, 2001; Schulze et al., 2002). In fact, some have argued that differences in parents' expectations are more attributable to SES differences within a culture than differences across cultural groups (Hoff, Laursen, & Tardif, 2002).

Finally, much of the research on parents' goals and expectations has focused on goals related to school achievement. Several researchers have argued that cultural differences in expectations for children's school achievement, along with general beliefs about the value and role of education, contribute to cross-national differences in children's school achievement. For example, in a series of multinational studies, Stevenson and his colleagues found that Chinese and Japanese mothers set higher expectations for their child's school performance as compared to American mothers (e.g., Chen & Uttal, 1988; Stevenson, Chen, & Lee, 1993; Stevenson & Lee, 1990; Stevenson, Lee, & Stigler, 1986). These differences in parents' expectations have been attributed to differences in broader cultural values and beliefs. For example, Chen and Uttal (1988) posited that Chinese parents set high expectations for their children's intellectual performance because of the high value placed on education both historically and in contemporary China, the cultural emphasis on self-improvement, and the strong cultural belief in human malleability.

According to Ho (1994), Confucian ethics emphasizing obligation to others rather than individual rights have provided a foundation for parent–child relationships in China, Japan, and Korea and find expression in parent–child relationships through the notion of filial piety.

> Among the filial precepts are: obeying and honoring one's parents, providing for the material and mental well-being of one's aged parents, performing the ceremonial duties of ancestral worship, taking care to avoid harm to one's body, ensuring the continuity of the family line, and in general conducting oneself so as to bring honor and not disgrace to the family name. (p. 287)

These underlying values may be reflected in parents' ideas about what it means to be a good parent and what constitutes a good or virtuous child. One interpretation of Asian parents' high expectations is that the expectations emerge from the belief that good parents will expect their children to obey and gain honor for the family.

Within the United States, similar differences are found across ethnic groups. For instance, in a study of Asian American, Latino, and European American families with fourth- and fifth-grade children (Okagaki & Frensch, 1998), Asian American parents had higher expectations for their child's educational attainment as compared to other parents. Of course, differences in parents' expectations may reflect differences in children's prior performance (e.g., Entwisle & Hayduk, 1978; Seginer, 1983). A hierarchical regression in which the previous year's grades and parents' perceptions of their child's ability were used to partial out differences in actual and perceived school performance still resulted in ethnic group differences in parents' expectations for their child's school attainment. This finding supports the hypothesis that differences in parental expectations are not simply a response to children's prior achievements, but may reflect differences in broader cultural values.

To understand parents' goals and expectations, we need to consider more than what parents would ideally like to happen. We can learn about parents' goals by examining what they set as minimum expectations for their children. In their study of Asian American, European American, and Latino parents, Okagaki and Frensch (1998) asked parents to indicate how

much education they ideally wanted their child to attain; how much education they expected their child to receive; and the minimum amount of education they would allow their child to receive before the child could termi-
nate his or her education. In all three conditions, Asian American parents
had higher expectations than Latino and European American parents.
Asian American parents ideally wanted their child to earn a graduate or
professional degree. They expected their child to receive a college degree,
and the minimum education that would satisfy the parents was a college degree. In contrast, European American parents ideally wanted their child to
obtain a college degree, expected their child to receive some college education, and minimally required their child to graduate from high school. Parents' expectations for the grades the child received followed a similar pattern. Although all parents indicated that they would be pleased if their
child received an A, Asian American parents were less satisfied if their child
received a B or a C than Latino or European American parents were. In a
related study of high-achieving and low-achieving (as determined by school
achievement test scores) children of Mexican descent (Okagaki, Frensch, &
Gordon, 1995), parents of both high-achieving and low-achieving children
valued education, wanted their children to obtain good educations, and
held similar expectations for the amount of schooling they expected their
children to obtain. Parents of high-achieving and low-achieving children,
however, differed in the minimum educational attainment level that they
set for their children and in their responses to grades of Cs and Ds. Parents
of high achievers set a higher minimum boundary for their children's
grades and educational attainment. Although about half of the parents in
each group wanted their child at least to complete college, of those who
would be satisfied with less than a college degree, the parents of high
achievers were more likely to want their child to complete at least some college or vocational training after high school. Parents of high achievers were
also less satisfied with Cs and Ds than were parents of low achievers. Again,
difference in parents' responses to grades may reflect children's prior performance. However, when only the responses of parents who reported that
their children normally received As and Bs were examined, parents of low
achievers were still more likely to be satisfied with Cs and Ds than parents of
high achievers. In short, parents' expectations are multifaceted. They are,
at least, comprised of parents' ideals, parents' realistic assessments of what
might happen, and what Goodnow (2002) has called the "bottom line"—
that is, the minimum acceptable performance.

Summary

In this section, we have described ways in which parents' social cognitions
vary across social contexts. Although the field has described variation in
parents' social cognitions across groups, the research is limited in three im-

portant ways. First, although researchers have posited that differences in broad cultural values or orientation lead to differences in specific parental social cognitions, by and large researchers have not specifically measured those broad cultural values (e.g., collectivistic and individualistic perspectives) and examined the relations between those values and measures of parents' social cognitions. Second, when Western psychologists have examined parents' social cognitions across cultural groups, they generally have done so using a Western psychological model rather than attempting to incorporate constructs based on appropriate non-Western psychological theories. As a result, we are prone to misunderstanding the social cognitions of parents from other cultural groups. Third, because the research is correlational and cross-sectional, it does not demonstrate that social context influences parents' social cognitions. Establishing a causal link between contextual influences and parents' social cognitions is particularly important given previous research and theory suggesting the possibility that parents' behaviors may influence their parenting beliefs.

PARENTS' SOCIAL COGNITIONS
AND THEIR CHILDREARING BEHAVIORS

Developmental researchers have primarily examined parents' social cognitions because they have been hypothesized to be the underlying force directing parents' childrearing strategies and behaviors (Sigel & McGillicuddy-De Lisi, 2002). Whereas most of the other chapters in this volume consider the influence that factors outside of the parent have on parental behaviors, this chapter—like Vondra, Sysko, and Belsky's (chap. 2, this volume) discussion of the relations between personality and childrearing—is a consideration of the relations between characteristics of parents and their childrearing behaviors. In this section, we examine research exploring the relations between parents' social cognitions and their behaviors.

Parental Beliefs and Behaviors

A number of research studies document the relation between various parents' beliefs and their self-reported or observed childrearing behaviors (e.g., DeBarysche, 1995; Kinlaw, Kurtz-Costes, & Goldman-Fraser, 2001; Stevens, 1984). For example, the degree to which mothers believe that children's development can be facilitated by their social environment is positively correlated with the amount and type of language that mothers use during mother–child interactions (Donahue, Pearl, & Herzog, 1997). In this study, mothers who more strongly believed that the social environment played an important role in children's development were more likely to use questions (e.g., requiring the child to think about categories or relation-ships), as opposed to other forms of communication, to help focus their child's attention on important details of a picture while completing a refer-ential communication task. Other research has demonstrated that moth-ers' and fathers' beliefs about the importance of teaching children mathe-matics are positively correlated with parents' self-reports of engaging in mathematics-related activities with their child (e.g., encouraging the child to count; Musun-Miller & Blevins-Knabe, 1998).

Although correlations have been obtained between parents' beliefs and their behaviors, it is not necessarily clear how to interpret these findings. In many studies, the correlations between parents' beliefs and behaviors have been relatively weak ($r < .30$) or nonsignificant, particularly when measured over time (Coleman & Karraker, 2003; Mantizicopoulos, 1997; Sigel & McGillicuddy-De Lisi, 2002). In other studies, the correlation between par-ents' beliefs and behaviors may be a methodological artifact resulting when parents' self-reports are used to measure both parents' beliefs and their behaviors. One problem inherent in a self-report approach to measuring parents' ideas about children and their behaviors toward children is that it may overestimate the relation between the variables being studied. This may occur as a result of parents' failure to adequately report their actual practices (Goodnow, 2002). Parents may, knowingly or unknowingly, re-port what they believe to be ideal parenting practices, which may be more strongly correlated with their beliefs about parenting. A second problem in interpreting correlations based on parents' self-report of beliefs and behav-iors is that correlations between two measures are always stronger when a single source reports on both measures than correlations between meas-ures originating from different sources (i.e., shared method variance; Mil-ler, 1987).

The strength of the correlation between parents' beliefs and behaviors de-pends, in part, on the closeness of the match between the content of the be-liefs and the type of behavior that is measured. A study by Sigel (1992) pro-vides an illustration of the possible effects of shared method variance and of the degree of congruence between the content of the beliefs and the type of observed behavior. Sigel examined relations between parents' beliefs and their behaviors using multiple methodologies. During a semistructured in-terview, fathers and mothers responded to vignettes designed to tap their ideas about how children learn in four knowledge domains: physical knowl-edge (dealing with space, time, and distance), social knowledge (knowledge of social rules), moral knowledge (dealing with right-and-wrong issues, such as cheating), and understanding of self (awareness of inner feelings and emotional states). Parents' responses were coded into four categories: (1) children learn by thinking and reasoning through problems, (2) children learn through direct instruction, (3) children learn through positive feedback and reinforcement, and (4) children learn through negative feedback and punishment. Parents were also asked to describe how they would help their child learn or solve the problems presented in the vignettes, and these responses were coded in a similar fashion. Finally, parents were observed helping their child learn how to tie a knot. Their behaviors were coded to reflect the type of teaching strategy they used by indicating the degree to which the parent required the child to think through the problem himself. Behaviors were coded as (a) high cognitive demands (i.e., requiring the child to think abstractly and consider alternatives), (b) low demands (i.e., requiring the child to answer focused, concrete questions that require minimal representational thinking), or (c) structuring (i.e., facilitating or defining the task for the child to help move the task along).

In Sigel's study (1992), parents' beliefs about how children learn were related to their descriptions of what they would do if they were helping their child solve the same problems posed in the vignettes. As expected, mothers who believed that children learn by thinking through problems themselves were more likely to report strategies that involved asking questions that required children to think abstractly and consider alternative solutions and were less likely to report giving children explicit instructions for solving the problem ($r = .72$ and $r = -.60$, respectively). On the other hand, mothers who believed that children learn through direct instruction were less likely to report that they would ask questions to help their child think through the problem and more likely to report giving explicit instructions ($r = -.60$ and $r = .56$, respectively). The degree to which fathers believed that children learn by thinking through problems on their own was positively correlated with fathers' reports of asking questions ($r = .77$); but the degree to which fathers believed that children learn through direct instruction was not related to fathers' reported use of this strategy. Meanwhile, fathers' beliefs about direct instruction were negatively related to their reported use of distancing strategies ($r = -.37$). In general, the correlations between beliefs and self-reported behaviors were moderately strong.

Examinations of the relation between parents' reported beliefs and their observed parenting behaviors revealed weaker associations. First, the degrees to which mothers and fathers believed that children learn by thinking through problems were unrelated to the frequency with which they asked their child questions during the knot-tying task. However, the degree to which fathers believed that children learn through direct instruction was negatively correlated with the degree to which fathers asked questions that required their child to think through the problem ($r = -.34$). The degree to which mothers believed that children learn through direct instruction was positively related to how they talked to their child about the steps that were necessary to complete the task (i.e., structured the task for the child; $r = .27$).

The difference in the strength of the correlations between self-reported beliefs and self-reported behaviors and between self-reported beliefs and observed behaviors illustrates, first, that correlations tend to be stronger when the measurement method is similar (i.e., shared method variance). Second, the difference may reflect the lack of correspondence in the type of problem used in the observed parent–child interaction (i.e., the knot-tying task) and the types of problems used to elicit parents' beliefs about children's cognitive development (e.g., physical, social, moral, and emotional knowledge). As Sigel (1992) observed, parenting strategies may be context sensitive. The same vignettes were used to elicit parents' beliefs and their self-reported behaviors. However, the knot-tying task used for observing parents' teaching behaviors was entirely different in content and structure to the vignettes.

In contrast to Sigel's study, the following study provides an example of a closer match between the content of the beliefs and the observed child-rearing behavior, and stronger correlations were obtained. DeBaryshe (1995) examined the relation between mothers' early literacy beliefs (e.g., mothers' beliefs about the importance of reading to young children, their role as educator, and the importance of making reading a fun experience for the child) and the frequency of mothers' questions and mother–child conversations during joint book reading interactions. A moderately strong correlation was obtained between mothers' early literacy beliefs and the quality of mother–child joint book reading interactions ($r = .48$). Given these findings, one explanation for variation in the strength of belief–behavior correlations is the degree to which the content of the belief being measured matches the nature of the observed parenting behavior.

Parental Attitudes and Behavior

Much of the research on the relations between parents' attitudes and their behaviors has focused either on parenting style (e.g., Daggett, O'Brien, Zanolli, & Peyton, 2000; Gorman, 1998; Holden & Miller, 1999) or the quality of the home environment (e.g., Benasich & Brooks-Gunn, 1996; Iverson & Segal, 1992; Kochanska, Kuczynski, & Radke-Yarrow, 1989). For example, Benasich and Brooks-Gunn (1996) found that maternal childrearing attitudes were positively related to the quality of the home environment, as measured by the Home Observation Measurement of the Environment.

In a study of Puerto Rican mothers and their preschool-age child, mothers' attitudes toward authoritative parenting behaviors (e.g., encouraging child to talk about feelings) and authoritarian parenting behaviors (e.g., parents should control parenting) were correlated with mothers' behaviors during a mother–child teaching task (Vargas & Busch-Rossnagel, 2003). Mothers were asked to teach their child how to build two Tinkertoy models.

The frequencies with which mothers asked questions, gave direct instructions, praised, scolded or showed verbal disapproval, modeled or demonstrated what to do, were physically affectionate, and used physical control were coded. Significant, but weak, correlations were obtained between mothers' childrearing attitudes and their teaching behaviors. The degree to which mothers endorsed authoritative childrearing beliefs was positively correlated with asking questions and praising their child during the teaching task. However, there was no correlation between authoritarian childrearing attitudes and parenting behaviors.

Parental Perceptions and Behavior

Although researchers for decades have recognized that both parents and their children are active agents in the socialization process, only recently have examinations of parenting behavior begun to seriously consider potential influences of the child on parents' behaviors (Grusec, Goodnow, & Kuczynski, 2000). One mechanism by which children may influence their parents' behaviors is through parents' perceptions of children's characteristics and behaviors. For example, previous research has linked parents' perceptions of difficult temperaments (Dadds, 1987), discipline problems (Bates, Bayles, Bennet, Ridge, & Brown, 1991; Nix et al., 1999), and inattentiveness or impulsivity (Russell, 1997) to childrearing behavior and the quality of the parent–child relationship.

Parents appear to adapt their childrearing strategies to account for their perceptions of their child's abilities or special needs. In families with typically developing children, researchers have examined the ways in which childrearing changes according to the developmental needs of the child. For example, Cicognani and Zani (1998) found that parents of adolescents often adopt a more flexible parenting style in order to cope with their perceptions of their child's changing developmental needs. Research on children with special needs has linked parents' perceptions of children's ability to family functioning (Blacher, Nihira, & Meyers, 1987) and childrearing behaviors (Marks & Dollahite, 2001).

One limitation of the research examining the relations between parents' perceptions of their child to their childrearing behavior is that most of it is correlational and limited to data collected at one point in time. Few studies have examined whether parents' perceptions of children's abilities or characteristics are related to subsequent parental behavior. A notable exception is a study of the relation between parents' perceptions of their child's shyness and their subsequent parenting style (Rubin, Nelson, Hastings, & Asendorpf, 1999). At 2 years of age, children's behavioral inhibition was observed in a laboratory setting and mothers' and fathers' ratings of child shyness and their own parenting style were collected via self-report. At 4 years of age, mothers and fathers completed additional self-report measures of child shyness and parenting style.

Mothers' and fathers' perceptions of their child's early shyness at age 2 directly predicted their reports of parenting behaviors that encouraged child independence 2 years later. Mothers and fathers who perceived their child as being shy at age 2 were less likely to encourage the child's independent behavior at age 4. However, the relation between early shyness and self-reported parenting practices was not replicated when observers' ratings of child shyness at age 2 were substituted for parents' reports of shyness in the analysis. These data are consistent with the hypothesis that it appears to be parents' perceptions of their young child's temperament, rather than the child's observed level of inhibition, that directly influences parents' self-reported behaviors over time (Rubin et al., 1999).

Because parents' perceptions of child temperament and their child-rearing behaviors were both assessed using self-report measures, the obtained relations may be a methodological artifact (i.e., shared method variance). The researchers, however, argued that by using structural equation modeling, they were able to control for shared method variance better than with other types of analyses and therefore have stronger support for parents' perceptions mediating the relation between child's characteristics and parent's behaviors.

Perception of parental efficacy has also been posited to influence parenting behaviors (e.g., Coleman & Karraker, 1998). For example, mothers and fathers who were more confident about their ability to use specific parenting strategies have been found to be more likely to use those strategies when managing conflict between their children (Perozynski & Kramer, 1999). Mothers who felt more confident in their ability to perform control strategies (e.g., threatening to punish children) were more likely to use these strategies. Mothers were more likely to use a passive nonintervention approach (e.g., ignored the conflict, let the children work out conflict) when they believed that this was an effective strategy for managing sibling conflicts and when they believed that they could effectively use this technique. The results for fathers were not as straightforward. Fathers' perceptions of their ability to use control strategies or passive nonintervention strategies were not related to their use of these strategies. Rather, the only relation that emerged was between fathers' use of control strategies and their perception of their inability to implement child-centered strategies. Fathers who viewed child-centered strategies as an effective way to resolve sibling conflict but who doubted their ability to use such strategies were more likely to use control strategies, rather than child-centered strategies, during the observed sibling conflicts.

Parental Attributions and Behavior

Much of the research on parental attributions has focused on understanding the attributions of parents who are at risk for abusing their children
(Bugental & Happaney, 2002; Coplan, Hastings, Lagace-Seguin, & Moulton, 2002). For example, Dadds, Mullins, McAllister, and Atkinson (2003)
examined the relation between maternal attributions about children's behavior, reported parenting practices, and observed mother–child interactions in a study of mothers and their preschool-age child. Two groups of
mothers were included in this study, mothers who were at risk for abusing
their child—defined as those having children with behavioral problems—
and mothers of typically developing children. Mothers were videotaped interacting with their children in a laboratory setting and then interviewed regarding their emotions and attributions while watching videotaped interactions of themselves and their child.

Dadds and colleagues (2003) found that the two groups of mothers differed in their attributions and reported parenting behaviors. Upon viewing
the videotape segments, mothers at risk for abusing their child were more
likely to attribute their child's positive behaviors to external causes (e.g.,
the child was happy because of all the toys), reported being less happy
about their child's behavior, and reported that they would use more coercive strategies (e.g., threaten or enact physical punishment) in response to
the child's behaviors than mothers of typically developing children. In contrast, mothers of typically developing children were more likely to attribute
positive behaviors to internal characteristics of the child (e.g., child's personality). Examinations of the relation between the attributions of at-risk
mothers and their self-reported parenting behaviors revealed that mothers'
attributions predicted behavior in ambiguous situations (e.g., child's behavior is neither overtly positive or negative) only. In these settings, the
more the mother attributed ambiguous child behavior to internal factors
and saw the child as naughty, the more likely the mother was to report a coercive parenting response. This finding suggests that at-risk mothers appear
to attribute negative intentions to rather innocent or ambiguous child behavior and as a result are more likely to respond with more coercive
parenting strategies. Although Dadds and colleagues (2003) found no relation between parenting attributions and actual parenting behavior, other
research suggests that parents' attributions play an important role in parents' disciplinary practices.

In an experiment with 44 middle-class, European American mothers of
2-year-old children, Slep and O'Leary (1998) provided evidence of a causal
relation between maternal attributions and actual parenting behavior. During the first laboratory visit, mothers completed questionnaires and a short
interview. Before the second visit, mothers were randomly assigned to one

of two groups—the child-responsible group or the child-not-responsible group. During the second visit, mothers in the child-responsible group were taught that children were responsible for their own behaviors and that they misbehave to get their way and attract attention. Mothers in the not-responsible group were told that children's misbehavior is generally unintentional—young children, for example, lack the developmental maturity or have not yet developed self-control skills to handle situations. Mothers were then observed while they played with their child and as they helped their child clean up after the activity. After the play period, mothers were shown two short videotaped segments of this interaction and were asked questions regarding their emotional state and indirect and direct attributional assessments of their child.

No differences on outcome measures existed between mothers in the child-not-responsible and child-responsible groups before participation in the experiment. After the experimental intervention, mothers in the child-responsible condition attributed higher levels of control and more negative intentions to their child in response to their child's misbehavior than did mothers in the child-not-responsible group—indicating that the experimental manipulation worked to change mothers' beliefs about the reasons for children's misbehavior. More important, observers blind to the experimental condition judged the child-responsible mothers as being harsher and displaying more anger when they disciplined their child than mothers in the child-not-responsible condition. These data provide evidence that parents' attributions can affect their behaviors.

Parental Expectations and Behaviors

Intuitively one would expect parents' goals and expectations for their child to be related to parents' childrearing behaviors. Relatively little research, however, has directly assessed the relation between parents' goals and expectations and their behaviors. In a series of studies, Hastings and Grusec (1998) tested the hypothesis that parents' goals are related to their self-reported disciplinary strategies. In one of these studies, mothers and fathers were presented with a series of vignettes describing parent–child interactions (e.g., behaving badly in a grocery store, wanting to watch television before chores are completed) and were asked what they would do in each situation. Parents were then given a pregenerated list of goals and were asked to rate how important each goal was in the context of each vignette. The goals reflected the degree to which parents (a) wanted their child to obey and comply with their requests within a specific situation, (b) wanted to teach their child important values, and (c) wanted to develop and maintain a close parent–child relationship. As hypothesized, parents who focused on obedience and compliance were more likely to report using coercive strategies and less likely to use reasoning or responsive parenting strategies. On the other hand, parents who emphasized teaching broad values were less likely to use control tactics. A limitation to this study, of course, is that there was no measure of parents' actual behaviors, and the significant correlations between self-reported beliefs and behaviors may be due to shared method variance.

One reason for not finding strong relations between parents' goals and their behaviors is that parents' hopes and expectations may not be accompanied by an accurate knowledge of how to make them achievable (e.g., Okagaki, Frensch, & Gordon, 1995). Such a gap may be more likely to occur when parents want their children to obtain a goal that lies outside their usual routines and the tacit knowledge of their social group (Goodnow, 2002). For example, in their study of African American and European American first- and second-grade students' reading and math achievement, Alexander and Entwisle (1988) found that over time African American mothers' expectations for their child's reading and math achievement were less in tune with children's actual attainment than those of European American mothers. When reporting academic expectations, African American mothers failed to attend to indications of child preparedness, previous test performance, and maturity. Alexander and Entwisle (1988) argued that although the African American mothers highly valued schooling, they appeared to lack the experience, knowledge base, and personal resources for effective academic follow-through.

Summary

In this section, we examined the relation between parents' social cognitions and their parenting behaviors. In general, the research reviewed to this point shows low to moderate correlations between parents' beliefs, attitudes, perceptions, attributions, and expectations and their parenting behavior. A major limitation of many studies is their correlational nature. The Slep and O'Leary (1998) study is the notable exception to correlational studies of the relations between parents' social cognitions and behaviors.

The ability to understand and establish a causal connection between parents' social cognitions and parenting behaviors has important implications for parenting intervention and education programs. As parenting interventions seek to change parents' behaviors, one mechanism by which this may occur is through parents' cognitions. Consequently, if an intervention program can change parents' beliefs, one could then look for a corresponding change in parenting behavior. Studies like that of Slep and O'Leary are of significance because they give evidence that parents' beliefs can be manipulated to some degree and this manipulation does, in fact, influence parenting behaviors. More research that seeks to causally connect parenting beliefs and behaviors in this manner is necessary next step.

MOVING FORWARD IN RESEARCH ON PARENTS' SOCIAL COGNITIONS

In the past decade, researchers have begun to take a more complex view of parents' social cognitions and use more sophisticated approaches to examine the relations between parents' social cognitions and their childrearing behaviors. In this final section, we discuss new research developments and highlight the types of changes that we believe will move the field forward.

Complexity of Parents' Social Cognitions

Parents' social cognitions and their relations to parenting behaviors are more complex than researchers initially acknowledged, whether one studies parents' beliefs, attitudes, perceptions, attributions, or expectations. One of the most obvious ways in which the complexity of parents' social cognitions emerges and subsequently complicates identifying the relations between social cognitions and parenting behaviors has to do with the relations among parents' social cognitions. Current theorists (e.g., McGillicuddy-De Lisi & Sigel, 1995; Sigel & McGillicuddy-De Lisi, 2002) posit that parents' social cognitions do not function as separate, distinct factors that have a one-to-one effect on childrearing behaviors. Rather, social cognitions are thought to be interrelated such that some social cognitions may act together to potentially direct a childrearing behavior or one might moderate the effect of another on a specific behavior.

Brody, Flor, and Gibson (1999) found this to be the case in their study of African American families. In this study, mothers' perceptions of adequate family finances and their parental efficacy and their developmental goals were interrelated. When mothers perceived family resources to be more adequate, mothers were more likely to perceive their parenting as being efficacious. Parental efficacy was, in turn, related to mothers' goals for their child. The degree to which mothers perceived themselves as being effective parents was correlated with the degree to which mothers set higher expectations for their child.

Second, researchers have begun to consider the ways in which parents' social cognitions develop over time—to recognize that parents' social cognitions are not static. Researchers have suggested that when individuals first become parents, their beliefs and attitudes about childrearing are largely a function of their childhood experiences with their own parents (Daggett et al., 2000). After parents begin to accumulate experiences with their own child, with the success or failure of childrearing strategies, and with unanticipated parenting situations, they may refine their initial beliefs and acquire new ideas and attitudes related to childrearing. Goodnow (2002) has hypothesized that it is during transitions in parenthood (e.g., when one first becomes a parent, when the child becomes an adolescent, when the adolescent becomes a young adult and leaves the home) that parents are most open to new ideas about parenting and to advice from others.

In a study of first-time mothers-to-be, Scott and Hill (2001) examined mothers' beliefs prior to and 6 months after the birth of the infant. Among other findings, after 6 months of parenting, the mothers were less likely to believe that infants' behavior should be controlled by parents and more likely to believe that nurturing behaviors (e.g., showing love and affection toward child) were important. In addition, mothers' attitudes toward breastfeeding were less positive after the birth than prior to the birth. This finding suggests mothers may have preferred to breastfeed their infant, but that interaction with their infant or the experience of breastfeeding itself contributed to a change in these attitudes. It may simply have been that mothers' initial conceptions of breastfeeding their infant were unrealistic and romanticized and that after the experience of breastfeeding their infant, their attitudes toward breastfeeding were based on a more realistic understanding of what it entails.

Another illustration of change and development in parents' social cognitions comes from a study of mothers' attitudes toward corporal punishment (Holden et al., 1997). Researchers asked mothers of a 3-year-old child questions about their attitudes toward corporal punishment and if their attitude was the same as it had been before they were parents. Because the data were retrospective, the evidence for change is weaker than in the previous study, but nonetheless interesting. About two thirds of the mothers reported that their attitudes towards spanking had changed since they had become a parent. About half of these mothers indicated that they went from having a positive attitude toward spanking to being against spanking. The other half changed from being against spanking to becoming more positive toward it. Almost all of the mothers (87%) who reported developing a more positive attitude toward spanking indicated that experiences with their child had led to the change in attitude. For example, mothers reported they began to use spanking as a disciplinary strategy because they needed to use a stronger response to get their child's attention or they perceived their child as being very independent and determined such that the child needed a strong disciplinary strategy in order for the parent to gain some control over the child. Among those mothers who became less in favor of spanking, the majority (65%) reported that something about the child led them to change their attitude. For example, mothers indicated that they did not think that spanking worked with their child or the child responded so negatively to being spanked that the mother was motivated to try other methods of discipline.

A third way in which researchers have begun to recognize the complexity of parents' social cognitions and their relations to parents' behaviors is by attending to the congruence between the content of the social cognition and the type of behavior being measured. Haight, Parke, and Black (1997), for example, examined parents' beliefs about children's pretend play and a play session involving the parents with their child. In this study, parents were observed playing with their child at 24, 30, and 36 months of age and were interviewed about their preferred type of parent–child interaction (e.g., pretend, rough and tumble, and book reading) and their beliefs about the developmental significance of such activities. The results reveal that mothers' beliefs about the importance of pretend play in promoting their child's development and ratings of the importance of parental partici-pation in this type of play predicted the proportion of parent–child play time spent in pretend play ($r = .34$ and $r = .36$, respectively). Although the correlations between beliefs and behaviors for mothers were modest, when compared to previous findings suggesting weak or no relation between mothers' beliefs and behaviors, they appear to support the assertion that examining the congruence between the content of the social cognition and the type of behavior being measured is important.

Methodological Developments

Over a decade ago, developmental researchers were challenged to utilize work by social and cognitive psychologists in order to forward our under-standing of parents' social cognitions (e.g., Goodnow, 1988; Goodnow & Collins, 1990; Holden & Edwards, 1989). To date, our progress has not taken advantage of many innovative approaches from other psychological sciences, and exhortations to strengthen the methodologies used by par-enting researchers continue (e.g., Goodnow, 2002; Holden & Buck, 2002). Data on parents' social cognitions, for example, have generally been ob-tained through self-report questionnaires. Much empirical evidence has ac-cumulated documenting the pitfalls to creating good items and good in-struments for obtaining reliable, valid, and interpretable data (e.g., see Schwarz, 1999). Inconsistent results across studies may result, in part, from the use of different instruments and a lack of attention, for instance, to how rating scales, reference periods, question format, and surrounding ques-tions can affect parents' responses.

Social and cognitive psychologists have used experimental paradigms to determine the effects of social cognitions on the ways in which individuals process information, make decisions, and behave. Using priming tech-niques, social psychologists have determined, for example, that stereotypes about an individual's social group can affect performance in domains that are important to the individual's self-concept—a phenomenon that Steele has labeled *stereotype-threat* (Steele, 1997). Evoking negative stereotypes in experimental settings has been shown to lower math performances of women (Spencer, Steele, & Quinn, 1999) and of European American men (where the negative stereotype was a comparison to Asian students; Aronson et al., 1999). General stereotypes about fathers' ineptness with infants, for instance, might affect fathers' caregiving behaviors with their infant.

Social psychologists have long known that preexisting social cognitions about a person or situation affect the way in which individuals process new information relevant to that person or situation (Fiske & Taylor, 1991). Initially, when people are in the process of developing beliefs, perceptions, and attitudes about a person—a schema of that person—they are open to new information. Over time, however, that schema or view of the person becomes established, and anomalous information tends to be disregarded or made to fit with the existing view. For example, in experimental conditions using priming techniques, evoking positive or negative attitudes about a person diminishes an individual's ability to perceive change in that person (Fazio, Ledbetter, & Towles-Schwen, 2000). Consider the parent who has been struggling to encourage his adolescent son to behave more responsibly, to act more maturely, and to conform to what the father sees as being more conventional ways of presenting oneself in public. If the father's conception or schema of his son is set, is the father less likely to notice and support the small changes in the son's behavior as the son moves toward adulthood?

Finally, we consider work on implicit social cognition. Greenwald and Banaji (1995) have applied an implicit memory or implicit cognition model to understanding social cognition. Implicit memory refers to instances in which the memory of an experience is not accessible to the individual at the level of conscious recall of the experience, but it affects performance. One hypothesis for explaining the lack of consistent, strong correlations between self-report of social cognitions and observed behaviors is that social cognitions may affect behavior at a subconscious level—that is, when individuals cannot directly recall or are not consciously aware of drawing on those social cognitions to inform their behavior. In experimental studies, for example, when people judge individuals who are physically attractive and unattractive, they generally attribute more positive characteristics to and rate more favorably the work of those who are attractive (e.g., Eagly, Ashmore, Makhijani, & Longo, 1991). However, those who are making these judgments are not consciously aware that their judgments are influenced by their stereotypes of attractive and unattractive people—that they are affected by implicit social cognitions. The previous examples of stereotype threat and of instances in which preexisting schemas interfere with the processing of anomalous data are also consistent with an implicit social cognition framework. Greenwald and Banaji suggest that social cognitions may generally be expressed in behavior through an implicit mode. Research on implicit social cognitions and parenting behaviors may result in stronger and more consistent relations between the two.

CONCLUSION

In this chapter we have considered the development and maintenance of parents' social cognitions with a specific focus on how these cognitions are related to parenting behavior. Our examination of research on parents' social cognitions is in three areas. First, we considered how ecological factors serve as a source for the development of parents' social cognitions. Given the limitations of space in this chapter, we focused our discussion on macro-level factors, culture and SES, that appear to impact the development and maintenance of parents' social cognitions. Our review suggests that parents' ideas appear to be related to broader cultural values. However, our knowledge of the role that culture and SES play in the formation of beliefs is limited. Few studies have specifically measured these broader cultural values and explicitly correlated them with measures of parents' social cognitions. Researchers have also relied too heavily on Western psychological perspectives and theories when studying non-Western cultures. Finally, given the correlational and cross-sectional nature of the majority of research on parents' social cognitions, our understanding of actual causal influences on the development and maintenance of parents' social cognitions is limited.

Second, we considered research that connects parents' social cognitions to their parenting behaviors. One overarching theme of this research is that, although parents' social cognitions have been linked with parenting behavior, the majority of these links are weak. Further, research on parents' social cognitions and behaviors has generally failed to verify a causal relation between the two. Another limitation of current belief–behavior research is the way in which parents' social cognitions are measured (e.g., mixing different types of social cognitions into a single scale, low reliability of scales). Much research relies on parents' reports to measure both social cognitions and behaviors, which may inflate the relation between the two.

Third, progress is being made in better conceptualization and measurement of parents' social cognitions. Promising methodologies and theoretical perspectives have emerged from social cognitive research. These approaches should prove useful in helping us gain a better understanding of the interrelated nature of parents' social cognitions, as well as a clearer picture of the degree to which social cognitions connect to parenting behaviors, particularly over time.

Identifying the relations among parents' social cognitions, and between social cognitions and childrearing behaviors, may provide keys to understanding what drives parenting behaviors. Theoretically this type of work also addresses the broader psychological questions of how different social cognitions are related to each other and how competing (or related) social cognitions may affect a specific behavior. Pragmatically a better understanding of the relation between social cognitions and behavior should strengthen our ability to develop effective parent intervention programs.

ACKNOWLEDGMENTS

We would like to thank Tom Luster and Marc Bornstein for their helpful editorial comments with previous drafts of this manuscript.

REFERENCES

Alexander, K. L., & Entwisle, D. R. (1988). Achievement in the first two years of school: Patterns and processes. *Monographs for the Society for Research in Child Development, 53*(Serial No. 218).

Aronson, J., Lustina, M. J., Good, C., Keough, K., Steele, C. M., & Brown, J. (1999). When white men can't do math: Necessary and sufficient factors in stereotype threat. *Journal of Experimental Social Psychology, 35*, 29–46.

Bartkowski, J. P., & Ellison, C. G. (1995). Divergent models of childrearing in popular manuals: Conservative Protestants vs. the mainstream experts. *Sociology of Religion, 56*(1), 21–34.

Bates, J., Bayles, K., Bennet, D. S., Ridge, B., & Brown, M. (1991). Origins of externalizing behavior problems at eight years of age. In D. J. Pepler & K. H. Rubin (Eds.), *The development and treatment of childhood aggression* (pp. 93–120). Hillsdale, NJ: Lawrence Erlbaum Associates.

Benasich, A. A., & Brooks-Gunn, J. (1996). Maternal attitudes and knowledge of child-rearing: Associations with family and child outcomes. *Child Development, 67*, 1186–1205.

Blacher, J., Nihira, K., & Meyers, C. E. (1987). Characteristics of home environment of families with mentally retarded children: Comparisons across levels of retardation. *American Journal of Mental Deficiency, 91*, 313–320.

Bornstein, M. H., Haynes, O. M., Azuma, H., Galperin, C., Maital, S., Ogino, M., et al. (1998). A cross-national study of self-evaluations and attributions in parenting: Argentina, Belgium, France, Israel, Italy, Japan, and the United States. *Developmental Psychology, 34*, 662–676.

Bornstein, M. H., Tamis-LeMonda, C. S., Pascual, L., Haynes, O. M., Painter, L. M., Galperin, C. Z., et al. (1996). Ideas about parenting in Argentina, Belgium, France, and the United States. *International Journal of Behavioral Development, 19*, 347–367.

Brody, G. H., Flor, F. L., & Gibson, N. M. (1999). Linking maternal efficacy beliefs, developmental goals, parenting practices, and child competence in rural single-parent African American families. *Child Development, 70*, 1197–1208.

Bronfenbrenner, U. (1979). *The ecology of human development: Experiments by nature and design.* Cambridge, MA: Harvard University Press.

Bugental, D. B., & Happaney, K. (2002). Parental attributions. In M. H. Bornstein (Ed.), *Handbook of parenting: Vol. 3. Status and social conditions of parenting* (pp. 509–535). Mahwah, NJ: Lawrence Erlbaum Associates.

Chao, R. K. (1994). Beyond parental control and authoritarian parenting style: Understanding Chinese parenting through the cultural notion of training. *Child Development, 65,* 1111–1119.

Chao, R. K. (1996). Chinese and European American mothers' beliefs about the role of parenting in children's school success. *Journal of Cross-Cultural Psychology, 27,* 403–423.

Chao, R. K. (2000). The parenting of immigrant Chinese and European American mothers: Relations between parenting styles, socialization goals, and parental practices. *Journal of Applied Developmental Psychology, 21,* 233–248.

Chen, X., Hastings, P. D., Rubin, K. H., Chen, H., Cen, G., & Stewart, S. L. (1998). Childrearing attitudes and behavioral inhibition in Chinese and Canadian toddlers: A cross-cultural study. *Developmental Psychology, 34,* 677–686.

Chen, Z. Y., & Uttal, D. H. (1988). Cultural values, parents' beliefs, and children's achievement in the United States and China. *Human Development, 31,* 351–358.

Chiang, T., Barrett, K. C., & Nunez, N. N. (2000). Maternal attributions of Taiwanese and American toddlers' misdeeds and accomplishments. *Journal of Cross-Cultural Psychology, 31,* 349–368.

Cicognani, E., & Zani, B. (1998). Parents' educational style and adolescent autonomy. *European Journal of Psychology of Education, 13,* 485–502.

Coleman, P. K., & Karraker, K. H. (1998). Self-efficacy and parenting quality: Findings and future applications. *Developmental Review, 18,* 47–85.

Coleman, P. K., & Karraker, K. H. (2003). Maternal self-efficacy beliefs, competence in parenting, and toddlers' behavior and developmental status. *Infant Mental Health Journal, 24,* 126–148.

Coplan, R. J., Hastings, P. D., Lagace-Seguin, D. G., & Moulton, C. E. (2002). Authoritative and authoritarian mothers' parenting goals, attributions, an emotions across different childrearing contexts. *Parenting: Science & Practice, 2,* 1–26.

Cote, L. R., & Bornstein, M. H. (2003). Cultural and parenting cognitions in acculturating cultures: 1. Cultural comparisons and developmental continuity and stability. *Journal of Cross-Cultural Psychology, 34,* 323–349.

Crouter, A. C. (1984). Participative work as an influence on human development. *Human Development, 5,* 71–90.

Dadds, M. R. (1987). Families and the origins of child behavior problems. *Family Process, 26,* 341–357.

Dadds, M. R., Mullins, M. J., McAllister, R. A., & Atkinson, E. (2003). Attributions, affect, and behavior in abuse-risk mothers: A laboratory study. *Child Abuse and Neglect, 27,* 21–45.

Daggett, J., O'Brien, M., Zanolli, K., & Peyton, V. (2000). Parents' attitudes about children: Associations with parental life histories and child-rearing quality. *Journal of Family Psychology, 14,* 187–199.

Danso, H., Hunsberger, B., & Pratt, M. (1997). The role of parental religious fundamentalism and right-wing authoritarianism in child-rearing goals and practices. *Journal for the Scientific Study of Religion, 36,* 496–511.

DeBaryshe, B. D. (1995). Maternal belief systems: Linchpin in home reading process. *Journal of Applied Developmental Psychology, 16,* 1–20.

Dix, T. (1992). Parenting on behalf of the child: Empathic goals in the regulation of responsive parenting. In I. E. Sigel, A. V. McGillicuddy-De Lisi, & J. J. Goodnow (Eds.), *Parental belief systems: The psychological consequences for children* (2nd ed., pp. 319–346). Hillsdale, NJ: Lawrence Erlbaum Associates.

Donahue, M. L., Pearl, R., & Herzog, A. (1997). Referential communication with preschoolers: Effects of children's syntax and mothers' beliefs. *Journal of Applied Developmental Psychology, 18,* 133–147.

Dornbusch, S. M., Ritter, P. L., Leiderman, P. H., Roberts, D. F., & Faleigh, M. J. (1987). The relation of parenting style to adolescent school performance. *Child Development, 58,* 1244–1257.

Eagly, A. H., Ashmore, R. D., Makhijani, M. G., & Longo, L. C. (1991). What is beautiful is good, but . . . : A meta-analytic review of research on the physical attractiveness stereotype. *Psychological Bulletin, 110,* 109–128.

Ellison, C. G., & Sherkat, D. E. (1993). Obedience and autonomy: Religion and parental values reconsidered. *Journal for the Scientific Study of Religion, 32*(4), 313–329.

Entwisle, D. R., & Hayduk, L. A. (1978). *Too great expectations: The academic outlook of young children.* Baltimore, MD: Johns Hopkins University Press.

Fazio, R. H., Ledbetter, J. E., & Towles-Schwen, T. (2000). On the costs of accessible attitudes: Detecting that the attitude object has changed. *Journal of Personality and Social Psychology, 78,* 197–210.

Fiske, S. T., & Taylor, S. E. (1991). *Social cognition.* New York: McGraw-Hill.

Gershoff, E. T., Miller, P. C., & Holden, G. W. (1999). Parenting influences from the pulpit: Religious affiliation as a determinant of parental corporal punishment. *Journal of Family Psychology, 13,* 307–320.

Goodnow, J. J. (1988). Parents' ideas, actions, and feelings: Models and method from developmental and social psychology. *Child Development, 59,* 286–320.

Goodnow, J. J. (1995). Parent's knowledge and expectations. In M. H. Bornstein (Ed.), *Handbook of parenting: Vol. 3. Status and social conditions of parenting* (pp. 305–332). Mahwah, NJ: Lawrence Erlbaum Associates.

Goodnow, J. J. (2002). Parents' knowledge and expectations: Using what we know. In M. H. Bornstein (Ed.), *Handbook of parenting: Vol. 3. Being and becoming a parent* (pp. 439–460). Mahwah, NJ: Lawrence Erlbaum Associates.

Goodnow, J. J., & Collins, W. A. (1990). *Development according to parents: The nature, sources, and consequences of parents' ideas.* Hillsdale, NJ: Lawrence Erlbaum Associates.

Gorman, J. C. (1998). Parenting attitudes and practices of immigrant Chinese mothers of adolescents. *Family Relations, 47,* 73–80.

Greenberger, E., O'Neil, R., & Nagel, S. K. (1994). Linking workplace and homeplace: Relations between the nature of adults' work and their parenting behaviors. *Developmental Psychology, 30,* 990–1002.

Greenwald, A. G., & Banaji, M. R. (1995). Implicit social cognitions: Attitudes, self-esteem, and stereotypes. *Psychological Review, 102,* 4–27.

Grusec, J. E. Goodnow, J. J., & Kuczynski, L. (2000). New directions in analyses of parenting contributions to children's acquisition of values. *Child Development, 71,* 205–211.

Haight, W. L, Parke, R. D., & Black, J. E. (1997). Mothers' and fathers' beliefs about and spontaneous participation in their toddlers' pretend play. *Merrill-Palmer Quarterly, 43,* 271–290.

Hao, L., & Bornstead-Bruns, M. (1998). Parent–child differences in educational expectations and the academic achievement of immigrant and native students. *Sociology of Education, 71,* 175–198.

Harkness, S., & Super, C. (Eds.). (1996). *Parents' cultural belief systems: Their origins, expressions, and consequences.* New York: Guilford.

Harrison, A. O., Wilson, M. N., Pine, C. J., Chan, S. Q., & Buriel, R. (1990). Family ecologies of ethnic minority children. *Child Development, 61,* 347–362.

Harwood, R. L. (1992). The influence of culturally derived values on Anglo and Puerto Rican mothers' perceptions of attachment behavior. *Child Development, 63,* 822–839.

Harwood, R. L., Handwerker, W. P., Schoelmerich, A., & Leyendecker, B. (2001). Ethnic category labels, parental beliefs, and the contextualized individual: An exploration of the individualism–sociocentrism debate. *Parenting: Science and Practice, 1,* 217–236.

Harwood, R. L., Schoelmerich, A., & Schulze, P. A. (2000). Homogeneity and heterogeneity in cultural belief systems. In S. Harkness & C. Raeff (Eds.), *Variability in social construction of the child* (pp. 41–57). San Francisco, CA: Jossey-Bass.

Hastings, P. D., & Grusec, J. E. (1998). Parenting goals as organizers of responses to parent–child disagreement. *Developmental Psychology, 34,* 465–479.

Hess, R. D., Chih-Mei, C., & McDevitt, T. M. (1987). Cultural variations in family beliefs about children's performance in mathematics: Comparisons among People's Republic of Chinese, Chinese American, and Caucasian American families. *Journal of Educational Psychology, 79,* 179–188.

Ho, D. Y. F. (1994). Cognitive socialization in Confucian heritage cultures. In P. M. Greenfield & R. R. Cocking (Eds.), *Cross-cultural roots of minority child development* (pp. 285–313). Hillsdale, NJ: Lawrence Erlbaum Associates.

Hoff, E., Laursen, B., & Tardif, T. (2002). Socioeconomic status and parenting. In M. H. Bornstein (Ed.), *Handbook of parenting: Vol. 2. Biology and ecology of parenting* (pp. 231–252). Mahwah, NJ: Lawrence Erlbaum Associates.

Holden, G. W., & Buck, M. J. (2002). Parental attitudes toward childrearing. In M. H. Bornstein (Ed.), *Handbook of parenting: Vol. 3. Being and becoming a parent* (pp. 537–562). Mahwah, NJ: Lawrence Erlbaum Associates.

Holden, G. W., & Edwards, J. (1989). Parental attitudes toward child rearing: Instruments, issues, and implications. *Psychological Bulletin, 125,* 223–254.

Holden, G. W., & Miller, P. C. (1999). Enduring and different: A meta-analysis of the similarity in parents' child rearing. *Psychological Bulletin, 125,* 223–254.

Holden, G. W., Thompson, E. E., Zambarano, R. J., & Marshall, L. A. (1997). Child effects as a source of change in maternal attitudes toward corporal punishment. *Journal of Social and Personal Relationships, 14,* 481–490.

Iverson, T. J., & Segal, M. (1992). Social behavior of maltreated children: Exploring links to parent behavior and beliefs. In I. E. Sigel, A. McGillicuddy-De Lisi, & J. J. Goodnow (Eds.), *Parental beliefs systems: The psychological consequences for children* (2nd ed., pp. 267–289). Hillsdale, NJ: Lawrence Erlbaum Associates.

Jambunathan, S., Burts, D. C., & Pierce, S. (2000). Comparisons of parenting attitudes among five ethnic groups in the United States. *Journal of Comparative Family Studies, 31,* 395–406.

Joe, J., & Malach, R. S. (1992). Families with Native American roots. In E. W. Lynch & M. J. Hanson (Eds.), *Developing cross-cultural competence: A guide for working with young children and their families* (pp. 89–119). Baltimore: Paul H. Brookes Publishing.

Kinlaw, C. R., Kurtz-Costes, B., & Goldman-Fraser, J. (2001). Mothers' achievement beliefs and behaviors and their children's school readiness: A cultural comparison. *Applied Developmental Psychology, 22,* 493–506.

Kochanska, G., Kuczynski, L., & Radke-Yarrow, M. (1989). Correspondence between mothers' self-reported and observed child-rearing practices. *Child Development, 60,* 56–63.

Kohn, M. L. (1963). Social class and parent–child relationships: An interpretation. *American Journal of Sociology, 18,* 471–480.

Kohn, M. L. (1969). *Class and conformity: A study in values.* Homewood, IL: The Dorsey Press.

Kohn, M. L. (1979). The effects of social class on parental values and practices. In D. Reiss & H. Hoffman (Eds.), *The American family: Dying or developing* (pp. 45–68). New York: Plenum.

Kohn, M. L., & Schooler, C. (1983). *Work and personality: An inquiry into the impact of social stratification.* Norwood, NJ: Ablex.

LeVine, R. A. (1988). Human parental care: Universal goals, cultural strategies, and individual behavior. In W. Damon (Series Ed.) & R. A. Levine, P. M. Miller, & M. M. West (Vol. Eds.), *New directions for child development: Parental behavior in diverse societies* (Vol. 40, pp. 3–11). San Francisco: Jossey-Bass.

Machamer, A. M., & Gruber, E. (1998). Secondary school, family, and educational risk: Comparing American Indian adolescents and their peers. *Journal of Educational Research, 91,* 357–369.

Mansbach, I. V., & Greenbaum, C. W. (1999). Developmental maturity expectations of Israeli fathers and mothers: Effects of education, ethnic origin, and religiosity. *International Journal of Behavioral Development, 23,* 771–797.

Mantizicopoulos, P. Y. (1997). The relationship of family variables to Head Start children's preacademic competence. *Early Education and Development, 8,* 357–375.

Marks, L. D., & Dollahite, D. C. (2001). Religion, relationships, and responsible fathering in Latter-day Saint families of children with special needs. *Journal of Social and Personal Relationships, 18,* 625–650.

McGillicuddy-De Lisi, A. V., & Sigel, I. E. (1995). Parental beliefs. In M. H. Bornstein (Ed.), *Handbook of parenting: Vol. 3. Status and social conditions of parenting* (pp. 333–358). Mahwah, NJ: Lawrence Erlbaum Associates.

Miller, J., Schooler, C., Kohn, M. L., & Hiller, K. A. (1979). Women and work: The psychological effects of occupational conditions. *American Journal of Sociology, 85,* 66–94.

Miller, S. A. (1987). *Developmental research methods.* Englewood Cliffs, NJ: Prentice-Hall.

Musun-Miller, L., & Blevins-Knabe, B. (1998). Adults' beliefs about children and mathematics. *Early Development and Parenting, 7,* 191–202.

Nix, R. L., Pinderhughes, E. E., Dodge, K. A., Bates, J. E., Pettit, G. S., & McFadyen-Ketchum, S. A. (1999). The relation between mothers' hostile attribution tendencies and children's externalizing behavior problems: The mediating role of mothers' harsh discipline practices. *Child Development, 70,* 896–909.

Ogbu, J. U. (1981). Origins of human competence: A cultural-ecological perspective. *Child Development, 52,* 413–429.

Okagaki, L., & Divecha, D. J. (1993). Development of parental beliefs. In T. Luster & L. Okagaki (Eds.), *Parenting: An ecological perspective* (1st ed., pp. 35–67). Hillsdale, NJ: Lawrence Erlbaum Associates.

Okagaki, L., & Frensch, P. A. (1998). Parenting and children's school achievement: A multiethnic perspective. *American Educational Research Journal, 35,* 123–144.

Okagaki, L., Frensch, P. A., & Gordon, E. W. (1995). Encouraging school achievement in Mexican American children. *Hispanic Journal of Behavioral Sciences, 17,* 160–179.

Okagaki, L., & Sternberg, R. J. (1991). *Directors of development: Influences on the development of children's thinking.* Hillsdale, NJ: Lawrence Erlbaum Associates.

Papoušek, H., & Papoušek, M. (1995). Intuitive parenting. In M. H. Bornstein (Ed.), *Handbook of parenting: Vol. 2. Biology and ecology of parenting* (pp. 117–136). Mahwah, NJ: Lawrence Erlbaum Associates.

Perozynski, L., & Kramer, L. (1999). Parental beliefs about managing sibling conflict. *Developmental Psychology, 35,* 489–499.

Rose, G. M., Dalakas, V., & Kropp, F. (2002). A five-nation study of developmental timetables, reciprocal communication and consumer socialization. *Journal of Business Research, 55,* 943–949.

Rubin, K. H., Nelson, L. J., Hastings, P., & Asendorpf, J. (1999). The transaction between parents' perceptions of their children's shyness and their parenting styles. *International Journal of Behavioral Development, 23,* 937–958.

Russell, A. (1997). Individual and family factors contributing to mothers' and fathers' positive parenting. *International Journal of Behavioral Development, 21,* 111–132.

Schulze, P. A., Harwood, R. L., & Schoelmerich, A. (2001). Feeding practices and expectations among middle-class Anglo and Puerto Rican mothers of 12-month-old infants. *Journal of Cross-Cultural Psychology, 32,* 397–406.

Schulze, P. A., Harwood, R. L., Schoelmerich, A., & Leyendecker, B. (2002). The cultural structuring of parenting and universal developmental tasks. *Parenting: Science & Practice, 2,* 151–178.

Scott, D. A., & Hill, J. (2001). Stability and change in parenting beliefs in first-time mothers from the pre- to postnatal period. *Journal of Reproductive and Infant Psychology, 19,* 105–119.

Schwarz, N. (1999). Self-reports: How the questions shape the answers. *American Psychologist, 54,* 93–105.

Seginer, R. (1983). Parents' educational expectations and children's academic achievements: A literature review. *Merrill-Palmer Quarterly, 29,* 1–23.

Sigel, I. E. (Ed.). (1985). *Parental belief systems: The psychological consequences for children.* Hillsdale, NJ: Lawrence Erlbaum Associates.

Sigel, I. E. (1992). The belief behavior connection: A resolvable dilemma? In I. E. Sigel, A. V. McGillicuddy-De Lisi, & J. J. Goodnow (Eds.), *Parental belief systems: The psychological consequences for children* (2nd ed., pp. 433–456). Hillsdale, NJ: Lawrence Erlbaum Associates.

Sigel, I. E., & McGillicuddy-De Lisi, A. V. (2002). Parental beliefs are cognitions: The dynamic belief systems model. In M. H. Bornstein (Ed.), *Handbook of parenting: Vol. 3. Status and social conditions of parenting* (pp. 333–358). Mahwah, NJ: Lawrence Erlbaum Associates.

Slep, A. M. S., & O'Leary, S. G. (1998). The effects of maternal attributions on parenting: An experimental analysis. *Journal of Family Psychology, 12,* 234–243.

Spence, J. T. (1985). Achievement American style: The rewards and costs of individualism. *American Psychologist, 40,* 1285–1295.

Spencer, S. J., Steele, C. M., & Quinn, D. M. (1999). Stereotype threat and women's math performance. *Journal of Experimental Social Psychology, 35,* 4–28.

Steele, C. M. (1997). A threat in the air: How stereotypes shape intellectual identity and performance. *American Psychologist, 52,* 613–629.

Steinberg, L., Dornbusch, S. M., & Brown, B. B. (1992). Ethnic differences in adolescent achievement: An ecological perspective. *American Psychologist, 47,* 723–729.

Steinberg, L., Mounts, N. S., Lamborn, S. D., & Dornbusch, S. M. (1991). Authoritative parenting and adolescent adjustment across varied ecological niches. *Journal of Research on Adolescence, 1,* 19–36.

Stevens, J. H. (1984). Child development knowledge and parenting skill. *Family Relations, 33,* 237–244.

Stevenson, H. W., Chen, C., & Lee, S. (1993). Mathematics achievement of Chinese, Japanese, and American children: Ten years later. *Science, 259,* 53–58.

Stevenson, H. W., & Lee, S. (1990). Contexts of achievement. *Monographs of the Society for Research in Child Development, 55*(Serial No. 221).

Stevenson, H. W., Lee, S., & Stigler, J. W. (1986). Mathematics achievement of Chinese, Japanese, and American children. *Science, 231,* 693–699.

Triandis, H. C. (1995). The self and social behavior in differing cultural contexts. *Psychological Review, 96,* 506–520.

Triandis, H. C., Bontempo, R., Villareal, M. H., Asai, M., & Lucca, N. (1988). Individualism and collectivism: Cross cultural perspectives on self–ingroup relationships. *Journal of Personality and Social Psychology, 54,* 323–338.

Vargas, M., & Busch-Rossnagel, N. A. (2003). Teaching behaviors and styles of low-income Puerto Rican mothers. *Applied Developmental Science, 7,* 229–238.

von der Lippe, A. L. (1999). The impact of maternal schooling and occupation on child-rearing attitudes and behaviors in low income neighborhoods in Cairo, Egypt. *International Journal of Behavioral Development, 23,* 703–729.

Williams, P. D., Williams, A. R., Lopez, M., & Tayko, N. P. (2000). Mothers' developmental expectations for young children in the Philippines. *International Journal of Nursing Studies, 37,* 291–301.

2

Developmental Origins of Parenting: Personality and Relationship Factors

Joan Vondra
University of Pittsburgh

Helen Bittmann Sysko
Mercy Behavioral Health
Pittsburgh, PA

Jay Belsky
Birkbeck University of London

INTRODUCTION

The premise and starting point for this, and probably any, discussion of parenting is a simple one. Individual differences in parenting depend on who the parent is, first, as an individual psychological agent and, second, as a partner in close relationships. All the intrinsic qualities that shape an individual's psychological functioning—his or her personality and temperament, physical and mental health, intelligence, maturity, gender, physical attractiveness and so on—will also shape what kind of partner he or she is in close relationships. These same qualities will also influence what kind of partner he or she chooses for close relationships, as well as the quality of the relationship the two co-create. Every close relationship, in turn, has important effects on the Psychological well-being and functioning of each partner.

These points have several implications for a discussion of the developmental origins of parenting. First, there is an inherent confound in any ex post facto investigation of parenting: Psychological functioning and relationship functioning are inextricably interconnected. One cannot take the "person" out of the parent any more than one can separate the "person" from the relationship in which he or she is a partner. This is as true of a parent in a parent–child relationship as it is of a parent in his or her adult intimate relationships. Therefore, when we choose to discuss personality at one point, relationship history at another, and developmental and experiential effects at still another, the distinction is, in many ways, an artificial one. Every association studied between past or current parent psychological functioning, relationship behavior, relationship quality, and child functioning reflects some of the same key psychological differences between people, as well as differences in how their relationships are played out.

Second, it would be presumptuous to consider only experiential factors that contribute to individual differences in parenting. Obviously, both individual and relationship functioning, and even the effects on the individual of relationship functioning, have a greater or lesser basis in parent physiology and genetic inheritance (Reiss & Neiderhiser, 2000). Associations and group differences that are reported and discussed in this chapter should always be viewed from the lens of biology and genetics as well as that of socialization and experience. An even-tempered individual who responds to crying infants and squabbling siblings with calmness and equanimity, is more likely to be a spouse who doesn't fly off the handle in the face of some irritable criticism by his or her partner. This may be an adult with more consistency in ambient levels of hormones across the day (Jacklin, 1989) which is, in turn, a product of genetic predisposition, a generally calm and relaxed home environment when growing up, selection of a reasonably well-adjusted partner, current family circumstances, and so forth. It seems quite clear from recent research that one's physiology (and therefore psychological functioning) reflects current environment as well as genetics and past experience (Reiss & Neiderhiser, 2000).

We begin our analysis with a summary of evidence suggesting that personality characteristics and relationship attributes contribute to individual differences in parenting. We also discuss hypothesized processes of influence linking personality and relationships with parenting functioning. We then examine theoretical and research models of the impact of developmental history on individual and dyadic functioning in adulthood. We attempt to highlight work that elaborates both conditions of continuity and discontinuity across generations and over time. It is worth noting that evidence for either inoculating or cataclysmic effects of early parenting— when within the normal range—is sparse. Instead, the interplay of genes, physiology, and experience continually shapes and reshapes the developing individual, even as familiar patterns of functioning often re-emerge, but also re-form over time.

PERSONALITY AND PARENTING

Some two decades ago, Belsky proposed a model of the determinants of parenting that assigns to personality a central role in filtering sociocontextual influences on parenting (Belsky, 1984; Belsky & Vondra, 1985). In essence, he argued that the impact of marriage, work, social support, and developmental history on parenting are, in part, mediated through their effects on individual psychological functioning. For example, a conflicted marital relationship may alter parental (and child) functioning directly, as when disagreement about childrearing interferes with effective child guidance. But much of the impact may be expressed through changes in parental psychological functioning. Increased parental distress, irritability, and depression resulting from marital conflict may lead to impatience, inconsistency, and/or emotional unavailability as a parent. In the long run, experiences of victimization, emotional coercion, powerlessness in a relationship, and a host of other emotional lessons may alter how a parent understands and adapts in relationships, even reshaping how he or she relates to his or her children over time. In the earlier edition of this volume (Vondra & Belsky, 1993), we devoted the section on personality and parenting to three general topics: parental psychological differentiation, negative affectivity, and psychological impairment. In this edition, we focus more exclusively on personality characteristics as they are conceptualized within the *Big Five* factor model of personality, described below. This is not to deny the critical influence of psychological health and maturity on parenting. Work based on clinical samples of depressed mothers (Carter et al., 2001; Murray & Cooper, 1997; Radke-Yarrow, 1998), parents battling alcoholism (Eiden, Chavez, & Leonard, 1999; Whipple, Fitzgerald, & Zucker, 1995; Zucker & Gomberg, 1986) and drug use (Beckwith, Howard, Espinosa, & Tyler, 1999; Burns, Chethik, Burns, & Clark, 1997; Dunn et al., 2001), and parents with other forms of mental illness (Hipwell, Goossens, Melhuish, & Kumar, 2000) continues to demonstrate associations between chronicity and severity of psychological disturbance and impairment in parental caregiving. Those forms of mental illness that most interfere with parent attentional and emotional responsiveness to their children appear most disruptive to their capacity to provide supportive care. Likewise, psychological maturity or immaturity, intelligence, and level of empathy—qualities broadly captured within the construct of *psychological differentiation*—are also fairly consistently implicated in correlational studies of parenting differences (McGroder, 2000; van Bakel & Riksen-Walraven, 2002).

Across the continuum from psychological differentiation and maturity to psychological disturbance and mental illness, the story line is similar. As personal psychological resources increase, so does a parent's ability to take the perspective of the child, avoid attributing negative intent to child transgressions, and provide sensitive care. Parent personality and adjustment are, in some sense, the most proximal determinants of parenting. Thus, parent psychological functioning is arguably the linchpin for a host of contextual factors that affect parenting.

We choose in this edition to focus more exclusively on variation in major characteristics of personality that have been identified through studies of nonclinical populations. Thus, we shift our lens away from the health/pathology dimension of psychological functioning to the personality dimension. However, in both cases, it is important to think in terms of bi-directional influence. That is, both psychological health and personality shape and are shaped by a person's physiology (e.g., neural reactivity and regulation), as well as by his or her choices: whether to stay on or leave school, what jobs to pursue and how to behave in the workplace, which friends and intimates to select and how to contribute to those relationships, whether or not to plan for pregnancy, and so forth. To varying degrees, a person chooses and alters his or her context, but the experiences that ensue then alter the person (e.g., Kim, Conger, Elder, & Lorenz, 2003).

In this section, we describe major facets of adult personality and their connections to parenting. We organize discussion of personality and parenting around these core dimensions of personality, then consider psychological mechanisms that may account for how personality comes to be related to parenting.

The Big Five Model of Personality

Despite early interest by psychoanalytically oriented investigators in parental personality characteristics and their effects on parenting behavior, the study of these issues was interrupted by important shifts within the field of personality psychology during the 1970s and into the 1980s (see Caspi, 1998, for review). A major contribution to the re-emergence of personality as an important area of inquiry came from acknowledging and embracing The Big Five factor model of personality, which did much to organize a rather disparate area of inquiry. The Big Five factors—neuroticism, extraversion, openness to experience, agreeableness, and conscientiousness—were identified first by Tupes and Christal (1961), who found through factor analytic techniques that long lists of personality variables compiled by Cattell (1943, 1945) could be reduced to five broad-band personality factors. This five-factor structure has since been replicated in diverse samples and across numerous raters, including self, peers, and clinicians (John & Srivastava, 1999).

Neuroticism. Neuroticism reflects adjustment versus emotional instability, and measures of neuroticism identify individuals prone to psychological distress, unrealistic ideas, excessive cravings or urges, and maladaptive coping responses. A person scoring high on this trait worries a lot, is nervous, emotional, insecure, and feels inadequate, whereas a person scoring low is calm, relaxed, unemotional, hardy, secure and self-satisfied. Because factor analytic studies indicate that indices of the negative emotions of anxiety, hostility and depression all load on a single factor (Costa & McCrae, 1992)—whether measured as states or traits—some prefer to use the term *negative affectivity* rather than neuroticism (Tellegen, Watson, & Clark, 1999; Watson & Clark, 1984). The important point is less what this trait is called than what this trait reflects. And the fact that it reflects the proclivity or disposition to experience anxiety and hostility as well as depression raises important questions about all the work carried out on depression and mothering in the field of developmental psychology over the past two decades. One is forced to wonder whether studies in which only depressive symptoms are measured report data pertaining only to depression and mothering or, instead, capture negative affectivity more generally, including anxiety and hostility. Until these other negative-emotion facets of neuroticism are examined in studies (of normal and clinical samples) that also include measures of depressive symptoms or even diagnoses of clinical depression, it will be impossible to address this issue.

The fact that the empirical literature is the way it is means that much of the work to be considered in this section deals with depressive symptomatology. But we restrict ourselves here to research dealing with depressive symptoms measured as a continuous variable in nonclinical samples because it is highly likely that higher and lower scores on measured depression also reflect higher and lower scores, respectively, on the broader construct of neuroticism/negative affectivity. We begin with investigations focused on parents of infants and proceed developmentally from that point forward.

During the infancy period, (maternal) depression has been the facet of neuroticism receiving the most empirical attention. Although the evidence is not always consistent, there is repeated indication, even in nonclinical samples, that mothers experiencing more symptoms of depression provide less sensitive care to their infants. This was the case in the work of the NICHD Early Child Care Research Network (1999), in which depressive symptoms and sensitivity were repeatedly measured in a sample of more than 1,000 mothers across the first three years of their child's life. Similarly, Crockenberg (1987) reported in a study of teenage mothers that those reporting more psychological distress engaged in simple custodial and unstimulating care of their infants more often than other mothers. And when Zaslow and associates (1985) examined relations between mothers feeling "blue" on eight or more days since the birth of their 4-month-old children and maternal behavior, they observed that increased sadness predicted less smiling at, less speaking with, and less touching of the infant. In addition to undermining active involvement with the infant, negative affectivity may also promote negative and intrusive maternal behavior, as Diener and colleagues' (1995; Goldstein, Diener, & Mangelsdorf, 1996) correlational data on adolescent Latino mothers and infants suggested.

During the preschool and middle-childhood years similar results obtain. In one investigation of rural African-American and European-American families, for example, high levels of emotional distress (i.e., anxiety, depression, irritability) among mothers were related to low levels of positive parenting (e.g., hugs, praise) and high levels of negative parenting (e.g., threats, slaps, derogatory statements) during the course of structured parent–child interactions, and also to strong endorsement of authoritarian childrearing values (Conger et al., 1984). When Zelkowitz (1982) studied low-income African-American and European-American mothers of 5- to 7-year-olds, she further observed that high levels of anxiety and depression predicted high expectations for immediate compliance on the part of the child, but inconsistency in following up when the child did not comply. Furthermore, high levels of psychological distress were associated with more hostile and dominating behavior, less reliance on reasoning and loss of privileges when disciplining the child, and more intensive demands for the child's involvement in household maintenance (Longfellow, Zelkowitz, & Saunders, 1982).

During the teenage years, neuroticism or negative affectivity continues to be associated with problematic parenting. For example, Gondoli and Silverberg (1997) reported that mothers who experienced emotional distress (i.e., depression, anxiety, low self-efficacy) were less accepting of their teen's behavior during problem solving discussions and were less supportive of the youth's psychological autonomy than other mothers. In an analysis of almost 1,000 mothers and fathers of 10- to 17-year-olds interviewed as part of a national survey, Voydanoff and Donnelly (1998) found that feeling sad, blue, tense, tired, and overwhelmed was related to parents not participating in activities with their children, though such negative affectivity proved unrelated to parental monitoring. In a series of studies, Conger and associates (1992, 1993, 1995; Simons, Beaman, Conger, & Chao, 1993) investigated family interaction patterns in a large sample of Iowa farm families and posited both direct and indirect effects of negative affectivity on maternal and paternal behavior. Depressive symptoms predicted more harsh and inconsistent discipline on the part of both mothers and fathers (Conger, Patterson, & Ge, 1995; Simons et al., 1993) and less nurturant behavior by both parents when interacting with sons (Conger et al., 1992), though not daughters (Conger et al., 1993). Furthermore, for both mothers and fathers and sons and daughters, elevated levels of parental depressive symptoms predicted increased marital conflict and, thereby, lower levels of nurturant parenting (Conger et al., 1992, 1993). Such indirect pathways of possible influence of parental psychological functioning on their parenting are consistent with Belsky's (1984) process model of the determinants of parenting. Finally, Brody and associates (2002) showed that higher levels of depressive symptoms (in concert with lower levels of optimism and self-esteem) predict less involved/vigilant parenting and lower quality mother–teen discussions in their short-term longitudinal study of 150 African-American families living in single-parent families in the rural South.

In sum, whether one considers research on infants, toddlers, preschoolers, school-age children, or adolescents, there is repeated evidence that high levels of depressive symptoms—even in nonclinical samples—and of other facets of neuroticism, including anxiety and irritability/hostility, are related to less competent parenting. This statistical effect can take the form of less active and involved parenting, as well as more negative, intrusive, and overcontrolling parenting.

Extraversion. Extraversion reflects the quantity and intensity of interpersonal interaction, activity level, need for stimulation and capacity for joy that characterize individuals. A person scoring high on extraversion is considered sociable, active, talkative, person-oriented, optimistic, fun loving, and affectionate, whereas a low scoring individual is reserved, sober, unexuberant, aloof, task oriented, retiring, and quiet. One might anticipate, on the basis of this description, that extraverted individuals might function better as parents than less extraverted parents, if only because parenting is a social task involving another, though dependent, person. On the other hand, one might imagine that high levels of extraversion and especially of sociability predispose one to be interested in more adult social exchange than is often experienced by a parent, particularly one who remains home all day with children.

Although the database is by no means extensive, in general the evidence is supportive of the first prediction, namely that of a positive association between extraversion and sensitive, responsive, emotionally engaged, and stimulating parenting. Levy-Shiff and Israelashvilli (1988) found that Israeli men scoring high on extraversion showed more positive affect and engaged in more toy play and teaching with their 9-month-olds in their homes than men scoring low on extraversion. Mangelsdorf and her colleagues (1990) detected similar personality-parenting associations when studying mothers of 9-month-olds. Belsky, Crnic, and Woodworth (1995) replicated both sets of results during the course of naturalistic home observations with mother, father, and their 15- and 21-month-old toddlers, finding that mothers and fathers alike who were more extraverted expressed more positive affect toward their children and were more sensitive and cognitively stimulating when observed at home. Finally, in a study of mothers, fathers, and their children up to 8 years of age, more extraverted parents reported engaging in more positive supportive parenting, such as displaying positive affection and encouraging independence (Losoya, Callor, Rowe, & Goldsmith, 1997). Apparently, the link between extraversion and positive parenting is not restricted to the infant–toddler period. To date, however, there are no studies linking this personality trait with parenting during the adolescent years.

Agreeableness.   Agreeableness reflects one's interpersonal orientation along a continuum from compassion to antagonism in thoughts, feelings, and actions. A person scoring high on this trait is soft-hearted, good-natured, trusting, helpful, forgiving, gullible, and straightforward, whereas a person scoring low is cynical, rude, suspicious, uncooperative, vengeful, ruthless, irritable, and manipulative. Clearly, the prediction regarding parenting is that more agreeable individuals would make better parents—at least from the child's perspective. As it turns out, only four studies have examined the relation between this particular personality trait and parenting, two of which have been noted. In the aforementioned toddler work by Belsky et al. (1995), higher levels of agreeableness predicted greater maternal (but not paternal) positive affect and sensitivity and lower levels of negative affect and intrusive–overcontrolling behavior. Consistent with these findings, Losoya et al. (1997) found in their study of parents with children as old as 8 that agreeableness was positively associated with supportive parenting and inversely associated with negatively controlling parenting. Kochanska, Clark, and Goldman (1997) observed that lower levels of agreeableness were related to more power-assertive and less responsive parenting in their study of toddlers, although in other work by the same research team, only the agreeableness–responsiveness association was replicated (Clark, Kochanska, & Ready, 2000). Thus, preliminary evidence shows some consistency with the hypothesis advanced.

Openness to Experience.   The person who is open to experience tends to enjoy new experiences, has broad interests, and is very imaginative; in contrast, a person scoring low on this trait is down-to-earth, practical, traditional, and pretty much set in his ways. Predictions from this trait to parenting are less straightforward than was the case with respect to the other Big Five traits considered to this point. Only two investigations of parenting have explored openness to experience, with one showing that Israeli fathers who were more open to experience engaged in more physical caregiving of their infants than fathers less open to experience (Levy-Shiff & Israelashvilli, 1988), perhaps because the father role itself is a new experience worth exploring for these kinds of men. The other study found that openness was related to more supportive parenting among mothers and fathers alike (Losoya et al., 1997).

Conscientiousness.   Conscientiousness reflects the extent to which a person is organized and has high standards, always striving to achieve his or her goals. An individual who scores low on conscientiousness is easygoing, not very organized, somewhat careless, and not especially planful. Once again, it is not exactly clear how this trait should relate to parental behavior, as it seems possible that, however attractive high conscientious may appear—especially to an employer—it could prove too demanding to a child. At the same time, disorder and chaos, in contrast to organization, are typically not in children's best interests, so one could imagine low levels of conscientiousness also predicting parental behavior that might not be especially supportive of children's functioning. The aforementioned study by Losoya et al. (1997) that examined this trait in relation to the childrearing attitudes and practices of mothers and fathers with children under 8 years of age found conscientiousness to be positively related to supportive parenting and inversely related to negative, controlling parenting. Clark and associates (2000) chronicled similar relations when looking at mothers of toddlers, finding that more conscientious mothers are more responsive and less power assertive than less conscientious mothers. However limited, the evidence to date suggests that conscientiousness and positive parenting go together.

Processes Linking Personality and Parenting

This brief examination of research on personality and parenting suggests that, if one could choose one's parents, the most beneficial choice would be parents who are low in neuroticism, high in extraversion and agreeableness, and perhaps high in openness to experience and conscientiousness. These individuals seem more supportive, sensitive, responsive, and intellectually stimulating, apparently irrespective of the child's age. But it is one thing to observe, as we have, that a parent's personality is predictive of his or her parenting, and quite another to understand the mechanisms responsible for this relation. Two possibilities have received some limited attention in the literature, but deserve more. The first involves attributions, the second, mood and emotion.

There is increasing appreciation in developmental research that attributions play an important role in close relationship processes, including those in the parent–child relationship (MacKinnon-Lewis, Castellino, Brody, & Fincham, 2001). Models of social cognition that have been advanced in the marital, developmental, and social psychology literatures (e.g., Bradbury & Fincham, 1990; Dix, Ruble, & Zambarano, 1989; Dodge, 1986) have been applied to the study of parenting (e.g., Nix et al., 1999). For example, parents who think their child is whining because he is tired are inclined to respond to the child in a manner quite different (i.e., sensitively) than when they believe the child is trying to manipulate them. Bugental and Shennum (1984) showed that mothers with more dysfunctional attributional styles responded to children in ways that maintained or enhanced difficult behavior, a finding that was experimentally reproduced by Slep and O'Leary (1998), who manipulated parent attributions in a challenging situation. Johnston and Patenaude (1994) found that parents were more likely to regard oppositional–defiant child behavior as under the child's control than inattentive–overreactive behavior, and this accounted for why the former evoked more negative parental reactions than the latter.

The fact that such attributions predict much the same parenting behavior that personality characteristics predict raises the possibility that one means by which personality shapes parenting is via attributions: Personality→Attributions→Parenting. Is it the case, for example, that neurotic rather than agreeable parents are most likely to attribute negative intent to their young children's negative affect and behavior? If so, does this dynamic account for why these personality traits predict parenting in the ways they do?

Because attributions themselves are linked to emotion, it is reasonable to wonder further about the role that emotion plays in mediating effects of personality on parenting. After all, in the aforementioned study by Slep and O'Leary (1998), manipulating mothers' attributions affected the degree to which they felt angry at their children. Emotion is central to the personality traits of neuroticism (negative affectivity) and extraversion (sometimes viewed as positive affectivity).

Two studies to date have examined the mediating role of emotion in accounting for personality–parenting relations. In a German investigation of almost 300 families with 8- to 14-year-old sons, Engfer and Schneewind (1982) showed, via path analysis, that maternal irritability and nervousness (i.e., neuroticism) were statistically linked to harsh punishment of their children via mother's proneness to anger. Belsky and his colleagues (1995) tested and found correlational results consistent with an *affect-specific* process—whereby personality could potentially affect mood and, thereby, parenting—in their home-observational study of families with toddler sons. Whereas extraversion, with its emphasis on the experience of positive emotions, predicted mothers' expressions of positive but not negative affect toward their toddlers, neuroticism, with its emphasis on the experience of negative emotions, predicted mothers' expressions of negative but not positive affect. In light of these results and those concerning attributions, it seems appropriate to encourage further work examining the potential mediating role of attributions and emotionality in accounting for some personality–parenting linkages, including the proposition that Personality→ Emotions→Attributions→Parenting.

Interestingly, attributions and emotions are at the very core of the construct of "internal working models" that Bowlby (1969/1982) proposed to understand how infants and children come to experience and internalize attachment relationships with primary caregivers. Internal working models are a developmental construct because they are conceived in constructivist terms, shaping what is perceived and interpreted, but also changing in response to what is experienced—literally over the life span. They are proving a useful tool for understanding how personality and relationship experiences might interface across development, particularly around parenting (e.g., Cassidy & Berlin, 1994; Cassidy & Kobak, 1988).

We turn now to consider close relationship functioning in adulthood and how it relates both to personality and to parenting. We argue that parenting is an adult's contribution to the close relationship he or she co-creates with his or her child, but that all of an adult's close relationships have relevance and meaning for each other. We return to the concepts of personality and the attachment internal working model when we invoke the latter as a developmental mechanism to link early and continuing social experiences with the style of relationships an adult establishes, whether with other adults or with his or her own children.

QUALITY OF CLOSE RELATIONSHIPS

Probably in much the same way that personality—and psychological functioning more broadly—appear to play a role in parenting and, consequently, in the nature and style of the parent–child relationship, personality and psychological functioning affect both how parents relate to other social partners and what kind of relationship emerges. In this section, we consider the many ways in which adult psychological, social, and parental functioning interface.

Personality and Relationship Quality

Correlational data indicate a solid link between individual and relationship functioning in adulthood. Distressed or dissatisfying marriages, for example, tend to involve relatively more distressed or less well-adjusted individuals (Kim & Mckenry, 2002; O'Leary, Christian, & Mendell, 1994). As early as the 1930s, research on the self-descriptions of spouses in happy and unhappy marriages established this (Terman, 1938). Happily married women appeared to possess "kindly attitudes toward others" and "expected kindly attitudes in return," were "cooperative," "self-assured," and "optimistic," whereas unhappily married women were emotionally tense, moody, aggressive, irritable, and egocentric (Terman, 1938, pp. 145–146). Within a normative adult sample, Beach and O'Leary (1993) reported that a subset of "chronically dysphoric" marital partners were especially likely to report an increase in depressive symptoms that accompanied downward shifts in early marital adjustment. But individual and marital adjustment tend to covary across all levels of functioning (Gotlib, Lewinsohn, & Seeley, 1998; Sarason, Sarason, & Gurung, 1997).

What is very much unclear in these correlational data is the direction of effects. Do anxious, depressed, defended, and angry individuals select partners and create relationships that reflect these personality characteristics, or do distressed, conflicted, and abusive relationships create less agreeable and more troubled partners? We feel comfortable in arguing that the process of influence undoubtedly works in both directions. Long-range longitudinal data suggest that this is the case, at least among clinical populations. Back in 1966, Robins (see also Robins, 1986) reported that children with greater antisocial behavior in childhood were more likely in adulthood to be unemployed, lack social support, experience rejection by friends and have repeated marital break-ups. Similar findings were documented by Champion, Goodall, and Rutter in 1995. Bardone and her colleagues (1996) found that adolescent girls with conduct disorder and, to a lesser extent, those with depression left school earlier, were more likely to be cohabiting with a partner, to have cohabited with multiple partners, to have become pregnant, and to report violence in their relationship by age 21 than comparison girls without mental illness (and presumably the family circumstances that accompany it). Comparable findings have been reported by Kessler, David, and Kendler (1997) and by Gotlib and colleagues (1998), who reported earlier and less satisfying marriages among individuals with a history of adolescent depression. Quality of close relationships in adulthood, in other words, is predicted by psychological adjustment in childhood and adolescence.

Perhaps even more compelling for the Personality→Relationship path is the association between childhood problems and selection of a teenage or adult partner with various mental health problems. Quinton, Rutter, and their colleagues (Quinton, Pickles, Maughan, & Rutter, 1993; Rutter, Quinton, & Hill, 1990) found that children removed from their homes as a result of problems in parenting were more likely than their peers to have a partner in adulthood with mental health problems or a criminal history. Referring specifically to depression, Petersen et al. (1993, p. 161) observed that, "once in a depressed trajectory in development, an individual becomes more likely to stay on this course because of the tendency to both alienate and withdraw from the very social supports that can minimize negative effects." Rutter (2000) argued that this observation is applicable in general to individuals with psychopathology.

However, when an individual with problems or at high risk of problems during youth manages to select a better-adjusted partner and co-create a more supportive relationship, he or she demonstrates better than expected psychosocial functioning in adulthood, suggesting the opposite causal path: Relationships→Personality and Personal Adjustment. Laub and colleagues (Laub, Nagin, & Sampson, 1998) found this true of adults with a criminal history, and Quinton and Rutter (Quinton & Rutter, 1988; Rutter, Quinton, & Hill, 1990) documented such life course changes in their sample of urban, low-income women and men who had been institutionalized as children due to parenting breakdown in their families. As Rutter (2000) pointed out, "experiences that people bring about through their own actions can nevertheless constitute a major risk or protective influence on their subsequent behavior" (p. 391). The extent to which these actions can be attributed to genetic inheritance should not, however, be underestimated.

Even studies of parenting interventions testify to a *relationship self-selection* effect. In reviewing social support interventions for families in need, Thompson and Ontai (2000; see also Gomby, Culross, & Behrman, 1999; Reichman & McLanahan, 2001) discussed the pervasive problem of lack of participation, lack of engagement, and attrition in all kinds of interventions—including home visitation—when parents are stressed, depressed, defended, addicted, or otherwise troubled (e.g., DePanfilis & Zuravin, 2002; Gaudin, Wodarski, Arkinson, & Avery, 1990–1991). A parent who has problematic relationships with children, partners, parents, and/or friends is especially likely to have problems developing a relationship—therapeutic or otherwise—with service providers. Without engagement and alliance, the intervention is unlikely even to take place, let alone be effective (Fraiberg, 1980; Krupnick et al., 1996).

Conversely, intervention efficacy appears to be concentrated among those parents who, to a large extent, self-select themselves into the group of better attending, more involved, and more responsive participants (Gomby et al., 1999; Thompson & Ontai, 2000) and/or when the intervention involves frequent home visiting sustained for at least a year or more (i.e., with those parents who have chosen not to drop out), using highly trained home visitors with low turnover rates (who are presumably more effective in building therapeutic relationships with less adjusted parents; Brooks-Gunn, 2001). In other words, the link between service intensity and client improvement (e.g., Erickson Warfield et al., 2000; Reichman & McLanahan, 2001) may be as much or more a product of client adjustment and motivation (choosing or being able to participate more fully in the intervention) than of service efficacy. Better adjusted adults tend to provide better quality parenting and to make better use of parenting interventions.

Among nonclinical populations, well-adjusted adults tend to have and perceive supportive relationships both within and outside their homes (Blum & Mehrabian, 1999; Contreras et al., 1999). But supportive relationships may also foster greater adjustment in those who experience them (Collins, Dunkel-Schetter, Lobel, & Scrimshaw, 1993; Sarason et al., 1997). Bost and her colleagues (2002) interviewed rural, working class, European-

American couples four times over their transition to parenthood. Those husbands and wives who reported relatively more satisfaction with their friends prenatally and at three months postpartum reported fewer symptoms of depression. This association tended to increase in strength over time from birth through age 2. A similar pattern was observed between satisfaction with one's spouse and depressive symptoms, with the association also increasing in strength over the first two years of parenthood. Apparently, as adjustment to a first child unfolds, feelings of support from partner and friends become more closely bound to feeling good about oneself and one's experience.

Relationship Quality and Parenting

If the quality of marital or other close relationships is linked with psychological functioning, and psychological functioning is linked to quality of parental care, it should come as no surprise that marital and social network support are also associated with individual differences in parenting (cf. Cochran & Walker, chap. 8, this volume). Among a sample of 62 low-income, African-American mothers, Burchinal, Follmer, and Bryant (1996) found no effects of a home visiting program on quality of home environment or maternal interaction, but consistent associations of the latter with social network size. Mothers reporting larger social networks had more developmentally supportive homes across early childhood (6 months to 4½ years) and were warmer, more involved, and less directive with their 1½-year-olds.

The associations between mothers' naturally occurring social support and their parenting raise several different causal possibilities. First, the same person with the same psychological functioning is a partner in both kinds of relationships. One would expect that parents who listen to, share with, and trust their spouses and friends would generally show greater respect for, involvement in, and patience with their children. At the same time, one arguably becomes more effective in dealing with emotionally demanding situations like parenting when personal and situational needs are met through a supportive close relationship. Still, the parent who believes in him or herself, feels deserving of love, has an understanding of relationships as mutually supportive, and holds a belief in his or her own ability to make personal changes, is probably more likely to leave unsatisfactory relationships, help create positive relationships, and express greater satisfaction with supportive relationships.

Does research demonstrate the specific kinds of developmental links among beliefs, social skills, relationship models, social relationships, and parenting that are argued above? We have already reviewed some of the simple (zero order) correlations between personality factors, marital relations, and quality of caregiving. However, only experimental and quasi-experimental studies begin to demonstrate causal connections and to rule out connections that are incidental to the key causal influences. Fortunately, a small body of such research, along with a large number of generally supportive correlational investigations, does exist. This research considers the significance of developmental history for adult functioning most relevant to parenting.

THE ROLE OF DEVELOPMENTAL HISTORY

Development History and Adult Psychological Functioning

In this section, we use two areas of research—the developmental origins of depression and of aggression—to illustrate links researchers are uncovering from developmental history to adult psychological functioning. The increasing emphasis in both areas is on likely mechanisms connecting early experiences with adult behavior and adjustment. Both highlight the potential importance of cognitive processes and their accompanying emotional responses within the Genetic Risk + Environmental Stress + Poor Parenting link to emerging psychopathology.

Origins of Depression.   Beginning in the 1940s with studies by Spitz (1945, 1946; see also Skodak & Skeels, 1949), who documented features of a depressive syndrome (termed *hospitalism*) in infants who had been separated from their mothers and institutionalized, there have been numerous efforts to link experiences of interpersonal loss in childhood and adolescence with later depression and other dysfunction in adulthood (Frommer & O'Shea, 1973; Harris, Brown, & Bifulco, 1986, 1990). When loss is accompanied, as it often is, by poor alternative caregiving, children are considerably more likely to evidence psychological problems in subsequent development (Rutter, 1999). According to psychoanalytic—and, later, attachment principles—such loss can produce intense and unresolved anxiety, guilt, and anger (see Hesse & Main, 1999, 2000; Main & Hesse, 1990). Without open communication and psychological processing (Kobak, 1999), these negative reactions are believed to make an individual emotionally vulnerable to similar feelings later in development in the face of perceived loss, lack of caring, or perhaps simply major psychological transitions such as becoming a parent. Vulnerability to depressive symptoms and a tendency to experience strong negative emotions, it should be recalled, represent core features of negative affectivity, and key personality factors associated with parenting. Thus, evidence to suggest that early experiences contribute to adult negative affectivity is pertinent to understanding the developmental origins of parenting behavior.

Experimental evidence supports the notion that a key mechanism underlying and/or exacerbating depressive episodes is negative attributions ("It's my fault Tom had that dreadful accident"), negative thoughts ("He's just never going to be the same again"), and the ensuing connection to negative emotions. Cognitive behavior therapy designed to prevent depression (Clarke et al., 1995; Gillham, Reivich, Jaycox, & Seligman, 1995; Muñoz et al., 1995) decreases self-reported depressive symptoms. These interventions help participants understand connections between thoughts and feelings, generate alternative explanations for negative events, use evidence to select the best-fitting explanation, and gain skill in coping with conflict and solving problems. Research indicates that positive intervention effects of cognitive behavior therapy are mediated by a decrease in participants' negative thoughts (Cardemil, Reivich, & Seligman, 2002) and/or attributional or explanatory style (Gilham et al., 1995). In other words, the same mechanisms proposed for linking the Big Five personality characteristics to parenting—parental attributions and emotions—have also proven valuable as a way to understand and alter the psychological dynamics underlying depression.

Recent research is further clarifying and enriching this model of environmental stress. It appears that those children and adolescents most likely to respond to loss (or other major negative life events, parental psychopathology, or troubled family relationships) with adult mental illness are those already at genetic risk for psychopathology. For example, a research team headed by Cadoret (Cadoret et al., 1995, 1996) found that both adult depression and adult substance abuse were linked to serious problems in adoptive homes (in this case, parental psychopathology) only among those adopted children who had alcoholism documented in their birth parents. Adoption or twin studies have also established that connections between family conflict and/or negative life events and later schizophrenia (Tienari et al., 1985, 1994), alcohol abuse (Cloninger et al., 1981, 1996), and depression (Silberg et al., 2001) primarily exist or are notably stronger when there is a genetic background of psychopathology (as assessed in the biological parents). In other words, two individuals with the same genes (i.e., identical twins) show different rates of adult psychopathology if only one is exposed to severe or chronic stress. Likewise, the same problematic home experiences appear to provoke psychopathology only in those individuals (or siblings) with a genetic vulnerability to mental illness.

Noting the critical qualifying role of genetic vulnerability need not, however invalidate developmental models that propose a Life Stress/Poor Parenting→Cognitive or Emotional Dysfunction→Adult Psychopathology path of causality. For those at genetic risk, stress—probably especially in the context of poor parenting—may exacerbate the tendency toward pessimism, self-blame, helplessness, and hopelessness that appears to trigger (and, in part, defines) episodes of depression (Cardemil et al., 2002; Muñoz et al.,

1995; Seligman, Schulman, DeRubeis, & Hollon, 1999). Normative variation in neuroticism and clinical levels of depression and anxiety, as we have seen, appear to undermine effective parenting across all developmental periods. Thus, genetic transmission, modeling of maladaptive cognitive/emotional responses, and less nurturant, responsive, and consistent care place children of depressed parents at higher risk for problems of their own in both psychological and interpersonal (e.g., parenting) adjustment.

Origins of Aggression. A comparable model of Poor Parenting and Environmental Stress→Cognitive/Emotional Dysfunction→Later Aggression/Conduct Problems has been developed in the study of serious aggressive behavior. The linkages begin with genetic inheritance. Both twin (e.g., Eaves et al., 1997; Edelbrock, Rende, Plomin, & Thompson, 1995) and adoption studies (e.g., Deater-Deckard & Plomin, 1999; Van den Oord, Boomsma, & Verhulst, 1994) have established *moderate to substantial* genetic variation in externalizing (i.e., acting out and aggressive) behavior problems. At the same time, frightened or frightening behavior by caregivers—probably in the context of spousal conflict and aggression (Cummings & Davies, 2002) or parent–child aggression (Crittenden, 1999; Youngblade & Belsky, 1990)—has been linked and may lead to disorganized attachment in toddlerhood (see Lyons-Ruth & Jacobvitz, 1999). Disorganized attachment, in turn, is one of many risk factors for externalizing and other behavior problems (see van IJzendoorn, Schuengel, & Bakermans-Kranenburg, 1999).

The kind of hostile, physically punitive parenting associated in maltreatment samples with attachment disorganization is also linked directly to disruptive, aggressive problems in the child, particularly those problems showing early onset (Patterson & Yoerger, 1997). Campbell and her colleagues (1996) used a laboratory clean-up task with about 100 mothers of preschool boys who were or were not identified as having symptoms of Attention Deficit Disorder by their preschool teachers. Those mothers who showed greater negative affect and intrusive control during the clean-up task at age 4 described their sons as having more externalizing problems both concurrently and subsequently at ages 6 and 9. Negative maternal interaction statistically mediated the association between a variety of maternal-reported stressors (marital dissatisfaction, negative life events, and maternal depressive symptoms) and boys' acting out behavior problems.

Both the presence of negative parenting practices (Campbell, Shaw, & Gilliom, 2000) and the absence of a warm, close relationship between parent(s) and child (Stattin & Kerr, 2000) predict externalizing problems, but this is especially true among multi-risk families where parental mental health problems and family ecological risk are high, such as in maltreating families. It seems likely, once again, that genetic vulnerability interacts with parenting problems and family stress to create longstanding problems with aggression. Twin and adoption studies underscore the dual contribution of genetic susceptibility and family environment (Eley, Lichtenstein, & Stevenson, 1999; van den Oord et al., 1994).

Interestingly again, in light of the hypothesized role of parent attributions and emotions in relating personality to parenting, maternal hostile attributions about children's ambiguous problem behavior appear to provide part of the context for the harsh discipline and hostility that is, in turn, associated with child externalizing behavior. Using a community sample of 277, mostly European-American families of varying socioeconomic status, Nix and his colleagues (1999) found shared variance between maternal hostile attributions to ambiguous child behavior vignettes and children's acting-out behavior (as rated by teachers and peers) over the transition to school. Much of this variance could be accounted for by mothers' harsh discipline practices (see also MacKinnon-Lewis et al., 1992). Children may, in fact, model both hostile parental attributions and parental aggression; they may be provoked more often to aggression as a result of hostile attributions; and/or they may inherit dispositional tendencies toward greater hostility in their thought processes and behavior.

Recent research has been devoted to documenting some of the distorted perceptions and attributions of aggressive children and adolescents. Dodge (1985, 1986; Crick & Dodge, 1994) provided the conceptual basis and initial empirical support for expecting aggressive children to have inaccurate perceptions about and hostile attributions in ambiguous social situations. In a meta-analytic review of studies on aggression and hostile attributions in community and clinical samples, Orobio de Castro and his colleagues (2002) found a robust association between the two. Older children (ages 8 to 12), more aggressive children, and those who had been rejected by peers showed the strongest links between hostile attributions and aggressive behavior. The connection to peer rejection appears to be an important one. Aggression not only predicts peer rejection (Coie, 2004), but when the two co-occur, the likelihood of long-term conduct problems and maladjustment is particularly high (Bierman & Wargo, 1995; Dodge et al., 2003).

Externalizing behavior shows a fair degree of stability, especially among the subset of children with early onset of these problems (i.e., those with disorganized attachment and harsh parenting experiences), accumulating adjustment problems over time, school failure, and delinquency by early adolescence (Stattin & Magnusson, 1996). It is associated not only with conduct problems and criminality in adulthood, but also substance dependence. For girls, continuing conduct problems are also associated with school failure, early pregnancy, unstable relationships, and partner aggression (Bardone et al., 1996). The significance for later problems in parenting is obvious. Indeed, these cases of long-term externalizing/conduct problems probably represent one pathway for the intergenerational transmission of child abuse and neglect.

In the next section, we consider more direct evidence that experiences in the family of origin help explain individual differences in parenting, bearing in mind two points. First is that the impact of those experiences depends upon a person's genetic vulnerabilities, protective factors, and characteristics (Kim-Cohen, Moffitt, Caspi, & Taylor, 2004). If one is not prone to panic, for example, successfully negotiated crisis experiences can even have a competence-enhancing effect. But among individuals who react with overwhelming emotion, crises may promote dysregulation and dysfunction. A second point is recognizing that experiences after childhood can play a marked role in determining how neatly early experiences map onto later parenting. In general, expecting simple connections between developmental history and styles of parenting is wishful thinking; more complicated connections have emerged in research that tests specific developmental processes leading to particular kinds of parenting outcomes.

Developmental History and Parenting

Child Maltreatment. The desire to link experiences in the family of origin to parent–child relationships in adulthood is much apparent in the field of child maltreatment. In their efforts to understand the etiology of child abuse and neglect, researchers examined the incidence of maltreatment and other instances of parenting breakdown in abusive parents' own childhoods (e.g., Hanson, Lipovsky, & Saunders, 1994; Milner & Chilamkurti, 1991; Muller, Hunter, & Stollak, 1995). Results suggest that abusive and neglectful mothers are unable to mobilize what few resources they have in support of their child's development until their own history of attachment disturbances is acknowledged and addressed (Cicchetti & Toth, 1995; Fraiberg, 1980; Lieberman & Zeanah, 1999). Although the associations are by no means perfect (Kaufman & Zigler, 1993), there is ample evidence that a high proportion of parents who maltreat and/or have a child removed from their care have experienced disturbances and disruptions in relations with their own parents, without necessarily having suffered the form of maltreatment they themselves perpetrate.

There are enough methodological limitations in these studies, however, to argue that a history of parent–child relationship dysfunction is a key risk factor, rather than a necessary and sufficient cause, in the etiology of maltreatment. When combined with other risk factors such as troubled adult relationships, lack of education, teen pregnancy, poverty, and life event stress, the probability of child maltreatment increases substantially (National Research Council, 1993).

Perhaps just as informative have been studies of adults with a history of child maltreatment who (up to the time of the study) fail to reenact child victimization in the next generation. A good relationship with the non-maltreating parent or a parent surrogate, opportunities at home or at school to demonstrate competence, talent, and/or leadership that, in turn, attracts supportive relationships, psychotherapy, and/or a better adjusted, long-term intimate partner have all been implicated as potential change factors in a history of child maltreatment (Egeland, Jacobvitz, & Sroufe, 1988; Rutter & Quinton, 1984). In other words, the maltreatment literature suggests that developmental history may set the stage for parenting in the next generation, but intervening events can change the scenery, sometimes dramatically.

Fathering.   A still emerging field of research investigating the role of developmental history in shaping later parenting is work on fatherhood (see Parke, chap. 4, this volume). The potential influence of the father–child relationship should not, however, be examined in isolation of the family context in which it functions. Dynamics of the marriage, extended kinship relationships, and other parent–child and sibling relationships together shape how a child comes to experience his or her relationship with each parent. Elder and his colleagues (Elder, Caspi, & Downey, 1986; Elder, Liker, & Cross, 1984) used unique longitudinal data sets originating just prior to the Great Depression to document intergenerational connections between family income loss, irritable and arbitrary behavior by fathers, and problem behavior and relationships in the next generation. Intergenerational (but still correlational) data on both fathers (Elder, Nguyen, & Caspi, 1985) and mothers (Caspi & Elder, 1988) showed that quarrelsome, irritable children tended to become irritable, explosive adults with conflicted marriages. Particularly in the context of economic stress, these adults tended to parent in arbitrary, overreactive, and rejecting ways, which was, in turn, associated with behavior problems in the next generation.

More recently, using a sample of struggling farm families from Iowa, Conger and Elder demonstrated that serious economic pressures were linked to depression and demoralization of both parents, which in turn predicted marital conflict and also irritable, less skillful parenting, sibling conflict and, ultimately, more depressive symptoms, aggression, and drinking by offspring in the middle school years (Conger et al., 1991, 1992; Elder, Conger, Foster, & Ardelt, 1992; Skinner, Elder, & Conger, 1992). The link from economic problems to adolescent distress was strongest for fathers', rather than mothers', negativity in the family (Elder et al., 1992).

Summary.   Using the two examples of child maltreatment and fathering, it is apparent that research on parenting has had some success in highlighting links between experiences in the family of origin and characteristics and functioning in the next generation of adults and, more specifically, parents. A consistent theme in this research is that parent personality and quality of relationships may play key roles as mechanisms of transmission. We conclude this chapter with discussion about how this may transpire.

SPECIFYING DEVELOPMENTAL PROCESS

In the remainder of the chapter we elaborate and extend the empirical and conceptual ideas raised about the developmental origins of parenting, with an emphasis on understanding: (a) the processes by which developmental history shapes both personality and patterns of relationship—and thereby parenting—and (b) the conditions under which both continuity and discontinuity are predicted and documented. To do this, we consider two important research directions: first, studies about the development of psychological and interpersonal functioning in childhood, with an emphasis on the notion of an internal working model of attachment, and second, studies about continuity and discontinuity of functioning into adulthood.

Development of Psychological Functioning in Childhood

Attachment theory advances the concept of internal working models—affect-laden mental representations of self, others, and relationships. Bowlby (1980) proposed that internal working models are derived from early social experiences and that they function (mostly outside of conscious awareness) to direct attention (e.g., toward or away from separations with loved ones), alter emotional experience (e.g., heighten or suppress feelings of vulnerability), and organize memory (e.g., integrate or split off comforting and distressing memories of a caregiver). These effects on attention, emotional experience, and memory are, in turn, believed to shape attributions about oneself (e.g., as vulnerable or impervious to being hurt), guide interpersonal behavior (e.g., seeking out or avoiding those who are hurtful), and alter the interpretation of social experience (e.g., interpreting a slap as appropriate punishment or abuse). Like personality factors, internal working models are believed to alter behavior by shaping attributions and affect (as well as attentional processes). There is obvious conceptual interface between personality and attachment models, although attachment models consider individual differences along a more circumscribed dimension than do, for example, the Big Five personality factors. In this section, we consider developmental findings of relevance to adult personality and psychological functioning drawn from literature on child and adult attachment.

Meta-analysis of the many studies examining associations between attachment security in toddlerhood and functioning in early to middle childhood indicates that although there are discernible patterns of prediction (Thompson, 1996), the patterns are not necessarily those initially hypothesized, nor are they necessarily replicated across laboratories (Cohen, 1999; Thompson, 1999). Some of the themes that emerge from these studies are that (a) attachment security and both current and subsequent *emotion regulation* often (but certainly not always) share some common variance (Cassidy & Berlin, 1994; Vondra et al., 2001), (b) attachment security can predict competence in other *social relationships*, though effect sizes are small to moderate (see Schneider, Atkinson, & Tardif, 2001, for a meta-analysis), (c) patterns of attachment correspond with, and occasionally forecast, some differences in *self-concept and social cognition* (Cassidy, Kirsh, Scolton, & Parke, 1996; Laible & Thompson, 1998; Verschueren, Marcoen, & Schoefs, 1996), and (d) among those at ecological risk due to poverty, parental psychopathology, negative life events, and so forth, attachment disorganization helps identify those children most likely to show *behavior problems* over time (Lyons-Ruth & Jacobvitz, 1999; van IJzendoorn et al., 1999).

These data offer a route for theorizing about developmental processes that underlie parenting. They do so by helping to build a bridge between attachment security, its psychological correlates in childhood, and adult psychological and interpersonal functioning. Increasingly, studies are examining how children and adolescents evidencing different working models of attachment appear to differentially shape their own experience in ways likely to affect later psychosocial adjustment. Two illustrative studies give a flavor of the work being done to identify the mechanisms by which attachment working models have their hypothesized effects.

Using a sample of three-year-olds, Belsky, Spritz, and Crnic (1996) found that children classified as secure in attachment at age 1 showed better recall of positive events in a puppet show, whereas those classified as insecure showed better recall of negative events. These data are consistent with Bowlby's argument that working models alter what kinds of affective information one notices. In the realm of social attributions, Cassidy and her colleagues (Cassidy et al., 1996) reported that children whose attachment appeared secure in kindergarten and first grade tended to assume that characters were not trying to cause problems in stories about negative peer experiences. Those children judged insecure, in contrast, were more likely to infer hostile intentions from the same characters.

These data suggest that attachment insecurity is, or can be, associated with both a bias to focus on negative affective events (as in neuroticism) and a bias to make hostile attributions in problem situations when a person's motivations are not clear (as in lack of agreeableness). Recall that both cognitive biases have been described earlier in the developmental origins of depression and aggression, as well as in the Big Five personality factors. It should not come as a surprise, therefore, that attachment insecurity—more specifically, disorganized (or, in childhood, *controlling*) attachment—is associated with a greater number of behavior problems throughout childhood (see Lyons-Ruth & Jacobvitz, 1999, for a review). Attachment disorganization has been associated with both internalizing (anxiety, depression, social withdrawal) and externalizing (aggression, noncompliance, peer provocation) problems.

One caveat in nearly all correlational studies of attachment and development is the possibility that genetic or physiological factors play a significant role in the tendency (a) to display various components of attachment/relationship security, (b) to score higher or lower on correlated indices of psychosocial functioning, and even (c) to exhibit more or less stable patterns of security and adjustment over time. In adolescence, particularly, genetic effects generally account for more than half the covariation between parent–child (and other family) relationships and adolescent adjustment (Reiss, Neiderhiser, Hetherington, & Plomin, 2000).

Genetic studies focusing on specific patterns of attachment are equivocal (van IJzendoorn et al., 2000; Lakatos et al., 2000). Perhaps we are best informed at present by the hundreds of studies conducted on mother–infant relationship styles in Rhesus monkeys (see Suomi, 1999, for a review), the latter of which offer "compelling parallels . . . to each of the major human attachment types" (Suomi, 1999, p. 188). Intergenerational studies of Rhesus monkey mothers and their offspring suggest that (a) maternal temperament observed from infancy, (b) style of mother's relationship with her own mother in her infancy, and (c) offspring temperament all contribute to Rhesus mother–infant attachment. Genetic transmission, in other words, need not occur through relationship functioning directly, but through temperamental characteristics that alter both the quality and experience of maternal care.

Regardless of the relative contribution of genes and experience, the internal working model construct—and personality more generally—works as a developmental mechanism for links from childhood psychological functioning to parenting in adulthood only if there is evidence that both continuity and lawful discontinuity take place across development. Such evidence is beginning to emerge, although it is clear that the working model construct can account for only a part of the developmental process that underlies the development of relationship functioning and parenting. A wider lens that incorporates physiological and genetic factors, the ecological contexts of development, *and* attachment experiences, begins to capture the complexity that is involved. In the next section, we take the attachment construct and its implications for parenting into the longitudinal framework of development.

CONDITIONS OF CONTINUITY AND DISCONTINUITY

Continuity, change, and the conditions under which each is likely to prevail
have received considerable attention within the attachment arena. An internal working model, after all, is a working model that should not necessarily demonstrate stability over time, but should come to reflect new experiences, particularly when those experiences involve strong emotion and/
or are repeated. Bowlby (1973) argued that working models would evolve
and respond to experience. Although much of the research on this topic involves a considerable degree of inference, recent work helps articulate how
and when early working models might demonstrate continuity over time
and thus correlate with later patterns of functioning, including personality
and parenting.

Stability of Attachment

Attachment security can be surprisingly stable across childhood (90% from
ages 1 to 6 years; Wartner et al., 1994; see Thompson, 1996, for a review of
early studies). However, it is just as common to find stability rates that vary
between 46% and 68% just within the second year of life (Belsky, Campbell,
Cohn, & Moore, 1996; Mangelsdorf et al., 1990; Rauh, Ziegenhain, Muller,
& Wijnroks, 2000; Vondra, Hommerding, & Shaw, 1999). Thus, even quite
early, there appears to be a substantial amount of change in indices of a
child's internal working model of attachment.

Associations between change in security and the presence of stressful
family circumstances or events are a relatively consistent finding. Maternal
psychological functioning (Egeland & Farber, 1984; Vondra et al., 1999),
quality of caregiving (Rauh et al., 2000; Vaughn, Egeland, Sroufe, & Waters,
1979), and birth of a younger sibling (Teti et al., 1996; Touris, Kromelow, &
Harding, 1995) have all been linked to changes in childhood attachment.
Some of the changes in attachment security from infancy to late adolescence have also been linked to intervening experiences (Hamilton, 2000;
Weinfield, Sroufe, & Egeland, 2000; Zimmerman, Fremmer-Bombik,
Spangler, & Grossman, 1997) such as severe illness or loss of a parent
through death or divorce (Cox & Owen, 1993; Lewis, Feiring, & Rosenthal,
2000; Waters et al., 2000). Experience, it appears, may lead a child or adolescent to conclude that close relationships are more or less reliable and enduring than previously understood.

Interventions for Attachment

Even more compelling as an argument for the role of experience—in particular, caregiving experience—in maintaining or altering the attachment
working model are the handful of intervention studies that have, overall,

documented moderate effects of therapy on maternal sensitivity and modest (less consistent) effects on early attachment security (see van IJzendoorn, Juffer, & Duyvesteyn, 1995, for a meta-analysis and Lieberman & Zeanah, 1999, for a review).

Dozier (Dozier, Stovall, Albus, & Bates, 2001; Dozier, Albus, Fisher, & Sepulveda, 2002) spearheaded critical research and theory on both developmental psychopathology among foster children and interventions to assist foster parents in developing healthy attachments with infants removed from their biological parent(s). Foster infants, she noted, are particularly likely to show behavioral dysregulation and to form disorganized attachment relationships with nonnurturing foster parents. However, preliminary evidence suggests not only that some foster parents (those with secure working models themselves; Dozier et al., 2001) can become more effective in caring for these often difficult-to-nurture infants, but also that the infants themselves then show more secure behaviors toward their foster parent(s) and more typical patterns of self-regulation.

Toth and her colleagues (Cicchetti, Toth, & Rogosch, 1999; Toth et al., 2002) have been able to demonstrate changes in both infant attachment security and child representations of self and mother in their program of intervention for maltreated children and their caregivers, using parent–child psychotherapy. In the second of two intervention studies (the first, with depressed mothers), Toth and her colleagues (2002) assessed the effects of approximately one year of parent–child psychotherapy or psychoeducational home visits, versus standard community services only, provided to mothers of preschool-aged children with a documented history of maltreatment within the family. Baseline (age 4) and outcome (age 5) representations of self, mother, and their relationship were assessed using narrative story stems with the study children. Parent–child psychotherapy (see Fraiberg, 1980; Lieberman, Silverman, & Pawl, 2000) was most effective in reducing maladaptive child representations of self and mother and increasing positive representations of mother and expectations of the mother–child relationship.

Interestingly, the psychoeducational home visits, which adopted an ecologically informed, but didactic approach to intervention (i.e., "How can we help improve your financial/social/residential situation?"), proved no more effective than (and added no substantial improvement on) standard community services. As noted earlier, psychoeducational and social support home visiting approaches have, in general, not proven particularly effective in making lasting changes in quality of parenting (Gomby et al., 1999; Lieberman & Pawl, 1988; Thompson & Ontai, 2000). If attachment-focused parent–child psychotherapy proves more effective, it suggests the need to target a troubled parent's working model of attachment and self to foster long-term change within the mother–child relationship.

Summary

In summary, the effects of a troubled and/or problematic childhood on parenting appear to depend on opportunities to rework poor relationship experiences. When children have alternative relationship models available to them and/or can participate in a supportive relationship amidst childhood stressors and crises, when adolescents and young adults can rework relationship issues by their long-term involvement with a caring and supportive individual, when adults are able to select mentally healthy partners and build and maintain constructive relationships over time, the relationships they subsequently create with their own children need not mirror the hardships of their upbringing.

It becomes moot, at this stage, to argue how much personality or psychological adjustment versus supportive relationships contribute to parental outcomes; the two are inextricably linked. As Bowlby (1973) argued in his attachment work and Sullivan (1953) argued in his clinical work, individuals define themselves very much in terms of their interpersonal relationships. Relationships (attachment working models) that are conflicted, insecure, and/or troubled not only undermine individual well-being, but also undermine positive conceptions about oneself (or reinforce negative ones). Individuals with adjustment or personality problems usually exhibit greater than average difficulties developing and maintaining supportive relationships. The two combined are clearly proximal determinants of caregiving and the quality of parental care.

To the extent that both personality and relationship problems appear to be set in motion on developmental trajectories that begin in infancy and childhood (not to mention in a genotype that shapes experiences even before birth and in changing rhythms across the life span), they represent important process variables for understanding how developmental history is played out in later parenting. And to the degree that both personality and relationship functioning demonstrate malleability on the basis of later experiences, they represent key mechanisms for understanding how contextual factors shape parenting as well. If we are to gain a full understanding of the determinants of parenting, it is obvious that both constructs—personality/psychological adjustment and supportive relationships—and both kinds of dynamics—influences of developmental history and of ecological context—must be taken into account.

CONCLUSIONS

We have summarized data in this chapter attesting to the significance of genes and of both early and continuing experiences for development, including individual differences in parenting. By no means, however, have we argued for simple linkages, either from genes to personality/behavior, or from childhood to adulthood. Genetic inheritance, combined with early and contemporaneous experiences within the family, help to select and shape a child's experiences in school, with peers, and ultimately, in adult relationships. They do so through the medium of social and psychological competence and adjustment. But in no case can one assume a simple *main effects* model. Whether the childhood legacy is documented maltreatment, institutionalization, or unconditional love, intervening experiences hold the power to deflect early developmental trajectories. Process-oriented empirical work on parenting that considers the interplay of individual, relational, and environmental factors brings us closer to understanding the mechanisms underlying both developmental continuity and discontinuity.

We conclude this discussion with recognition of the rapprochement that has been emerging between clinical and empirical efforts to understand adult functioning and, in particular, individual differences in caregiving. The analysis we have undertaken in this chapter is predicated on advances that have been made in applying clinical theory to research settings, providing greater specification of developmental process within clinical theory, using tools that quantify—or at least classify—clinical constructs, and adopting research designs that more effectively capture genetic influence and developmental change. As a result, empirical support for clinical constructs and mechanisms has grown, but at the same time research in this area has gained a notable measure of depth and relevance. The consequence of each has been better understanding of both the factors and the processes involved in the evolution of differences in parental care.

REFERENCES

Bardone, A. M., Moffitt, T. W., Caspi, D., Dickson, N., & Silva, P. A. (1996). Adult mental health and social outcomes of adolescent girls with depression and conduct disorder. *Development and Psychopathology, 8,* 811–829.

Beach, S. R., & O'Leary, K. D. (1993). Marital discord and dysphoria: For whom does the marital relationship predict depressive symptomatology? *Journal of Social and Personal Relationships, 10*(3), 405–420.

Beckwith, L., Howard, J., Espinosa, M., & Tyler, R. (1999). Psychopathology, mother–child interaction, and infant development: Substance-abusing mothers and their offspring. *Development and Psychopathology, 11,* 715–725.

Belsky, J. (1984). The determinants of parenting: A process model. *Child Development, 55,* 83–96.

Belsky, J., Campbell, S. B., Cohn, J. F., & Moore, G. (1996). Instability of infant–parent attachment security. *Developmental Psychology, 32,* 921–924.

Belsky, J., Crnic, K., & Woodworth, S. (1995). Personality and parenting: Exploring the mediating role of transient mood and daily hassles. *Journal of Personality, 63,* 905–931.

Belsky, J., Spritz, B., & Crnic, K. (1996). Infant attachment security and affective–cognitive information processing at age 3. *Psychological Science, 7,* 111–114.

Belsky, J., & Vondra, J. (1985). Characteristics, consequences, and determinants of parenting. In L. L'Abate (Ed.), *Handbook of family psychology and therapy* (pp. 523–536). Homewood, IL: The Dorsey Press.

Bierman, K. L., & Wargo, J. B. (1995). Predicting the longitudinal course associated with aggressive–rejected, aggressive (nonrejected), and rejected (nonaggressive) status. *Development and Psychopathology, 7*, 669–682.

Blum, J. S., & Mehrabian, A. (1999). Personality and temperament correlates of marital satisfaction. *Journal of Personality, 67*(1), 93–125.

Bost, K. K., Cox, M. J., Burchinal, M. R., & Payne, C. (2002). Structural and supportive changes in couples' family and friendship networks across the transition to parenthood. *Journal of Marriage and the Family, 64*(2), 517–531.

Bowlby, J. (1969/1982). *Attachment and loss: Vol. 1. Attachment.* New York: Basic Books.

Bowlby, J. (1973). *Attachment and loss: Vol. 2. Separation.* New York: Basic Books.

Bowlby, J. (1980). *Attachment and loss: Vol. 3. Loss: Sadness and depression.* New York: Basic Books.

Bradbury, T., & Fincham, F. (1990). Attributions in marriage. *Psychological Bulletin, 107*, 3–33.

Brody, G., Murry, V., Kim, S., & Brown, A. (2002). Longitudinal pathways to competence and psychological adjustment among African American children living in rural single-parent households. *Child Development, 73*, 1505–1516.

Brooks-Gunn, J. (2001). What are the components of successful early childhood programs? (Society for Research in Child Development). *Social Policy Report, 15*(2), 9.

Bugental, D., & Shennum, W. (1984). Difficult children as elicitors and targets of adult communication patterns. *Monographs of the Society for Research in Child Development, 49*(1, Serial No. 205).

Burchinal, M., Follmer, A., & Bryant, D. (1996). The relations of maternal social support and family structure with maternal responsiveness and child outcomes among African American families. *Developmental Psychology, 32*, 1073–1083.

Burns, K., Chethik, L., Burns, W. J., & Clark, R. (1997). The early relationship of drug-abusing mothers and their infants. An assessment at eight to twelve months of age. *Journal of Clinical Psychology, 53*, 279–287.

Cadoret, R. J., Winokur, G., Langbehn, D., & Troughton, E. (1996). Depression spectrum disease I: The role of gene–environment interaction. *American Journal of Psychiatry, 153*, 892–899.

Cadoret, R. J., Yates, W. R., Troughton, E., Woodworth, G., & Stewart, M. A. (1995). Adoption study demonstrating two genetic pathways to drug abuse. *Archives of General Psychiatry, 52*, 42–52.

Campbell, S. B., Pierce, E. W., Moore, G., Marakovitz, S., & Newby, K. (1996). Boys' externalizing problems at elementary school age: Pathways from early behavioral problems, maternal control, and family stress. *Development and Psychopathology, 8*(4), 701–719.

Campbell, S. B., Shaw, D. S., & Gilliom, M. (2000). Early externalizing behavior problems: Toddlers and preschoolers at risk for later maladjustment. *Development and Psychopathology, 12*(3), 467–488.

Cardemil, E. V., Reivich, K. J., & Seligman, M. E. P. (2002, May 8). The prevention of depressive symptoms in low-income, minority middle-school students. *Prevention and Treatment, 5.* Retrieved January 4, 2005, from http://gateway1.ma.ovid.com/ovidweb.cgi.

Carter, A., Garrity-Roukous, F., Chazan-Cohen, R., Little, C., & Briggs-Gowan, M. (2001). Maternal depression and comorbidity: Predicting early parenting, attachment security, and toddler social–emotional problems and competencies. *Journal of the American Academy of Child and Adolescent Psychiatry, 40*, 18–26.

Caspi, A. (1998). Personality development across the life course. In W. Damon (Series Ed.) & R. B. Cattell (Vol. Ed.). The description of personality: Basic traits resolved into clusters. *Journal of Abnormal and Social Psychology, 38*, 476–506.

Caspi, A., & Elder, G. H., Jr. (1988). Emergent family patterns: The intergenerational construction of problem behavior and relationships. In R. A. Hinde & J. Stevenson-Hinde (Eds.), *Relationships within families: Mutual influences* (pp. 218–240). Oxford, England: Clarendon.

Cassidy, J., & Berlin, L. J. (1994). The insecure/ambivalent pattern of attachment: Theory and research. *Child Development, 65*, 971–991.

Cassidy, J., Kirsh, S. J., Scolton, K. L., & Parke, R. D. (1996). Attachment and representations of peer relationships. *Developmental Psychology, 32*, 892–904.

Cassidy, J., & Kobak, R. R. (1988). Avoidance and its relation to other defensive processes. In J. Belsky & T. Nezworski (Eds.), *Clinical implications of attachment* (pp. 300–323). Hillsdale, NJ: Lawrence Erlbaum Associates.

Cattell, R. B. (1943). The description of personality: Basic traits resolved into clusters. *Journal of Abnormal and Social Psychology, 38*, 476–506.

Cattell, R. B. (1945). The principal trait clusters for describing personality. *Psychological Bulletin, 42*, 129–161.

Champion, L. A., Goodall, G. M., & Rutter, M. (1995). Behavioural problems in childhood and stressors in early adult life: A 20-year follow-up of London school children. *Psychological Medicine, 25*, 231–246.

Cicchetti, D., & Toth, S. L. (1995). Child maltreatment and attachment organization: Implications for intervention. In S. Goldberg, R. Muir, & J. Kerr (Eds.), *Attachment theory: Social, developmental, and clinical perspectives.* Hillsdale, NJ: Analytic Press.

Cicchetti, D., Toth, S. L., & Rogosch, F. A. (1999). The efficacy of toddler–parent psychotherapy to increase attachment security in offspring of depressed mothers. *Attachment and Human Development, 1*, 34–66.

Clark, L. A., Kochanska, G., & Ready, R. (2000). Mothers' personality and its interaction with child temperament as predictors of parenting behavior. *Journal of Personality and Social Psychology, 79*, 274–285.

Clarke, G. N., Hawkins, W., Murphy, M., Sheeber, L. B., Lewinsohn, P. M., & Seeley, J. R. (1995). Targeted prevention of unipolar depressive disorder in an at-risk sample of high school adolescents: A randomized trial of a group cognitive intervention. *Journal of The American Academy of Child and Adolescent Psychiatry, 34*(3), 312–321.

Cloninger, C. R., Bohman, M., & Sigvardsson, S. (1981). Inheritance of alcohol abuse: Cross-fostering analysis of adopted men. *Archives of General Psychiatry, 38*, 861–868.

Cloninger, C. R., Sigvardsson, S., & Bohman, M. (1996). Type I and type II alcoholism: An update. *Alcohol Health and Research World, 20*, 18–23.

Cohen, M. M. (1999). *A meta-analysis of the predictive ability of infant attachment: Is the emperor wearing any clothes?* Unpublished doctoral dissertation, University of Pittsburgh.

Coie, J. D. (2004). The impact of negative social experiences on the development of antisocial behavior. In J. B. Kupersmidt & K. A. Dodge (Eds.), *Children's peer relations: From development to intervention.* Washington, DC: American Psychological Association.

Collins, N. L., Dunkel-Schetter, C., Lobel, M., & Scrimshaw, S. (1993). Social support in pregnancy: Psychosocial correlates of birth outcomes and postpartum depression. *Journal of Personality and Social Psychology, 65*, 1243–1258.

Conger, R., Conger, K., Elder, G., Lorenz, F., Simons, R., & Whitbeck, L. (1992). A family process model of economic hardship and adjustment of early adolescent boys. *Child Development, 63*(3), 526–541.

Conger, R., Conger, K., Elder, G., Lorenz, F., Simons, R., & Whitbeck, L. (1993). Family economic stress and adjustment of early adolescent girls. *Developmental Psychology, 29*, 206–219.

Conger, R., Lorenz, F., Elder, G., Melby, J., Simons, R., & Conger, K. (1991). A process model of family economic pressure and early adolescent alcohol use. *Journal of Early Adolescence, 11*(4), 430–449.

Conger, R., McCarthy, J., Yang, R., Lahey, B., & Kropp, J. (1984). Perception of child, childrearing values, and emotional distress as mediating links between environmental stressors and observed maternal behavior. *Child Development, 54,* 2234–2247.

Conger, R., Patterson, G., & Ge, X. (1995). It takes two to replicate: A mediational model for the impact of parents' stress on adolescent adjustment. *Child Development, 66,* 80–97.

Contreras, J. M., Lopez, I. R., Rivera-Mosquera, E. T., Raymond-Smith, L., & Rothstein, K. (1999). Social support and adjustment among Puerto Rican adolescent mothers: The moderating effect of acculturation. *Journal of Family Psychology, 13*(2), 228–243.

Costa, P. T., & McCrae, R. R. (1992). *NEO PI-R Professional manual.* Odessa, FL: Psychological Assessment Resources.

Cox, M. J., & Owen, M. T. (1993, March). *Marital conflict and conflict negotiation: Effects on infant–mother and infant–father relationships.* Paper presented at the Biennial Meeting of the Society for Research in Child Development, New Orleans, LA.

Crick, N. C., & Dodge, K. A. (1994). A review and reformulation of social information processing mechanisms in children's social adjustment. *Psychological Bulletin, 115,* 74–101.

Crittenden, P. M. (1999). Danger & development: The organization of self-protective strategies. In J. I. Vondra & D. Barnett (Eds.), Atypical patterns of attachment in infancy and early childhood. *Monographs of the Society for Research in Child Development* (Serial No. 258). Malden, MA: Blackwell.

Crockenberg, S. (1987). Support for adolescent mothers during the postnatal period. In C. Boukydis (Ed.), *Research on support for parents and infants in the postnatal period* (pp. 3–24). Norwood, NJ: Ablex.

Cummings, E. M., & Davies, P. T. (2002). Effects of marital discord on children: Recent advances and emerging themes in process-oriented research. *Journal of Child Psychology and Psychiatry, 43,* 31–63.

Deater-Deckard, K., & Plomin, R. (1999). An adoption study of the etiology of teacher and parent reports of externalizing behavior problems in middle childhood. *Child Development, 70*(1), 144–154.

DePanfilis, D., & Zuravin, S. J. (2002). The effect of services on the recurrence of child maltreatment. *Child Abuse and Neglect, 26*(2), 187–205.

Diener, M., Mangelsdorf, S., Contrerae, J., Hazelwood, L., & Rhodes, J. (1995, March). *Correlates of parenting competence among Latina adolescent mothers.* Paper presented at the Biennial Meeting of the Society for Research in Child Development, Indianapolis, IN.

Dix, T., Ruble, D., & Zambarano, R. (1989). Mothers' implicit theories of discipline. *Child Development, 60,* 1373–1391.

Dodge, K. A. (1985). Attributional bias in aggressive children. In P. C. Kendall (Ed.), *Advances in cognitive–behavioral research and therapy* (pp. 73–110). Orlando, FL: Academic Press.

Dodge, K. A. (1986). A social information processing model of social competence in children. In M. Perlmutter (Ed.), *Minnesota symposia on child psychology* (Vol. 18, pp. 77–125). Hillsdale, NJ: Lawrence Erlbaum Associates.

Dodge, K. A., Lansford, J. E., Burks, V. S., Bates, J. E., Pettit, G. S., Fontaine, R., & Price, J. M. (2003). Peer rejection and social information-processing factors in the development of aggressive behavior problems in children. *Child Development, 74*(2), 374–393.

Dozier, M., Albus, K., Fisher, P. A., & Sepulveda, S. (2002). Interventions for foster parents: Implications for developmental theory. *Development and Psychopathology, 14*(4), 843–860.

Dozier, M., Stovall, K. C., Albus, K. E., & Bates, B. (2001). Attachment for infants in foster care: The role of caregiver state of mind. *Child Development, 72,* 1467–1477.

Dunn, M. G., Mezzich, A., Janiszewski, S., Kirisci, L., & Tarter, R. (2001). Transmission of neglect in substance abuse families: The role of child dysregulation and parental SUD. *Child and Adolescent Substance Abuse, 10*(4), 126–134.

Eaves, L. J., Silberg, J. L., Meyer, J. M., Maes, H. H., Simonof, E., Pickles, A., Rutter, M., Neale, M. C., Reynolds, C. A., Erikson, M. T., Heath, A. C., Loeber, R., Truett, K. R., & Hewitt, J. K.

(1997). Genetics and developmental psychopathology: 2. The main effects of genes and environment on behavioral problems in the Virginia Twin Study of Adolescent Behavioral Development. *Journal of Child Psychology and Psychiatry, 38*, 965–980.

Edelbrock, C., Rende, R., Plomin, R., & Thompson, L. A. (1995). A twin study of competence and problem behavior in childhood and early adolescence. *Journal of Child Psychology and Psychiatry, 36*, 775–785.

Egeland, B., & Farber, E. (1984). Infant–mother attachment: Factors related to its development and changes over time. *Child Development, 55*, 753–771.

Egeland, B., Jacobvitz, D., & Sroufe, L. A. (1988). Breaking the cycle of abuse: Relationship predictors. *Child Development, 59*, 1080–1088.

Eiden, R. D., Chavez, F., & Leonard, K. E. (1999). Parent–infant interactions among families with alcoholic fathers. *Development and Psychopathology, 11*, 745–762.

Elder, G. H., Jr., Caspi, A., & Downey, G. (1986). Problem behavior and family relationships: Life course and intergenerational themes. In A. Sorensen, F. Weinert, & L. Sherrod (Eds.), *Human development and the life course* (pp. 293–340). Hillsdale, NJ: Lawrence Erlbaum Associates.

Elder, G. H., Jr., Conger, R. D., Foster, E. M., & Ardelt, M. (1992). Families under economic pressure. *Journal of Family Issues, 13*(1), 5–37.

Elder, G. H., Jr., Liker, J. K., & Cross, C. E. (1984). Parent–child behavior in the Great Depression: Life course and intergenerational influences. In P. B. Baltes & O. G. Brim, Jr. (Eds.), *Life-span development and behavior* (Vol. 6, pp. 109–158). New York: Academic Press.

Elder, G. H., Jr., Nguyen, T. V., & Caspi, A. (1985). Linking family hardship to children's lives. *Child Development, 56*(2), 361–375.

Eley, T. C., Lichtenstein, P., & Stevenson, J. (1999). Sex differences in the etiology of aggressive and nonaggressive antisocial behavior: Results from two twin studies. *Child Development, 70*(1), 155–168.

Engfer, A., & Schneewind, K. (1982). Causes and consequences of harsh parental punishment. *Child Abuse and Neglect, 6*, 129–139.

Erickson Warfield, M., Hauser-Cram, P., Wyngaarden Krauss, M., Shonkoff, J. P., & Upshur, C. C. (2000). The effect of early intervention services on maternal well-being. *Early Education and Development, 11*, 499–518.

Fraiberg, S. (1980). *Clinical studies in infant mental health*. New York: Basic Books.

Frommer, E., & O'Shea, G. (1973). The importance of childhood experiences in relation to problems of marriage and family building. *British Journal of Psychiatry, 123*, 157–160.

Gaudin, J. M., Wodarski, J. S., Arkinson, M. K., & Avery, L. S. (1990–1991). Remedying child neglect: Effectiveness of social network interventions. *Journal of Applied Social Sciences, 15*, 97–123.

Gillham, J., Reivich, K., Jaycox, L., & Seligman, M. E. P. (1995). Prevention of depressive symptoms in schoolchildren: Two-year follow-up. *Psychological Science, 6*, 343–351.

Goldstein, L., Diener, M., & Mangelsdorf, S. (1996). Maternal characteristics and social support across the transition to motherhood: Associations with maternal behavior. *Journal of Family Psychology, 10*, 60–71.

Gomby, D. S., Culross, P. L., & Behrman, R. E. (1999). Home visiting: Recent program evaluations—Analysis and recommendations. *The Future of Children, 9*, 4–26.

Gondoli, D., & Silverberg, S. (1997). Maternal emotional distress and diminished responsiveness. *Developmental Psychology, 33*, 861–868.

Gotlib, I. H., Lewinsohn, P. M., & Seeley, J. R. (1998). Consequences of depression during adolescence: Marital status and marital functioning in early adulthood. *Journal of Abnormal Psychology, 107*, 686–690.

Hamilton, C. E. (2000). Continuity and discontinuity of attachment from infancy through adolescence. *Child Development, 71*(3), 690–694.

Hanson, R. F., Lipovsky, J. A., & Saunders, B. E. (1994). Characteristics of fathers in incest families. *Journal of Interpersonal Violence, 9*(2), 155–169.

Harris, T., Brown, G. W., & Bifulco, A. (1986). Loss of parent in childhood and adult psychiatric disorder: The role of lack of adequate parental care. *Psychological Medicine, 16*, 641–659.

Harris, T., Brown, G. W., & Bifulco, A. (1990). Loss of parent in childhood and adult psychiatric disorder: A tentative overall model. *Development and Psychopathology, 2*, 311–328.

Hesse, E., & Main, M. (1999). Second generation effects of unresolved trauma in nonmaltreating parents: Dissociated, frightened, and threatening parental behavior. In D. Diamond & S. J. Blatt (Eds.), Psychoanalytic theory and attachment research I: Theoretical considerations. *Psychoanalytic Inquiry, 19*, 481–540.

Hesse, E., & Main, M. (2000). Disorganized infant, child and adult attachment: Collapse in behavioral and attentional strategies. *Journal of the American Psychoanalytic Association, 48*(4), 1097–1127.

Hipwell, A. E., Goossens, F. A., Melhuish, E. C., & Kumar, R. (2000). Severe maternal psychopathology and infant–mother attachment. *Development and Psychopathology, 12*(2), 157–175.

Jacklin, C. N. (1989). Female and male: Issues of gender. *American Psychologist, 44*, 127–133.

John, O. P., & Srivastava, S. (1999). The Big Five trait taxonomy: History, measurement, and theoretical perspectives. In L. A. Pervin & O. P. John (Eds.), *Handbook of personality: Theory and research* (2nd ed., pp. 102–138). New York: Guilford Press.

Johnston, C., & Patenaude, R. (1994). Parent attributions for inattentive–overreactive and oppositional–defiant child behaviors. *Cognitive Therapy and Research, 18*, 261–275.

Kaufman, J., & Zigler, E. (1993). The intergenerational transmission of abuse is overstated. In R. J. Gelles & D. R. Loseke (Eds.), *Current controversies on family violence.* Newbury Park, CA: Sage.

Kessler, R. C., David, C. G., & Kendler, K. S. (1997). Childhood adversity and adult psychiatric disorder in the US National Comorbidity Survey. *Psychological Medicine, 27*, 1101–1119.

Kim, H. K., & Mckenry, P. C. (2002). The relationship between marriage and psychological well-being: A longitudinal analysis. *Journal of Family Issues, 23*(8), 885–911.

Kim, K. J., Conger, R. D., Elder, G. H., Jr., & Lorenz, F. O. (2003). Reciprocal influences between stressful life events and adolescent internalizing and externalizing problems. *Child Development, 74*(1), 127–143.

Kim-Cohen, J., Moffitt, T. E., Caspi, A., & Taylor, A. (2004). Genetic and environmental processes in young children's resilience and vulnerability to socioeconomic deprivation. *Child Development, 75*(3), 651–668.

Kobak, R. (1999). The emotional dynamics of disruptions in attachment relationships. In J. Cassidy & P. R. Shaver (Eds.), *Handbook of attachment: Theory, research, and clinical application* (pp. 21–43). New York: Guilford.

Kochanska, G., Clark, L., & Goldman, M. (1997). Implications of mothers' personality for parenting and their young children's developmental outcomes. *Journal of Personality, 65*, 389–420.

Krupnick, J. L., Sotsky, S. M., Simmens, D., Moyer, J., Elkin, I., Witkins, J., & Pilkonis, P. A. (1996). The role of the therapeutic alliance in psychotherapy and pharmacotherapy outcome: Findings in the National Institute of Mental Health Treatment of Depression Collaborative Research Program. *Journal of Consulting and Clinical Psychology, 64*, 532–539.

Laible, D. J., & Thompson, R. A. (1998). Attachment and emotional understanding in preschool children. *Developmental Psychology, 34*, 1038–1045.

Lakatos, K., Toth, I., Nemoda, Z., Ney, K., Sasvari-Szekely, M., & Gervai, J. (2000). Dopamine D4 receptor (DRD4) gene polymorphism is associated with attachment disorganization in infants. *Molecular Psychiatry, 5*(6), 633–637.

Laub, J. H., Nagin, D. S., & Sampson, R. J. (1998). Trajectories of change in criminal offending: Good marriages and the desistance process. *American Sociological Review, 63*, 225–238.

Levy-Shiff, R., & Israelashvilli, R. (1988). Antecedents of fathering. *Developmental Psychology, 24*, 434–441.

Lewis, M., Feiring, C., & Rosenthal, S. (2000). Attachment over time. *Child Development, 71*(3), 707–720.

Lieberman, A. F., & Pawl, J. H. (1988). Clinical applications of attachment theory. In J. Belsky & T. Nezworski (Eds.), *Clinical implications of attachment* (pp. 325–351). Hillsdale, NJ: Lawrence Erlbaum Associates.

Lieberman, A. F., Silverman, R., & Pawl, J. (2000). Infant–parent psychotherapy: Core concepts and current approaches. In C. Zeanah (Ed.), *Handbook of infant mental health* (2nd ed., pp. 472–484). New York: Guilford Press.

Lieberman, A. F., & Zeanah, C. H. (1999). Contributions of attachment theory to infant–parent psychotherapy and other interventions with infants and young children. In J. Cassidy & P. R. Shaver (Eds.), *Handbook of attachment: Theory, research, and clinical applications* (pp. 555–574). New York: Guilford Press.

Longfellow, C., Zelkowitz, P., & Saunders, E. (1982). The quality of mother–child relationships. In D. Belle (Ed.), *Lives in stress* (pp. 163–176). Beverly Hills, CA: Sage.

Losoya, S., Callor, S., Rowe, D., & Goldsmith, H. (1997). Origins of familial similarity in parenting. *Developmental Psychology, 33*, 1012–1023.

Lyons-Ruth, K., & Jacobvitz, D. (1999). Attachment disorganization: Unresolved loss, relational violence, and lapses in behavioral and attentional strategies. In J. Cassidy & P. R. Shaver (Eds.), *Handbook of attachment: Theory, research, and clinical applications* (pp. 520–554). New York: Guilford Press.

MacKinnon-Lewis, C., Castellino, D., Brody, G., & Fincham, F. D. (2001). A longitudinal examination of the associations between fathers' and children's attributions and negative interactions. *Social Development, 10*, 473–487.

MacKinnon-Lewis, C., Lamb, M. E., Arbuckle, B., Baradaran, L. P., & Volling, B. L. (1992). The relationship between biased maternal and filial attributions and the aggressiveness of their interactions. *Development and Psychopathology, 4*, 403–415.

Main, M., & Hesse, E. (1990). Parents' unresolved traumatic experiences are related to infant disorganized attachment status: Is frightened and/or frightening parental behavior the linking mechanism? In M. T. Greenberg, D. Cicchetti, & E. M. Cummings (Eds.), *Attachment in the preschool years: Theory, research, and intervention* (pp. 161–182). Chicago: University of Chicago Press.

Mangelsdorf, S., Gunnar, M., Kestenbaum, R., Lang, S., & Andreas, D. (1990). Infant proneness-to-distress temperament, maternal personality, and mother–infant attachment: Associations and goodness of fit. *Child Development, 61*, 820–831.

McGroder, S. M. (2000). Parenting among low-income, African American single mothers with preschool-age children: Patterns, predictors, and developmental correlates. *Child Development, 71*(3), 752–771.

Milner, J. S., & Chilamkurti, C. (1991). Physical child abuse perpetrator characteristics: A review of the literature. *Journal of Interpersonal Violence, 6*, 345–366.

Muller, R. T., Hunter, J. E., & Stollak, G. (1995). The intergenerational transmission of corporal punishment: A comparison of social learning and temperament models. *Child Abuse and Neglect, 19*(11), 1323–1335.

Muñoz, R. F., Ying, Y., Bernal, G., Perez-Stable, E. J., Sorenson, J. L., Hargreaves, W. A., Miranda, J., & Miller, L. S. (1995). Prevention of depression with primary care adults: A randomized control trial. *American Journal of Community Psychology, 23*, 199–222.

Murray, L., & Cooper, P. J. (Eds.). (1997). *Postpartum depression and child development.* New York: Guilford Press.

National Research Council. (1993). *Understanding child abuse and neglect.* Washington, DC: National Academy Press.

NICHD Early Child Care Research Network. (1999). Chronicity of maternal depressive symptoms, maternal sensitivity, and child functioning at 36 months: Results from the NICHD Study of Early Child Care. *Developmental Psychology, 35,* 1297–1310.

Nix, R. L., Pinderhughes, E. E., Dodge, K. A., Bates, J. E., Pettit, G. S., & McFadyen-Ketchum, S. A. (1999). The relation between mothers' hostile attribution tendencies and children's externalizing behavior problems: The mediating role of mothers' harsh discipline practices. *Child Development, 70*(4), 986–909.

O'Leary, D. A., Christian, J. L., & Mendell, N. R. (1994). A closer look at the link between marital discord and depressive symptomatology. *Journal of Social and Clinical Psychology, 13,* 33–41.

Orobio de Castro, B., Veerman, J. W., Koops, W., Bosch, J. D., & Monshouwer, H. J. (2002). Hostile attribution of intent and aggressive behavior: A meta-analysis. *Child Development, 73*(3), 916–934.

Patterson, G. R., & Yoerger, K. (1997). A developmental model for late-onset delinquency. *Nebraska Symposium on Motivation, 44,* 119–177.

Peterson, A. C., Compas, B. E., Brooks-Gunn, J., Stemmler, M., Ey, S., & Grant, K. E. (1993). Depression in adolescence. *American Psychologist, 48,* 155–186.

Quinton, D., Pickles, A., Maughan, B., & Rutter, M. (1993). Partners, peers, and pathways: Assortative pairing and continuities in conduct disorder. *Development and Psychopathology, 5,* 763–783.

Quinton, D., & Rutter, M. (1988). *Parenting breakdown: The making and breaking of intergenerational links.* Aldershot, UK: Avebury.

Radke-Yarrow, M. (1998). *Children of depressed mothers.* New York: Cambridge University Press.

Rauh, H., Ziegenhain, U., Muller, B., & Wijnroks, L. (2000). Stability and change in infant–mother attachment in the second year of life: Relations to parenting quality and varying degrees of daycare experience. In P. M. Crittenden & A. H. Claussen (Eds.), *The organization of attachment relationships: Maturation, culture, and context.* New York: Cambridge University Press.

Reichman, N. E., & McLanahan, S. S. (2001). Self-sufficiency programs and parenting interventions: Lessons from New Chance and the Teenage Parent Demonstration. Society for Research in Child Development. *Social Policy Report, 15*(2).

Reiss, D., & Neiderhiser, J. M. (2000). The interplay of genetic influences and social processes in developmental theory: Specific mechanisms are coming into view. *Development and Psychopathology, 12*(3), 357–374.

Reiss, D., Neiderhiser, J. M., Hetherington, E. M., & Plomin, R. (2000). *The relationship code: Deciphering genetic and social patterns in adolescent development.* Cambridge, MA: Harvard University Press.

Robins, L. N. (1966). *Deviant children grow up.* Baltimore: Williams & Wilkins.

Robins, L. N. (1986). The consequence of conduct disorder in girls. In D. Olweus, J. Block, & M. Radke-Yarrow (Eds.), *Development of antisocial and prosocial behavior: Research, theories, and issues* (pp. 385–414). Orlando, FL: Harcourt, Brace, Jovanovich.

Rutter, M. (1999). Psychosocial adversity and child psychopathology. *British Journal of Psychiatry, 174,* 480–493.

Rutter, M. (2000). Psychosocial influences: Critiques, findings, and research needs. *Development and Psychopathology, 12,* 375–405.

Rutter, M., & Quinton, D. (1984). Long-term follow-up of women institutionalized in childhood: Factors promoting good functioning in adult life. *British Journal of Developmental Psychology, 2,* 191–204.

Rutter, M., Quinton, D., & Hill, J. (1990). Adult outcome of institution-reared children: Males and females compared. In L. Robins & M. Rutter (Eds.), *Straight and deviant pathways from childhood to adulthood* (pp. 135–157). New York: Cambridge University Press.

Sarason, B. R., Sarason, I. G., & Gurung, R. A. (1997). Close personal relationships and health outcomes: A key to the role of social support. In S. W. Duck (Ed.), *Handbook of personal relationships: Theory, research and interventions* (2nd ed., pp. 547–573). Chichester, UK: Wiley.

Schneider, B. H., Atkinson, L., & Tardif, C. (2001). Child–parent attachment and children's peer relations: A quantitative review. *Developmental Psychology, 37*(1), 86–100.

Seligman, M. E. P., Schulman, P., DeRubeis, R. J., & Hollon, S. D. (1999). The prevention of depression and anxiety. *Prevention and Treatment, 2.* Retrieved on January 5, 2005, from http://gateway1.ma.ovid.com/ovidweb.cgi.

Silberg, J., Rutter, M., Neale, M., & Eaves, L. (2001). Genetic moderation of environmental risk for depression and anxiety in adolescent girls. *British Journal of Psychiatry, 179,* 116–121.

Simons, R., Beaman, J., Conger, R., & Chao, W. (1993). Childhood experience, conceptions of parenting, and attitudes of spouse as determinants of parental behavior. *Journal of Marriage and the Family, 55,* 91–106.

Skinner, M. L., Elder, G. H., Jr., & Conger, R. D. (1992). Linking economic hardship to adolescent aggression. *Journal of Youth and Adolescence, 21*(3), 259–276.

Skodak, M., & Skeels, H. M. (1949). A final follow-up study of one hundred adopted children. *Journal of Genetic Psychology, 75,* 85–125.

Slep, A., & O'Leary, S. (1998). The effects of maternal attributions on parenting. *Journal of Family Psychology, 12,* 234–243.

Spitz, R. A. (1945). Hospitalism: An inquiry into the genesis of psychiatric conditions in early childhood. *Psychoanalytic Study of the Child, 1,* 53–74.

Spitz, R. A. (1946). Anaclitic depression: An inquiry into the genesis of psychiatric conditions in early childhood, II. *Psychoanalytic Study of the Child, 2,* 313–324.

Stattin, H., & Kerr, M. (2000). Parental monitoring: A reinterpretation. *Child Development, 71*(4), 1072–1085.

Stattin, H., & Magnusson, D. (1996). Antisocial development: A holistic approach. *Development and Psychopathology, 8*(4), 617–645.

Sullivan, H. S. (1953). *The interpersonal theory of psychiatry.* New York: Norton.

Suomi, S. J. (1999). Attachment in Rhesus monkeys. In J. Cassidy & P. R. Shaver (Eds.), *Handbook of attachment: Theory, research, and clinical applications* (pp. 181–197). New York: Guilford Press.

Tellegen, A., Watson, D., & Clark, L. (1999). On the dimensional and hierarchichal structure of affect. *Psychological Science, 10,* 297–303.

Terman, L. (1938). *Psychological factors in marital happiness.* New York: McGraw-Hill.

Teti, D. M., Saken, J. W., Kucera, E., Corns, K. M., & Eiden, R. D. (1996). And baby makes four: Predictors of attachment security among preschool-age firstborns during the transition to siblinghood. *Child Development, 67,* 579–596.

Thompson, R. A. (1996). Early sociopersonality development. In W. Damon (Series Ed.) & N. Eisenberg (Vol. Ed.), *Handbook of child psychology: Vol. 3. Social, emotional, and personality development* (5th ed.). New York: Wiley.

Thompson, R. A. (1999). Early attachment and later development. In J. Cassidy & P. R. Shaver (Eds.), *Handbook of attachment: Theory, research, and clinical applications* (pp. 265–286). New York: Guilford Press.

Thompson, R. A., & Ontai, L. (2000). Striving to do well what comes naturally: Social support, developmental psychopathology, and social policy. *Development and Psychopathology, 12,* 657–675.

Tienari, P., Sorri, A., & Lahti, I. (1985). Interaction of genetic and psychosocial factors in schizophrenia. *Acta Psychiatric Scandinavica, 71,* 19–30.

Tienari, P., Wynne, L. C., Moring, J., Lahti, I., Maarala, M., Sorri, A., Wahlberg, K. E., Saarento, O., Seitamaa, M., Kaleva, M., & Laksy, K. (1994). The Finnish Adoption Family Study of Schizophrenia: Implications for family research. *British Journal of Psychiatry, 164,* 20–26.

Toth, S. L., Maughan, A., Manly, J. T., Spagnola, M., & Cicchetti, D. (2002). The relative efficacy of two interventions in altering maltreated preschool children's representational models: Implications for attachment theory. *Development and Psychopathology, 14*, 877–908.

Touris, M., Kromelow, S., & Harding, C. (1995). Mother–firstborn attachment and the birth of a sibling. *American Journal of Orthopsychiatry, 65*, 293–297.

Tupes, E. C., & Christal, R. C. (1961). *Recurrent personality factors based on trait ratings* (Tech. Rep.). Lackland Air Force Base, TX: USAF.

van Bakel, H. J. A., & Riksen-Walraven, J. M. (2002). Parenting and development of one-year-olds: Links with parental, contextual, and child characteristics. *Child Development, 73*(1), 256–273.

Van den Oord, E. J., Boomsma, I., & Verhulst, F. C. (1994). A study of problem behavior in 10- to 15-year-old biologically related and unrelated international adoptees. *Behavior Genetics, 24*, 193–205.

van IJzendoorn, M. H., Juffer, F., & Duyvesteyn, M. G. C. (1995). Breaking the intergenerational cycle of insecure attachment: A review of the effects of attachment-based interventions on maternal sensitivity and infant security. *Journal of Child Psychology and Psychiatry, 36*, 225–248.

van IJzendoorn, M. H., Moran, G., Belsky, J., Pederson, D., Bakermans-Kranenburg, M. J., & Kneppers, K. (2000). The similarity of siblings' attachments to their mother. *Child Development, 71*(4), 1086–1098.

van IJzendoorn, M. H., Schuengel, C., & Bakermans-Kranenburg, M. J. (1999). Disorganized attachment in early childhood: Meta-analyses of precursors, concomitants, and sequelae. *Development and Psychopathology, 11*, 225–249.

Vaughn, B., Egeland, B., Sroufe, L. A., & Waters, E. (1979). Individual differences in infant–mother attachment: Stability and change in families under stress. *Child Development, 50*, 971–975.

Verschueren, K., Marcoen, A., & Schoefs, V. (1996). The internal working model of the self, attachment, and competence in five-year-olds. *Child Development, 67*, 2493–2511.

Vondra, J., & Belsky, J. (1993). Developmental origins of parenting: Personality and relationship factors. In T. Luster & L. Okagaki (Eds.), *Parenting: An ecological perspective* (1st ed., pp. 1–33). Hillsdale, NJ: Lawrence Erlbaum Associates.

Vondra, J. I., Hommerding, K. D., & Shaw, D. S. (1999). Stability and change in infant attachment in a low-income sample. In J. I. Vondra & D. Barnett (Eds.), Atypical patterns of attachment in infancy and early childhood. *Monographs of the Society for Research in Child Development* (Serial No. 258, pp. 119–144). Malden, MA: Blackwell.

Vondra, J. I., Shaw, D. S., Swearingen, L., Cohen, M., & Owens, E. B. (2001). Attachment stability and emotional and behavioral regulation from infancy to preschool age. *Development and Psychopathology, 13*, 13–33.

Voydanoff, P., & Donnelly, B. (1998). Parents' risk and protective factors as predictors of parental well-being and behavior. *Journal of Marriage and the Family, 60*, 344–355.

Wartner, U. G., Grossmann, K., Fremmer-Bombik, E., & Suess, G. (1994). Attachment patterns at age six in South Germany: Predictability from infancy and implications for preschool behavior. *Child Development, 65*, 1014–1027.

Waters, E., Merrick, S., Treboux, D., Crowell, J., & Albersheim, L. (2000). Attachment security in infancy and early adulthood: A twenty-year longitudinal study. *Child Development, 71*(3), 684–689.

Watson, D., & Clark, L. (1984). Negative affectivity. *Psychological Bulletin, 95*, 465–490.

Weinfield, N. S., Sroufe, L. A., & Egeland, B. (2000). Attachment from infancy to early adulthood in a high-risk sample: Continuity, discontinuity, and their correlates. *Child Development, 71*(3), 695–702.

Whipple, E. E., Fitzgerald, H. E., & Zucker, R. A. (1995). Parent–child interactions in alcoholic and non-alcoholic families. *American Journal of Orthopsychiatry, 65*, 153–159.

Youngblade, L. M., & Belsky, J. (1990). The social and emotional consequences of child maltreatment. In R. Ammerman & M. Hersen (Eds.), *Children at risk: An evaluation of factors contributing to child abuse and neglect* (pp. 109–146). New York: Plenum Press.

Zaslow, M., Pedersen, F., Cain, R., Suwalsky, J., & Kramer, E. (1985). Depressed mood in new fathers. *Genetic, Social, and General Psychology Monographs, 111*, 133–150.

Zelkowitz, P. (1982). Parenting philosophies and practices. In D. Belle (Ed.), *Lives in stress* (pp. 154–162). Beverly Hills, CA: Sage.

Zimmerman, P., Fremmer-Bombik, E., Spangler, G., & Grossman, K. E. (1997). Attachment in adolescence: A longitudinal perspective. In W. Koops, J. B. Hoeksema, & D. C. van den Boom (Eds.), *Development of interaction and attachment: Traditional and non traditional approaches* (pp. 281–291). Amsterdam: North-Holland.

Zucker, R. A., & Gomberg, E. S. L. (1986). Etiology of alcoholism reconsidered: The case for a biopsychosocial process. *American Psychologist, 41*, 783–793.

3

Adolescent Mothers and Their Children: An Ecological Perspective

Tom Luster
Michigan State University

Julie Laser Haddow
University of Denver

INTRODUCTION

During the 1990s, there was a decline in the birthrate among adolescent females in the United States. The number of births per 1,000 females ages 15 to 19 was 42.9 in 2002 compared to 62.1 per 1,000 in 1991 (Child Trends, 2003). A number of factors contributed to this decline in the birthrate. The percentage of high school students who were sexually active decreased (Centers for Disease Control, 2001), and the use of contraception generally increased (Terry & Manlove, 2000). In addition, longer-term forms of birth control, such as Depo Provera and the birth control patch, became available.

Although fewer teens are becoming parents, there were still 431,988 births to adolescents in the U.S. in 2002 (Child Trends, 2003). Moreover, the birthrate to adolescents in the U.S. continues to be much higher than it is in most other developed countries (Child Trends, 2001). Countries with very low birthrates (e.g., Japan, Italy, Spain) have fewer than 10 births per 1,000 teenage females. Teens in the U.S. are less likely to use contraception consistently than teens in most other developed countries, and that is the primary reason why other developed countries have lower birthrates among teens than the U.S. (Alan Guttmacher Institute, 2002).

During the past several decades, numerous studies have been conducted to determine the antecedents of early childbearing and the effects of early childbearing on the adolescents and their children. Other studies focused on factors that influence the way in which adolescents parent their children. In this chapter, we summarize the results of some of the key studies in these areas. The chapter is divided into four parts. In the first section, we examine factors associated with early sexual activity and childbearing. In what ways do adolescents who become mothers differ from adolescents who do not? It is important to consider selection factors when discussing the outcomes of adolescent mothers and their children, and when examining the parenting practices of adolescent mothers. The second section focuses on the outcomes of adolescent mothers in areas such as education and income. In this section, we review research that has addressed two related questions: (a) How do adolescent mothers differ from peers who delay childbearing on these outcomes? and (b) To what extent are these outcomes due to early childbearing, and to what extent can they be explained by selection factors? In the third section, we consider the consequences of early childbearing for the children. The questions of interest are: (a) How do the children of adolescent mothers fare compared to children born to older mothers? and (b) What factors contribute to successful outcomes among children born to adolescent mothers? The fourth section examines research concerned with individual differences in parenting practices among adolescents mothers. Some adolescent mothers provide very supportive environments for their children, while other mothers provide less optimal environments. Based on Belsky's (1984) model of the determinants of parenting, the influences on parenting of interest to us include characteristics of the young mothers, contextual sources of stress and support, and characteristics of their children. We are especially interested in adolescent mothers who are functioning well in their role as parents. Knowledge about why they adapt successfully to the challenges of early parenthood should be useful to those who design programs for adolescent mothers and their children.

FACTORS ASSOCIATED WITH EARLY CHILDBEARING

Adolescent mothers are diverse. They come from all racial, ethnic, and income groups. There are adolescent mothers who are National Merit Scholars and others who are in special education classes. Some adolescent mothers are well adjusted, and others are troubled or depressed. Because of this diversity, it is important not to stereotype adolescent mothers. On the other hand, we must also recognize that adolescent mothers are not representative of adolescent females in the population. For example, birthrates differ by race. The birthrate in the United States in 2001 was highest for Latina adolescents (84 per 1,000), followed by African American (74 per 1,000) and Non-Hispanic Whites (30 per 1,000) (Child Trends, 2003). In this section of the chapter, we examine factors associated with becoming an adolescent mother. In general, these studies show that adolescents who become parents are more likely than their peers to come from relatively disadvantaged circumstances (e.g., low-income families and impoverished neighborhoods), experience a variety of risk factors (e.g., sexual abuse) and have limited internal (e.g., educational aptitude) and external assets (e.g., parents who closely monitor their activities; appealing options in the area of education and employment) (Hotz, McElroy, & Sanders, 1997; Luker, 1991; Small & Luster, 1994; Manlove et al., 2002; Miller, 2002; Moore, Miller, Glie, & Morrison, 1995; Musick, 1993).

Comparisons of adolescents who become parents and those who do not show that the two groups differ, on average, on several characteristics. Adolescents who are struggling in school, score low on tests of educational aptitude, or who have dropped out of school are at risk for early childbearing (Hotz et al., 1997; Jaffee, Caspi, Moffitt, Belsky, & Silva, 2001; Moore, Miller, Glie, & Morrison, 1995; Rauch-Elnekave, 1994). Those who become adolescent parents are more likely than their peers to have a history of sexual abuse, to abuse alcohol and other drugs, and to engage in other problematic behaviors (Butler & Burton, 1990; Boyer & Fine, 1992; Luster & Small, 1997; Moore et al., 1995; Musick, 1993). Conduct disorders in childhood are also predictive of teenage pregnancy (Kessler et al., 1997; Kovacs, Krol, & Voti, 1994; Miller-Johnson et al., 1999; Zoccolillo, Meyers, & Assiter, 1997; Zoccolillo & Rogers, 1991). This is not to suggest that most adolescent mothers have these characteristics; these characteristics are just found more often in adolescent mothers than in the overall population of adolescent females.

Similarly, on average, adolescent mothers differ from their peers in terms of family background characteristics. A disproportionate number of teenage mothers live in single-parent households, in families living below the poverty line, with parents who obtained low levels of education, and with mothers who had their first children as teenagers (Hotz et al., 1997; Kahn & Anderson, 1992; Luker, 1991). In our longitudinal study in Flint, Michigan, we were also struck by how many of the adolescent mothers had troubled relationships with their parents (Luster, 1998). Although the problems may have been due, at least in part, to having an infant as a teenager or the normal conflicts that adolescents have as they push for independence, many of the adolescents reported long-standing relationship problems with their parents or between their parents. Another possible family influence on adolescent parenthood is the behavior of older siblings; it increases the risk of early pregnancy among the younger adolescent siblings when older siblings have their first children as teenagers (East & Jacobson, 2001).

Adolescents who become mothers are also more likely to come from impoverished neighborhoods and to attend schools where rates of adolescent pregnancies are high (Brewster, 1994; Musick, 1993). Adolescents may be less likely to postpone having children if the future they envision for themselves does not include opportunities for postsecondary educations and high paying jobs. The future they envision for themselves may be strongly influenced by what they observe about the lives of those who live in their neighborhoods and communities.

Adolescents may also be influenced by the behavior of their peers and partners. Some researchers have proposed a social contagion model of adolescent sexuality with peers strongly influencing the sexual attitudes and behavior of adolescents (Rodgers & Rowe, 1993). In addition, early parenthood may seem more appealing if friends gain status and attention from having a baby. Male partners may also pressure adolescents into having a child early.

Looking across numerous studies on factors related to early childbearing, Moore and her colleagues (1995) concluded, "Perhaps the clearest conclusion that can be drawn across the myriad of studies examined is that the youth most at risk for becoming parents during their teen years are those least well-situated to raise a healthy, well-adjusted and high achieving child" (p. 148). These selection factors also have implications for the life-course outcomes of adolescent mothers.

OUTCOMES FOR ADOLESCENT MOTHERS

Given what is known about selection factors that are associated with becoming a teenage parent, it is not surprising that adolescent mothers tend to fare less well than their peers on a variety of life-course outcomes. For example, adolescent mothers are less likely than women who delay having children to finish high school or obtain a GED (Hotz et al., 1997; Klepinger, Lundberg, & Plotnick, 1995). By age 30, 61% of women who had their first child by age 18 had a high school diploma or GED compared with 91% of women who did not have a child during their teen years (Hotz et al., 1997). Researchers have been trying to determine if early childbearing is the reason why adolescent mothers obtain lower level of education or if the lower level of education is due to characteristics of the young mothers (e.g., low academic aptitude) or family background characteristics (e.g., low parental education, poverty). Many approaches have been used to tease apart the influence of early childbearing and selection factors on educational attainment.

One approach is to control for characteristics of the women and their families in the analysis when examining the relation between early childbearing and educational attainment. Klepinger and his colleagues (1995) used this approach and found that having a child before age 20 reduced the level of education attained by almost three years for Whites, Blacks, and

Hispanics at age 25. The variables they controlled included such things as parental education, parental divorce, and attending religious services.

Some researchers have argued that it is difficult to control statistically for all relevant background characteristics and have used other creative approaches to address this issue. Hotz and his colleagues (1997) compared females who had their first child before age 18 with females who became pregnant before age 18 but had a miscarriage and, therefore did not have their first child until later; on average, those who had a miscarriage had their first children three to four years later than the teenage mothers. Given that both groups had become pregnant as teenagers, the researchers concluded that females who had miscarriages as teenagers provided an ideal comparison group for teenage mothers. The two groups were not likely to differ markedly in terms of family background characteristics and other factors associated with becoming pregnant at an early age. Hotz found that teen mothers were much less likely than those who had miscarriages to receive a standard high school diploma (41% vs. 61%), but they were more likely to obtain a GED (23% vs. 2%). Overall there was no effect of early childbearing on obtaining a high school level education if high school diplomas and GEDs are treated as equivalent.

By age 30, the annual earnings of women who had their first children before age 18 is only 58% of the annual earnings of all other women who delayed having children (Hotz et al., 1997). The earnings gap is due both to the lower wages teenage mothers earn and the fewer hours that they work per year. Once again researchers have tried to determine if the earnings gap is due to early childbearing per se or selection factors associated with early childbearing. Hotz and colleagues compared the annual earnings of teenage mothers and women who had miscarriages prior to age 18. The annual earnings of both groups were low, but those who had their first births before age 18 earned significantly more from their mid 20s through mid 30s than those who had miscarriages. Hotz and his colleagues explained this surprising finding by noting that both groups of women ended up in jobs that did not require special educational credentials; job skills were acquired on the job and higher compensation was obtained through the acquisition of these skills and through continuity on the job. Women who completed their childbearing in their early 20s had an advantage over women from similar backgrounds who had children later; the women who had miscarriages delayed their entry into the labor force or moved in and out of jobs as they had their children during their 20s.

Geronimus and Korenman (1992) also used a creative approach to disentangle the effects of early childbearing and selection factors on socioeconomic status outcomes. Utilizing three national data sets, they compared women who had their first children during their teenage years with their sisters who had their children after their teen years; the sisters were about five years older, on average, than the teenage mothers when they had their first child. Presumably the sisters have similar family background characteristics and exposure to other risk factors such as substandard schools or neighborhoods with high concentrations of impoverished families. As expected, differences in family income, family income-to-needs ratio, and poverty rates were less pronounced when the sisters were compared than when a cross section of early childbearers and women who delayed childbearing were compared and family background characteristics were statistically controlled. (This was true for two out of three national data sets; for the Panel Study of Income Dynamics, differences between the sisters were comparable to differences between early and later childbearers in the cross-sectional sample.) What differences there were between the sisters in their family income-to-needs ratio could be explained by the higher level of education obtained by the sister who delayed childbearing and by the fact that the later childbearers were more likely to be married at the time that family income was measured.

The studies by Hotz et al. (1997) and Geronimus and Korenman (1992) indicate that simple comparisons (i.e., those that do not control for selection factors) of teenage mothers and females who delay childbearing until their 20s tend to overestimate the effects of early childbearing per se on outcomes such as educational attainment, income, and poverty status. Nevertheless, whatever the cause of the disadvantage, the fact remains that children of teenage mothers are more likely than other children to be raised by parents with low educational levels and low levels of income.

Another outcome of interest is the marital status of the young mothers. Approximately four out of five teen births are nonmarital (Child Trends, 2003); among women of all ages in the US, about one third of births are nonmarital. Thus, children of teenage mothers are more likely than other children to live with a never-married mother for at least part of their lives. Hotz et al. (1997) compared teenage mothers and women who had miscarriages during their teen years on the percentage of time spent as a single mothers from age 14 to 30. Teenage mothers spent more time as single mothers during those years than those who had miscarriages as teens and had their children three to four years later on average. Part of the concern about teenage parenthood results from the knowledge that a disproportionate number of their children grow up in homes without their fathers. Moreover, among adolescent mothers who marry the fathers, divorce rates tend to be high (Furstenberg, Brooks-Gunn, & Morgan, 1987).

In addition to interest in the marital status of adolescent mothers, there is growing interest in the quality of relationships they have with their male partners or spouses. Leadbeater and Way (2001) conducted one of the few studies of domestic violence among adolescent mothers in their sample from New York City. They interviewed the mothers six years after their children were born and asked about physical abuse, sexual abuse, and controlling behavior by male partners (e.g., telling them when they could leave the house). Of the 93 young mothers in the sample, 41% had experienced abuse by a male partner. Another 31% had experienced or were currently involved in relationships with male partners that were viewed primarily as negative and conflicted. Only 28% described their former or current relationships as positive or neutral. Mothers who were abused by their partners experienced more depressive symptoms and were more likely to be self-critical than mothers involved in positive relationships with their partners. They also tended to change residences more frequently than other mothers over the six years of the study. Maternal depressive symptoms and frequent changes in residence were associated with more problem behaviors in children at age 6.

Some studies have compared adolescent mothers and older mothers (i.e., 20 or older) on measures of depression or other indicators of psychological well-being. Several studies have shown that adolescent mothers exhibit more depressive symptoms than mothers who are older, but often these comparison are made without controlling for possible confounding variables (Osofsky, Hann, & Peebles, 1993). Whitman, Borkowski, Keogh, and Weed (2001) assessed depression levels in their sample at three and five years after the children were born. Approximately 10% of their sample exhibited moderate to severe levels of depression at each assessment and another quarter of the sample experienced mild depression levels. The adolescent mothers also had self-esteem scores that were low relative to adolescents in the general population. Given the troubled histories of some adolescent mothers and the challenges of their current circumstances, it is not surprising that some adolescent mothers exhibit signs of psychological distress.

However, the young age of the mother may be less important for predicting depression in later years than her marital status and background characteristics. Using data from the National Longitudinal Survey of Youth (NLSY), Kalil and Kunz (2002) found that women who had their first children as teenagers had higher depression scores at ages 27 to 28 than women who had their first child at age 20 or later. However, the effect of age at first birth was reduced to nonsignificance when marital status at the time of the birth was controlled. Mothers who were unmarried had more depressive symptoms in young adulthood than mothers who were married. Further analyses suggested that prebirth individual and family characteristics (i.e., selection factors) were stronger predictors of depressive symptoms in young adulthood than either marital status or age at first birth. Women with more depressive symptoms were more likely to have lived with a stepfather at age 14 and to have scored low on the Armed Forces Qualification Test (AFQT), a measure of educational aptitude.

To summarize, research shows that adolescent mothers are more likely than mothers in the general population to achieve lower levels of education, have low paying jobs, and to be single parents. Thus a disproportionate number of their children live in poverty and experience the risks associated with poverty. However, it is also clear that these outcomes cannot be completely explained by early childbearing per se; characteristics of the teens who become parents and of their contexts (family, neighborhood) contribute to these outcomes as well. The research also shows that adolescent mothers are diverse. Some young mothers achieve high levels of education, obtain good jobs, enjoy high levels of support from their partners and their parents, and live in safe neighborhoods with the infrastructure to support young families (e.g., day care, medical services, parks, good schools).

OUTCOMES FOR CHILDREN BORN
TO ADOLESCENT MOTHERS

As teenage mothers are quite diverse in their competencies, environmental context, level of social support, and intellectual abilities, their children are also wide-ranging in their level of functioning. There has been keen interest in following these children as they develop. Many longitudinal studies have monitored these children as they negotiated important developmental milestones (Furstenberg et al., 1987; Jaffee, Caspi, Moffitt, Belsky, & Silva, 2001; Leadbeater & Way, 2001; Luster, Bates, Fitzgerald, Vandenbelt, & Key, 2000; Moore, Morrison, & Greene, 1997; Seitz & Apfel, 1993; Whitman, Borkowski, Keogh, & Weed, 2001). In this section, we summarize the findings from these longitudinal studies and other key studies.

Although there are different life scenarios for each of these children, some common issues for children born to adolescent mothers have emerged from the data. Many researchers have found that these children achieve lower scores in assessments of cognition, social development, emotional development, and language proficiency as compared to children born to adult mothers (Furstenberg et al., 1987; Jaffee et al., 2001; Luster et al., 2000; Moore & Brooks-Gunn, 2002; Moore et al., 1997; Whitman et al., 2001).

Developmental Assessments

Although most infants born to adolescent mothers are healthy at birth, developmental delays become notable shortly thereafter for a disproportionate number of these children (Whitman et al., 2001). At 1 year of age, children born to adolescent mothers made fewer vocalizations than infants of adult mothers (Culp, Osofsky, & O'Brien, 1996). Children of adolescent mothers also had lower scores on receptive language assessments than their peers born to adult mothers in the Notre Dame longitudinal study (Whitman et al., 2001). At 3 years of age, nearly three fourths of the children born to adolescent mothers in the Notre Dame study experienced delays in one domain of development, and nearly one half of the children had delays in two domains of development.

Academic Difficulties

Investigators have found that these developmental delays extend past the earliest years of life. It has been noted that children born to adolescent mothers are at risk for low school readiness (Furstenberg et al., 1987; Luster et al., 2000). This is a troublesome finding because school readiness is predictive of academic outcomes in elementary school, as well as educational attainment in adulthood (Luster & McAdoo, 1996).

Academic difficulties continue for many children born to adolescent mothers throughout their school years (Furstenberg et al., 1987; Whitman et al., 2001). Furthermore, high rates of special education placement have been documented for these students (Furstenberg et al., 1987; Whitman et al., 2001). By adolescence, nearly fifty percent of children born to adolescent mothers who participated in the Baltimore Longitudinal Project had repeated a school grade (Furstenberg et al., 1987). Not surprisingly, low educational aspirations have also been found in these youth (Furstenberg et al., 1987). Thus, school achievement is an area of concern for children born to adolescent mothers.

There are both selection factors and environmental factors that predispose the children born to adolescent mothers to do less well in school than their peers born to adult mothers (Jaffee et al., 2001). Levine, Pollack, and Comfort (2001) found that most of the relation between early childbearing and academic and behavioral outcomes of children born to adolescent mothers can be explained by individual and family background factors of the adolescent mother. Adolescent mothers who participated in Whitman and colleagues' (2001) Notre Dame study had an average full scale IQ of 87, well below 100, the average IQ score for the population. Low intellectual ability on the part of the mothers was predictive of poor school performance by the children.

It has also been documented that many of children born to adolescent mothers did not grow up in enriched environments in which they were being stimulated by adult interaction and had developmentally appropriate toys and activities (Dubow & Luster, 1990; Moore et al., 1997; Whitman et al., 2001). In addition, Whitman and his colleagues (2001) found that children born to adolescent mothers were more likely than their peers born to adult mothers to exhibit insecure attachment, which may reduce their problem-solving ability by undermining their ability to self-regulate (Borkowski & Dukewich, 1996). Low maternal intellectual ability, the quantity and quality of their interaction with adults, rates of insecure attachment, and unstimulating environments may be some of the underlying reasons why the children born to adolescent mothers have more academic problems than children born to adult mothers.

Behavior Problems

Higher levels of internalizing problems have also been documented in children born to adolescent mothers relative to those born to adult mothers (Moore et al., 1997; Whitman et al., 2001). Internalizing problems are turning feelings of frustration, embarrassment, and anger inwardly upon oneself in the form of depression, low self-esteem, helplessness, or self-loathing.

In addition, many children born to adolescent mothers have exhibited behavior problems at home or at school (Dubow & Luster, 1990; Furstenberg et al., 1987; Levine et al., 2001; Moore et al., 1997; Seitz & Apfel, 1993; Whitman et al., 2001). When they reach their teen years, the offspring of adolescent mothers have higher rates of delinquency than those born to adult mothers (Furstenberg et al., 1987; Grogger, 1997; Jaffee et al., 2001). Similarly, higher rates of incarceration have been found in children born to adolescent mothers (Grogger, 1997). However, Nagin, Pogarsky, and Farrington (1997) found that higher rates of criminality in the offspring of adolescent mothers were explained by such factors as paternal criminal behavior, poor or neglectful parenting, poor role modeling, and diminished resources. Nagin, Pogarsky, and Farrington (1997) concluded that "early childbearing is not a cause of subsequent problem behavior but rather a marker for a set of behaviors and social forces that give rise to adverse consequences for the life chances of children" (p. 147).

Child Outcomes: The Importance of Selection
Factors Versus Young Maternal Age

Children of adolescent mothers perform less well than children born to older mothers on a variety of indicators including measures of receptive vocabulary, achievement, and behavior problems. Much like the studies that have compared the outcomes of adolescent and older mothers (e.g., income and education), some researchers have tried to determine if the poor outcomes observed in children born to adolescent mothers are largely due to the young age of the mother or selection factors, such as the family background characteristics of the teens who become mothers. Adapting the approach that Geronimus and her colleagues used to study the effects of early childbearing on the outcomes of the mothers, some researchers have compared the children born to adolescent mothers with the children born to the sisters of adolescent mothers who had their first child after their teen years (Geronimus, Korenman, & Hillemeier, 1994; Turley, 2003). In this approach, cousins are compared so that the family background characteristics of their mothers are similar.

Using data from the NLSY, Geronimus, Korenman, and Hillemeier (1994) found that children born to the teenage mothers did not fare any worse than their cousins on measures that assessed outcomes in the area of receptive vocabulary, academic achievement, verbal memory and behavior problems. In contrast, more conventional analyses that compared children born to teenage mothers and children born to older mothers while controlling for family background characteristics suggested that children of teenage mothers generally fared somewhat worse than comparison children. Geronimus and her colleagues argued that their comparison of cousins controls for family background characteristics more comprehensively, including characteristics that are not measured and controlled in more traditional analyses. Based on these analyses, they concluded ". . . our findings suggest that the heightened risk of poor performance on developmental indicators may be common to children of disadvantaged mothers in general, not peculiar to those with teenage mothers" (p. 604).

In a similar study by Turley (2003) comparing the performance of first cousins with more recent waves of NLSY data, there was not a significant effect of maternal age at first birth on math achievement, vocabulary, or behavior problems; however, there was an effect of maternal age at first birth on reading. Turley also reran the analysis limiting the sample to children born to sisters who began childbearing at least five years apart, and the results were the same. Maternal age at first birth was also unrelated to how children's scores on the NLSY measures (e.g., achievement test scores) changed from the first assessment to the last assessment (a span of 2 to 12 years). Overall, these results support the view that the poor outcomes for the children can be largely explained by selection factors rather than the mother's age when the children were born.

Jaffee, Caspi, Moffitt, Belsky, and Silva (2001) used data from a 20-year longitudinal study in Dunedin, New Zealand to examine the effects of early childbearing on four outcomes measured when the children ranged in age from 15 to 21. The outcomes were: (1) early school leaving, (2) unemployment, (3) early parenthood, and (4) violent offending. Children born to teenage mothers showed poorer outcomes on each of these four measures than children born to mothers who did not have their first child as a teenager. Next, the investigators attempted to determine the extent to which the poorer outcomes could be explained by social selection factors and the extent to which they could be explained by the social circumstances in which the children were reared. Variables identified as social selection variables included maternal IQ, maternal reading ability, school certification, maternal conviction history and paternal conviction history. Several family variables were used as indicators of social circumstances including several measures of parent–child interaction, SES, household composition, and residential instability.

The results showed that both selection factors and social circumstances explain the poorer outcomes of children born to adolescent mothers. Maternal characteristics, such as low IQ scores or poor reading ability, accounted for approximately 18% of the effect of teen childbearing on children's outcomes. On average, family circumstances accounted for about 21% of the teen childbearing effect on the outcomes after controlling for maternal characteristics; the unique effect of family circumstances was smallest for unemployment (12%) and largest for early school leaving (32%). Jaffee and her colleagues concluded that both selection factors and family circumstances that result from early childbearing explain the poorer outcomes observed in children of adolescent mothers.

The findings regarding child outcomes are similar to the findings regarding the outcomes for the mothers. There is a strong association between early childbearing and child outcomes when there are no controls for other factors. When there are controls for social selection factors, the relation between early childbearing and child outcomes is greatly reduced and in some cases is no longer significant. However, for some outcomes, selection factors do not fully account for the relation between early childbearing and child outcomes. It is also noteworthy that later-born children of mothers who had their first children as adolescents have outcomes that are similar to those of their siblings who were born when the mothers were still teenagers (Jaffee et al., 2001; Moore, Morrison, & Greene, 1997; Turley, 2003). Whatever is accounting for the poorer outcomes of first-born children of adolescent mothers seems to be having the same effect on their later-born children, who are born when these mothers are in their 20s.

Victims of Child Abuse

Research has also demonstrated that children of adolescent mothers are at greater risk for becoming victims of child abuse (Bolton, 1990; Goerge & Lee, 1997; McCullough & Scherman, 1998; Whitman et al., 2001) and have higher rates of foster care placement than children of adult mothers (Goerge & Lee, 1997). This higher rate of child abuse has been partially attributed to adolescent mothers' lack of child development knowledge, immature interaction styles between mother and child, and reliance on punitive physical discipline for child misbehaviors (Whitman et al., 2001).

Intergenerational Adolescent Parenting

Being a child of an adolescent mother is predictive of early sexual experience and becoming an adolescent parent (Furstenberg et al., 1987; Haveman, Wolfe, & Peterson, 1997; Jaffee et al., 2001; Levine et al., 2001). Therefore, adolescent parenthood is a recurring pattern for some families (Moore & Brooks-Gunn, 2002).

Resilient Teen Mothers

Although the outcomes for some children of adolescent mothers seem bleak, many of these children are competent, high achievers and well-adjusted. It is useful to study these thriving offspring to investigate factors that promote resilient children. In addition, it is useful to explore factors that contribute to resilience among adolescent mothers and linkages between the development of the mothers and children.

Based on their longitudinal study, Werner (1990, 1994) and Werner and Smith (1989, 1992, 2001) discuss protective characteristics of the adolescent mothers that are associated with positive outcomes in their children. These protective factors included: strong attachment to the infant, positive interactions between mother and infant, feelings of responsibility and flexibility on the part of the mother, post-secondary education of the mother, a supportive partner, fewer subsequent children, and social support from family and friends. Werner and Smith also acknowledged that the outcomes of the young mothers improved with the passage of time; typically the adolescent mothers' situation (e.g., financial security) improved in their thirties and forties.

Furstenberg and colleagues (1987) found that the most economically successful adolescent mothers limited further childbearing and were motivated to continue their education and to become self-supported. However, the strongest predictor of mother's involvement with welfare by participants in the Baltimore study was the educational attainment of the maternal grandparents; teen mothers who had parents who had more education spent less time on welfare. Moore and Brooks-Gunn (2002) concluded that the factors predicting positive functioning for adolescent mothers were being on grade level at the time of pregnancy, having a parent with at least a tenth-grade education, attending a school for pregnant teens, having future educational aspirations, and finishing high school. They defined positive functioning as a family income of $25,000 or more, lack of involvement with welfare for over a year, and having fewer than three children.

Leadbeater and Way (2001) found some recurring themes in their interviews with resilient inner-city adolescent mothers. Regarding the family of origin of these mothers, they often stated that they had been reared in strict and disciplined homes, had family members who valued education and who were positive role models. Many successful adolescent mothers acknowledged that support by family members had been provided conditionally, with an understanding that the parents had clear expectations for the young mothers. Frequently, these mothers' internal characteristics included an optimistic attitude, autonomy, tenacity, and a strong desire to succeed. Leadbeater and Way also found that these young women often had access to and support for post-secondary education.

The psychological well-being of the mother has a profound effect on the parenting of the child (Belsky, 1984). Maternal depression has been associated with problematic child behaviors and continued dependence on welfare (Almgren, Yamashiro, & Ferguson, 2002). Crockenberg (1988) found that higher levels of maternal social support increased both feelings of maternal self-esteem and positive parenting of her child. Furthermore, high maternal self-esteem has been found to be predictive of children's social competence (Hubbs-Tait, Osofsky, Hann, & Culp, 1994). Similarly, it has been reported that adolescent mother's parenting skills are related to her self-esteem (Hurlbut, Culp, & Jambunathan, 1997). In sum, the evidence suggests that greater maternal psychological well-being contributes to positive outcomes for her child.

Resilient Mothers and Children

Whitman and colleagues (2001) separated adolescent mothers and children into four categories: resilient mothers with resilient children, vulnerable mothers with resilient children, resilient mothers with vulnerable children, and vulnerable mothers with vulnerable children. Maternal resiliency was defined as graduation from or currently enrolled in high school, current employment, higher self-esteem scores and lower scores on inventories of depression and anxiety. Resilience in the children was defined as average intellectual functioning, average adaptive behaviors, and nonclinical levels of behavioral problems. Overall, children were two times more likely to be resilient, if their mothers were resilient.

Eighteen percent of the Notre Dame Project sample was categorized as resilient mothers with resilient children. These mothers were characterized as "more cognitively ready for their maternal roles" (p. 185). This included meeting the child's needs with greater empathy and listening to the child. These mothers also were more openly affectionate to their children. Furthermore, these mothers were more aware of the appropriate developmental milestones than other young mothers. The young women were more accepting of their children and more involved in their daily care. A supportive partner was often present in the lives of the mother and the child. These mothers also reported that their children had easy temperaments.

Academically, the young women had more education than any of the other subgroups and were more likely to be at grade level. This group of adolescent mothers was also characterized as being socially competent and high in self-esteem.

Resilient mothers with vulnerable children accounted for nearly 20% of the Notre Dame Project sample. In general, this subgroup of mothers had high academic attainment and good social competence. However, this subgroup differed from the previous subgroup in their ability to transition to the role of mother, and the level of emotional support that they received from their partners. The investigators reported that the mothers of this subgroup were either less able or less willing to perform the role of mother. Many were unaware of the developmental needs of their children and were not child-centered in their focus. Most adolescent mothers in this group also had conflicted or nonexistent relationships with the child's father.

Vulnerable mothers with resilient children comprised nearly 14% of the overall sample. Vulnerable mothers tended to be younger, to have completed less education, and were less likely to be at grade level. Many of these mothers also had difficulty accepting their maternal role and often had little child development knowledge. The vulnerable mothers who had resilient children often reported positive relationships with the child's father. Interestingly, the children of this subgroup spent the greatest amount of time in their grandparents' care; these resilient children had surrogates to provide for them.

The remaining 50% of the mother–child dyads of the Notre Dame Project were categorized as vulnerable mothers and vulnerable children.

Resilient Children Born to Teen Mothers

In our longitudinal study in Flint, we separated our sample of children born to adolescent women into quartiles based on their receptive vocabulary scores at age 54 months, and compared the experiences of the children who had scored in the highest quartile with those of children in the bottom quartile (Luster et al., 2000). The most successful children had experienced much more supportive care throughout the duration of the study, were frequently read to, had mothers who had higher academic attainment and who were more likely to be employed, were living with a father or father figure as well as their mother, were the only child in the family, and had maternal grandmothers who had completed high school. Furthermore, when these children were in first grade, high scores on achievement tests were related to authoritative parenting practices (Vandenbelt, Luster, & Bates, 2001). In particular, children who performed better on first grade achievement tests had mothers who were child centered, read to them, demonstrated warmth, limit-setting, and praise, and communicated effectively about household rules during the preschool years.

Summary of Results Regarding Resilience

Some common themes emerge in studies focusing on relatively successful adolescent mothers and their children. Adolescent mothers who are more cognitively and emotionally prepared to parent make better parents. Knowledge of child development and parenting techniques that show both warmth and concern for the child's feelings but also limit-setting and logical consequences for misbehavior are predictive of successful outcomes in children of adolescent mothers. Likewise, maximizing educational attainment for the adolescent mothers is beneficial for them, as well as their children. Moreover, limiting further childbearing is associated with positive outcomes for both the mothers and their children.

The father of the child has the opportunity to be a positive role model in the life of the child, as well as a source of support for the mother. Furthermore, accessing formal as well as informal sources of social support is important for young mothers. Various types of support can influence their educational advancement, career paths, parenting information, emotional well-being, and parenting practices.

FACTORS RELATED TO INDIVIDUAL DIFFERENCES IN THE PARENTING PRACTICES OF ADOLESCENT MOTHERS

Adolescent mothers, like older mothers, differ markedly in their parenting practices. Some young mothers provide excellent care for their children whereas others abuse or neglect their children. Most provide care that is somewhere between those two extremes. Many researchers have been interested in factors that are related to individual differences in the quality of care that adolescent mothers provide their children.

Theories regarding the determinants of parenting have focused on influences in three domains: (1) characteristics of the parent; (2) characteristics of the child; and (3) contextual sources of stress and support (Belsky, 1984; Schellenbach, Whitman, & Borkowski, 1992). The developmental history of the teen, which refers the experiences she had in the years prior to the time that she became a parent, is also viewed as an important influence on parenting. In the following sections, we will review research that has examined potential influences on parenting in each of those categories. It is important to keep in mind that nearly all of these studies used correlational designs; these studies determine what factors are associated with the parenting practices of young mothers, but cannot determine if the relations are causal. Therefore, caution must be used in drawing conclusions about the determinants of parenting practices.

Characteristics of the Parent

Several studies have focused on individual differences among adolescent mothers in their levels of depression, cognitive readiness for parenting, and educational attainment or intellectual competence. Of these three characteristics, the characteristic of the mothers that has been studied most frequently is depressive symptoms. As expected, the results from these studies show that mothers with more depressive symptoms tend to provide less supportive care for their children. In studies of adolescent mothers, higher levels of depressive symptoms are associated with child neglect (Zuravin & DiBlasio, 1996), fewer contingent responses in free-play interactions (Leadbeater, Bishop, & Raver, 1996), more negative feeding interactions with infants (Panzarine, Slater, & Sharps, 1995), lower levels of sensitivity (Cassidy, Zoccolillo, & Hughes, 1996), less positive mother–infant interaction (Whitman et al., 2001), and lower levels of maternal involvement (Reis & Herz, 1987). In our research, depressive symptoms were predictive of home visitors' ratings of the adolescents' parenting behavior; the ratings of parenting behavior were completed after the home visitors had worked with the young mothers for more than four years (Luster, 1998).

A second characteristic of the young mothers that has been examined is cognitive readiness for parenting (Schellenbach et al., 1992). Cognitive readiness includes childrearing beliefs, attitudes, and knowledge of child development. Although parents may not always act in accordance with their beliefs and knowledge, it is reasonable to expect that parents' ideas exert some influence on how they care for their children. Evidence from several studies is consistent with that expectation. Early studies showed that mothers with punitive attitudes tended to provide less supportive home environments for their infants, as measured with the HOME inventory (Luster & Rhoades, 1989; Reis & Herz, 1987). Mothers who worried about spoiling their infants by being affectionate and responsive also tended to have lower HOME scores (Luster & Rhoades, 1989). Higher HOME scores were associated with beliefs that it was important to provide verbal stimulation to infants and that infants should be given considerable leeway in exploring their environments. In another study, mothers with responsive attitudes exhibited more smiling and eye contact with their infants but responsive attitudes were not related to how quickly the mothers responded to their crying infants (Crockenberg, 1987b).

One limitation of the early studies was that beliefs and behaviors were measured at the same time. Although most researchers have presumed that beliefs influence behavior, cognitive dissonance (Festinger, 1957) and self-perception theorists (Bem, 1972) argue that behavior may also influence beliefs. Parents may change their beliefs so that they are in accord with their behaviors. To address the temporal ordering problem, we measured adolescents' beliefs before their children were born and related their beliefs to subsequent parenting behaviors (Luster, 1998). We measured prenatal beliefs with the Adult–Adolescent Parenting Inventory (AAPI; Bavolek, 1984) which assesses beliefs in four domains that may influence whether or not the mother engages in abusive behavior (i.e., empathy, corporal punishment, role reversal, and inappropriate expectations). More favorable scores on the AAPI were associated with higher HOME scores at 36 months (Chen, 1997) and more favorable ratings of parenting by home visitors at 54 months (Luster, 1998). These results were consistent with the view that beliefs influence behavior.

Sommer and her colleagues (1993) constructed a measure they called cognitive readiness for parenting that included the four AAPI subscales, a 40-item measures of child development knowledge, and other items to measures attitudes regarding authoritarianism, nurturance, rejection, and independence. Cognitive readiness scores assessed during the prenatal period were predictive of individual differences in parenting by adolescent mothers six months after their children were born; mothers who were more cognitively prepared displayed a more competent interactional style than their peers who received lower cognitive readiness scores. However, the relation between cognitive readiness and maternal behavior was not significant when IQ, SES, race, and education were controlled. This study demonstrates the need for further studies that examine the relation between parental beliefs and behavior while controlling for other factors.

The final characteristic of adolescent mothers that has been widely studied is educational attainment or intellectual competence. With regard to educational attainment, one hypothesis is that young mothers who are competent in the classroom are likely to be relatively competent in caring for their children. An alternative hypothesis is that young mothers who focus their time and energy on school may do so at the expense of their children. They may spend less time with them and be less attuned to their needs. Studying the relation between educational attainment and parenting is difficult with adolescent mothers because many mothers are still going to school when their parenting is being assessed. Because of this, we examined the relation between educational attainment when the mothers were approximately 20 years old and measures of caregiving behavior assessed in various ways throughout our study. Our findings were consistent with the first hypothesis that young mothers who went farther in school also tended to receive higher scores on measures of parenting. We also found that mothers who repeated a grade in school prior to having their first child were rated as less supportive caregivers by home visitors (Luster, 1998). Unfortunately, we did not have a measure of IQ, so we could not determine if educational attainment was predictive of parenting when intellectual ability was controlled.

Zuravin and DiBlasio (1996) found that adolescent mothers who neglected their children achieved lower levels of education than adolescents mothers who did not neglect their children. However educational attainment was unrelated to whether or not the child had been physically abused. The lack of association between maternal education and physical abuse may be due to the fact that the mothers were often not the perpetrators of the abuse. The perpetrators were sometimes fathers, boyfriends, babysitters, or unidentified people.

Whitman and colleagues (2001) assessed the intelligence of the young mothers in their study with the Wechsler Adult Intelligence Scale–Revised (WAIS–R). The mothers who scored higher on the vocabulary and block design subtests of the WAIS–R received more favorable scores on videotaped interactions with their children. Similarly, in a sample of African American mothers, most of whom were adolescents when their children were born, mothers with low scores on the Peabody Picture Vocabulary Test (PPVT) were more likely to exhibit problematic parenting while working with their preschoolers on puzzles (Wakschlag, Chase-Lansdale, & Brooks-Gunn, 1996). However, mothers' educational attainment was not a significant predictor of parenting when PPVT scores and other background characteristics were controlled.

Looking across studies, the findings are consistent with the view that maternal cognitive competence is associated with more supportive caregiving practices. However, more research is needed to determine the processes involved, if indeed there is a causal relation. Maternal intellectual ability could have a direct effect on parenting given that parenting involves a fair amount of problem solving, especially with uncommunicative infants. Brighter or better educated mothers may also value education more and work harder to promote the intellectual growth of their children than mothers who struggled in school. Alternatively intellectual ability could affect parenting or the home environment indirectly via family income or poverty status.

Characteristics of the Children

Although it is generally accepted that children and parents influence each other, there has been far less attention paid to the role that child characteristics play in the care they receive in the adolescent parenting literature. It seems reasonable to expect that infants who are relatively difficult to care for will, on average, elicit less supportive parenting. However, evidence to support this hypothesis is limited. The child characteristics that have been examined most include difficult temperament and low birth weight.

Some studies have found that irritable or difficult babies elicit less supportive caregiving than their easier peers (e.g., Luster, 1998), but other studies report no relation between the two variables (e.g., Hess, Papas, & Black, 2002). Inconsistent results have also been found in studies of older mothers (Crockenberg, 1986). As Crockenberg explained, the effect of infant temperament on parenting may depend on characteristics of the mother (e.g., patience, her interpretation of the behavior) or contextual factors (e.g., level of support the mother receives or other stressors she is dealing with). Thus, simple correlations between temperament and parenting measures may not be very informative. We are likely to learn more by examining the goodness-of-fit between the infant and parent characteristics (Lerner, 1993) while considering the influence of other contextual factors, such as other stressors and the mother's level of social support.

Low birth weight and the health of the infant have been the focus of researchers' attention even less often than temperament. Two early studies reported that preterm and low birth weight infants were at greater risk for poor parenting by adolescent mothers during the newborn period (Field, 1980; Wise & Grossman, 1980). In our longitudinal study, we found that low birth weight was associated with lower HOME scores when the infants were 12 months old, but was unrelated to subsequent measures of the home environment. We speculated that low birth weight infants may be more difficult to care for than their peers early in life, but differences in behavior may largely disappear if there are no lingering medical complications.

Contextual Sources of Stress and Support

Being a parent is a demanding task at any age. Parenting as an adolescent is especially difficult given the other developmental tasks that adolescents are dealing with, such as going to school, starting jobs, establishing an identity, and developing relationships with partners and peers. Being an adolescent parent is even more difficult than usual for young mothers who are dealing with other stressors and/or have limited support from parents or partners. Stressors that may directly influence their children or indirectly influence children via parenting include poverty, unsafe neighborhoods, and domestic violence.

Poverty. Poverty is likely to affect adolescent mothers and their children in many ways. One way in which poverty affects family is the toll that it takes on parents' psychological well-being (McLoyd, 1990). Chronic stress can cause some parents to be irritable, depressed, or too preoccupied to be child-centered. Poverty has been linked to lower HOME scores (Luster &

Dubow, 1990) and neglect (Zuravin & DiBlasio, 1996). A precarious financial situation is also associated with frequent changes of residence which can be problematic for children, especially when they reach school age (Bates, Luster, & Vandenbelt, 2003). Most adolescents have difficulty making ends meet if they must depend on income from their typically low-paying jobs. Therefore, much depends on the financial support they receive from their parents or partners. In many cases, the father of the baby or their current partner have low incomes and provide limited financial support.

Neighborhood Characteristics. Families in poverty face many challenges, but neighborhood poverty rates may also be important (Duncan, Brooks-Gunn, & Klebanov, 1994). Unfortunately, there is very little research on adolescent mothers that has explored this potential influence. In our research, poverty rates at the census tract level were correlated with measures of parenting during the preschool years (Bates, Luster, & Vandenbelt, 2003). Home visitors also rated the neighborhoods of the young mothers in terms of safety and overall quality of life at various points in the longitudinal study. Young mothers who lived in unsafe neighborhoods and those rated low in quality of life tended to score low on various measures of caregiving that we used (Luster, 1998). Further research is needed to determine if there is an effect of neighborhood quality on caregiving when characteristics of the mother and poverty status are controlled.

Domestic Violence. Another area in need of further study is the effect of domestic violence on adolescent mothers and their children. As noted earlier, Leadbeater and Way (2001) found that mothers who were abused by their partners had considerably higher scores on a measure of depressive ymptoms than mothers who had more positive relationships with their partners. They also scored high on a measure of stressful life events and tended to be self-critical. The children tended to have more behavior problems if the mother exhibited depressive symptoms and had high stressful life events scores. In qualitative interviews with our home visitors, we also found that some of the children who were having the greatest difficulties in first grade had mothers who were in abusive relationships (Luster, Bates, Vandenbelt, & Nievar, 2004). Further research is needed to determine if maternal parenting behavior mediates the relation between domestic violence exposure and child outcomes or if the effect of domestic violence on children's behavior is largely a direct effect.

Social Support. How well adolescents deal with the challenges of parenting and the other stressors they face is likely to depend on their personal strengths and the amount of support that they receive from others. Several studies have examined the relation between the social support young mothers receive from their families and the parenting they provide. These studies have produced mixed results with some studies showing that mothers with higher levels of support providing more supportive care for their children and other studies showing no relation between perceived support and caregiving. In some cases, the lack of relationship between social support and parenting may be due to the fact that the mothers who are having the greatest difficulty adjusting to parenting are receiving the most support from their families; the support is being offered by family members in response to a perceived need on the part of the mother (Barratt, Roach, Morgan, & Colbert, 1996). In these instances, social support may be helpful to the mothers receiving it, but they would not necessarily receive high marks on measures of parenting when compared to other adolescent mothers. Moreover, in some cases support from family members has a direct effect on the child rather than being mediated by the caregiving of the adolescent mothers. Some of the children in our study who were doing very well in first grade had been cared for primarily by their grandparents for most of their lives (Luster et al., 2004).

The other key person in the young mother's social network is likely to be the father of the child or current partner. Potentially the male partner could influence the mother and child by providing financial support for the family, emotional support for the mother, and care for the child. However, there is surprisingly limited research on the relation between level of support from the male partner and maternal caregiving or child outcomes. The studies that have been done have produced mixed results with some showing level of partner support having a positive effect on maternal parenting at least some of the time (Unger & Wandersman, 1985) and others reporting no relation (Voight, Hans, & Bernstein, 1996). The importance of support from the male partner may depend on other factors such as how much support the mother is receiving from her family or on her own developmental history (Crockenberg, 1987b; Quinton & Rutter, 1988).

Developmental History

The developmental history of a teen can influence parenting in a number of ways. Experiences in the years before the adolescent gave birth could influence characteristics of the mother such as her psychological well-being, values, childrearing beliefs, level of education, and sense of self-efficacy. For example, adolescents with a history of abuse experience more depressive symptoms (Stevens-Simon & McAnarney, 1994). In addition, the way that adolescent mothers were parented could influence the way they care for their children. In some cases, young mothers may use some of the same practices that were used in their family of origin, and in other cases, they may make a conscious choice to do things differently (e.g., be less harsh when disciplining their children). Certainly adolescent mothers who experienced poor parenting in the family of origin will not inevitably follow the same path. However, it may be difficult to provide optimal care for children if abusive or neglectful parenting is all that the young mothers have experienced.

Unfortunately, there is relatively little research on the developmental history of young mothers, in part because it is a difficult topic to study. Developmental history encompasses many things and the aspects of developmental history that may be important for one adolescent may be less important for another. Moreover, studies of adolescent mothers typically begin around the time that the first child is born; therefore, measures of developmental history are likely to be retrospective which raises questions about the validity of the measures.

A few studies have examined the developmental history of adolescent mothers who were involved with Child Protective Services (CPS) because their children were abused or neglected. Mothers who neglected their children were more likely than other adolescent mothers to have experienced frequent changes in the caregivers they lived with while growing up. Adolescent mothers who had children who were physically abused were more likely to have had mothers with emotional problems while growing up (Zuravin & DiBlasio, 1996). Spieker and her colleagues (1996) found that mothers with a history of sexual abuse were more likely to have preschool children involved in CPS than mothers without a history of sexual abuse. Boyer and Fine (1992) reported similar findings.

Ward and Carlson (1995) examined the relation between adolescent mothers' relationships in the family of origin and how they related to their infants. Young mothers who were rated as having more secure relationships with their families tended to be more sensitive in their interactions with their infants, and their infants were more likely to be rated as securely attached in Ainsworth's Strange Situation procedure at 15 months. Crockenberg (1987) assessed teenage mothers' recollections of their relationships with their parents. Mothers who experienced rejection in the family of origin tended to be more angry and punitive with their toddlers than mothers with more favorable experiences during childhood. However, the link between poor parenting in one generation and poor parenting in the next was not found if the adolescent mother was in a supportive relationship with a male partner.

When the children in our study were 54 months old, we asked the young mothers if they could name someone who had been a strong, positive role model for them. We were interested in whether or not they identified their mothers as role models. We found that those who selected their mothers received more favorable parenting ratings from the home visitors than those who selected someone else or no one at all (Luster, 1998). We also asked them about their relationship history with men. Our interest in this topic was due to the advocates' report that many of these young mothers had been in abusive, controlling, or exploitive relations with men since childhood. Young mothers who reported having more positive relationships with men also tended to receive higher parenting ratings from the home visitors. Although these questions did not focus solely on the period before the focal child was born, the findings suggest that the relationship history of adolescent mothers is relevant for understanding their approach to parenting.

CONCLUSIONS

This chapter is divided into four parts. The first section is concerned with factors related to becoming an adolescent mother. The research shows that early parenthood occurs in all demographic groups in the U.S., but higher birth rates are found among teens who struggle in school, come from low-income or multi-problem families, live in neighborhoods with high concentrations of poverty, and are exposed to other risk factors. Teens are less likely to become parents if their vision of their future includes going to school beyond high school and establishing a career before having children.

In the second section, we examined the impact of early childbearing on the life course of the mother. Adolescent mothers are more likely than peers who delay having children to: achieve low levels of education, live in poverty, exhibit depressive symptoms, and rear their children as single parents. At one time it was thought that these outcomes were largely the consequence of early childbearing, and the research still suggests that early childbearing affects the life course of the mothers and their children. However, recent research has considered the effect of selection factors on these outcomes, and has contributed to a more balanced view about the combined influence of selection factors and the effects of early childbearing on the life-course outcomes of the mother.

In the third section, we focus on the children of adolescent mothers. Given selection factors and the context in which many of these children are being reared, it is not surprising that children of adolescents fare less well than other children in various developmental domains. However, many children of adolescent mothers are competent and well-adjusted. Typically these children have received supportive care from their mothers and/or other caregivers such as fathers and grandparents that set them on a positive developmental trajectory during the early years of life. Many of their mothers are intelligent, child-centered individuals who are determined to create a better life for their children.

Adolescent mothers, like older mothers, differ markedly in the way that they parent their children. In the final section, we examined factors related to individual differences in the caregiving practice of young mothers. Correlational studies show that differences in caregiving are related to characteristics of the young mothers, characteristics of the children, and the context in which the relationship is evolving. The experiences of the young mothers prior to the time that they have children also influence parental behavior.

The research that we have reviewed shows that much has been learned about adolescent mothers and their children since the first edition of this book was published a decade ago (Luster & Okagaki, 1993). Given the continuing interest in this topic, we expect the next decade of research to add considerably to our understanding of these families. Insights gained from these efforts are likely to be useful to those who work directly with young mothers and their children, program planners, and policymakers.

ACKNOWLEDGMENTS

Our research on adolescent mothers and their children was supported by grants from the Mott Children's Health Center in Flint, Michigan, and the Spencer Foundation. Support for preparing this chapter was provided to the first author by the Michigan Agricultural Experiment Station.

REFERENCES

Alan Guttmacher Institute. (2002). *Facts in brief. Teenager's sexual and reproductive health.* Retrieved December 8, 2004, from http://www.agi-usa.org

Almgren, G., Yamashiro, G., & Ferguson, M. (2002). Beyond welfare or work: Teen mothers, household subsistence strategies, and child development outcomes. *Journal of Sociology and Social Welfare, 29*(3), 125–149.

Barratt, M. S., Roach, M. A., Morgan, K. M., & Colbert, K. K. (1996). Adjustment to motherhood by single adolescents. *Family Relations, 45*, 209–215.

Bates, L. V., Luster, T., & Vandenbelt, M. (2003). Factors related to social competence in elementary school among children of adolescent mothers. *Social Development, 12*(1), 107–124.

Bavolek, S. (1984). *The Adult–Adolescent Parenting Inventory.* Schaumburg, IL: Family Development Resources.

Belsky, J. (1984). The determinants of parenting: A process model. *Child Development, 55*, 83–96.

Bem, D. J. (1972). Self-perception theory. In L. Berkowitz (Ed.), *Advances in experimental social psychology* (Vol. 6, pp. 2–62). New York: Academic Press.

Bolton, F. (1990). The risk of child maltreatment in adolescent parenting. *Advances in Adolescent Mental Health, 4*, 223–237.

Borkowski, J., & Dukewich, T. (1996). Environmental covariations and intelligence: How attachment influences self-regulation. In D. Determan (Ed.), *Current topics in human intelligence* (Vol. 5, pp. 3–15). Norwood, NJ: Ablex.

Boyer, D., & Fine, D. (1992). Sexual abuse as a factor in adolescent pregnancy and child mal-treatment. *Family Planning Perspectives, 24,* 4–11.

Brewster, K. (1994). Race differences in sexual activity among adolescent women: The role of neighborhood characteristics. *American Sociological Review, 59,* 408–424.

Butler, J., & Burton, L. (1990). Rethinking teenage childbearing: Is sexual abuse a missing link? *Family Relations, 39,* 73–80.

Cassidy, B., Zoccolillo, M., & Hughes, S. (1996). Psychopathology in adolescent mothers and its effects on mother–infant interactions: A pilot study. *Canadian Journal of Psychiatry, 41,* 379–384.

Centers for Disease Control. (2001). *Youth risk behavior surveillance system.* Retrieved June 2003, from http://www.cdc.gov/nccdphp/dash/yrbs/

Chen, F. (1997). *Factors related to adolescent mothers' caregiving practices for their three-year-old children.* Paper presented at the Biennial Meeting of the Society for Research in Child Development, Washington, DC.

Child Trends. (2001). *Facts at a glance.* Washington, DC. Retrieved December 8, 2004, from http://www.childtrends.org

Child Trends. (2003). *Facts at a glance.* Washington, DC. Retrieved December 8, 2004, from http://www.childtrends.org

Crockenberg, S. (1986). Are temperamental differences in babies associated with predictable differences in caregiving. In J. V. Lerner & R. M. Lerner (Eds.), *Temperament and child development: New directions for child development* (pp. 53–73). San Francisco: Jossey-Bass.

Crockenberg, S. (1987). Predictors and correlates of anger toward and punitive control of toddlers by adolescent mothers. *Child Development, 58,* 964–975.

Crockenberg, S. (1988). Social support and parenting. In H. Fitzgerald, B. Lester, & M. Yogman (Eds.), *Theory and research in behavioral pediatrics* (Vol. 4, pp. 141–174). New York: Plenum.

Culp, A., Osofsky, J., & O'Brien, M. (1996). Language patterns of adolescent and older mothers. *First Language, 16,* 61–75.

Dubow, E., & Luster, T. (1990). Adjustment of children born to teenage mothers: The contribution of risk and protective factors. *Journal of Marriage and the Family, 52,* 393–404.

Duncan, G. J., Brooks-Gunn, J., & Klebanov, P. K. (1994). Economic deprivation and early childhood development. *Child Development, 65,* 296–318.

East, P., & Jacobson, L. (2001). The younger siblings of teenage mothers: A follow-up of their pregnancy risk. *Developmental Psychology, 37,* 254–264.

Field, T. M. (1980). Interaction of preterm and term infants with their lower and middle-income teenage and adult mothers. In T. M. Field, S. Goldberg, D. Stern, & E. Sostek (Eds.), *High-risk infants and children: Adult and peer interaction* (pp. 113–132). New York: Academic Press.

Festinger, L. (1957). *A theory of cognitive dissonance.* Evanston, IL: Row Peterson.

Furstenberg, F., Brooks-Gunn, J., & Morgan, S. (1987). *Adolescent mothers in later life.* New York: Cambridge University Press.

Geronimus, A., & Korenman, S. (1992). The socioeconomic consequences of teenage child-bearing reconsidered. *Quarterly Journal of Economics, 107,* 1187–1214.

Geronimus, A., Korenman, S., & Hillemeier, M. (1994). Does young maternal age adversely affect child development? Evidence from cousin comparisons in the United States. *Population and Developmental Review, 20,* 585–609.

Goerge, R., & Lee, B. J. (1997). Abuse and neglect of the child. In R. Maynard (Ed.), *Kids having kids: Economic costs and social consequences of teen pregnancy* (pp. 205–230). Washington, DC: Urban Institute Press.

Grogger, J. (1997). Incarceration-related costs of early childbearing. In R. Maynard (Ed.), *Kids having kids: Economic costs and social consequences of teen pregnancy* (pp. 231–255). Washington, DC: Urban Institute Press.

Haveman, R., Wolfe, B., & Peterson, E. (1997). Children of early child-bearers as young adults. In R. Maynard (Ed.), *Kids having kids: Economic costs and social consequences of teen pregnancy* (pp. 257–284). Washington, DC: Urban Institute Press.

Hess, C. R., Papas, M. A., & Black, M. M. (2002). Resilience among African American adolescent mothers: Predictors of positive parenting in early infancy. *Journal of Pediatric Psychology, 27*, 619–629.

Hotz, V. J., McElroy, S. W., & Sanders, S. G. (1997). The impacts of teenage childbearing on the mothers and the consequences of those impacts for government. In R. A. Maynard (Ed.), *Kids having kids: Economic costs and social consequences of teen pregnancy* (pp. 55–94). Washington, DC: Urban Institute Press.

Hubbs-Tait, L., Osofsky, J., Hann, D., & Culp, A. (1994). Predicting behavior problems and social competence in children of adolescent mothers. *Family Relations, 43*, 439–446.

Hurlbut, N., Culp, A., & Jambunathan, S. (1997). Adolescent mothers' self-esteem and role identity and their relationship to parenting skill knowledge. *Adolescence, 32*, 639–654.

Jaffee, S., Caspi, A., Moffitt, T. E., Belsky, J., & Silva, P. (2001). Why are children born to teen mothers at risk for adverse outcomes in young adulthood? Results from a 20-year longitudinal study. *Development and Psychopathology, 13*, 377–397.

Kahn, J. R., & Anderson, K. E. (1992). Intergenerational patterns of teenage fertility. *Demography, 29*, 39–57.

Kalil, A., & Kunz, J. (2002). Teenage childbearing, marital status, and depressive symptoms in later life. *Child Development, 73*, 1748–1760.

Kessler, R. C., Berglund, P. A., Foster, C. L., Saunders, W. B., Stang, P. E., & Walters, E. E. (1997). Social consequences of psychiatric disorders II: Teenage parenthood. *American Journal of Psychiatry, 154*, 1405–1411.

Klepinger, D. H., Lundberg, S., & Plotnick, R. D. (1995). Adolescent fertility and educational attainment of young women. *Family Planning Perspectives, 27*, 23–28.

Kovacs, M., Krol, R. M., & Voti, L. (1994). Early onset psychopathology and the risk for teenage pregnancy among clinically referred girls. *Journal of the American Academy of Child and Adolescent Psychiatry, 33*, 106–113.

Leadbeater, B. J., Bishop, S. J., & Raver, C. C. (1996). Quality of mother–toddler interactions, maternal depressive symptoms, and behavior problems in preschoolers of adolescent mothers. *Developmental Psychology, 32*, 280–288.

Leadbeater, B., & Way, N. (2001). *Growing up fast: Transitions to early adulthood of inner-city adolescent mothers.* Mahwah, NJ: Lawrence Erlbaum Associates.

Lerner, J. V. (1993). The influence of child temperamental characteristics on parent behaviors. In T. Luster & L. Okagaki (Eds.), *Parenting: An ecological perspective* (1st ed., pp. 101–120). Hillsdale, NJ: Lawrence Erlbaum Associates.

Levine, J., Pollack, H., & Comfort, M. (2001). Academic and behavioral outcomes among children of young mothers. *Journal of Marriage and the Family, 63*, 355–369.

Luker, K. (1991, Spring). Dubious conceptions: The controversy over teen pregnancy. *The American Prospect*, 73–83.

Luster, T. (1998). Individual differences in the caregiving behavior of teenage mothers: An ecological perspective. *Clinical Child Psychology and Psychiatry, 3*, 341–360.

Luster, T., Bates, L., Fitzgerald, H., Vandenbelt, M., & Key, J. P. (2000). Factors related to successful outcomes among preschool children born to low-income adolescent mothers. *Journal of Marriage and the Family, 62*, 133–146.

Luster, T., Bates, L., Vandenbelt, M., & Nievar, M. A. (2004). Family advocates' perspectives on the early academic success of children born to low-income adolescent mothers. *Family Relations, 53*, 68–77.

Luster, T., & Dubow, E. (1990). Predictors of the quality of the home environment that adolescent mothers provide for their school-aged children. *Journal of Youth and Adolescence, 19*, 475–494.

Luster, T., & McAdoo, H. (1996). Family and child influences on educational attainment: A secondary analysis of the High/Perry Preschool data. *Developmental Psychology, 32*, 26–39.

Luster, T., & Okagaki, L. (1993). *Parenting: An ecological perspective* (1st ed.). Hillsdale, NJ: Lawrence Erlbaum Associates.

Luster, T., & Rhoades, K. (1989). The relation between childrearing beliefs and the home environment in a sample of adolescent mothers. *Family Relations, 38*, 317–322.

Luster, T., & Small, S. A. (1997). Sexual abuse history and number of sex partners among female adolescents. *Family Planning Perspectives, 29*(5), 204–211.

Manlove, J., Terry-Humen, E., Papillo, A. R., Franzetta, K., Williams, S., & Ryan, S. (2002). *Preventing teenage pregnancy, childbearing, and sexually transmitted diseases: What the research shows.* Washington, DC: Child Trends.

McCullough, M., & Scherman, A. (1998). Family-of-origin interaction and adolescent mothers' potential for child abuse. *Adolescence, 33*, 375–384.

McLoyd, V. (1990). The impact of economic hardship on Black families and children: Psychological distress, parenting, and socioemotional development. *Child Development, 61*, 311–346.

Miller, B. C. (2002). Family influences on adolescent sexual and contraceptive behavior. *Journal of Sex Research, 39*(1), 22–26.

Miller-Johnson, S., Winn, D. M., Coie, J., Maumary-Gremaud, A., Hyman, C., Terry, C., & Lochman, J. (1999). Motherhood during the teen years: A developmental perspective on risk factors for childbearing. *Development and Psychopathology, 11*, 85–100.

Moore, K. A., Miller, B. C., Glie, D., & Morrison, D. R. (1995). *Adolescent sex, contraception, and childbearing: A review of recent research.* Washington, DC: Child Trends.

Moore, K., Morrison, D., & Greene, A. (1997). Effects on children born to adolescent mothers. In R. Maynard (Ed.), *Kids having kids: Economic costs and social consequences of teen pregnancy* (pp. 145–180). Washington, DC: Urban Institute Press.

Moore, M., & Brooks-Gunn, J. (2002). Adolescent parenthood. In M. Borstein (Ed.), *Handbook of parenting: Vol. 3. Being and becoming a parent* (pp. 173–214). Mahwah, NJ: Lawrence Erlbaum Associates.

Musick, J. S. (1993). *Young, poor, and pregnant: The psychology of teenage motherhood.* New Haven: Yale University Press.

Nagin, D., Pogarsky, G., & Farrington, D. (1997). Adolescent mothers and the criminal behavior of their children. *Law and Society Review, 31*(1), 137–162.

Osofsky, J. D., Hann, D. A., & Peebles, C. (1993). Adolescent parenthood: Risks and opportunities for mothers and infants. In C. H. Zeanah (Ed.), *Handbook of infant mental health* (pp. 106–119). New York: Guilford Press.

Panzarine, S., Slater, E., & Sharps, P. (1995). Coping, social support, and depressive symptoms in adolescent mothers. *Journal of Adolescent Health, 17*, 113–119.

Quinton, D., & Rutter, M. (1988). *Parenting breakdown: The making and breaking of intergenerational bonds.* Aldershot, UK: Avebury.

Rauch-Elnekave, H. (1994). Teenage motherhood: Its relationship to undetected learning problems. *Adolescence, 29*, 91–103.

Reis, J. S., & Herz, E. J. (1987). Correlates of adolescent parenting. *Adolescence, 22*, 599–609.

Rodgers, J. L., & Rowe, D. C. (1993). Social contagion and adolescent sexual behavior: A developmental EMOSA model. *Psychological Review, 100*(3), 479–510.

Schellenbach, C. J., Whitman, T. L., & Borkowski, J. G. (1992). Toward an integrative model of adolescent parenting. *Human Development, 35*, 81–99.

Seitz, V., & Apfel, N. (1993). Adolescent mothers and repeated child-bearing: Effects of a school-based intervention program. *American Journal of Orthopsychiatry, 63*, 572–581.

Sommer, K., Whitman, T. L., Borkowski, J. G., Schellenbach, C., Maxwell, S., & Keogh, D. (1993). Cognitive readiness and adolescent parenting. *Developmental Psychology, 29*, 389–398.

Spieker, S. J., Bensley, L., McMahon, R., Fung, H., & Ossiander, E. (1996). Sexual abuse as a factor in child maltreatment by adolescent mothers of preschool aged children. *Development and Psychopathology, 8*, 497–509.

Small, S., & Luster, T. (1994). Adolescent sexual activity: An ecological, risk-factor approach. *Journal of Marriage and Family, 56*, 181–192.

Stevens-Simon, C., & McAnarney (1994). Childhood victimization: Relationship to adolescent pregnancy outcome. *Child Abuse and Neglect, 18*, 569–575.

Terry, E., & Manlove, J. (2000). *Trends in sexual activity and contraceptive use among teens.* Washington, DC: Child Trends.

Turley, R. N. L. (2003). Are children of young mothers disadvantaged because of their mother's age or family background? *Child Development, 74*, 465–474.

Unger, D., & Wandersman, L. P. (1985). Social support and adolescent mothers: Action research contributions to theory and application. *Journal of Social Issues, 41*, 29–45.

Vandenbelt, M., Luster, T., & Bates, L. (2001). Caregiving practices of low-income adolescent mothers and the academic competence of their first-grade children. *Parenting Science and Practice, 1*, 185–215.

Voight, J. D., Hans, S. L., & Bernstein, V. J. (1996). Support networks of adolescent mothers: Effects on parenting experiences and behavior. *Infant Mental Health Journal, 17*, 58–73.

Wakschlag, L. S., Chase-Lansdale, P. L., & Brooks-Gunn, J. (1996). Not just "Ghosts in the Nursery": Contemporaneous intergenerational relationships and parenting in young African-American families. *Child Development, 67*, 2131–2147.

Ward, M. J., & Carlson, E. A. (1995). Associations among adult attachment representations, maternal sensitivity, and infant–mother attachment in a sample of adolescent mothers. *Child Development, 66*, 69–79.

Werner, E. (1994). Overcoming the odds. *Journal of Developmental and Behavioral Pediatrics, 15*(2), 131–136.

Werner, E. (1990). Protective factors and individual resilience. In S. J. Meisels & J. P. Shonkoff (Eds.), *Handbook of early intervention: Theory, practice and analysis* (pp. 97–116). Cambridge, England: Cambridge University Press.

Werner, E., & Smith, R. (1989). *Vulnerable but invincible.* New York: Adams, Bannister & Cox.

Werner, E., & Smith, R. (1992). *Overcoming the odds: High risk children from birth to adulthood.* Ithaca, NY: Cornell University Press.

Werner, E., & Smith, R. (2001). *Journeys from childhood to midlife.* Ithaca, NY: Cornell University Press.

Whitman, T., Borkowski, J., Keogh, D., & Weed, K. (2001). *Interwoven lives: Adolescent mothers and their children.* Mahwah, NJ: Lawrence Erlbaum Associates.

Wise, S., & Grossman, F. K. (1980). Adolescent mothers and their infants: Psychological factors in attachment and interaction. *American Journal of Orthopsychiatry, 50*, 454–468.

Zoccolillo, M., Meyers, J., & Assiter, S. (1997). Conduct disorder, substance dependence, and adolescent motherhood. *American Journal of Orthopsychiatry, 67*, 152–157.

Zoccolillo, M., & Rogers, K. (1991). Characteristics and outcomes of hospitalized adolescent girls with conduct disorders. *Journal of the American Academy of Child and Adolescent Psychiatry, 30*, 973–981.

Zuravin, S. J., & DiBlasio, F. A. (1996). The correlates of child physical abuse and neglect by adolescent mothers. *Journal of Family Violence, 11*, 149–166.

4

Fathers: Cultural and Ecological Perspectives

Ross D. Parke
Jessica Dennis
Mary L. Flyr
Kristie L. Morris
Melinda S. Leidy
Thomas J. Schofield
University of California, Riverside

For decades parenting was typically operationalized as mothering. A variety of factors contributed to this narrow definition of parenting including assumptions about the critical caregiving role of mothers, the presumed inadequacy and disinterest of fathers in caregiving activities, and at least historically, the relatively greater breadwinner role assumed by fathers. Much has changed since Lamb (1975) made his famous pronouncement that fathers were the "forgotten contributors to child development" (p. 245). In this century, fathers are clearly recognized as central players in the family and are no longer relegated to the socialization sidelines. The goal of this chapter is to highlight the father's parenting role and to examine the determinants and consequences of fathers' roles in the family for children, for mothers and for fathers themselves. Since this topic covers a relatively vast terrain, a caveat is in order. Our review will be selective with the goals being to highlight both major advances and remaining puzzles and problems that still confront this relatively recent domain. For comprehensive overviews of this topic, a variety of recent chapters and books are available (Coltrane, 1996; Lamb, 2004; Parke, 1996, 2002; Parke & Brott, 1999; Tamis-LeMonda & Cabrera, 2002).

INTRODUCTION: GUIDING ASSUMPTIONS

Several assumptions guide this chapter. First and most critical is our assumption that the nature of the father–child relationship is best understood in terms of a family systems perspective. Just as mothering cannot be fully appreciated as an independent subsystem, fathers can only be fully understood as part of the family system as well (Cox & Paley, 1997; Parke, 2004). Therefore, to understand fathers, the complimentary family subsystems of the mother–child relationship, the sib–sib relationship, and the marital relationship need to be considered. Second, and consistent with a family systems viewpoint, mothers, fathers, and children influence one another both directly and indirectly (Parke, Power, & Gottman, 1979; Parke, 1996). For example, a father's harsh disciplinary tactics directed toward his child may lead to compensatory protective behavior by the mother toward the child. Alternatively, marital conflict may alter the level of co-parental cooperation that in turn may modify the father–child relationship (Cummings & O'Reilly, 1997). Third, different levels of analysis—individual, dyadic and family level—are needed to fully appreciate the father's role. Fourth, fathers as members of families are embedded in a variety of formal and informal social systems, such as extended families and work-related institutions. Fifth, culture shapes fathering and it is critical to recognize similarities and differences across fathers of various cultural backgrounds. Although much of our knowledge about fathers is based on European-American samples, recent work from other cultures, as well as intra-cultural variations in our own culture, is serving as a corrective to our assumptions about the universality of fathering processes. Our focus on cultural factors is consistent with the ecological theme of the volume that recognizes the embeddedness of fathers in a variety of ecological subsystems from the family to the wider society and culture. Finally, in light of the clear links between research and policy, it is important to offer policy guidelines that may aid in altering fathers' level of involvement in families.

Do Mothers and Fathers Play Distinctive Roles in the Family?

There is clear evidence that mothers and fathers contribute through different pathways to their children's development. Perhaps the most well established difference between parents of different genders is their relative investment in play and caregiving. Fathers participate less than mothers in caregiving but spend a greater percentage of the time available for interaction in play activities than mothers do. In the U.S. Kotelchuck (1976) found that fathers spent a greater percentage of their time with their infants in play (37.5%) than mothers did (25.8%), although in absolute terms mothers spent more time than fathers in play with their children. Similar findings have been reported from a longitudinal investigation of parent–infant interaction in England (Richards, Dunn, & Antonis, 1977). At both 30 and 60 weeks of age, playing with their infants was the most common activity of fathers, and over 90% of the fathers played regularly with their infants. Lamb (1977) observed interactions among mother, father, and infant in their homes at 7 to 8 months and again at 12 to 13 months. Marked differences emerged in the reasons that fathers and mothers pick up infants. Fathers were more likely to hold the babies simply to play with them, whereas mothers were far more likely to hold them for caregiving purposes. It is not only the quantity of time in play that discriminates between mother and father involvement in infancy; the quality of play activity does so as well. Power and Parke (1982) observed mothers and fathers interacting with their 8-month-old infants in a laboratory playroom. Fathers played more bouncing and lifting games, especially with boys, than mothers. In contrast, mothers played more watching games in which a toy is presented and made salient by moving or shaking it. Observations of father–and mother–infant interactions in unstructured home contexts with older infants reveals similar mother–father differences in play style (Clarke-Stewart, 1980; Lamb, 1977).

Nor are these effects evident only in infancy. MacDonald and Parke (1984), in an observational study of the play interaction patterns between mothers, fathers, and 3- and 4-year-olds, found that fathers engaged in more physical play with their children than mothers, while mothers engaged in more object-mediated play than fathers. However, according to MacDonald and Parke (1986), the father's distinctive role as physical play partner changes with age. Physical play was highest between fathers and 2-year-olds, and between 2 and 10 years of age there was a decreased likelihood that fathers engaged their children physically.

In spite of the decline in physical play across age, fathers are still more often physical play partners than mothers. In an Australian study of parents and their 6- to 7-year-old children (Russell & Russell, 1987), fathers were more involved in physical/outdoor play interactions and fixing things around the house and garden than mothers. In contrast, mothers were more actively involved in caregiving and household tasks and in school work. Mothers were also involved in more reading, playing with toys, and helping with arts and crafts.

In all studies reviewed, a reasonably consistent pattern emerges: Fathers are tactile and physical, and mothers tend to be verbal, didactic, and toy-mediated in their play. Clearly, infants and young children experience a qualitatively different stimulatory pattern from their fathers and mothers.

Is There a Universal Father Play Style?

Some cross-cultural studies support the generality of this pattern of mother–father differences in play style. Parents in England and Australia show similar sex differences (Russell & Russell, 1987; Smith & Daglish, 1977). However, other evidence suggests that this pattern of mother–father differences in play style may be, in part, culture bound. Specifically, neither in Sweden (Lamb et al., 1982) nor among Israeli kibbutz families (Sagi, 1982; Sagi et al., 1985) were there clear sex-of-parent differences in the tendency to engage in play or in the types of play initiated.

Similarly, Chinese Malaysian, Taiwanese, and Thai mothers and fathers reported that they rarely engage in physical play with their children (Sun & Roopnarine, 1996). Among middle-class Indian families in New Delhi, fathers and mothers are more likely to display affection than to play with infants while holding them. Although mothers engaged in more object-mediated play than fathers, there were no other differences in the play styles of mothers and fathers. Most interesting was the finding that the frequency of rough physical play was very low—less than once per hour (Roopnarine, Hooper, Ahmeduzzaman, & Pollack, 1981). Observations of Aka pygmies of Central Africa (Hewlett, 1991) are consistent with this pattern. In this culture, mothers and fathers rarely, if ever, engage in physical play in spite of plenty of close physical contact. In other cultures, such as Italy, it is neither mothers nor fathers, but other women in the extended family or within the community who are likely to play physically with infants (New & Benigni, 1987).

Whether these distinctively female and male play styles are due to cultural influences or biological factors, remains a puzzle for future researchers to solve. However, the fact that male monkeys show the same rough-and-tumble physical style of play as human fathers suggests that we cannot ignore a possible biological component in play styles of mothers and fathers (Parke & Suomi, 1981; Lovejoy & Wallen, 1988). Moreover, male monkeys tend to respond more positively to bids for rough and tumble play than do females (Meany, Stewart, & Beatty, 1985). Together, these threads of the puzzle suggest that predisposing biological differences between females and males may play a role in the play patterns of mothers and fathers (Maccoby, 1998). At the same time, the cross-cultural data clearly underscore the ways in which cultural and environmental contexts shape play patterns of mothers and fathers and remind us of the high degree of plasticity of human social behaviors.

Involvement by Mothers and Fathers With Children

It is not only stylistic differences in interaction patterns that differentiate mothers and fathers; the amount of involvement distinguishes opposite-gender parents as well. The most influential conceptualization of types of involvement was offered by Lamb and his colleagues (Lamb, 1987; Lamb, Pleck, & Levine, 1985), who suggested three components: interaction, availability, and responsibility.

Interaction refers to the father's direct contact with his child through care-giving and shared activities. Availability is a related concept concerning the father's potential availability for interaction, by virtue of being present or accessible to the child whether or not direct interaction is occurring. Responsibility refers to the role the father takes in ascertaining that the child is taken care of and arranging for resources to be available for the child. (Lamb, Pleck, Charnov, & Levine, 1987, p. 125)

As several previous authors (e.g., Palkovitz, 2002; Parke, 2000) found, the focus of research on fathers has been primarily on face-to-face parent–child interaction. To a large degree this emphasis reflects the common assumption that parental influence takes place directly through face-to-face contact or indirectly through the impact of the interaction on another family member. Similarly, the availability issue has been addressed, but largely through the research on father absence which is a consequence of either divorce or unwed parenthood (Mott, 1994; Garfinkel, McLanahan, Meyer, & Seltzer, 1998). Less is known about the determinants or consequences of availability of fathers among residential fathers. Only recently have researchers and theorists begun to recognize the managerial function of parents (Lamb et al.'s *responsibility* notion) and to appreciate the impact of variations in how this managerial function influences the child's development (Parke & O'Neil, 2000). By managerial, we refer to the way in which parents organize and arrange the child's home environment and set limits on the range of the home setting to which the child has access and the opportunities for social contact with playmates and socializing agents outside the family. The managerial role may be just as important as the parent's role as stimulator, because the amount of time that children spend interacting with the inanimate environment far exceeds their social interaction time (White, Kaban, Shapiro, & Attonucci, 1976).

It is important to distinguish among domains of involvement, since fathers and mothers vary in their distribution of time across different child and household activities. Several distinctions have been made in the prior literature including personal care activities, involvement in play, leisure and affiliative activities with children (Beitel & Parke, 1998; Radin, 1993). More recently Yeung, Sandberg, Davis-Kean, and Hofferth (2001) expanded the domain list to include not just personal care and play but achievement-related activities (i.e., homework, reading), household activities (i.e., housework, shopping), social activities (i.e., conversation, social events) and other activities, and examined how the determinants of involvement in these domains vary across fathers. Finally, recent estimates of father involvement have usefully distinguished between weekdays and weekends since both the types of activities and levels of father involvement vary as a function of the time period being assessed (Yeung et al., 2001).

In spite of current shifts in cultural attitudes concerning the appropriateness and desirability of shared roles and equal levels of participation in routine caregiving and interaction for mothers and fathers, the shifts toward parity are small, but nonetheless real. In a recent review, Pleck and Masciadrelli (2004) cited a range of studies which document that father involvement has increased, albeit slowly. For example, Robinson (1988) compared levels of child care by fathers in a small American city in 1966 and 1988 and found an increase. Employed fathers' time with children increased from 1.21 to 1.53 hours per week. This trend appears to be continuing. As Pleck (1997) noted: "Averaging across studies from the 1980s and 1990s, fathers' proportional engagement is somewhat over two-fifths of mothers' (43.5%) and their accessibility is two-thirds of mothers (65.6%)" (p. 71). These figures are higher than reports from the 1970s and early 1980s, which averaged one third for proportional engagement and one half for accessibility. Moreover, more recent work overcomes limitations of the small and unrepresentative samples used in earlier studies. Sandberg and Hofferth (2001) used a nationally representative sample of children in two parent families in the United States in 1997. The sample included children aged 0–12 and therefore allowed an assessment of the nature of paternal involvement across different developmental periods. Finally, by collecting the data in 1997, the study permitted a comparison of father involvement in the 1960s and 1980s and the late 1990s to determine if there had been a historical shift in level of father involvement. Sandberg and Hofferth (2001) found that the relative time fathers in intact families were directly engaged with children was 67% of the time that mothers were involved on weekdays and 87% of mothers' engagement on weekends. Accessibility showed similar shifts across time and, in accord with earlier estimates (Pleck, 1997), were higher than levels of engagement. Finally Sandberg and Hofferth (2001) found relatively few differences in level of father involvement (engagement or accessibility) as a function of ethnicity (African American, European American and Latin American). In a related study, Bianchi (2000) compared 1965–66 and 1998 levels of father involvement and found that fathers' engagement and accessibility increased.

Cross-cultural evidence supports these trends as well. Studies in Canada, Finland, the Netherlands, and Norway found increases in the last two decades in father engagement as well (Pleck & Masciadrelli, 2004). These trends are less clear for paternal responsibility but some evidence suggests a modest shift toward greater responsibility. One survey of men's childcare responsibility found that the percentage of children whose fathers cared for them during their mothers' work hours rose from 15% in 1985 to 20% in 1991 (O'Connell, 1993). Other evidence supports this picture. For example, the NICHD Early Child Care Research Network (1997) found that fathers function as the primary caregivers about 23% of the time. Pleck and Masciadrelli (2004) noted:

> Fathers were the primary care arrangement (23%) as often as child care cen-
> ters and preschools combined (24%), as often as family day care homes
> (23%), and more often than grandparents (16%). The fact that fathers are
> the primary caregivers during mothers' working hours in more than one out
> of five dual-career families with preschool children suggests that a much
> higher proportion of fathers have significant childcare responsibility than is
> usually thought. Some estimate that fathers' involvement in all aspects of
> child care, not just during their wives' working hours, is nearly a third of the
> total child-care by U.S. dual-career couples in the 1990s. (p. 242)

Although more mothers are entering the work force, current occupational arrangements still mean that the vast majority of fathers have less opportunity for interaction with their children than mothers.

Differences Across Development

These patterns of relative involvement of mothers and fathers are evident in infancy and continue into middle childhood and adolescence (Collins & Russell, 1991). In a study of middle childhood (6- to 7-year-olds), Russell and Russell (1987) found that Australian mothers were available to children 54.7 hours/week compared to 34.6 hours/week for fathers. Mothers also spent more time alone with children (22.6 hours/week) than did fathers (2.4 hours/week). However, when both parents and children were together, mothers and fathers initiated interactions with children with equal frequency and children's initiations toward each parent were similar. Adolescents spend less time with their parents than younger children and less time alone with their father than with their mother (Larson & Richards, 1994). Montemayer (1982), in a study of 15- to 16-year-olds, reported that more than twice as much time was spent with mother alone than with father alone each day. Similar findings were reported for 14- to 18-year-olds by Montemayer and Brownlee (1987). In summary, mothers and fathers clearly differ in terms of their degree of involvement with their offspring from infancy through adolescence.

Although the relative difference in mother and father involvement is not markedly different across development, the absolute level of father involvement decreases as the child develops, and the types of activities in which fathers and children interact also vary across development. In the Yeung et al. (2001) survey, for example, in the case of infants and toddlers (aged 0–2) fathers interact directly or are accessible to their children for approximately 3 hours a day. By ages 9 to 12, the level of involvement has decreased to 2 hours, 15 minutes. Activities vary across age as well. Time in personal care with fathers (either interaction or accessibility) drops from one hour per day for infants to 30 minutes for 9–12-year-olds. Play/companionship activities with fathers are more common among infants and toddlers (44 minutes/day) than at later ages (23 minutes for 9–12-year-olds). While indoor games and toy play as well as outdoor activities and sports decrease, T.V. and video watching increases across age. Achievement-related activities which include reading, educational play, and studying increases from 7 to 27 minutes from toddlerhood to pre-adolescence. The pattern is similar on weekends but the absolute amount of time in which fathers are either involved or accessible nearly doubles. Not unexpected is the rise in household activities (i.e., shopping) and social activities (i.e., religious services) on weekends for fathers and their children. As the Yeung et al. study clearly underscores, both age and type of activity need to be considered in descriptions of father involvement.

DETERMINANTS OF FATHER INVOLVEMENT

The importance of examining the determinants of father involvement stems from the view that the paternal role is less culturally scripted and determined than the maternal role and few clear role models for defining fatherhood exist (Daly, 1995; Marsiglio, 1993). It is assumed that a multi-factor approach to father involvement is necessary because a variety of factors determines the degree of father involvement with children. It is useful to distinguish individual, familial and societal levels of analysis in assessing the determinants of father involvement (Doherty, Kouneski, & Erikson, 1998; Parke, 1996). This structure is consistent with the ecological model that underlies the theme of the volume and our approach to the issue of fatherhood.

Biological Factors in Paternal Behavior

It has long been recognized that females undergo a variety of hormonal changes during pregnancy and childbirth which may facilitate maternal behavior. Rosenblatt (2002), using the rat as an experimental model, showed that hormonal changes elicited maternal behavior, and other studies show similar effects for human mothers (Fleming, Ruble, Krieger, & Wong, 1997). It was long assumed that hormones play an unimportant role in paternal behavior because exposure to rat pups increases paternal activity without any changes in hormone levels (Fleming & Li, 2002). More recent evidence has challenged the assumption that hormonal levels are unimportant determinants of paternal behavior by examining this issue in species other than the rat, which is not a natural paternal species. In naturally paternal species, such as candid species that constitute less than 10% of mammalian species (Storey, Walsh, Quinton, & Wynne-Edwards, 2000), researchers have found that males experience hormonal changes including increases in prolactin and decreases in testosterone prior to the onset of parental behavior and during infant contact (Rosenblatt, 2002; Fleming & Li, 2002). Human fathers, too, undergo hormonal changes during pregnancy and childbirth. Storey et al. (2000) found that men experienced significant pre, peri, and postnatal changes in each of these hormones—prolactin, cortisol, and testosterone—a pattern of results which was similar to the women in their study. Specifically, prolactin levels were higher for both men and women in the late prenatal period than in the early prenatal period, and cortisol levels increased just before and decreased in the postnatal period for both men and women. Testosterone levels were lower in the early postnatal period, which corresponds to the first opportunity for interaction with their infants. Hormonal levels and changes were linked with a variety of social stimuli as well. Men with lower testosterone held test baby dolls longer and were more responsive to infant cues (crying) than men with higher testosterone. Men who reported a greater drop in testosterone also reported more pregnancy or couvade symptoms. Together these findings suggest that lower testosterone in the postnatal period may increase paternal responsiveness, in part by reducing competitive nonnurturing behavior (Storey et al., 2000). Similarly, prolactin levels were higher in men showing greater responsiveness to infant cries and in men reporting more couvades symptoms during pregnancy. Finally, Storey et al. (2000) argue that the "cortisol increases in late pregnancy and during labor may help new fathers focus on and become attached to their newborns" (p. 91). Men's changes in hormonal levels are linked not only with baby cries and the time in the pregnancy birth cycle but also to the hormonal levels of their partners. Women's hormonal levels were closely linked with the time remaining before delivery, and men's levels were linked with their partner's hormone levels, not with time until birth. This demonstrates that contact with the pregnant partner may play a role in paternal responsiveness, just as the quality of the marital relationship is linked with paternal involvement in later infancy. This suggests that social variables need to be considered in understanding the operation of biological effects. Perhaps intimate ties between partners during pregnancy stimulate hormonal changes, which in turn, are associated with more nurturance toward babies.

Other evidence is consistent with a psychobiological view of paternal behavior. Fleming and her colleagues (Fleming, Corter, Stallings, & Steiner, 2002) found that fathers with lower baseline levels of testosterone are more sympathetic and show a greater need to respond when presented with infant cries than men with higher baseline testosterone levels. Moreover, fathers with higher baseline prolactin levels are more positive and alert in response to infant cries. Since similar links between androgen levels and responsiveness to cries are evident for non-fathers as well, it suggests that "human fathers' androgen levels at baseline are associated with a nurturant style and are predictive of responsiveness to infant cries" (Corter & Fleming, 2002, p. 167). However, experience does appear to play a role as well. At 2 days after the birth of a baby, fathers in contrast to non-fathers show lower levels of testosterone. Moreover, fathers with more experience with babies have lower testosterone and higher prolactin levels than first time fathers (Corter & Fleming, 2002)—even after controlling for paternal age. This perspective recognizes the dynamic or transactional nature of the links between hormones and behavior in which behavior changes can lead to hormonal shifts and vice versa. In contrast to the myth of the biologically unfit father, this work suggests that men may be more prepared even biologically for parenting than previously thought. Finally, it is critical to underscore that these hormonal changes are not necessary for the elicitation of fathering behavior in either animals or humans (Fleming & Li, 2002; Corter & Fleming, 2002). In humans, for example, studies of father–infant relationships in the cases of adoption clearly suggest that hormonal shifts are unnecessary for the development of positive father–infant relationships (Brodzinsky & Pinderhughes, 2002). Next, we turn to a discussion of the social determinants of father involvement.

Social Determinants of Paternal Behavior

There are a host of individual, family background and marital relationship factors that influence father involvement. These determinants have been extensively reviewed elsewhere (see Pleck & Masciadrelli, 2004; Parke, 2002) and will be only briefly examined here.

Maternal and Paternal Attitudes. At the individual level, paternal attitudes, role identity, and perceived competence predict levels of father involvement (Beitel & Parke, 1998; Rane & McBride, 2000). Individual factors are not the only determinants of father involvement. Maternal attitudes concerning father involvement and the marital relationship are both family level factors which require examination. Consistent with a family systems view, maternal attitudes need to be considered as a determinant of paternal participation in childcare. In spite of advances in women's participation in the workplace, many women still feel ambivalent about father involvement in domestic issues (Coltrane, 1996; Dienhart & Daly, 1997). As Allen and Hawkins (1999) suggest, their ambivalence "may be because increased paternal involvement intrudes on a previously held monopoly over the attentive and intuitive responsibilities of family work which if altered may compromise female power and privilege in the home" (p. 202). These maternal attitudes may lead to behavior which, in turn, limit father involvement and constitute a form of gatekeeping (Beitel & Parke, 1998; Bonney et al., 1999). However, two qualifications to our discussion of gatekeeping are needed. First, the term is gender neutral and fathers as well as mothers engage in gatekeeping activities in other domains of family life (Allen & Hawkins, 1999). Second, gates can open as well as close and the term needs to be broadened to recognize that parents—mothers and fathers—can facilitate as well as inhibit the type and level of domestic involvement of each other. Work on parental gatekeeping needs to include gate opening as well as gate closing in order to underscore the dual nature of the inhibitory and facilatory processes that are in part of the co-parenting enterprise (Parke, 2002).

Marital Relationships and Father–Child Relationships. Models that limit examination of the effects of interaction patterns to only the father–child and mother–child dyads and the direct effects of one individual on another are inadequate for understanding the impact of social interaction patterns in families (Belsky, 1984; Parke, 1988, 1996; Parke et al., 1979). From a family systems viewpoint, the marital relationship needs to be considered as well. Several studies in both the United States (Dickie & Matheson, 1984; Pedersen, 1975) and other cultures (e.g., Japan; Durrett, Otaki, & Richards, 1984) support the conclusion that the degree of emotional/social support that fathers provide mothers is related to both indices of maternal caregiving competence as well as measures of the quality of infant–parent attachment. Other evidence suggests that the quality of the marital relationship is related to father–child interaction patterns (Booth & Amato, 1994; Coley & Chase-Lansdale, 1999; Cummings & O'Reilly, 1997). Moreover, the evidence suggests that the father–child relationship is altered more than the mother–child relationship by the quality of the marriage (Belsky, 1984; Belsky et al., 1991). A number of factors may aid in explaining this relation. First, there is prior evidence that the father's level of participation is, in part, determined by the extent to which the mother permits participation (Beitel & Parke, 1998; Allen & Hawkins, 1999). Second, because the paternal role is less well articulated and defined than the maternal role, spousal support may serve to help crystallize the boundaries of appropriate role behavior. Third, men have fewer opportunities to acquire and practice skills that are central to caregiving activities during socialization and therefore may benefit more than mothers from informational (e.g., cognitive) support (Parke & Brott, 1999).

Ecological Determinants of Father Involvement. Fatherhood needs to be viewed as embedded in a set of contexts including work and culture. In this section, shifts in work patterns of both mothers and fathers will be considered as well as cultural background as contextual factors that organize both the amount and type of fathering behavior. In terms of work, two issues are relevant. First, does father involvement shift with increases in maternal employment? Second, how does the quality of work alter fathering behavior? Maternal employment is a robust predictor of paternal involvement (Pleck & Masciadrelli, 2004). For example, Bonney, Kelley, and Levant (1999) found that among European Americans, father participation in childcare was higher when mothers were employed outside the home. Similar findings are evident for African-American and Mexican-American fathers as well. Fagan (1998) found that, as the number of hours that wives work increases, the amount of time African American fathers spend playing, reading, and directly interacting with their preschoolers increases. Evidence suggests that the relation between maternal employment and father involvement is, in part, dependent on fathers' childbearing beliefs (NICHD Child Care Research Network, 2000). When mothers do not work or work only part-time, fathers were more likely to participate in care giving if they held non-traditional views of parenting; when mothers were employed full time, father participation in care giving is higher regardless of fathers' beliefs. However, there are exceptions to this overall pattern. Yeung et al. (2001), in their national sample, found no evidence of an increase in fathers' child care responsibilities on weekdays as a function of the number of hours of maternal employment.

Although there has been an increase in recent years in the number of parents who are employed, many workers experienced increases in work hours, a decrease in job stability, a rise in temporary jobs, and especially among low wage workers, a decrease in income (Mishel, Bernstein, & Schmitt, 1999). As a result of these changes, the theoretical questions have shifted. More recently, instead of examining whether or not one or both parents are employed, researchers have begun to address the issue of the impact of the quality and nature of work on the parenting of both mothers and fathers (Perry-Jenkins, Repetti, & Crouter, 2000). Both how much and when parents work matter for children. Not only are heavy parental work schedules associated with negative outcomes for children (Parcel & Menaghan, 1994), but non-overlapping work hours for husbands and wives have negative effects on marital relationships (White & Keith, 1990). Job loss and underemployment have serious effects on family life, including marital relationships, parent–child relationships, and child adjustment (Conger & Elder, 1994; Conger et al., 2002; White & Rogers, 2000).

In terms of the impact of work on families, Crouter (1994) suggests two types of linkage. One type of research focuses on work as an emotional climate that, in turn, may have carryover effects to the enactment of roles in home settings. The focus is generally on short-term or transitory effects. A second type of linkage focuses on the types of attitudes and values that adults acquire in the workplace and on how these variations in job experience alter their behavior in family contexts. In contrast to the short-term perspective of the spillover of emotional climate research, this second type examines more enduring and long-lasting effects of work on family life.

Work in the first tradition has been conducted by Repetti (1994), who studied the impact of working in a high stress job (air-traffic controller) on subsequent family interaction patterns. She found that male air traffic controllers were more withdrawn in marital interactions after high-stress shifts and tended to be behaviorally and emotionally withdrawn during interactions with their children as well. Although high workload is associated with withdrawal, negative social experiences in the work place have a different effect. Distressing social experiences at work were associated with higher expressions of anger and greater use of discipline during interaction with the child later in the day. Repetti and Wood (1997) found similar effects for mothers who withdrew from their preschoolers on days when the mothers experienced greater workloads or interpersonal stress on the job. Repetti views this as a spillover effect in which there is transfer of negative feeling across settings. Similarly, Crouter, Bumpus, Maguire, and McHale (1999) found that parents who reported high work pressure and role overload had more conflicts with their adolescents.

Research in the second tradition of family–work linkages, namely the effects of the nature of men's occupational roles on their fathering behavior, dates back to the classic work of Kohn (1995). Men who experience a high degree of occupational autonomy value independence in their children, recognize children's intentions when considering discipline, and use reasoning and withdrawal of rewards instead of physical punishment. In contrast, men who are in highly supervised jobs with little autonomy value conformity and obedience, focus on consequences rather than intentions and use more physical forms of discipline. In short, they repeat their job-based experiences in their parenting roles. Several researchers extended this work by focusing on the outcomes of job characteristics for children's development. Cooksey, Menaghan, and Jokielek (1997) found that children had fewer behavior problems when their mothers' work involved more autonomy, working with people, and more problem-solving opportunities. Similarly, others found that fathers with greater job complexity and autonomy were less authoritarian (Grimm-Thomas & Perry-Jenkins, 1994), responded with greater warmth to their children, and provided more verbal explanations (Greenberger, O'Neil, & Nagel, 1994).

As these studies clearly suggest, fathers' and mothers' work experiences impact their parenting behavior. However, the process probably operates in both directions in which parents' home experience affects their job performance as well. In fact, arguments at home with a wife or with a child were negatively related to father's work performance (Frone, Yardley, & Markel, 1997). Perhaps, a positive home-based experience would create a positive mood and possibly enhance one's workday. These studies underscore the importance of moving beyond employment status per se to a detailed exploration of the nature of work in our future investigations of family–work linkages.

Cultural Factors in Fathering

Cultural factors also play an important role in determining both the amount and quality of father involvement. In spite of this recognition there is relatively little knowledge about the cultural aspects of fatherhood.

Reasons for the Neglect of Other Cultural Groups in Fathering Research. There are a variety of reasons for our neglect of other cultural groups in the fathers' area. First, there is a universalist assumption that underlies much of the theorizing in the social sciences. This assumes that the processes noted in studies of Western fathers or more narrowly middle-class European American fathers will be generalizable to both other cultures and other non European American groups in the United States. In the last several decades, this assumption has been challenged on several fronts. Theoretically, there has been a revival of interest in cross-cultural and intra-cultural variations in large part due to the re-discovery of Vygotskian theory with the strong focus on the cultural embeddedness of families (Rogoff, 2003). This is reflected in renewed interest in cross-cultural variations in parenting more generally (Bornstein, 1991; Parke & Buriel, 1998) and fathering more specifically (Hewlett, 1991; Lamb, 1987). Second, demographic shifts in North America have fueled interest in intra-cultural variation. In 2003, 31% of the population belonged to a racial minority group. Currently, 13% of the U.S. population are Hispanic (37 million), 12.7% are African-Americans (36.2 million), 3.9% are Asian-American (11 million), 1% are Indian or Alaska Natives (2.7 million) and another 4.1% are of two or more races (4.1 million) (U.S. Census Bureau, 2003). In view of these demographic shifts there is an opportunity to evaluate the generalizability of our assumptions about fathering. At the same time we have a moral obligation to better understand large segments of our population in order to be able to develop and provide culturally sensitive services, and programs and policies on behalf of children and families of diverse cultural backgrounds. In recognition of intra-cultural diversity within the United States, there has been a shift away from the cultural deficit model in which the focus was on majority–minority differences in parenting behavior. Instead, the field has moved toward an understanding of intra-group variation with a focus on understanding the adaptive strategies ethnic minority fathers and families develop in response to their ecological circumstances and cultural traditions. This new paradigm recognizes the value of within-group analyses involving a single ethnic group and re-focuses attention away from merely documenting group differences.

In spite of the importance of addressing these cultural variations in fathering processes and practices, there are barriers that have limited the amount of work that has been devoted to these minority groups. Not only are fathers more difficult to recruit for research participation relative to mothers, recruitment of members of ethnic minority groups is especially difficult to enlist in our research projects (Parke et al., 2003). Members of minority groups are often skeptical about participation in scientific studies for a variety of reasons, including the past history of mistreatment of minority research participants. Moreover, in the case of Hispanic-American and Asian-American groups, some of whom are recent immigrants—sometimes illegal—there is a healthy wariness of official institutions and a distrust of unfamiliar individuals. As a result, many of our minority samples are often biased and unrepresentative. Moreover, due to the biased samples there is a tendency to pathologize fathers and/or families who do not conform to either the structure, role arrangements, or child-rearing practices and values of the majority culture (Gadsen, 1999). Many samples of African-American fathers, for example, are poor and unmarried and not living with their partner, and therefore fathers from intact African-American families are underrepresented in our studies. Moreover, this sampling bias not only leads to a distorted portrait of the full range of African-American fathers' involvement, but makes comparisons with Euro-American fathers problematic since most of this work involves intact, middle class fathers. A second problem is the establishment of scalar equivalence across fathers in different ethnic groups. Progress has been made on this front but more on mothers than fathers (Knight et al., 2002). Another problem is interpretative validity (Maxwell, 1992) or the need to insure that our interpretations of fathers' behaviors and utterances are, in fact, consistent with their own understanding of those displays. The increased use of focus groups (Silverstein & Auerbach, 1999) with fathers of different ethnic backgrounds has been valuable in addressing these issues. Next, we examine the role of fathers in families of different ethnic groups—African-American, Hispanic-American, Asian-American and Native-American.

African-American Fathers. A body of literature has developed in recent years regarding African-American fathers, that has shown the relation between the fathering role and the well-being of family members, including both mothers and children (Cooper, Holman, & Braithwaite, 1983; Gorman-Smith, Tolan, Zelli, & Huesmann, 1996). Moreover, the links between a variety of demographic and attitudinal characteristics within the African-

American family and adolescent psychological adjustment (Dancy & Handal, 1984), academic achievement (Heiss, 1996; Lamborn, Dornbusch, & Steinberg, 1996), violence and delinquency (Gorman-Smith et al., 1996), and self-esteem (Mandara & Murray, 2002) have emerged. The traditional portrait of the absent or uninvolved father within a pathological family unit is no longer present, but rather a picture of fathers who play a significant role in family life has emerged (Gadsen, 1999; McAdoo, 1988).

Most of the work on African-American fathers has focused on poor, noncustodial nonresidential fathers. This focus stems from the policy concerns about the effects of father absence on children's development that has accompanied the rise in the number of single mother families over the last several decades. In 1970, 68% of African-Americans with children were married, while 28% of households were headed by women with no spouse present and 4% were male parent only households. In contrast, by the mid 1990s only 47% of African Americans with children were married, while 48% of households were female-headed with no spouse present and 6% were male parent households with no spouse present (U.S. Census Bureau, 1995). Many scholars have attributed the increase in female-headed families to the economic marginalization of African-American males (Mason, 1996; Lerman & Ooms, 1993). Because men often link their ability to provide for their families with the fathering role, the chronic economic problems encountered by African-American men contribute to their limited participation in the rearing of children compared to white middle class fathers (Gadsen, 1999). At the same time, there have been challenges to traditional approaches to assessing involvement of nonresidential African-American fathers, because the patterns of contact and involvement may be different for these men than for men in intact families (Lamb, 2002). Although more sporadic than in intact families, contact between nonresident fathers and their children is important, and high-quality relationships are associated with positive outcomes for the child.

Although the focus has been on father absence and nonresidential fathers in studies of African-American families (Gadsen, 1999), when the role of fathers in intact African-American families has been examined, the psychopathological portrait of black fathers is clearly challenged. In one of the earliest studies of middle class intact African-American families, McAdoo (1981) found that among 40 middle-class African-American fathers, verbal interaction with their preschoolers was warm, loving, and supportive, and their behaviors demonstrated a sensitivity toward the children's needs. When questioned regarding child rearing, fathers endorsed the view that fathers should be actively involved in the socialization of their children. Child-rearing attitudes were further elucidated in a study of 135 fathers by Hyde and Texidor (1988) where 99.3% expressed the view that fathers and mothers are equally responsible for child care. Further, 80%

had taken an active role in rule setting, teaching morals, and disciplining, and 87% felt that as fathers, they had the unique characteristics that would best serve the needs of their children.

More recently, Hofferth (2003) has provided an even clearer portrait of African-American fathers using a nationally representative sample of African American, Caucasian, and Hispanic fathers. In comparison to White fathers, African-American fathers spend less time with their children on a regular basis, although the differences are relatively modest (12.76 hours per week vs. 15.35 hours per week for African-American and White fathers respectively). This finding is in part due to family size, family structure and employment patterns. "Black fathers have larger families, are less likely to be the biological father and are more likely to be unemployed living with a female breadwinner, all of which by themselves, would result in less time spent with children" (Hoffreth, 2003, p. 211). In spite of these differences in level of involvement, African-American fathers assumed greater responsibility for routine care of their children than white fathers. This level of responsibility is consistent with the less traditional attitudes of Black fathers toward maternal roles than White fathers. African-American fathers are less likely to endorse such views, as "preschool children are likely to suffer if their mother is employed." In terms of child-rearing style, Black fathers rate themselves as lower on warmth and more controlling than white fathers—a finding consistent with earlier work (McAdoo, 1988; Gadsen, 1999). Finally, African-American fathers were higher in monitoring their children than White fathers. As others (Deater-Deckard & Dodge, 1997) have argued neighborhood characteristics may account for these patterns. African-American fathers control and monitor their children more because their neighborhoods are more dangerous. Family size may explain this difference as well since African-Americans have larger families than Caucasian families and larger families require more parental control.

Several studies have focused on the determinants of involvement for African-American fathers (Hofferth, 2003; Toth & Xu, 1999). As in the case of White fathers, higher numbers of work hours is linked with less father involvement. When spouses are employed outside the home, Black fathers spend more time with their children—a pattern found in earlier studies of White fathers (Coltrane, 1996). Neighborhood characteristics are important as well. Black fathers who live in predominantly African-American neighborhoods exhibit higher levels of warmth than those who reside in more heterogeneous neighborhoods (Hofferth, 2003). In sum, while there are differences in style and level of involvement, the determinants of variation in involvement in African-American families and White families are similar.

Although it is important to understand differences between African-Americans and other cultural groups, it is also necessary to recognize that there is considerable variability within African-American families as well.

Recently several investigators have applied a person-oriented or typology approach to the study of fathers and families. For example, Jain, Belsky, and Crnic (1996) described different types of White fathers including care-takers, playmates, teachers, disciplinarians and disengaged fathers. Following in their tradition, Mandara and Murray (2002) recently developed a typology of middle class African-American families. This study demon-strates how demographic and attitudinal characteristics give form to a fam-ily structure and create well-functioning constituents. Many of the features in this typology can be used across racial and ethnic groups as can Baum-rind's (1991) seminal work. Three family types were identified: Cohesive-Authoritative, Conflictive-Authoritarian, and Defensive-Neglectful. The Co-hesive-Authoritative family is expressive and exhibits a very low level of fam-ily conflict. Personal growth is emphasized and there is much participation in recreational activities; family members are encouraged to be assertive, and are high on proactive racial socialization and low in defensive racial so-cialization. The Conflictive-Authoritarian family is high on internal con-flict, lack concern and commitment for family members, and parents ex-hibit an overbearing authoritarian discipline style. Family relationships are distressed and children do not feel they can express emotions. There is a strong emphasis on achievement and competition but not on intellectual stimulation. Their focus on racial socialization is relatively moderate. The Defensive-Neglectful family is at the greatest risk for becoming dysfunctional. Children are socialized to dislike other racial groups, but are also taught not to be proud of being African American. There is a high level of neglectful parenting where parents are not nurturing or supportive, but very critical. There is low emphasis on achievement and no active participation in recre-ational activities or religious affiliations. While this study did not deal with the predictors of various outcome variables, it provides a more accurate de-scription of the various forms of African-American families.

In sum, the findings of current literature demonstrate that African-American fathers' involvement is a function of the interplay between social and economic conditions and gender role ideology. By focusing on intact rather than single-parent families, many of the assumed differences between African-American and European-American fathers are less evident. Instead of being viewed as irresponsible and uninvolved, African-American fathers are, in fact, central players in family life in intact families. A focus on the op-portunities and constraints associated with jobs and education is providing more insight into African-American male involvement in fathering activities.

Hispanic-American Fathers.   Although commonly held notions of Latino fathers might expect that they would be less involved, those who study La-tino families have hypothesized that Latino fathers may be more likely than fathers of other ethnicities to be involved with their children due to the cultural values found amongst Latinos. One such value is familism which emphasizes family cohesion, cooperation, and closeness (Cauce & Domenech-Rodriguez, 2002). Other cultural values that are hypothesized to be related to father involvement include the concept of machismo, which in recent years has been revised from earlier, largely misguided notions of manly self-reliance and sexuality to include masculine loyalty and responsibility (Mirandé, 1997). Empirical research has indeed found that Latino fathers spend similar lengths of time involved in caring for their children as fathers of other ethnicities. Specifically, some studies have found that Latino fathers are more likely to be engaged in caretaking than European Americans (Bartkowski & Xu, 2000; Toth & Xu, 1999; Yeung, Sandberg, Davis-Kean, & Hofferth, 2001). Others have found no difference in the amount of father engagement between fathers of different ethnicities (Hofferth, 2003; Hossain, Field, Malphurs, Valle, & Pickens, 1995; NICHD Early Child Care Research Network, 2000).

When focusing on different types of engagement activities with their children, researchers have found both patterns of similarity and differences between Latino fathers and other ethnicities. Similar to other types of fathers, Latino fathers spend more time in play with their children relative to mothers (Toth & Xu, 1999; Yeung et al., 2001). Latino fathers have been found to be more involved in household and personal care activities than European-American fathers (Yeung et al., 2001). Finally, Latino fathers show similar levels of affection and warmth to their children as fathers of other ethnicities (Hofferth, 2003; Toth & Xu, 1999).

Studies of responsibility in Latino fathers have mostly focused on the extent to which Latino fathers monitor or restrict their children's behavior. Toth and Xu (1999) found that Latino fathers reported increased restriction of their children's behavior over European-American fathers. Hofferth (2003) found that Latino fathers report less monitoring of their children's behavior than European-American fathers. Hofferth did, however, find that Latino fathers report more responsibility for care of their children than White fathers in spite of the fact that she found no difference in level of involvement between Latino and White fathers. Discrepancies between these two studies in the extent to which Latino fathers monitor their children relative to other ethnicities may be due to sample characteristics in each study; clearly more work is needed on the level of responsibility taken by fathers in Latino families.

Several studies have examined factors related to increased paternal involvement for Latinos. Among relevant demographic variables, high income, maternal employment, and maternal hours of work have been related to increased paternal involvement in Latino families (Fagan, 1998). Similarly, Coltrane, Parke, and Adams (2004) have found that fathers were more involved with their children in families where mothers earned a greater share of the income relative to other families. Neighborhood characteristics have also been related to father involvement. Specifically, living in poorer neighborhoods and in neighborhoods that are largely comprised of other Latinos is associated with more father responsibility (Hofferth, 2003). These neighborhood characteristics account for part of the variance in the relation between Latino fathers and increased responsibility for childcare. Father attitudes and beliefs that are related to involvement include non-traditional gender role orientations (Coltrane et al., 2004; Coltrane & Valdez, 1993; Hofferth, 2003; Toth & Xu, 1999), positive attitudes towards parenting (Hofferth, 2003), commitment to the parenting role (Toth & Xu, 1999), and value of child obedience (Toth & Xu, 1999). One paradoxical issue that must be explained is why Latino fathers have been found to hold more traditional gender role ideologies and yet are often found to be similarly, if not more involved in childrearing than fathers of other ethnicities. It has been speculated that commitment to family and to the parenting role (Toth & Xu, 1999) might account for this discrepancy, but more work must be done to untangle these effects.

Native American Fathers. In spite of the fact that there are 1.5 million Native Americans in the United States, the role of Native American fathers has been largely neglected in research. It is important to note that one cannot generalize across all Native Americans since there are 280 different tribal groups and 161 linguistic groups (Staples, 1988). Some Native Americans live on reservations, some do not. Thus, the terms *Native Americans* or *American Indians* refer to a variety of cultures, languages, nationalities, and family systems (Mirandé, 1991), just as in the case of other groups.

While no one group can be considered typical, Mirandé (1991) has used the Navajo as a way of illustrating some common features of Native American families and how the family structure has been altered by contact with the dominant, Euro-American society. Traditionally, Navajo women were equal to, if not greater than, men, in terms of family roles. Women were responsible for the care and maintenance of children. Many teaching and disciplinary functions were carried out by the mother's brothers, not the father. As the society came in contact more with Euro-American culture, the father became increasingly important within the family and the mother lost much of her influence (Mirandé, 1991).

Native American families rely heavily on the community as a whole. Children are protected, loved, and nurtured not only by parents, but also by siblings, aunts, uncles, grandparents, cousins, and other extended family (Mirandé, 1991). Therefore, fathering in the traditional Native-American community is best examined in the context of the extended family (Burgess, 1980). The extended family network partakes in child rearing, which provides a safeguard and protection for children and parents do not have absolute or even primary authority over children (Mirandé, 1991). Cross (1986) asserted that community opinion governs parents' childrearing behavior, and parents who do not comply are often ridiculed into compliance. In some Native American tribes, the role of disciplinarian is assigned to a specific tribal member or sometimes even a mythological figure, thus removing the burden of physical discipline from parents and placing it on a "wise one." In fact, adults seldom, if ever, strike children, nor do they talk loudly or yell at children, especially when correcting them. Native-American children do not expect praise for doing what is required of them. Parents occasionally praise children for doing well, and indicate their approval through a smile, pleasant tone of voice, or friendly pat (Burgess, 1980). Burgess (1980) claimed that for children, knowledge of approval and disapproval is undoubtedly a powerful means of social control in Native American societies.

In one of the few studies of paternal involvement among Native American fathers, Williams, Radin, and Coggins (1996) examined childrearing and school performance among the Ojibwa children. Higher amounts of father involvement were associated with better academic functioning and better Native American adaptive functioning. Native American functioning assessed adaptive traits that researchers believed to be important in most Native American populations. For sons in particular, increased amounts of father involvement were associated with better academic functioning, lower levels of internalization, and better Native-American adaptive functioning. Fathers who expected higher community leadership for their children spent a higher percentage of their time as primary caregivers. It was also surprising that children of more nurturant fathers appeared to be less competent in school. However, Williams et al. suggest that this could be a result of the father responding to a child who is struggling in a primarily Euro-American classroom with individualistic and competitive atmosphere, which is very different from the tribal society to which the child is accustomed. Overall, this study indicated that there is a strong relation between fathers' greater presence and sons' better cognitive and social development.

While the role of the father in Native American families is still poorly understood, it is clear that in traditional Native-American society, ultimate power and authority is vested in neither the father nor the mother, but rather in the community as a whole (Mirandé, 1991). Fathers have been found to influence child academic achievement, especially for sons. However, more research is needed to examine the particular amount of involvement and responsibility Native-American fathers have in childrearing, and, in turn, how this is changing across generations as a consequence of assimilation.

Asian Fathers. Asian fathers have typically been viewed as aloof and uninvolved with their children. Again, this stereotype has some historical basis, but the portrait of the modern Asian father is changing due to both patterns of immigration and acculturation as well as shifting economic conditions in some Asian countries (for a detailed discussion see Ishii-Kuntz, 1993, 2000; Chao & Tseng, 2002). In both Asian American and Asian families, there are two general findings that characterize the father's role in the family. First, the strong commitment to the breadwinner role among Asian fathers has resulted in men's limited involvement with the care of their children (Ishii-Kuntz, 2000) compared to other cultures. For example, Japanese fathers are less involved with their children than fathers in other countries. While Japanese fathers, according to a 1994 survey, spend 3.8 hours per day with their young children (3 years or younger), fathers in other cultures were higher (US: 5.35 hours; Korea 4.12 hours; Thailand, 7.17 hours; UK 6.45 hours). As in many countries, Japanese fathers engaged in play more than routine physical care (Ishii-Kuntz, 2000). However, both fathers themselves as well as their children and wives view their involvement in work as valuable. In one survey (Miwa, 1995) over 90% of 5th graders saw outside work as fathers' primary responsibility while over 80% viewed mothers as best suited to be primary caregivers. Consistent with these findings, the amount of time that Japanese children spent with their fathers did not greatly affect their perceptions of their fathers (Ishii-Kuntz, 1995). Similar low levels of father involvement have been reported for Chinese families (Jankowiak, 1992) as well as Taiwanese families (Sun & Roopnarine, 1996). Taiwanese fathers were less involved in child care with their infants than Euro-American fathers, and in China fathers were not viewed as sufficiently competent or trustworthy to care for infants. Instead, in Chinese families, father's role was focused on children's education when children entered middle school.

However, as Ishii-Kuntz (2000) notes, the centrality of the men's breadwinning role among Japanese fathers is changing. In one recent study, 81% of Japanese fathers ranked the paternal role as first or second in importance among five paternal roles—evidence that the importance of the worker role is lessening (Shwalb, Kawai, Shoji, & Tsunetsugu, 1997). Second, the economic recession in Japan, in combination with an increase in the labor force participation of women, has contributed to this decline as well. Although not universal, there are trends among some segments of Japanese society for men to become more involved in fathering (Ishii-Kuntz, 2000). Similarly, in the United States as Asian families become more acculturated, there is a trend toward greater equality in the division of household labor including more equity in child-care responsibilities (Ishii-Kuntz, 2000). However, the patterns are not uniform across Asian subgroups that vary in terms of immigration patterns and levels of economic participation.

Stylistic differences as well as level of involvement need to be considered. As Chao and Tseng (2002) recently observed, "Parenting differences purported between Asian fathers and mothers have been based on the traditional adage 'strict father, kind mother'—wherein fathers exert high degrees of authoritarian control and mothers manifest high degrees of warmth" (p. 73). Consistent with this view, Shek (2000) found that Chinese adolescents perceived maternal parenting as being more positive than paternal parenting. Adolescents stated that fathers showed less concern, less responsiveness, and higher levels of harshness than mothers. Also, father–adolescent communication was perceived less positively and as occurring less frequently than mother–adolescent communication. However, Jankowiak (1992) reported that fathers spoke to their children, from ages 1 to 6, in a softer tone than mothers. Fathers were actually very affectionate.

In contrast to the general picture that emerges for East Asian families, studies of Asian immigrant families in the United States have found few differences between mothers and fathers in levels of authoritarian parenting control and warmth (Chao & Kim, 2000). Again, acculturation clearly plays a role in helping to understand differences in mother–father childrearing styles. These patterns present a clear challenge to our stereotype of the maternal and paternal childrearing styles among Asian-American families. Diversity among Asian Americans needs to be recognized in light of the differences in the recency of entry of some groups (e.g., Hmong, Vietnamese) relative to other groups (e.g., Chinese, Japanese) into the United States. As in the case of fathers in other cultural minorities, there is a gap between cultural stereotypes and reality.

Consequences of Variations in Fathering for Fathers, Marriage and Children

Consequences for Men's Development. Becoming a father impacts a man's own psychological development and well-being. As Parke (1981) noted, "the father–child relationship is a two-way process and children influence their fathers just as fathers alter their children's development" (p. 9). There is extensive work on the impact of fatherhood on marital relationships. As Cowan and Cowan (2000) and others (Belsky, Rovine, & Fish, 1989) have documented, the transition to parenthood signals marked changes in marital relationships. Some couples experience a drop in marital satisfaction, others show an increase, while still others show no change. Moreover, both fathers and mothers are affected by the shift from couple to family status. Several lines of evidence suggest that discrepancies in expectations on the part of mothers and fathers concerning the relative roles that each will play may be an important determinant of post-partum marital satisfaction. The Cowans (2000) found that, when there was a larger discrepancy between the wives' expectations of their husbands' involvement in infant care and his level of actual participation, there was a greater decline in wives' marital satisfaction between late pregnancy and 18 months. Belsky,

Ward, and Levine (1986) found a similar decrease in marital satisfaction when mother's expectations about father involvement were not met. Men show a similar effect of a discrepancy between attitudes and behavior. McDermid, Huston, and McHale (1990) found greater negative impact of the onset of parenthood when there was a discrepancy between spouses' sex role attitudes and the division of household and childcare labor. McBride (1989) found that traditional fathers who held conservative sex-role attitudes, but were nonetheless involved in child care, had lower levels of satisfaction. In summary, research suggests that discrepancies in parental expectations about roles, rather than the level of change per se, may be a key correlate of men's marital satisfaction after the onset of fatherhood. However, it is important to underscore that marital relationships are both determinants as well as a consequence of paternal involvement, as noted above (Pleck & Masciadrelli, 2004). Even though marital satisfaction decreases for men (and women) after the onset of parenthood, marital stability (i.e., the likelihood of staying in the marriage) increases relative to childless couples (Cowan & Cowan, 2000). As the Cowans (1992) noted:

> The marital stability of couples who have preschool children is protected. Although new parents may be experiencing increase tension or dissatisfaction as couples, their joint involvement with managing the baby's and the family's needs may lead them to put off, or possibly work harder on, the problems in their marriage—at least while the children are young. (p. 110)

Less is known about the impact of being a father on marital satisfaction after the transition to parenthood. An exception is the longitudinal study by Heath and Heath (1991) that followed a cohort of college men born in the 1930s into their 30s and mid-40s and found that competent fathers were in satisfying marriages. However, these two indices (paternal competence and marital satisfaction) are also related to psychological maturity, leaving open the possibility that fathering activities lead to marital satisfaction and maturity or that maturity is the common correlate of being both a competent father and husband. Due to limitations in sample size, reliance on qualitative indices, and the lack of adequate statistical analyses, these results remain suggestive rather than definitive. However, Snarey (1993) found support for the relation between paternal involvement in childhood or adolescence on marital satisfaction. In a follow-up longitudinal study of men originally studied in the 1940s and 1950s, Snarey assessed the marital success of these men at mid-life (age 47). "Fathers who provided high levels of social-emotional support for their offspring during the childhood decade (0–10 years) and high levels of intellectual, academic and social emotional support during the adolescent decade (11–21 years) were themselves as men at mid-life, more likely to be happily married" (Snarey, 1993, p. 111).

In sum, it is clear that there are long-term positive effects of father involvement on marriage, even though there may, in some cases, be a decline in satisfaction accompanying the transition to fatherhood.

Does fatherhood alter men's own development? First, men's self-identity changes after the onset of parenthood. The Cowans (2000) assessed role shifts during the transition to fatherhood and found that men who become fathers decreased the partner/lover aspect of their self and increased the parent percentage of their self-rating over the 21-month assessment period. Self-esteem, however, was not affected by the transition to parenthood for either fathers or mothers in the Cowans' project. Grossman (1987), who studied men's transition to parenthood, found that first time fathers who were both more affiliative (i.e., importantly connected to others, enjoying empathetic relationships) and more autonomous (viewing themselves as separate and distinct from others) had significantly higher life adaptation scores. Fathers of firstborns who were more affiliative at 1 year also reported being higher in emotional well-being. These findings suggest that "separateness and individuation are not sufficient for men's well-being; they need connections as well" (Grossman, 1987, p. 107).

Does fatherhood have a longer-term impact on men's psychological development? Heath and Heath (1991), in a longitudinal study of college men, found that fatherhood related to men's ability to understand themselves, to understand others sympathetically, and to integrate their own feelings. Second, just as women have difficulty balancing work and parenting, there is evidence that men experience role strain between family and occupational demands as well (Parke & Brott, 1999; Levine & Pittinsky, 1998). For example, several studies report that more involved fathers feel that they have less time for their careers and that their family obligations interfere with their occupational demands (Baruch & Barnett, 1986). Similarly, Greenberger and O'Neil (1990) found that work–family role strain is lowest when there is low work commitment and high parental involvement. Although policy debates (e.g., Hochschild, 1989) usually involve role conflicts for mothers, there has been increased recognition that in dual-career families, balancing work and family obligations is clearly an issue that affects parents of both genders (Parke & Brott, 1999).

Does fatherhood affect generativity, a concept derived from Erikson's (1975) theoretical writings? Snarey (1993) provided a succinct summary:

> The psychosocial task of middle adulthood, Stage 7 (in Erikson's Stage theory) is the attainment of a favorable balance of generativity over stagnation and self-absorption . . . Most broadly, Erikson (1975) considers generativity to mean any caring activity that contributes to the spirit of future generations, such as the generation of new or more mature persons, products, ideas, or works of art . . . generativity's psychosocial challenge to adults is to create, care for, and promote the development of others from nurturing the growth

of another person to shepherding the development of a broader community. (pp. 18–19)

Snarey (1993) described three types that apply to fathers, namely (1) biological generativity (indicated by the birth of a child), (2) parental generativity (indicated by child rearing activities), and (3) societal generativity (indicated by caring for other younger adults; serving as a mentor, providing leadership, and contributing to generational continuity). Is men's societal generativity at mid-life related to the level of care and support they provide their children?

Snarey (1993) found that men who nurtured their children's social-emotional development during childhood (0–10 years) and who also contributed to both social-emotional and intellectual-academic development during the second decade (11–21 years) were at mid-life more likely to become generative in areas outside their family. Again this contribution of father participation to societal generativity was evident after controlling for a variety of background variables. Snarey offered several interpretations of these findings. First, a disequilibrium explanation suggests that parental child-rearing responsibility results in demands that are difficult to meet, and that, in turn, promote "increased complexity in the fathers' cognitive emotional and behavioral repertoire. . . . This commitment beyond the self, in turn, prepares the way for societal generativity which involves a commitment beyond the family" (pp. 117–118). Second, perhaps a nurturing predisposition may underlie both parenting and societal generativity and account for the continuity across time. Third, the arrival of children often leads to increases in men's participation in neighborhood and community organizations on behalf of children, which, in turn, may continue into the mid-life years. In summary, although the processes are not yet well understood, it is clear that involved fathering relates in positive ways to other aspects of men's lives. As Snarey (1993) noted, "men who are parentally generative during early adulthood usually turn out to be good spouses, workers, and citizens at mid-life" (p. 119).

Others have found support for these links between childrearing involvement (e.g., taking child on routine errands and jobs; consulting with teachers, supervising homework) and generativity (McKeering & Pakenham, 2000). Moreover, paternal engagement is related to civic engagement in a large representative sample (Eggebeen & Knoester, 2001). At the same time, other studies report only small or marginal links between care giving involvement and generativity (Bailey, 1992; Christiansen & Palkovitz, 1998). Clearly more work is needed before strong conclusions about the caregiving–generativity link can be firmly established (Pleck & Masciadrelli, 2004).

Implications of Father Involvement for Children's Development

Two types of approaches to the issue of the impact of father involvement on children's social, emotional, and cognitive development can be distinguished. First, in a modern variant of the earlier father-absence theme, sociologists, in particular, have recently examined the impact of nonresident fathers' frequency and quality of contact on children's development. The second, or normative approach, focuses on the consequences of the quality and quantity of father–child interaction on children's development in intact families.

Contact Between Nonresident Fathers and Their Children. Research has focused on large national samples of fathers and children, such as the National Longitudinal Survey of Youth (NLSY), the National Survey of Children (NSC), and the National Survey of Families and Households (NSFH). These surveys reveal a high level of disengagement on the part of nonresident fathers but at the same time sufficient variability to permit an examination of the issue of the impact of contact on children's development. A meta-analysis of 63 studies of the associations between nonresident fathers' contact and children's well-being was reported by Amato and Gilbreth (1999). Although they found weak associations between contact and academic success and internalizing problems, there was no link between contact and externalizing problems. In general, frequency of contact with nonresident fathers was not linked to child outcomes. This conclusion is consistent with other scholarly evaluations of the evidence (Eggebeen, 2002; McLanahan & Sandefur, 1994).

However, quality and not presence/absence alone, is important in assessing the impact of nonresident fathers. In a follow-up study of 18- to 21-year-old children of African-American adolescent mothers, Furstenberg and Harris (1993) found little impact of contact alone on young adults' outcomes but clear beneficial effects if the quality of the relationship was taken into account. Those who reported a strong bond or attachment with their father during adolescence had higher educational attainment, were less likely to be imprisoned, and were less depressed. These effects were especially evident in the case of children living with the father and were only marginally evident for nonresident biological fathers. The data suggest that both presence and quality matters; but quality is especially important because fathers' presence is unrelated to outcomes when quality (degree of attachment to father) is controlled. The Amato and Gilbreth (1999) meta-analysis confirms these earlier findings; a measure of the affective relationship between the father and child (feeling close) was positively associated with academic success, and negatively with internalizing and externalizing problems. The effect sizes were modest in magnitude. Second, father's authoritative parenting was associated with academic success, and negatively related to internalizing and externalizing problems. Authoritative parenting was a better predictor than either frequency of contact or the "feeling close" measure. In addition to quality of involvement, the amount of father's payment of child support was a significant predictor of children outcomes, including academic success and children's externalizing behavior. Internalizing behavior was not linked with fathering indices. This finding is not surprising, because "fathers financial contributions provide wholesome food, adequate shelter in safe neighborhoods, commodities (such as books, computers, and private lessons) that facilitate children's academic success and support for college attendance" (Amato & Gilbreth, 1999, p. 559). Finally, this effect was evident for both boys and girls and African-American and European American families. This work reflects earlier and recurring themes in the parent–child literature, namely that quality is the critical factor in determining children's development (Wachs, 2000). One of the lingering questions concerns the determinants of continual involvement of nonresident fathers, and interesting links among child support, contact, and child well-being are emerging (Eggebeen, 2002). For example, Garfinkel and McLanahan (1995) found that fathers will spend more time with their children as child support increases which, in turn, benefits the children. More work is needed to more fully understand this important policy issue.

Impact of Normal Variations in Intact Families on Children's Development. A voluminous literature has emerged over the last three decades that clearly demonstrates relations between quality of paternal involvement and children's social, emotional, and cognitive development (Pleck & Masciadrelli, 2004; Parke, 1996, 2002). At the same time, considerable evidence shows a good deal of redundancy between fathers' and mothers' impact on children. There is less evidence that fathers make a unique contribution to children's development.

In a review of the effects of fathers on children, Marsiglio, Amato, Day, and Lamb (2000) reviewed 72 studies published in the 1990s with the majority involving young children or adolescents and the remaining concerning young adults. Their review revealed moderate negative associations between authoritative fathering and internalizing and externalizing problems. The relations held for children and adolescents regardless of age. Moreover, Amato and Rivera (1999) found a similar positive influence on children's behavior for European American, African American and Latino fathers. Marsiglio et al. (2000) offer three important caveats to their conclusion that "positive father involvement is generally beneficial to children"

(p. 1183). First, most studies rely on a single data source which raises the problem of shared method variance. Second, many researchers do not control for the quality of the mother–child relationship when examining father effects. Since the behavior and attitudes of parents are often highly related, this step is critical. Only 8 of the 72 studies reviewed by Marsiglio et al. (2000) did, in fact, control for the quality of the mother–child relationship; however, five of the eight studies continued to show a father effect after taking into account mother–child effects. For example, Isley, O'Neil, and Parke (1996) found that fathers' level of affect and control predicted children's social adaptation with peers both concurrently and one year later after controlling for maternal effects (see also Mosley & Thompson, 1995; Hart, Nelson, Robinson, Olsen, & McNeilly-Choque, 1998).

Pleck and Masciadrelli (2004) cited several other recent studies that controlled for maternal involvement and avoided the same reporter problem. For example, Aldous and Mulligan (2002) using a national data set found that positive paternal engagement is linked to lower frequency of later behavior problems for boys and for difficult-to-rear children. Similarly, in a large sample of British teenagers, positive paternal engagement predicted positive school attitudes (Flouri, Buchanan, & Bream, 2002). Pleck and Masciadrelli (2004) concluded that in over 70% of the studies that were methodologically sound (controlling for maternal effects and independent data sources), there were positive correlations between child outcomes and paternal involvement. Although there is overlap between the effects of mothers and fathers on their children's academic, emotional, and social development, evidence is emerging that fathers make a unique contribution to their children's development (Parke, 2002; Rohner, 1998).

A third caveat concerns problems of inferring direction of causality because studies are correlational and involve concurrent rather than longitudinal assessments (Marsiglio et al., 2000). However, two strands of evidence suggest that the direction of effects can plausibly flow from paternal behavior to child outcomes. First, longitudinal studies support the view that fathers influence their children (see Amato & Rivera, 1999; Parke, 1996, 2002; Pleck & Masciadrelli, 2004, for reviews). For example, Gottman, Katz, and Hooven (1997) found that fathers' acceptance of and assistance with their children's emotions (sadness, anger) at 5 years of age were related to higher levels of social acceptance with peers at age 8. Positive father engagement in tenth grade was related to fewer behavior problems one year later (Zimmerman, Salem, & Notaro, 2000). Nor are the effects of fathering on developmental outcomes restricted to childhood. In a follow-up of the classic childrearing study of Sears, Maccoby, and Levin (1957), Koestner, Franz, and Weinberger (1990) reassessed a sample of the original children when they were 31 years old. The most powerful predictor of empathy in adulthood for both men and women was paternal child-rearing involvement at age 5. This paternal factor was a better predictor than several other maternal variables. In a further study (Franz, McClelland, & Weinberger, 1991), at age 41, men and women with better social relationships (marriage quality; extra-familial ties) in mid-life had experienced more paternal warmth as children. Although these studies support a father effects perspective, it is likely that reciprocal relationships will become evident, in which children and fathers mutually influence each other across the life course (Parke, 2002).

Beyond Description: Processes Which Link Fathering and Child Outcomes. Recent work that has focused on fathers' special style of interaction, namely play, has begun to reveal the processes through which fathers influence over children's development is achieved (see Parke, 1996; Parke et al., 2002, for reviews). Parke and his colleagues, for example, examined the relation between father–toddler play and children's adaptation to peers. In one study (MacDonald & Parke, 1984), fathers and their 3- and 4-year-old girls and boys were observed in 20 minutes of structured play in their homes. Teachers ranked these children in terms of their popularity among their preschool classmates. For both girls and boys, fathers who were rated as exhibiting high levels of physical play with their children, and eliciting high levels of positive affect from their children during the play sessions, had children who received the highest peer popularity ratings. For boys, however, this pattern was qualified by the father's level of directiveness. Boys whose fathers were both highly physical and low in directiveness received the highest popularity ratings, and the boys whose fathers were highly directive received lower popularity scores. Possibly, children who interact with a physically playful father and at the same time have an opportunity to regulate the pace and tempo of the interaction, a characteristic of low-directive fathers, learn how to recognize and send emotional signals during social interactions. Later studies confirmed these findings and showed a link between children's emotional encoding and decoding abilities that are presumably acquired, in part, in these playful interchanges and children's social adaptation to peers (Parke & O'Neil, 2000). In addition, fathers' affect displays, especially father anger, seem to be a potent correlate of children's social acceptance. In studies in both the laboratory (Carson & Parke, 1996) and the home (Boyum & Parke, 1995), fathers' negative affect is inversely related to preschool and kindergarten children's sociometric status. Mize and Pettit (1997) found that preschool children whose play with fathers is characterized by mutuality or balance in making play suggestions and following partners' suggestions were less aggressive, more competent, and better liked by peers. Similarly Hart and his colleagues (Hart et al., 1998, 2000) found that greater playfulness, patience, and understanding with children, especially on the part of the father, are associated with less aggressive behavior with peers. Later work has isolated other emotional processes such as emotional regulation (McDowell, Kim, O'Neil, & Parke, 2002) and knowledge and use of display rules (McDowell & Parke, 2000) that, in turn, are influenced by paternal (as well as maternal) interaction patterns and are predictive of children's social acceptance.

Although father involvement in infancy and childhood is quantitatively less than mother involvement, the data suggest that fathers nevertheless do have an important impact on their offspring's development.

APPLIED AND POLICY PERSPECTIVES

In light of the evidence it is clear that strategies aimed at increasing father involvement are worthwhile. Since, fathering is multi-determined, suggestions and policies aimed at facilitating fathers involvement need to be multi-level in nature as well. Parke and Brott (1999) provide some guidelines for increasing father involvement, by noting various steps that men, women, the government and the private sector can take to increase father involvement. Men themselves can increase their involvement in various ways. These include taking the initiative more rather than waiting to be asked. "If men are going to be fully involved, they are going to have to share responsibility for the household and childcare in an active fashion" (Parke & Brott, 1999, p. 193). This means being a partner not merely a helper. Second, men need to get more practice in parenting skills. Whatever women know about raising children they learned by doing and men can learn to improve their parenting as well. Programs are available to help fathers learn the basics of childcare, but men have to be willing to take advantage of these opportunities (Fagan & Hawkins, 2000). While many women gained these critical childcare experiences while they were growing up (Parke, 2000), many men have to catch up when they become fathers. Third, men need to be emotionally available to their children if they are going to be fully effective parents. As Gottman (1994) wisely notes: "Men must allow themselves to be aware of their feelings so they can empathize with their children. Then they must take whatever steps necessary to make themselves available to their kids. They must structure their lives so they give more time and attention to their children" (p. 183). And nonresidential fathers need to stay involved if they are single, separated or divorced. To achieve this goal fathers need to know their legal rights as a noncustodial parent, but also be aware of their responsibilities to continue to play an active role in their children's lives and to meet their financial support obligations.

As we noted earlier, fathering is a negotiated set of activities and mothers play an important part in determining how much fathers are involved. Just as men need to rethink their family roles as "assistants" to mothers, women need to change their expectations about their partners as well and communicate that parenting is a shared enterprise, not just a mother's responsibility. "Asking for help makes it seem as if what he's (fathers) helping with is really the women's job and that she should be grateful" (Parke & Brott, 1999, p. 197). Second, women should be gate openers, not gate closers. As research has shown, when women function as gate closers men's participation is less (Allen & Hawkins, 1999; Beitel & Parke, 1998). To increase father participation, women need to be facilitators and encourage men to play a part in family caregiving routines. Third, and closely related to the gate-keeper issue is the need to adjust standards. Women need to recognize that men and women may have different standards, if fathers are going to be full participants. As Parke and Brott (1999) wryly observed, "No child ever suffered long term trauma by having her diaper put on a bit looser than mother would like" (p. 196). Modifying standards in non-critical domains may encourage greater father participation.

In view of our ecological systems perspective, it is clear that individuals and couples cannot be expected to achieve changes in father involvement without support from societal institutions. Schools can play a role in this process by providing parenting education for both boys and girls, beginning in elementary school. This is not a new idea; the National PTA recommended that parenthood education be included in the curriculum as early as 1925. Second, physicians need to treat fathers as parents. Too often hospitals and doctors treat fathers—even expectant fathers—as second class citizens whose primary usefulness is to pay the bills. Fathers need opportunities to learn about the care and feeding of new babies in the hospital and to have programs that are sensitive to their needs and roles (Fagan & Hawkins, 2000). Pediatricians can encourage men to be present at well-baby checkups and to make evening appointment available so fathers can be there. The government can play a role too by funding public awareness campaigns by federal, state, and local governments about the importance of fathers in the lives of children, and government can overhaul welfare practices to encourage father involvement by not reducing maternal welfare benefits when fathers are active residential partners. Government policies, such as the Family and Medical Leave Act which gives fathers the same right as mothers to take time off after the birth of their children, need to be upheld and extended. At present, this law does not provide wages for the parents and by offering a financial safety net, more men (and women) would take advantage of these opportunities. On the legal front a policy of encouraging joint custody is an important tool for keeping more fathers involved in their children's lives and reducing some of the negative effects of divorce on children. The media can encourage father involvement by portraying fathers realistically and not as inept, uninvolved, and unimportant. Instead television can help shape our visions of men as partners for their wives and as involved and equal contributors to the care and up bringing of their children.

It is imperative that these policies and programs be carefully crafted and organized to appeal to fathers of different ethnic backgrounds. This kind of cultural sensitivity is crucial to attracting and retaining fathers in these programs and for these men to appreciate the relevance of these policies to their lives.

As Parke and Brott (1999) conclude:

> Promoting a cultural change in the ways that society views fathers and the ways that men view themselves in this role is no easy task. Just as there are many real barriers that converge and conspire to limit fathers' involvement, it will take a coordinated effort by men, women, the media, government and the private sector to bring about a new and more involved era of fatherhood. It's no easy task, but children, women, and men themselves will all benefit if we can increase father's involvement as we enter the twenty-first century. (p. 204)

One goal of this chapter is to extend an invitation to join this effort and to provide the scholarly foundation that underlies such an undertaking.

CONCLUSIONS

Our review suggests that fathers play important roles in the family and their involvement has significant consequences for children, mothers, and men themselves. Father involvement is multiply determined and a variety of influences, including individual, familial, marital, institutional, and cultural factors, need to be considered in order to understand variations in level of involvement. By recognizing fathers' embeddedness in community and culture as well as in family contexts, we will more fully understand the father's role and be better positioned to design intervention efforts to increase fathers' level of involvement in the lives of their children.

ACKNOWLEDGMENTS

Thanks to Faye Harmer for her assistance in the preparation of the manuscript. Support from NIMH grant RO1MH54154 to Parke, in part, facilitated the work described in this chapter.

REFERENCES

Aldous, J., & Mulligan, G. M. (2002). Fathers' child care and children's behavior problems. *Journal of Family Issues, 54,* 699–707.

Allen, J., & Hawkins, A. (1999). Maternal gatekeeping: Mothers' beliefs and behaviors that inhibit greater father involvement in family work. *Journal of Marriage and the Family, 61,* 199–212.

Amato, P. A., & Gilbreth, J. G. (1999). Nonresident fathers and children's well-being: Meta analysis. *Journal of Marriage and the Family, 61,* 15–73.

Amato, R. R., & Rivera, F. (1999). Paternal involvement and children's behavior. *Journal of Marriage and the Family, 61,* 375–384.

Bailey, W. T. (1992). Psychological development in men: Generativity and involvement with young children. *Psychological Reports, 71,* 929–930.

Bartkowski, J. P., & Xu, X. (2000). Distant patriarchs or expressive dads?: The discourse and practice of fathering in conservative Protestant families. *Sociological Quarterly, 41,* 465–485.

Baruch, G. K., & Barnett, R. C. (1986). Fathers' participation in family work and children's sex-role attitudes. *Child Development, 57,* 1210–1223.

Baumrind, D. (1991). The influence of parenting style on adolescent competence and substance abuse. *Journal of Early Adolescence, 11,* 56–94.

Beitel, A., & Parke, R. D. (1998). Paternal involvement in infancy: The role of maternal and paternal attitudes. *Journal of Family Psychology, 12,* 268–288.

Belsky, J. (1984). The determinants of parenting: A process model. *Child Development, 55,* 83–96.

Belsky, J., Rovine, M., & Fish, M. (1989).The developing family system. In M. Gunnar & E. Thelen (Eds.), *Systems and development: Vol. 22. Minnesota symposia on child psychology* (pp. 119–166). Hillsdale, NJ: Lawrence Erlbaum Associates.

Belsky, J., Ward, H. J., & Levine, M. (1986). Prenatal expectations, postnatal experiences and the transition to parenthood. In R. Ashmore & D. Brodzinsky (Eds.), *Perspectives on the family* (pp. 111–146). Hillsdale, NJ: Lawrence Erlbaum Associates.

Belsky, J., Youngblood, L., Rovine, M., & Volling, B. (1991). Patterns of marital change and parent–child interaction. *Journal of Marriage and the Family, 53,* 487–498.

Bianchi, S. M. (2000). Maternal employment and time with children: Dramatic change or surprising continuity? *Demography, 37,* 401–414.

Bonney, J. F., Kelley, M. L., & Levant, R. F. (1999). A model of fathers' involvement in child care in dual-earner families. *Journal of Family Psychology, 13,* 401–415.

Booth, A., & Amato, P. (1994). Parental marital quality, divorce and relations with offspring in young adulthood. *Journal of Marriage and the Family, 56,* 21–34.

Bornstein, M. H. (Eds.). (1991). *Cultural approaches to parenting.* Hillsdale, NJ: Lawrence Erlbaum Associates.

Boyum, L., & Parke, R. D. (1995). Family emotional expressiveness and children's social competence. *Journal of Marriage and Family, 57,* 593–608.

Brodzinsky, D. M., & Pinderhughes, E. (2002). Parenting and child development in adoptive families. In M. Bornstein (Ed.), *Handbook of parenting* (2nd ed., Vol. 1, pp. 279–312). Mahwah, NJ: Lawrence Erlbaum Associates.

Burgess, B. J. (1980). Parenting in the Native-American community. In M. R. Fantini & R. Cárdenas (Eds.), *Parenting in a multicultural society* (pp. 63–73). New York: Longman.

Carson, J., & Parke, R. D. (1996). Reciprocal negative affect in parent–child interactions and children's peer competency. *Child Development, 67,* 2217–2226.

Cauce, A. M., & Domenech-Rodriquez, M. (2002). Latino families: Myths and realities. In J. M. Contreras, K. A. Kerns, & A. M. Neal-Barnett (Eds.), *Latino children and families in the United States* (pp. 3–25). Westport, CT: Praeger.

Chao, R. K., & Kim, K. (2000). Parenting differences among immigrant Chinese fathers and mothers in the United States. *Journal of Psychology in Chinese Societies, 1,* 71–91.

Chao, R., & Tseng, V. (2002). Parenting of Asians. In M. Bornstein (Ed.), *Handbook of parenting* (2nd ed., Vol. 4, pp. 59–94). Mahwah, NJ: Lawrence Erlbaum Associates.

Christiansen, S. L., & Palkovitz, R. (1998). Exploring Erikson's psychosocial theory of development: Generatively and its relationship to paternal identity, intimacy, and involvement in childcare. *Journal of Men's Studies, 7*, 133–156.

Clarke-Stewart, K. A. (1980). The father's contribution to children's cognitive and social development in early childhood. In F. Pedersen (Ed.), *The father–infant relationship.* New York: Praeger.

Coley, R. L., & Chase-Lansdale, P. L. (1999). Stability and change in paternal involvement among urban African-American fathers. *Journal of Family Psychology, 13*, 416–435.

Collins, W. A., & Russell, A. (1991). Mother–child and father–child relationships in middle childhood and adolescence. *Developmental Review, 11*, 99–136.

Coltrane, S. (1996). *Family man.* New York: Oxford.

Coltrane, S., Parke, R. D., & Adams, M. (2004). Complexity of father involvement in low income Mexican-American families. *Family Relations, 53*, 179–189.

Coltrane, S., & Valdez, E. (1993). Reluctant compliance: Work–family role allocation in dual earner Chicano families. In J. Hood (Ed.), *Men, work, and family* (pp. 151–174). Newbury Park, CA: Sage.

Conger, R., & Elder, G. (1994). *Families in troubled times.* New York: Aldine de Gruyter.

Conger, R. D., Wallace, L. E., Sun, Y., Simons, R. L., McLoyd, V. C., & Brody, G. H. (2002). Economic pressure in African-American families: A replication and extension of the family stress model. *Developmental Psychology, 38*, 179–193.

Cooksey, E. C., Menaghan, E. G., & Jokielek, S. M. (1997). Life course effects of work and family circumstances on children. *Social Forces, 76*, 637–667.

Cooper, J. E., Holman, J., & Braithwaite, V. A. (1983). Self-esteem and family cohesion: The child's perspective. *Journal of Marriage and the Family, 45*, 153–159.

Corter, C., & Fleming, A. S. (2002). Psychobiology of maternal behavior in human beings. In M. Bornstein (Ed.), *Handbook of parenting* (2nd ed., Vol. 2, pp. 141–182). Mahwah, NJ: Lawrence Erlbaum Associates.

Cowan, C. P., & Cowan, P. A. (1992). *When parents become partners.* New York: Basic Books.

Cowan, C. P., & Cowan, P. A. (2000). *When parents become partners.* Mahwah, NJ: Lawrence Erlbaum Associates.

Cox, M. J., & Paley, B. (1997). Families as systems. *Annual Review of Psychology, 45*, 243–267.

Cross, T. L. (1986). Drawing on cultural tradition in Indian child welfare practice. *Social Casework, 67*, 283–289.

Crouter, A. C. (1994). Processes linking families and work: Implications for behavior and development in both settings. In R. D. Parke & S. Kellam (Eds.), *Exploring family relationships with other contexts* (pp. 9–28). Hillsdale, NJ: Lawrence Erlbaum Associates.

Crouter, A. C., Bumpus, M. F., Maguire, M. C., & McHale, S. M. (1999). Linking parents' work pressure and adolescents' well being: Insights into dynamics in dual-earner families. *Developmental Psychology, 35*, 1453–1461.

Cummings, E. M., & O'Reilly, A. W. (1997). Fathers in family context: Effects of marital quality on child adjustment. In M. E. Lamb (Ed.), *The father's role in child development* (3rd ed.). New York: Wiley.

Daly, K. (1995). Reshaping fatherhood: Finding the models. In W. Marsiglio (Ed.), *Fatherhood: Contemporary theory, research and social policy* (pp. 21–40). Thousand Oaks, CA: Sage.

Dancy, B., & Handal, P. (1984). Perceived family climate, psychological adjustment, and peer relationship of Black adolescents: A function of parental marital status or perceived family conflict. *Journal of Community Psychology, 12*, 222–229.

Deater-Deckard, K., & Dodge, K. (1997). Externalizing behavior problem and discipline revisited: Nonlinear effect and variation by culture, context and gender. *Psychological Inquiry, 8*, 161–175.

Dickie, J. R., & Matheson, P. (1984, August). *Mother–father–infant: Who needs support?* Paper presented at the meeting of the American Psychological Association, Toronto.

Dienhart, A., & Daly, K. (1997). Men and women co-creating father involvement in a nongenerative culture. In A. J. Hawkins & D. C. Dollahite (Eds.), *Generative fathering* (pp. 147–164). Thousand Oaks, CA: Sage.

Doherty, W. E. J., Kouneski, E. F., & Erikson, M. (1998). Responsible fathering: An overview and conceptual framework. *Journal of Marriage and the Family, 60,* 277–292.

Durrett, M. E., Otaki, M., & Richards, P. (1984). Attachment and the mother's perception of support from the father. *International Journal of Behavioral Development, 7,* 167–176.

Eggebeen, D. J. (2002). Sociological perspectives on fatherhood: What do we know about fathers from social surveys? In C. S. Tamis-LeMonda & N. Cabrera (Eds.), *Handbook of father involvement* (pp. 189–210). Mahwah, NJ: Lawrence Erlbaum Associates.

Eggebeen, D. J., & Knoester, C. (2001). Does fatherhood matter for men? *Journal of Marriage and Family, 63,* 381–393.

Erikson, E. (1975). *Life history and the historical moment.* New York: Norton.

Fagan, J. (1998). Correlates of low-income African American and Puerto Rican fathers' involvement with their children. *Journal of Black Psychology, 24,* 351–367.

Fagan, J., & Hawkins, A. J. (Eds.). (2000). *Clinical and educational interventions with fathers.* New York: Haworth Press.

Fleming, A. S., Corter, C., Stallings, J., & Steiner, M. (2002). Testosterone and prolactin are associated with emotional responses to infant cues in new fathers. *Hormones and Behavior, 43,* 399–413.

Fleming, A. S., & Li, M. (2002). Psychobiology of maternal behavior and its early determinants in nonhuman mammals. In M. Bornstein (Ed.), *Handbook of parenting* (2nd ed., Vol. 2, pp. 61–98). Mahwah, NJ: Lawrence Erlbaum Associates.

Fleming, A. S., Ruble, D., Krieger, H., & Wong, P. Y. (1997). Hormonal and experimental correlates of maternal responsiveness during pregnancy and the puerperium in human mothers. *Hormones and Behavior, 31,* 145–158.

Flouri, E., Buchanan, A., & Bream, V. (2002). Adolescents' perceptions of their fathers' involvement: Significance to school attitudes. *Psychology in the Schools, 39,* 575–582.

Franz, C. E., McClelland, D., & Weinberger, J. (1991). Childhood antecedents of conventional social accomplishment in midlife adults: A 26-year prospective study. *Journal of Personality and Social Psychology, 58,* 709–717.

Frone, M. R., Yardley, J. K., & Markel, K. S. (1997). Developing and testing an integrative model of the work–family interface. *Journal of Vocational Behavior, 50,* 145–167.

Furstenberg, F. F., & Harris, K. M. (1993). When and why fathers matter: Impacts of father involvement on children of adolescent mothers. In R. I. Lerman & T. J. Ooms (Eds.), *Young unwed fathers* (pp. 117–138). Philadelphia: Temple University Press.

Gadsen, V. (1999). Black families in intergenerational and cultural perspective. In M. E. Lamb (Ed.), *Parenting and child development in "nontraditional" families* (pp. 221–246). Mahwah, NJ: Lawrence Erlbaum Associates.

Garfinkel, I., & McLanahan, S. S. (1995). The effects of child support reform on child well being. In J. Brooks-Gunn & L. Chase-Lansdale (Eds.), *Escape from poverty: What a difference for children?* New York: Cambridge University Press.

Garfinkel, L., McLanahan, S., Meyer, D., & Seltzer, J. (1998). *Fathers under fire: The revolution of child support enforcement.* New York: Russell Sage Foundation Press.

Gorman-Smith, D., Tolan, P. H., Zelli, A., & Huesmann, R. L. (1996). The relations of family functioning to violence among inner-city minority youths. *Journal of Family Psychology, 10,* 115–129.

Gottman, J. M. (1994). *Why marriages succeed or fail.* New York: Simon & Schuster.

Gottman, J. M., Katz, L., & Hooven, C. (1997). *Meta-emotion.* Mahwah, NJ: Lawrence Erlbaum Associates.

Greenberger, E., & O'Neil, R. (1990). Parents' concerns about their child's development: Implications for fathers' and mothers' well-being and attitudes toward work. *Journal of Marriage and Family, 52,* 621–635.

Greenberger, E., O'Neil, R., & Nagel, S. K. (1994). Linking workplace and home place: Relations between the nature of adults' work and their parenting behaviors. *Developmental Psychology, 30*, 990–1002.

Grimm-Thomas, K., & Perry-Jenkins, M. (1994). All in a day's work: Job experiences, self-esteem and fathering in working-class families. *Family Relations, 43*, 174–181.

Grossman, F. K. (1987). Separate and together: Men's autonomy and affiliation in the transition to parenthood. In P. W. Berman & F. A. Pedersen (Eds.), *Men's transition to parenthood* (pp. 89–114). Hillsdale, NJ: Lawrence Erlbaum Associates.

Hart, C. H., Nelson, D. A., Robinson, C. C., Olsen, S. F., & McNeilly-Choque, M. K. (1998). Overt and relational aggression in Russian nursery-school-age children: Parenting style and marital linkages. *Developmental Psychology, 34*, 687–697.

Hart, C. H., Nelson, D. A., Robinson, C. C., Olsen, S. F., McNeilly-Choque, M. K., Porter, C. L., & McKee, T. R. (2000). Russian parenting styles and family processes: Linkages with subtypes of victimization and aggression. In K. A. Kerns, J. M. Contreras, & A. M. Neal-Barnett (Eds.), *Family and peers: Linking two social worlds*. Westport, CT: Praeger.

Heath, D. H., & Heath, H. E. (1991). *Fulfilling lives; Paths to maturity and success*. San Francisco: Jossey-Bass.

Heiss, J. (1996). Effects of African American family structure on school attitudes and performance. *Social Problems, 43*, 246–265.

Hewlett, B. S. (1991). *Intimate fathers*. Ann Arbor, MI: University of Michigan Press.

Hochschild, A. (1989). *The second shift: Working parents and the revolution at home*. New York: Viking Press.

Hofferth, S. L. (2003). Race/ethnic difference in father involvement in two-parent families: Culture, context, or economy? *Journal of Family Issues, 24*, 185–216.

Hossain, T., Field, I., Malphurs, J. E., Valle, C., & Pickens, J. (1995). *Father caregiving in low income African-American and Hispanic American families*. Unpublished manuscript, University of Miami Medical School, Miami, Florida.

Hyde, B. L., & Texidor, M. S. (1988). A description of the fathering experience among Black fathers. *Journal of Black Nurses Association, 2*, 67–78.

Ishii-Kuntz, M. (1993). Japanese fathers: Work demands and family roles. In J. C. Hood (Ed.), *Men, work, and family* (pp. 45–67). Newbury Park: Sage Publications.

Ishii-Kuntz, M. (1995). Paternal involvement and perception toward fathers' roles: A comparison between Japan and the United States. In W. Marsiglio (Ed.), *Fatherhood: Contemporary theory, research, and social policy* (pp. 102–118). Newbury Park: Sage Publications.

Ishii-Kuntz, M. (2000). Diversity within Asian American families. *Handbook of family diversity* (pp. 274–292). New York: Oxford University Press.

Isley, S., O'Neil, R., & Parke, R. D. (1996). The relation of parental effect and control behavior to children's classroom acceptance: A concurrent and predictive analysis. *Early Education and Development, 7*, 7–23.

Jain, A., Belsky, J., & Crnic, K. (1996). Beyond fathering behavior: Types of dads. *Journal of Family Psychology, 10*, 431–442.

Jankowiak, W. (1992). Father–child relations in urban China. In B. S. Hewlett (Ed.), *Father–child relations: Cultural and biosocial contexts* (pp. 345–363). New York: Aldine De Gruyter.

Knight, G., Tein, J., Prost, J. H., & Gonzales, N. A. (2002). Measurement equivalence and research on Latino children and families: The importance of culturally informed theory. In J. M. Contreras, K. K. Kerns, & A. M. Neal-Barnett (Eds.), *Latino children and families in the United States* (pp. 181–202). Westport, CT: Praeger.

Koestner, R., Franz, C., & Weinberger, J. (1990). The family origins of empathic concern: A 26-year longitudinal study. *Journal of Personality and Social Psychology, 58*, 709–717.

Kohn, M. (1995). Social structure and personality through time and space. In P. Moen, G. H. Elder, & K. Luscher (Eds.), *Examining lives in context: Perspectives on the ecology of human development* (pp. 141–168). Washington, DC: American Psychological Association.

Kotelchuck, M. (1976). The infant's relationship to the father: Experimental evidence. In M. E. Lamb (Ed.), *The role of the father in child development.* New York: Wiley.

Lamb, M. E. (1975). Fathers: Forgotten contributors to child development. *Human Development, 18,* 245–266.

Lamb, M. E. (1977). Father–infant and mother–infant interaction in the first year of life. *Child Development, 48,* 167–181.

Lamb, M. E. (Ed.). (1987). *The father's role: Cross-cultural perspectives.* Hillsdale, NJ: Lawrence Erlbaum Associates.

Lamb, M. E. (2002). Nonresidential fathers and their children. In C. S. Tamis-LeMonda & N. Cabrera (Eds.), *Handbook of father involvement* (pp. 169–184). Mahwah, NJ: Lawrence Erlbaum Associates.

Lamb, M. E. (Ed.). (2004). *The role of the father in child development* (4th ed.). New York: Wiley.

Lamb, M. E., Frodi, A. M., Hwang, C. P., Frodi, M., & Steinberg, J. (1982). Effects of gender and caretaking role on parent–infant interaction. In R. M. Emde & R. J. Harmon (Eds.), *Attachment and affiliative systems.* New York: Plenum.

Lamb, M. E., Pleck, J., Charnov, E. L., & Levine, J. A. (1987). A biosocial perspective on paternal behavior and involvement. In J. B. Lancaster, J. Altmann, A. Rossi, & L. R. Sherrod (Eds.), *Parenting across the life span: Biosocial perspectives.* Chicago: Aldine.

Lamb, M. E., Pleck, J. H., & Levine, J. A. (1985). The role of the father in child development: The effects of increased paternal involvement. In B. Lahey & E. E. Kazdin (Eds.), *Advances in clinical child psychology* (Vol. 8). New York: Plenum.

Lamborn, S. D., Dornbusch, S. M., & Steinberg, L. (1996). Ethnicity and community context as moderators of the relations between family decision making and adolescent adjustment. *Child Development, 67,* 283–301.

Larson, R., & Richards, M. (1994). *Divergent realities.* New York: Basic Books.

Lerman, R., & Ooms, T. (Eds.). (1993). *Young unwed fathers.* Philadelphia, PA: Temple University Press.

Lovejoy, J., & Wallen, K. (1988). Sexually dimorphic behavior in group-house rhesus monkeys (Macaca mulatto) at 1 year of age. *Psychobiology, 16,* 348–356.

Levine, J. A., & Pittinsky, T. L. (1998). *Working fathers.* Reading, MA: Addison-Wesley.

Maccoby, E. E. (1998). *The two sexes: Growing up apart, coming together.* Cambridge, MA: Harvard University Press.

MacDonald, K., & Parke, R. D. (1984). Bridging the gap: Parent–child interaction and peer interactive competence. *Child Development, 55,* 1265–1277.

MacDonald, K., & Parke, R. D. (1986). Parent–child physical play: The effects of sex and age of children and parents. *Sex Roles, 78,* 367–379.

Mandara, J., & Murray, C. B. (2002). Development of an empirical typology of African American family functioning. *Journal of Family Psychology, 16,* 318–337.

Marsiglio, W. (1993). Contemporary scholarship on fatherhood: Culture, identity and conduct. *Journal of Family Issues, 14,* 484–509.

Marsiglio, W., Amato, P., Day, R. D., & Lamb, M. E. (2000). Scholarship on fatherhood in the 1990s and beyond. *Journal of Marriage and the Family, 62,* 1173–1191.

Mason, P. L. (1996). *Joblessness and unemployment among African American men and fathers: A review of the literature* (Monograph L. R., 96-3). Philadelphia: University of Pennsylvania.

Maxwell, J. A. (1992). Understanding and validity in qualitative research. *Harvard Educational Review, 62,* 279–300.

McAdoo, J. L. (1981). Black fathers and child interaction. In L. E. Gary (Ed.), *Black men* (pp. 115–130). Beverly Hills: Sage.

McAdoo, J. L. (1988). The roles of Black fathers in the socialization of Black children. In H. P. McAdoo (Ed.), *Black families* (pp. 257–269). Newbury Park, CA: Sage.

McBride, B. A. (1989). Stress and fathers' parental competence: Implications for family life and parent educators. *Family Relations, 38,* 385–389.

McDermid, S. M., Huston, T., & McHale, S. (1990). Changes in marriage associated with the transition to parenthood: Individual differences as a function of sex-role attitudes and changes in the division of household labor. *Journal of Marriage and the Family, 52,* 475–486.

McDowell, D. J., & Parke, R. D. (2000). Differential knowledge of display rules for positive and negative emotion: Influence from parents, influences on peers. *Social Development, 9,* 415–432.

McDowell, D. J., Kim, M., O'Neil, R., & Parke, R. D. (2002). Children's emotional regulation and social competence in middle childhood: The role of maternal and paternal interactive style. *Marriage and Family Review, 34,* 345–364.

McKeering, H., & Pakenham, K. I. (2000). Gender and generativity issues in parenting: Do fathers benefit more than mothers from involvement in child care activities? *Sex Roles, 43,* 459–480.

McLanahan, S. S., & Sandefur, G. (1994). *Growing up with a single parent: What helps, what hurts.* Cambridge, MA: Harvard University Press.

Meany, M. J., Stewart, J., & Beatty, W. W. (1985). Sex differences in social play: The socialization of sex roles. In J. S. Rosenblatt, C. Bear, C. W. Bushnell, & P. Slater (Eds.), *Advances in the study of behavior* (Vol. 15, pp. 1–58). New York: Academic Press.

Mirandé, A. (1991). Ethnicity and fatherhood. In F. W. Bozett & S. M. H. Hanson (Eds.), *Fatherhood and families in cultural context* (pp. 53–82). New York: Springer Publishing Company.

Mirandé, A. (1997). *Hombres et machos: Masculinity and Latino culture.* Boulder, CO: Westview.

Mishel, L., Bernstein, J., & Schmitt, J. (1999). *The state of working America.* Ithaca, NY: Cornell University Press.

Miwa, S. (1995). Parent–child relationships from the child's viewpoint. In L. Nagoyaka (Ed.), *Contemporary child rearing and parent–child relationships.* Nagoya: Nagayaki.

Mize, J., & Pettit, G. S. (1997). Mothers social coaching, mother–child relationship style and children's peer competence: Is the medium the message? *Child Development, 68,* 312–332.

Montemayer, R. (1982). The relationship between parent–adolescent conflict and the amount of time adolescents spend alone with parents and peers. *Child Development, 68,* 312–332.

Montemayer, R., & Brownlee, J. (1987). Fathers, mothers, and adolescents: Gender based differences in parental roles during adolescence. *Journal of Youth and Adolescence, 16,* 281–291.

Mosley, J., & Thompson, E. (1995). Fathering behavior and child outcomes: The role of race and poverty. In W. Marsigllo (Ed.), *Fatherhood: Contemporary theory, research and social policy* (pp. 158–165). Thousand Oaks: Sage.

Mott, F. L. (1994). Sons, daughters and fathers' absence: Differentials in father-leaving probabilities and in home environments. *Journal of Family Issues, 5,* 97–128.

New, R., & Benigni, L. (1987). Italian fathers and infants: Cultural constraints on paternal behavior. In M. E. Lamb (Ed.), *The father role: Cross-cultural perspectives.* New York: Wiley.

NICHD Early Child Care Research Network. (1997). Child care in the first year of life. *Merrill-Palmer Quarterly, 43,* 340–360.

NICHD Early Child Care Research Network. (2000). Factors associated with fathers' caregiving activities and sensitivities with young children. *Journal of Family Psychology, 14,* 200–219.

O'Connell, M. (1993). *Where's Papa? Father's role in child care.* Washington, DC: Population Reference Bureau.

Palkovitz, R. (2002). *Involved fathering and men's adult development.* Mahwah, NJ: Lawrence Erlbaum Associates.

Parcel, J. L., & Menaghan, E. G. (1994). *Parents' jobs and children's lives.* New York: Aldine de Gruyter.

Parke, R. D. (1981). *Fathers.* Cambridge, MA: Harvard University Press.

Parke, R. D. (1988). Families in life-span perspective: A multi-level developmental approach. In E. M. Hetherington, R. M. Lerner, & M. Perlmutter (Eds.), *Child development in life span perspective* (pp. 159–190). Hillsdale, NJ: Lawrence Erlbaum Associates.

Parke, R. D. (1996). *Fatherhood*. Cambridge, MA: Harvard University Press.

Parke, R. D. (2000). Father involvement: A developmental psychological perspective. *Marriage and Family Review, 29*, 43–58.

Parke, R. D. (2002). Fathers and families. In M. Bornstein (Ed.), *Handbook of parenting* (2nd ed., Vol. 3, pp. 27–73). Mahwah, NJ: Lawrence Erlbaum Associates.

Parke, R. D. (2004). Development in the family. *Annual Review of Psychology, 55*, 365–400.

Parke, R. D., & Brott, A. (1999). *Throwaway dads*. Boston: Houghton-Mifflin.

Parke, R. D., & Buriel, R. (1998). Socialization in the family: Ecological and ethnic perspectives. In W. Damon (Ed.), *Handbook of child psychology*. New York: Wiley.

Parke, R. D., Coltrane, S., Borthwick-Duffy, S., Powers, J., Adams, M., Fabricius, W., Braver, S., & Saenz, D. (2003). Assessing father involvement in Mexican-American families. In R. Day & M. E. Lamb (Eds.), *Conceptualizing and measuring paternal involvement* (pp. 17–38). Mahwah, NJ: Lawrence Erlbaum Associates.

Parke, R. D., McDowell, D. J., Kim, M., Killian, C., Dennis, J., Flyr, M. L., & Wild, M. N. (2002). Fathers contribution to children's peer relationships. In C. S. Tamis-LeMonda & N. Cabrera (Eds.), *Handbook of father involvement* (pp. 141–168). Mahwah, NJ: Lawrence Erlbaum Associates.

Parke, R. D., & O'Neil, R. (2000). The influence of significant others on learning about relationships: From family to friends. In R. Mills & S. Duck (Eds.), *The developmental psychology of personal relationships* (pp. 15–47). London: Wiley.

Parke, R. D., Power, T. G., & Gottman, J. M. (1979). Conceptualization and quantifying influence patterns in the family triad. In M. E. Lamb, S. J. Suomi, & G. R. Stephenson (Eds.), *Social interaction analysis: Methodological issues*. Madison: University of Wisconsin Press.

Parke, R. D., & Suomi, S. J. (1981). Adult male–infant relationships: Human and non-human primate evidence. In K. Immelmann, G. Barlow, M. Main, & L. Petrinovich (Eds.), *Behavioral development: The Bielefeld Interdisciplinary Project* (pp. 700–725). New York: Cambridge University Press.

Pedersen, F. A. (1975, September). *Mother, father and infant as an interactive system*. Paper presented at the annual convention of the American Psychological Association, Chicago.

Perry-Jenkins, M., Repetti, R. L., & Crouter, A. C. (2000). Work and family in the 1990's. *Journal of Marriage and the Family, 62*, 981–989.

Pleck, J. H. (1997). Paternal involvement: Levels, sources and consequences. In M. E. Lamb (Ed.), *The role of the father in child development* (3rd ed., pp. 66–103). New York: Wiley.

Pleck, J. H., & Masciadrelli, B. P. (2004). Paternal involvement: Levels, sources and consequences. In M. E. Lamb (Ed.), *The role of the father in child development* (4th ed., pp. 222–273). New York: Wiley.

Power, T. G., & Parke, R. D. (1982). Play as a context for early learning: Lab and home analyses. In I. E. Sigel & L. M. Laosa (Eds.), *The family as a learning environment*. New York: Plenum.

Radin, N. (1993). Primary caregiving fathers in intact families. In A. Gottfried & A. Gottfried (Eds.), *Redefining families* (pp. 11–54). New York: Plenum.

Rane, T. R., & McBride, B. A. (2000). Identity theory as a guide to understanding fathers' involvement with their children. *Journal of Family Issues, 21*, 347–366.

Repetti, R. L. (1994). Short-term and long-term processes linking perceived job stressors to father–child interactions. *Social Development, 3*, 1–15.

Repetti, R., & Wood, J. (1997). Effects of daily stress at work on mothers interactions with preschoolers. *Journal of Family Psychology, 11*, 90–108.

Richards, M. P. M., Dunn, J. F., & Antonis, B. (1977). Caretaking in the first year of life: The role of fathers' and mothers' social isolation. *Child: Care, Health, and Development, 3*, 23–26.

Robinson, J. (1988). Who's doing the housework? *American Demographics, 10,* 24–28.

Rogoff, B. (2003). *The cultural nature of human development.* New York: Oxford University Press.

Rohner, R. P. (1998). Father love and child development; History and current evidence. *Current Directions in Psychological Science, 1,* 157–161.

Roopnarine, J. C., Hooper, F. H., Ahmeduzzaman, M., & Pollack, B. (1993). Gentle play partners: Mother–child, father–child play in New Delhi, India. In K. MacDonald (Ed.), *Parent–child play* (pp. 287–304). Albany: State University of New York Press.

Rosenblatt, J. (2002). Hormonal basis of parenting in mammals. In M. Bornstein (Ed.), *Handbook of parenting* (Vol. 2, pp. 3–25). Mahwah, NJ: Lawrence Erlbaum Associates.

Russell, G., & Russell, A. (1987). Mother–child and father–child relationships in middle childhood. *Child Development, 58,* 1573–1585.

Sagi, A. (1982). Antecedents and consequences of various degrees of paternal involvement in childrearing: The Israeli project. In M. E. Lamb (Ed.), *Nontraditional families: Parenting and child development* (pp. 205–232). Hillsdale, NJ: Lawrence Erlbaum Associates.

Sagi, A., Lamb, M. E., Shoham, R., Dvir, R., & Lewkowicz, K. S. (1985). Parent–infant interaction in families on Israeli kibbutzim. *International Journal of Behavioral Development, 8,* 273–284.

Sandberg, J. F., & Hofferth, S. L. (2001). Changes in children's time with parents: United States, 1981–1997. *Demography, 38,* 423–436.

Sears, R. R., Maccoby, E. E., & Levin, H. (1957). *Patterns of childrearing.* Evanston, IL: Row Peterson.

Shek, D. L. T. (2000). Differences between fathers and mothers in the treatment of, and relationship with, their teenage children: Perceptions of Chinese adolescents. *Adolescence, 35,* 135–146.

Shwalb, D. W., Kawai, H., Shoji, J., & Tsunetsugu, K. (1997). The middle class Japanese father: A survey of parents of preschoolers. *Journal of Applied Developmental Psychology, 18,* 497–511.

Silverstein, L. B., & Auerbach, C. F. (1999). Deconstructing the essential father. *American Psychologist, 54,* 397–407.

Smith, P. K., & Daglish, L. (1977). Sex differences in parent and infant behavior in the home. *Child Development, 48,* 1250–1254.

Snarey, J. (1993). *How fathers care for the next generation.* Cambridge, MA: Harvard.

Staples, R. (1988). The Black American family. In C. H. Mindel, R. W. Habenstein, & R. W. Wright, Jr. (Eds.), *Ethnic families in America: Patterns and variations* (pp. 173–195). New York: Elsevier.

Storey, A. E., Walsh, C. J., Quinton, R. L., & Wynne-Edwards, K. E. (2000). Hormonal correlates of paternal responsiveness in new and expectant fathers. *Evolution and Human Behavior, 21,* 79–95.

Sun, L. C., & Roopnarine, J. L. (1996). Mother–infant, father–infant interaction and involvement in child care and household labor among Taiwanese families. *Infant Behavior and Development, 19,* 121–129.

Tamis-LeMonda, C. S., & Cabrera, N. (Eds.). (2002). *Handbook of father involvement.* Mahwah, NJ: Lawrence Erlbaum Associates.

Toth, J. F., & Xu, X. (1999). Ethnic and cultural diversity in fathers' involvement: A racial/ethnic comparison of African American, Hispanic, and White fathers. *Youth and Society, 31,* 76–99.

U.S. Census Bureau. (1995). *Population reports.* Washington, DC: Government Printing Office.

U.S. Census Bureau. (2003). *Population reports.* Washington, DC: Government Printing Office.

Wachs, T. (2000). *Necessary but not sufficient.* Washington, DC: American Psychological Association.

White, B. L., Kaban, B., Shapiro, B., & Attonucci, J. (1976). Competence and experience. In I. C. Uzgiris & F. Weizmann (Eds.), *The structuring of experience* (pp. 115–152). New York: Plenum.

White, L., & Keith, B. (1990). The effect of shift work on the quality and stability of marital relations. *Journal of Marriage and the Family, 52,* 453–462.

White, L., & Rogers, S. L. (2000). Economic circumstances and family outcomes: A review of the 1990's. *Journal of Marriage and the Family, 62,* 1035–1051.

Williams, E., Radin, N., & Coggins, K. (1996). Paternal involvement in childrearing and the school performance of Ojibwa children: An exploratory study. *Merrill-Palmer Quarterly, 42,* 578–595.

Yeung, W. J., Sandberg, J. F., Davis-Kean, P. E., & Hofferth, S. L. (2001). Children's time with fathers in intact families. *Journal of Marriage and the Family, 63,* 136–154.

Zimmerman, M. A., Salem, D. A., & Notaro, P. C. (2000). Make room for daddy II: The positive effects of fathers' role in adolescent development. In R. D. Taylor & M. C. Wang (Eds.), *Resilience across contexts: Family, work, culture, and community* (pp. 233–258). Mahwah, NJ: Lawrence Erlbaum Associates.

II

CHARACTERISTICS
OF THE CHILD

5

The Effects of Child Characteristics on Parenting

Katherine Hildebrandt Karraker
West Virginia University

Priscilla K. Coleman
Bowling Green University

INTRODUCTION

The broad topic of parenting has received substantial research attention in recent years (e.g., Bornstein, 1995; 2002). Studies have been devoted to increasing our understanding of the many personal and environmental influences on parenting, of the impact of variations in parenting on child developmental outcomes, and of the processes by which parenting interacts with other aspects of family life. Based on the accumulating empirical and theoretical work on this topic, contemporary parenting researchers have developed a keen awareness of the inherent complexity of this area of study. Not only are multiple factors involved in determining parenting and its effects, but many relations among the relevant factors are bi-directional, multi-directional, and nonlinear. In this chapter, we examine one relatively neglected aspect of parenting, the effects of child characteristics on parenting, while attempting to maintain sensitivity to the broader literature on parenting and to the myriad relations between parenting and other variables.

Despite awareness of the complexity of parenting dynamics, most of the studies of parenting conducted over the last several decades have adopted a unidirectional perspective in which variations in parenting behavior have been assumed to operate as causes of various indicators of child adjustment and development. When correlational relations between some aspect of parenting and some aspect of child development have been identified, the predominant interpretation has been that variations in parenting produce variations in child outcomes. Other possible causal or noncausal relations between these classes of variables, such as the possibility that the child outcomes actually elicit the observed parenting behaviors, often are not discussed or are given minimal consideration.

Some recent studies of parenting effects on children have expanded on this assumption of unidirectional causality by assessing the joint role of parenting and child characteristics in determining child outcomes. However, the interpretation of findings continues to emphasize parenting effects on children, albeit with recognition that these parenting effects may vary for different types of children. Again, minimal attention has been paid to the notion that dissimilar children may systematically elicit differential parenting.

Variations among parents in how they behave toward their children are likely related to parents' personality, prior experiences, and social/environmental conditions as well as to the eliciting effects of children's characteristics and behavior. Disentangling these influences can be challenging. One source of evidence that individual children elicit different parenting behaviors comes from comparisons of parenting behavior directed to different children by the same adult, such as in families with more than one child. As a hypothetical example, a parent might be likely to use milder discipline techniques in response to the misbehavior of a very sensitive and eager-to-please child who rarely misbehaves compared to a less sensitive child who is prone to pushing limits. Such variations in parenting behavior undoubtedly play a strong role in defining the non-shared environments leading to behavioral and developmental differences among children in the same home (Feinberg & Hetherington, 2001; Kowal & Kramer, 1997; McGuire, Dunn, & Plomin, 1995; McHale & Pawletko, 1992). Even when physical and psychological differences between siblings are minimal, as in the case of identical twins, mothers engage in differential parenting with more positive parenting behaviors associated with more positive child outcomes (Deater-Deckard et al., 2001). One challenge is to identify the factors within the parent and within the child that lead to such differential parenting.

Children's moment-to-moment behavior tends to be highly variable, with their moods and levels of agreeableness fluctuating frequently in response to situational events and interactions with others. Although these transitory behavioral variations clearly have an impact on parent behavior, stable characteristics and behavioral propensities of children are of most concern to our understanding of differential parenting and its outcomes. The primary goal of this chapter is, therefore, to explore mechanisms by which children's relatively enduring characteristics are likely to influence the qualitative nature of the parenting they receive. Although we will draw from examples related to gender, age, physical appearance, and a few other characteristics, most of our discussion will revolve around child temperament, as it has long been considered to be a relevant factor in many studies of parenting. We begin the chapter with a discussion of historical and theoretical considerations in understanding parenting and children's effects on parenting. We then consider the mechanisms by which children affect parenting and parenting affects children. We then summarize the literature concerning the effects of particular child characteristics on parenting, with an emphasis on temperament. We conclude by considering implications of the literature reviewed for our understanding of parenting and child development.

HISTORICAL AND THEORETICAL VIEWS
OF CHILD EFFECTS ON PARENTING

Acknowledgment of child contributions to parenting processes dates back to early research on socialization (Bell, 1968; Sears, Maccoby, & Levin, 1957) and temperament (Thomas, Chess, Birch, Hertzig, & Korn, 1963). Although the concept of bi-directionality in socialization processes was formally introduced by Sears et al. in 1957, acceptance of reciprocal determinism (effects flowing from child to parent as well as from parent to child) did not receive extensive attention until the publication of Bell's 1968 review of the limitations of the unidirectional approach. Further, Sameroff and Chandler's (1975) seminal paper effectively highlighted the transactional process wherein organismic and contextual elements in combination determine child outcomes. This paper also promoted a conceptualization of the environment as dynamic, capable of both influencing and being influenced by the child. This transactional model can be illustrated in a simplified form using a single child temperament characteristic such as shyness. Parenting a shy child is likely to elicit particular parenting cognitions (e.g., "Have I sheltered my child too much?" "Will my child be lonely and isolated as shy children often are?" "How can I help my child to become more outgoing?") and emotions (e.g., "I worry that my child isn't happy at school." "I really feel compassion for my child as I was just like him." "I get frustrated when my child won't jump into activities like other children do."). These internal parental responses may lead to increased sensitivity to the child's comfort level in social situations, more concerted efforts to help the child identify compatible friends and maintain relationships, or alternatively to behaviors such as enabling the child to avoid social situations or engaging in criticism of the child. These parent behaviors may then lead to positive or negative child outcomes depending on how the behaviors are perceived and acted upon by the individual child. For instance, one shy child may appreciate parental compassion and assistance in becoming more social and may respond by putting forth an extra effort to change, while another shy child may resent the attention and insist on being left alone. The child's responses to the parent's behaviors then influence the parent's subsequent cognitions, emotions, and behaviors, which then affect the child's responses, and so on.

Dialectical and contextualistic theoretical developments over the last several decades have also supported the view of an active child. For example, Vygotsky (1978) argued that development proceeds through the process of internalization whereby externally experienced events are translated into personal, mental activity. The view of the child as capable of influencing his or her own development is further exemplified by the concept of constructive epigenesis (Bidell & Fischer, 1997), which focuses on the primary role of self-organizing activity in the development of new abilities. Bronfenbrenner (1979) also advanced a bioecological model (most recently termed the Process-Person-Context-Time Model; Bronfenbrenner & Morris, 1998), which offers a theoretical perspective within a contextual framework for understanding how particular processes involving environmental components interact with characteristics of the individual child to differentially impact development. In this model, parenting is viewed as a proximal process in development. The influence of parenting on development is conceptualized as one that varies in relation to child characteristics. Belsky's (1984) widely cited discussion of the primary influences on the quality of parenting extends some of Bronfenbrenner's earlier notions. Belsky proposed that the main influences on the quality of parenting include parents' psychological resources, child characteristics, and sociocultural or environmental factors.

Very little scholarly work explored child effects on others until results from the New York Longitudinal Study (Thomas et al., 1963) effectively challenged the dominant belief that parents were solely responsible for their children's development. Child behavior problems were reported to emerge occasionally despite the presence of positive parenting practices, and adaptive child behaviors were sometimes evident when children were exposed to dysfunctional parenting behavior. Moreover, components of children's temperament and particular aspects of their rearing environments were found to combine to produce positive and negative outcomes (Chess, Thomas, & Birch, 1965).

Despite the current prevailing consensus that children do have powerful effects on others, there are surprisingly few studies devoted specifically to examining the role of such effects in parent–child relations. Researchers, parents, and society more generally persist in assuming that parent-to-child effects represent the most salient causal path in the socialization process. With this assumption rooted heavily in classic theories of development, tradition in the field, intuition, and conventional wisdom (Harris, 1998; Patterson & Fisher, 2002), other explanations for correlations between parent behavior and child outcomes are not as actively researched as might be expected. Many behavioral geneticists (e.g., Plomin, 1990; Scarr, 1988) and environmentalists (e.g., Wachs, 1992; Wachs & Kohnstamm, 2001) have attempted to examine the child's role in models of environmental influence. Nevertheless, many contemporary examples suggest that researchers are not taking child effects seriously. For example, in an extensive recent review of literature on parenting related to child and parent psychopathology by Berg-Nielsen, Vikan, and Dahl (2002), the unidirectional bias is quite obvious. Although child effects are alluded to at the beginning of the report, they are not mentioned again until the last page under a segment devoted to future research.

The tendency to ignore or minimize the effects of the child on parenting in particular and the childrearing environment more generally cannot be attributed to declining interest in the study of parenting as the number of empirically based studies of parenting has increased dramatically in recent years (Bornstein, 1995, 2002; Patterson & Fisher, 2002). The outpouring of scholarly work crossing numerous disciplines including psychology, sociology, social work, and nursing, among others, is undoubtedly tied to the increased complexity and multiple pressures characterizing the lives of contemporary parents (Patterson & Fisher, 2002). Because much parenting research is motivated by the desire to identify ways that parents can positively influence their children, the research agenda tends to be biased toward examining parent effects rather than child effects.

As we explore the merits of including child effects in the study of parenting processes, an examination of the definitions used in the literature is a logical starting point. Berg-Nielsen and colleagues (2002) offer a very straightforward definition of parenting when they define it as everyday parental behavior (including cognitions, emotions, and attributions) directed toward children in addition to relevant attitudes and values. Most contemporary researchers define the construct similarly; however, as noted by O'Connor (2002), different scholars have emphasized distinct components (e.g., behavior over socio-cognitive processes) and have adopted different assessment strategies designed to measure parent and child variables separately or to examine dyadic behaviors such as synchrony, mutuality, or reciprocity. Efforts have also been made to define competent and less competent or dysfunctional parenting, with competent parenting typically referring to internal attributes and behaviors believed to promote positive physical, emotional, cognitive, and social development in children and dysfunctional parenting referring to internal attributes and behaviors believed to adversely impact the child's development (Berg-Nielsen et al., 2002).

MECHANISMS RELATING PARENTING TO CHILD
CHARACTERISTICS AND BEHAVIOR

An abundance of correlational research has accumulated suggesting strong
associations between various parenting behaviors and child characteristics
and behaviors. For example, the importance of parental warmth/support,
conflict or hostility/rejection, and monitoring and control of children's behavior as predictors of discrete child outcomes has been well documented in
the literature (Baumrind, 1991; O'Connor, 2002). In addition, we know that
parenting variations are associated with particular child temperamental characteristics (see discussion later). However, the majority of individual studies
devoted to examining associations between parent behavior and children's
behavior or adjustment has not tackled the question of causality in a systematic and controlled manner. In this section of the chapter, we describe a general model of parent–child influence followed by examination of the underlying mechanisms that can account for parent–child correlations.

A Model of Parent–Child Influence

The model we endorse is relatively simple and is based on the transactional
model of development. Most basically, we maintain that children influence
their parents, and parents influence their children. These influences take
place simultaneously and continually, and changes in either parents or children resulting from these processes then impact future interactions and
paths of influence. However, the model becomes somewhat more complex
when we recognize the role of internal processes (various cognitions and
emotions) in addition to overt behavioral interactions. Child characteristics, such as physical appearance or gender, can influence parents by affecting the child's behavior, the parent's cognitions, or both. Parents' behaviors toward the child may therefore be affected by their stereotypes,
expectations, perceptions, or beliefs about the child as well as by the child's
actual behavior. Similar processes may take place in the child, although
many of these internal processes may be simplified or nonexistent in younger children.

Because the majority of studies of parenting and child characteristics are
correlational rather than experimental in design, it is not possible to know
whether a particular correlation between a parenting variable and a child
variable represents a causal relation. There are a number of reasons why assumptions of causality based on naturally occurring, correlational relations
between variables may be ill-founded. First, many of the observed associations between parents' and children's behavior are artificially inflated due
to shared method variance (O'Connor, 2002). Measures of both parenting
and child behavior frequently are obtained from the same source (typically

the parent) using the same methodology (typically questionnaires). The resulting correlations between the two sets of measures may be inflated as a result of having the same person provide both measures. Second, correlations observed between parent behavior and child characteristics or behaviors may very well be due to third variables in the environment. For example, an association observed between inconsistent parenting and aggressive child behavior may be the result of stress or parental divorce causing both the inconsistency and the aggression. Third, research suggesting that parent behaviors cause variations in child outcomes often ignores explanations based on shared genes. For instance, an association between frequent parental verbal stimulation and children's academic achievement could very easily be based on a shared genetic endowment that leads to both verbal and academic competence.

Many observed correlations between parenting cognitions and behaviors and child characteristics and outcomes probably do represent the result of a causal relation. The difficulty lies in determining whether the parenting variable causes the child variable or the child variable causes the parenting variable. The remainder of this section describes the possible mechanisms underlying each of these causal paths, as well as the potential roles of genetic and contextual factors in determining or identifying causation.

Parent Influences on Children

Influences on children's behavior and development extend from the immediate family to schools, friendship networks, relatives, neighborhoods, communities, and geographical locations, all of which are embedded in dynamic economic, cultural, and political systems that are operative during particular historical periods (Bronfenbrenner, 1979). However, based on the time, energy, and emotional investment parents have in their children's lives, the study of parenting behavior has logically occupied the central focus of studies designed to explore environmental influences on child outcomes. Virtually all of the parenting research prior to the 1960s and a great deal of the more recent research has been devoted to the study of parent effects on children's adjustment and development. Subsequent related studies have naturally focused on individual and environmental determinants of those parenting behaviors that are likely to place children at risk for negative outcomes or that serve to promote children's optimal development.

O'Connor (2002) evaluated evidence for parenting effects in animal studies, intervention studies, and various types of longitudinal studies. He concluded that, although there is definitive support for the existence of parent effects on children, three issues require further attention. First, the influence of parents is too frequently studied without attention to the larger psychosocial context. Second, checks for genetic mediation of environmental processes have generally been omitted. Finally, the uni-directional assumption that effects flow only from parent to child remains pervasive in the study of parenting. The problem with the uni-directional approach is the notion that parenting resides within the parent rather than representing a process defined by the parent, the child, relationships within the family, and contextual elements.

Although it is well accepted that parents do, at least in some realms, influence their children's development, the precise mechanisms by which these influences occur are not always known. Proposed mechanisms range from the purely behavioral (parents reinforce desired child behavior and punish undesired child behavior, leading to child behavior change) to the highly cognitive or affective (children change their behavior in response to their parents' actual or presumed thoughts and feelings). Parent behaviors are often clustered into behavioral styles or patterns, such as sensitivity, hostility, authoritativeness, coercive control, warmth, and disturbed communication. Although many of these patterns of parenting behavior appear to have an impact on child functioning, based on both correlational and experimental evidence (O'Connor, 2002), little is known about how this impact occurs.

Child Influences on Parents

The most compelling evidence for child effects on parents comes from experimental and quasi-experimental studies in which adults' responses to children whose target characteristics systematically vary are compared. For example, research by Barkley and colleagues (cited in Patterson & Fisher, 2002) revealed that when children with ADHD were medicated, and therefore demonstrated less hyperactivity than when they were unmedicated, their mothers' behavior became less aversive. Similarly, a study by Anderson, Lytton, and Romney (1986) showed that women exhibited more negative behavior when interacting with boys diagnosed with conduct disorder than when interacting with their own boys who did not have the disorder. Stern and Hildebrandt (1986) illustrated that women interacted differently with unfamiliar infants who were labeled as having been born prematurely and infants labeled as having been born at full term, independent of the infants' actual birth status.

Experimental manipulation of children's characteristics or behavior is often not possible, so again, most of our information about the effects of children on parents is inferred from correlational data. The mechanisms underlying the presumed effects of children's characteristics and behaviors on parenting behavior include both direct and mediated effects of child characteristics and behaviors on parenting behavior. The most commonly identified mediators are parent cognitions, such as beliefs, attitudes, values, perceptions, expectations, stereotypes, knowledge, and desires (Holden, 1995), and parent emotions (Dix, 1991). These cognitions or emotions occur in response to children's characteristics or behaviors, and then the cognitions or emotions guide parents' subsequent behaviors. Genetic factors in both the parent and child, the goodness-of-fit between child and parent characteristics, and contextual factors also all play a role in determining how children can influence their parents. The possibility that parent and child behaviors are correlated due to shared genes, rather than the effect of one individual on the other, must always be considered as well.

Children obviously influence their parents directly via their immediate behavior. Children can affect their parents' behavior directly by engaging in reinforcing or punishing responses to their parents' actions. For example, most parents are reinforced by children's smiles and approach and are punished by children's negative emotions and refusals to cooperate. In addition, many child behaviors elicit particular adult responses; for instance, child distress commonly elicits parent behaviors intended to calm or distract the child, child misbehavior often elicits punishing or redirecting parental behaviors, and child quiet play usually elicits parental encouragement or inattention.

Mediated effects of children on parents occur when enduring child characteristics, such as child gender or appearance, or persistent temperament qualities, like high activity level, function to influence parents' perceptions of the child or to reinforce or modify previously formed parental cognitions or prevailing ways of responding emotionally, which in turn impact parents' child-directed behavior. For example, if a mother enters into the experience of parenting believing that little girls are generally calm and passive, and she finds herself with a daughter who craves activity and is perpetually on the go, she may experience emotional and cognitive shifts that eventually lead her to adapt her approach to parenting. This parent may come to an understanding that children vary considerably along the activity dimension regardless of gender, and she is likely to realize that she needs to provide opportunities for her child to engage in positive energy outlets (e.g., through sports or dance). She may also learn effective ways to encourage her child to sit long enough to do her homework, possibly through negotiation (e.g., one hour of play outside for one-half hour of homework). If the parenting strategies adopted succeed in enabling the child's activity needs to be fulfilled while participating fully in other life experiences, positive outcomes are probable. Another parent surprised by an unusually active child may be less inclined to change her beliefs, becoming convinced that she can change her child's disposition instead, which would likely produce frustration and negative behavior in both the parent and the child. Evidence that child gender can influence parents' expectations and the manner in which a child's behavior is interpreted by the parent (Okagaki &

Divecha, 1993) is exemplified by Rubin, Provenzano, and Luria's (1974) demonstration of parents' use of masculine adjectives to describe their new-born sons and feminine adjectives to describe their newborn daughters (see also Karraker, Vogel, & Lake, 1995). Such perceptions are likely to greatly influence the nature of parents' interaction with their children (Stern & Karraker, 1989). For example, if a father believes female infants are more fragile than male infants, he is likely to handle a female child more gently.

Another illustration of the mediating role of parental cognitions comes from studies indicating that parents with atypically demanding children (those with difficult temperaments or behavior disorders) tend to have lower self-efficacy beliefs compared to parents of nonproblem children (e.g., Teti and Gelfand, 1991). Parents with low self-efficacy are inclined to have trouble putting their parenting knowledge into action and typically do not show high levels of persistence in parenting (Grusec, Hastings, & Mammone, 1994). Mothers with low self-efficacy also are more likely to ex-perience postpartum depression (Cutrona & Troutman, 1986), which then may further compromise their parenting behavior.

Child characteristics may also influence the nature of parenting by im-pacting other relationships in the parent's life (such as with a spouse, other children, friends, relatives, or co-workers) or by detracting from a parent's competence at work, energy level, or general well-being. For example, the stress associated with having a very reticent child who engages in frequent school refusal may cause parents who are feeling powerless to argue and blame each other in addition to missing time from work. If the situation persists, the pressure they are under may result in decreased sensitivity to the child and less effective parenting.

The Role of Genetic Factors

Identifying the true effects of biological children on their parents is compli-cated by the influence of genetic factors. As mentioned previously, shared genes may underlie some of the observed correlations between parent and child behaviors. Comparisons of parent–child correlations for adopted and nonadopted children can help to identify the effects of shared genes. A stronger correlation for nonadopted vs. adopted children suggests that shared genes underlie a relation between parent and child behaviors. Simi-larly, stronger correlations between parenting behaviors directed to non-adoptive siblings (biological siblings reared in the same family) than to adoptive siblings (biologically unrelated children adopted into the same family) also suggest the functioning of shared genes. Several studies have identified such differences in correlations. For instance, using this method-ology with a sample of infants tested at 12 and 24 months, Plomin, DeFries, and Fulker (1988) found higher correlations for nonadoptive than for adoptive siblings on measures of parental provision of toys and parental restriction–punishment. Similarly, Dunn and Plomin (1986) reported higher correlations for nonadoptive than for adoptive siblings on a measure of maternal affection derived from observations of mother–child interaction from infancy to early childhood. Plomin, Loehlin, and DeFries (1985) also reported higher correlations in nonadoptive siblings than in adoptive siblings for relations between Home Observation for the Measurement of the Environment (HOME) scores and 2-year-olds' Bayley mental scores as well as scores on a measure of language development. There are also research findings to suggest that the level of genetic influence on child and adolescent perceptions of parenting differs depending on the aspect of parenting measured, with support for genetic effects related to measures of warmth but not control (Braungart, 1994; Elkins, McGue, & Iacono, 1997; Goodman & Stevenson, 1989). Finally, results from a study of families containing both biological and adoptive children between the ages of 12 and 18 years revealed stronger associations between parent reports of family functioning and adolescent reports of behavioral adjustment for the biological children (McGue, Sharma, & Benson, 1996).

All of the above examples of evidence for genetic influence illustrate what is referred to as a passive genotype-environment correlation (Scarr & McCartney, 1983; Towers, Spotts, & Neiderhiser, 2001) presumably based on genetic relatedness. Unfortunately the studies conducted to examine the effects of shared genes have not been able to specify exactly how these effects operate (Towers et al., 2001), and the ability to describe such mechanisms is confounded by the numerous ways that parent–child genetic similarity might be expressed through parenting. There have been recent efforts to identify particular candidate genes among family members using DNA samples (Plomin & Rutter, 1998; Towers et al., 2001). This methodology basically involves associating specific genes with behaviors using statistical methods such as regression analysis. These studies have also begun to examine the role of family relationship factors in mediating or moderating the behavioral expression of candidate genes (Towers et al., 2001).

A child's genetic endowment may also impact parenting behavior through nonpassive genotype-environment correlations (Scarr & McCartney, 1983; Towers et al., 2001). These correlations result from the impact of the child's genetically determined characteristics on the parent, regardless of the parent's genetic makeup. There are two forms of nonpassive genotype-environment correlations. First, there are evocative gene-environment correlations which are defined as reactions of others to a genetically influenced trait of the individual. For example, a mother of a child with a short attention span is likely to find herself providing many different types of materials (books, art supplies, games, and so forth) and opportunities to keep her child content and may become very creative in strategies to help the child remain focused for increasing time intervals. Second, there are active gene-environment correlations, which involve the individual seeking out a particular environment or experience as a function of genetically based traits. For example, a child with high verbal aptitude may seek opportunities to exercise her talent through social experiences, writing, drama, or a debate club. Parenting will undoubtedly be influenced as the child pursues support to engage in such activities.

Genetic processes clearly are an important mechanism underlying some relations between parenting behavior and child characteristics or behavior. However, these processes have only been studied in limited contexts and often are not recognized as a possible influence on parent–child correlations.

The Role of Contextual Factors

Relations between parent and child characteristics are rarely consistent across all individuals and all contexts. A variety of contextual factors may influence the strength of the association between individual parent and child attributes as well as the underlying causal factors that produce the association in any particular dyad.

Thomas and Chess's (1977) goodness-of-fit model helps to explain how child characteristics and features of the environment can work together to detract from or optimize development. According to this model, adaptive child outcomes are most probable when the child's physical and behavioral characteristics are compatible with the requirements of his or her physical and social environment. As related to parenting, a child's physical distinctiveness and psychological individuality will prompt varying reactions in parents based on the parents' attitudes, values, stereotypes, and behavioral style, and on the physical characteristics of the setting (Lerner, 1993). Children will naturally differ in the extent to which they are able to meet the many demands of their parents and the environment.

According to the goodness-of-fit model, positive development is not simply the product of particular child characteristics nor the specific nature of demands made by the environment, but instead results when there is a good match between the child's unique qualities and the demands imposed (Lerner, 1993). For example, a difficult child temperament and harsh and inconsistent parental discipline produces a poor fit that may result in a steady escalation of the child's problematic behavior. In contrast, when parents of difficult children provide warm and stable rearing with appropriate and consistently applied discipline, the child's behavior is likely to become less challenging over time.

Beyond contributing to goodness-of-fit, features of the environment can also serve as mediators and moderators of relations between child characteristics and parents and parenting processes. Bronfenbrenner's (1979) ecological model describes a series of layers of influence on children's development ranging from immediate or proximal influences within the family to more distal influences originating in the neighborhood, community, and broader society. One of the basic tenets of this theoretical model is the notion that there are numerous connective links among the forms and levels of influence with many of the more distal factors influencing children through their effects on parents. Although a good portion of the work on parenting has been examined in isolation without adequate consideration of the multiple interacting layers of environmental influence, there have been many studies designed to examine the moderating effects of particular environmental factors such as exposure to various cultures and subcultures, as well as multiple neighborhood characteristics, on parenting behavior and children's development (O'Connor, 2002). For example, a study by Chen et al. (1998) revealed that the associations between toddler inhibition and maternal acceptance and encouragement of achievement were positive in a Chinese sample and negative in a Canadian sample. Studies of this sort provide crucial data pertaining to how relations between various aspects of temperament differentially impact parenting processes depending on the belief, economic, and social systems characterizing particular cultures. Studies have also demonstrated that parenting variables mediate the impact of certain environmental factors such as economic adversity (e.g., stress on parents reduces their competence) and peer relationships (e.g., parents encourage and facilitate some relationships but not others) on child outcomes (O'Connor, 2002).

Unfortunately, most of the studies devoted to understanding how aspects of the environment are related to parenting processes seldom consider more than a few variables, and studies have only recently begun to consider how other familial relationships or extra-familial factors modify the effects that children have on their parents. For example, the presence or absence of siblings can alter the effects of parents on children and children on parents. Research has revealed distinct child adjustment outcomes associated with relatively more positive or more negative parental behavior directed toward individual siblings within a family (McGuire et al., 1995; Pike, McGuire, Hetherington, Reiss, & Plomin, 1996), motivating exploration of various causes including child effects on parental tendencies to treat one child more or less well than another. Variations in birth order, parental preferences for one child over another based on child characteristics, one child being more effective at eliciting attention from the parent than another, the congruence between parent and child personalities, and a child's similarity (or lack of similarity) in appearance or behavior to someone the parent knows can influence parents' differential responding to their children (Karraker & Coleman, 2002). Other studies have found that financial and relationship stressors including marital conflict and family size increase differential treatment by parents (Crouter, McHale, & Tucker, 1999; Deal, 1996; Jenkins, Rasbash, & O'Connor, 2003; Volling & Elins, 1998); however, the extent to which these environmental factors interact with child effects to predict differential treatment has not been adequately explored.

With widespread acceptance of the transactional model of child development, one of the largest challenges facing researchers today will be to find effective methods to tease apart parent–child and child–parent effects that are complexly intertwined with each other and with other factors that influence parenting (Patterson & Fisher, 2002). For example, a correlation between child rebelliousness and maternal withdrawal behavior may reflect a causal relation between the two variables flowing from child to mother or from mother to child, effects of additional child, maternal, genetic, or environment variables, or some combination of all of these. More precise specifications of the causal factors involved in the parenting of children should follow as research moves from simple correlational studies to designs involving experimental factors, complex correlational designs that take advantage of sophisticated statistical modeling techniques, and adoption or other designs that allow identification of the role of genetic factors.

EVIDENCE FOR CHILD INFLUENCES ON PARENTING

Several child characteristics are particularly likely candidates to influence parenting. These include temperament, age, gender, and physical attractiveness. The predominant evidence to be reviewed is correlational in nature, and thus susceptible to alternate causal interpretations. However, these child characteristics are difficult or impossible to change and therefore the likelihood that a correlation indicates an effect of these characteristics on parenting is at least logically plausible.

Our focus is on child temperament because a large literature base has explored the structure and function of temperament from the infancy period throughout childhood and adolescence, including its role in influencing parent–child relationships and determining child outcomes. After defining temperament, we provide examples of findings that can be interpreted as support for both direct and moderated effects of child temperament on parenting.

Definition of Temperament

Numerous definitions of temperament involving a variety of distinct dimensions have been proposed by Thomas and Chess (1977) and others. Most conceptualizations define temperament as encompassing individual differences in three broad areas: (a) reactivity or negative emotionality reflecting negative mood or irritability, inflexibility, and intensely negative reactions to limitations and/or novelty, (b) self-regulation, or the degree of effortful control of attentional and emotional processes, and (c) approach/withdrawal, inhibition, or sociability (Sanson, Hemphill, & Smart, 2002). Many studies also refer to difficult temperament, which involves some combination of socially undesirable scores on indexes of these three dimensions or which, in some cases, is simply equated with high irritability. Temperament is believed to be constitutionally based and relatively stable across childhood, although environmental modification of temperament traits or the manner in which they are expressed is sometimes possible (Sanson et al., 2002). Temperament is typically measured via parental report, although occasionally it is assessed through independent observations of children's behavior.

Parents typically become aware of distinct temperament qualities in their children soon after birth; however, parents usually do not understand the powerful effect of temperament on their own behavior until after the birth of a second child (Dunn & Plomin, 1990; Putnam, Sanson, & Rothbart, 2002). Parents of more than one child with different temperaments increasingly recognize that their own behavior is not always the strongest influence on their children's development and discover that they are inclined to parent each of their children differently in response to the children's temperamental individuality.

Effects of Child Temperament on Parenting

The focus of many contemporary parenting studies that include measures of child temperament is on the individual or combined effects of parenting and temperament on child outcomes, with findings related to temperament effects on parenting considerably less common. Oftentimes data on temperament-parenting associations are buried in reports with a primarily uni-directional focus on child outcomes. Although a few studies have explicitly reported a failure to find relations between temperament and parenting (e.g., Rothbart, 1986; Vaughn, Taraldson, Crichton, & Egeland, 1981; Wachs & Grandour, 1983), the majority of studies that have reported assessments of both of these variables have found significant associations. A particularly common finding is that parenting stress accompanies parenting a child with difficult temperament qualities (Gelfand, Teti, & Radin Fox, 1992; Mash & Johnston, 1983; McBride, Schoppe, & Rane, 2002; Mulsow, Caldera, Pursley, & Reifman, 2002). As a result of this general finding, much of the research devoted to understanding how children's temperament-driven behavior impacts parenting in more specific ways has focused on those temperament qualities that are hard to manage.

One longitudinal investigation that examined correlations between difficult temperament and aggressive social behavior of children from early to middle childhood revealed that difficult children were exposed to harsher parenting and had poorer quality relationships with their parents than did easier children (Kingston & Prior, 1995). Similarly, data from the Bloomington Longitudinal study revealed associations between 3-year-olds' resistance to control or low manageability and concurrent conflicts with parents (Bates, Bayles, Bennett, Ridge, & Brown, 1991). Further, in a study by Clark, Kochanska, and Ready (2000), negative child emotionality measured between 8 and 10 months was found to predict maternal power assertion 5 months later. Research with parents of young children who exhibited early social fearfulness and inhibition suggested that this temperament style tended to elicit overprotective and overcontrolling parental behavior, which in turn lead to more fearfulness and peer rejection once the children entered school (Rubin & Stewart, 1996; Rubin, Stewart, & Chen, 1995).

Findings with children in early middle childhood indicated that maternal reports of children's high irritable distress and low effortful control were associated with children's reports of maternal hostility (Morris et al., 2002). Similarly, research by Braungart-Rieker, Garwood, and Stifter (1997) revealed that mothers of toddlers with high negative reactivity showed a tendency to use harsh forms of behavioral control rather than gentler methods. Several other studies have likewise identified correlations between temperamental difficulty and low levels of maternal warmth and responsiveness and more conflict-ridden, less emotionally close parent–child relationships (Mangelsdorf, Gunnar, Kestenbaum, Lang, & Andreas, 1990; Stocker, 1995; van den Boom & Hoeksma, 1994). These findings suggest that the challenges inherent in parenting a temperamentally difficult child may cause many parents to invest minimal energy in parenting and emotionally withdraw from the relationship.

Although the studies cited above have generally found associations between aspects of child difficulty and negative parenting behaviors, a number of studies have indicated that in some cases having children with challenging temperaments can lead to the development of skillful parenting behavior. For example, Crockenberg (1986) reviewed six studies showing that the amount of crying engaged in by infants and the amount of time required to soothe them at 1 and 3 months was positively associated with active caregiving and social interaction between mothers and infants at 9 months. In addition, a study by Park, Belsky, Putnam, and Crnic (1997) showed that parents exhibit more sensitive and affectionate and less intrusive behavior toward socially inhibited children compared to less inhibited children.

Another study found a similar result with socially inhibited child behavior eliciting responsive behavior in parents (Belsky, Rha, & Park, 2000). In a study designed to examine the interaction between child fearfulness and parental use of gentle forms of discipline at age 2 on conscience development at age 4, child fearfulness and parental use of gentle forms of discipline were found to be significantly correlated (Fowles & Kochanska, 2000). Finally, significant relations were observed between social fearfulness and a general index of parenting quality after controlling for various parental and child characteristics (van Bakel & Riksen-Walraven, 2002).

A few studies also have shown simultaneous positive and negative associations between parenting and difficult child temperament. One study with toddlers demonstrated associations between dysregulated temperament and both maternal warmth and negative dominance (Rubin, Hastings, Chen, Stewart, & McNichol, 1998). Another study, which also involved toddlers, revealed that temperamental difficulty was associated with both maternal assistance and disapproval during a cognitive task (Gauvain & Fagot, 1995). These findings suggest that some child characteristics can elicit complex behavioral patterns from parents. Some parent behaviors may reflect the parent's irritation with the child's undesirable behavior whereas others may represent the parent's attempts to positively redirect or change the child's behavior.

As indicated previously, the vast majority of studies that have assessed associations between child temperament and parenting behaviors have emphasized negative or demanding child characteristics. However, some studies also have found that children with more adaptable, sociable, and easy-to-soothe temperaments are likely to elicit warm and responsive parenting (Putnam et al., 2002). Moreover, several studies have indicated that certain positive temperament traits (such as high sociability, adaptability, and positive emotionality, and low impulsivity and negative emotionality) operate as resiliency factors when children are exposed to high levels of familial psychosocial stress (e.g., due to parental mental illness or alcoholism, abuse, neglect, or poverty; Hetherington, 1989; Masten, 1989; Putnam et al., 2002; Werner & Smith, 1982). Werner and Smith suggest that children with these qualities are able to elicit more care and concern from parents and other individuals in their lives.

Most of the studies reviewed thus far have examined only mothers' parenting behavior. However, a few studies of both mothers and fathers have revealed some interesting similarities and differences. One study identified associations between difficult temperament and less affectionate and responsive parenting by fathers (Volling & Belsky, 1991); yet, other studies indicated no significant associations between child temperament and paternal behavior (Jain, Belsky, & Crnic, 1996; Woodworth, Belsky, & Crnic, 1996). Further, high child activity tends to be associated with less positive maternal behavior, whereas child activity levels tend not to predict paternal behavior (Buss, 1981; McBride et al., 2002).

In addition to these observed linkages between measures of temperament and specific measures of parenting behavior, associations have been detected between difficult temperament and internal parenting responses such as dissatisfaction or discomfort with the parenting role and low parenting self-efficacy (Coleman & Karraker, 1998; Gross, Conrad, Fogg, & Wothke, 1994; Sheeber & Johnson, 1992). In one study (Leve, Scaramella, & Fagot, 2001), child distress to limitations was found to be negatively correlated with both mothers' and fathers' reports of pleasure in everyday parenting activities. In the same study, child fearfulness correlated negatively with mothers' but not fathers' reports of pleasure in parenting. Rubin, Nelson, Hastings, and Asendorpf (1999) conducted a longitudinal study of mothers, fathers, and their children at 2 and 4 years designed to examine associations between child wariness/inhibition and parents' beliefs regarding the most appropriate means for socializing their children. The results indicated that parent perceptions of child social wariness at 2 years predicted preferences for socialization strategies that limited opportunities for their children to develop independent thinking and behavior. Parents of inhibited children who frightened easily seemed to believe that their job was to shield their children from stressful emotions whenever possible and may have viewed their children as too anxious and potentially excitable to make good decisions that would protect them from psychological and/or physical risks.

The contention that child characteristics can affect parenting is supported by this selective review of studies that have found relations between child temperament characteristics and parenting behavior. However, most of the studies reviewed use correlational methodologies, and thus the possibility exists that observed relations between temperament and parenting could be a function of the operation of method variance or other third variables such as genetic relatedness, or the effects of parenting on child temperament. Longitudinal studies that identify relations between earlier child characteristics and later parenting also provide some support for the idea that children affect parents, rather than the reverse, but even these conclusions could be flawed by the operation of third variables. Definitive evidence will require future experimental study.

Moderators of the Effects of Child Temperament on Parenting

Along with the many direct associations between characteristics of child temperament and parenting, temperament may interact with parent characteristics, other child characteristics, and/or contextual factors to impact parenting behavior. As illustrated above, relations between child temperament and parenting are not always simple or intuitive (i.e., negative temperament qualities do not always predict negative parenting practices), suggesting that other factors may function to determine the nature of the relation between these two variables in some cases. Most studies of temperament interactions with other variables are directed toward predicting child outcomes rather than parenting behavior, but a few studies have illustrated how the effects of temperament on parenting can be moderated by other variables.

Although focused on determinants of child outcomes rather than determinants of parenting behavior, Rubin and colleagues' *temple of doom* model provides an excellent example of a moderator effect (Rubin, LeMare, & Lollis, 1990; Rubin & Stewart, 1996). In this model, early child inhibition leads to negative parenting behavior (insensitivity, overprotection, and/or overcontrol) only when linked with other family stressors. The negative parenting behavior then increases the probability of child insecure attachment, social withdrawal, and peer rejection. In this scenario, the effect of temperament on parenting is moderated by family stress.

Other moderators of relations between child temperament and parenting have been reported. For example, Clark et al. (2000) found that difficult child temperament was related to the use of power assertion among mothers who were high in extraversion and low in empathy but not among mothers low in extraversion or high in empathy. The authors interpreted these findings as indicating that some correlates of extraversion, such as dominance, as well as lowered ability to take another person's perspective (low empathy) sensitized mothers to the effects of difficult child behavior, leading to increased power assertion. This study illustrates the importance of considering both parent and child characteristics and their interaction in predicting parent behavior.

In a study involving level of conflict in sons' and daughters' relationships with each parent among seventh graders, mother–son conflict was highest with the combination of a less adaptable mother and a low activity son (Galambos & Turner, 1997). On the other hand, mother–daughter conflict was highest with the combination of a less adaptable mother and a high activity daughter. Low adaptability in fathers and daughters was associated with high conflict between daughters and both parents as well as greater use of paternal psychological control. This pattern was not apparent with male children. Finally, in a study by Kawaguchi, Welsh, Powers, and Rostosky (1998), difficult temperament in adolescent girls was correlated with low support and depth in the father–daughter relationship; whereas difficult temperament in boys was associated with greater conflict in mother–son dyads.

Crockenberg (1986) proposed the idea that relations between child temperament and parenting are moderated by age because parents of difficult children may invest a great deal of time and energy during infancy, but later find themselves worn out, frustrated, and unable to maintain the stamina needed to continue to adequately meet their difficult child's demands. Empirical data support the notion of declining emotional and verbal responsiveness, reduced teaching efforts, and increased negativity among parents of difficult children with increasing child age (Peters-Martin & Wachs, 1984; Maccoby, Snow, & Jacklin, 1984).

An emerging literature is devoted to describing and understanding how the effects of temperament on parenting and child outcomes might be modified by environmental factors. For example, a study by Jenkins et al. (2003) revealed that associations between difficult temperament and parent negativity were considerably stronger among families with low socioeconomic status (SES) compared to families with high socio-economic status. As noted by the authors, parents with high SES may be less reactive to their children's difficult temperament because they have lower levels of stress generally or because they have different ways of attributing child misbehavior, with higher SES parents adopting explanations that tend to be constitutionally based. Contrasting results were reported by Prior, Sanson, Carroll, and Oberklaid (1989), who found nearly twice as many significant correlations between measures of temperament and parenting among high-SES participants compared to low-SES participants, with the authors suggesting that high-SES parents may be more aware of their children's individual qualities.

Effects of Other Child Characteristics on Parenting

Several other child characteristics besides temperament also appear to have influences on parenting. A brief summary of evidence for the effects of child age, gender, and physical attractiveness will be provided, although other characteristics may also be influential.

In view of the rapid growth in the parenting literature across the last several decades, it is rather surprising how little research has been devoted to documenting differences in parenting based on the age of the child, with most of the available studies focusing on transition periods of relatively short duration (O'Connor, 2002). Work by Dunn and Plomin (1990) suggests that parenting behavior directed toward individual children does show considerable variability over child age during infancy and early childhood. Parental monitoring or control seems to play an increasingly important role in models of adaptive parenting during late childhood; however control becomes less effective and less central to positive parenting during adolescence (Hetherington & Clingempeel, 1992). Maintaining a positive relationship and not restricting the adolescent's growing desire for independence are apparently key components of effective parenting during adolescence (Allen, Hauser, Bell, & O'Connor, 1994). A few studies have also explored possible differences in parenting behavior corresponding to birth order. For example, research by Jenkins et al. (2003) revealed that the oldest child tended to receive the most positive behavior from parents followed by youngest and then middle children.

More attention has been paid to the influence of child gender on parenting than to the influence of child age. Child gender can influence the caregiving environment in a variety of ways. For example, differential behavior based on gender might impact the behavior and cognitions of parents. Nevertheless, most literature reviews (e.g., Beal, 1994; Maccoby, 1998) indicate few and relatively minor gender differences in behavior during infancy, with differences increasing in early childhood, presumably as a function of socialization pressure and children's increased understanding of gender roles. A recent study by Jenkins et al. (2003) revealed that male children between the ages of 2 and 11 were exposed to more parental negativity than female children. Results of another recent investigation by Smetana and Daddis (2002) revealed that adolescent daughters were the recipients of higher levels of parental monitoring and psychological control than adolescent sons.

Perhaps the most probable means though which child gender is likely to impact parenting behavior is through the process of gender stereotyping. Studies have clearly demonstrated that parents perceive male and female newborns differently (Karraker et al., 1995; Rubin et al., 1974) and that differences in adults' behavior toward male and female infants is due to stereotypes rather than infant behavioral differences (Stern & Karraker, 1989). These studies and others indicating that parents behave differently with male and female infants and toddlers (reviewed by Beal, 1994) suggest that the environments of boys and girls differ from early infancy.

The results pertaining to differential parenting based on gender are conflicting, however, as evidenced by a meta-analysis conducted by Lytton and Romney (1991) revealing very few differences in the parenting of boys and girls with the exception of encouragement of sex-typed activities. The authors point out that this difference may actually reflect a biological substrate that is reinforced rather than created by parents. Unfortunately, as Putnam et al. (2002) point out, the review by Lytton and Romney did not take into consideration interactions between child gender and temperament in predicting differential parenting responses, and as the studies reviewed earlier suggest, gender can operate as a strong moderator of relations between temperament and parenting. According to Putnam et al. (2002), with only a few exceptions, the literature generally suggests more parental acceptance of irritability and negative affect from male children and more acceptance of shyness in female children. These gender-based differences in tolerance for particular temperament characteristics associated with gender are undoubtedly related to stereotypical beliefs regarding acceptable male and female behavior. The available evidence seems to indicate that as a result of this differential parental treatment, inborn gender differences, and children's cognitive processing of gender role information, boys and girls can be expected to behave differently and to elicit differential responses from others. However, in an extensive review of the gender literature, Fagot (1995) concluded that the central question pertaining to whether parents treat male and female children differently has not been sufficiently answered. She further notes that differential child outcomes based on parenting may be tied more to attitudes than behavior and the study of internal responses of parents to the parenting role has just emerged in recent years.

Physical attractiveness is another child characteristic that may lead to differential parenting behavior. For example, Langlois, Ritter, Casey, and Sawin (1995) found that mothers of more attractive newborns demonstrated more warmth and interest in playing with their newborns when compared to mothers of less attractive newborns. Adults also tend to look longer at and pay more attention to attractive infants and toddlers compared to their less attractive peers (Hildebrandt & Cannan, 1985; Hildebrandt & Fitzgerald, 1978). In view of the high value placed on physical attractiveness in contemporary society (Hatfield & Sprecher, 1986), the environments of more and less attractive children may differ in other ways as well.

Summary of Effects of Child Characteristics on Parenting

The studies reviewed previously provide evidence that certain child characteristics may elicit differential responding from parents. Much of the available evidence for these effects is necessarily correlational rather than experimental, and thus susceptible to alternate causal and noncausal explanations. In addition, from a transactional perspective, our understanding of the parenting process would be enhanced by simultaneous consideration of alternate causal pathways, mediators, and moderators. As Putnam et al. (2002) noted, investigations of complex interactive effects have not always been theory driven, and more theory-based model development would enhance our understanding of the parenting process.

IMPLICATIONS AND CONCLUSIONS

Expansion of the study of parenting to include child effects in combination with parent and contextual factors has resulted in a much more sophisticated picture of the parenting process with considerable potential to one day offer very useful information to parents as they face the challenges of rearing very different children under widely varying circumstances in a rapidly changing and complex world. Efforts to include more variables in parenting research with enhanced sensitivity to bi-directional and interactional effects are increasing, although at this point the findings generated often raise more questions than they answer. Nevertheless, some central themes are emerging that should provide clear direction as this area of study matures.

First, our knowledge of parenting cannot be reasonably developed when examined in isolation from a full understanding of both parents and children as individuals, as partners in a dyadic relationship, and as members of a family, community, and society. Consideration of both interpersonal dynamics beyond the dyad and situational factors will be critical to advancing our understanding of the parenting process. Researchers must also remember that attention to internal processes such as perceptions and cognitions facilitate comprehension of parenting.

Second, both children and parents are constantly changing as they engage in the ongoing process of impacting each other's behavior and development and in response to familial and broader contextual changes. Therefore, it is essential for studies of parenting to adopt longitudinal designs with frequent assessments that carry the potential to capture these dynamics and provide clarity regarding issues of directionality.

Third, specification of causal relations between parenting and other variables will require the use of multiple methodologies. O'Connor (2002) emphasized the need to include different types of designs tailored to particular research questions. The use of a rich combination of methodologies (e.g., controlled experiments, naturally occurring experiments, twin and adoption studies, comparisons of siblings, structural equation modeling, case studies of single dyads, and so on) should not only foster greater fit between research questions and designs, but will also enable more focused effort to explore the generalizability of findings detected at higher levels of constraint. Particular attention to the role of genetic factors in the parenting process is crucial.

Finally, recent research on parenting has in many ways underscored the centrality of parents in the lives of their children. However, studies that include child characteristics have also strongly suggested that much of the variance once believed to be attributable to the power of parents to influence the lives of their children may actually represent responses elicited by or at least constrained by child characteristics. As data revealing the critical role that children's individual qualities play in their own development accumulate, parents will grow to understand that their behavior is impacted by factors outside their personal control and that each child is unique. This knowledge is likely to relieve some of the pressure and guilt experienced by parents. A substantive understanding of how children with different qualities affect parents with different qualities on a daily basis and over extended periods of time should also lead to more effective parenting strategies, more positive child outcomes, and enhanced parent satisfaction with the role as the knowledge is made publicly available and used to inform training and intervention efforts. As the study of parenting expands in this direction, researchers need to make a concerted effort not to fall into a pattern described by O'Connor (2002) as occurring when "efforts to demonstrate the child's contribution to the parent–child relationship ('child effects') sometimes ignore the parent's contribution—rather missing the bi-directionality idea and replacing one uni-dimension with its inverse" (p. 563).

The knowledge gained by more fully considering interactive child, parent, and contextual contributions to parenting should further lead to considerably more effective parenting intervention strategies with parents who are currently engaging in or are at risk for maladaptive parenting. As noted by Putnam et al. (2002), "Any program giving prescriptions about 'the right way to do it' will clearly be deficient if it does not also direct parents' attention to individuality and to the need to be flexible in their approach to parenting" (p. 270). A number of temperament-based parent intervention programs are available that emphasize general information about temperament, feedback regarding individual children's dispositions, specific recommendations for effective parenting of children with different temperaments, and use of parent support groups (Sheeber & McDevitt, 1998). Evaluation of the programs has thus far been limited, but preliminary data indicate that parents tend to report high levels of satisfaction with their participation, satisfaction in parenting, perceptions of competence and mental health, as well as lowered levels of family disruption (Sheeber & McDevitt, 1998). The goal of these programs is typically to reduce the stress in the parent–child system created by a lack of synchrony between child and parenting behavior. However, very few if any of the existing programs also consider the parent as a unique individual with a history of experiences, personality characteristics, attitudes, and beliefs that play a role in the goodness-of-fit between child temperament and parenting behavior. Hopefully as these programs are developed in the future, the greater sensitivity to the child exhibited recently will be coupled with enhanced awareness of the individuality of parents.

When the study of parenting is conducted in a manner that is true to the transactional perspective, the opportunities to understand the mysteries of parents' subjective responses to the role and potential for personal growth and satisfaction become much richer. For example, use of this perspective should be able to substantively highlight the mechanisms behind the commonly voiced experience of parents in which they describe the parenting of one child as involving predominantly positive emotions and experiences, while care for another child is reported to involve a constant struggle coupled with feelings of helplessness and anger. Parenting research adopting the transactional perspective should likewise lead to answers to many of the complex questions related to the dynamics of parenting and child development that have challenged scholars for years and were simply unanswerable using the circumscribed uni-directional perspective. Moreover, as our knowledge expands, the utility of our efforts to offer the tangible, directly applicable information that parents need to understand their children and enhance their contributions to their children's well-being should remarkably improve.

REFERENCES

Allen, J. P., Hauser, S. T., Bell, K. L., & O'Connor, T. G. (1994). Longitudinal assessment of autonomy and relatedness in adolescent–family interactions as predictors of adolescent ego development and self-esteem. *Child Development, 65,* 179–194.

Anderson, K. E., Lytton, H., & Romney, D. M. (1986). Mothers' interactions with normal and conduct-disordered boys: Who affects whom? *Developmental Psychology, 22,* 604–609.

Bates, J. E., Bayles, K., Bennett, D. S., Ridge, B., & Brown, M. M. (1991). Origins of externalizing behavior problems at eight years of age. In D. Pepler and K. Rubin (Eds.), *Development and treatment of childhood aggression* (pp. 93–120). Hillsdale, NJ: Lawrence Erlbaum Associates.

Baumrind, D. (1991). Effective parenting during the early adolescent transition. In P. A. Cowan & E. M. Hetherington (Eds.), *Family transitions* (pp. 111–163). Hillsdale, NJ: Lawrence Erlbaum Associates.

Beal, C. R. (1994). *Boys and girls: The development of gender roles.* New York: McGraw-Hill.

Bell, R. Q. (1968). A reinterpretation of the direction of effects in studies of socialization. *Psychological Review, 75,* 81–95.

Belsky, J. (1984). The determinants of parenting: A process model. *Child Development, 55,* 83–96.

Belsky, J., Rha, J., & Park, S. (2000). Exploring reciprocal parent and child effects in the case of child inhibition in US and Korean samples. *International Journal of Behavioral Development, 24,* 338–347.

Berg-Nielsen, T. S., Vikan, A., & Dahl, A. A. (2002). Parenting related to child and parental psychopathology: A descriptive review of the literature. *Clinical Child Psychology and Psychiatry, 7,* 529–552.

Bidell, T. R., & Fischer, K. W. (1997). Between nature and nurture: The role of human agency in the epigenesis of intelligence. In R. J. Sternberg & L. L. Grigorenko (Eds.), *Intelligence, heredity, and environment* (pp. 193–242). New York: Cambridge University Press.

Bornstein, M. H. (Ed.). (1995). *Handbook of parenting.* Mahwah, NJ: Lawrence Erlbaum Associates.

Bornstein, M. H. (Ed.). (2002). *Handbook of parenting* (2nd ed.). Mahwah, NJ: Lawrence Erlbaum Associates.

Braungart, J. M. (1994). Genetic influences on "environmental" measures. In J. C. DeFries, R. Plomin, & D. W. Fulker (Eds.), *Nature and nurture during middle childhood* (pp. 233–248). Cambridge, MA: Blackwell.

Braungart-Rieker, J., Garwood, M. M., & Stifter, C. (1997). Compliance and noncompliance: The roles of maternal control and child temperament. *Journal of Applied Developmental Psychology, 18,* 411–428.

Bronfenbrenner, U. (1979). *The ecology of human development: Experiments by nature and design.* Cambridge, MA: Harvard University Press.

Bronfenbrenner, U., & Morris, P. (1998). The ecology of developmental processes. In W. Damon (Series Ed.) & R. M. Lerner (Vol. Ed.), *Handbook of child psychology: Vol. 1. Theoretical models of human development* (5th ed., pp. 993–1028). New York: Wiley.

Buss, D. M. (1981). Predicting parent–child interaction from children's activity level. *Developmental Psychology, 17,* 59–65.

Chen, X., Hastings, P. D., Rubin, K. H., Chen, H., Cen, G., & Stewart, S. L. (1998). Child rearing practices and behavioral inhibition in Chinese and Canadian toddlers: A cross-cultural study. *Developmental Psychology, 34,* 677–686.

Chess, S., Thomas, A., & Birch, H. G. (1965). *Your child is a person.* New York: Viking.

Clark, L. A., Kochanska, G., & Ready, R. (2000). Mothers' personality and its interaction with child temperament as predictors of parenting behavior. *Journal of Personality and Social Psychology, 79,* 274–285.

Coleman, P. K., & Karraker, K. H. (1998). Self-efficacy and parenting quality: Findings and future applications. *Developmental Review, 18,* 46–85.

Crockenberg, S. B. (1986). Are temperamental differences in babies associated with predictable differences in care giving? In J. V. Lerner and R. M. Lerner (Eds.), *New Directions for Child Development: Vol. 31. Temperament and social interaction during infancy and childhood* (pp. 53–73). San Francisco: Jossey-Bass.

Crouter, A. C., McHale, S. M., & Tucker, C. J. (1999). Does stress exacerbate parental differential treatment of siblings? A pattern analytic approach. *Journal of Family Psychology, 13,* 286–299.

Cutrona, C., & Troutman, B. (1986). Social support, infant temperament, and parenting self-efficacy. *Child Development, 57,* 1507–1518.

Deal, J. (1996). Marital conflict and differential treatment of siblings. *Family Process, 35,* 333–346.

Deater-Deckard, K., Pike, A., Petrill, S. A., Cutting, A. L., Hughes, C., & O'Connor, T. G. (2001). Nonshared environmental processes in social-emotional development: An observational study of identical twin differences in the preschool period. *Developmental Science, 4,* F1–F6.

Dix, T. (1991). The affective organization of parenting: Adaptive and maladaptive processes. *Psychological Bulletin, 110,* 3–25.

Dunn, J. F., & Plomin, R. (1986). Determinants of maternal behavior toward three-year-old siblings. *British Journal of Developmental Psychology, 57* 348–356.

Dunn, J., & Plomin, R. (1990). *Separate lives: Why siblings are so different.* Basic Books.

Elkins, I. J., McGue, M., & Iacono, W. G. (1997). Genetic and environmental influences on parent–son relationships. Evidence for increasing genetic influence during adolescence. *Developmental Psychology, 33,* 351–353.

Fagot, B. I. (1995). Parenting boys and girls. In M. H. Bornstein (Ed.), *Handbook of parenting: Vol. 1: Children and parenting* (pp. 163–183). Mahwah, NJ: Lawrence Erlbaum Associates.

Feinberg, M., & Hetherington, E. M. (2001). Differential parenting as a within-family variable. *Journal of Family Psychology, 15,* 22–37.

Fowles, D. C., & Kochanska, G. (2000). Temperament as a moderator of pathways to conscience in children: The contribution of electrodermal activity. *Psychophysiology, 37,* 788–795.

Galambos, N. L., & Turner, P. K. (1997, April). Shaping parent–adolescent relations: Goodness-of-fit in parent–adolescent temperaments. Poster presented at the biennial meeting of the Society for Research in Child Development, Washington, DC.

Gauvain, M., & Fagot, B. (1995). Child temperament as mediator of mother–toddler problem solving. *Social Development, 4,* 257–276.

Gelfand, D. M., Teti, D. M., & Radin Fox, C. E. (1992). Sources of parenting stress for depressed and non-depressed mothers. *Journal of Clinical Child Psychology, 21,* 262–272.

Goodman, R., & Stevenson, J. (1989). A twin study of hyperactivity-II. The aetiological role of genes, family relationships and perinatal adversity. *Journal of Child Psychology and Psychiatry, 30,* 691–709.

Gross, D., Conrad, B., Fogg, L., & Wothke, W. (1994). A longitudinal model of maternal self-efficacy, depression, and difficult temperament in toddlerhood. *Research in Nursing & Health, 17,* 207–215.

Grusec, J. E., Hastings, P., & Mammone, N. (1994). Parenting cognitions and relationship schemas. In J. G. Smetana (Ed.), *Beliefs about parenting: Origins and developmental implications* (pp. 5–19). San Francisco: Jossey-Bass.

Harris, J. R. (1998). *The nurture assumption.* New York: Free Press.

Hatfield, E., & Sprecher, S. (1986). *Mirror, mirror . . . The importance of looks in everyday life.* Albany, NY: State University of New York Press.

Hetherington, E. M. (1989). Coping with family transitions: Winners, losers, and survivors. *Child Development, 60,* 1–14.

Hetherington, E. M., & Clingempeel, W. G. (1992). Coping with marital transitions. *Monographs of the Society for Research in Child Development, 57*(2–3, Serial No. 227).

Hildebrandt, K. A., & Cannan, T. (1985). The distribution of caregiver attention in a group program for young children. *Child Study Journal, 15,* 43–55.

Hildebrandt, K. A., & Fitzgerald, H. E. (1978). Adults' responses to infants varying in perceived cuteness. *Behavioral Processes, 3,* 159–172.

Holden, G. W. (1995). Parental attitudes toward childrearing. In M. H. Bornstein (Ed.), *Handbook of parenting: Vol. 3. Status and social conditions of parenting* (pp. 359–392). Mahwah, NJ: Lawrence Erlbaum Associates.

Jain, A., Belsky, J., & Crnic, K. (1996). Beyond fathering behaviors: Types of dads. *Journal of Family Psychology, 10,* 431–442.

Jenkins, J. M, Rasbash, J., & O'Connor, T. G. (2003). The role of the shared family context in differential parenting. *Developmental Psychology, 39,* 99–113.

Karraker, K. H., & Coleman, P. (2002). Infants' characteristics and behaviors help shape their environments. In H. E. Fitzgerald, K. Karraker, & T. Luster (Eds.), *Infant development: Ecological perspectives* (pp. 165–191). New York: Garland.

Karraker, K. H., Vogel, D. A., & Lake, M. A. (1995). Parents' gender-stereotyped perceptions of newborns: The eye of the beholder revisited. *Sex Roles, 33,* 687–701.

Kawaguchi, M. C., Welsh, D. P., Powers, S. I., & Rostosky, S. S. (1998). Mothers, fathers, sons, and daughters: Temperament, gender, and adolescent–parent relationships. *Merrill-Palmer Quarterly, 44,* 77–96.

Kingston, L., & Prior, M. (1995). The development of patterns of stable, transient, and school-age onset aggressive behavior in young children. *Journal of the American Academy of Child and Adolescent Psychiatry, 34,* 348–358.

Kowal, A., & Kramer, L. (1997). Children's understanding of parental differential treatment. *Child Development, 68,* 113–126.

Langlois, J. H., Ritter, J. M., Casey, R. J., & Sawin, D. B. (1995). Infant attractiveness predicts maternal behaviors and attitudes. *Developmental Psychology, 31,* 464–472.

Lerner, J. V. (1993). The influence of child temperamental characteristics on parent behaviors. In T. Luster & L. Okagaki (Eds.), *Parenting: An ecological perspective* (1st ed., pp. 101–120). Hillsdale, NJ: Lawrence Erlbaum Associates.

Leve, L. D., Scaramella, L. V., & Fagot, B. I. (2001). Infant temperament, pleasure in parenting, and marital happiness in adoptive families. *Infant Mental Health Journal, 22,* 545–558.

Lytton, H., & Romney, D. M. (1991). Parents' sex-related differential socialization of boys and girls: A meta-analysis, *Psychological Bulletin, 109,* 267–296.

Maccoby, E. E. (1998). *The two sexes.* Cambridge, MA: Harvard University Press.

Maccoby, E. E., Snow, M. E., & Jacklin, C. N. (1984), Children's dispositions and mother–child interaction at 12 and 18 months: A short-term longitudinal study. *Developmental Psychology, 20,* 459–472.

Mangelsdorf, S., Gunnar, M., Kestenbaum, R., Lang, S., & Andreas, D. (1990). Infant proneness to distress temperament, maternal personality, and mother–infant attachment: Associations and goodness-of-fit. *Child Development, 61,* 820–831.

Mash, E. J., & Johnston, C. (1983). Parental perceptions of child behavior problems, parenting self-esteem, and mothers' reported stress in younger and older hyperactive and normal children. *Journal of Consulting and Clinical Psychology, 51,* 86–99.

Masten, A. S. (1989). Resilience in development: Implications of the study of successful adaptation for developmental psychopathology. In D. Cicchetti (Ed.), *The emergence of a discipline: Rochester Symposium on Developmental Psychopathology* (Vol. 1, pp. 261–294). Hillsdale, NJ: Lawrence Erlbaum Associates.

McBride, B. A., Schoppe, S. J., & Rane, T. R. (2002). Child characteristics, parenting stress, and parental involvement: Fathers versus mothers. *Journal of Marriage and Family, 64,* 998–1011.

McGue, M., Sharma, A., & Benson, P. (1996). The effect of common rearing on adolescent adjustment: Evidence from a U.S. adoption cohort. *Developmental Psychology, 32,* 604–613.

McGuire, S., Dunn, J., & Plomin, R. (1995). Maternal differential treatment of siblings and children's behavioral problems: A longitudinal study. *Development and Psychopathology, 7,* 515–528.

McHale, S. M., & Pawletko, T. M. (1992). Differential treatment in two family contexts. *Child Development, 63,* 68–81.

Morris, A. S., Silk, J. S., Steinberg, L., Sessa, F. M., Avenevoli, S., & Essex, M. J. (2002). Temperamental vulnerability and negative parenting as interacting predictors of child adjustment. *Journal of Marriage and Family, 64,* 461–471.

Mulsow, M., Caldera, Y. M., Pursley, M., & Reifman, A. (2002). Multilevel factors influencing maternal stress during the first three years. *Journal of Marriage and Family, 64,* 944–956.

O'Connor, T. G. (2002). Annotation: The 'effects' of parenting reconsidered: Findings, challenges, and applications. *Journal of Child Psychology and Psychiatry, 43,* 555–572.

Okagaki, L., & Divecha, D. J. (1993). Development of parental beliefs. In T. Luster & L. Okagaki (Eds.), *Parenting: An ecological perspective* (1st ed.). Hillsdale, NJ: Lawrence Erlbaum Associates.

Park, S., Belsky, J., Putnam, S., & Crnic, K. (1997). Infant emotionality, parenting, and 3-year inhibition: Exploring stability and lawful discontinuity in a male sample. *Developmental Psychology, 33,* 218–227.

Patterson, G. R., & Fisher, P. A. (2002). Recent developments in our understanding of parenting: Bidirectional effects, causal models, and the search for parsimony. In M. H. Bornstein (Ed.), *Handbook of parenting: Vol. 5. Practical issues in parenting* (2nd ed., pp. 59–88). Mahwah, NJ: Lawrence Erlbaum Associates.

Peters-Martin, P., & Wachs, T. D. (1984). A longitudinal study of temperament and its correlates in the first 12 months. *Infant Behavior and Development, 7,* 285–298.

Pike, A., McGuire, S., Hetherington, E. M., Reiss, D., & Plomin, R. (1996). Family environment and adolescent depression and antisocial behavior: A multivariate genetic analysis. *Developmental Psychology, 32,* 590–603.

Plomin, R. (1990). *Nature and nurture: An introduction to human behavioral genetics.* Belmont, CA: Brooks/Cole.

Plomin, R., DeFries, J. C., & Fulker, D. W. (1988). *Nature and nurture during infancy and early childhood.* New York: Cambridge University Press.

Plomin, R., Loehlin, J. C., & DeFries, J. C. (1985). Genetic and environmental components of "environmental" influences. *Developmental Psychology, 21,* 391–402.

Plomin, R., & Rutter, M. (1998). Child development and molecular genetics. What do we do with genes once they are found? *Child Development, 69,* 1225–1242.

Prior, M., Sanson, A., Carroll, R., & Oberklaid, F. (1989). Social class and differences in temperament ratings of pre-school children. *Merrill Palmer Quarterly, 35,* 239–248.

Putnam, S. P., Sanson, A. V., & Rothbart, M. K. (2002). Child temperament and parenting. In M. H. Bornstein (Ed.), *Handbook of parenting: Vol. 1. Children and parenting* (2nd ed., pp. 255–277).

Rothbart, M. K. (1986). Longitudinal observation of infant temperament. *Developmental Psychology, 22,* 356–365.

Rubin, K. H., Hastings, P., Chen, X., Stewart, S., & McNichol, K. (1998). Interpersonal and maternal correlates of aggression, conflict, and externalizing problems in toddlers. *Child Development, 69,* 1614–1629.

Rubin, K. H., LeMare, L. J., & Lollis, S. (1990). Social withdrawal in childhood: Developmental pathways to peer rejection. In S. R. Ashey & J. D. Coie (Eds.), *Peer rejection in childhood* (pp. 217–249). New York: Cambridge University Press.

Rubin, K. H., Nelson, L. J., Hastings, P., & Asendorpf, J. (1999). The transaction between parents' perceptions of their children's shyness and their parenting styles. *International Journal of Behavioral Development, 23,* 937–957.

Rubin, J. Z., Provenzano, F. J., & Luria, Z. (1974). The eye of the beholder: Parents' views on sex of newborns. *American Journal of Orthopsychiatry, 44,* 47–55.

Rubin, K. H., & Stewart, S. L. (1996). Social withdrawal and inhibition in childhood. In E. Mash & R. Barkley (Eds.), *Child psychopathology* (pp. 277–307). New York: Guilford Press.

Rubin, K. H., Stewart, S. L., & Chen, X. (1995). Parents of aggressive and withdrawn children. In M. Bornstein (Ed.), *Handbook of parenting: Vol. 1. Children and parenting* (pp. 255–284). Hillsdale, NJ: Lawrence Erlbaum Associates.

Sameroff, A., & Chandler, M. (1975). Reproductive risk and the continuum of caretaking casualty. In F. Horowitz (Ed.), *Review of child development research* (Vol. 4, pp. 303–331). Chicago: University of Chicago Press.

Sanson, A., Hemphill, S. A., & Smart, D. (2002). Temperament and social development. In P. K. Smith & C. H. Hart (Eds.), *Blackwell handbook of childhood social development* (pp. 97–115). Malden, MA: Blackwell.

Scarr, S. (1988). How genotypes and environments combine: Development and individual differences. In N. Bolger, A. Caspi, G. Downey, & M. Moorehouse (Eds.), *Persons in context: Developmental processes* (pp. 217–244). Cambridge, England: Cambridge University Press.

Scarr, S., & McCartney, K. (1983). How people make their own environments: A theory of genotype-environment effects. *Child Development, 54,* 424–435.

Sears, R. R., Maccoby, E. E., & Levin, H. (1957). *Patterns of child rearing.* Evanston, IL: Row, Peterson.

Sheeber, L. B., & Johnson, J. H. (1992). Child temperament, maternal adjustment, and changes in family lifestyle. *American Journal of Orthopsychiatry, 62,* 178–185.

Sheeber, L. B., & McDevitt, S. C. (1998). Temperament-focused parent training. In J. M. Briesmeister & C. E. Schaefer (Eds.), *Handbook of parent training* (pp. 479–507). New York: Wiley.

Smetana, J. G., & Daddis, C. (2002). Domain-specific antecedents of parental psychological control and monitoring: The role of parenting beliefs and practices. *Child Development, 73,* 563–580.

Stern, M., & Hildebrandt, K. A. (1986). Prematurity stereotyping: Effects on mother–infant interaction. *Child Development, 57,* 308–315.

Stern, M., & Karraker, K. H. (1989). Sex stereotyping of infants: A review of gender labeling studies. *Sex Roles, 20,* 501–522.

Stocker, C. M. (1995). Differences in mothers' and fathers' relationships with siblings: Links with children's behavior problems. *Development and Psychopathology, 7,* 499–513.

Teti, D. M., & Gelfand, D. M. (1991). Behavioral competence among mothers of infants in the first year: The mediational role of maternal self-efficacy. *Child Development, 62*, 918–929.

Thomas, A., & Chess, S. (1977). *Temperament and development.* New York: Brunner/Mazel.

Thomas, A., Chess, S., Birch, H. G., Hertzig, M. E., & Korn, S. (1963). *Behavioral individuality in early childhood.* New York: New York University Press.

Towers, H., Spotts, E. L., & Neiderhiser, J. M. (2001). Genetic and environmental influences on parenting and marital relationships: Current findings and future directions. *Marriage and Family Review, 33*, 11–29.

van Bakel, H. J. A., & Riksen-Walraven, J. M. (2002). Parenting and development of one-year-olds: Links with parental, contextual, and child characteristics. *Child Development, 73*, 256–273.

van den Boom, D. C., & Hoeksma, J. B. (1994). The effect of infant irritability on mother–infant interaction: A growth curve analysis. *Developmental Psychology, 31*, 581–590.

Vaughn, B. E., Taraldson, B. J., Crichton, L., & Egeland, B. (1981). The assessment of infant temperament: A critique of the Carey Infant Temperament Questionnaire. *Infant Behavior and Development, 4*, 1–17.

Volling, B. L., & Belsky, J. (1991). Multiple determinants of father involvement during infancy in dual-earner and single-earner families. *Journal of Marriage and the Family, 53*, 461–474.

Volling, B. L., & Elins, J. L. (1998). Family relationships and children's emotional adjustment as correlates of maternal and paternal differential treatment: A replication with toddler and preschool siblings. *Child Development, 69*, 1640–1656.

Vygotsky, L. S. (1978). *The mind in society: The development of higher psychological processes.* Cambridge, MA: Harvard University Press.

Wachs, T. D. (1992). *The nature of nurture.* Newbury Park, CA: Sage Publications.

Wachs, T. D., & Grandour, M. J. (1983). Temperament, environment, and six-month cognitive-intellectual development: A test of the organismic specificity hypotheses. *International Journal of Behavioral Development, 6*, 135–152.

Wachs, T. D., & Kohnstamm, G. A. (Eds.). (2001). The bidirectional nature of temperament-context links. In T. D. Wachs & G. A. Kohnstamm (Eds.), *Temperament in context* (pp. 201–222). Mahwah, NJ: Lawrence Erlbaum Associates.

Werner, E., & Smith, R. (1982). *Vulnerable but invincible.* New York: McGraw-Hill.

Woodworth, S., Belsky, J., & Crnic, K. (1996). The determinants of fathering during the child's second and third years of life: A developmental analysis. *Journal of Marriage and the Family, 58*, 679–692.

6

Parenting Children with Developmental Disabilities

Robert M. Hodapp
Vanderbilt University

Tran M. Ly
University of California–Los Angeles

INTRODUCTION

To understand the ecology of parenting children with disabilities, one must first appreciate certain societal changes. Since the 1970s, changes have arisen in most Western societies in the conceptualization of disabilities, in the nature and amount of services offered to children and their families, and in the roles that adults with disabilities play in the society at large. So, too, have major advances occurred in various sciences associated with disabilities; we now know much more about the causes and consequences of many disability conditions.

To give a flavor of societal changes, compare American disability policy today as opposed to the 1960s and early 1970s. In the 1970s, many more persons—including children—resided in large, often impersonal institutions. In 1967, almost 200,000 Americans lived in institutions, including 91,000 children. By 1997, that number had fallen to 56,161, including fewer than 3,000 children (Anderson, Lakin, Mangan, & Prouty, 1998; Lakin, Prouty, Braddock, & Anderson, 1997). Of those children who remained at home during the 1960s and early 1970s, access to formal education varied widely, depending mainly on the generosity of their particular town or state. Only in 1974, with the passage of the (federal) Education for All Handicapped Children Act (PL 94-142), were U.S. states and towns required to provide a "free, appropriate public education" to all students, including those with disabilities (Hallahan & Kauffman, 2002). Each of these events constitutes part of the changing macro-environment of parenting children with disabilities (Glidden, 2002).

Equally striking advances have occurred in the science of disability. Consider the example of mental retardation. On the one hand, the professional study of mental retardation dates to the founding of the field's main professional organization, the American Association on Mental Retardation, in 1876 (Scheerenberger, 1983). Around the same time, physicians such as J. Langdon Down began identifying specific syndromes that cause mental retardation (Down, 1866; see also Dunn, 1991). But the scientific study of mental retardation has blossomed only during the past several decades. From the discovery in 1959 that Down syndrome is caused in most cases by an extra chromosome 21 (Lejeune, Gautier, & Turpin, 1959), we now know that mental retardation is associated with more than 1,000 different genetic conditions (Dykens, Hodapp, & Finucane, 2000). Over the past two decades, increased numbers of behavioral studies have appeared on such disorders as fragile X syndrome, Prader-Willi syndrome, and Williams syndrome (Hodapp & Dykens, 2004). See Table 6.1 for a brief description of some prominent genetic forms of mental retardation.

When examining parenting issues for children with mental retardation, then, recent years have seen changes on a variety of levels. On the macro-environmental level, the number, variety, and quality of services have all increased or improved dramatically. Parents and families have both initiated and benefited from these changes. How researchers have conceptualized families of children with disabilities has also changed over time. During the same period, the field has learned much more about behavioral characteristics of the children themselves, thereby allowing for more thoughtful, complex investigations of parenting issues. How all of these changes go together is in many ways the topic of this chapter.

Although we focus on societal and scientific advances that are specific to the field of disabilities, we also feel that studying the parenting of children with disabilities is important to all researchers, not only to those interested in children with disabilities. Our approach in this chapter thus emphasizes the use of children with disabilities as experiments of nature. Just as twins, children of divorce, or children adopted from orphanages can inform us about basic processes of human development (Rutter, Pickles, Murray, & Eaves, 2001), children with different genetic disorders can also inform us about typical parenting reactions and behaviors. Such issues are discussed in more detail later, but suffice it to say that we view issues and findings of parenting children with disabilities as both applying and informing parenting studies more generally.

This chapter, then, surveys the state of the art on parenting children with disabilities. For the most part, we limit our scope to the study of children with mental retardation, leaving aside most other disability conditions. We

TABLE 6.1
Prominent Genetic Forms of Mental Retardation

Disorder	Genetics	Prevalence	Prominent Behavioral Features
Down syndrome	95% involve trisomy 21	1–1.5/1,000	Moderate MR: slowing rate of development as child gets older; social strengths; weaknesses in grammar & speech
Fragile X syndrome	Fragile site on X-chromosome	.73–.92/1,000	Moderate MR; more males than females; strength in simultaneous processing & weakness in sequential processing; slowed development from puberty; hyperactivity and autistic-like behaviors
Prader-Willi syndrome	2/3 involve deletions on chromosome 15; 1/3 involve both chromosome 15s from mother	1/15,000	Mild MR; failure to thrive in infancy followed by hyperphagia; proneness to obesity, food foraging, and compulsive behaviors; strength in jigsaw puzzles; stubbornness; skin picking
Smith-Magenis syndrome	Deletion on chromosome 17	1/25,000–50,000	Mild to moderate MR; minor physical and facial anomalies; sleep disturbance; self-injurious behaviors and high levels of many maladaptive behaviors
Williams syndrome	Deletion on chromosome 7	1/7,500	Mild to moderate MR; strengths in language and facial recognition; difficulties in visual-spatial construction tasks; interest in (and sometimes fairly talented in) music; sociable but difficulty in making and keeping friends; very high rates of anxiety, fears, and phobias
5p- syndrome (Cri du Chat)	Deletion on short arm of chromosome 5	1/50,000	Severe MR; high-pitched, infantile, cat-like cry; better developed receptive than expressive language; self-stimulatory and repetitive behaviors; hyperactivity and inattention

begin with a brief history, emphasizing the ways that family researchers have changed in how they view parents of children with disabilities. We then describe some parenting studies of children with different genetic mental retardation syndromes, before discussing such remaining issues as: who affects whom in parent–child interactions; what parents know and how parental knowledge relates to parental behaviors; and the ways in which various levels of the environment might be linked when discussing the parenting of children with disabilities.

Old and New Perspectives on Parenting Children With Disabilities

In the field of disabilities, family studies are not new. The sociologist Bernard Farber's (1959; 1960) early work dates to the late 1950s and early 1960s, and families have been an area of research within the disabilities field for over 100 years (Blacher & Baker, 2002). But earlier studies—those up to the early 1980s—differ from more modern studies in several ways. Five changes illustrate the movement from old to new studies of families of children with disabilities.

From Pathology-Negative Perspectives to Stress-Coping Perspectives. Most early studies considered only the negative consequences that might arise from parenting a child with disabilities. Using Freud's (1917/1957) model of mourning in response to losses of any kind, Solnit and Stark (1961) described what they called *maternal mourning.* In this view, upon the birth of their child with disabilities, mothers mourn, as in a death, the loss of the perfect child. Mothers were thought to go through a grief process that was characterized by a specific, stage-like process (see Blacher, 1984 for a review).

In line with Solnit and Stark's (1961) formulation, family studies of the 1960s and 1970s mainly examined depression, neuroticism, role tensions, and other adverse psychological effects. Some researchers examined depression in mothers (Cummings, Bayley, & Rie, 1966; Friedrich & Friedrich, 1981) and in fathers (Cummings, 1976). Others examined siblings, noting that the oldest nondisabled daughters may be most at-risk for psychological problems due to the role tensions associated with being the child in the family most often saddled with increased household or childcare responsibilities (Lobato, 1983). Throughout, the perspective of early researchers was that bad things happen to families of children with disabilities.

Beginning in the early 1980s, however, researchers began to adopt a more balanced view of these families. In a seminal article, Crnic, Friedrich, and Greenberg (1983) proposed that the experiences of these parents and families were better thought of in terms of stress and coping. In stress and coping models, the child with disabilities is considered an increased stressor on the family, but one that could be handled differently by different parents and families. Parenting the child with disabilities thus became like handling any stressor—for example, like coping with the illness of a parent or child, or of one or both parents losing their jobs, or of the family moving. Like reactions to all stressors, parents and families can react either positively or negatively. As we discuss below, the search for risk and protective factors—within children, parents, or families—has increasingly characterized research on families of children with disabilities.

From More General to More Specific Disability Groups. Older family studies also lacked attention to the child's type of disability. To some extent, this inattention to child problems also stems from Solnit and Stark (1961). If parents are reacting to the loss of the idealized infant, then any violation of expectations, involving any type of child problem, might bring about maternal mourning. Solnit and Stark (1961) even speculated that mothers of twins might suffer from maternal-mourning reactions.

A good example of this approach can be seen in a study by Drotar, Baskiewicz, Irvin, Kennell, and Klaus (1975). In that study, the authors interviewed 20 mothers and 5 fathers of children with disabilities to examine a stage theory of the mourning reaction. But within their group with disabilities were children with cleft lip and palate, spina bifida, Down syndrome, and multiple congenital malformations. In line with the thinking of the time, mothers were reacting to parenting a child with disabilities; the exact nature of the disability seemed unimportant.

As recent findings demonstrate, however, children with different disabilities may differentially affect their parents. In mental retardation, for example, we now know that children with different genetic mental retardation disorders show different, etiology related maladaptive behaviors, profiles of cognitive-linguistic strengths and weaknesses, and periods of faster or slower development (Dykens & Hodapp, 2001). Such child behaviors, in turn, may elicit different reactions and behaviors from parents. In contrast to the perspectives used in early family work, then, later family researchers concluded that specific characteristics of the child matter for how parents and families cope with parenting the child with mental retardation. As we mention later, children with Down syndrome may elicit better coping from their parents, siblings, and families; children with syndromes that predispose children to perform higher or lower on specific intellectual tasks may also elicit different reactions from their parents.

From Between-Group to Between- and Within-Group Comparisons. Given the earlier, dominant view that parents and families coped poorly and that various child characteristics were unimportant, most early family research adopted a group-difference perspective. Thus, most studies of the 1960s and 1970s compared parents of children with disabilities to parents of same-aged children without disabilities.

With the change to a stress and coping perspective, this group-difference approach began to be complemented by studies using a within-group approach. If parents and families differ widely in how they cope, which factors might predispose certain parents to cope well and others poorly? The identification of such factors—in children, parents, and families as a whole—has now become a major focus of disability family research. By identifying protective or risk variables, family researchers are also attempting to understand the mechanisms by which adaptation occurs (Hodapp, 2002).

Although between-group studies continue to be performed, newer family research is increasingly characterized by more attention to within-group issues. Consider research on the problem-solving styles of mothers of children with disabilities. Several studies have now documented that those parents who engage in active, problem-based styles of coping experience less depression than those who either deny their emotional feelings or who engage in what has been called *emotion-based coping* (e.g., Essex, Seltzer, & Krauss, 1999).

From Mothers Alone to Mothers, Fathers, and Others.   In most early studies, mothers were the sole parent considered. This emphasis on mothers was due to a variety of factors. First, mothers were (and remain) the primary caregivers for most children. In addition, particularly until approximately 1980, lower percentages of mothers worked outside the home, and these percentages were likely even lower for mothers of children with disabilities. Finally, given a predominant Freudian perspective, there may have been an implicit emphasis on mothers as the child's main parent. For example, even those who disagreed with Solnit and Stark's (1961) model—feeling that maternal reactions were a series of ups and downs, depressive and nondepressive reactions (Olshansky, 1962)—were still implicitly using Freud as their touchstone and mothers as their focus.

Although fathers remain underexamined in modern studies, most researchers nevertheless acknowledge the important role that fathers play in families of children with disabilities. Moreover, various researchers are discovering that the needs of fathers may differ from those of mothers. More than fathers, mothers express needs for more social and familial support, information to explain the child's disability to others, and help with child care (Bailey, Blasco, & Simeonsson, 1992). In contrast, fathers are particularly concerned about the costs of caring for a child with disabilities and what the child will mean to the family as a whole (Price-Bonham & Addison, 1978). Comparing factors affecting mothers versus fathers of young children with mental retardation, Krauss (1993) noted, "mothers reported more difficulty than did fathers in adjusting to the personal aspects of

parenting and parenthood (parental health, restrictions in role, and relations with spouse). . . . fathers reported more stress related to the child's
temperament (e.g., child's mood and adaptability) and their relationship
to the child (such as feelings of attachment and of being reinforced by the
child)" (p. 401).

From Older to More Modern Cultural Views of Disability.   A final issue dis-
tinguishing older from more modern studies involves the culture itself.
American culture has changed dramatically in its reactions to children with
disabilities. As a result, over the past several decades the lives of these children and of their parents have changed dramatically.

The first area of change involves the timing of services to children and
parents. In addition to school services from age 3 through 21 years, states
now provide early intervention services during the 0- to 3-year period. And
later, after the school-age years, services help young adults with disabilities
to work and live as independently as possible during adulthood (Hallahan
& Kauffman, 2002). Services for individuals and their families are thus life-
long, and one must consider the interplay between children–parents–families and the service–delivery system from a life-span perspective. Changing
services constitute one important level of the overall ecology of that person's life.

A second change relates to how services are conceptualized. Partly due
to the change from pathological to stress-and-coping models, service delivery is now considered in terms of supporting families. No longer are parents, siblings, and families conceptualized as patients who need to be
cured, but instead as persons—or consumers—who require long- or short-
term support to enable themselves to cope more effectively. One family
may require more information about a range of state-supported services,
another respite care (i.e., short term out-of-family care) in order that the
family can get a break from the full-time care of the offspring with disabilities. Still other parents may need to be put in touch with parents of children
with similar problems, or parents who have dealt with the same school dis-
trict, or who can otherwise help in their particular situation. This support
revolution has changed the nature of services and how such services are understood by families and professionals (Hallahan & Kauffman, 2002).

Third, knowledge about many disorders has changed dramatically in recent years, and many family-based services transmit knowledge to parents
and families. Considering genetic mental retardation disorders, parent-
professional groups exist for most every disorder (see Table 6.2 for a list of
some helpful Web sites). Organizations such as NORD—the National Organization of Rare Disorders—run informational Web sites that provide up-
to-date information about the disorder and about the relevant parent-
professional groups and their annual or biennial meetings. The National

TABLE 6.2
Web Sites of Parent-Professional Groups

Syndrome-Specific Organizations	
Down syndrome	
National Down syndrome Society	http://www.ndss.org
National Down syndrome Congress	http://www.ndsccenter.org
National Association for Down syndrome	http://www.nads.org
National Fragile X Foundation	http://www.nfxf.org
Prader-Willi syndrome Association (USA)	http://www.pwsausa.org
PRISMS: Parents and Researchers Interested in Smith-Magenis syndrome	http://www.smithmagenis.org
Williams syndrome	http://www.williams-syndrome.org
	http://www.wsf.org
	http://www.liliclairefoundation.org
5p- syndrome Society (Cri du Chat)	http://www.fivepminus.org
Support and Informational Organizations	
Alliance of Genetic Support Groups	http://www.medhelp.org/www/agsg2.htm
The Arc of the United States	http://www.thearc.org
National Organization for Rare Disorders (NORD)	http://www.rarediseases.org
Special Olympics International	http://www.specialolympics.org

Institutes of Health (NIH) also offers consumer-friendly information on the web, and some disorders also feature local or state chapters, discussion groups, chat rooms, and other supports. Many hospitals and each state's University Centers of Excellence (formerly called University Affiliated Programs, or UAPs) provide family resource centers, support groups for parents and siblings, conferences, and advocacy services to deal with schools or regional centers. Compared to only a few decades ago, families can access an almost bewildering amount of supportive services, contacts, and educational or medical information. This exponential increase in potential knowledge and support that parents might access constitutes an important change in the culture of disabilities. More knowledge and supportive services exist every day, and parents are both helped and challenged by these vast information and service systems.

Family studies in disabilities, then, have changed markedly over the past 20 years. From pathology to stress and coping; from little to much attention to child characteristics and within-group correlates of family functioning; from mothers alone to all family members; from older to more modern cultural views and service changes—all serve as the background within which family studies in disability need to be considered. We now turn to one aspect of family studies—the ways in which families might react differently when children have various genetically-based mental retardation disorders.

Parenting Children with Different Genetic Mental Retardation Syndromes

In discussing the many ways in which the ecology of parenting has changed over the past few decades, one important advance concerns knowledge. Simply put, we now know much more about the behaviors of children with many different etiologies or causes of mental retardation (Dykens & Hodapp, 2001). Indeed, a new area of *behavioral phenotypes* has arisen (Dykens, 1995), a field that examines the ways in which particular genetic disorders affect behaviors. Although not every affected person necessarily shows that disorder's characteristic behaviors, genetic syndromes do appear to influence the behaviors of most children in many areas. To give a few examples, compared to other children with mental retardation:

1. Children with Down syndrome are considered by their parents as demonstrating sociable, upbeat personalities (Hornby, 1995; Wishart & Johnston, 1990). Intellectually, these children show relative strengths in visual versus auditory short-term memory (Hodapp, Evans, & Gray, 1999; Pueschel, Gallagher, Zartler, & Pezzullo, 1986), as well as weaknesses in expressive language and in grammar (Chapman & Hesketh, 2000; Miller, 1999).

2. In addition to obsessions–compulsions (Dykens, Leckman, & Cassidy, 1996) and to life-threatening hyperphagia (i.e., overeating), children with Prader-Willi syndrome solve jigsaw puzzles at levels well above both MA-matched children with mental retardation and CA-matched, typically developing children (Dykens, 2002).

3. Children with Williams syndrome show extreme weaknesses in many visuo-spatial tasks, even as they show relative strengths in several areas of language (Bellugi, Mills, Jernigan, Hickok, & Galaburda, 1999; Mervis, Morris, Bertrand, & Robinson, 1999).

Although more examples could be provided, these behavioral characteristics highlight the ways that different syndromes predispose children to show specific maladaptive behaviors, personalities, and cognitive-linguistic profiles. On a more basic level, each also shows the ways in which genetic disorders have direct effects on the behaviors of affected individuals (Hodapp, 1997). Presently, we do not know the pathways from specific genetic disorder to particular brain structures, to ultimate behavioral outcomes (at different ages and with different experiences). Still, there seems a strong predisposition for persons with one versus another genetic syndrome to show particular, etiology related behavioral outcomes.

Such etiology related behaviors may also influence others. In line with influences from parent-to-child and vice-versa (Bell, 1968), children with different genetic disorders, by their etiology related behaviors, may elicit predictable responses and behaviors from their mothers, fathers, siblings, teachers, peers, and others in their environments. Genetic disorders thus directly predispose children to show etiology related behaviors, which in turn indirectly lead to certain reactions and behaviors from others (Hodapp, 1999).

Although potential indirect effects have only begun to be examined in the mental retardation field, we provide below two tentative examples. We conclude this chapter by discussing future issues and problems.

Down Syndrome Advantage

Compared to several different comparison groups and using a range of measures, parents of children with Down syndrome appear to experience less stress and to feel more rewarded by their child. We first present the few available studies that examine stress and rewardingness in parents of children with Down syndrome, before discussing possible reasons for this *Down syndrome advantage.*

Parental Stress.   In studies that examine parents of children with or without disabilities, stress is examined using a variety of measures. Probably the most used of these measures include Abidin's Parenting Stress Index (PSI) (Abidin, 1995) and the Questionnaire on Resources and Stress, in its original (QRS; Holroyd & MacArthur, 1976) or Freidrich (QRS-F) editions (Friedrich, Greenberg, & Crnic, 1983). Some studies have also used the Beck Depression Inventory (Beck, Rush, Shaw, & Emery, 1971) as an indicator of psychological distress.

Despite using different measures of stress, studies of parents of children with Down syndrome generally report less stress compared to parents of children with such severe disabilities as autism. In an early study comparing same-aged children with autism and with Down syndrome, Holroyd and MacArthur (1976) found that parents of children with Down syndrome reported less stress on the QRS. Similarly, compared to children with autism, parents reported less child-related stress on the PSI (Kasari & Sigman, 1997). Using the QRS-F, Sanders and Morgan (1997) found that, relative to parents of children with autism, both mothers and fathers of children with Down syndrome experienced similar levels of parental pessimism but fewer parent and family problems.

Other studies compared stress levels in parents of children with Down syndrome to levels in parents of children and adults with other types of mental retardation. Fidler, Hodapp, and Dykens (2000) found that parents of 3- to 10-year-old children with Down syndrome reported less stress on the QRS-F relative to parents of children with Williams syndrome or Smith-

Magenis syndrome. In another study comparing mothers of children with heterogeneous causes of mental retardation as opposed to Down syndrome, mothers of children with Down syndrome reported lower total child-related stress levels (Hodapp, Ricci, Ly, & Fidler, 2003). This *Down syndrome advantage* was also present when Seltzer, Krauss, and Tsunematsu (1993) compared parenting stress in mothers of 35-year-old adults with Down syndrome to stress in mothers of adults with other forms of mental retardation.

In contrast, over a three-year span Hanson and Hanline (1990) did not find a consistent trend when comparing mother–child pairs of children with Down syndrome, with neurological impairments, and with hearing impairments. Specifically, mothers of children with Down syndrome reported less stress than did mothers of children with neurological impairments, but more than mothers of children with hearing impairments on some subscales of the PSI. Similarly, Cahill and Glidden (1996) did not find a Down syndrome advantage on the QRS when children with Down syndrome and children with other types of mental retardation were matched on several demographic variables.

Overall, then, most (but not all) studies find a Down syndrome advantage when parents of children with Down syndrome are compared to parents of children with autism, psychiatric disorders, or other forms of mental retardation. For the most part, such an advantage is not seen when comparisons are made to parents of children with same-aged, typically developing children (Scott, Atkinson, Minton, & Bowman, 1997; Roach, Orsmond, & Barratt, 1999; although see also Sanders & Morgan, 1997, and Wolf, Noh, Fisman, & Speechley, 1989). Thus, although parents of children with Down syndrome reported less stress than did parents of children with various disabilities, they usually reported slightly more stress when compared to parents of typically-developing age-mates.

Parental Rewardingness. Consistent with the changing emphasis from negative to positive outcomes in family research, some studies also examine parental rewardingness in parents of children with Down syndrome. Parents of children with Down syndrome do seem more rewarded by their children, and perhaps as rewarded as parents of typically developing children.

Using the PSI, studies showed that, when compared to parents of children with other types of disorders, parents of children with Down syndrome were more rewarded by their children. (In these studies, less PSI Reinforcement stress was considered as evidence that parents considered the child as more rewarding.) Hoppes and Harris (1990) found that, relative to parents of children with autism, parents of children with Down syndrome regarded their children as more rewarding. Noh, Dumas, Wolf, and Fisman (1989) also found the same pattern when contrasting parents of children with Down syndrome to parents of children with autism or with conduct disorder. Likewise, Hodapp et al. (2003) found that, relative to parents of children with heterogeneous causes of mental retardation, mothers of children with Down syndrome considered their child more acceptable and more rewarding.

It may even be the case that parents of children with Down syndrome experience equal levels of rewardingness as parents of typically developing children. Interestingly, these low levels of PSI Reinforcement stress occurred even when parents reported higher levels of stress overall. Such was the case in the study by Roach et al. (1999). Mothers and fathers reported more stress on most of the PSI subscales compared to their counterparts of same-aged typically developing children. On the PSI Reinforcement subscale, however, no group differences emerged (and the means of parents of typical children and of children with Down syndrome were almost identical). Similarly in Noh et al. (1989), although parents of children with Down syndrome rated their children as less attractive, socially appropriate, and intelligent, they regarded "their children as happier and as a greater source of positive reinforcement than the parents of normal children" (p. 460).

Indirect Effects or Associated Characteristics? Two explanations account for the Down syndrome advantage to parents. The first concerns what we have called *associated characteristics*, or aspects of Down syndrome that do not concern the behavior of these children themselves and that may make parenting children with Down syndrome different from parenting children with other types of disabilities. For example, Down syndrome is the most well known disorder to parents, professionals, and educators alike. It is also the most studied syndrome, with almost as many studies as all other genetic mental retardation syndromes combined (Hodapp, 1996). Parents of children with Down syndrome also have the option of joining the many active parent support and advocacy groups (Hodapp, Ly, Fidler, & Ricci, 2001).

Other parent- or family-related characteristics may also underlie the Down syndrome advantage. These include the higher likelihood of children with Down syndrome being born to older mothers (Olsen, Cross, Gensburg, & Hughes, 1996), who are more likely to have had one or more children already (and thus are more experienced in parenting). Likewise, older parents are more likely to have worked longer, and thus may be of slightly higher SES.

Apart from this set of associated characteristics, however, certain etiology related behaviors may also predispose parents of children with Down syndrome to display lower stress levels and to feel more rewarded by their child. For example, although researchers debate whether a *Down syndrome personality* exists (Wishart & Johnston, 1990), children with Down syndrome are often perceived to be sociable because of their ability to share and integrate emotions and attention with others. Compared to mental age-matched typical controls, children with Down syndrome look more often to the experimenter's face and less often to toys (Kasari, Mundy, Yirmiya, & Sigman, 1990; Ruskin, Kasari, Mundy, & Sigman, 1994). Further, children with Down syndrome tend to look to adults and engage in social behaviors, particularly during difficult problem-solving tasks (Kasari & Freeman, 2001; Pitcairn & Wishart, 1994). Thus, these children often smile when looking at others, thereby indicating their eagerness to interact with others and supporting the long-held belief that children with Down syndrome have an easygoing, pleasant, and sociable personality (Gibson, 1978; Wishart & Johnston, 1990).

Possibly due to these sociable behaviors, parents often find their child with Down syndrome to be positive and easygoing. Most fathers (Hornby, 1995) and mothers (Carr, 1995) spontaneously described their child with Down syndrome as "affectionate," "lovable," and "sociable." In addition to their positive personalities, children with Down syndrome also exhibit less etiology related maladaptive problems (Dykens & Kasari, 1997; Meyers & Pueschel, 1991). Parents, in turn, may be reacting positively to such positive behaviors from their children. Thus, when parents perceive their children with Down syndrome to have more sociable and positive personalities (and lower levels of maladaptive behaviors), mothers were more likely to normalize their child's noncompliant behaviors (Ly & Hodapp, 2002) and to experience less child-related stress and more reward from their children (Hodapp et al., 2003).

At this point, it remains unknown how the Down syndrome advantage operates—even whether this advantage is mainly due to child behaviors or to parental (and societal) knowledge and expectations about the syndrome. Also remaining to be examined are a variety of issues concerning what one might call the ecology of both knowledge and support. How, for example, is any Down syndrome advantage influenced by what parents know about the syndrome, by their level of participation in parent groups, by parental educational levels or work status, parent-teacher connections, or the parents' and family's degree of formal (e.g., therapists) or informal (extended family or friends) supports? Each issue remains open to future research.

Interactive Behaviors Within Interactions Tapping Etiology Related High versus Low Abilities

A second example of indirect effects can be seen in parental behaviors in response to a specific interaction, such as putting together a novel jigsaw puzzle, involving children with two other genetic forms of mental retardation, Prader-Willi syndrome and Williams syndrome. These two syndromes were chosen because, as a group, children with each of these two disorders are either exceptionally strong (Prader-Willi syndrome) or exceptionally weak (Williams syndrome) in puzzles and other visuospatial tasks. Thus, Dykens (2002) has recently found that, even compared to typical children of similar chronological ages, children with Prader-Willi syndrome perform exceptionally well in putting together jigsaw puzzles. In contrast, children with Williams syndrome perform particularly poorly (i.e., below mental age-levels) on a wide variety of visuospatial tasks (Bellugi, Mills, Jernigan, Hickok, & Galaburda, 1999; Mervis, Morris, Bertrand, & Robinson, 1999).

In one study, Ly and Hodapp (2003) examined child effects on parents' behaviors in parent–child dyads of 20 children with Prader-Willi syndrome and 21 children with Williams syndrome. We measured parents' amount of helping and reinforcement behaviors in response to interacting with their child to complete a jigsaw puzzle task. The jigsaw puzzle task was used to capitalize on the strength of Prader-Willi syndrome and the weakness of Williams syndrome. From attribution theory (Graham, 1991), parents of children with Williams syndrome (vs. with Prader-Willi syndrome) were hypothesized to provide more help and reinforcement during the jigsaw puzzle interaction task.

Prior to the interaction task, children completed a jigsaw puzzle independently to obtain an objective measure of the child's puzzle abilities. Although children with Prader-Willi syndrome, on average, completed more jigsaw puzzle pieces than children with Williams syndrome, each group showed a fair amount of within-syndrome variability. Two groups were therefore created—low and high puzzle ability.

Findings showed that, compared to parents of children with Prader-Willi syndrome, parents of children with Williams syndrome provided both more helping and more reinforcement behaviors. Within the 5-minute interaction session, parents of children with Williams syndrome helped their child 49 times, compared to slightly less than 24 times for the Prader-Willi parents. Similarly, parents of children with Williams syndrome reinforced their children over twice as often (Ms = 14.14 and 5.75, SDs = 8.46 and 5.41 for Williams and Prader-Willi syndromes, respectively). Although parents did not differ in the amount of reinforcement behaviors in children with higher versus lower puzzle abilities, parents provided more instances of help when their children had lower (M = 45.96, SD = 23.43) versus higher (M = 24.89, SD = 20.10) puzzle abilities.

These findings show that different genetic mental retardation syndromes may have indirect effects on parents, and possibly on others in the child's environment. If, indeed, parents of children with Down syndrome are reacting to the child's more pleasant personalities (and general lack of maladaptive behaviors), and those of children with Prader-Willi and Williams syndromes are reacting to high versus low puzzle abilities (respectively), then different genetic disorders may indirectly affect surrounding adults. Just how such influences occur, however, remains unclear, and we now turn to five intriguing, unresolved issues in this regard.

Five Remaining Questions

(1) What Is the Direction of Effects? In introducing the concept of interaction between mothers and their children, R. Q. Bell (1968) entitled his groundbreaking article "A reinterpretation of the direction of effects in studies of socialization." In that article, Bell reinterpreted the direction of effects, arguing that, for many studies of socialization (in which mothers presumably affected—or socialized—their children), one could equally argue that the direction of effects instead ran from children to adults. Since the 1970s, researchers of both typical and atypical development have struggled with the issue of direction of effects. Do parents affect children, do children affect parents, do both occur, and, if so, in what ways and at what points during development?

Similarly with regard to dyads of parents and children with disabilities, the direction-of-effects question remains. For example, do the more pleasant personalities and relative lack of psychopathology of children with Down syndrome elicit less stress and more reward from their parents, or, conversely, are less stressed, happier parents producing children with more pleasant personalities (who also have lower amounts of maladaptive behavior)?

Although disability studies of parenting remain unclear about the direction of effects, some preliminary evidence points to children influencing their parents. In a study examining children with mental retardation when children were 3, 7, and 11 years old, Keogh, Garnier, Bernheimer, and Gallimore (2000) found that the more likely direction of effects was from child to parent. Using path analyses, the child's higher levels of behavior problems, greater degrees of cognitive impairment, and lower levels of personal-social competence affected parent and family adaptation. In contrast, parental changes and accommodations of the family routine usually did not influence later child behaviors. Although the question remains open for many aspects of parent–child interaction, some evidence supports a child-affects-parents direction of effect. Obviously, more studies using longitudinal designs and more complex statistical analyses will be needed in future work.

(2) Can One Use Genetic Disorders as Behavioral Proxies? In many studies examining the direct effects of genetic disorders on children themselves, researchers emphasize how this or that genetic syndrome can serve as a model for a particular gene–brain–behavior pathway. In research on indi-

rect effects as well, researchers are implicitly using genetic disorders as a model. In this case, however, we are using a specific genetic disorder as a proxy for a particular, etiology related behavior (Hodapp, 2004). In the parent stress and reward studies mentioned above, we use Down syndrome as a stand-in for a pleasant personality and relative lack of psychopathology. In the study examining parental behaviors in the puzzle task, we use children with Prader-Willi syndrome to represent *good puzzlers* and children with Williams syndrome as proxies for *poor puzzlers.*

However, as shown by the listing of etiology-related behaviors in Down, Prader-Willi, and Williams syndromes, children with each syndrome are prone to several behaviors. Children with Prader-Willi syndrome are generally good at jigsaw puzzles, but also show hyperphagia, obsessions–compulsions, and other maladaptive behaviors. Compared to others with mental retardation, children with Down syndrome may display sociable personalities, but they also show relatively strong visual versus auditory short-term memory, as well as relative weaknesses in expressive language and in grammar. A genetic disorder predisposes individuals to a variety of behavioral characteristics.

Given that a genetic syndrome predisposes individuals to many behavioral outcomes, one must be careful when thinking about indirect effects. When judging the reactions or interactive behaviors of mothers of children with Down syndrome, which aspects of behavior are mothers reacting to? Are mothers more attuned to their child's sociable personalities, weak language abilities, or strong visual short-term memory? Mothers may also react differently from fathers, siblings, or teachers. In the same way, the interactional situation itself may matter. Thus, when putting together a jigsaw puzzle, parents seem likely to be responding to their child's jigsaw puzzle abilities. But in other situations, the child's puzzle abilities are probably not foremost in parents' minds. Which behavior matters to parents, in which specific circumstances, with which particular parent or other interactor?

A variety of ecological concerns also come into play. For example, how might attributions of their children's success or failure differ when parents come from different cultural groups (e.g., Euro-American vs. Asian-American)? Are any of these attributions and attribution-based behaviors related to whether mothers are married, divorced, or single, or to those with different educations, incomes, or levels of formal and informal support? At present, such ecological issues remain totally unexamined.

(3) Are Indirect Effects Etiology-Specific or Etiology-General? In considering the ways that genetic disorders indirectly affect others, our original thinking proposed what might be called an *etiology general approach* (Hodapp, 1997, 1999). That is, a genetic disorder predisposes children to show one or

more etiology related behaviors, which in turn lead parents to certain, predictable responses. The parent's response was to the child's behavior, not to the child's etiology per se. Considering cases in which the behavior of an individual child ran counter to the general etiology related profile, then, parents should essentially react to the behavior, not to the etiology. Thus, if a specific child with Down syndrome is not particularly pleasant or has many behavior problems, parents should feel more stressed and less rewarded. If a specific child with Prader-Willi syndrome is poor at puzzles, parents should react with more help. Conversely, if a certain child with Williams syndrome is good at puzzles, parents should offer less help. In effect, then, an etiology general approach assumes that parents react to the child's behavior, and that any child showing that behavior should elicit similar parental reactions and behaviors, regardless of the etiology of mental retardation.

In several studies, however, parents react to the child's behavior, but mainly in the context of what parents know or perceive of their child's syndrome. In one study, Ly and Hodapp (2002) asked parents of children with Down syndrome versus with other forms of mental retardation to make causal attributions in response to hypothetical vignettes in which their child performed each of two common, noncompliant behaviors. Parents of children considered more sociable and outgoing attributed their child's noncompliant behaviors as due to normative concerns ("my child is acting like other children his age"). But such connections between child personality and normalizing behaviors were found only within the Down syndrome group. Thus, among parents of children with Down syndrome, those who saw their child as more sociable, also rated more highly normalizing as the reason for their child's noncompliance, $r = .43$, $p < .01$. But among parents of children with mixed forms of mental retardation, no such connections existed between child personality and parental ratings of normalizing attributions, $r = .05$, ns.

A similar, maybe even more extreme, finding occurred in the jigsaw puzzle study (Ly & Hodapp, in press). In addition to comparing parental help and reward behaviors to children with Williams syndrome versus with Prader-Willi syndromes, we also divided children into high and low puzzlers. Given the usual amount of within-syndrome variance, dividing children at the overall median score for the two groups combined produced some children in each etiological group who were *against the etiology*. Some children with Prader-Willi syndrome were therefore poor puzzlers, and some with William syndrome were good puzzlers. To separate the contributions of the child's level of puzzle ability and parents' knowledge of the child's etiological diagnosis on parental behaviors, we then performed stepwise multiple regressions, using both etiology group and puzzle ability as independent predictors. When looking at parents' helping behaviors, the child's etiology accounted for 28% of the variance, with the child's puzzle ability accounting for an additional 12%. For reinforcement behaviors, only the child's etiology emerged as a significant predictor, accounting for 27% of the variance.

Such findings suggest a complex interplay between the child's behavior, on one hand, and parental knowledge or perceptions of etiology related behavior on the other. In the case of Down syndrome, increasing amounts of etiology related personality elicited greater degrees of parental normalizing attributions. More etiology related behavior was associated with a particular parental reaction, but only within the Down syndrome group. In the puzzle study, the important issue seemed to be parents' perceptions of what that etiology means, less so the child's behavior per se. There seems, then, to be a complex interaction between the behaviors themselves and the child's type of mental retardation. Sometimes both are important, sometimes etiology trumps behavior, and sometimes behavior matters, but only within the context of what parents know or think that they know about etiology related behaviors of their child's etiology. We again return to Bell, and his idea that reactions and behaviors must be considered within the context of a "thinking parent" (Bell, 1979).

(4) What Do Parents Know and How Do They Know It?   If parental perceptions and knowledge of their child's etiology are so important, what do parents know? This involves the issue of parental beliefs and their origins (Okagaki & Divecha, 1993; Okagaki & Bingham, chap. 1, this volume), a significant area within parenting studies of typically developing children, which is relatively unexplored among parents of children with disabilities.

In a few syndromes, however, we do have some sense of what parents know about their child's etiology. In one study, Fidler, Hodapp, and Dykens (2002) asked parents of children with Prader-Willi syndrome, Down syndrome, and Williams syndrome about several education-related aspects of their child's behavioral characteristics and school accommodations. Whereas parents of children with Down syndrome were aware of their child's cognitive-linguistic strengths (e.g., visual short-term memory) and weaknesses (e.g., expressive language), parents in the two other groups knew much less. Among parents of children with Prader-Willi syndrome, parents knew of their child's extreme overeating and tantrums, but were less aware of their child's strong visuospatial abilities. In Williams syndrome, parents were aware of the many fears and anxieties shown by these children (Dykens, 2003), but less aware of these children's general propensity to have relatively strong linguistic skills and relatively weak visuospatial skills.

Another, somewhat unexpected finding concerned delivery of etiology related information into the classroom setting. Thus, one of our questions asked parents about who among ten different people (the parent and nine different school professionals) brought information about their child's syndrome into the classroom. In Down syndrome, an average of 3.38 people—including mothers themselves, school psychologists, teachers, and speech-language pathologists—all brought Down syndrome-related information into the school setting. In contrast, an average of only 1.52 persons brought Prader-Willi-related information into the school, and 1.25 people brought Williams syndrome-related information into the school. Stated another way, only 9.5% of mothers of children with Down syndrome were the sole providers of etiology based information to their child's school personnel, but 52% and 66.7% of parents of children with Prader-Willi syndrome and Williams syndrome, respectively, were the sole *etiology-information-providers* to their child's school.

Though suggestive, these findings leave unanswered countless other questions. Where do mothers receive their information, when do they receive it, and to what extent are mothers good information providers about their child's condition? How might such information be related to parental access to and abilities in searching the Internet, or to a parent's degree of involvement with an etiology related parent group? Are there ethnic differences in information gathering or use? How do schools and other service-systems relate to parents who present etiology based information, particularly given the general disregard of etiology-related information that has historically characterized the field of special education (see Hodapp & Fidler, 1999, for a review)? To these and other questions, we remain woefully uninformed.

(5) How Do We Link Various Levels of the Environment?   As the many unexplored questions imply, the field of parenting studies in mental retardation—and even in disabilities in general—has not yet joined the various levels of the child's environment (e.g., parents and families, schools, neighborhoods). Although an ecological approach to parenting is a booming enterprise for parents of typically developing children, our knowledge of Bronfenbrenner's (1979) many different levels, or of how such levels interrelate is almost non-existent for children with mental retardation.

And yet, as shown above, if we are to understand parenting children with different genetic disorders, we need to know how children with these disorders live within their families, with friends, and in their schools, neighborhoods, and other environments. In addition to knowing about each level separately, we will also need to know how the various levels of ecology go together. To follow our example above, we will need to know when and how parents access information, how such information might be gathered or used differently by parents who are of different ages, ethnicities, SES levels, or who live in different geographic locales or types of locale (urban, suburban, rural).

To further complicate this interplay of various levels of the ecology, parents of children with disabilities confront service and scientific worlds that are changing rapidly. As noted earlier, the disabilities field has changed enormously over the past few decades. Parents are now simultaneously faced with learning about and accessing services for their child with mental retardation; rearing their child with mental retardation while simultaneously rearing other, nondisabled children; and taking care of their own needs as individuals and as a couple. The increasing amount of research information adds a further complication. To give a single example, more and more children with disorders such as Williams and Prader-Willi syndromes have only recently been diagnosed at early ages, and an explosion of knowledge has occurred in these and other syndromes (Dykens & Hodapp, 2001). Keeping up with this knowledge explosion is a challenge, particularly when most parents do not start out as experts in any area of child development, genetics, psychiatry, or social service systems. The world has changed, and the field is only now catching up in its understanding of how parents of children with different genetic syndromes cope within this changing world, this moving target.

CONCLUSIONS

In conceptualizing parenting children with disabilities, we grope for a metaphor that might do justice to the various changes in society, family, and child. If Bronfenbrenner's (1979) ecological model is, in a visual sense, a series of circles-within-circles, those circles-within-circles must become more dynamic when considering the parenting of children with disabilities. As Glidden (2002) notes, the entire macro-environment of parenting has changed for these parents, even as the very objects of their parenting—the children—have changed, at least in terms of what professionals know about children's behavior and those interventions and supports that might help. How such field-related knowledge reaches (or does not reach) parents and interventionists is yet another complicated, dynamic issue. Everything, it seems, is changing at all times.

We end this chapter with the sense that, for all our advances, we know too little about these families. Moreover, when we do have knowledge, such findings often appear piecemeal and unconnected. Although such a state of affairs may simply be the hallmark of any field that has a relatively small research community, the number and size of our gaps remain alarming.

Still, even with these problems, one can judge as successful the changes in both society and science as those changes pertain to parenting children with disabilities. Parents and children do benefit from the major societal advances seen in the services and conceptualization of children with disabilities. So, too, have advances occurred in how these families are understood by researchers and practitioners, as represented by the movement from more pathological and less differentiated views to more stress-and-coping perspectives. Scientific advances have also helped us know much more about the biomedical and behavioral characteristics of children with a wide variety of genetic syndromes. Although we have far to go, we remain hopeful that we will continue to learn more about parenting children with disabilities, thereby benefiting the families themselves as well as the larger parenting field in general.

ACKNOWLEDGMENTS

We would like to thank Tom Luster, Lynn Okagaki, Marc Bornstein, and Elisabeth Dykens for their comments on earlier drafts of this chapter. The support of NSF post-doctoral fellowship #0310013 to the second author is also gratefully acknowledged.

REFERENCES

Abidin, R. (1995). *Parenting Stress Index: Professional manual* (3rd ed.). Odessa, FL: Psychological Assessment Resources.

Anderson, L. L., Lakin, K. C., Mangan, T. W., & Prouty, R. W. (1998). State institutions: Thirty years of depopulation and closure. *Mental Retardation, 36*, 431–443.

Bailey, D., Blasco, P., & Simeonsson, R. (1992). Needs expressed by mothers and fathers of young children with disabilities. *American Journal on Mental Retardation, 97*, 1–10.

Beck, A. T., Rush, A. J., Shaw, B. F., & Emory, G. (1971). *Cognitive theory of depression*. New York: Guilford Press.

Bell, R. Q. (1968). A reinterpretation of direction of effects in studies of socialization. *Psychological Review, 75*, 81–95.

Bell, R. Q. (1979). Parent, child, and reciprocal influences. *American Psychologist, 34*, 821–826.

Bellugi, U., Mills, D., Jernigan, T., Hickok, G., & Galaburda, A. (1999). Linking cognition, brain structure, and brain function in Williams syndrome. In H. Tager-Flusberg (Ed.), *Neurodevelopmental disorders* (pp. 111–136). Cambridge: MIT Press.

Blacher, J. (1984). Sequential stages of parental adjustment to the birth of the child with handicaps: Fact or artifact? *Mental Retardation, 22*, 55–68.

Blacher, J., & Baker, B. (Eds.). (2002). *Best of AAMR: Families and mental retardation. A collection of notable AAMR journal articles across the 20th century*. Washington, DC: American Association on Mental Retardation.

Bronfenbrenner, U. (1979). *The ecology of human development*. Cambridge, MA: Harvard University Press.

Cahill, B. M., & Glidden, L. M. (1996). Influence of child diagnosis on family and parent functioning: Down syndrome versus other disabilities. *American Journal on Mental Retardation, 101*, 149–160.

Carr, J. (1995). *Down's syndrome: Children growing up*. Cambridge: Cambridge University Press.

Chapman, R. S., & Hesketh, L. J. (2000). Behavioral phenotype of individuals with Down syndrome. *Mental Retardation and Developmental Disabilities Research Reviews, 6,* 84–95.

Crnic, K., Friedrich, W., & Greenberg, M. (1983). Adaptation of families with mentally handicapped children: A model of stress, coping, and family ecology. *American Journal of Mental Deficiency, 88,* 125–138.

Cummings, S. (1976). The impact of the child's deficiency on the father: A study of fathers of mentally retarded and chronically ill children. *American Journal of Orthopsychiatry, 46,* 246–255.

Cummings, S., Bayley, H., & Rie, H. (1966). Effects of the child's deficiency on the mother: A study of mentally retarded, chronically ill, and neurotic children. *American Journal of Orthopsychiatry, 36,* 595–608.

Down, H. L. (1866). Observations of an ethnic classification of idiots. *London Hospital Clinical Lecture and Report, 3,* 259–262.

Drotar, D., Baskiewicz, A., Irvin, N., Kennell, J., & Klaus, M. (1975). The adaptation of parents to the birth of an infant with congenital malformation: A hypothetical model. *Pediatrics, 56,* 710–717.

Dunn, P. M. (1991). Dr. Langdon Down (1828–1896) and "mongolism." *Archives of Disease in Childhood, 66,* 827–828.

Dykens, E. M. (1995). Measuring behavioral phenotypes: Provocations from the "New Genetics." *American Journal on Mental Retardation, 99,* 522–532.

Dykens, E. M. (2002). Are jigsaw puzzle skills spared in persons with Prader-Willi syndrome? *Journal of Child Psychology and Psychiatry, 43,* 343–352.

Dykens, E. M. (2003). Anxiety, fears, and phobias in persons with Williams syndrome. *Developmental Neuropsychology, 23,* 291–316.

Dykens, E. M., & Hodapp, R. M. (2001). Research in mental retardation: Toward an etiologic approach. *Journal of Child Psychology and Psychiatry, 42,* 49–71.

Dykens, E. M., Hodapp, R. M., & Finucane, B. (2000). *Genetics and mental retardation syndromes: A new look at behavior and treatments.* Baltimore: Paul H. Brookes Publishing Company.

Dykens, E. M., & Kasari, C. (1997). Maladaptive behavior in children with Prader-Willi syndrome, Down syndrome, and non-specific mental retardation. *American Journal on Mental Retardation, 102,* 228–237.

Dykens, E. M., Leckman, J. F., & Cassidy, S. B. (1996). Obsessions and compulsions in Prader-Willi syndrome. *Journal of Child Psychology and Psychiatry, 37,* 995–1002.

Essex, E. L., Seltzer, M. M., & Krauss, M. W. (1999). Differences in coping effectiveness and well-being among aging mothers and fathers of adults with mental retardation. *American Journal on Mental Retardation, 104,* 454–563.

Farber, B. (1959). The effects of the severely retarded child on the family system. *Monographs of the Society for Research in Child Development, 24,* no. 2.

Farber, B. (1960). Family organization and crisis: Maintenance of integration in families with a severely mentally retarded child. *Monographs of the Society for Research in Child Development, 25,* no. 1.

Fidler, D. J., Hodapp, R. M., & Dykens, E. M. (2000). Stress in families of young children with Down syndrome, Williams syndrome, and Smith-Magenis syndrome. *Early Education and Development, 11,* 395–406.

Fidler, D. J., Hodapp, R. M., & Dykens, E. M. (2002). Behavioral phenotypes and special education: Parent report of educational issues for children with Down syndrome, Prader-Willi syndrome, and Williams syndrome. *Journal of Special Education, 36,* 80–88.

Freud, S. (1917). Mourning and melancholia. (Reprinted from *A general selection from the works of Sigmund Freud,* pp. 124–140, by J. Rickman, Ed., 1957, Garden City, NY: Doubleday)

Friedrich, W. L., & Freidrich, W. N. (1981). Psychosocial assets of parents of handicapped and nonhandicapped children. *American Journal of Mental Deficiency, 85,* 551–553.

Friedrich, W. N., Greenberg, M. T., & Crnic, K. (1983). A short-form of the Questionnaire on Resources and Stress. *American Journal on Mental Deficiency, 88,* 41–48.

Gibson, D. (1978). *Down syndrome: The psychology of mongolism.* Cambridge: Cambridge University Press.

Glidden, L. M. (2002). Parenting children with developmental disabilities: A ladder of influence. In J. L. Borkowski, S. L. Ramey, & M. Bristol-Powers (Eds.), *Parenting and the child's world: Influences on academic, intellectual, and socio-emotional development* (pp. 329–344). *Monographs in Parenting.* Mahwah, NJ: Lawrence Erlbaum Associates.

Graham, S. (1991). A review of attribution theory in achievement contexts. *Educational Psychology Review, 3,* 5–39.

Hallahan, D. P., & Kauffman, J. M. (2002). *Exceptional children: Introduction to Special Education* (9th ed.). Boston: Allyn & Bacon.

Hanson, M., & Hanline, M. F. (1990). Parenting a child with a disability: A longitudinal study of parental stress and adaptation. *Journal of Early Intervention, 14,* 234–248.

Hodapp, R. M. (1996). Down syndrome: Developmental, psychiatric, and management issues. *Child and Adolescent Psychiatric Clinics of North America, 5,* 881–894.

Hodapp, R. M. (1997). Direct and indirect behavioral effects of different genetic mental retardation disorders. *American Journal on Mental Retardation, 102,* 67–79.

Hodapp, R. M. (1999). Indirect effects of genetic mental retardation disorders: Theoretical and methodological issues. *International Review of Research in Mental Retardation, 22,* 27–50.

Hodapp, R. M. (2002). Parenting children with mental retardation. In M. Bornstein (Ed.), *Handbook of parenting, 2nd ed.: Vol. 1. How children influence parents* (pp. 355–381). Mahwah, NJ: Lawrence Erlbaum Associates.

Hodapp, R. M. (2004). Studying interactions, reactions, and perceptions: Can genetic disorders serve as behavioral proxies? *Journal of Autism and Developmental Disorders, 34,* 29–34.

Hodapp, R. M., & Dykens, E. M. (2004). Studying behavioral phenotypes: Issues, benefits, challenges. In E. Emerson, C. Hatton, T. Parmenter, & T. Thompson (Eds.), *International handbook of applied research in intellectual disabilities* (pp. 203–220). New York: John Wiley & Sons.

Hodapp, R. M., Evans, D. W., & Gray, F. L. (1999). Intellectual development in children with Down syndrome. In J. Rondal, J. Perera, & L. Nadel (Eds.), *Down syndrome: A review of current knowledge* (pp. 124–132). London: Whurr.

Hodapp, R. M., & Fidler, D. J. (1999). Special education and genetics: Connections for the 21st century. *Journal of Special Education, 33,* 130–137.

Hodapp, R. M., Ly, T. M., Fidler, D. J., & Ricci, L. A. (2001). Less stress, more rewarding: Parenting children with Down syndrome. *Parenting: Science and Practice, 1,* 317–337.

Hodapp, R. M., Ricci, L. A., Ly, T. M., & Fidler, D. J. (2003). The effects of the child with Down syndrome on maternal stress. *British Journal of Developmental Psychology, 21,* 137–151.

Holroyd, J., & MacArthur, D. (1976). Mental retardation and stress on parents: A contrast between Down's syndrome and childhood autism. *American Journal on Mental Deficiency, 80,* 431–436.

Hoppes, K., & Harris, S. (1990). Perceptions of child attachment and maternal gratification in mothers of children with autism and Down syndrome. *Journal of Child Clinical Psychology, 19,* 365–370.

Hornby, G. (1995). Fathers' views of the effects on their families of children with Down syndrome. *Journal of Child and Family Studies, 4,* 103–117.

Kasari, C., & Freeman, S. F. N. (2001). Task related social behavior in children with Down syndrome. *American Journal on Mental Retardation, 106,* 253–264.

Kasari, C., Mundy, P., Yirmiya, N., & Sigman, M. (1990). Affect and attention in children with Down syndrome. *American Journal on Mental Retardation, 95,* 55–67.

Kasari, C., & Sigman, M. (1997). Linking parental perceptions to interactions in young children with autism. *Journal of Autism and Developmental Disorders, 27,* 39–57.

Keogh, B. K., Garnier, H. E., Bernheimer, L. P., & Gallimore, R. (2000). Models of child-family interactions for children with developmental delays: Child-driven or transactional? *American Journal on Mental Retardation, 105*, 32–46.

Krauss, M. (1993). Child-related and parenting stress: Similarities and differences between mothers and fathers of children with disabilities. *American Journal on Mental Retardation, 97*, 393–404.

Lakin, C., Prouty, B., Braddock, D., & Anderson, L. (1997). State institution populations: Smaller, older, more impaired. *Mental Retardation, 35*, 231–232.

Lejeune, J., Gautier, M., & Turpin, R. (1959). Etudes des chromosomes somatique de neuf enfants mongoliens. *Comptes Rendus de l'Academie des Sciences, 48*, 1721.

Lobato, D. (1983). Siblings of handicapped children: A review. *Journal of Autism and Developmental Disorders, 13*, 347–364.

Ly, T. M., & Hodapp, R. M. (2002). Maternal attribution of child noncompliance in children with mental retardation: Down syndrome versus other etiologies. *Journal of Developmental and Behavioral Pediatrics, 23*, 322–329.

Ly, T. M., & Hodapp, R. M. (in press). Children with Prader-Willi syndrome vs. Williams syndrome: Indirect effects on parents during a jigsaw puzzle task. *Journal of Intellectual Disability Research.*

Mervis, C. B., Morris, C. A., Bertrand, J. M., & Robinson, B. F. (1999). Williams syndrome: Findings from an integrated program of research. In H. Tager-Flusberg (Ed.), *Neurodevelopmental disorders* (pp. 65–110). Cambridge: MIT Press.

Meyers, B. A., & Pueschel, S. M. (1991). Psychiatric disorders in persons with Down syndrome. *Journal of Nervous and Mental Disease, 179*, 609–613.

Miller, J. (1999). Profiles of language development in children with Down syndrome. In J. F. Miller, M. Leddy, & L. A. Leavitt (Eds.), *Improving the communication of people with Down syndrome* (pp. 11–39). Baltimore, MD: Paul H. Brookes Publishing Company.

Noh, S., Dumas, J. E., Wolf, L. C., & Fisman, S. N. (1989). Delineating sources of stress in parents of exceptional children. *Family Relations, 38*, 456–461.

Okagaki, L., & Divecha, D. J. (1993). Development of parental beliefs. In T. Luster & L. Okagaki (Eds.), *Parenting: An ecological perspective* (pp. 35–67). Hillsdale, NJ: Lawrence Erlbaum Associates.

Olsen, C. L., Cross, P. K., Gensburg, L. J., & Hughes, J. P. (1996). The effects of prenatal diagnosis, population aging, and changing fertility rates on the live birth prevalence of Down syndrome in New York State, 1983–1992. *Prenatal Diagnosis, 16*, 991–1002.

Olshansky, S. (1962). Chronic sorrow: A response to having a mentally defective child. *Social Casework, 43*, 190–193.

Pitcairn, T. K., & Wishart, J. G. (1994). Reactions of young children with Down's syndrome to an impossible task. *British Journal of Developmental Psychology, 12*, 485–489.

Price-Bonham, S., & Addison, S. (1978). Families and mentally retarded children: Emphasis on the father. *The Family Coordinator, 27*, 221–230.

Pueschel, S. R., Gallagher, P. L., Zartler, A. S., & Pezzullo, J. C. (1986). Cognitive and learning profiles in children with Down syndrome. *Research in Developmental Disabilities, 8*, 21–37.

Roach, M. A., Orsmond, G. I., & Barratt, M. S. (1999). Mothers and fathers of children with Down syndrome: Parental stress and involvement in childcare. *American Journal on Mental Retardation, 104*, 422–436.

Ruskin, E. M., Kasari, C., Mundy, P., & Sigman, M. (1994). Attention to people and toys during social and object mastery in children with Down syndrome. *American Journal on Mental Retardation, 99*, 103–111.

Rutter, M., Pickles, A., Murray, R., & Eaves, L. (2001). Testing hypotheses on specific environmental causal effects on behavior. *Psychological Bulletin, 127*, 291–324.

Sanders, J. L., & & Morgan, S. B. (1997). Family stress and adjustment as perceived by parents of children with autism or Down syndrome: Implications for intervention. *Child and Family Behavior Therapy, 19*, 15–32.

Scheerenberger, R. C. (1983). *A history of mental retardation.* Baltimore: Paul H. Brookes Publishing Company.

Scott, B. S., Atkinson, L., Minton, H. L., & Bowman, T. (1997). Psychological distress of parents of infants with Down syndrome. *American Journal on Mental Retardation, 102,* 161–171.

Seltzer, M. M., Krauss, M. W., & Tsunematsu, N. (1993). Adults with Down Syndrome and their aging mothers: Diagnostic group differences. *American Journal on Mental Retardation, 97,* 496–508.

Solnit, A., & Stark, M. (1961). Mourning and the birth of a defective child. *The Psychoanalytic Study of the Child, 16,* 523–537.

Wishart, J. G., & Johnston, F. H. (1990). The effects of experience on attribution of a stereotyped personality to children with Down's syndrome. *Journal of Mental Deficiency Research, 34,* 409–420.

Wolf, L. C., Noh, S., Fisman, S. N., & Speechley, M. (1989). Psychological effects of parenting stress on parents of autistic children. *Journal of Autism and Developmental Disorders, 19,* 157–166.

III

CONTEXTUAL INFLUENCES
ON PARENTING

7

Parenting and the Marital Relationship

Frank D. Fincham
Florida State University

Julie H. Hall
University at Buffalo, The State University of New York

INTRODUCTION

Parent and spouse roles are characterized by numerous expectations and responsibilities that tend to be fulfilled simultaneously as partners in a marriage are often partners in parenting as well. Thus, it can be quite difficult to disentangle marital and parenting processes, and to determine how one relationship impacts the other. Considerable attention has been devoted to exploring how becoming a parent affects the marital relationship; the birth of a child is associated with an increase in marital conflict and a decrease in marital satisfaction, but an increased sense of partnership (Belsky, Lang, Rovine, 1985; Cowan, Cowan, Heming, Garrett, Coysh, Curtis-Boles, & Boles, 1985). Yet at the same time, marital relationships also exert a considerable influence on parenting processes and behaviors. Given the nature of this book, we focus on this aspect of the association between marriage and parenting.

In Bronfenbrenner's (1979, 1992) ecological model, the marital relationship constitutes part of a child's microsystem, and thus directly influences the child. Behavioral exchanges between spouses are one of the major vehicles through which the immediate environment directly affects a child's psychological growth (Bronfenbrenner, 1979, 1992). Beyond the direct effects of the marital relationship on child development, Bronfenbrenner also highlighted how marriage impacts children indirectly, through the parenting relationship. Such indirect influence, defined as second-order effects, points out how the marital relationship can affect interactions between parent and child (Bronfenbrenner, 1979). The ecological model also emphasizes the importance of the marital relationship as a support system for parenting; Bronfenbrenner (1986) reviewed evidence that mothers who felt supported by their husbands tended to have higher marital satisfaction and more positive attitudes toward parenting. This research helped lay the foundation for much current work on marital and parenting processes, and illustrated the importance of the environment in such processes.

In keeping with Bronfenbrenner's ecological model, this chapter explores the direct effects of the marital relationship on child development, as well as the indirect effects that occur through parenting. We review briefly direct effects, before turning to the primary focus of the chapter, how marital and parenting processes interact to influence child development. Following consideration of the major research in this area, the next section identifies promising avenues for future research. The chapter concludes with a summary of the main arguments.

DIRECT EFFECTS OF THE MARITAL RELATIONSHIP ON CHILD DEVELOPMENT

There is a robust association between marital conflict and child behavior problems. For example, the meta-analysis by Buehler, Anthony, Krishnakumar, and Stone (1997) of 68 studies testing the association between marital conflict and child adjustment showed that the average effect size for this association was .32, midway between a small (.20) and medium (.50) effect as described by Cohen (1977). According to social learning theory, negative marital interactions lead children to adopt similar maladaptive behaviors through the processes of modeling. Children who are repeatedly exposed to marital conflict may acquire negative strategies of conflict resolution and affective expression through observing their parents' behavior (Easterbrooks & Emde, 1988), and they are at greater risk for externalizing disorders (Cummings & Davies, 1994). Children also tend to be more aggressive towards peers after observing an angry argument between adults (Cummings, Iannotti, & Zahn-Walker, 1985), and are more likely to have social problems with siblings and peers (Stocker & Youngblade, 1999).

There is also a direct relation between marital conflict and disorganized-disoriented infant attachment behavior (Owen & Cox, 1997). It has been suggested that exposure to negative marital interactions adversely affects the organization of children's emotional response to stressful situations (Davies & Cummings, 1994). Owen and Cox (1997) argued that exposure to chronic marital conflict leads infants to experience their parents as frightening, and to have limited options for alleviating accompanying distress. In contrast, marital satisfaction is associated with secure attachment in toddlers (Goldberg & Easterbrooks, 1984).

Specific aspects of marital conflict appear to have differential effects on child adjustment; Buehler and colleagues (1997) showed that effect sizes differed depending on how conflict was expressed. Studies assessing overt conflict, defined as direct expressions of hostile behavior and affect, produced a larger effect size (.35) than studies examining covert conflict (.28), in which hostility is expressed indirectly, withdrawal from conflict (.27), or studies simply measuring conflict frequency (.19). These differences suggest that the way parents manage conflict, rather than its occurrence per se, determines its impact on children.

The direct relation between marital conflict and child adjustment can also be understood by conceptualizing conflict as a stressor on children (Fincham, Grych, & Osborne, 1994; Wilson & Gottman, 1995). Children report that observing interparental conflict is a significant stressor (Lewis, Siegal, & Lewis, 1984), and observational studies show that children typically exhibit distress when exposed to angry or aggressive interactions involving their parents (see Cummings, Davies & Campbell, 2000). Even at a young age, children become distressed when observing family conflict (Cummings, Zahn-Walker, Radke-Yarrow, 1981), and that distress increases with more frequent exposure to anger and aggression (Cummings et al., 1985). Exposure to conflict has also been found to threaten children's sense of safety and emotional security (Davies & Cummings, 1994).

However, as noted, interparental conflict may not be intrinsically damaging to children; rather, *how* conflict is handled may determine whether the interaction will serve as a stressor for the child. Frequent conflicts that are intense, unresolved, and child-related tend to be more distressing to children than non-child related conflicts that are resolved constructively and nonaggressively (Grych & Fincham, 1992). It has also been suggested that children are more affected by marital conflict when parent-to-child hostility is expressed during the course of the conflict (Gordis, Margolin, & John, 2001).

Although some scholars have argued that the relation between conflict and child adjustment is due to the effects of marital conflict on parenting (e.g., Fauber & Long, 1991), others have argued that this relation cannot be reduced to variations in parenting. In support of this position it is noted that overt marital conflict has a greater impact on children than covert conflict (Emery, Fincham, & Cummings, 1992) and that children's perceptions of marital conflict tend to be related to their adjustment (Cummings, Davies, & Simpson, 1994; Harold, Fincham, Osborne, & Conger, 1997). Such findings would be unlikely if parenting processes accounted for all of the variance in child adjustment.

INDIRECT EFFECTS OF THE MARITAL RELATIONSHIP
ON CHILD DEVELOPMENT

Parenting has consistently been shown to play a mediating role in the relation between marital quality and child functioning. High marital quality is
associated with sensitive parenting and optimal toddler functioning (e.g.,
Goldberg & Easterbrooks, 1984), whereas marital discord undermines and
disrupts effective parenting practices and is associated with poor child adjustment (Belsky, 1984; Fauber & Long, 1991; Reid & Crisafulli, 1990).
However, before one can fully explore such associations, it is critical to examine central constructs. For example, Erel and Burman (1995) were not
able to test adequately whether relevant variables moderated the association between the marital and parent–child relationships owing to the heterogeneity of effect sizes within categories of the moderator variables that
they examined (e.g., different operationalizations of marital quality).

Marital Quality Is Not Marital Quality Is Not Marital Quality

Much of the literature regarding the marriage–parenting association has
focused on the general concept of marital quality, and how it relates to
parenting practices. As noted by Erel and Burman (1995) and Goldberg
and Easterbrooks (1984), however, studies have varied widely in the conceptualization and measurement of marital quality. The emergence of a
replicable association between marital quality and the quality of parenting
is noteworthy. But both of these constructs are multidimensional. Thus, it is
important to distinguish among their dimensions and to consider how specific aspects of the marital relationship are associated with specific aspects
of parenting. The importance of such conceptual development is emphasized by the fact that even the most sophisticated statistical analyses cannot
clarify ambiguous constructs.

Erel and Burman (1995) identified three conceptualizations of marital
quality used by researchers: general marital satisfaction, overt marital conflict, and marital coalition. Before we consider the first two of these in
greater detail, it is important to note that parenting can be conceptualized
along numerous dimensions, including global quality, satisfaction, covert
control, discipline, or within/between parent consistency. However, the
majority of the studies in Erel and Burman's (1995) meta-analysis measured
marital quality in terms of marital satisfaction and the parent–child relationship in terms of global quality. Nevertheless, it is important to consider
these distinctions when reviewing the literature, as a general association between marital quality and parenting could reflect several different relationships.

What is Marital Satisfaction?   This is not the context in which to offer a definitive answer to this question, and we therefore limit ourselves to two observations. First, two of the most commonly used measures of marital satisfaction, the Marital Adjustment Test (MAT; Locke & Wallace, 1959) and Dyadic Adjustment Scale (DAS; Spanier, 1976), combine heterogeneous question types, including general evaluative questions and specific descriptive questions about behavior (e.g., communication, affection). As a result, these scales may overestimate associations between marital quality and self-reported interpersonal processes within marriage because of item overlap (Bradbury, Fincham, & Beach, 2000; Feeney, Noller, & Ward, 1997). This has led some researchers to suggest that global, evaluative measures of marital satisfaction (e.g., Quality Marriage Index, QMI; Norton, 1983; Kansas Marital Satisfaction Scale, KMSS; Schumm, Paff-Bergen, Hatch, Obiorah, Copeland, Meens, & Bugaighis, 1986) are more appropriate when seeking to capture an individual's overall sentiment toward the marriage (Fincham, 1998; Fincham & Bradbury, 1987). However, global measures are only appropriate when the researcher is seeking to measure marital quality as an overall evaluative judgment, and they are less useful when information is sought about specific dimensions of marital quality.

Second, it is important to note that marital satisfaction is not the mere absence of dissatisfaction, and that satisfaction and dissatisfaction are not necessarily inversely related (Bradbury et al., 2000). In actuality, it is possible for an individual to evaluate his or her marriage as both positive and negative (Fincham, Beach, & Kemp-Fincham, 1997; Fincham & Linfield, 1997). Conceptualizating marital quality as bi-dimensional allows researchers to distinguish between people who may score similarly on measures of global marital satisfaction, despite the fact that some are high in positivity and negativity (i.e., ambivalent), whereas others are low on both dimensions (i.e. indifferent; see Fincham & Linfield, 1997). Few researchers have so far adopted this bi-dimensional approach.

In summary, then, marital quality has been operationalized in different ways. The vast majority of studies have used the MAT, DAS or some variant of these measures. Increasingly, however, researchers are limiting marital satisfaction to global judgments of the marriage and using separate measures to assess different aspects of marriage (e.g., communication, consensus) that are also tapped by instruments such as the MAT and DAS.

What Is Marital Conflict?   Marital conflict has been conceptualized in several different ways, with most sharing the common themes that conflict can be overt or covert, can arise from the perceived conflict of interests, goals, wishes, expectations, or interference with behavior, and that conflict behaviors vary across time and situation (Fincham & Beach, 1999). Couples can be differentiated based on their marital conflict styles, including physical aggression, verbal aggression, withdrawal, and nondistressed/low levels of conflict (Burman, Margolin, & John, 1993). Marital conflict can also be considered in terms of process, by exploring cycles of escalation and resolution within couples. For example, Burman et al. (1993) found that physically aggressive and nondistressed couples display similar negative conflict behavior patterns, but nondistressed couples are able to exit from negative exchanges more quickly. As with measures of marital satisfaction, measures of marital conflict vary according to the specific dimensions of interest to the researcher.

Overlap Between Satisfaction and Conflict. Although we have discussed marital satisfaction and marital conflict as separate constructs, empirical evidence suggests that conflict directly affects satisfaction in well established relationships (Christensen & Walczynski, 1997). When compared to nondistressed couples, distressed couples experience more frequent conflict (Christensen & Margolin, 1988), engage in more criticism and disagreement, and are more likely to reciprocate negative behaviors. In fact, negative reciprocity is more consistent across different types of situations than is the amount of negative behavior, making it the most reliable overt signature of a dissatisfied marriage. Both frequency and reciprocity of negative behavior are more pronounced in couples where physical aggression is found (Fincham, 2003). Marital conflict also predicts deterioration in relationship satisfaction over time (Karney & Bradbury, 1995). Nevertheless, they are distinct constructs, as it is possible for marriages to be high in conflict and satisfaction or low in both. Furthermore, marital satisfaction and conflict have unique effects on parenting and parent–child behavior. Thus, we continue to consider them separately.

Models of the Association Between Marriage and Parenting

Erel and Burman (1995) found a positive association between marital quality and parenting (the composite mean weighted effect size was .46). Thus, on the whole, harmonious marriages tend to be associated with effective parenting, whereas troubled marriages are linked to maladaptive parenting. This finding supports a spillover model whereby the affective tone of the marriage spills over into the parent–child relationship; it stands in sharp contrast to the alternative compensatory model in which marital quality and parenting quality are posited to be negatively related (Erel & Burman, 1995; Goldberg & Easterbrooks, 1984).

However, there is some empirical support for the compensatory model in which parents are hypothesized to compensate for marital frustration and dissatisfaction by channeling these negative emotions into positive parenting behaviors (Amato, 1986; Belsky, Youngblade, Rovine, & Volling,

1991). Parents may attempt to fill the void left by their unhappy marriage by establishing fulfilling relationships with their children. Nevertheless, Cox, Paley, and Harter (2001) point out that it is difficult to differentiate between genuinely positive parenting and parent–child relationships that seem positive but actually serve to meet the needs of the parent. As a whole, support for the compensatory model is limited and difficult to interpret.

Krishnakumar and Buehler's (2000) meta-analysis of interparental conflict and parenting behaviors suggests a third model, compartmentalization, in which parents are able to maintain the boundaries between their spousal and parenting roles. Such a model requires partners to contain their feelings about the marriage and to not let them contaminate the parent–child relationship. This model implies that there is no relationship between marital quality and parenting. However, neither Erel and Burman (1995) nor Krisnakumar and Buehler (2000) found support for this model in their meta-analyses. In fact the latter authors found an average weighted effect size of –.62 between interparental conflict and positive parenting behaviors which lends further support to the spillover model.

What Processes Account for the Spillover Effect?   Grych (2002) reviewed several conceptual models that might explain the association between marital and parenting domains. Family systems theory accounts for this association through the idea of circular causality in which relationships within the family are reciprocally related. From a stress and coping perspective, the marital relationship is conceptualized as a source of stress or support for parenting processes. Third, the affective spillover model posits that emotional experiences in the marriage carry over to affective expression in parent–child relationships. A fourth conceptual model proposes that spouses in distressed marriages withdraw from their children, leading to problems in parenting. However, it is also possible that a third variable influences behavior in both marital and parenting domains. Although each of these models is theoretically sound, it is difficult to distinguish among them empirically because the processes described in each lead to the same outcomes.

A general theoretical framework would facilitate research on the interrelationship of marriage and parenting, but it is equally important to explore empirically specific associations to identify which elements of marital functioning are linked to parenting. As noted, one important association supported by empirical research is the link between marital satisfaction and quality of parenting.

Marital Satisfaction/Adjustment and Parenting

High marital satisfaction/adjustment is related to parenting that is sensitive, responsive, warm, and accepting (Goldberg & Easterbrooks, 1984; Grych, 2002), whereas lower marital satisfaction is related to permissive parenting and more negative parent–child relationships (DeVito & Hopkins, 2001; Easterbrooks & Emde, 1988). However, the direction of causality in such relationships is uncertain since most data are cross-sectional.

However, there is a handful of relevant longitudinal studies. Kurdek (1998) found that marital adjustment in the first year of marriage was not predictive of parenting satisfaction eight years later. Similarly, Lindahl, Clements, and Markman (1997) showed that parents' affective responsiveness to their children was not predicted by prechild marital satisfaction, but was related to current marital satisfaction. Prebirth marital adjustment also does not predict cognitive and verbal stimulation of the infant (Heinicke, 1995).

In contrast, Shek (1998) found that marital adjustment was longitudinally associated with parent–child relational quality and perceived demands from children, and suggested that marital quality predicted change in parent–child relational quality. Cowan and Cowan (2000) also found that greater marital satisfaction during pregnancy was associated with parenting that was warm, responsive, and structuring when children reached preschool age, whereas marital dissatisfaction predicts more authoritarian and less authoritative parenting (Cowan & Cowan, 1992). Thus, further research is needed to determine the strength of the longitudinal relationship between marital satisfaction/adjustment and parenting. This is an especially interesting area of research because marital satisfaction changes across the life cycle and is generally believed to follow a U-shaped pattern of declining in the early years of parenthood and increasing in the later years (Emery & Tuer, 1993).

In the past decade, efforts to understand the association between marital processes and child development increasingly have focused on how couples express and manage conflict in their relationship. It is now clear that marital conflict is more important for understanding child development than satisfaction (Grych & Fincham, 2001).

Marital Conflict and Parenting

Several studies show that ineffective parenting partially or fully mediates the relation between marital conflict and children's maladjustment (Osborne & Fincham, 1996; Vandewater & Lansford, 1998; Webster-Stratton & Hammond, 1999). Three processes have been suggested to account for such indirect effects; marital conflict disrupts parental discipline, diminishes the affective quality of parent–child interactions, and increases parent–child aggression (Fincham et al., 1994).

Discipline and Affect in Parent–Child Interactions. A meta-analysis suggested that the parenting behaviors impacted most by interparental conflict are harsh discipline and parental acceptance (Krishnakumar & Buehler,

2000). Marital conflict is also related to child rejection, low parental involvement, and low emotional responsivity (Buehler & Gerard, 2002; Fauber, Forehand, Thomas, & Wierson, 1990; Webster-Stratton & Hammond, 1999). Parents often become so consumed by marital conflicts that their parenting behavior grows less effective and more inconsistent (Fauber & Long, 1991). Indeed, marital conflict may drain parent resources to the point that it reduces parents' ability to recognize and respond to the child's emotional needs (Goldberg & Easterbrooks, 1984). Children may perceive parental inattention as rejection, leading to emotional and behavioral problems (Fincham et al., 1994). In addition to diminishing the quantity of parent–child interactions, marital conflict may also influence the quality of these exchanges. Negative affect from the marital context may spillover into parent–child relationships (Kerig, Cowan, & Cowan, 1993), leading to disciplinary techniques that are harsh, critical, and rely on guilt and anxiety induction (Buehler & Gerard, 2002; Fauber et al., 1990; Fincham et al., 1994; Gable, Belsky, & Crnic, 1992; Webster-Stratton & Hammond, 1999). When compared to nondistressed families, tension in distressed families endures for a longer period of time, and marital conflict increases the probability of parent–child conflict (Christensen & Margolin, 1988; Margolin, Christensen, & John, 1996).

Parent–Child Aggression.   Children whose parents engage in physical violence toward one another are at increased risk of being abused by their parents; the median base rate of co-occurrence in clinical samples is 40% (Appel & Holden, 1998). In a nationally representative sample, the conditional probability of child abuse given the presence of partner abuse is 31% (O'Leary, Slep & O'Leary, 2000). Appel and Holden (1998) identified five models that may underlie this association. The simplest is a single perpetrator model, in which one parent (stereotypically the father) aggresses toward spouse and child. This pattern can also be sequential, such that the victim of marital violence becomes aggressive toward the child, or follow a dual model in which one spouse is violent toward his/her partner, and both are violent toward the child.

The remaining two models are bi-directional and thus incorporate the child and victimized partner as active agents in the system. In the marital violence model, both partners are abusive toward one another and towards the child, whereas the family dysfunction model includes a pathway in which the child aggresses towards both parents. Although the single perpetrator model has received the most empirical support, these models have not been empirically contrasted with one another and thus their relative utility remains uncertain. However, some researchers have cautioned that marital conflict and parent–child aggression may not lead to one another; rather, both may arise from a third factor, such as the individual characteristics of one or both parents (e.g., antisocial personality; Fincham et al., 1994).

As noted earlier, a more fine-grained examination of the dimensions of conflict is necessary to advance our understanding of the impact of interparental conflict on parenting, parent–child relationships, and child development. The impact of conflict is likely to depend on the intensity, frequency, resolution, content, and context of the dispute (Cummings & Davies, 1994; Fincham, 2003; Fincham et al., 1994; Zimet & Jacob, 2001). Children's understanding and appraisals of the conflict are also likely to influence its impact as there is already evidence that stable and global attributions for interparental conflict and/or blaming the self leads to negative consequences for the child (Davies & Cummings, 1994; Grych & Fincham, 1990).

In a similar vein there is a small body of research that emphasizes the importance of spousal appraisals, particularly attributions or explanations for marital conflict, for parenting and parent–child relationships.

The Role of Marital Attributions

Maritally distressed couples tend to attribute their difficulties to causes that are stable or unchanging, global (affect many areas of the relationship), and located within the other spouse (see Fincham, 2001). Negative attributions such as these serve to exacerbate and maintain marital difficulties and have been shown to predict behavior in marital interactions (Bradbury & Fincham, 1992). The relation between such conflict promoting attributions and behavior holds across different levels of marital satisfaction (Bradbury, Beach, Fincham, & Nelson, 1996) and is not due to general negative affectivity (Karney, Bradbury, Fincham, & Sullivan, 1994).

Maladaptive marital attributions are also associated with negative attributions for child behavior (Fincham & Grych, 1991). Thus, spouses who interpret their partner's negative behavior as internal, stable, and global tend to perceive their children's misbehavior in the same way, and such attributions influence subsequent behavior. Parents' attributional styles are related to how coercive, harsh, and authoritarian their interactions are with their children (Bugental & Johnston, 2000). Slep and O'Leary (1998) found that mothers who believe that their child is to blame for his/her misbehavior are angrier and more overreactive in their disciplinary responses when compared to mothers who believe their child is not to blame. There is also an association between attributions for child behavior and parental maltreatment of children. Abusive/neglectful mothers tend to make more internal (to the child) and stable attributions for their children's negative behavior than do non-abusive mothers (Larrance & Twentyman, 1983). Similarly, Bugental, Blue, and Cruzcosa (1989) found that parents who perceive themselves as lacking power are most likely to use coercive control tactics with their children.

Brody, Arias, and Fincham (1996) further explored how marital attributions are related to parenting, and also examined the link with children's attributions for negative parental behavior. Consistent with prior research, they found that husbands' and wives' conflict promoting attributions were related to negativity in the marital context, which was associated with harsh, punitive parenting, less involved communicative parenting, and ineffective parent–child communication. Harsh, punitive parenting tends to be associated with conflicted and distant parent–child relationships, whereas involved communicative parenting is associated with harmonious and cohesive parent–child relationships (Collins, 1990). The direct effects of attributions on parent–child relationships were also stronger for fathers than for mothers. Brody et al. (1996) also found that parenting behavior was related to children's attributions for negative parental behavior. Involved communicative parenting was negatively related to children's conflict promoting attributions, and harsh, punitive parenting was positively related (Brody et al., 1996).

Implicit in our discussion thus far is the assumption that the processes discussed are gender neutral. But the same behavior performed by a father versus a mother may be experienced quite differently. Not only might responses differ because boys and girls develop different relationships with fathers and mothers, but factors such as size and strength differences can make a slap delivered with the same force more or less threatening depending on whether the mother slaps the father or vice versa. We therefore turn to consider the role of gender.

Gender Matters

There has been a great deal of controversy as to whether there are systematic differences in the association between marital quality and fathering versus mothering. Several studies have suggested that fathering is more affected by marital quality than is mothering (Belsky et al., 1991; Coiro & Emery, 1998; Easterbrooks & Emde, 1988; Goldberg & Easterbrooks, 1984; Kitzmann, 2000). Some researchers have posited that this is because male familial roles are less defined than those of females, and/or that mothers are better able to maintain boundaries between familial roles (Belsky et al., 1991).

Marital satisfaction and conflict also have been linked to gender differences in parenting behaviors and attitudes. Marital satisfaction is positively related to fathers' childrearing attitudes but is unrelated to the attitudes of mothers (Easterbrooks & Emde, 1988). Fathering is also more likely to be affected by marital conflict than mothering (Coiro & Emery, 1998), with fathers being more likely to withdraw from their wives and children following marital conflict or when in distressed marriages (Christensen & Heavey, 1990; Howes & Markman, 1989). There is an especially strong link between destructive forms of marital conflict and negative fathering behaviors (Lindahl & Malik, 1999). Fathers tend to be less supportive and engaged when interacting with their sons after a conflictual marital discussion whereas mothers do not show such an effect (Kitzmann, 2000). There is also evidence of gender specific longitudinal associations between marital quality and parenting, as deterioration in marital quality over time is associated with more negative and intrusive fathering behavior but facilitative mothering behavior (Belsky et al., 1991).

While these findings may suggest that there is a null or compensatory relation between marital quality and maternal parenting behavior, there is evidence that marital distress is linked to lower maternal involvement and increased negativity (Erel & Burman, 1995; Grych & Fincham, 1990). Furthermore, Osborne and Fincham (1996) found that boys' perceptions of interparental conflict were more strongly associated with mother–child relationships than father–child relationships, and that there was no difference in the associations for girls. As these findings show, it is insufficient merely to introduce gender at the parental level. Only by considering both parent and child gender is it possible to show that interparental conflict is especially deleterious for cross-gender parent child relationships (e.g., Kerig, Cowan, & Cowan, 1993) which, unlike same-sex relationships, predict child outcome even though boys and girls report similar levels of exposure to interparental conflict (Osborne & Fincham, 1996). Despite the considerable attention given to child gender, our understanding of the impact of the interparental relationship on boys versus girls remains limited (see Davies & Lindsay 2001).

Kerig, Cowan, and Cowan (1993) found that, overall, both fathers and mothers tend to respond negatively towards daughters more often than sons. Also, less maritally adjusted fathers behave most negatively towards daughters, whereas mothers in less satisfied marriages are the least accepting of daughter's assertiveness and are more likely to reciprocate their sons' negative affect. However, Reid and Crisafulli (1990) found that there is a stronger association between marital conflict and externalizing child behavior for sons than for daughters. Similarly, Gordis, Margolin, and John (2001) showed that parent-to-child hostility increases the effects of marital hostility on child adjustment among boys but not among girls. This could be due to the fact that boys are less shielded from family conflict than girls (Grych & Fincham, 1990), or that girls are more likely to react with internalizing behaviors than externalizing behaviors. Thus, evidence of gender effects in the association between marriage and parenting is somewhat mixed. It is important that future research examine not only the effects of parent and child gender, but also their interaction (Grych, 2002; Snyder, 1998).

In sum, consideration of parent and child gender is likely to yield a more textured picture of the associations among the marital relationship, parenting and child development. Moving beyond consideration of family dyads is similarly likely to yield a more sophisticated understanding. We therefore turn to briefly consider triadic family interactions.

Triadic Family Interactions

In recent years, it has become increasingly apparent that parents treat their children differently when their spouse is present than they do when alone with their children. However, triadic interactions are extremely complex to study, as they require a focus on three different dyadic relationships, as well as an examination of how the third person influences each of these dyads. Vuchinich, Emery, and Cassidy (1988) found that in situations with dyadic conflict, a third family member intervened more than one-third of time, and often in a way that formed an alliance with one of the parties. Children tended to use distraction tactics to intervene, and girls were more likely than boys to intervene in all family disputes except marital conflicts. Fathers tended to use authority strategies to intervene, whereas mothers used mediational tactics, but mothers and fathers were unlikely to side against each other when intervening in dyadic conflicts.

Early studies showed that parents tend to have less physical contact and talk less to their infants when in triadic situations than they do in dyadic parent–child interactions (Belsky, 1979). However, when looking at adolescents, Gjerde (1986) found that both the quantity and the quality of parenting behaviors changed across contexts, as well as by gender. The quality of mother–son interactions improved when the father was present, with mothers becoming more engaged, secure, consistent, and affective than they were when they were alone with their sons. However, father–son interactions deteriorated in quality when in the presence of the mother, with fathers decreasing in involvement, engagement, and egalitarianism, and increasing in criticism and antagonism. In contrast, Johnson (2001) found that both parents displayed less negative affect and were less engaged with their children in triadic interactions than in dyadic parent–child interactions, but that parental warmth and responsiveness were stable across contexts. There also tends to be greater role differentiation between mothering and fathering in triadic interactions than in dyadic parent–child interactions. Mothers are more at ease and traditional in their mothering role when in the presence of the father. In contrast, fathers are more likely to withdraw from a primary parenting role when in the presence of their wives (Gjerde, 1986; Johnson, 2001).

Marital Conflict and Triadic Interaction. Marital conflict has a negative impact upon triadic family interactions. Kerig (1995) found that marital conflict and dissatisfaction are positively associated with triangulation (cross-generational coalitions) in triadic interactions. Similarly, destructive marital conflicts are associated with parental withdrawal during triadic interactions, and fathering behaviors that are rejecting, coercive, and less emotionally supportive (Lindahl & Malik, 1999). Marital hostility is also associated with fathers being more intrusive and less positively involved in triadic interactions, and mothers displaying more derisive humor (Katz & Gottman, 1996). However, when husbands withdraw from the marriage, mothers are more intrusive and critical in triadic interactions (Katz & Gottman, 1996). There is also a longitudinal association between marital conflict and triadic interaction, as negative escalation of marital discussions before children are born is predictive of coalition formation and low family cohesion, as well as father's triangulation of the child into marital conflict (Lindahl et al., 1997).

Marital Power and Triadic Interaction. Lindahl and Malik (1999) examined how the balance of power within marriage relates to parenting in triadic situations, and classified marriages as balanced, male dominant, or power struggle. The results varied according to gender, level of marital distress, and ethnicity. Mothers from male-dominant marriages were more emotionally supportive in triadic interactions than mothers from power struggle marriages, but only when they were European American and were not maritally distressed. However, maritally distressed fathers from male-dominant marriages were more coercive with sons than fathers from balanced or power struggle marriages. Hispanic American fathers from balanced marriages were more emotionally supportive of sons in triadic interactions than fathers from male-dominant or power struggle marriages. Meanwhile, European American fathers from power struggle marriages were more withdrawn than fathers from the other power groups. These results illustrate the complexity of triadic interactions, and the variety of ways in which marital processes can interact with parenting behavior.

In sum, it is clear that the marital relationship–parenting association cannot be adequately understood without consideration of the broader context of triadic family processes. At the same time, it is apparent that work on triadic family processes is in its infancy. In the next section of the chapter we turn explicitly to identifying directions for future research that might provide a more complete understanding of marriage, parenting, and child development.

FUTURE DIRECTIONS

As emphasized throughout this chapter it is crucial to pinpoint specific aspects of the marital relationship that are associated with specific dimensions of parenting. However, identification of such associations begs the important question of why such associations exist. What processes or mechanisms give rise to the associations? We therefore discuss one particularly promising mechanism before exploring the implications of current marital research for future research on the link between marriage and parenting.

The Search for Mechanism: Coparenting

Coparenting refers to how mothers and fathers function together in their roles as parents, and reflects discrepancies in parenting involvement, as well as the extent to which parents support or undermine one another. Coparenting has been conceptualized bidimensionally, in terms of mutual support in parenting and mutual involvement with the child (McHale, 1995) and has been broken down into four dimensions: family integrity, disparagement, conflict, and reprimand (McHale, 1997). Using this definition, McHale (1997) found evidence of five types of coparenting families: disconnected, supportive, average, distressed–conflicted, and passionate. An alternative conceptualization of coparenting is offered by Margolin, Gordis, and John (2001) who identified three coparenting dimensions: conflict over parenting issues, cooperation, and triangulation. Further distinctions have been drawn between overt and covert coparenting processes, with the former referring to triadic interactions in which both parents and the child are present, whereas the latter refers to dyadic (parent–child) interactions involving family issues when the other partner is not present (Margolin et al., 2001; McHale, 1997). Covert processes illustrate how coparenting continues even in one partner's absence; such behaviors can either strengthen or undermine a child's sense of family integrity (McHale, Lauretti, Talbot, & Pouquette, 2002). McHale and Rasmussen (1998) found that mothers' verbal and nonverbal messages about fathers in the fathers' absence have a powerful influence on the child; children whose mothers engage in negative covert coparenting behavior (e.g., disparagement of the father) are rated by teachers as showing more behavior problems then peers (McHale & Rasmussen, 1998). Thus, both overt and covert coparenting processes may influence child adjustment.

How Is Coparenting Related to Marriage, Parenting, and Child Adjustment?

Co-operative coparenting is positively associated with marital satisfaction and parenting quality. However, it is important to note that coparenting and marital relationships are distinct, because the former is motivated by concern for the child, whereas the latter is motivated by concern for the self, the partner, and/or the dyad (Margolin et al., 2001). Nevertheless, positive coparenting behaviors, such as supporting the other parent's disciplinary attempts, are related to higher marital satisfaction and more effective parenting. In contrast, negative coparenting behaviors, such as disparagement and conflict, are associated with lower marital satisfaction and marital discord (Christensen & Margolin, 1988; McHale, 1997). Belsky, Crnic, and Gable (1995) found that greater differences between spouses (e.g., in terms of demographic factors, personality, and so forth) were associated with unsupportive coparenting, and that this association was strongest in families with high levels of stress. As regards different types of coparenting, supportive coparenting families tend to display high marital satisfaction, whereas disconnected and distressed–conflicted coparenting families express low marital satisfaction (McHale, 1997).

Coparenting is also related to marital conflict. Katz and Gottman (1996) found that marital hostility was associated with hostile and competitive coparenting, lower partner responsiveness and interaction, and greater father withdrawal from children. Coparenting styles are also less democratic after a conflictual marital discussion (Kitzmann, 2000). It has also been suggested that positive coparenting strengthens individual parenting (e.g., Margolin et al., 2001). These findings suggest that marital conflict impairs a couples' abilities to be supportive coparents.

Coparenting is also associated with child adjustment, even after controlling for other factors such as parental well-being and marital quality (McHale, Kuersten-Hogan, Lauretti, & Rasmussen, 2000; McHale & Rasmussen, 1998), parent–child relationship quality (Belsky, Putnam, & Crnic, 1996), and marital conflict (Frosch, Mangelsdorf, & McHale, 2000). Unsupportive coparenting predicts child externalizing behavior, low inhibition, and the severity of child behavior problems (Bearss & Eyberg, 1998; Belsky et al., 1996; Floyd & Zmich, 1991; Schoppe, Mangelsdorf, & Frosch, 2001). McHale and Rasmussen (1998) found that larger parenting discrepancies are predictive of greater child anxiety, whereas more hostile-competitive coparenting and lower harmony predicts higher child aggression. Coparenting is also related to negative peer behavior (McHale, Johnson, & Sinclair, 1999) and children's classroom adjustment, as it predicts attention, passivity/dependence, and grades, even after controlling for child gender and parents' rejection (Stright & Neitzel, 2003).

Gender Differences. Among maritally distressed families, the association between marital quality and coparenting differs by child gender. Marital conflict has been associated with hostile–competitive coparenting in triadic interactions with sons, whereas a link between marital distress and discrepant levels of parental involvement is more characteristic of parent–daughter interactions (McHale, 1995). These findings are consistent with research suggesting that boys are at greater risk for exposure to interparental conflict and childrearing disputes (e.g., Block, Block, & Morrison, 1981), whereas maritally distressed fathers are more likely to withdraw from their daughters (Amato, 1986). However, several other studies, including Margolin et al. (2001) found that child gender did not affect the way that coparenting mediated the link between marital conflict and parenting.

Nevertheless, parent gender may influence coparenting, as Katz and Gottman (1996) found that the spillover from marital to parenting/coparenting processes differed for fathers and mothers. Marital hostility was associated with greater father withdrawal from children in subsequent triadic interactions. On the other hand, husbands' withdrawal from marital conflict was associated with fathers being more positively involved with children in triadic interactions. However, husbands' withdrawal from marital conflict was associated with mothers being less positively involved with children in subsequent triadic interactions. Thus, spousal behavior also plays a role in gendered parenting.

Coparenting as a Mediator. Coparenting lies at the intersection of marital and parent–child relationships, and several studies suggest that coparenting is more proximally and strongly associated with parenting and child adjustment than is the marital relationship (Abidin & Brunner, 1995; Bearss & Eyberg, 1998; Feinberg, 2002; McHale & Rasmussen, 1998). This lends support to the view that coparenting is the mechanism that explains the link between marriage and parenting. Margolin et al. (2001) presented evidence suggesting that coparenting mediates the relation between marital functioning and parenting. More specifically, they found that reports of one's spouse's coparenting mediated the association between spouse reports of marital conflict and one's own parenting practices and stress. The authors suggested that this occurs because "conflict in the marriage may spill over and be reflected in the coparenting relationship, which, in turn, affects the level of efficacy and the amount of stress experienced in the parenting relationship" (p. 4). Margolin et al. (2001) further explained that coparenting may represent a risk mechanism, whereas marital processes are actually risk indicators (Rutter, 1994). Floyd, Gilliom, and Costi-gan (1998) also found that coparenting (parenting alliance) mediated the effects of marital quality on parenting and did not find evidence of a recip-rocal relation (i.e., parenting → marital quality).

Parenting behavior may have a particularly strong influence on child be-havior when coparenting is unsupportive; parental rejection plays an espe-cially important role in predicting attention, passivity/dependence, and grades when supportive coparenting is low (Stright & Neitzel, 2003). Simi-larly, unsupportive coparenting influences externalizing behavior when family structure is less adaptive (Schoppe et al., 2001). This interaction also extends to positive affect in the family—when positive affect is low, suppor-tive coparenting protects against the development of externalizing prob-lems, but when positive affect is high, supportive coparenting is not associ-ated with such problems (Schoppe et al., 2001).

As research on coparenting as a mechanism continues, it will be neces-sary to explore what aspects of marriage are related to coparenting, and which aspects of coparenting are related to parenting. Nevertheless, it is im-portant to recognize that coparenting is only one of several likely mecha-nisms operating in the relation between marriage and parenting. Other possibilities include parent's own adjustment (Cowan & Cowan, 2002; Seifer & Dickstein, 2000), individual personality differences (Belsky et al., 1995), and/or disrupted sibling relationships (Deal, Hagan, Bass, Hether-ington, & Clingempeel, 1999). The field will benefit from further explora-tion of possible mechanisms in this relationship.

Causal Pathways in Relations Among Marriage, Coparenting, and Parenting. The findings described earlier lend further support to a model in which marital conflict affects parenting through changes in coparenting. One dif-ficulty in interpreting such findings is that both coparenting and parenting are, in part, a response to child behavior. As a consequence, they will always covary more with each other than with factors (e.g., marital discord) that may also potentially explain parenting but which are not necessarily direct responses to child behavior. In light of such observations it is perhaps not surprising to note that the relation between marriage and coparenting may be a reciprocal one, in which coparenting styles can also influence marital relations. But virtually no attempt has been made to examine possible bi-directional causal relations.

Two relatively simple steps can be taken to increase confidence in causal inference. First, a temporal dimension can be introduced into correlational studies to determine whether marital conflict (a) precedes the onset of dele-terious coparenting practices and (b) predicts later coparenting independ-ently of earlier coparenting. The converse temporal relations can also be ex-amined allowing investigation of bi-directional relations. Although data from such longitudinal studies are still correlational, they do permit one to make slightly stronger causal inferences. Second, intervention studies allow experimental manipulation and thus stronger causal inference. We therefore highlight the role of intervention research in the next section.

Intervention Research

Although longitudinal studies are informative, they cannot answer questions of causality. Instead, the most powerful way to address the question of directionality in the relations among marriage, coparenting, parenting, and child adjustment is to conduct intervention research.

Coparenting Interventions. A growing body of research suggests that marital quality influences coparenting and one study suggests that the converse may also be true. Belsky and Hsieh (1998) found that unsupportive coparenting predicted a later deterioration in marital quality. Should future research show that coparenting mediates the relation between marriage and parenting, interventions targeted at coparenting could be valuable.

Feinberg (2002) suggested that the coparenting relationship is a more malleable intervention target than the marital relationship and has the potential to bring about greater improvements in parenting processes. Positive coparenting appears to help buffer the deleterious effects of marital distress and conflict on parenting (Feinberg, 2002; Margolin et al., 2001). Such findings have led researchers to suggest that improving the quality of coparenting will enhance parenting sensitivity, warmth, and consistency, which will in turn lead to positive emotional consequences for children (Feinberg, 2002). Thus, coparenting interventions may be a powerful way to control the negative effects of marriage on parenting and determine the nature of potential causal relations between the two variables.

Marital and Parenting Intervention Research. Intervention research can also explore whether marital/parenting therapy benefits child adjustment and/or whether family therapy improves marital relations and parenting. Cowan and Cowan (2002) point out that, if a family-based intervention "produces a positive change in parent–child or marital relationship quality, *and if change in these two central family relationships is associated with improvement in the child's adaptation,* that would constitute strong support, though not absolute proof, of the causal relevance of family relationship patterns to the child outcomes under study" (pp. 733–734). These issues are important in choosing the most effective course of treatment for child behavior problems, and can also inform preventive interventions. Cowan and Cowan (2002) acknowledge that even with random assignment to intervention condition, intervention studies establish associations between risk and outcome, but do not address the issue of etiology.

There is very little existing research examining the interplay of marital quality, parenting, and child adjustment in family interventions. However, it has been demonstrated that parenting interventions are associated with improved child adjustment (see Cowan & Cowan, 2002). Parent training is also associated with improved marital satisfaction—but only for troubled couples, not those who are satisfied (Brody & Forehand, 1985). As regards the link between marital quality and child adjustment, Dadds, Schwartz, and Sanders (1987) explored how marital discord affects treatment outcome in behavioral treatment of child conduct disorders. They compared child management (CMT) to a combination of CMT and partner support training that focused on marital issues such as conflict and communication. At follow-up, children whose parents received the treatment combination performed significantly better than children whose parents received only CMT, but again only for couples with marital discord.

Few marital interventions have looked beyond how the intervention affects the marriage, to explore its affects on parenting, coparenting, and child adjustment. Cowan, Cowan, Ablow, Johnson, and Measelle (in press) recently conducted a study in which maritally focused couples groups and parenting focused couples groups were compared to controls, and found that the interventions affected the appropriate mediators (i.e., marital vs. parenting quality), and that these mediators were associated with child adjustment one to two years later. However, couples in the parenting focused groups showed improvements in parenting but not in marital interaction, whereas couples in the maritally focused groups showed improvement in both areas. This suggests a marriage → parenting → child adjustment pathway, rather than vice versa. Consistent with such a model, Oltmanns, Broderick, and O'Leary (1977) found that improvements in child behavior were not associated with improvements in marital satisfaction, and Margolin and Christensen (1981) showed that marital therapy improves both marital and parent–child problems, but family therapy does not help marital problems. These findings are consistent with Bronfenbrenner's (1979) observations about second order effects in that improving the marriage had a salutary impact on parenting.

Cowan and Cowan (2002) make several suggestions for the future of intervention research. They first highlight the importance of linking theories of development and theories of intervention explicitly rather than implicitly. They also proposed that researchers test a wider variety of theories and attempt to narrow the gap between correlational data and results of intervention studies. Research will further benefit from including fathers in intervention studies and focusing on moderators and mediators. Finally, these authors suggested that we emphasize developmental outcomes rather than just child adaptation. The bottom line is that the field of intervention research on parenting and coparenting needs to move beyond asking if an intervention works, to ask whom it works for and under what conditions, and to focus on specific intervention targets (Cowan & Cowan, 2002).

In addition to an increased focus on intervention our understanding of the relation among marital processes, parenting, and child development will benefit from attention to recent advances in marital research, a topic that we now briefly address.

Recent Developments in Marital Research

Recent calls have been made to reconsider the role of conflict in marriage (e.g., Bradbury, Rogge & Lawrence, 2001; Fincham, 2003). These calls reflect, in part, recognition of the fact that couple conflict varies according to contextual factors. For example, conflictual marital interactions occur more frequently in couples' homes on days of high general life stress (e.g., Repetti, 1989), and at times and places associated with multiple competing demands (e.g., Halford, Gravestock, Lowe, & Scheldt, 1992). Similarly the interior context of the marriage is important for understanding marital conflict. For example, in the context of poor support communication, conflict produces the greatest risk of marital deterioration (Pasch & Bradbury, 1998; see also Carels & Baucom, 1999; Saitzyk, Floyd, & Kroll, 1997), whereas in the context of high levels of affectional expression between spouses, the inverse correlation between negative spouse behavior and marital satisfaction decreases significantly (Huston & Chorost, 1994).

As a result, greater attention is being paid to positive aspects of marriage, a development further facilitated by the emergence of positive psychology (Sheldon & King, 2001), with its emphasis on shifting attention from repairing distressed marriages to building up happy, satisfying marriages (Seligman, 2002). This shift is paralleled in the more general family literature. As noted by McHale, Kuersten, and Lauretti (1996), much of the current research on family processes focuses on conflict, and we must look beyond that in order for the field to progress.

The implications are relatively straightforward. First, the ecological niche of the couple—their life events, family constellation, socioeconomic standing, and stressful circumstances—can no longer be ignored. For example, Conger, Rueter, and Elder (1999) found that economic pressure in a sample of predominantly rural families at Time 1 predicted individual distress and observed marital conflict at Time 2, which in turn predicted marital distress at Time 3. Such findings have lead to the argument that it may be "at least as important to examine the struggle that exists between the couple . . . and the environment they inhabit as it is to examine the interpersonal struggles that are the focus of our work" (Bradbury et al., 2001, p.76). To the extent that work on marriage and parenting takes into account the broader ecological niche of the couple it is likely to be more informative.

Second, it is important to recognize the processes that promote and maintain good marriages, and examine how they relate to parenting. Focusing on positive marital processes and strengths will allow researchers to broaden their conceptual frameworks and look at a range of emotions, not solely negative ones. It has become increasingly apparent that marital satisfaction and marital conflict are not mutually exclusive, and that positive, satisfying marital processes reflect much more than the absence of negative processes (Fincham, 1998; Reis & Gable, 2003). However, at the same time, we must not conclude that marital conflict is wholly negative; there are no doubt constructive elements that might even be beneficial (e.g., in building resilience in the couple, providing children with a model of conflict resolution). The field will benefit from incorporating into research on parenting and marriage these and other constructive variables such as positive affect (Dix, 1991), communication (McHale et al., 1996), marital intimacy (O'Brien & Peyton, 2002), and spousal supportive behavior (Pasch & Bradbury, 1998).

CONCLUSIONS

In this chapter we map the terrain that stands at the interface of marital and parenting research. Our initial brief review of the direct effects of marital processes on child development serves as a springboard for an extended discussion of how the marital relationship may be linked to child development via parenting behavior. We consider several models of the association between marital processes and parenting before examining specific ways in which marital conflict might influence parent behavior. This, in turn, highlights the need to consider marital attributions, child gender and triadic interactions to gain a more complete understanding of the marital relationship–parenting association. In the penultimate section of the chapter, we offer some signposts that might guide future exploration, focusing in particular on coparenting as a process that links marital processes to mothering and fathering and, to a lesser extent, the implications of recent developments in marital research. Although our map is far from complete, we hope it will provide a heuristic stepping stone for cartographers as they develop a more detailed map of the ecology of parenting and its implications for understanding child development.

ACKNOWLEDGMENTS

This chapter was written while the first author was supported by a grant from the National Institute on Alcohol Abuse and Alcoholism (R21AA013690).

REFERENCES

Abidin, R., & Brunner, J. (1995). Development of a parenting alliance inventory. *Journal of Clinical Child Psychology, 24,* 31–40.

Amato, P. (1986). Marital conflict, the parent–child relationship, and child self-esteem. *Family Relations, 35,* 403–410.

Appel, A. E., & Holden, G. W. (1998). The co-occurrence of spouse and physical child abuse: A review and appraisal. *Journal of Family Psychology, 12*(4), 578–599.

Bearss, K., & Eyberg, S. (1998). A test of the parenting alliance theory. *Early Education and Development, 9,* 179–185.

Belsky, J. (1979). Mother–father–infant interaction: A naturalistic observational study. *Developmental Psychology, 15*(6), 601–607.

Belsky, J. (1984). The determinants of parenting: A process model. *Child Development, 55,* 83–96.

Belsky, J., Crnic, K., & Gable, S. (1995). The determinants of coparenting in families with toddler boys: Spousal differences and daily hassles. *Child Development, 66*(3), 629–642.

Belsky, J., & Hsieh, K. (1998). Patterns of marital change during the early childhood years: Parent personality, coparenting, and division-of-labor correlates. *Journal of Family Psychology, 12,* 511–528.

Belsky, J., Lang, M. E., & Rovine, M. (1985). Stability and change in marriage across the transition to parenthood: A second study. *Journal of Marriage and the Family, 47,* 855–865.

Belsky, J., Putnam, S., & Crnic, K. (1996). Coparenting, parenting and early emotional development. In J. P. McHale & P. A. Cowan (Eds.), *Understanding how family-level dynamics affect children's development: Studies of two-parent families* (pp. 45–56). San Francisco: Jossey-Bass.

Belsky, J., Youngblade, L., Rovine, M., & Volling, B. (1991). Patterns of marital change and parent–child interaction. *Journal of Marriage and Family, 53,* 487–498.

Block, J., Block, J., & Morrison, A. (1981). Parental agreement–disagreement on child-rearing orientations and gender-related personality correlates in children. *Child Development, 52,* 965–974.

Bradbury, T. N., Beach, S. R., Fincham, F. D., & Nelson, G. M. (1996). Attributions and behavior in functional and dysfunctional marriages. *Journal of Consulting & Clinical Psychology, 64,* 569–576.

Bradbury, T. N., & Fincham, F. D. (1992). Attributions and behavior in marital interaction. *Journal of Personality & Social Psychology, 63,* 613–628.

Bradbury, T. N., Fincham, F. D., & Beach, S. R. (2000). Research on the nature and determinants of marital satisfaction: A decade in review. *Journal of Marriage and the Family, 62*(4), 964–980.

Bradbury, T. N., Rogge, R., & Lawrence, E. (2001). Reconsidering the role of conflict in marriage. In A. Booth, A. C. Crouter, & M. L. Clements (Eds.), *Couples in conflict* (pp. 59–81). Mahwah, NJ: Lawrence Erlbaum Associates.

Brody, G. H., Arias, I., & Fincham, F. D. (1996). Linking marital and child attributions to family processes and parent–child relationships. *Journal of Family Psychology, 10*(4), 408–421.

Brody, G. H., & Forehand, R. (1985). The efficacy of parent training with maritally distressed and nondistressed mothers: A multimethod assessment. *Behaviour Research and Therapy, 23,* 291–296.

Bronfenbrenner, U. (1979). *The ecology of human development.* Cambridge: Harvard University Press.

Bronfenbrenner, U. (1986). Ecology of the family as a context for human development: Research perspectives. *Developmental Psychology, 22*(6), 723–742.

Bronfenbrenner, U. (1992). Ecological systems theory. In R. Vasta (Ed.), *Six theories of child development: Revised formulations and current issues* (pp. 187–249). London: Jessica Kingsley Publishers.

Buehler, C., Anthony, C., Krishnakumar, A., & Stone, G. (1997). Interparental conflict and youth problem behaviors: A meta-analysis. *Journal of Child & Family Studies, 6,* 223–247.

Buehler, C., & Gerard, J. M. (2002). Marital conflict, ineffective parenting, and children's and adolescents' maladjustment. *Journal of Marriage and Family, 64,* 78–92.

Bugental, D. B., Blue, J., & Cruzcosa, M. (1989). Perceived control over caregiving outcomes: Implications for child abuse. *Developmental Psychology, 25*(4), 532–539.

Bugental, D. B., & Johnston, C. (2000). Parental and child cognitions in the context of the family. *Annual Review of Psychology, 51,* 315–344.

Burman, B., Margolin, G., & John, R. S. (1993). America's angriest home videos: Behavioral contingencies observed in home reenactments of marital conflict. *Journal of Consulting and Clinical Psychology, 61*(1), 28–39.

Carels, R. A., & Baucom, D. H. (1999). Support in marriage: Factors associated with on-line perceptions of support helpfulness. *Journal of Family Psychology, 13,* 131–144.

Christensen, A., & Heavey, C. L. (1990). Gender and social structure in the demand/withdraw pattern of marital conflict. *Journal of Personality & Social Psychology, 59*(1), 73–81.

Christensen, A., & Margolin, G. (1988). Conflict and alliance in distressed and non-distressed families. In R. Hinde & J. Stevenson-Hinde (Eds.), *Relationships within families* (pp. 263–282). Oxford: Clarendon Press.

Christensen, A., & Walczynski, P. T. (1997). Conflict and satisfaction in couples. In R. J. Sternberg & M. Hojjat (Eds.), *Satisfaction in close relationships* (pp. 249–274). New York: The Guilford Press.

Cohen, J. (1977). *Statistical power analysis for the behavioral sciences.* New York: Academic Press.

Coiro, M. J., & Emery, R. E. (1998). Do marriage problems affect fathering more than mothering? A quantitative and qualitative review. *Clinical Child and Family Psychology Review, 1*(1), 23–40.

Collins, W. A. (1990). Parent–child relationships in the transition to adolescence: Continuity and change in interaction, affect, and cognition. In R. Montemayor, G. Adams, & T. Gullotta (Eds.), *Advances in adolescent development: Vol. 2. From childhood to adolescence: A transitional period?* (pp. 85–106). Beverly Hills, CA: Sage.

Conger, R. D., Rueter, M. A., & Elder, G. H., Jr. (1999). Couple resilience to economic pressure. *Journal of Personality and Social Psychology, 76,* 54–71.

Cowan, C. P., & Cowan, P. A. (1992). *When partners become parents: The big life change for couples.* New York: Basic Books.

Cowan, C. P., & Cowan, P. A. (2000). *When partners become parents: The big life change for couples.* Mahwah, NJ: Lawrence Erlbaum Associates.

Cowan, P. A., & Cowan, C. P. (2002). Interventions as tests of family systems theories: Marital and family relationships in children's development and psychopathology. *Development and Psychopathology, 14,* 731–759.

Cowan, P. A., Cowan, C. P., Ablow, J., Johnson, V. K., & Measelle, J. (Eds.). (in press). *The family context of parenting in children's adaptation to elementary school.* Mahwah, NJ: Lawrence Erlbaum Associates.

Cowan, C. P., Cowan, P. A., Heming, G., Garrett, E., Coysh, W. S., Curtis-Boles, H., & Boles, A. J. (1985). Transition to parenthood: His, hers, and theirs. *Journal of Family Issues, 6,* 451–481.

Cox, M. J., Paley, B., & Harter, K. (2001). Interparental conflict and parent–child relationships. In J. H. Grych & F. D. Fincham (Eds.), *Interparental conflict and child development: Theory, research, and applications* (pp. 249–272). Cambridge: Cambridge University Press.

Cummings, E. M., & Davies, P. (1994). *Children and marital conflict: The impact of family dispute and resolution.* New York: The Guilford Press.

Cummings, E. M., Davies, P. T., & Campbell, S. B. (2000). *Developmental psychopathology and family process.* New York: Guilford Press.

Cummings, E. M., Davies, P. T., & Simpson, K. S. (1994). Marital conflict, gender, and children's appraisals and coping efficacy as mediators of child adjustment. *Journal of Family Psychology, 8*(2), 141–149.

Cummings, E. M., Iannotti, R. J., & Zahn-Walker, C. (1985). The influence of conflict between adults on the emotions and aggression of young children. *Developmental Psychology, 21*, 495–507.

Cummings, E. M., Zahn-Walker, C., & Radke-Yarrow, M. (1981). Young children's responses to expressions of anger and affection by others in the family. *Child Development, 52*, 1274–1282.

Dadds, M. R., Schwartz, S., & Sanders, M. R. (1987). Marital discord and treatment outcome in behavioral treatment of child conduct disorders. *Journal of Consulting and Clinical Psychology, 55*, 396–403.

Davies, P. T., & Cummings, E. M. (1994). Marital conflict and child adjustment: An emotional security hypothesis. *Psychological Bulletin, 116*(3), 387–411.

Davies, P. T., & Lindsay, L. L. (2001). Does gender moderate the effects of marital conflict on children? In J. H. Grych & F. D. Fincham (Eds.), *Interparental conflict and child development: Theory, research, and applications* (pp. 64–97). Cambridge: Cambridge University Press.

Deal, J. E., Hagan, M. S., Bass, B., Hetherington, E. M., & Clingempeel, G. (1999). Marital interaction in dyadic and triadic contexts: Continuities and discontinuities. *Family Process, 38*(1), 105–115.

DeVito, C., & Hopkins, J. (2001). Attachment, parenting, and marital dissatisfaction as predictors of disruptive behavior in preschoolers. *Development and Psychopathology, 13*, 215–231.

Dix, T. (1991). The affective organization of parenting: Adaptive and maladaptive processes. *Psychological Bulletin, 110*, 3–25.

Easterbrooks, M. A., & Emde, R. N. (1988). Marital and parent–child relationships: The role of affect in the family system. In R. Hinde & J. Stevenson-Hinde (Eds.), *Relationships within families* (pp. 83–103). Oxford: Clarendon Press.

Emery, R. E., Fincham, F. D., & Cummings, E. M. (1992). Parenting in context: Systemic thinking about parental conflict and its influence on children. *Journal of Consulting and Clinical Psychology, 60*, 909–912.

Emery, R. E., & Tuer, M. (1993). Parenting and the marital relationship. In T. Luster & L. Okagaki (Eds.), *Parenting: An ecological perspective* (pp. 121–148). Hillsdale, NJ: Lawrence Erlbaum Associates.

Erel, O., & Burman, B. (1995). Interrelatedness of marital relations and parent–child relations: A meta-analytic review. *Psychological Bulletin, 118*, 108–132.

Fauber, R., Forehand, R., Thomas, A. M., & Wierson, M. (1990). A mediational model of the impact of marital conflict on adolescent adjustment in intact and divorced families: The role of disrupted parenting. *Child Development, 61*, 1112–1123.

Fauber, R. L., & Long, N. (1991). Children in context: The role of the family in child psychotherapy. *Journal of Consulting and Clinical Psychology, 59*, 813–820.

Feeney, J. A., Noller, P., & Ward, C. (1997). Marital satisfaction and spousal interaction. In R. J. Sternberg & M. Hojjat (Eds.), *Satisfaction in close relationships* (pp. 160–189). New York: The Guilford Press.

Feinberg, M. E. (2002). Coparenting and the transition to parenthood: A framework for prevention. *Clinical Child and Family Psychology Review, 5*(3), 173–195.

Fincham, F. D. (1998). Child development and marital relations. *Child Development, 69*, 543–574.

Fincham, F. D. (2001). Attributions and close relationships: From balkanization to integration. In G. J. Fletcher & M. Clark (Eds.), *Blackwell handbook of social psychology* (pp. 3–31). Oxford: Blackwells.

Fincham, F. D. (2003). Marital conflict: Correlates, structure, and context. *Current Directions in Psychological Science, 12*, 23–27.

Fincham, F. D., & Beach, S. R. (1999). Conflict in marriage: Implications for working with couples. *Annual Review of Psychology, 50,* 47–77.

Fincham, F. D., Beach, S. R., & Kemp-Fincham, S. I. (1997). Marital quality: A new theoretical perspective. In R. J. Sternberg & M. Hojjat (Eds.), *Satisfaction in close relationships* (pp. 275–304). New York: The Guilford Press.

Fincham, F. D., & Bradbury, T. N. (1987). The assessment of marital quality: A reevaluation. *Journal of Marriage and the Family, 49,* 797–809.

Fincham, F. D., & Grych, J. H. (1991). Explanations for family events in distressed and nondistressed couples: Is one type of explanation used consistently? *Journal of Family Psychology, 4,* 341–353.

Fincham, F. D., Grych, J. H., & Osborne, L. N. (1994). Does marital conflict cause child maladjustment? Directions and challenges for longitudinal research. *Journal of Family Psychology, 8,* 128–140.

Fincham, F. D., & Linfield, K. J. (1997). A new look at marital quality: Can spouses feel positive and negative about their marriage? *Journal of Family Psychology, 11,* 489–502.

Floyd, F. J., Gilliom, L. A., & Costigan, C. L. (1998). Marriage and the parenting alliance: Longitudinal prediction of change in parenting perceptions and behaviors. *Child Development, 69,* 1461–1479.

Floyd, F. J., & Zmich, D. E. (1991). Marriage and the parenting partnership: Perceptions and interactions of parents with mentally retarded and typically developing children. *Child Development, 62,* 1434–1448.

Frosch, C., Mangelsdorf, S., & McHale, J. (2000). Marital behavior and the security of preschooler-parent attachment relationships. *Journal of Family Psychology, 14,* 144–161.

Gable, S., Belsky, J., & Crnic, K. (1992). Marriage, parenting, and child development: Progress and prospects. *Journal of Family Psychology, 5*(3/4), 276–294.

Gjerde, P. F. (1986). The interpersonal structure of family interaction settings: Parent–adolescent relations in dyads and triads. *Developmental Psychology, 22*(3), 297–304.

Goldberg, W. A., & Easterbrooks, M. A. (1984). Role of marital quality in toddler development. *Developmental Psychology, 20,* 504–514.

Gordis, E. B., Margolin, G., & John, R. S. (2001). Parents' hostility in dyadic marital and triadic family settings and children's behavior problems. *Journal of Consulting and Clinical Psychology, 69,* 727–734.

Grych, J. H. (2002). Marital relationships and parenting. In M. Bornstein (Ed.), *Handbook of parenting: Vol. 4. Social conditions and applied parenting* (pp. 203–225). Mahwah, NJ: Lawrence Erlbaum Associates.

Grych, J. H., & Fincham, F. D. (1990). Marital conflict and children's adjustment: A cognitive-contextual framework. *Psychological Bulletin, 108,* 267–290.

Grych, J. H., & Fincham, F. D. (1992). Interventions for children of divorce: Toward greater integration of research and action. *Psychological Bulletin, 111,* 434–454.

Grych, J. H., & Fincham, F. D. (2001). *Interparental conflict and child development: Theory, research, and applications.* Cambridge: Cambridge University Press.

Halford, W. K., Gravestock, F. M., Lowe, R., & Scheldt, S. (1992). Toward a behavioral ecology of stressful marital interactions. *Behavioral Assessment, 14,* 199–217.

Harold, G. T., Fincham, F. D., Osborne, L. N., & Conger, R. D. (1997). Mom and dad are at it again: Adolescent perceptions of marital conflict and adolescent psychological distress. *Developmental Psychology, 33,* 333–350.

Heinicke, C. M. (1995). Determinants of the transition to parenting. In M. H. Bornstein (Ed.), *Handbook of parenting: Vol. 3. Status and social conditions of parenting* (pp. 277–303). Hillsdale, NJ: Lawrence Erlbaum Associates.

Howes, P., & Markman, H. J. (1989). Marital quality and child functioning: A longitudinal investigation. *Child Development, 60,* 1044–1051.

Huston, T. L., & Chorost, A. F. (1994). Behavioral buffers on the effect of negativity on marital satisfaction: A longitudinal study. *Personal Relationships, 1,* 223–239.

Johnson, V. K. (2001). Marital interaction, family organization, and differences in parenting behavior: Explaining variations across family interaction contexts. *Family Process, 40,* 333–342.

Karney, B. R., & Bradbury, T. N. (1995). The longitudinal course of marital quality and stability: A review of theory, method, and research. *Psychological Bulletin, 118,* 3–34.

Karney, B. R., & Bradbury, T. N. (1997). Neuroticism, marital interaction, and the trajectory of marital satisfaction. *Journal of Personality and Social Psychology, 72,* 1075–1092.

Karney, B. R., Bradbury, T. N., Fincham, F. D., & Sullivan, K. T. (1994). The role of negative affectivity in the association between attributions and marital satisfaction. *Journal of Personality & Social Psychology, 66*(2), 413–424.

Katz, L. F., & Gottman, J. M. (1996). Spillover effects of marital conflict: In search of parenting and coparenting mechanisms. In J. P. McHale & P. A. Cowan (Eds.), *Understanding how family-level dynamics affect children's development: Studies of two-parent families* (pp. 57–76). San Francisco: Jossey-Bass.

Kerig, P. K. (1995). Triangles in the family circle: Effects of family structure on marriage, parenting, and child adjustment. *Journal of Family Psychology, 9,* 28–43.

Kerig, P. K., Cowan, P. A., & Cowan, C. P. (1993). Marital quality and gender differences in parent–child interaction. *Developmental Psychology, 29,* 931–939.

Kitzmann, K. M. (2000). Effects of marital conflict on subsequent triadic family interactions and parenting. *Developmental Psychology, 36,* 3–13.

Krishnakumar, A., & Buehler, C. (2000). Interparental conflict and parenting behaviors: A meta-analytic review. *Family Relations, 49,* 25–44.

Kurdek, L. A. (1998). Prospective predictors of parenting satisfaction for fathers and mothers with young children. *Journal of Family Psychology, 12,* 56–65.

Larrance, D. T., & Twentyman, C. T. (1983). Maternal attributions and child abuse. *Journal of Abnormal Psychology, 92*(4), 449–457.

Lewis, C. E., Siegal, J. M., & Lewis, M. A. (1984). Feeling bad: Exploring sources of distress among pre-adolescent children. *American Journal of Public Health, 74,* 117–122.

Lindahl, K. M., Clements, M., & Markman, H. (1997). Predicting marital and parent functioning in dyads and triads: A longitudinal investigation of marital processes. *Journal of Family Psychology, 11,* 139–151.

Lindahl, K. M., & Malik, N. M. (1999). Observations of marital conflict and power: Relations with parenting in the triad. *Journal of Marriage and the Family, 61,* 320–330.

Locke, H. J., & Wallace, K. M. (1959). Short marital adjustment prediction tests: Their reliability and validity. *Marriage and Family Living, 21,* 251–255.

Margolin, G., & Christensen, A. (1981). *The treatment of families with marital and child problems.* Paper presented at the meeting of the Association for Advancement of Behavior Therapy, Toronto.

Margolin, G., Christensen, A., & John, R. S. (1996). The continuance and spillover of everyday tensions in distressed and nondistressed families. *Journal of Family Psychology, 10,* 304–321.

Margolin, G., Gordis, E. B., & John, R. S. (2001). Coparenting: A link between marital conflict and parenting in two-parent families. *Journal of Family Psychology, 15,* 3–21.

McHale, J. P. (1995). Coparenting and triadic interactions during infancy: The roles of marital distress and child gender. *Developmental Psychology, 31,* 985–996.

McHale, J. P. (1997). Overt and covert parenting processes in the family. *Family Process, 36,* 183–201.

McHale, J. P., Johnson, D., & Sinclair, R. (1999). Family dynamics, preschoolers' family representations, and preschool peer relationships. *Early Education & Development, 10,* 373–401.

McHale, J. P., Kuersten, R., & Lauretti, A. (1996). New directions in the study of family-level dynamics during infancy and early childhood. In J. P. McHale & P. A. Cowan (Eds.), *Under-*

standing how family-level dynamics affect children's development: Studies of two-parent families (pp. 5–26). San Francisco: Jossey-Bass.

McHale, J. P., Kuersten-Hogan, R., Lauretti, A., & Rasmussen, J. L. (2000). Parental reports of coparenting and observed coparenting behavior during the toddler period. *Journal of Family Psychology, 14*, 220–236.

McHale, J. P., Lauretti, A., Talbot, J., & Pouquette, C. (2002). Retrospect and prospect in the psychological study of coparenting and family group process. In J. P. McHale & W. S. Grolnick (Eds.), *Retrospect and prospect in the psychological study of families* (pp. 127–165). Mahwah, NJ: Lawrence Erlbaum Associates.

McHale, J. P., & Rasmussen, J. L. (1998). Coparental and family group-level dynamics during infancy: Early family precursors of child and family functioning during preschool. *Development & Psychopathology, 10*, 39–59.

Norton, R. (1983). Measuring marital quality: A critical look at the dependent variable. *Journal of Marriage and the Family, 45*, 141–151.

O'Brien, M., & Peyton, V. (2002). Parenting attitudes and marital intimacy: A longitudinal analysis. *Journal of Family Psychology, 16*, 118–127.

O'Leary, K. D., Slep, A., & O'Leary, S. (2000). Co-occurrence of partner and parent aggression: Research and treatment implications. *Behavior Therapy, 31*, 631–648.

Oltmanns, T. F., Broderick, J. E., & O'Leary, K. D. (1977). Marital adjustment and the efficacy of behavior therapy with children. *Journal of Consulting & Clinical Psychology, 45*(5), 724–729.

Osborne, L. N., & Fincham, F. D. (1996). Marital conflict, parent–child relationships, and child adjustment: Does gender matter? *Merrill-Palmer Quarterly, 42*(1), 48–75.

Owen, M. T., & Cox, M. J. (1997). Marital conflict and the development of infant–parent attachment relationships. *Journal of Family Psychology, 11*(2), 152–164.

Pasch, L. A., & Bradbury, T. N. (1998). Social support, conflict, and the development of marital dysfunction. *Journal of Consulting & Clinical Psychology, 66*(2), 219–230.

Reid, W. J., & Crisafulli, A. (1990). Marital discord and child behavior problems: A meta-analysis. *Journal of Abnormal Child Psychology, 18*(1), 105–117.

Reis, H. T., & Gable, S. L. (2003). Toward a positive psychology of relationships. In C. L. Keyes & J. Haidt (Eds.), *Flourishing: Positive psychology and the life well-lived* (pp. 129–159). Washington, DC: American Psychological Association.

Repetti, R. (1989). Effects of daily workload on subsequent behavior during marital interaction: The roles of social withdrawal and spouse support. *Journal of Personality and Social Psychology, 57*, 651–659.

Rutter, M. (1994). Family discord and conduct disorder: Cause, consequence, or correlate? *Journal of Family Psychology, 8*, 170–186.

Saitzyk, A. R., Floyd, F. J., & Kroll, A. B. (1997). Sequential analysis of autonomy-interdependence and affiliation-disaffiliation in couples' social support interactions. *Personal Relationships, 4*, 341–360.

Schoppe, S. J., Mangelsdorf, S. C., & Frosch, C. A. (2001). Coparenting, family process, and family structure: Implications for preschoolers' externalizing behavior problems. *Journal of Family Psychology, 15*(3), 526–545.

Schumm, W. R., Paff-Bergen, L. A., Hatch, R. C., Obiorah, F. C., Copeland, J. M., Meens, L. D., & Bugaighis, M. A. (1986). Concurrent and discriminant validity of the Kansas Marital Satisfaction Scale. *Journal of Marriage and the Family, 48*, 381–387.

Seifer, R., & Dickstein, S. (2000). Parental mental illness and infant development. In C. H. Zeanah, Jr. (Ed.), *Handbook of infant mental health* (2nd ed., pp. 145–160). New York: Guilford Press.

Seligman, M. E. (2002). Positive psychology, positive prevention, and positive therapy. In C. R. Snyder & S. J. Lopez (Eds.), *Handbook of positive psychology* (pp. 3–9). London: Oxford University Press.

Shek, D. T. (1998). Linkage between marital quality and parent–child relationship: A longitudinal study in the Chinese culture. *Journal of Family Issues, 19*(6), 687–703.

Sheldon, K. M., & King, L. (2001). Why positive psychology is necessary. *American Psychologist, 56*(3), 216–217.

Slep, A. S., & O'Leary, S. (1998). The effects of maternal attributions on parenting: An experimental analysis. *Journal of Family Psychology, 12*(2), 234–243.

Snyder, J. R. (1998). Marital conflict and child adjustment: What about gender? *Developmental Review, 18*, 390–420.

Spanier, G. B. (1976). Measuring dyadic adjustment: New scales for assessing the quality of marriage and similar dyads. *Journal of Marriage and the Family, 38*, 15–28.

Stocker, C. M., & Youngblade, L. (1999). Marital conflict and parental hostility: Links with children's sibling and peer relationships. *Journal of Family Psychology, 13*(4), 598–609.

Stright, A. D., & Neitzel, C. (2003). Beyond parenting: Coparenting and children's classroom adjustment. *International Journal of Behavioral Development, 27*(1), 31–39.

Vandewater, E. A., & Lansford, J. E. (1998). Influences of family structure and parental conflict on children's well-being. *Family Relations, 47*(4), 323–330.

Vuchinich, S., Emery, R. E., & Cassidy, J. (1988). Family members and third parties in dyadic family conflict: Strategies, alliances, and outcomes. *Child Development, 59*(5), 1293–1302.

Webster-Stratton, C., & Hammond, M. (1999). Marital conflict management skills, parenting style, and early-onset conduct problems: Processes and Pathways. *Journal of Child Psychology and Psychiatry and Allied Disciplines, 40*, 917–927.

Wilson, B. J., & Gottman, J. M. (1995). Marital interaction and parenting. In M. Bornstein (Ed.), *Handbook of parenting: Vol. 4. Applied and practical parenting* (pp. 33–55). Mahwah, NJ: Lawrence Erlbaum Associates.

Zimet, D. M., & Jacob, T. (2001). Influences of marital conflict on child adjustment: Review of theory and research. *Clinical Child and Family Psychology Review, 4*, 319–335.

8

Parenting and Personal Social Networks

Moncrieff Cochran
Cornell University

Susan K. Walker
University of Maryland, College Park

INTRODUCTION

In this chapter, we examine the effects of parents' personal networks on their parenting attitudes and behaviors. To limit ourselves to that single connection—between personal networks and parenting—would, however, run counter to the ecological perspective guiding this book, because personal networks are, in part, social lines of transmission, carrying the influences of the larger society into the life-space of the individual and family. Thus, to a significant degree, a parent's network reflects her or his position in the social structure of a given society. For that reason, the impacts of that network on parenting attitudes and behavior must be understood as the impacts of that social structure, and his or her location in it.

In order to capture the ecology of parents' networks, and so do justice to ecological influences on parenting, we have organized this chapter around a conceptual framework that includes articulation of the forces influencing the development of parents' networks as well as specification of those network dimensions affecting parenting attitudes and behavior. Using this framework we begin with a definition of the network of interest, and then review studies that illustrate the effects of culture, structural position (class, race, family structure), and neighborhood ecology on the network membership potential available to parents. Then, we examine ways that personal initiatives by the parents themselves might also contribute to the form and content of their networks. Next, there is consideration of evidence bearing on the processes by which network membership influences parenting, and the parenting outcomes that are affected. This is followed by the presentation of evidence suggesting that the size and composition of parents' networks can combine with other influences to affect the ways that children develop, both directly and also indirectly as they affect parenting. Examples from parenting programs are introduced to illustrate how personal social network structural dimensions and interactions can affect parents' participation and receptiveness to external supports, and impact the accomplishment of program goals. Finally we discuss some of the policy implications that flow from what has been learned about the societal factors affecting network development, and the effects of those networks on parents and children.

WHAT ARE PERSONAL SOCIAL NETWORKS?

Social networks are specific sets of linkages among defined sets of people (Mitchell, 1969). The type of social network of particular interest to the readers of this chapter is *personal,* that is, anchored to a specific person or family. In this case our focus is on the personal networks of parents or children, or the whole family. These networks consist of those relatives, neighbors, co-workers, and other friends who are directly linked to a family member, and who may be linked to one another as well.

Some years ago, in an article linking child development with personal social networks, Cochran and Brassard (1979) defined the network of interest as consisting of "those people outside the household who engage in activities and exchanges of an affective and/or material nature with the members of the immediate family" (p. 601). In that original formulation the spouse and children were specifically excluded from the parent's personal network, and siblings from the child's, so long as they lived together with the parent or child anchoring the network. Bryant (1985), examining sources of support in middle childhood, defined the network as including the family members in the child's household, explicitly rejecting this earlier definition.

From a conceptual standpoint the important distinction here is between the nuclear family and the personal network. Bott (1957), in her networks study *Family and Social Network,* emphasized the distinction to show that the definition of roles in a marital relationship is a function in part of the structure of the personal networks that each person brings to the new family. In so doing she distinguished membership in the nuclear family from membership in the networks of husband and wife. Study of nuclear families has a long tradition in sociology and anthropology, and the subdiscipline of family sociology has become well established during the past half century. Family historians and others conceive of the family as an emotional entity resting on sentimental ties between husband and wife and parents and children, and as a social unit with economic significance (Haraven, 1984). Thus, the nuclear family is a concept that has meaning in the real world and significance for the development of the individual, separate from the impacts of other kin, associates and friends.[1]

There is empirical evidence that spousal and parent–child relations are qualitatively different from those relationships maintained by parents or children with people living outside the household. Brassard (1982) applied the in versus outside the family distinction in the design of her own study of mother–child interaction and personal social networks, by comparing stress and support in one- and two-parent families and measuring the contributions of the father separately from those of other kin and nonkin. She found that the effects of a supportive father on mother–child relations were quite different from the effects of a supportive network. Her research underscores the value of making a distinction between members of the nuclear family and the rest of the personal network. Others have also identified the independent effect of a supportive partner on the parenting behavior of the mother (Quinton & Rutter, 1985; Crockenberg, 1987). For instance, Simons, Lorenz, Wu, and Conger (1993) used a sample of 451 two-parent families to examine a number of possible determinants of parenting behavior, including economic pressure, parental depression (mother and father), spouse support, and social network support. The LISREL statistical model-building technique was used to examine how the significant relations between economic pressure and supportive parenting might be mediated by spouse support, network support, and depression. Best fit models showed no significant association between spouse support and network support and the two variables demonstrated differential relationships to parenting. Spouse support had a positive, direct influence on parenting, and an indirect influence through depression. Network support was only indirectly influential on parenting through mothers' emotional well-being. There was some evidence that spousal support was especially salient when social support was low, again suggesting that the two kinds of support should be considered independent of one another.

SOCIAL NETWORKS AND SOCIAL SUPPORT

When defining the social networks concept it is also important to distinguish it from social supports. Most of those using the social support concept refer to the work of Cobb (1976), who defined such support as information that

---

[1]We recognize that the distinction between nuclear and extended families may not be valid beyond societies in North America and Europe.

leads an individual to believe that he or she is cared for and loved, valued, and a member of a network of mutual obligation. Crockenberg (1988) stated that social support refers to the emotional, instrumental, or informational help that other people provide to an individual. She went on to say that:

> With respect to families, emotional support refers to expressions of empathy and encouragement that convey to parents that they are understood and capable of working through difficulties in order to do a good job in that role. Instrumental support refers to concrete help that reduces the number of tasks or responsibilities a parent must perform, typically household and child care tasks. Informational support refers to advice or information concerning child care or parenting. (p. 141)

The personal social network has been defined earlier as a specific set of linkages among a defined set of persons. The content of those linkages ranges from information of various kinds (where to find work, how to rear your child, which day care arrangement to choose) to emotional and material assistance and access to role models (Cochran & Brassard, 1979; Mitchell, 1969). Thus the social support concept focuses primarily on the types of support provided (emotional, instrumental, informational) and the psychological state of the receiving individual (cared for and loved, valued), whereas with the personal network the emphasis is both on the characteristics of the set of linkages (structure) and on a broader range of types of exchanges between the anchoring individual and members of the network (content).

Researchers interested only in support have tended to map the networks of their respondents with the use of probes that are oriented explicitly to support, like "Please give me the names of all the people who provide you with emotional support." These particular defining characteristics lead to identification of a partial network, excluding all of those people in a person's life who are not thought of primarily in terms of support. Such other people are more likely to be included in response to an orienting question like "Please give me the names of all the people who make a difference to you in one way or another." This more inclusive approach was the one adopted in the Cornell studies described later in this chapter.

The emphasis by social support theorists and researchers on function (what is provided) much more than on role (the socially proscribed parameters of the relationship) helps to explain why they include partners as members of the social support network along with friends and relatives living outside the household. Those interested in the broader social network concept are as concerned with the limits imposed by society on personal relationships as we are on the content of those relationships. For this reason we assign spouses and partners living with the mother to the immediate family, and reserve network membership for those living outside the household.

Both the social network and the social support concepts are valuable. The distinction can be maintained, in part, by acknowledging that network relations are stressful as well as supportive, and that network members can influence parenting in ways that extend well beyond those included in the support concept.[2] In her study of low-income mothers with young children Belle (1982) was interested in the costs as well as the benefits of social ties, and concluded that "one cannot receive support without also risking the costs of rejection, betrayal, burdensome dependence, and vicarious pain" (p. 143). Research has documented the negative consequences for development in adolescence and early adulthood of network membership that is a source of conflict as well as support (see for example, Crockenberg, 1987). Based on their study of the support networks of 25 African-American adolescent first-time mothers, Voight, Hans, and Bernstein (1996) concluded that "when support is provided by someone who is also a source of stress, the combination of support and conflict may be related to poor maternal adjustment" (p. 70). Wellman (1981) wrote an entire chapter on the application of network analysis to the study of support, in which he articulated the various ways that the concept of social support can oversimplify the nature of social networks:

> Its focus on a simple "support/nonsupport" dichotomy de-emphasizes the multi-faceted, often contradictory nature of social ties. Its assumption that supportive ties form a separate system isolates them from a person's overall network of interpersonal ties. Its assumption that all of these supportive ties are connected to each other in one integrated system goes against empirical reality and creates the dubious expectation that solitary systems are invariably more desirable. Its assumption that there are no conflicts of interest between "supporters" invokes the false premise of a common good. (p. 173)

PERSONAL NETWORKS AND PARENTING: A MODEL

What forces and factors influence how personal networks develop? What determines their size and shape, and how they change over time? What is the role of the individual parent in the network-building process? How do the resulting networks affect parenting attitudes and behaviors? A framework for addressing these questions is provided in Fig. 8.1, as a summarizing model. A detailed presentation of the model and empirical evidence on which the framework is based are presented elsewhere (Cochran, Larner, Riley, Gunnarsson, & Henderson, 1990). The model incorporates the forces constraining or shaping network development, the factors stimulat-

---

[2]Perhaps the most powerful articulation of network influences that are distinct from social support can be found in Granovetter's 1973 article "The strengths of weak ties."

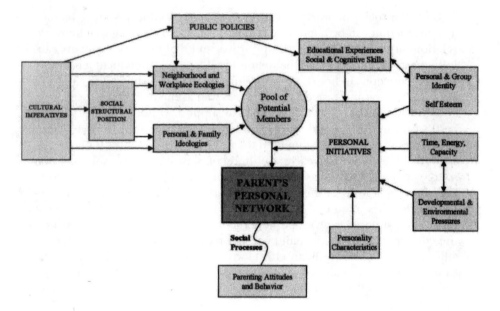

From Cochran, Larner, Riley, Gunnarsson, and Henderson, 1990

FIG. 8.1.   Personal networks and parenting: a conceptual framework.

ing individual initiatives at network-building, the parent's network itself, and reference to the resultant parenting processes and outcomes.

It is very important to project the dynamic qualities of the processes driving this model. Most of the potential for network change comes from the forces and factors shown on the right side of the figure; shifts in developmental stage, level of knowledge and skill, and personal identity all affect the amount and direction of social initiatives taken by the parent. Initiatives themselves can take two forms: (a) the selection of network members from the pool of individuals available to the parent, and (b) maintenance activities undertaken within the existing network.

A pool of eligibles distinguishes between the people actually available to the parent for inclusion in the network and those included as members. The pool of eligibles consists of those people to whom the parent has access for potential inclusion in the network. Use of this concept permits definition of the constraints on the left side of the model as establishing the boundaries for the size and content of the pool, and at the same time provides the individual parent with a role in building a network from that pool.

Selection of the term *constraints* to characterize the factors included on the left side of the model draws upon the terminology of Fischer and other sociologists doing network research (Fischer, 1982; Wellman, 1979). This term connotes restraint on individual action. The emphasis here is on the ways in which parents may be restrained by societal forces beyond their control from establishing social relations that are crucial to their development as parents. At the same time, we also recognize that many of the constraints by societies placed on individual behavior are constructive. Limits placed on violence against children, for example, and on the right of parents to relinquish responsibility for financial support of their children are positive constraints.

It is also important to note the use of the word *initiatives*, rather than Fischer's (1982) *choices*, to characterize the behavioral contribution of the individual parent to the construction of his or her network. Initiatives rather than choices is preferred because the word conveys action without necessarily assuming that alternatives exist. That is, a parent can initiate the act of including or excluding a person available in the "pool of eligibles" without necessarily choosing among alternatives available in the pool.

Evidence presented later in this chapter indicates that a substantial number of parents experience severe constraints on free choice because of the structural forces arraying on the left hand side of the figure. Fischer (1982) wrote early in *To Dwell Among Friends* that, "In general, we each construct our own networks" (p. 4). The evidence presented in this chapter, taken as a whole, indicates: (a) that it is inappropriate to generalize across ecological niches, and (b) that the networks of poor and undereducated parents—who make up 20% to 25% of all parents in the United States—are largely constructed for them by their life circumstances. The model in Fig. 8.1 conveys the power struggle between cultural and social structural forces on the one hand and the individual on the other for control over the content of the personal social network. For any given adult the tilt in the power balance is determined by that person's location in the social structure of the society to which he or she belongs. Recent studies indicate, for instance, that in the United States an unemployed, poor, African-American, single mother has far less control over who is included in her personal network than does a European-American, married, middle-income mother working outside the home (Cochran et al., 1990). Wilson and Tolson (1990), in a review of the structural, functional, and interactional aspects of African-American familial networks, attribute the depletion of network resources (jobs, father presence, stable family membership) to social and economic opportunities. They cited generational poverty, ongoing racial discrimination, and differences in the economic status of African-American and European-American families as some primary contributors to network vulnerability.

Stability and Change Over Time

During the past decade there has been an expansion of knowledge related to stability and change in the social networks of parents over time. The inaugural longitudinal study of parents' networks, reported by Larner

(1990), showed that the networks of parents with young children show stability in structural characteristics such as overall size and kin/nonkin distribution, but that considerable change can occur at the level of the individual network member, as one friend is replaced by another, for instance. Manetti and Schneider (1996) have since replicated those findings with an Italian sample of parents with 4- and 5-year-olds, examining social networks with children's school transition over two years. Bost, Cox, Burchinal, and Payne (2002) focused on parents' networks during the transition to parenthood, gathering networks and support data during the prenatal period and over three time points until the firstborn's second birthday. They also found considerable stability in network size and amount of support during that transition, yet noted important dynamic changes across networks during this period.

PERSONAL NETWORKS AND LARGER SOCIAL SYSTEMS

Toward the end of his chapter Wellman (1981) reminded the reader that personal networks operate within and must be influenced by the attributes of larger social systems. He referred in that regard to the social and spatial division of labor, the ways that bureaucracies are organized, and the social classes to which respondents belong. These more macro-level constraints were included on the left side of the model shown in Fig. 8.1. They represent aspects of the social ecology surrounding families and children that shape their social and economic opportunities. In Fig. 8.2 they are shown in greater detail. We discuss only certain of these constraint factors, given the limited space available in a single chapter and our desire to illustrate other aspects of the overall model.

Social Class

Family income, the educational level of parents, and the status and complexity of the occupations parents engage in are thought of by sociologists as contributing to determination of the social class in which a family is located. The first sociologist to provide empirical evidence for the relations between dimensions of social class and network ties was Fischer (1982), in his book *To Dwell Among Friends: Personal Networks in Town and City*. Fischer's team interviewed slightly more than 1,000 people in a 20 county area around San Francisco about their personal social networks. These people were all English-speaking, at least 18 years old, and permanent residents. Some were parents, others were not. They reflected rather well the diversity in educational, occupational, economic, gender and life-cycle characteris-

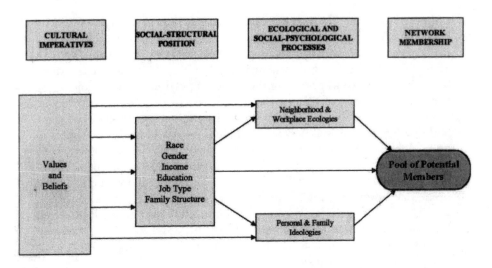

From Cochran, Larner, Riley, Gunnarsson, and Henderson, 1990

FIG. 8.2. Personal networks and larger social systems.

tics of that part of California. It is these variations that are of particular importance to us, because Fischer was able to consider the extent to which various aspects of the personal networks described by the people in his study were associated with such social structural factors. Of these factors, Fischer found that educational level had the most consistent effect upon the personal networks. He stated:

> Other things being equal, the more educational credentials respondents had, the more socially active they were, the larger their networks, the more companionship they reported, the more intimate their relations, and the wider the geographic range of their ties. In general, education by itself meant broader, deeper, and richer networks. (p. 252)

Fischer also found that household income made a sizeable difference in the networks reported, even with education held constant. People with more income included more nonkin in their networks, and were more likely to report adequate amounts of companionship and practical support than were the poor. In considering the meaning of these relations between socioeconomic factors and network ties Fischer offered three, not necessarily contradictory, possibilities. Perhaps, he suggested, certain kinds of personalities result in both higher socioeconomic status and greater sociability. Another explanation, and the one he seemed to prefer, emphasized the social skills and concrete resources that come with more education and income, and the ways that these skills and resources can be used to build and maintain network ties. The third explanation, which he thought of as operating "in a straightforward structural manner" (p. 252), is one in which schooling is viewed as providing the direct opportunity to meet and make friends with people of like mind.

Fischer's work also provided insight into the impacts of life cycle stage and gender on personal networks. Married people named more relatives and neighbors than did those who were unmarried, whereas single people were more involved with nonkin. Children restricted the social involvement of their parents, and especially of their mothers. "Women with children at home had fewer friends and associates, engaged in fewer social activities, had less reliable social support, and had more localized networks than did otherwise similar women without children" (p. 253). From the gender perspective, women tended to be more involved with kinfolk and to report more intimate ties than did men.

Culture, Class and Race

Some years ago Gunnarsson and the first author participated with Welsh and West German colleagues in a coordinated set of studies of mothers' social networks, which extended Fischer's general approach to a comparison of networks across cultures (Sweden, the United States, Wales, West Germany), social class (blue collar vs. white collar), and family structure (one vs. two parent families; Cochran & Gunnarsson, 1990). The mothers in all four countries were Caucasian, and each had a 3-year-old child when first interviewed. Concentrating first on mothers in two-parent families, the researchers found in all four countries that mothers in white-collar families reported larger networks than did women in blue-collar households. Interestingly, the magnitude of the difference proved to be about the same in every country except the United States, where the differences by occupational status were larger. Network size however, differed by culture. Networks of mothers in the United States and in Sweden were larger than those of mothers in West Germany and in Wales. Looking beyond simply network size for the functions performed by network members, again differences by class were readily apparent. Mothers in the white-collar families reported involvement with a higher number of network members in every category of social support. This difference was most visible for social and recreational activities. The data suggested, as a hypothesis, that mothers in white-collar families had more leisure time at their disposal (especially in Sweden and the United States), and spent some of that extra time in social and recreational activities with network members. Across cultures, network support differed as well. Mothers in the United States and in Sweden identified greatly higher percentages of network members whom they could call on for all types of social support, compared with the mothers in Germany and Wales.

Within the United States, MacPhee and colleagues (MacPhee, Fritz, & Miller-Heyl, 1996) compared the social networks of Latin-American, Native-American and European-American parents. Their sample included 500 low-income parents of 2 to 5 year old children (74% mothers) living in urban and rural areas in a western state. The three ethnic groups were equally likely to identify a domestic partner, children and parents in their social networks. Though overall network size was similar across ethnic groups (each mentioning approximately 15 persons), Native Americans had significantly more extended kin and siblings in their networks than did European Americans. More friends were found in the European-American reports of network membership. Even with socioeconomic status held constant, ethnic differences appeared in network density and contact.

The authors characterized Native-American caregivers as having a close knit social system, one with which they felt satisfaction with support and frequency of contact. The authors suggested that closeness of the Native-American network may be a cultural phenomenon, but may also be due to reservation dynamics and a response to local prejudice. Latin-American parents also had large, close-knit networks yet relied on smaller numbers of immediate and extended kin for emotional support. Offers of babysitting as practical assistance were more prevalent within the larger network. A site difference was noted within this ethnic group. Urban Latin Americans had smaller, more cohesive networks with more expression of emotional support. MacPhee and his colleagues observed that urban areas afford more opportunities for interaction and the formation of subcultures. The Latin American families in this particular geographic area also showed relatively little migration, suggesting residential stability as a potential factor in cohesive networking. European-American parents, on the other hand, had more diffuse networks in terms of contact and connectedness, yet reported more offers of emotional support within the network. The authors suggested that this may be due to geographic mobility or a preference to turn to a wider range of different individuals for support and assistance.

Roschelle (1997), using data from the National Survey of Families and Households (NSFH) looked at the structure and function of social support across culture, gender, and class. In particular, Roschelle was interested in determining if culture and/or economic need dominate in determining participation in support networks and whether such differences are the result of cultural or gendered attitudes, economic resources, or a combination of these structural factors. Limitations of the data set precluded an analysis of network size. Rather, Roschelle was able to examine the proximity of network members (specifically at least one parent, siblings, and adult children) by distance from the respondent, the presence of extended family living in the home, and the exchange of support functions (child care, monetary resources, and household assistance received from and given to network members). The sample included 13,017 individuals 19 and older, living in a household, and was divided by race/ethnicity to include European Americans, African Americans, Chicanos, and Puerto Ricans.

The examination of household help revealed that European Americans were significantly more likely to be involved with their social networks in offers of help than were the other three race/ethnic subgroups. Yet, examination of the receipt of assistance did not find this group's participation with their networks greater than the others. In fact, no predictable pattern emerged across the race/ethnic groups on the type of support or source within the network with whom support was exchanged. However, within gender lines, offers of child care (for women) and household assistance (for men) cut across all race/ethnic categories.

Looking at offers of child care to women by their families and extended networks and by women to their networks, Roschelle found unexpected race or ethnic differences across the four groups. In fact, she found that European-American women, especially as compared with African American mothers, were more likely than women in other groups to offer and receive child care help. Economic circumstances, the proximity of extended family members, and migration status played a part in the dynamics. As women's economic situations improved, so did their offers of child care to and from family members. It was also determined that the closer a respondent lived to family members, the greater the amount of child-care exchange. That non U.S.-born Puerto Rican mothers exchanged less child care with family members was believed to reflect the back and forth migration patterns of immigrant parents. Roschelle observed that the lack of participation in social network exchanges of child care may not indicate that cultural norms toward familism are irrelevant, rather that limited resources may prevent poor women from these exchanges.

When she shifted her attention to the household help men contribute to other family members, as well as the help they receive from family and extended family, Roschelle again found an impact based on economic conditions. African American, Chicano, and Puerto Rican men were not more likely than non-Latin American men to offer or receive household assistance. Puerto Rican men's assistance was similarly affected by their migration status. The relation between exchanges of household assistance and Puerto Rican ethnicity disappeared when migration status was controlled for. Roschelle considered her results a replication of those of the first author and his colleagues (p. 177) and suggested that more impoverished families do not have the time and resources necessary to become involved in offering or receiving support from others in their family and extended family networks. She suggested that the finding of limited availability of kin networks with declining economic conditions dispels a common belief that in tough times, and in the face of fewer public services, families can turn to each other.

Limited resources also affect mothers' satisfaction with support. If, as Roschelle asserted, network participation is based on exchange reciprocity, it would make sense that satisfaction with support from the network would be tied to socioeconomic status and the ability to return assistance and support. Miller-Loncar and colleagues (Miller-Loncar, Erwin, Landry, Smith, & Swank, 1998) examined the social network differences among low-income African-American, Latin-American and European-American mothers and determined that across all ethnic groups, mothers higher in socioeconomic status were more likely to be satisfied with help from family and friends than were those of lower SES.

Immigration status among non-U.S. parents also can affect the structure and function of their network relations. In Roschelle's analyses she found a clear relation between migration status and participation of social networks among Latin American mothers. Chicano and Puerto Rican respondents born in the United States were far more active participants with their networks than were those not born in the United States. This was due to proximity; second and third generation mothers had more access to family members. First generation mothers had to rely on visits to or from family members who were in their native countries, and thus offered less support overall and less offers of instrumental support specifically. Yet even this phenomenon may be tied to economic status and motivation. Some racial–ethnic groups may choose to live near family as a way to maintain cultural and familial ties. Others may choose to move away from kin and nonkin, including migration to another country as a means to seek greater access to economic resources. Roschelle also noted that for Puerto Ricans circular migration patterns may lead to the perception among network members of their unavailability to participate in network exchanges and fulfill obligations. Therefore, migration among Puerto Ricans in the United States may discourage connections to kin and nonkin in both countries.

Societies, and classes within societies, differ in terms of the roles women are permitted or encouraged to adopt (mother vs. worker, for instance), and the extent to which they can develop identities beyond those roles. From a developmental perspective, one can distinguish between development as a parent (parent role) and development as a person (personal identity). Network members can be thought of as contributing more or less to one or another of these developmental trajectories. It is reasonable to suggest, for instance, that kinfolk contribute heavily to definition and reinforcement of the parental role, whereas other friends are more likely to contribute to "development of self as person" or personal identity.

Our general understanding of class differences indicates that blue-collar expectations are somewhat more conservative than those of white-collar workers regarding the roles of men and women. This pattern was reflected in the network data presented by Cochran and colleagues, and Roschelle. Cutting across cultures was the picture of lower-SES networks as somewhat smaller, more kin-dominated, less geographically dispersed and more child-related and practical in content than their higher income, more highly educated counterparts. The overall impression from the Cornell networks study is that cultural expectations regarding the woman's place override those of class; that is, the network differences were greater between pairs of countries than among occupational levels within country. Adding to this, Roschelle suggested that stereotypical behaviors about gender roles extend beyond culture, race and socioeconomic status. In her analysis of the NSFH data, she determined that men and women, across race and ethnic groups, taught their like-gendered offspring skills that maintain traditional male (occupational) and female (nurturing) skills.

Cross (1990) examined the personal networks of African-American single and married mothers, and compared the size and functioning of those networks with the social ties reported by White ethnic and nonethnic mothers from similar socioeconomic circumstances living in the same city. His study included a dimension of cross race membership in networks of the mothers, testing the likelihood that at least one opposite race contact would appear at the functional level of the network. The results of this analysis showed that 21% of the African American mothers and 16% of the White parents in one-parent families had at least one opposite race friend. This modest disparity by race increased as family structure changed and socioeconomic level became higher; within the two-parent sample 41% of the African American women but only 11% of the European Americans reported friends of the opposite race.

Cross postulated a relation between the relative lack of African-American people in the networks of European-American mothers and the smaller number of other friends reported by the African-American women. On the one hand, he suggested that the exclusion of African Americans as potential friends would not have much of an effect on the overall size of European-American networks (reduce the pool of eligibles very much), since the large numbers of European Americans in all sectors of everyday life provide numerous opportunities to meet and incorporate new European-American nonkin contacts. On the other hand, he pointed out that this is not the case for African-American people living in the same community. In the northeastern city where this study was conducted only about 12% of the population was African American. So the pool of potential same-race network members was much smaller for African American than for European-American mothers, meaning that any cross-race avoidance that might have occurred would have placed the African American women at a relative disadvantage.

The evidence that Cross assembled strongly suggests that in the United States race continues to be a social divide. He questions what the consequences of such segregation might be for the development of children in these families, and points for evidence to studies of group identity showing that African-American children develop a much more bi-racial orientation than European-American children, and so are better equipped to function in a truly multi-racial society.

In this section of the chapter we present evidence that structural factors operating at the levels of culture, class, race, ethnicity, and family structure constrain the network-building opportunities of some parents more than of others. That is, the pool of network eligibles available to some parents is smaller than that available to others. African-American parents, parents with relatively little education, first generation immigrants, and parents living in cultures shaped by beliefs that lead to narrow definitions of the woman's role all have a smaller pool of potential network membership available to them than do their more socioeconomically and socially advantaged counterparts. Constraints accumulate for single parents, who often have less access to relatives, to further education, to jobs paying a decent salary, and to housing in neighborhoods that are supportive of neighboring activities.

One-Parent Families

In the Cornell networks study, interest in a cross-cultural examination of solo parenting and network relations led to the oversampling of single parent families by the Swedish and U.S. teams (Gunnarsson & Cochran, 1990). Forty-three Swedish mothers and 48 of the U.S. mothers were Caucasian single parents. Comparisons of these mothers' networks with those of mothers in two-parent families showed that they were smaller, regardless of culture or class. There was also a remarkably large difference in the American sample between the average number of network members reported by white- and blue-collar single mothers (18 vs. 12). As mentioned earlier, this difference was found also in the U.S. two-parent sample. Differentiation by social class was not nearly as evident in the Swedish sample; in fact, there the tendency was for white-collar, single mothers to have somewhat smaller networks than their blue-collar counterparts.

One major factor accounting for the difference in total size of the networks was a smaller number of relatives in the networks of single mothers. In the U.S. sample there was an average difference of more than four relatives between mothers in two-parent families and single mothers, regardless of social class. In Sweden, where the networks of mothers in two-parent families were themselves smaller and less kin-centered than in the United States, there was still an average of two more relatives in the networks of the coupled women than in those of the single mothers.

In the other friends sector, single mothers in white-collar families included more membership than mothers in blue-collar families, both in Sweden and in the United States. The marked differences between the sizes of the total network reported by the U.S. white- and blue-collar single mothers was largely explained by this greater number of other friends. The average of eight nonkin friends in the networks of American white-collar single mothers outranked all the other subgroups of women by a substantial margin, and was nearly twice as large as in the case of U.S. blue-collar single mothers.

It is important to understand that other friends are acquired rather than ascribed network members. Such acquisition requires access to people, interest and motivation to build and maintain such relationships, and the social and material resources with which to initiate and sustain the process. The white-collar single mothers in the U.S. sample were working outside the home to a much larger degree than were the blue-collar single mothers, and so had access to workmates. White-collar jobs are likely to provide more opportunities for socializing than is the case with jobs in the blue-collar sector. Training for such jobs usually involves educational situations where opportunities to meet people are present and social interaction and development of social skills encouraged. Finally, financial and material resources are likely to be more available to the white-collar single mothers in the sample; their jobs pay better.

It is interesting to note that in Sweden more than 70% of the neighbors included in the networks of single mothers were themselves mothers with young children, whereas in the United States the corresponding figures were only 48 to 59%. This cultural difference was especially extreme for blue-collar single parents (86% vs. 48%). The difference may stem from the fact that in the United States such families are often forced by financial disadvantage to live in high-crime areas with substandard housing, where parents are suspicious of their neighbors and are afraid to allow their children to play outside, whereas in Sweden income redistribution has made it possible to ensure that all families can live in safe, relatively child-friendly neighborhoods.

Swedish women in two-parent families lived further from their network ties than did mothers in any of the other three countries. This cultural difference was reinforced and extended by the data from Swedish single mothers, whose networks were still more dispersed geographically. Only about half the membership in the networks of the Swedish single mothers lived within 10 miles, compared with more than three quarters of American membership. In fact, in the United States single mothers lived in closer proximity to network members than did their two-parent counterpart, whereas in Sweden the reverse was true.

What prompts a mother, and especially a single mother, to live closer to or further from her relatives or friends? One reason might be economic necessity. Some single mothers in the U.S. sample were actually living with their parents, because they could not afford to live elsewhere. Beyond housing there are other ways of relieving stress that require rather close proximity: child care, housework, transportation, and babysitting. Knowing of the greater need by single parents for these services, it was not surprising to find in the U.S. data that they were living closer to their network contacts than were mothers living with their spouses. Therefore, it was puzzling to find the opposite pattern in the Swedish data. One hypothesis is that the sharp difference in proximity patterns is due to the much larger set of formal supports available to such mothers in Sweden—parental leave, housing allowance, child allowance, subsidized child care arrangements—supports that may well reduce the need to live together with or right next to relatives or friends.

Roschelle (1997) made an interesting observation about the exchanges of social support involving different types of single mothers in the NSFH data set. With single, never-married mothers she found fewer exchanges of child care than in two-parent families. Single mothers were far less likely to offer child care services to family members, suggesting that the presence of a spouse enabled married women to offer care for others. This may also have been due to co-residence of single mothers with other single mothers, keeping the exchange of child care help within the household. Yet, when the one parent family was headed by a woman who was divorced, separated or widowed, exchanges of child care between the parent and her non-family social network were more frequent than in two-parent families. The social network membership of these women featured more relationships with friends and neighbors. Roschelle hypothesized that divorced, separated or widowed women with young children may bond in a friendship network, or an intimate community of shared experiences. This may not be as common or available to single, never-married mothers.

THE NETWORK-BUILDING PROCESS

The underlying thesis of the previous section was that cultures are structured in ways that may limit the range of social relations available to some, and perhaps many, of their members. Equally important to acknowledge is the role played by the individual in challenging those limits. One key feature of the ecological orientation is its recognition that influence is bi-directional. Not only are individuals and families shaped by the larger forces within which they are embedded, but they also play active, initiating roles in altering those larger systems to fit their needs. In his preface to *Network Analysis: Studies in Human Interaction* (Boissevain & Mitchell, 1973), Boissevain refers to "the concept of man as an interacting social being capable of manipulating others as well as being manipulated by them" (p. viii). This concept of the human organism as a proactive participant in construction of the social environment implies a need to know how humans, and in this case parents, develop network-building skills, and whether different social, ethnic, and cultural groupings are more or less likely to promote such behavior by their members. Cochran and Brassard devoted a section of their 1979 article to development in the child of such skills, and identified reciprocal exchange as the key cognitive process underlying network-building developed during childhood. They also acknowledged the part that individual temperament and personality characteristics might play in affecting the propensity to initiate relationships, and pointed to the importance of studying children across developmental time for an understanding of network-building processes. The first author and colleagues (Cochran et al., 1990) carried this thinking further in relation to parents, as summarized below in Fig. 8.3. There the reader sees nine factors proposed as contributors to the propensity of the parent to engage actively in network building; that is, to recruit network membership from the pool of potentials provided by the society of which she is a part. Much of this model is speculation, pure and simple, because the studies needed to examine these factors systematically have yet to be carried out. Again, space does not permit discussion of every possible element in the model, so we limit ourselves to some key illustrations.

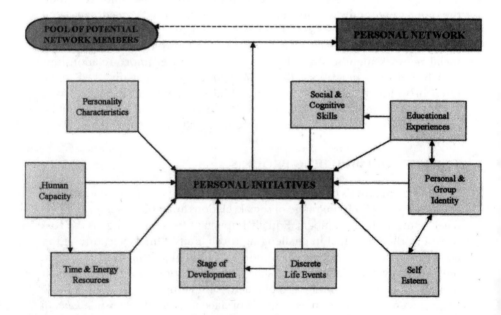

From Cochran, Larner, Riley, Gunnarsson, and Henderson, 1990

FIG. 8.3.   The network-building process.

Personal Identity

McLanahan and her colleagues were the first researchers to link personal identity with personal social networks (McLanahan, Wedemeyer, & Adelberg, 1981). Working with data gathered through in-depth interviews with 45 divorced mothers, they distinguished women who wished to maintain their existing identity after the divorce from those trying to create a different and less traditional identity for themselves. These researchers suggested that a close-knit network may be especially supportive to those interested in retaining their pre-divorce identity, and a loose-knit network can be helpful to those seeking change. In practice, involvement in a close-knit network typically meant that the mother had frequent contact with her own mother and other female relatives, who usually lived nearby. Women wishing to transition from one role orientation to another—for instance, from homemaker to working outside the home—seemed to be better served by more extended networks, which included significant numbers of nonkin, female friends.

The study by McLanahan and colleagues alerted us to the fact that different kinds of network resources are useful to women with differing definitions of their own roles, and different future orientations. The differing identities of the women studied translated into greater or lesser expectations for change. Where role transition was sought, some kinds of social resources were more helpful than others. Implied by the findings, but not studied directly, is the notion that when the needed resources are not present in the network, women desiring change will seek them elsewhere, and attempt to recruit them into their networks.

This reference to networks fitting with psychosocial needs serves as a reminder that the relations between personal identity and the network are dynamic. Alcalay (1983) summarized the differing functions of high and low density networks under different conditions in this way:

> Social networks can be both a source of direct help and a source of linkage to other resources. In crises a small, dense network with strong ties may be most valuable. At times of psychosocial transition, a low density network with weak ties . . . may be most useful. Under these circumstances social support networks provide a much needed sense of identity, a feeling of belonging, of being wanted and worthwhile. (p. 73)

Networks contribute to a sense of identity, just as changes in identity may contribute to modifications in network composition and function.

Stage of Development

There is growing evidence that both biological changes in the organism and changes in the expectations of significant others compel the developing person to periodically reassess the resource potential represented by members of the existing network. For instance, adult relatives seem to be especially salient for young children. In an American study of the networks and school performance of first graders Cochran and Riley (1990) found that the number of adult kinfolk (other than parents) engaging in task-oriented interactions with these six-year-olds was a strong predictor of how well they were performing in school.

Bryant (1985) focused on middle childhood, with a particular interest in possible relations between sources of social support and socioemotional functioning during middle childhood. She found that there was a positive relation between the support variables and socioemotional functioning for 10-year-olds but not for 7-year-olds. Bryant suggested, among several possible explanations, that a certain amount of parental distancing in middle childhood may nudge the 10-year-olds from the parental nest, thereby giving other supports more salience. Thus it may not be that the amount of network resources change from one developmental stage to the next, but that many of the same resources have different meaning, and are used differently, because the press for social relations is different at the succeeding stage.

In adolescence, nonkin come to the fore; analysis of Norwegian data indicated that it was the number of nonkin adults in the networks reported by 16-year-old boys that predicted their school performance (Cochran & Bø, 1989). Again, a reasonable explanation for the shift in importance from kin to nonkin adults involves developmental press. The extended family provides a secure base from which to develop new relations in the neighborhood and school, and at the same time permitting the younger child to experience the behavior and expectations of adults different enough from the parents to require development of some new social skills and expansion of cognitive frames. In adolescence, when the transition into adulthood and work roles looms large, nonkin adults provide models for the future, challenge the teenager to accept increased responsibility for self, significant others and the community, and provide information about where to obtain services, training, and paid work. Finally, for the young adults (parents) in the Cornell networks study both kin and nonkin were important, but for different purposes in different roles (Cochran et al., 1990). Kinfolk had particular salience for perceptions and activities of these adults in their childrearing roles, whereas nonrelatives were especially relevant to the work role, and for personal self-regard.

Discrete Life Events

It is important to distinguish developmental press from those presses caused by life events. Significant, time-limited life events like birth or death of a family member, marriage or divorce, or job acquisition, change, or loss, create social presses for the individual that are different from the demands stemming from developmental change. The causes of these events may be independent of the individual. However, they are not necessarily direct extensions of the environmental constraints discussed earlier (see Fig. 8.2). The interest here is in how such occurrences might stimulate networking initiatives by the individual.

The transition to parenthood is a major life event for adults, with high potential for change in both network composition and function. Bost et al. (2002) examined patterns of change in couples' social networks in the months during their first child's birth through 24 months postpartum. One hundred and thirty-seven primarily European-American, working-class couples from rural prenatal clinics in North Carolina participated in the study. Network dimensions of size, composition and frequency of contact, satisfaction with support, depression and adjustment scores for husbands and wives were examined separately prenatally and three times postpartum (3 months, 12 months and 24 months). All social network and support dimensions remained relatively stable over the two years for both parents, with network size the most consistent variable. At various points across the years, some flux in network dimensions was observed. For example, although family network size decreased after the birth of the children, the frequency of contact with family members increased. Yet, as the authors observed, amidst great change, and over time, social network characteristics can remain stable.

Depression and adjustment scores were also found to be stable across time for husbands and wives. Variability in these indicators of well-being related to mothers' and fathers' interactions with and the size of their social networks. Increased network size was related to parental adjustment, yet more frequent contact was associated with decreased adjustment. The authors suggested that less adjusted parents may feel the need for more contact with family members with the onset of parenting. Depression was negatively linked to perceived reciprocity and satisfaction with network support, particularly from friends, and the importance of this relationship increased over time. Bost and her colleagues concluded that social relationships and the support they offer remain critical aids to adjustment and well-being during the transition to parenthood. They recommended however, that the dynamic nature of social structures and support should be examined more closely to determine their roles in familial adaptation over time.

The research by McLanahan and her associates and by Roschelle discussed earlier underscore the importance of the divorcing woman's personal identity in determining the utility of existing network ties. Thus it is plausible to suggest, pending better evidence, that separation or divorce acts as a stimulus to network reorganization primarily in combination with an interest in establishing a new identity and use of resources.

In the Cornell networks study a family support program provided home visitors, neighborhood parenting support groups, or a combination of these two types of support to 160 of the 225 families that participated in the American portion of the overall longitudinal study. Thus involvement in the support program over a three year period could be viewed as a discrete event in the lives of those families. Participation in this program stimulated network-building activity on a conditional basis, with the conditions in this case involving race and family structure. European-American single parents in the program added a significant number of nonkin to their networks over a three year period, when compared with a *no program* comparison group, whereas with African-American single parents the additions were both kin and nonkin. Married women showed no increases in the size of their networks as a function of the program, but assigned greater importance at follow-up than at baseline to people already in their networks.

Personality Characteristics

Researchers believe that personality traits like responsiveness, persistence, and introversion are temperamental, biologically wired into a child at birth, and affecting that person throughout life (Thomas & Chess, 1977; Chess & Thomas, 1984; Hinde, Stevenson-Hinde, & Tamplin, 1985). Whether or not this is the case, it is reasonable to propose that shy or introverted parents may be less likely to take advantage of social opportunities than are parents who are gregarious or extroverted.

Other characteristics of a parent's personality develop through experiences during childhood and adolescence. The body of research in this domain focuses not on why some parents and not others engage in network building, but instead on why some parents are much more socially isolated than others. This interest stems from evidence linking this social isolation with child abuse and neglect. Crockenberg (1988), in summarizing these findings, introduced the possibility that "characteristics of the mothers account both for their low support and their abusive parenting" (p. 160). Polansky, Gaudin, Ammons, and Davis (1985) carried out a comparison of neglectful with nonneglectful mothers that supports this hypothesis. These researchers used a comparison group that was similar to the neglectful families not only in socioeconomic and family characteristics, but also regarding the geographic accessibility of relatives and proximity to where they grew up. One innovative feature of the study involved interviewing a neighbor of every neglectful and control family to determine perceptions of the friendliness and helpfulness of people in the neighborhood, whether there were people one could call on for help, and whether there were people who needed help in raising their children. Polansky and colleagues found first, that neglectful mothers described their neighborhoods as less supportive and friendly than did parents in the control group or neighbors of the parents in either group. Thus they described a different psychological reality, although there was no evidence from the neighbors of differences in the objective support potential (the size of what is referred to in Figs. 8.1–8.3 as the pool of potential network members). Second, there was evidence that neglectful parents were less helpful than control parents to others in the neighborhood, based both on their own reports and the reports of their neighbors. The researchers concluded from their data that "inadequacies of ability, and perhaps motivation, cut them off from helping networks dependent on mutuality. Related inadequacies lead to their being stigmatized and held at a distance socially" (p. 274).

Crittenden (1981, 1985a) conducted research that provides greater understanding of what the inadequacies referred to by Polansky et al., might consist of, and some indication of their origins. She drew on the work of attachment theorists to propose that adults have internalized working models of social relationships that are developed from experiences in early childhood, and then modified over time based on the social relations experienced during later childhood and adolescence. Crittenden documented that maltreating mothers have deviant patterns of interaction with their children, and inferred that these patterns result from working models of what a social relationship can and should be that are very different from those of mothers not maltreating their children. She showed that these deviant interaction patterns were leading, in turn, to more difficult and more passive child behaviors. The proposal is that the behavioral differences found in the children reflected the beginnings of working models for social interaction similar to those carried by their mothers.

Applying this conceptual orientation to network relations, Crittenden (1985b) proposed that "on the basis of her working model, a mother may influence her relationship with her network, just as she appears to do in her relationship with her child, through the processes of generalization and repetition of ingrained patterns of behavior" (p. 1301). This proposal received support from her comparison of the networks and parent–professional relationships of adequate mothers with those of neglectful and abusive/neglectful mothers. She found that mothers in the adequate group had far more supportive and satisfying network relationships than the mothers in either of the other two groups. This was true despite the fact that the adequate and maltreating mothers were often living in the same neighborhoods. The adequate mothers were also more cooperative in the parent–professional relationship, and less defensive or withdrawn. Crittenden then examined the relations of the network and parent-professional variables with the security of attachment between the mothers and their 1-

to 4-year-old children. She found that a cooperative approach to the parent–professional relationship was substantially more powerful than network typology in predicting a secure attachment. Crittenden concluded that her data are "highly consistent with the notion that the mothers' approach to relationships of all kinds was reflected both in their relationships with their children and in their relationships with network members" (p. 1311). The terms she used to characterize the interaction styles of these women—cooperative, defensive, withdrawn—can be thought of as learned personality characteristics. Crittenden argued that these characteristics reflect internalized working models of relationships, and result in greater or lesser openness to and capacity for the establishment and maintenance of satisfying and supportive network relations.

Rogosch, Mowbray and Bogat (1992) studied mothers with severe psychopathology and examined the link between mothers' relational experiences in childhood and their current perceptions of emotional support and parenting practices. Their findings paralleled those of mentally healthy mothers and provided further evidence to support the notion of working models of social relationships continuing to influence socialization and parenting into adulthood. Mothers who had difficulties in their childhood relational experiences had fewer persons in their current lives on whom they could rely for emotional support. Mothers' self-esteem was tied to their perception of emotional support from the social network and sensitivity in their orientation toward parenting. Mothers with low emotional support showed less adaptive parenting attitudes.

PERSONAL NETWORK INFLUENCES ON PARENTS

In the first section of this chapter we focus on the structural constraints defining the pool of network potential available to parents in differing ecological niches. In the second section we identify some of the factors that might determine the propensity of parents to actively seek out relationships with people in the pool of potential membership. We shift now to the question of how networks with differing characteristics, once they are in place and functioning, affect parenting attitudes and behavior. (See *social processes*, in Fig. 8.1.)

Network Size

Network dimensions of size, density, and frequency of contact have been examined as structural influences on parents' attitudes and behaviors. Most commonly, larger social networks have been associated with more positive parenting. For example, Jennings, Stagg and Connors (1991) examined network size, cohesion, and satisfaction as influences on mothers' play interactions with their 4-year-old children. Consistent with other research, mothers with smaller, more cohesive networks tended to be less satisfied with their personal network relations. A clear relationship emerged between dimensions of mothers' networks and their parenting behavior. Mothers with larger networks and those who were more satisfied with their network relations showed a warmer, less intrusive style of interaction. Similarly, this parenting style was associated with less cohesive maternal networks. The authors acknowledged that the relation between mothers' social networks and parenting may not be due to structural dynamics, but that more socially competent mothers may be more skilled in parenting. Yet, they speculated about the influence of processes underlying the structural dynamics of the mothers' relationships, and suggested that mothers whose own needs are met by a quantity of supportive others are better able to meet and respond to the emotional and developmental needs of their children. Mothers in smaller, more tightly knit networks may experience more power and control in their relationships and be more likely to utilize these strategies with their children. Frequent contact may increase exposure to relationships that reinforce negative parenting practices.

Emotional and Instrumental Support

Studies of parents' social networks conducted during the 1980s revealed that assistance with child care, unconditional emotional support and advice about how to maintain authoritative control over the child's behavior prove particularly helpful to young mothers, especially when the women are single, divorced or separated (Brassard, 1982; Colletta, 1981). Work by Belle (1982), cited earlier, provides important evidence in this regard. Belle studied the costs and benefits of social ties identified as important by 43 low-income mothers with young children. Although her work is within the broader *social support and health outcomes* tradition of Cobb, with particular interest in personal mastery and depression in adults, she was also interested in the quality of interaction between the mothers and their children. Belle found that it was not network size, proximity of membership, or frequency of contact that was associated with emotional well-being, but rather the number of people reported as engaged specifically in providing child care assistance and "someone to turn to." This greater provision of concrete assistance and support seemed to carry over positively to the quality of the interactions between these mothers and their children.

Recent studies alluded to earlier in the chapter convey the importance of recognizing the stresses as well as the supports in network relations. Voight and colleagues (1996), for instance, studied the support networks of 25 low-income, African-American teenage mothers and found that network size and offers of support were associated with perception of the parenting experience and observations of parenting behavior. Having more friends in her social network was positively related to the quality of the adolescent's interactions with her one-year-old child, as was the number of types of supports that her mother offered (though the latter was negatively related to the parenting experience). The relationship effect was conditional on the source of the network support (more siblings and more sibling support related to poorer parenting behavior, support from male partners was not significant), and on support from the network being positive. The authors determined that larger network membership was related to the quality of the parenting experience if the quality of the relationship was marred by conflict. More sources of conflicted support were negatively associated with parenting behavior.

The study by MacPhee and associates (1996) referred to previously also examined influences from social network structure and support on parenting practices, and was based on the premise that ethnic differences in the formation of and processes within personal social networks may help to explain subcultural variations in socialization practices of parents. As they noted in their review of cultural literature related to parenting, network exchanges convey childrearing norms through approval or criticism. More frequent exchanges with smaller numbers of individuals increase the opportunities for social sanctions, modeling, and reinforcement of behavior. Values of familism and interdependence frequently seen in collectivistic cultures, such as those associated with the Latin American and Native American groups represented in their study, can reinforce the reliance upon family members as the primary support network. As a result, parents' exposure to information outside the kin network may be potentially limited. Social support from the cultural network that increases personal well-being, and buffers parenting stress, may be most influential on parenting when psychosocial risk is greatest.

These authors were cautious about teasing out ethnic network influences from those by geographic area, population density and social stratification. Economic well-being is a critical dimension of ethnic differences in both social network composition and function and parenting practices. Often when economic variables such as income, education, and occupation are controlled, ethnic differences in social networks disappear. In fact, in this study, though some variation was noted surrounding parents' value for autonomy, controlling for socioeconomic variables lessened the impact of ethnicity on parenting.

Despite differences observed in structural aspects of the social networks in the three ethnic groups, MacPhee and colleagues found that the quality of emotional support proved to be a more important influence on parenting. Controlling for psychosocial risk in within-ethnicity regression analyses, satisfaction with support provided by others (for Latin Americans) and satisfaction and level of support (for Native Americans and European Americans) positively related to the parenting practice of limit setting. For Latin Americans and European Americans, quality of emotional support negatively related to harsh parenting. The relationship between emotional support and parenting was mediated by parental competence. Support provided by close attachment figures rather than distant network members appeared to be particularly important, leading the authors to suggest that "one's sense of competence in a specific role may be quite dependent on the regard of others who share that role" (p. 3292).

The stress-buffering hypothesis was not supported for Native American and Latin American parents. Parents in these groups with the least social integration showed more non-normative parenting practices. Native Americans with low psychosocial risk who were less satisfied with support received showed less parental efficacy and harsher parenting practices. Conversely, Latin American parents who received less support, and who were in less contact with their networks showed less punitive practices. The authors concluded that less contact with network members may have reduced the reinforcement and social modeling needed to regulate parenting practices within the cultural group.

Childrearing Advice and Other Informational Support

Riley (1990) broadened the discussion of networks and parenting to include men in the parenting role, by capitalizing on the fact that the Cornell networks study's data set included information about the networks of fathers. The question he asked of these data was: in what ways would a father utilize his social ties in the service of his childrearing efforts? One important way is to use network members for discussion of parenting concerns and to gather childrearing advice. To whom do the fathers turn for such advice? Do they favor advice from their own parents or siblings, or from other young parents? Are there fathers who report no one with whom they talk about childrearing? To answer these questions, Riley focused on the 70 married, non-African-American, employed fathers from two-parent households who participated in the follow-up portion of the study. The average network included 5.1 sources of childrearing advice. But there was great variation. Eleven of the 70 fathers reported 10 or more sources of advice, while 12 fathers (17%) reported no one.

Riley related aspects of the fathers' networks to those men's levels of involvement in the rearing of their six-year-old children, focusing on two areas of father involvement: participation in routine child care tasks and play interaction with the child. He was careful to distinguish families by maternal employment status. Thirty-seven of the 70 families had an employed mother. Analyses were carried out separately for families with and without an employed mother.

Riley found that in the two-earner families both nonkin allies and local female kin affected the child care participation of the father. Nonkin allies are those highly elective and supportive network members who provided three or more of the following six kinds of support to the father: practical borrowing, financial assistance, work-related support, a person to talk with about marital issues, emotional support, and social activities. Local female kin consisted of the number of adult female relatives (including in-laws) in the father's network who lived in the same section of town. Of these two sources of network support, the nonkin allies variable was a much stronger predictor than was the number of local female kin. Riley noted that the two were related; fathers with fewer local kinfolk had more nonkin allies. He suggested the intriguing possibility that today some men are substituting multiply-supportive nonkin bonds for the traditional extended family bonds sustained by other men.

In the case of the one-earner families the pattern was different: There was a powerful effect for what Riley called the *male network* variable, showing that as the percentage of men in the network increased, the father's share of parent–child play went down. The existence of local female relatives also decreased the father's play involvement. The local female kin seemed to re-duce the demand for the father's assistance in childrearing, and the male peer group to maintain activities and attitudes in competition with the father's home role. Riley concluded by emphasizing that in two-parent households maternal employment status appeared to represent a crucial ecological divide. His findings indicated that fathers are often pushed into childrearing involvement, or away from it, by situational demands. The ex-istence of a local female kin network appeared to relieve the pressure on the father to participate in childrearing (or it may have competed with him if he wanted more responsibility for his children). At the same time, there was evidence that fathers may to some extent select or construct the social environment that thereafter influences them. The male peer group and nonkin allies are highly amenable to active construction by the individual. This is especially true for the nonkin allies, since they represent social bonds encompassing diverse kinds of support content, often with an indi-vidual known through no regular role-context.

Cotterell (1986), working in rural towns of inland Australia, was inter-ested in the influences on childrearing of the father's workplace, the mother's social network, and the community itself. With a total of 96 mar-ried mothers he compared the personal networks of and the childrearing milieus provided by those with husbands regularly present with those whose partners' jobs routinely required periods of absence from home. Character-istics of the childrearing environment were measured with the Caldwell

HOME inventory, and the quality of maternal expectations and beliefs was assessed with the Parent as a Teacher (PAAT) inventory. Analysis of the network data indicated that mothers with absentee husbands relied more heavily on their neighbors than those with husbands regularly at home. When the *quality of childrearing* variables were analyzed by father presence/ absence and mother's amount of informational support from the network, the characteristics of the father's work exerted independent influence on only two of the variables, while the effects of support were statistically significant for six of the seven childrearing measures. In order to assess the separate and joint contributions of the three environmental dimensions, Cotterell entered them all with the childrearing variables in a regression equation. In his own words:

> Between 40% and 60% of the variance explained in the full model could be attributed to the factors of father absence, community characteristics, and mother's informational support. Of the three factors, the support factor had the greatest prominence in terms of its power to add significantly to the variance in the measures of childrearing quality. (p. 369)

Cotterell was careful to point out the danger of assuming that these three environmental forces—general character of the community, father's work situation and network support—operate independently and at the same level of influence. He suggested that "the chain of influence of father's work is connected to maternal behavior via the patterns of social relationships established by the mother" (p. 371). His evidence indicated that the wives of absentee husbands had smaller networks, and that these women had a more limited range of settings available for contacting network members.

It is important to keep in mind the effects of context on the value of support as an influence on parenting. Ceballo and McLloyd (2002) examined whether living under stressful neighborhood conditions influences social support's effects on parenting behavior. Their sample was 262 low income, African-American single mothers of middle school age children who resided in lower and working-class urban neighborhoods. As neighborhood quality decreased, based on mothers' perceptions, violent crime rate statistics, and levels of poverty by families in the area, emotional support from friends and relatives had less influence on mothers' nurturant parenting. Similarly, the negative relation between instrumental support and maternal punishment was also weakened as neighborhood quality diminished. The findings suggest that in certain conditions, social support may have limited value as a cushion to mothers' stress. The authors cautioned that a fuller understanding of parenting behavior should include the consideration of context as potential moderator of psychological relations.

Crockenberg (1988), in her review of the theories explaining how social support affects parental behavior, identified four processes by which benefits might be conveyed. First, support can reduce the sheer number of stressful events. The instrumental support described earlier probably operates largely in this manner. Babysitting, childrearing advice, and financial assistance simply provide relief from daily burdens that might otherwise accumulate to incapacitate the parent, or press her or him into inappropriate or even abusive behavior patterns.

It is possible that social support may not directly reduce the number of stressful events experienced by the parent, but may act as a buffer, preventing the parent from being as adversely affected by a stressful event, like divorce or job loss, and making it possible for parents to maintain satisfactory childrearing routines in the face of hard times. This second process is probably not an alternative to sheer reduction of stressful events, but rather operates in addition to it.

Crockenberg identified generation of active coping strategies as the third process by which social supports may have beneficial effects on parents. This process operates on the initiatives side of the model presented in Fig. 8.1; the mother's self confidence is bolstered by praise from a supportive and more experienced network member, and her skills improve as a result of suggestions from this person. The result is willingness and ability to take positive initiatives, rather than passivity generated by inexperience and self-doubt.

The fourth process identified by Crockenberg involves the emotional support that emerged from several of the studies reviewed earlier as an important predictor of more constructive parenting behaviors. She tied emotional support to the idea of working models of relationships outlined previously in relation to maltreating parents (Crittenden, 1985b), pointing out that "ongoing emotional support or nurturance may affirm this sense [of herself or himself as a person deserving of care and capable of caring for someone else] and in doing so encourage the individual's inclination to be nurturant to others" (p. 146).

THE PERSONAL NETWORKS OF MOTHERS, AND CHILD-RELATED OUTCOMES

It is important to go beyond relations between parents' networks and their childrearing attitudes and behaviors, to consider the question of whether the social resources available to parents actually have an impact on the development of their children. Space limitations permit the presentation of only four illustrative examples of the link to child development. Crockenberg (1981) was interested in ways that social support might affect the nature of the emotional bond between mother and infant. Her sample was middle- and working-class in socioeconomic composition. She stated her primary findings rather unambiguously:

> The adequacy of the mother's social support is clearly and consistently associated with the security of the infant–mother attachment: low social support was associated with high resistance, high avoidance, and with anxious attachment. Moreover, that support had its strongest effects on the irritable babies and their mothers suggests that the availability of social support is particularly critical when the family is under particular stress. (p. 862)

The fact that the positive relation between social support for the mother and the attachment behaviors of the child was obtained primarily in the case of irritable babies is important to note. An environmental demand, the irritable baby, appears to have created the conditions calling for mobilization of existing support.

Melson, Ladd, and Hsu (1993) tested a model of maternal network characteristics as direct influences on children's social and cognitive development and as indirect influences through mother's attributions about parenting. The sample was comprised of 69 primarily European-American, moderately high SES mothers and their preschool age children from a university preschool setting. Network size and quality (including components of contact frequency, duration, and perceived helpfulness, conflict, satisfaction and a willingness to seek help), directly predicted child cognitive performance. Children's exposure to stimulation and network influences on maternal interactions were cited as probable processes at play. Indirectly, network size positively influenced cognitive performance and peer acceptance through maternal attributions about helping the child. Network size was also related to differing patterns of attributions depending on the ease of the helping situation. Mothers who had larger social networks were more likely to attribute an easy situation of cognitive or social assistance to the child, and they were less likely to make a child attribution when the situation of assistance was difficult. The authors suggested that more support from a larger social network may expose mothers to more information about caring for their children, generate a greater sense of well-being in mothers, and help them feel more positive toward the children.

Manetti and Schneider (1996) examined the direct connection between the structure and satisfaction with parents' social networks and children's adjustment to the transition to elementary school. They studied an Italian sample of mothers, their spouses, and their children over a three-year period, beginning when the children were 4- and 5-year-olds. The size of the mothers' networks at year one predicted the adjustment of the children to school two years later, as measured by teacher ratings. Network support to mothers who experienced stressful life events showed a stronger impact. For these mothers, both network size and frequency of contact were predictive of children's school adjustment, at one point in time (year three) and over time (year one data predicting year three adjustment). The findings were related only to the mother's social network. The authors cautioned that the lack of findings for the fathers may be related to small numbers in the sample over time.

With an ethnically and economically diverse sample, Marshall and colleagues (Marshall, Noonan, McCartney, Marx, & Keefe, 2001) looked at the social networks of African-American, European-American and Latin-American parents with an elementary school age child (grades 1 to 4) to determine the relation, if any, between parents' social networks and several aspects of children's well-being. This study differed from others in that nonstandard measures of size and structure were used to measure the social network. Network homogeneity was determined by whether or not kin were within walking distance, and network size was determined by the number of neighbors the parent knew well enough to stop and talk with outside the home. Also, the children were involved by answering questions about the availability of adults to talk about their feelings.

There was no difference in emotional support provided by the social networks to parents of different races or ethnic backgrounds. European-American parents had less extended family nearby and were more involved with their neighbors. African-American parents were more likely to rely on relatives than on friends in aspects of caring for their children and, like Latin-American families, had more extended family nearby. Although neighborhood ties were positively associated with children's social competence and negatively associated with children's depression, when parent gender, maternal education and ethnicity were controlled, these direct relations were no longer detected. However, indirect effects of social networks on child outcomes were found through the influence of the network on parental behavior and efficacy. Parents with more heterogeneous networks demonstrated more responsive, warm parenting practices, and their children had fewer behavior problems. This outcome was also observed in the children of those parents who reported feeling more effective in their parenting role, which was influenced by the degree of emotional support from their networks. And, parents with heterogeneous networks also provided a more stimulating home environment for their children, who showed more positive social skills.

PERSONAL SOCIAL NETWORKS
AND PROGRAM IMPACTS

Acknowledging the potential impact of personal networks on parents, parenting programs have begun to explore how personal social networks relate to the accomplishment of program goals. The social and cognitive processes occurring through a parent's interaction with her social network—information gathering, cognitive stimulation, social integration—that result in changes in parenting perceptions or practices (Cochran, 1990) are also stimulated by a parent's participation in parent education and support programs. Such programs trigger personal social network interactions. For instance, Tracy, Whittaker, Kapp, and Overstreet (1994) suggested the value of understanding parents' social network membership and functions in meeting the goals of family preservation. Workers who are aware of families' social networks will discern a variety of supports available to families, and can identify gaps in their support needs. Understanding the membership and functions of the caregivers' social network could also enable workers to encourage the more timely mobilization of network resources. Encouraging parents to ask others for help widens their base of support and decreases dependency on the worker as the primary source of support.

Program and social network interactions can also operate conjointly. Sheldon (2002) examined how the structure of personal social networks might influence parent involvement with their children's education at home and at school. Helping children prepare and participate in school, complete homework and school assignments, learn school concepts, and advocating for students in the school system enhances student achievement and engagement in learning. Yet educators acknowledge that many parents are not as involved as they might be with their children's education, and seek to find ways to bolster their participation.

Sheldon asked a sample of urban and suburban parents of children in grades 1 to 5 to identify up to seven other parents at their child's school with whom they discussed issues related to the child's education, and up to five other adults outside the school with whom they talked a lot about the child's education. These other adults were identified as relatives, those who worked in education, or a parent of a child enrolled in a different school. His analysis included the number and types of adults in parents' school discussion networks. Including background characteristics and parents' beliefs about the importance of being active in children's education in the models, network size predicted parent involvement at home and at school, although the variance accounted for was small (about 4%) in both cases. In addition, involvement was related to whom parents interacted with about their children's education: involvement with other parents at school predicted participation at school; involvement with other adults out of the school predicted participation at home. Sheldon observed that in his sample of urban and suburban parents, one-third reported not talking to any other parents about the school or their child's education. He suggested that connecting these isolated parents to other parents would be a way to help them gain information about the child's school and empower them to

make decisions about their children's education. Community empowerment initiatives built on this idea have shown benefit to immigrant families
(Delgado-Gaitan, 1993).

Walker and Riley (2001) took the idea of social network involvement as
an indicator of program involvement a step further by exploring whether
involvement was a vehicle to observed changes in parent behavior. New parents' primary sources of information about the development and care of an
infant include family and friends, and the pediatrician. Evaluations of an
age-paced newsletter about infant caregiving delivered to parents consistently showed it to be a reliable, credible, and popular source of information as well, and demonstrated positive results in self-reported change of
parenting behavior. The authors investigated how new parents' social networks of informational support on childrearing intersected with the educational process of the newsletter intervention. They asked whether new parents' discussions of the content of an age-paced newsletter with members of
their personal social network would affect the degree of behavior and confidence change they would report from reading the newsletter. Instead of
constructing a supportive group or class setting typical of many parenting
education programs, the study capitalized on a natural phenomenon of
parenting—talking with family and friends. By using a one-way form of
mass communication as the intervention method, variability in program
stimulus (also likely with different instructors and settings) was eliminated.

A primarily European-American sample of first time and experienced
mothers ($n = 427$) was surveyed about their program participation (use of
the newsletter, or amount read), and the degree to which they involved others in their social networks (which and how many people with whom they
shared copies of the newsletter and discussed newsletter content). Behavior
change was measured by self-reports of degree of change in five areas of
parenting (for example, providing a stimulating environment, responding
to baby's cries and cues) and change in confidence. Mothers reported discussing newsletter content with an average of two other people (usually the
father plus one other). Topics of discussion focused primarily on development, nutrition and feeding, and behavior.

Examining degree of behavior change with social network involvement,
mothers who shared and/or discussed the newsletter content with more
people (five or more) reported the highest degree of change and the differences in change scores were significant. Using path analysis to test the
mediational hypothesis, reading the newsletter was associated with greater
parental change whether or not they discussed newsletter content with others. But sharing and discussing the newsletters with others was associated
with greater self-reported parental change. When the network involvement
variable was added to the model, it produced a small (2%) but significant
increase in the explained variance. The two processes, reading the newslet-

ter and discussing and sharing it with others in the social network were significantly linked, but not so strongly that network involvement mediated the effect of participation; they were largely separate processes. Walker and Riley concluded from the findings that social network processes and parenting education intervention may exist as parallel learning environments for new parents and function perhaps, as separate channels of information about childrearing. But the analyses also revealed that they operate conjointly. The authors observed that the processes were correlated and that the measure of network involvement referred only to interactions around program (newsletter) content. This research encourages the question whether other results reported by parenting programs may, in part, be the result of stimulated interaction with the parents' personal support network.

CONCLUSIONS

In this chapter we consider parenting and social networks in ecological context. Larger systems with particular influence on parents' social ties include higher education environments, the workplace, and the neighborhood. Evidence that personal networks influence the attitudes and behaviors of parents is accumulating slowly, but findings from recent studies are consistent with those done earlier, and the samples involved are becoming increasingly representative. Kinfolk certainly are important as primary supporters, and to reinforce traditional parenting values and childrearing practices. Nonrelatives also appear to play important roles as supplementary (and even in some cases primary) supports and as sources of new information for parents. There is growing evidence, coming from both the United States and abroad, that nonkin can, within supportive environmental circumstances, function like kin in their support of friends who are parents.

There are also a few studies indicating that the support and assistance provided to parents by their network membership translates into more constructive childrearing practices, and positive outcomes in the child. More fine-grained, process-oriented studies have been conducted in recent years, and additional studies are needed before we will be able to trace exactly how this support translates into parenting activities that produce more competent children.

If certain kinds of networks are more beneficial than others for parents, then it behooves us to better understand network development, because in those developmental processes lie the keys to identifying ways that local communities and the larger society can structure themselves to facilitate the functioning of families in their childrearing roles. The policy implications of the constraints identified on the left hand side of Fig. 8.1 deserve serious consideration. Polices that increase the availability of post-secondary education would appear to deserve highest priority, because those parents who had acquired such schooling were much richer in network resources than those who had not. College scholarships, student loans, and programs providing incentives to adolescents and young adults for continuation of schooling through high school and beyond would seem to be an especially good investment to society from this standpoint.

Policies that stimulate job creation and continuation would also deserve high priority from a *networks in context* perspective. The workplace has been seen in our studies to be an important context for network building, and the economic returns associated with working provide the resources needed to sustain network relations. Just as importantly, the absence of job security for much of today's semi- or unskilled and non-unionized work force reduces the capacity of the workplace to support the development of social relationships among co-workers. Economic instability also contributes to residential mobility as families leave the state to seek better fortune in another part of the country. The protection of job security and assurances of fair treatment for employees during hard times would support the social as well as the economic well-being of working families.

We would be remiss, however, if in closing we left the impression that enhancement of network development can come only through removal of societal constraints. Several of the factors contributing to parental initiative in developing their network relations are accessible to public policies and programs. Educational opportunity has already been mentioned. Home visiting and parent support groups, if carried out in an empowering way, enhance parental self-esteem, and thereby increase network-building potential. Any family support program that provides parents with respite, and more time to devote to family life, increases the capacity of parents to engage in the social activities that develop and maintain network ties. And initial research about the intersection of parenting program influences and parents' social networks suggests great potential for strengthening network ties and relations through parent education and support programs.

At the same time, the most important policy lesson to be learned from the various studies of networks and parenting is that it is not nearly enough simply to provide opportunities for social interaction, and the message that social ties are important, if parents are to be supported on behalf of their own development and that of their children. Public policies must give first priority to freeing parents, and those who will become parents, from the constraints of inequality and oppression, by insuring the provision of adequate and sufficient education, employment, and housing conditions. The evidence suggests that freedom to grow and develop, through schooling, work, and leisure activities, will lead in turn to the social network connections that form the basis for healthy, productive communities.

ACKNOWLEDGMENTS

Permission to use the material in Figs. 8.1–8.3 has been provided by Cambridge University Press.

REFERENCES

Alcalay, R. (1983). Health and social support networks: A case for improving interpersonal communication. *Social Networks, 4,* 71–88.

Belle, D. (1982). Social ties and social support. In D. Belle (Ed.), *Lives in stress: Women and depression* (pp. 223–241). Beverly Hills, CA: Sage Publications.

Boissevain, J., & Mitchell, J. C. (1973). *Network analysis: Studies in human interaction.* The Hague: Mounton.

Bost, K. K., Cox, M. J., Burchinal, M. R., & Payne, C. (2002). Structural and supportive changes in couples' family and friendship networks across the transition to parenthood. *Journal of Marriage and the Family, 64,* 517–531.

Bott, E. (1957). *Family and social networks.* London: Havistock.

Brassard, J. (1982). *Beyond family structure: Mother–child interaction and personal social networks.* Unpublished doctoral dissertation, Cornell University, Ithaca, New York.

Bryant, B. (1985). The neighborhood walk: Sources of support in middle childhood. *Monographs of the Society for Research in Child Development, 50*(3, Serial No. 210).

Ceballo, R., & McLloyd, V. (2002). Social support and parenting in poor, dangerous neighborhoods. *Child Development, 73,* 1310–1321.

Chess, S., & Thomas, A. (1984). *Origins and evolution of behavior disorders.* New York: Bruner/ Mazel.

Cobb, S. (1976). Social support as a moderator of life stress. *Psychosomatic Medicine, 39,* 300–314.

Cochran, M. (1990). The network as an environment for human development. In M. Cochran, M. Larner, D. Riley, L. Gunnarsson, & C. Henderson, Jr. (Eds.), *Extending families: The social networks of parents and their children* (pp. 265–276). London/New York: Cambridge University Press.

Cochran, M., & Brassard, J. (1979). Child development and personal social networks. *Child Development, 50,* 609–615.

Cochran, M., & Bø, I. (1989). The social networks, family involvement and pro- and anti-social behavior of adolescent males in Norway. *Journal of Youth and Adolescence, 18*(4), 377–398.

Cochran, M., & Gunnarsson, L. (1990). The social networks of married mothers in four cultures. In M. Cochran, M. Larner, D. Riley, L. Gunnarsson, & C. Henderson, Jr. (Eds.), *Extending families: The social networks of parents and their children* (pp. 86–104). London/New York: Cambridge University Press.

Cochran, M., & Riley, D. (1990). The social networks of six-year-olds: Context, content, and consequence. In M. Cochran, M. Larner, D. Riley, L. Gunnarsson, & C. Henderson, Jr. (Eds.), *Extending families: The social networks of parents and their children* (pp. 154–178). London/New York: Cambridge University Press.

Cochran, M., Larner, M., Riley, D., Gunnarsson, L., & Henderson, C., Jr. (1990). *Extending families: The social networks of parents and their children.* London/New York: Cambridge University Press.

Colletta, N. (1981). Social support and the risk of maternal rejection by adolescent mothers. *Journal of Psychology, 109,* 191–197.

Cotterell, J. (1986). Work and community influences on the quality of childrearing. *Child Development, 57,* 362–374.

Crittenden, P. (1981). Abusing, neglecting, problematic, and adequate dyads: Differentiating by patterns of interaction. *Merrill-Palmer Quarterly, 27,* 1–18.

Crittenden, P. (1985a). Maltreated infants: Vulnerability and resistance. *Journal of Child Psychology and Psychiatry, 26,* 85–96.

Crittenden, P. (1985b). Social networks, quality of child rearing, and child development. *Child Development, 56,* 1299–1313.

Crockenberg, S. (1981). Infant irritability, mother responsiveness, and social support influences on the security of infant–mother attachment. *Child Development, 52,* 857–865.

Crockenberg, S. (1987). Support for adolescent mothers during the postnatal period: Theory and research. In C. F. Z. Boukydis (Ed.), *Research on support for parents and infants in the postnatal period.* New York: Ablex.

Crockenberg, S. (1988). Social support and parenting. In H. Fitzgerald, B. Lester, & M. Yogman (Eds.), *Theory and research in behavioral pediatrics* (Vol. 4, pp. 67–92). New York/London: Plenum.

Cross, W. (1990). Race and ethnicity: Effects on social networks. In M. Cochran, M. Larner, D. Riley, L. Gunnarsson, & C. Henderson, Jr. (Eds.), *Extending families: The social networks of parents and their children* (pp. 67–85). London/New York: Cambridge University Press.

Delgado-Gaitan, C. (1993). Parenting in two generations of Mexican American families. *International Journal of Behavioral Development, 16*(3), 409–427.

Fischer, C. (1982). *To dwell among friends: Personal networks in town and city.* Chicago: University of Chicago Press.

Granovetter, M. (1973). The strength of weak ties. *American Journal of Sociology, 78,* 1360–1380.

Gunnarsson, L., & Cochran, M. (1990). The social networks of single parents: Sweden and the United States. In M. Cochran, M. Larner, D. Riley, L. Gunnarsson, & C. Henderson, Jr. (Eds.), *Extending families: The social networks of parents and their children* (pp. 105–116). London/New York: Cambridge University Press.

Haraven, T. (1984). Themes in the historical development of the family. In R. D. Parke (Ed.), *Review of child development research* (Vol. 7, pp. 86–101). Chicago: University of Chicago Press.

Hinde, R., Stevenson-Hinde, J., & Tamplin, A. (1985). Characteristics of 3- to 4-year-olds assessed at home and their interactions in pre-school. *Developmental Psychology, 21,* 130–140.

Jennings, K. D., Stagg, V., & Connors, R. (1991). Social networks and mothers' interactions with their preschool children. *Child Development, 62,* 966–978.

Larner, M. (1990). Changes in network resources and relationships over time. In M. Cochran, M. Larner, D. Riley, L. Gunnarsson, & C. Henderson, Jr. (Eds.), *Extending families: The social networks of parents and their children* (pp. 181–204). London/New York: Cambridge University Press.

MacPhee, D., Fritz, J., & Miller-Heyl, J. (1996). Ethnic variations in personal social networks and parenting. *Child Development, 67,* 3278–3295.

Manetti, M., & Schneider, B. H. (1996). Stability and change in patterns of parental social support and their relation to children's school adjustment. *Journal of Applied Developmental Psychology, 17,* 101–115.

Marshall, N., Noonan, A., McCartney, K., Marx, F., & Keefe, N. (2001). It takes an urban village. Parenting networks of urban families. *Journal of Family Issues, 22,* 163–182.

McLanahan, S., Wedemeyer, N., & Adelberg, T. (1981). Network structure, social support and psychological well-being in the single-parent family. *Journal of Marriage and the Family, 43,* 601–612.

Melson, G. F., Ladd, G. W., & Hsu, H. (1993). Maternal support networks, maternal cognitions, and young children's social and cognitive development. *Child Development, 64,* 1401–1417.

Miller-Loncar, C. L., Erwin, L. J., Landry, S. H., Smith, K. E., & Swank, P. R. (1998). Characteristics of social support networks of low socioeconomic status African American, Anglo American, and Mexican American mothers of full-term and preterm infants. *Journal of Community Psychology, 26,* 131–143.

Mitchell, J. C. (1969). *Social networks in urban situations.* Manchester, England: Manchester University Press.

Polansky, N., Gaudin, J., Ammons, P., & Davis, K. (1985). The psychological ecology of the neglectful mother. *Child Abuse & Neglect, 9,* 265–275.

Quinton, D., & Rutter, M. (1985). Parenting behavior of mothers raised "in care." In R. Nicol (Ed.), *Longitudinal studies in child psychology and psychiatry.* Chichester, England: Wiley.

Riley, D. (1990). Network influences on father involvement in childrearing. In M. Cochran, M. Larner, D. Riley, L. Gunnarsson, & C. Henderson, Jr. (Eds.), *Extending families: The social networks of parents and their children.* London/New York: Cambridge University Press.

Rogosch, F. A., Mowbray, C. T., & Bogat, G. A. (1992). Determinants of parenting attitudes in mothers with severe psychopathology. *Development and Psychology, 4,* 469–487.

Roschelle, A. (1997). *No more kin: Exploring race, class and gender in family networks.* Thousand Oaks, CA: Sage.

Sheldon, S. B. (2002). Parents' social networks and beliefs as predictors of parent involvement. *The Elementary School Journal, 102*(4), 301–316.

Simons, R. L., Lorenz, F. O., Wu, C., & Conger, R. D. (1993). Social network and marital support as mediators and moderators of the impact of stress and depression on parental behavior. *Developmental Psychology, 29*(2), 368–381.

Thomas, A., & Chess, S. (1977). *Temperament and development.* New York: Bruner/Mazel.

Tracy, E. M., Whittaker, A. P., Kapp, S., & Overstreet, E. J. (1994). Support networks for primary caregivers receiving family preservation services: An exploratory study. *Families in Society: The Journal of Contemporary Human Services, 75*(8), 481–489.

Voight, J. D., Hans, S. L., & Bernstein, V. J. (1996). Support networks of adolescent mothers: Effects on parenting experience and behavior. *Infant Mental Health Journal, 17*(1), 58–73.

Walker, S. K., & Riley, D. A. (2001). Involvement of the personal social network as a factor in parent education effectiveness. *Family Relations, 50,* 186–193.

Wellman, B. (1979). The community question: The intimate networks of East Yorkers. *American Journal of Sociology, 84,* 129–131.

Wellman, B. (1981). Applying network analysis to the study of support. In B. H. Gottlieb (Ed.), *Social networks and social support* (pp. 166–183). Beverly Hills, CA: Sage Publications.

Wilson, M. N., & Tolson, T. F. J. (1990). Familial support in the Black community. *Journal of Clinical Child Psychology, 19,* 347–355.

9

The Long Arm of the Job Revisited: Parenting in Dual-Earner Families

Ann C. Crouter
Susan M. McHale
The Pennsylvania State University

INTRODUCTION

In *Middletown*, the classic monograph about U.S. culture, Lynd and Lynd (1929) coined the phrase "the long arm of the job" to describe the considerable influence that fathers' employment situations had on their families. As the Lynds explained, the temporal rhythms of work life and the specter of unemployment helped to shape many aspects of family life in Middletown, including parents' childrearing activities. In the years since that publication, the phrase "the long arm of the job" has been borrowed by other scholars too. Waller (1938) used it as a chapter title in his book, *The family: A dynamic interpretation,* as did Komarovsky (1962) in *Blue Collar Marriage.* Menaghan (1991) used the term "the long reach of the job" in her chapter on work and family for the *Annual Review of Sociology*. We were pleased to join this tradition in our chapter (Crouter & McHale, 1993a) in the first edition of *Parenting: An Ecological Perspective* and to continue it in our current reassessment of the influences of parental work on childrearing.

In our 1993 chapter on the long arm of the job, we acknowledged that the influence of work on family life was no less important then than it was in the Lynds' day, but we noted that the relationship between these two social institutions had become more complex with the entrance of large numbers of mothers into the paid labor force. Indeed, the movement of women, especially mothers of young children, into the labor force is one of the most dramatic demographic trends of the twentieth century (Hernandez, 1997).

This trend shows no signs of abating in the early twenty-first century. In many families today, there are two long arms of the job, one reaching back to the father's world of work and the other to the mother's work setting. In this chapter we focus on the way this dual-earner lifestyle poses certain opportunities and constraints for contemporary parents.

In the ecological framework, mother's workplace and father's workplace constitute an important exosystem for their developing children (and for one another as well). According to Bronfenbrenner (1979), "An exosystem refers to one or more settings that do not involve the developing person as an active participant, but in which events occur that affect, or are affected by, what happens in the setting containing the developing person" (p. 25).

Parenting researchers have examined work–family relations from several angles. Some look at the work–family interface through the lens of the workplace, and others examine these interconnections through the lens of the family (Kline & Cowan, 1989). When researchers examine the work–parenting interface through the lens of the workplace, parents' jobs are seen as ecological settings with certain characteristics and features. Work may be conceptualized broadly or narrowly. A broad view would include issues of subsistence, that is, how adults in a culture or subculture provide for their families. A narrower view of work zooms in on proximal processes such as daily work loads and interactions with co-workers and supervisors that shape ebbs and flows in parents' psychological well-being. When seen through the lens of the workplace, the question for researchers becomes: How does parents' involvement in certain work ecologies, as defined by their roles, relationships, and activities in those settings, influence the ways in which they rear their children?

When the research lens focuses on families, specific characteristics of parents' jobs are often peripheral or even ignored. Instead the emphasis is on how families function as settings for childrearing and differ in terms of mothers' and fathers' roles in the paid labor force. An ecological approach involves an examination of those familial processes that are similar and different across families with different connections to the labor force. When developmental researchers first examined work and family issues, the dominant questions in this genre focused on the implications of mothers' employment status for parenting and child development (see review of early research in this area by Bronfenbrenner & Crouter, 1982). More recently, and in part in acknowledgment of the widespread nature of maternal employment, there is less attention to maternal employment status and more attention to how much time mothers and, to a lesser extent, fathers spend at work. In a sense, the interest in mothers' and fathers' work hours reflects the tendency of developmental researchers to equate parents' work time with absence from the family.

In this chapter, we describe research that examines the work–parenting interface through both lenses, noting the strengths, limitations, and unexplored territory in each. We begin by examining characteristics of parents' jobs that may affect their patterns of childrearing and then turn to consider how living in a dual-earner family may influence women's and men's activities as parents.

THROUGH THE LENS OF THE WORKPLACE: CHARACTERISTICS OF WORK THAT MATTER FOR CHILDREARING

When the impact of parental work on parenting is viewed through the lens of the workplace, there are three levels of analysis to consider. At the broadest level, work is adults' means of subsistence and, as such, is a central determinant of their world views (Kanter, 1977). Work informs parents' conceptualizations of how their environments operate and the qualities required to be successful in these environments (Kohn, 1977; Ogbu, 1981). These ideas in turn shape parents' values about the characteristics that are important to inculcate in their young.

At an intermediate level, the characteristics of parents' jobs and the organizations in which they are employed pose opportunities and constraints for parenting. For example, some jobs encourage the acquisition of skills that are applicable not only on the job but at home. Other work settings provide informal support to working parents via helpful co-workers and supervisors or access to formal workplace benefits and programs that enable parents to carry out their parenting roles more effectively. Jobs also come with characteristic stressors, such as low control, fast pace, or frequent deadlines, stressors that have implications over time for the quality of parenting.

Finally, the work–parenting system can be examined at a very proximal, immediate level, a view of work–family dynamics that focuses on daily work experiences. Although most jobs have fairly stable characteristics, such as a schedule, an assortment of supportive or unsupportive co-workers, and certain activities that make up the nature of the work itself, there are also daily fluctuations in work demands and interpersonal interactions that shape the daily emotional state of the employee. "How was your day?" is a familiar question in the post-reunion script of family members. The answer to that question usually is based on the unusual occurrences of that particular day and often has to do with how those events made the person feel. Here, work is seen as an influence on parents' emotional states, moods that in turn may be brought home to influence the tenor and content of parent–child and mother–father interactions.

Work and the Acquisition of Parenting Values

Anthropologist Ogbu (1981) argued that adults acquire ideas about what it takes to be successful in their culture by observing prevailing subsistence patterns, that is, by observing work roles in the culture that are associated with success. In a hunting and gathering society, for example, adults identify the characteristics of successful hunters (e.g., individualism, bravery, risk-taking, and independence) as those traits that they value and wish to inculcate in their children (Barry, Child, & Bacon, 1959). Ogbu (1981) explained that adults form theories of childrearing that correspond to those values and, in turn, they develop childrearing techniques designed to foster these desirable qualities in children. Miller and Swanson (1958) provided early evidence for this idea in their comparison of parental values of mothers whose husbands were employed in entrepreneurial versus bureaucratic work settings. The former group emphasized achievement and striving in their children, whereas their bureaucratic counterparts emphasized interpersonal skills and getting along well with others in their reports of childrearing values.

Note that the early work in this area simplified the picture considerably. The causal arrow was seen to run in one direction: from work (notably fathers' work) to parenting values. There was little recognition that powerful sorting mechanisms function to distribute people into jobs on a non-random basis, as is the case in western, industrialized societies. People select (and are selected for) jobs based on a complex set of variables including aptitudes, educational background, specific job related training, interests, skills, perceptions of opportunity, attraction to the lifestyle represented by the job, and so forth. Thus, before they even take their first jobs, future entrepreneurs and bureaucrats undoubtedly differ on many characteristics that may in turn have implications for parenting. The reciprocal linkages between work and the individual are rarely acknowledged in work and family research but are critically important. Jobs shape individual functioning, but individuals also actively select in and out of careers, occupations, and specific jobs.

One of the leading researchers in the area of work and parental values who has recognized the complex, reciprocal linkages between work and individual characteristics is sociologist Kohn. In *Class and Conformity*, Kohn (1977) argued that men who differ in their occupational position in the stratification system come to see the world differently and that the characteristics associated with success in men's occupational niches influence the qualities they value in their children and, consequently, the characteristics they will support or discourage in the context of daily childrearing activities. In a survey of more than 3,000 employed men, Kohn (1977) found that men in middle-class occupations tended to value independence and initiative in their offspring, whereas their working class counterparts tended to value obedience and conformity.

The mechanisms through which parents translate abstract childrearing values into daily childrearing activities are murky in Kohn's research. He found that middle-class fathers were more likely to report using reasoning and withdrawal of love as discipline techniques than were working-class fathers. Middle-class fathers also reported taking their child's intentions into account when determining disciplinary action; misbehavior seen as accidental thereby receives less severe punishment than misbehavior seen as intentional. Working-class fathers, on the other hand, reported using more physical punishment and indicated that they punished on the basis of the consequences of their child's misbehavior rather than the child's intentions. Compliance seemed to be the primary goal of working-class fathers, and an internalized standard could be seen as the goal for middle-class fathers. Nonetheless, a clear correspondence between values and childrearing strategy is missing in Kohn's research. Additional limitations of this early research were that it focused only on fathers and was based on fathers' self-reported practices in hypothetical situations. It is difficult to ascertain what their behavior would be in real life.

Parcel and Menaghan built on the occupational socialization tradition in a series of studies using data from the National Longitudinal Survey of Youth (NLSY) (Parcel & Menaghan, 1994; Menaghan, 1991; Menaghan & Parcel, 1995). They were particularly interested in the connections between parental work conditions and the nature of the home environment. A strength of their work has been the focus on the substantive complexity of jobs, a component of a more global construct Kohn and Schooler (1983) term "occupational self-direction." Parcel and Menaghan operationalized complexity by matching NLSY mothers' occupations with objective data on work demands provided by the *Dictionary of Occupational Titles.* Arguing that, "having a parent in a complex job can be a resource for children in that it sets a high level of expectation regarding self-direction and intellectual flexibility" (Parcel & Menaghan, 1994, p. 14), they found that, controlling for mothers' education, age, measured mental ability, income and other possible confounds, mothers employed in jobs with greater substantive complexity created more stimulating home environments for their children. The positive effects of high maternal job complexity were particularly important when the father held a job low in complexity.

Menaghan and Parcel's (1995) longitudinal analyses also illustrated the potential effects of movement in and out of jobs of varying complexity. Home environments deteriorated over time in the extent to which they offered stimulation and support for children if mothers moved into jobs low in substantive complexity but improved if mothers moved into more substantively complex jobs. Declines in the home environment were particularly pronounced for unmarried women who took on jobs low in complexity and low in wages. The quality of home environments in turn was related to children's receptive vocabulary at ages 3 to 6 and reading and math skills at ages 5 to 8 (Parcel & Menaghan, 1994). Interestingly, Parcel and Menaghan (1994) did not find statistical evidence that the quality of the home environment mediated the effects of occupational self-direction on child outcomes. Thus, the processes through which occupational complexity affects children's development remain unclear.

In a small scale study of 65 mother–infant dyads, Luster, Rhoades, and Haas (1989) focused more precisely on what the mechanisms might be that may link social class and parenting behavior during the first year of life. These researchers replicated the finding that social class is related to parents' values of conformity and self-direction in their children. They also identified a set of specific parental beliefs that mediated the relation between parental values and parenting behavior. Global parenting values were related to specific attitudes about spoiling the baby, giving babies freedom to explore the home environment, discipline, and the importance of verbal stimulation. These specific beliefs, in turn, were related to mothers' supportive and constraining behaviors toward their babies as reported by the mothers themselves and as rated by interviewers.

The dual-earner arrangement, so prevalent today, raises the issue that mothers and fathers, by virtue of their occupational positions, may identify different qualities as important and come to favor different childrearing practices. A mismatch in childrearing values and strategies may be unusual, however, given patterns of assortative mating in this culture (i.e., men and women who marry tend to have similar levels of education and thus would probably gravitate to jobs at similar levels in the occupational hierarchy) and given the fact that husbands and wives socialize one another throughout the life course (Gruber-Baldini, Schaie, & Willis, 1995). On the other hand, due to the prevalence of occupational segregation along gender lines, even within occupations, men and women tend to hold quite different jobs (Baron & Bielby, 1985). A hypothesis for future research is that incongruence in occupational position (and hence, world view) for husbands and wives is linked to differences in childrearing values and philosophy.

Workplace Opportunities and Constraints for Parenting

By virtue of the job that a parent holds and the nature of the specific workplace in which that job is carried out, mothers and fathers are exposed to certain opportunities and constraints with regard to their parenting role. In his review of the "determinants of parenting," Belsky (1984) conceptualized the influence of work on parenting in terms of stress and support. Although stress and support are important, a full consideration of the place of work in parents' lives requires thinking about dimensions of work experiences that are perhaps neither stressful nor supportive but serve to encourage parents to structure childrearing in qualitatively different ways.

Skill Development. Work has long been recognized as an important setting for adult socialization and development, but little research has focused on whether and how the skills and orientations attained at work make their mark on employed adults' behaviors in others settings, such as the family. If, for example, work-based training on stress management, communication, and administration result in the employed adult acquiring new skills, presumably these new capabilities generalize to other settings in which the adult spends time.

Crouter (1984) explored these issues in a qualitative study of employees in a manufacturing plant that was experimenting with new ways of involving blue-collar employees in managing their own work activities. Organized into small, semi-autonomous work teams, machinists and assembly workers participated in hiring fellow team members, monitoring work performance, ordering inventory, handling machine breakdowns, monitoring quality and safety, and interacting with external vendors and customers. Teams held meetings in which members were expected to voice their points of view constructively, listen to one another, problem solve, and make collective decisions. At various times, workers would leave the team area to participate in training exercises designed to improve teamwork. In semi-structured interviews, workers noted that they found themselves using the democratic approach to teamwork emphasized at work in their parenting. One employee described holding team meetings at home, adding, "After all, a family is kind of like a team" (Crouter, 1984, p. 82). A divorced mother made this analogy: "I say things to my daughter that I know are a result of the way things are at work. I ask her, 'What do you think about that?' or 'How would you deal with this problem?' I tend to deal with her the way we deal with people at work. The logic is the same" (Crouter, 1984, pp. 81–82). These quotes suggest that workers in this innovative setting favored a democratic or authoritative parenting style, an approach to childrearing that is characterized by "a high degree of warmth or acceptance, a high degree of psychological autonomy or democracy, and a high degree of behavioral control" (Steinberg, Elmen, & Mounts, 1989, p. 1425).

A direction for future research is to piggyback parenting research on to workplace experiments such as the introduction of semi-autonomous work teams in order to explore whether workers engaged in such new ways of organizing work change their parenting values, beliefs, or behaviors. Ideally, such a study would involve random assignment to work conditions to try to minimize the kinds of selection processes described above. Even with random assignment to traditional vs. innovative work settings, however, some selection effects are probably unavoidable. For example, employees told Crouter (1984) that younger workers found the transition to semi-autonomous work teams much easier than older workers, many of whom had become more entrenched in traditional ways of organizing work. Crouter's interviews were conducted with the survivors of this transition, the employees who had managed to adjust to the dramatic changes that occurred when the company switched from traditional assembly lines to semi-autonomous work teams. Her qualitative research did not include the perspectives of those workers who could not work effectively in work teams and either quit or lost their jobs.

Workplace Relationships.   Although work consumes a large portion of adults' time and is doubtless a setting in which many interpersonal relationships are formed, little systematic research has been conducted on personal relationships at work. This lacuna is particularly unfortunate in regard to employed parents of young children for whom work may provide an important source of peer interaction. Indeed, friends in the workplace may be an important source of advice to parents.

To learn more about day-to-day interactions between co-workers, Marks (1994) pored over the more than 1,000 pages of observer notes from the famous Hawthorne studies that were reported in Roethlisberger and Dickson's classic monograph, *Management and the Worker* (1939). He found the records about the women in the Relay Assembly Room particularly interesting:

> . . . for 5 years these women lived much of their lives together in that room. Their menial jobs did not deaden their vibrant personalities, and in their conversations with one another one can see a clear reflection of the totality of their lives. When I visit with these women through their conversations, I get to participate in their constant dramas, their continual flow of humor, their stories, their worries, their frivolity, their omnipresent planning for the next grand event, and above all, their intimacy . . . they talk in detail about their family members, especially if one of them is in any kind of difficulty. Here they reveal themselves not only as kin keepers but also as their coworkers' kin keepers. (pp. 160–161)

In one of the few empirical studies of parents to explicitly examine the role of co-workers, Greenberger, Goldberg, Hamill, O'Neil, and Payne (1989) surveyed more than 300 parents of preschool children about informal and formal sources of support in their work environments and the relationship between those workplace supports and parents' job-related attitudes (e.g., organizational commitment) and personal well-being (i.e., role strain, health). Controlling for background characteristics and other sources of workplace support, Greenberger et al. (1989) found that co-worker support was a significant correlate of role strain for married fathers and single mothers, although not for married mothers: the greater the perceived co-worker support, the less role strain married fathers and single mothers reported. Supervisor support was not associated with parents' reports of role strain in the Greenberger et al. study, although Repetti (1987) found that supervisor support mitigated depression in female bank tellers who experienced stressful work conditions. Future research is needed to examine whether co-worker support and supervisor support are linked to mothers' and fathers' actual parenting behavior.

Such research will have to grapple with the ubiquitous selection effects discussed earlier. Socially competent people may develop and engage in constructive relationships at work, and they may also develop and engage in constructive parent–child relationships. Finding a correlation between the two does not imply that workplace relationships cause effective parenting. This is another situation in which a workplace intervention, such as training supervisors to be supportive of workers' family roles, might be evaluated not only in terms of whether or not it reduces absenteeism and turnover or increased job satisfaction and productivity—traditional "outcomes" of interest to the workplace—but also in terms of whether it enhances employees' parenting.

Workplace Policies. In addition to the informal support provided by some supervisors and coworkers, work settings vary in terms of the extent to which they formally acknowledge or support employees' roles and responsibilities in the family. Workplace policies such as flexible scheduling (flextime), rules about the use of sick time and personal leave time, parental leave, and provisions for the care of employees' dependents presumably relieve the strain that results from balancing work and family roles, a support that ultimately may enhance parenting. The empirical evidence, however, is very scant (Friedman, 1990).

Evidence suggests that having some flexibility about work schedules is important for parents. For example, Gottfried, Gottfried, and Bathurst (2002), reviewing research from their Fullerton Longitudinal Study, reported no direct associations between mothers' work hours and child outcomes, although the correlation between mothers' work hours and mothers' attitudes toward the dual responsibilities of employment and parenting became stronger and more negative as children moved through the school-aged years. Having flexible schedules, in contrast, was consistently linked to less negative maternal attitudes toward work and family responsibilities which, in turn, predicted lower levels of behavior problems in children. Such findings suggest that mothers' flexible work hours may have indirect connections with child outcomes. Greenberger et al. (1989) found that mothers used formal benefits (e.g., flexible scheduling, parental leave policies, assistance with child care) more than fathers did and that, for single mothers, use of formal benefits was related to reduced role strain, even controlling for other sources of support at work.

Hyde and colleagues (Hyde, 1995; Hyde, Essex, Clark, Klein, & Byrd, 1996) have conducted research on maternity leave and its implications for mothers themselves as well as for the quality of their interactions with their children. Clark, Hyde, Essex, and Klein (1997), for example, compared the quality of mother–infant interaction when babies were about 4 months of age for mothers who had taken a maternity leave of about 6 weeks (*short*) vs. a leave of about 12 weeks (*long*). In general, mothers who experienced a short leave evidenced more negative affect and behavior than other mothers. Clark et al. (1997), however, also reported interaction effects. Mothers who experienced a short leave tended to interact with their offspring with less positive affect, responsiveness, and sensitivity if they also reported higher levels of depressive symptoms or perceived their baby as having a more difficult temperament.

Studying the effects of formal workplace policies should be relatively straightforward, but it is not. In some organizations, there is a discrepancy between the policies that are "on the books" and the behaviors that are informally encouraged or discouraged in the organization's culture: during lunch breaks, around the water cooler, and in hallway interactions. Parental leave may be technically available to employees, for example, but there may be strong informal discouragement of people actually taking that leave, discouragement that is hard to measure in surveys but may be detectable in qualitative research (see, for example, Fried, 1998). Likewise, long, inflexible work hours may not be a formal requirement of some organizations, but there may be subtle messages about the importance of "face time," messages that convey the difficulties of getting ahead in the organization if the employee does not put in long hours that are visible to coworkers and supervisors or go the extra mile to work on weekends and evenings.

Further complicating matters, the organization or larger cultural context may send different messages to men and women about taking advantage of workplace policies and benefits. Haas (1992) documents, for example, that, although both men and women are permitted by Swedish social policy to take a generous leave at the birth of a child, men are often informally discouraged from taking the time to which they are entitled. Thus, a careful examination of whether family friendly benefits and practices do in fact support parents in their childrearing roles would have to carefully assess not only the availability of the specific policies and practices but also the extent to which male and female workers are informally encouraged or discouraged from actually using them.

**Work Stress as an Influence on Parents' Emotional States
at Home**

A third level at which to examine the connections between parental work
and parents' childrearing behavior focuses on the work day as an influence
on parents' psychological states. This perspective recognizes that individuals experience considerable day-to-day variability in work demands, interpersonal dynamics at work, and work accomplishments that may influence
their mood at the end of the work day. The small but interesting body of research on the generalization of mood from work to family (and from family
to work) is part of a larger literature on emotional transmission (see review
by Larson & Almeida, 1999).

Studies linking mood at work to employed parents' behavior or mood at
home are challenging for a number of reasons. They require careful measurement of psychological states, repeatedly assessed over days or weeks, as
well as attention to the sequencing of mood and subsequent behavior.
Bolger, DeLongis, Kessler, and Wethington (1989), for example, asked
couples to complete a short questionnaire diary at the end of each day for
42 consecutive days and used the day as the unit of analysis, rather than the
individual. Researchers must also pay attention to the experiences that may
intervene between work and family. Fearing that long commutes would alter parents' work-based moods, Repetti and Wood (1997), for example, designed an ingenious study to collect data on parent–child reunion behavior
at workplace childcare centers. Parents in this situation have virtually no
commute, so researchers can be more confident that the mood the parent
exhibits as he or she walks into the center to pick up the child is the same
mood that he or she had several minutes ago when leaving the workplace.

Researchers also cannot assume that mothers and fathers will exhibit the
same patterns of work to family emotional transmission. Indeed, Larson and
Richards (1994) suggest that employed mothers and fathers of adolescents
experience work and family life quite differently. They used the *experience
sampling method*, an approach in which family members carry electronic beep-
ers throughout the day and are paged at random moments to complete brief
questionnaires about their activities, companions, and emotional states.
Larson and Richards found that employed wives recorded their most positive
moods while at work; indeed, wives' emotions were generally more positive
than were husbands' when they were paged on the job. Wives, however, experienced a decline in positive emotion at home during the evening hours
which were filled with housework and child care. Husbands, on the other
hand, recorded their most negative emotions in the workplace; at home,
their moods lightened, in part because non-work time provided a source of
leisure for them. Even when men performed housework or childcare, how-

ever, their moods during these tasks were more positive than was the case for their wives when they performed the same activities. Larson and Richards (1994) proposed that housework and child care elicit a more positive reaction from husbands than wives because it is seen as voluntary work by husbands. Men get involved when they are in the mood, and their efforts are noted and appreciated by wives, but wives are expected to handle these tasks whether or not they are in the mood to do them.

Much research on emotional transmission across the work–family interface has focused on stress. In a pioneering study, for example, Bolger et al. (1989) found an increased probability of arguments with spouse (but not children) after days in which the husband had had arguments at work. For wives, in contrast, there was no association between arguments at work and arguments with husbands (or children). Repetti (1989) examined the connections between work-induced stress and parents' behavior at home using a somewhat different strategy. She zeroed in on air traffic controllers, an occupation that is notoriously stressful, to take advantage of daily FAA records of work conditions and demands. Twenty seven air traffic controllers, all parents, completed daily reports on work stress and parent–child interactions on three consecutive days. Repetti found that parents tended to be more socially withdrawn and less emotionally expressive on days when work had been stressful.

To follow up Repetti's findings about parental withdrawal following stressful work days, Repetti and Wood (1997) collected mood data at the end of mothers' work shifts and self-report and observational parenting data during subsequent mother–child reunions at work-site child care centers. Consistent with their expectations, they found that mothers of preschoolers were more likely to withdraw from their children, both emotionally and behaviorally, on days during which they had experienced either overloads or negative interpersonal interactions at work. Interestingly, stress on the job generally was not followed by aversive mother–child interaction. Indeed, Repetti and Wood found some evidence in the observational component of their study that mothers were somewhat more patient with their children after high stress work days, a pattern they interpreted as part of the package of emotional and behavioral withdrawal. The extent to which mothers were able to refrain from engaging in negative interaction depended, however, on the mother's own general level of psychosocial functioning. Mothers characterized as high on Type A behavior were less able to refrain from interacting negatively with their children than were mothers with low scores on that measure. This finding is a good reminder that the effects of work conditions on parents are not uniform but undoubtedly depend on the individual strengths and vulnerabilities that parents bring to their work and family situations (Perry-Jenkins, Repetti, & Crouter, 2000).

A handful of studies has examined the connections between parents' global reports of stress or pressure on the job and parenting (see review by Crouter & Bumpus, 2001). This approach relies on mothers' and fathers' reports of their general levels of stress or pressure on the job, moving away from a focus on day-to-day variability in work conditions to generalizations about typical conditions. Crouter, Bumpus, Maguire, and McHale (1999), for example, examined the connections between mothers' and fathers' perceptions of work pressure (e.g., deadlines, fast pace) and conflict with their adolescents. They found that parental work pressure was linked to parents' feeling of being overloaded and that reports of overload in turn positively predicted parent–adolescent conflict. Unlike the literature on daily stress which suggests a pattern of parental withdrawal under high stress conditions, the literature on global work stress suggests a series of interrelated effects, much like a series of dominos. Work pressure exacerbates feelings of overload which in turn increase the likelihood of engaging in conflict with adolescent offspring.

In the future, researchers should consider asking questions that cut across the various areas we have reviewed here. For example, does emotional transmission from work to the family differ as a function of how responsive (formally or informally) the workplace is to family issues? Do supportive relationships at work buffer mothers' and fathers' parenting from the potentially negative effects of work-related pressure and stress?

THROUGH THE LENS OF THE FAMILY: PARENTING IN DUAL-EARNER FAMILIES

The second way researchers have examined the opportunities and constraints that working outside the home presents to parents pays little attention to the nature of the work that parents perform or to the setting in which that work is done but focuses instead on variations in family lifestyles as a function of parents' work-related choices. The first generation of studies in this area focused on the implications for two-parent families of having one or two parents working outside the home by comparing family processes or child outcomes in single-earner versus dual-earner families (see review by Bronfenbrenner & Crouter, 1982). Early studies in this tradition were often explicitly or implicitly designed to illuminate the potentially negative effects of maternal employment for parenting and, in turn, for children. We will briefly touch on this literature.

In recent years, however, the focus of this genre has shifted rather dramatically. As more and more mothers have moved into the paid labor force, with the concomitant trend that dual-earner families have become the most common form of two-parent family (Hernandez, 1997), and as the dual-earner lifestyle has become more widely accepted, researchers have paid less attention to maternal employment status and more attention to how much time mothers and fathers are spending at work. Like the old literature on employment status, the concern underlying some of the research on mothers' and fathers' work time is that long hours represent a risk factor for children because they reduce parents' temporal and (some worry) emotional availability to their children. As will be seen, however, the empirical evidence provides mixed support for these ideas.

Mothers' Employment and Work Hours

If we look simply at how much time parents spend with their children, the general picture is that, although there are minimal differences in involvement for mothers as a function of their employment status, maternal employment has the effect of pulling fathers into a more active parenting role.

Demographer Bianchi (2000) examined children's time with their parents from 1981 to 1997 and concluded that there has been surprisingly little change in the amount of time that mothers spend with their children across that period. In addition, she summarized evidence from several national studies showing that, after controlling for many of the variables that reflect parents' tendencies to select (or be selected) into one lifestyle or another, employed mothers today spend only slightly less time with their offspring, overall, than homemaker mothers do. The differences are modest. Bianchi suggests that rather than taking time away from parenting, employed mothers cut back "in other areas, reallocating priorities to protect time with children" (Bianchi, 2000, p. 406). Specifically, she notes that, during the historical period she studied, employed mothers reduced time spent in housework, volunteer work, personal care, leisure time, and even sleep!

Given that there are only small differences in maternal involvement with children as a function of earner status, it is perhaps not surprising that there is little consistent evidence that maternal employment has positive or negative implications for children's development. In an analysis of data from the National Longitudinal Survey of Youth, Parcel and Menaghan (1994) reported that, holding a variety of possible confounding variables constant, mothers' work hours have few consistent, direct effects on young children's cognitive and social outcomes, a conclusion underscored by Harvey's (1999) analyses of the same data set. In her review of the literature, Bianchi (2000) noted bits of evidence here and there that maternal employment may have some negative effects, for example in the first year of life or for children in certain family situations, but she underscored the paucity of significant outcomes for children:

... given the effort that has been devoted to searching for negative effects of maternal employment on children's academic achievement and emotional adjustment, coupled with the scarcity of findings (either positive or negative), it would appear that the dramatic movement into the labor force by women of childbearing age in the United States has been accomplished with relatively little consequence for children. (p. 401)

A number of studies document that fathers in dual-earner families increase their involvement with their children quite substantially when their wives hold jobs outside the home (Bianchi, 2000; Coltrane, 1996; Crouter, Helms-Erikson, Updegraff, & McHale, 1999). Bianchi (2000) summarized evidence that the time fathers contribute to childcare (relative to their wives) increased between 1965 and 1998. The factors that pull fathers into greater levels of involvement are complex and depend on a variety of other family circumstances in addition to the wife's work status and work hours. Coltrane (1996) reported, for example, that men increased their involvement in caring for their preschool aged children when they were employed fewer hours, had more children, held less traditional attitudes about gender roles, and when they became fathers at an older age.

The tendency for mothers' involvement in paid work to pull fathers into a more active caregiving role is mirrored in research on parents' knowledge of their children's daily activities. The construct of parental knowledge reflects the extent to which parents are informed on a daily basis about their children's activities, whereabouts, and companions (see review by Crouter & Head, 2002). Sometimes referred to as *parental monitoring*, parental knowledge is an important indicator of parenting, especially as children move into the school-age and adolescent years and spend less time in direct involvement in activities with their parents and more time with peers. Numerous studies indicate that children and adolescents tend to engage in higher levels of problem behavior when their parents are less informed about their daily experiences (Crouter & Head, 2002). Stattin and Kerr (2000; Kerr & Stattin, 2000, 2003), however, raised important questions about the direction of effect between parental knowledge and children's problem behavior. Although the field has tended to assume that children react poorly because their parents are out of touch and ill-informed, the arrow may go the other way: children who misbehave may tend to keep information from their parents. Indeed, in Stattin and Kerr's (2000) analysis of Swedish data, youths' tendency to self-disclose to their parents was a more powerful predictor of parental knowledge than was parents' solicitation (i.e., asking questions about their children's experiences and peer associations).

Regardless of the exact nature of these causal associations, parents' work involvement is related to parents' knowledge of their children's activities, whereabouts, and companions. Crouter et al. (1999) reported that, not sur-prisingly, mothers of school-aged children are more knowledgeable about their children's daily lives than fathers are. They also found that, although mothers did not differ in knowledge as a function of their level of involve-ment in paid work, fathers married to women who worked longer hours were more knowledgeable than their counterparts whose wives worked few hours.

Fathers' tendencies to respond to their wives' longer work hours with greater parental involvement and parental knowledge is suggested in a short-term longitudinal study conducted by Crouter and McHale (1993b) that capitalized on seasonal variability in mothers' work involvement. Using data on time use and daily parental knowledge collected during a series of evening telephone interviews with parents and children, they compared mothers and fathers at three time points: the school year, the following summer when children were not in school, and the following school year. They divided families into three groups on the basis of stability or change in mothers' work hours (all fathers were employed full-time). The three groups were (a) consistently dual-earner (both parents employed at all three time points); (b) consistently single-earner (fathers were consistently employed outside the home and their wives were employed very little or not at all); and (c) a group in which parents both worked during the school year but mothers cut their work hours way back or ceased working at all during the summer months. In comparison to the first two groups which were marked by stability in parents' work time the third group of families was characterized by substantial change from the winter to the summer in parenting processes. The division of parenting between mothers and fa-thers became significantly more traditional in the summer and then re-turned to a more egalitarian arrangement during the subsequent school year. In addition, although the fathers in the consistently dual-earner group maintained a relatively high level of knowledge about their chil-dren's daily activities throughout all three occasions of measurement, fa-thers in the group in which mothers cut way back in work involvement in the summer dropped substantially in their levels of knowledge in the sum-mer months and recovered again in the subsequent school year when mothers had returned to their prior levels of involvement in paid work.

Fathers' Employment and Work Hours

In comparison to the literature on maternal employment and work hours, less attention has been paid to fathers' work hours and the implications for parenting, probably because paternal employment is often seen as a given; being the good provider is an integral part of being a husband and father. On average, fathers work longer hours than mothers do (Jacobs & Gerson,

1998, 2001), so presumably there are more examples at the high end of fathers putting in extraordinarily long work weeks than of mothers doing so, but, with a few exceptions, paternal long hours have generally not been conceptualized as a social issue worthy of concern.

Parcel and Menaghan (1994) reported that, controlling for a variety of background and individual characteristics and for baseline levels of the quality of the home environment, the quality of children's home environments deteriorated over a two-year period when fathers worked part-time. This finding may reflect part-time employed men's tenuous position in the labor force. Parcel and Menaghan (1994) also underscored the importance of looking at the combination of fathers' and mothers' work hours, noting that when both parents held part-time work schedules they provided their children with lower quality home environments than was the case when only one parent worked part-time. Likewise, they found that the combination of two parents working overtime was associated with higher levels of problem behavior in children and lower levels of verbal competence (i.e., vocabulary) than was the case when only one parent worked overtime. In households in which both parents are putting in long hours, it may be harder to maintain consistent limit-setting, interact positively and contingently with children, and find time for conversations, story telling, songs, and other forms of verbal stimulation.

Crouter et al. (1999) found no connection between fathers' work hours and either fathers' or mothers' knowledge of their children's daily experiences. This may be due to the fact that fathers have a variety of different sources of information about their children's daily lives. Indeed, Bumpus and Crouter (2003) developed a typology of fathers based on their sources of knowledge about their children's daily experiences. One group of fathers was characterized by high levels of reliance on wives and other children in the family. Interestingly, these fathers tended to work long hours and to have close marital relationships. Mothers and fathers in two-parent families may catch their partners up on child-oriented events, another way in which children are buffered from the effects of long work hours. Under some conditions, however, long paternal work hours may erode the quality of father–child relationships. Crouter, Bumpus, Head, and McHale (2001) examined the connections among fathers' *overwork* (defined as paid employment of more than 60 hours a week), *overload* (e.g., fathers' subjective perceptions of being overwhelmed by having too much to do), and fathers' and adolescents' reports of the quality of their relationship. They found no associations between overwork or overload and the sheer amount of time fathers spent with their adolescent offspring in daily activities, data gathered through a series of seven evening telephone interviews about time use. In contrast, the combination of long paternal work hours and high paternal overload was consistently related to both fathers' and adolescents' subjective reports of lower levels of acceptance and perspective-taking and higher levels of conflict in their relationship. In other words, on their own, fathers' work hours were not related to the quality of father–adolescent relationships, but, coupled with high levels of subjective strain, they were linked to less positive father–adolescent relationship quality, as seen both by fathers and their sons and daughters. It is not possible to ascertain, however, whether fathers' hours exerted strain on the relationship or whether, in the face of less than positive father–adolescent relations, fathers increased their work hours. Both scenarios are possible.

Since the publication of the first edition of *Parenting: An Ecological Perspective* (Luster & Okagaki, 1993), there is a consensus that maternal employment in and of itself does not represent a risk factor for children. That does not mean, however, that future researchers should ignore the challenges men and women confront when they form a dual-earner family. In the conclusion of her presidential address to the Population of Association of America, Bianchi (2000) came to this sobering assessment:

> My one concern is that I have given the impression that women have found it quite easy to balance increased labor force participation with child rearing, to reduce hours of employment so as to juggle childcare, and to get their husbands more involved in child rearing; and that fathers have found it easy to add more hours with children to those they already commit to supporting children financially. I do not think these changes have been easy for American families, particularly for American women. (p. 412)

Bianchi's words echo the thoughts of Davis (1984), another demographer, who wrote about similar issues about 20 years ago. In his words:

> A century may seem a long time, but it is a short time to alter the basic structure of an institution. The new egalitarian system of sex roles still lacks normative guidelines. Each couple has to work out its own arrangement which means in practice a great deal of experimentation and failure. (p. 413)

CONCLUSIONS

For dual-earner families, mother's job and father's job constitute an important exosystem for the developing child. Scholars interested in the interrelationship between work and parenting have taken quite different approaches depending upon whether their focus is that of work, and the roles, activities, and relationships associated with employment, or family and the parenting dynamics associated with that context. Work influences childrearing via its effects on parents' views of the world, the opportunities and constraints jobs pose for parents who need to balance multiple roles, and the daily stresses (and exhilarations) of the work day that shape parents' emotional states as they leave their workplaces to resume their parenting roles. All three levels are important; the next challenge is to design research that bridges two or more. A second general approach researchers have taken to examining work and family life has been to focus primarily on whether and how family processes, such as parent–child involvement, parental knowledge, and parent–child closeness, differ in families that vary in terms of parents' connections to the paid labor force. Both perspectives are needed, alone and in tandem, to inform the next generation of research in this area.

A challenge for the future is to design studies that look in detail at the implications for parenting and parent–child relationships of the combination of mothers' and fathers' work situations. This means taking a dyadic approach to the study of work and parenting in two-parent families (see Crouter & Helms-Erikson, 1997). This can be done in at least two ways. A variable-oriented approach is to create interaction terms that combine variables reflecting "his and her" occupational conditions (e.g., Parcel & Menaghan, 1994). A pattern-analytic approach is to create typologies based on the patterning of mothers' and fathers' work characteristics (e.g., Bumpus, Crouter, & McHale, 1999; Crouter & Manke, 1997), using a statistical procedure like cluster analysis. Once interesting family groups have been identified and described, they can be examined in relation to parenting and parent–child relationships. Dyadic approaches will get us closer to a more holistic understanding of the diverse ecologies that are included under the rubric of dual-earner families—and hence to a more detailed, nuanced understanding of the work and family contexts of child development.

ACKNOWLEDGMENTS

We are grateful for the many insights provided by our current and former graduate students, Tom Luster, Lynn Okagaki, and Marc Bornstein, as well as for sustained funding for our work from the National Institute of Child Health and Human Development.

REFERENCES

Baron, J. N., & Bielby, W. T. (1985). Organizational barriers to gender equality: Sex segregation of jobs and occupations. In A. S. Rossi (Ed.), *Gender and the life course* (pp. 233–251). New York: Aldine.

Barry, H., Child, I. L., & Bacon, M. K. (1959). Relation of child training to subsistence economy. *American Anthropologist, 61,* 51–63.

Belsky, J. (1984). The determinants of parenting. A process model. *Child Development, 55*(1), 83–96.

Bianchi, S. M. (2000). Maternal employment and time with children: Dramatic change or surprising continuity? *Demography, 37,* 401–414.

Bolger, N., DeLongis, A., Kessler, R. C., & Wethington, E. (1989). The contagion of stress across multiple roles. *Journal of Marriage and the Family, 51,* 175–183.

Bronfenbrenner, U. (1979). *The ecology of human development: Experiments by nature and design.* Cambridge, MA: Harvard.

Bronfenbrenner, U., & Crouter, A. C. (1982). Work and family through time and space. In S. Kamerman & C. Hayes (Eds.), *Families that work: Children in a changing world* (pp. 39–83). Washington, DC: National Academy Press.

Bumpus, M. F., & Crouter, A. C. (2003, April). Fathers' strategies for acquiring knowledge about their adolescents' daily lives. Paper presented at the biennial meeting of the Society for Research in Child Development, Tampa Florida.

Bumpus, M. F., Crouter, A. C., & McHale, S. M. (1999). Work demands of dual-earner couples: Implications for parents' knowledge about children's daily lives in middle childhood. *Journal of Marriage and the Family, 61,* 465–475.

Clark, R., Hyde, J., Essex, M. J., & Klein, M. H. (1997). Length of maternity leave and quality of mother–infant interactions. *Child Development, 68,* 364–383.

Coltrane, S. (1996). *Family man.* New York: Oxford University Press.

Crouter, A. C. (1984). Participative work as an influence on human development. *Journal of Applied Developmental Psychology, 5,* 71–90.

Crouter A. C., & Bumpus, M. F. (2001). Linking parents' work stress to children's and adolescents' psychological adjustment. *Current Directions in Psychological Science, 10,* 156–159.

Crouter, A. C., Bumpus, M. F., Head, M. R., & McHale, S. M. (2001). Implications of overwork and overload for the quality of men's family relationships. *Journal of Marriage and Family, 63,* 404–416.

Crouter, A. C., Bumpus, M. F., Maguire, M. C., & McHale, S. M. (1999). Linking parents' work pressure to adolescents' well-being: Insights into dynamics in dual-earner families. *Developmental Psychology, 35,* 1453–1461.

Crouter, A. C., & Head, M. R. (2002). Parental monitoring and knowledge of children. In M. H. Bornstein (Ed.), *Handbook of parenting: Vol. 3. Being and becoming a parent* (2nd ed., pp. 461–483). Mahwah, NJ: Lawrence Erlbaum Associates.

Crouter, A. C., & Helms-Erikson, H. (1997). Work and family from a dyadic perspective: Variations in inequality. In S. Duck (Ed.), *Handbook of personal relationships.* New York: John Wiley.

Crouter, A. C., Helms-Erikson, H., Updegraff, K., & McHale, S. M. (1999). Conditions underlying parents' knowledge about children's daily lives in middle childhood: Between- and within-family comparisons. *Child Development, 70,* 246–259.

Crouter, A. C., & Manke, B. (1997). Development of a typology of dual-earner families: A window into differences between and within families. *Journal of Family Psychology, 11,* 62–75.

Crouter, A. C., & McHale, S. M. (1993a). The long arm of the job: Influences of parental work on childrearing. In T. Luster & L. Okagaki (Eds.), *Parenting: An ecological perspective.* Hillsdale, NJ: Lawrence Erlbaum Associates.

Crouter, A. C., & McHale, S. M. (1993b). Temporal rhythms in family life: Seasonal variation in the relation between parental work and family process. *Developmental Psychology, 29,* 198–205.

Davis, K. (1984). Wives and work: The sex role revolution and its consequences. *Population and Development Review, 10,* 397–417.

Fried, M. (1998). *Taking time: Parental leave policy and corporate culture.* Pennsylvania: Temple University Press.

Friedman, D. E. (1990). Corporate responses to family needs. In D. G. Unger & M. B. Sussman (Eds.), *Families in community settings: Interdisciplinary perspectives* (pp. 77–98). New York: Haworth.

Gottfried, A. E., Gottfried, A. W., & Bathurst, K. (2002). Maternal and dual-earner employment status and parenting. In M. H. Bornstein (Ed.), *Handbook of parenting: Vol. 2. Biology and ecology of parenting* (2nd ed., pp. 207–229). Mahwah, NJ: Lawrence Erlbaum Associates.

Greenberger, E., Goldberg, W. A., Hamill, S., O'Neil, R., & Payne, C. K. (1989). Contributions of a supportive work environment to parents' well-being and orientation to work. *American Journal of Community Psychology, 17,* 755–783.

Gruber-Baldini, A. L., Schaie, K. W., & Willis, S. L. (1995). Similarity in married couples: A longitudinal study of mental abilities and rigidity flexibility. *Journal of Personality and Social Psychology, 69,* 191–203.

Haas, L. (1992). *Equal parenthood and social policy.* New York: State University of New York Press.

Harvey, E. (1999). Short-term and long-term effects of early parental employment on children of the National Longitudinal Survey of Youth. *Developmental Psychology, 35,* 445–459.

Hernandez, D. J. (1997). Child development and the social demography of childhood. *Child Development, 68,* 149–169.

Hyde, J. S. (1995). Women and maternity leave: Empirical data and public policy. *Psychology of Women Quarterly, 19,* 299–313.

Hyde, J. S., Essex, M. J., Clark, R., Klein, M. H., & Byrd, J. E. (1996). Parental leave: Policy and research. *Journal of Social Issues, 52,* 91–110.

Jacobs, J. A., & Gerson, K. (1998). Who are the overworked Americans? *Review of Social Economy, 56,* 442–459.

Jacobs, J. A., & Gerson, K. (2001). Overworked individuals or overworked families? Explaining trends in work, leisure, and family time. *Work and Occupations, 28,* 40–63.

Kanter, R. M. (1977). *Work and family in the United States: A critical review and agenda for research and policy.* New York: Russell Sage Foundation.

Kerr, M., & Stattin, H. (2000). What parents know, how they know it, and several forms of adolescent adjustment: Further support for a reinterpretation of monitoring. *Developmental Psychology, 36,* 366–380.

Kerr, M., & Stattin, H. (2003). Parenting of adolescents: Action or reaction? In A. C. Crouter & A. Booth (Eds.), *Children's influence on family dynamics: The neglected side of family relationships* (pp. 121–151). Mahwah, NJ: Lawrence Erlbaum Associates.

Kline, M., & Cowan, P. A. (1989). Rethinking the connections among "work" and "family" and "well-being." *Journal of Social Behavior and Personality, 3,* 61–90.

Kohn, M. L. (1977). *Class and conformity: A study in values* (2nd ed.). Chicago: University of Chicago Press.

Kohn, M. L., & Schooler, C. (1983). *Work and personality: An inquiry into the impact of social stratification.* Norwood, NJ: Ablex.

Komarovsky, M. (1962). *Blue collar marriage.* New York: Random House.

Larson, R. W., & Almeida, D. M. (1999). Emotional transmission in the daily lives of families: A new paradigm for studying family process. *Journal of Marriage and the Family, 61,* 5–20.

Larson, R., & Richards, M. (1994). *Divergent realities: The emotional lives of mothers, fathers, and adolescents.* New York: Basic Books.

Luster, T., & Okagaki, L. (Eds.). (1993). *Parenting: An ecological perspective.* Hillsdale, NJ: Lawrence Erlbaum Associates.

Luster, T., Rhoades, K., & Haas, B. (1989). Relations between parenting values and parenting behavior. *Journal of Marriage and the Family, 51,* 139–147.

Lynd, R. S., & Lynd, H. M. (1929). *Middletown: A study in modern American culture.* New York: Harcourt, Brace & World.

Marks, S. R. (1994). Studying workplace intimacy: Havens at work. In D. L. Sollie & L. A. Leslie (Eds.), *Gender, families, and close relationships: Feminist research journeys* (pp. 145–168). California: Sage.

Menaghan, E. G. (1991). Work experiences and family interaction processes: The long reach of the job? *Annual Review of Sociology, 17,* 419–444.

Menaghan, E. G., & Parcel, T. L. (1995). Social sources of change in children's home environments: The effects of parental occupational experiences and family conditions. *Journal of Marriage and the Family, 57,* 69–84.

Miller, D. D., & Swanson, G. E. (1958). *The changing American parent: A study in the Detroit area.* New York: Wiley.

Ogbu, J. U. (1981). Origins of human competence: A cultural-ecological perspective. *Child Development, 52,* 413–429.

Parcel, T. L., & Menaghan, E. G. (1994). *Parents' jobs and children's lives.* New York: Aldine De Gruyter.

Perry-Jenkins, M., Repetti, R. L., & Crouter, A. C. (2000). Work and family in the 1990s. *Journal of Marriage and the Family, 62,* 981–998.

Repetti, R. L. (1987). Individual and common components of the social environment at work and psychology well-being. *Journal of Personality and Social Psychology, 52,* 710–720.

Repetti, R. L. (1989). Effects of daily workload on subsequent behavior during marital interaction: The roles of social withdrawal and spouse support. *Journal of Personality and Social Psychology, 57,* 651–659.

Repetti, R. L., & Wood, J. (1997). Effects of daily stress at work on mothers' interactions with preschoolers. *Journal of Family Psychology, 11,* 90–108.

Roethlisberger, F., & Dickson, W. J. (1939). *Management and the worker.* Cambridge, MA: Harvard University Press.

Stattin, H., & Kerr, M. (2000). Parental monitoring: A reinterpretation. *Child Development, 71,* 1072–1085.

Steinberg, L., Elmen, J. D., & Mounts, N. S. (1989). Authoritative parenting, psychosocial maturity, and academic success among adolescents. *Child Development, 60,* 1425.

Waller, W. W. (1938). *The family: A dynamic interpretation.* New York: Cordon.

10

Neighborhood and Community Influences on Parenting

James Garbarino
Cornell University

Catherine P. Bradshaw
Johns Hopkins University

Kathleen Kostelny
Erikson Institute for Advanced Study in Child Development

INTRODUCTION

Families are, to a certain degree, "open systems," and are thus influenced by the larger social context (Bronfenbrenner, 1986; Furstenberg, Cook, Eccles, Elder, & Sameroff, 1999; Leventhal & Brooks-Gunn, 2000; Minuchin, 1974; Stinnett, Chesser, & DeFrain, 1979). Families and environments continually negotiate and re-negotiate their relationships, each influencing, changing, and depending on the other. Although the effects are usually neither simple nor direct, there is a constant shifting and evolving interplay among the child's biology, the environment, and the parents' behavior. Consequently, the success of parents to a great extent depends on the difficulties posed by the children and the degree to which the social environment is toxic or nurturing to both children and their parents (Collins, Maccoby, Steinberg, Hetherington, & Bornstein, 2000; Garbarino, 1995). This interaction is particularly important to consider when examining how neighborhoods and communities influence parenting behaviors in modern societies.

In this chapter, we examine several aspects of neighborhoods and communities that have the potential to influence parents and the children they rear. We review some of the consequences of living in high-risk environments for both children and parents. A crucial indicator of successful parenting and family functioning is the absence of child maltreatment;

thus, it is important to consider how environmental factors can either support or work against high-risk parents (Garbarino & Crouter, 1978a; Garbarino & Sherman, 1980; Steinberg, Catalano, & Dooley, 1981). We follow with a discussion of some of the ways parents—both successfully and unsuccessfully—modify or adapt their parenting behavior to combat socially toxic forces (e.g., poverty, violence) present in the community and neighborhood. We also consider how the promotion of individual, family, school, and community based assets is associated with positive youth development. Because it is important to harness the strengths of parents and their communities when creating and implementing programs intended to benefit families, we conclude with a discussion of strategies for supporting parents in high-risk communities through programs and policies.

NEIGHBORHOOD AND COMMUNITY INFLUENCES ON FAMILIES

On the individual level, we know that one of the most important functions of parents is to provide stability and security. Parents are or should be a secure emotional base from which their children and adolescents explore the environment (Allen & Land, 1999). Similarly, parents serve as emotional and social buffers by creating boundaries for their children and deciding how permeable the boundaries will be to the flow of information, energy, and people in and out of the family system (Garbarino, 1995). Although parents play a significant role in promoting healthy development, socially toxic forces present in many American communities are often working against the goals of parents and impeding positive youth development.

Parenting and the Concentration of Poverty

The increasing number of high-risk families in a geographically concentrated underclass is exerting dramatic influences on the needs and the competence of many parents (Lehmann, 1986; Wilson, 1987, 1996). The concentration of poor families is relevant to parenting because it means that a disproportionately low percentage of parents are "free from drain" (Collins & Pancoast, 1976) and a high concentration of "needy" parents living in high-risk neighborhoods. Chronic impoverishment poses a serious threat to child welfare, but so does acute, episodic impoverishment—the much more common variety in the American system. Many researchers project that, unless there is some dramatic change in demography, policy, and the structure of the economy, one in four young children will continue to live in poverty. This trend appears particularly relevant to children living in single-parent households (Garbarino & Bedard, 2001), for single parenthood is a major correlate if not a direct cause of poverty. Furthermore, nearly 50% of children in America will live in a single-parent household at some point before turning eighteen, thus, single parenting is a feature of life for nearly half of all children (Amato, 2000).

Although there is considerable debate about the exact process by which poverty serves as a threat to parenting, there is consensus that acute economic deprivation represents a challenge to the coping resources of individuals, families, and communities (Klebanov, Brooks-Gunn, & Duncan, 1994; Wilson, 1991, 1996). Data from the nearly 900 families involved in the Infant Health and Development Program illustrate how the influences of neighborhood-level poverty differ from family level poverty (Klebanov et al., 1994). Even after controlling for family level poverty, neighborhood poverty was associated with less parental warmth and responsiveness, and a diminished quality of the home physical environment (e.g., unsafe play area, dimly lighted home interior). In contrast, family level risk factors (e.g., poverty, lower education, female-headed household), but not neighborhood-level factors, were associated with a diminished home learning environment (e.g., fewer developmentally appropriate educational toys). These findings provided some of the first empirical evidence of the process by which neighborhood poverty influences parenting behaviors, such as maternal characteristics and quality of the home environment provided by the parent or parents.

Unemployment is common among inner-city neighborhoods and compounds the effects of poverty. As Wilson describes in *When Work Disappears* (1996), there is a qualitative difference between being both poor and unemployed, from being poor but employed; for those with employment, there is the hope of greater economic stability and a more favorable set of attitudes and values regarding work, family, and community. As with the influence of poverty on parenting, the connection between unemployment and youth development crisis is mainly indirect (Wilson, 1991, 1995, 1996). Unemployment tends to diminish resources and precipitate problems in children's mental health and welfare, which presumably occurs through its effects on parents. Furthermore, male identity and parental status have traditionally been tied to occupational position, and unemployment diminishes that identity and can lead to role ambiguity, or even outright conflict in the family (Wilson, 1996).

The fact that employment is the principal source of basic health and welfare services only adds to the psychological and financial effects of unemployment. Unemployment thus simultaneously increases the vulnerability of children and decreases the likelihood that parents will attend and respond effectively to their children. This is particularly important for parents who are marginally employed and operate "one paycheck away from disaster." Their financial reserves are minimal or nonexistent.

Another consequence of deteriorating economic conditions is highly concentrated pockets of poverty, characterized by a high proportion (e.g.,

40% or more) of parents falling below the poverty level (Wilson, 1996). Studies indicate that child abuse and infant mortality rates are significantly higher in poverty stricken neighborhoods than in unafflicted communities. In Chicago, for example, the rates of child abuse in the poorest neighborhoods were four times higher than in the more affluent areas, and for infant mortality, the rate was higher by a factor of five (Garbarino, Dubrow, Kostelny, & Pardo, 1992). In the following section, we discuss research on child victimization and the numerous challenges posed to parents who live in high-risk communities as they struggle to keep their children physically safe while promoting positive youth development.

Community Influences on Child Victimization and Infant Mortality

Child victimization is a global concern and has even been characterized as a public health epidemic in the United States (Bell & Jenkins, 1993; Osofsky, 1997). The rate of violent victimization of children aged 12 to 17 in the United States is nearly three times that for adults (Snyder & Sickmund, 1995). The murder rate of juveniles increased 66% between 1985 and 1995 and the greatest increase was for older children. In 1997, approximately six juveniles were murdered each day in the United States, of which 70% were male and 47% were African American (Snyder & Sickmund, 1999). The number of juvenile murders reached its peak at 2,900 in 1993 (Sickmund, Snyder, & Poe-Yamagata, 1997), but has been declining since the mid-1990s (U.S. Department of Justice, 2002).

Whereas children over age 12 are more likely to be killed by someone other than a family member (95%), younger children are more likely to be killed by family members (57%) (National Clearinghouse on Child Abuse and Neglect Information, 2003; Sickmund et al., 1997). An estimated 1,300 children died in the U.S. in 2001 as the result of maltreatment (National Clearinghouse on Child Abuse and Neglect Information, 2003). Approximately one million cases of child maltreatment are substantiated each year; however, the National Incidence Study of Child Abuse and Neglect estimates that the actual rate is nearly three times that number (Sedlak & Broadhurst, 1996). In 2001, approximately 60% of the substantiated cases were for physical neglect, 19% for physical abuse, 10% for sexual abuse, and 7% for emotional or psychological maltreatment (U.S. Department of Health and Human Services, 2003).

Risk is more than simply the sum of child victimization rates, for there are two meanings of risk (Garbarino & Crouter, 1978b; Garbarino & Kostelny, 1992). In identifying high- and low-risk areas for child victimization, it is important to consider not only the absolute victimization rates (based on actual incidence in a given population), but also the rates of victimization that are higher or lower than would be expected in that community (given its socioeconomic and demographic composition). For example, consider two communities which have the same actual child maltreatment rates. One community might be labeled high-risk because its rate exceeds what it should be given its socioeconomic and demographic characteristics. In contrast, the other would be labeled low-risk because the rate is lower than expected, given its socioeconomic and demographic profile.

Building on this model, Garbarino and Kostelny (1992) examined community level factors as possible explanations for different patterns of infant mortality in Chicago's 77 communities during the mid-1980s. They predicted infant mortality rates for each community by computing a multiple regression analysis with nine socioeconomic and demographic variables, and then compared the predicted rates with the actual rates. Not surprisingly, there was a strong correlation between economically impoverished communities and high rates of infant mortality. However, closer examination of the data indicated more complex associations between other community level variables and infant mortality. Rates of infant mortality in 4 of the 77 communities were not adequately explained by either socioeconomic and demographic variables or the additional factors of low birth weight and births to teens. In these neighborhoods, idiosyncratic community factors, such as participation in the community's prenatal class, parenting education and support programs were associated with lower rates of infant mortality, whereas barriers to medical care, such as a hospital closure, were associated with higher rates.

This approach of comparing actual risks with expected risks illustrates how institutional policies and the concentration of poverty can have a negative influence on parents and childbearing. Conditions within poor communities (e.g., hospital closings) can exacerbate the problems faced by parents and increase the risk for children. In contrast, programs (e.g., community prenatal classes) for parents living in some impoverished communities have the potential to strengthen and support families, thereby reducing the actual risk of infant mortality. Comparing communities with similar predicted rates of risk factors, but different actual rates can provide useful insights for the development of intervention strategies in high-risk neighborhoods (Garbarino & Kostelny, 1992).

THE CHALLENGE TO PARENTS

The statistics on child and youth victimization summarized above illustrate the challenges posed to many children and parents who live in high-risk communities. These challenges can vary significantly and dramatically by neighborhood. Some communities have much more than their share of child victims. Approximately one quarter of all juvenile murders in the United States occur in only five out of the nearly 3,000 U.S. counties—these five counties include the cities of Los Angeles, Chicago, New York, Philadelphia, and Detroit (Sickmund et al., 1997). Poor, inner-city, minority neighborhoods are the sites for most of these murders and serious assaults. For example, the homicide rate in Chicago hovers around 22 per 100,000 and 17 for Los Angeles, when the national rate is only about 5.5 (Federal Bureau of Investigation, n.d.). Consequently, some children and their parents face environmental violence on a weekly, if not daily, basis. One study of children living in Chicago in the inner-city communities indicated that by age 17, 30% of the children had witnessed a homicide (Bell & Jenkins, 1991).

It is clear that children are sensitive and responsive to stressors in their environments; however, what parents do and say to their children can mediate these influences (Garbarino et al., 1992; Furstenberg et al., 1999). To a large degree, the effect of stressful neighborhoods and communities on children is influenced by the impact of that stress on the parents, most notably on mothers. Children in the care of their parents or familiar parent substitutes can cope with stressful life circumstances if parents are able to maintain their day-to-day routines, project high morale, and continue to be responsive to their children's basic physical and emotional needs (Richters & Martinez, 1993).

Parents' Own Emotional Responses to Stressful Environments

The way children respond to community violence depends at least in part on how their parents respond (Garbarino et al., 1992). Research and clinical observations indicate that parents' response to stress and trauma are one of the best predictors of how children will respond (Freud & Burlingham, 1943; Furstenberg et al., 1999; Groves, 2002; Osofsky, 1995). As long as parents are not pushed beyond their "stress absorption capacity," children will continue to cope with difficult environments. But once a parent's stress absorption capacity is exceeded, the well-being of young children deteriorates rapidly and markedly. These parents tend to deny or misinterpret their children's signals and needs, and thus are emotionally unavailable to their children. When parents begin to deteriorate or panic in response to stress and community violence, children suffer, as parents who are traumatized seldom offer their children what they need to cope successfully with these experiences (Osofsky, 1995). Without effective intervention or adaptation, day-to-day care breaks down and the risk of infant mortality, exploitation, or victimization increases.

Parents forced to cope with chronic danger in their community may adapt in ways that are dysfunctional for themselves and their families. The psychopathological dimensions of such adaptation are now widely recognized and can include Post-Traumatic Stress Disorder (PTSD) (Garbarino et al., 1992). The social dimensions are equally worthy of attention. Parents may cope with danger by adopting a world-view or persona that may be dysfunctional in nonviolent or normal situations. Some adaptations to chronic danger, such as emotional withdrawal or hypervigilance, may be socially adaptive in the short run, but become a danger to the next generation, when their children become parents. This response has been observed in studies of families of Holocaust survivors (Danieli, 1985) and in the parenting patterns of individuals who were abused as children (Egeland & Farber, 1984; Gelles & Lancaster, 1987).

Even in the absence of this intergenerational process, parental adaptations to dangerous environments may produce childrearing strategies that impede moral, social, or cognitive development. For example, a mother who does not allow her child to play on the floor because there is poison on the floor to kill the rats that infest the apartment may deprive the child of important opportunities for exploratory play. Likewise, a parent who prohibits the child from playing outside for fear of shooting incidents may be denying the child a chance to engage in social and athletic play, as an undesirable side effect of protecting the child from assault.

In more extreme environmental circumstances, studies indicate that parents living in urban areas may attempt to compensate for the unpredictability of their environment by setting greater restrictions on their children's behavior and using a slightly domineering or authoritarian parenting style, which sometimes includes the threat of physical punishment (Deater-Deckard, Dodge, Bates, & Pettit, 1996; Dunifon & Kowaleski-Jones, 2002; DuRant, Cadenhead, Pendergrast, Slavens, & Linder, 1994; Furstenberg et al., 1999; Leventhal & Brooks-Gunn, 2003). For example, interviews with mothers rearing children in the public housing projects of inner-city Chicago during the 1980s indicate that these mothers reported being more restrictive with their children and adolescents because they were concerned about their children's safety. These mothers stated that this was the only way they *felt* they could protect their children from the widespread gang activity and gunfire that was characteristic of their neighborhood (Dubrow & Garbarino, 1989). More recent studies indicate that these views and corresponding restrictive parenting behaviors are still prevalent among mothers living in public housing projects (Leventhal & Brooks-Gunn, 2003; Rymond-Richmond, 2003).

It is clear that these parents have good intentions and are struggling to ensure the physical well-being of their children, but at what cost? There is no empirical evidence indicating that authoritarian parenting and harsh parenting strategies (including the threat of physical punishment) are necessarily more effective in these contexts. To the contrary, previous research has shown that overly restrictive and controlling parenting practices are associated with increased behavior problems and greater affiliation with deviant peers among adolescents and pre-adolescents (Brody et al., 2001). This finding is particularly important, since several studies have shown that association with deviant peers is major risk factor for aggressive and delinquent behavior during adolescence (for a review see Thornberry & Krohn, 1997). It also illustrates the transactional nature of parenting, whereby ineffective parenting behavior leaves an open door to the influences of deviant peers (Patterson, DeBaryshe, & Ramsey, 1989).

An overly restrictive parenting style also likely heightens aggression on the child's part and models aggressive responses to threat. More restrictive parenting practices do appear to be somewhat effective in terms of reducing delinquency for younger African American children, but only when coupled with high levels of maternal warmth (Dunifon & Kowalski-Jones, 2002; Mason, Cauce, Gonzales, Hiraga, & Grove, 1994). Although these effects do not appear to hold for European American children, they remind us that the emotional context of any parenting behavior is extremely important (Steinberg, 2001).

In these examples, the parental adaptation was likely well-intentioned and may have appeared to be practically sensible, but its side effects may be detrimental in the long run. Attempts to shield the child from negative forces by punitive restrictiveness is generally much less successful as a strategy than expressing confidence in the child's capacities and promoting positive alternatives to the negative subculture feared by the parent (Scheinfeld, 1983). In the following section, we consider some of the other more successful strategies that parents use to mediate the negative influences of high-risk communities.

Mediating Environmental Influences

It is clear that the negative physical and psychological consequences of living in high-risk neighborhoods are great for both parents and children. There are however, strategies that individual parents, as well as communities, can utilize to cope with these problems and to minimize the negative developmental consequences for children. Several studies have shown that parents can—to a certain degree—alter their parenting behavior to compensate for the toxicity of their children's social environments (Beyers, Bates, Pettit & Dodge, 2003; Dishion & McMahon, 1998; Furstenberg et al., 1999; Garbarino, 1995).

Enhanced parental monitoring strategies, such as tracking and attending to the child's activities and whereabouts, are one way parents appear to be adapting to the risks posed by their environment. Well-monitored youth are at decreased risk for smoking, using drugs and alcohol, engaging in risky sexual behavior, becoming antisocial or delinquent, and socializing with deviant peers (Dishion & McMahon, 1998; Kerr & Stattin, 2000; Patterson & Stouthamer-Loeber, 1984). Although monitoring appears to be a protective factor, longitudinal studies indicate that parental monitoring typically decreases as youth become engaged in problem and delinquent behaviors (Paternoster, 1988). These youth are more difficult to monitor and less likely to disclose their activities and whereabouts to their parents. These and other similar studies suggest that certain youth are easier to monitor and may be more amenable to their parents' efforts at monitoring than others (Kerr & Stattin, 2000; Laird, Pettit, Dodge, & Bates, 2003). Parental monitoring appears to be most effective if initiated early and consistently throughout childhood and adolescence, rather than spontaneously after the youth has become delinquent or involved with drugs.

The effectiveness of parenting behaviors depends, to some extent, on the emotional context in which they occur (Laird et al., 2003). Related research indicates that it may be the youths' disclosure to the parents rather than parental monitoring that has the greatest impact on their problem behavior (Kerr & Stattin, 2000). Furthermore, youth who are securely attached to their parents are most likely to disclose to their parents (Armsden & Greenberg, 1987). This association illustrates the importance and profound effects of a secure parent–infant bond—one which is characterized by high levels of warmth, consistency, and responsiveness. Not only are secure attachments in early childhood associated with positive youth and parent relationships during adolescence, but they also are associated with positive social–emotional development and reduced stress reactivity for the youth (Sroufe, 1989).

More generally, an authoritative parenting style—including firmness, warmth, and psychological autonomy granting—is most effective for promoting positive behavior in children and adolescents (Baumrind, 1966; Steinberg, 2001). There also appear to be indirect effects of authoritative parenting which operate through peers, such that a youth may benefit simply from having friends whose parents are authoritative. It is likely that many of the positive attitudes and behaviors are passed onto the children of authoritative parents. More specifically, many of the qualities of an authoritative parent are also desirable in a good friend, such as being consistent and reliable (i.e., firm), supportive (i.e., warm), and being accepting and tolerant of individual or cultural differences (i.e., autonomy granting; Steinberg, 2001). Moreover, an entire community of authoritative parents also appears to have a cumulative effect, whereby the community has mutually agreed on norms of acceptable behavior for youth, and enforces and expects those behaviors in all youth (Fletcher, Darling, Steinberg, & Dornbusch, 1995).

Large-scale longitudinal studies have shown that neighbors' willingness to intervene on behalf of the common good is associated with reduced community violence (Sampson, Morenoff, & Earls, 1999; Sampson, Raudenbush, & Earls, 1997). This type of group effort requires that parents let go of the "American value" of individualism, a value which promotes closed family systems. Parents' effectiveness increases dramatically if they join forces with other parents to set norms and enforce expectations of acceptable behavior. In addition to establishing norms of parenting behaviors, adults should be willing to intervene when these norms are not meet. An example comes from the 161% increase in the number of maltreatment reports filed between 1980 and 1996. This dramatic jump in the number of cases reported is attributable, at least in part, to increased public awareness of the negative consequences of maltreatment and a greater willingness among adults to report suspected incidents (Sickmund et al., 1997).

The broader context also influences parents and parenting behaviors (Leventhal & Brooks-Gunn, 2000). Communities that are high in collective efficacy produce a carry over effect to individual children (Brody et al., 2001; Sampson et al., 1999; Sampson et al., 1997), which may help compensate—to some degree—for a less effective parent. This may be why some researchers (e.g., Harris, 1998) have argued that for low-risk children living in low-risk environments, slight variations in parenting behaviors only have a limited influence. However, this does not mean that parents do not matter in low-risk environments. Successful parenting behaviors appear to be particularly important when there are few neighborhood-level resources (e.g., low collective efficacy, social support) and many risks (e.g., neighborhood disorder, and high concentration of unemployed, low-SES residents; Beyers et al., 2003; Brody et al., 2001; Ceballo & McLoyd, 2002).

In contrast, there is a "double whammy" effect for children who live in communities with low social resources and have parents with poor parenting practices (Beyers et al., 2003; Brody et al., 2001). Under these conditions, children are at greatest risk for developing problem behaviors. One large-scale community based program has attempted to ameliorate the negative effects of neighborhood risks, such as low collective efficacy and high concentration of poverty, and better identify the mechanism by which neighborhoods influence both parents and children.

Moving to Opportunities Housing Demonstration Program. Moving to Opportunities (MTO) is a social and geographic mobility demonstration project sponsored by the U.S. Department of Housing and Urban Development (HUD); it was developed to alleviate some of the problems low income families face living in impoverished and disorganized neighborhoods (Orr et al., 2003; Shroder, 2001). In addition to providing more adequate housing, HUD is conducting a rigorous study to examine the effects of residential change and mobility counseling on family well-being, adult employment, family income, and children's academic performance.

The $70 million dollar MTO program is modeled after the smaller Gautreaux Program, in which African American families residing in public housing in inner-city Chicago were provided with a voucher to move to sub-sidized suburban or urban housing (Orr et al., 2003; Shroder, 2001). The families who moved to the suburbs demonstrated numerous gains in em-ployment and education. However, the program was not truly experimental (with random assignment to conditions), and thus it cannot be determined whether the changes resulted from the relocation or other factors (e.g., self-selection bias). To examine more specifically the influence of residen-tial mobility on parents and children, HUD developed the MTO program and utilized a controlled experimental design (Shroder, 2001).

Beginning in 1994, the MTO program identified 4,608 eligible families living in neighborhood with poverty rates of 40% or higher across five large cities: Baltimore, Boston, Chicago, Los Angeles, and New York (Orr et al., 2003). Approximately half of the sample consisted of African American families and another 39% were Hispanic. An average of 2.5 children under age 18 resided in each household, and the mean family income was just un-der $9,400; 75% of families received assistance through Aid to Families with Dependent Children (AFDC) or Temporary Assistances for Needy Families (TANF; Shroder, 2001).

The families were randomly assigned into one of three groups. Partici-pants in the experimental group were given a "Section 8" rental voucher to move to private-market rental housing and were provided counseling assis-tance in finding a new residence and working with prospective landlords. Their relocations were restricted, such that families were required to move into a community where no more than 10% of the population was below the poverty line. The families in the Section 8 only group also received a rental voucher for private-market housing, but there were no relocation re-strictions, nor were residential counseling services provided. Families in the comparison group continued residing in project-based housing (Orr et al., 2003). Approximately 48% of the experimental group (i.e., Section 8 voucher plus residential counseling) and 60% of the Section 8 only group "leased-up" through the use of the voucher system (Shroder, 2001). It is not clear why some families did not lease-up; some may have had a difficult time finding housing in low-poverty neighborhoods, whereas others may have simply chosen not to move.

A longitudinal study of the MTO program is currently underway to ex-amine the several aspects of mobility including, mental and physical health, educational achievement, delinquency and crime, employment, and earn-ings. The families in the experimental and Section 8 only groups who leased-up, moved to significantly better neighborhoods, as indicated by higher proportions of employed adults, high school graduates, and home-owners. The movers in the two voucher groups also reported greater satisfaction with the new neighborhood, greater perceptions of safety, less exposure to neighborhood disorder (e.g., litter, graffiti, public drinking), and reduced likelihood of witnessing or being victimized by violence in the neighborhood (Orr et al., 2003).

With regard to health outcomes, there was a reduced incidence of obesity among the parents in the experimental and Section 8 only groups, as well as reductions in psychological distress and depression for the parents in the experimental group. For the children in the two voucher groups, in contrast to the comparison group, there were no significant differences in the educational performance measures. The girls in the two voucher groups reported reductions in mental health problems (e.g., psychological distress, depression, anxiety), whereas the findings regarding the children's behavior problems (e.g., delinquency, risky behavior) were mixed. There is some indication that the effects of the move through the MTO voucher program yielded positive effects for girls, but some negative effects for boys (Orr et al., 2003).

Overall, the short-term findings from the first four years of the MTO demonstration are promising, despite the fact that only about half of the families in the experimental and Section 8 only groups actually moved (Shroder, 2001). Even with this limitation, the effects observed for families in the two voucher groups are positive, with those in the experimental group demonstrating the greatest improvements. And it is likely that the impacts will become stronger with time. These and other studies on neighborhood effects illustrate the role context can play in promoting healthy behaviors among parents and positive development among youth. In the following section, we highlight some of the other ways in which communities can support parents and contribute to the well-being of children.

THE ROLE OF COMMUNITIES IN SUPPORTING PARENTS

Strategies intended to promote positive youth development and effective parenting should incorporate an ecological orientation (Bronfenbrenner, 1986; Scales & Leffert, 1999). One such comprehensive approach examines children and adolescents' entire social and psychological environment in terms of the presence or absence of a series of assets. The Minnesota-based Search Institute has identified 40 such assets that are grouped into 8 categories: Support, Empowerment, Boundaries and Expectations, Constructive Use of Time, Commitment to Learning, Positive Values, Social Competencies, and Positive Identity. The more assets children or adolescents have the less likely they are to develop problems with aggression or violence, abuse alcohol, or use illicit drugs such as cocaine, heroin, or amphetamines (Scales, Benson, Leffert, & Blyth, 2000; Scales & Leffert, 1999).

The Boundaries and Expectations category emphasizes the "web of influence" that parents can collectively create to support positive development among the children in their neighborhoods (Price, Cioci, Penner, & Trautlein, 1993). This group of assets includes "neighbors take responsibility for monitoring young people's behavior" and "parent(s) and other adults model positive, responsible behavior" (Scales & Leffert, 1999, p. 2). These assets are based in part on research summarized above demonstrating a link between collective efficacy and reduced incidence of youth problem behaviors (e.g., Sampson et al., 1997).

Studies conducted by the Search Institute on these 40 developmental assets indicate that 61% of youth who had between zero and 10 developmental assets evidenced aggressive or violent behavior. This was compared to only 6% of youth with 31 to 40 assets (Scales & Leffert, 1999). A similar pattern occurred for substance abuse and other high-risk behaviors (see Table 10.1). Conversely, the greater the number of assets, the more likely youth are to demonstrate positive behaviors, such as school success, valuing diversity, maintaining good health, and delaying gratification. The Search Institute's research indicates that, although only 7% of youth with zero to 10 assets succeeded in school, 53% of those with 31 to 40 did. Similarly, whereas only 27% of those with zero to 10 assets delayed gratification, 72% of those with 31 to 40 did (Scales & Leffert, 1999). Although it is tempting to assume that simply adding assets would automatically replace positive for problem behaviors, the child development equation is far more complex. It is important to consider the role of family as well as community based assets. Parents who attempt to close off their family to community influences limit their children's opportunities for positive development, for only about 10

TABLE 10.1
Percent of Youth Demonstrating High-Risk
Behavior Grouped by Number of Assets

	Number of Assets			
	0–10	*11–20*	*21–30*	*31–40*
Alcohol Abuse	53	30	11	3
Tobacco Use	45	21	6	1
Illicit Drug Use	42	19	6	1
Sexual Intercourse	33	21	10	3
Depression/Suicide	40	25	13	4
Antisocial Behavior	52	23	7	1
Violence	61	35	16	6
School Problems	43	19	7	2
Drinking and Driving	42	24	10	4

Source: Scales, P., & Leffert, N. (1999). *Developmental assets: A synthesis of the scientific research on adolescent development.* Minneapolis, MN: Search Institute, p. 8. (N = 99,462 U.S. students.)

of the 40 assets are under the direct control of parents (e.g., "parent(s) are actively involved in helping young person succeed in school"; Scales & Leffert, 1999, p. 2). This means that the other 30 assets are primarily characteristics of the school or community (e.g., "school provides a caring, encouraging environment" and "young person experiences caring neighbors"; Scales & Leffert, 1999, p. 2). Assets found in contexts outside the family may complement those provided by the parents, and for some children, may help compensate for what parents cannot provide.

Quite a bit can be done to support children outside the actions of parents. Parents and the parent-oriented assets can benefit from social support provided by the larger community. Convergent findings from several studies of life course responses to stressful early experiences suggest a series of ameliorating factors that lead to prosocial and healthy adaptation (Losel & Bliesener, 1990):

1. Actively trying to cope with stress (rather than just reacting);
2. Cognitive competence (at least an average level of intelligence);
3. High levels of self-efficacy, self-confidence, and positive self-esteem;
4. Temperamental characteristics that favor active coping attempts and positive relationships with others (e.g., activity, goal orientation, sociability) rather than passive withdrawal;
5. A stable emotional relationship with at least one parent or other significant adult;
6. An open, supportive educational climate and parental model of behavior that encourages constructive coping with problems; and
7. Social support from persons outside the family.

Several of these factors involve community and neighborhood factors, both directly and as mediators of parenting. Community factors influence whether parents provide philosophical, moral, spiritual, and political support for the type of active coping, which helps children develop and express resilience. Communities can contribute to parents' efficacy by providing support and guidance and promoting positive youth/adult interaction. The Parents as Teachers (PAT) program is such an effort that seeks to involve and validate parents in active and developmentally enhancing relationships with their children from the first weeks of life (Parents as Teachers National Center, 2003). This program intends to reduce the child's risk of developmental delay and bolster resources for resilience. PAT originated in Missouri as a pilot project in the 1980s, but has become a national network including more than 2,500 programs. Recent evaluations of the Parents as Teachers program indicate that it can eliminate the disparity in school readiness scores between children living in high and low poverty communities (Pfannenstiel, Seitz, & Zigler, 2002).

For parenting to be successful in high-risk environments, parents must overcome powerful negative forces that include the depressive effects of living in chronic stress. Chicago's Center for Successful Child Development ("The Beethoven Project") is an effort which prevents developmental delays among an entire birth cohort in a public housing project (i.e., all the children born in one year who live in the same kindergarten catchment area; Barclay-McLaughlin, 1987; Center for Successful Child Development, 1998). The program provides several supportive services, such as home health visits, early developmental screening, prenatal health care, parent education, job training for parents, infant day care, child abuse prevention programming, and Head Start programming (Barclay-McLaughlin, 1987). When such efforts are conducted in the context of thoughtful evaluation research, they can serve as the kind of transforming experiments that advance an ecologically valid science of parenting (Bronfenbrenner, 1979).

Community influences also are important in providing the open, supportive educational climate, that is a source of resilience for children. Communities can help set the tone and the context of individual parenting decisions. For example, the growing campaign to end corporal punishment (i.e., physical assault as discipline) in U.S. schools is driven by the belief that this will help shape the context for disciplinary practices in the home. The informal nature of the community and neighborhood are an important source of resilience for children and, in a sense, are defined by the social support from individuals outside the family.

Informal social support, either through emotional support (e.g., someone to confide in) or instrumental support (e.g., someone to depend on), can be particularly important for parents, especially single parents. A study of 262 low-SES, African American single mothers indicated that emotional support was associated with greater warmth and more nurturing parenting behaviors (Ceballo & McLoyd, 2002). But these effects varied by context, such that within disordered neighborhoods, the association was weaker. Receipt of instrumental support by the mothers was associated with reductions in the single mothers' use of punitive parenting behaviors (e.g., yelling, hitting, threatening), but this association also weakened as the neighborhood conditions worsened (Ceballo & McLoyd, 2002). These findings suggest that parents may benefit less from social and instrumental support in disordered contexts. Furthermore, in these contexts, the costs of initiating or maintaining social networks may outweigh the benefits. Some parents may consciously withdraw—physically, emotionally, and socially—from the disorder present in their neighborhood as a way of protecting their children (Ceballo & McLoyd, 2002).

Maintaining a Minimum Standard of Care

The challenge to high-risk communities is to create an environment that helps maintain the integrity of the family, both through formal support services and informal neighborhood networking. Maintaining the minimum standard of care for young children in a society depends on how well that society sustains the basic infrastructure of family life. Parent–child attachment, parental self-esteem and identity, and stability of routine care-giving arrangements are three critical elements of this infrastructure (Bronfenbrenner, 1986).

If parents can sustain a strong attachment to their children, maintain a positive sense of self, and have access to rudimentary shelter, food, and medical care, then children will manage, although it may be at great cost to the psychological and physical welfare of those parents. Environments that maintain a stable infrastructure under stress have a different impact from situations of acute disaster, in which there is a dramatic and overwhelming destruction of the infrastructure of daily life. Erikson's study (1976) of an Appalachian community devastated by flood illustrated how children and their parents respond when confronted with vivid and concrete evidence of their vulnerability. Their homes were destroyed and their parents were demoralized and apparently socially powerless: "The major problem, for adults and children alike, is that the fears haunting them are prompted not only by the memory of past terrors but by a wholly realistic assessment of present dangers" (p. 238). When parents are emotionally incapacitated, children rightly fear for their future.

**Attenuating the Debilitating Effects of Community Level
Risk Factors Through Policy Changes**

The phenomenology of poverty is dominated by the experience of deprivation, and exacerbated by widespread promulgation of highly monetarized affluence as the standard. Low paying jobs can be interpreted as an affront in such a context, and the accoutrements of affluence a right. None of this contributes to the well-being of young children; all of it sustains rage and despair among parents. When you add to this the geographic concentration of economically marginal families, communities become more homogeneous (namely through clustering public housing), and the developmental effects on parenting—and thus on children—are profoundly disturbing. Large-scale community-based projects, such as the Moving to Opportunities Demonstration Program, are one way of ameliorate the stress of concentrated poverty on both parents and children.

In a nation where everything costs money and continues to cost more, most families need two incomes to keep up, although because of divorce and single-parenthood more and more families have only one potential wage earner. This was not the case at the outset of the economic depression of the 1930s, when most families with children contained two adults, and wives represented a largely untapped resource that had the potential to be, and in fact was, mobilized to generate cash income in response to the unemployment and income loss experienced by male workers (Elder, 1974). Now, this resource has already been tapped to meet basic family expenses, and therefore does not represent a reserve in the same sense that it did in the 1930s. Children are increasingly an economic burden, directly because of what it costs to rear them and indirectly because of what they "cost" in lost parental income (i.e., time away from the job that over a childhood comes to tens of thousands if not hundreds of thousands of dollars; Garbarino & Bedard, 2001).

Economic issues play quite a large role in the dynamics of early risk, for family structure and activities interact with the parents' participation in the workforce. To the degree to which the community's day-to-day life is monetarized, families will be drawn or driven into the cash economy. The greatest risks come when families lack the financial resources to purchase support services in the market place and are cut off from the informal helping relationships. This is seen most clearly in the urban underclass that has become the focal point for emergency intervention. Marginal or submarginal economic resources interact with diminished psychosocial resources born of violence, academic failure, exploitation, despair, fear, and deteriorated community infrastructure. In such environments most females experience their first pregnancy while still an unmarried teenager, living with little prospect of economic self-sufficiency or two-parent family status. Many of these pregnancies result from sexual exploitations by much older men (Barclay-McLaughlin, 1987). These are the environments in which prenatal care is inadequate, intervals between births are often too brief, beliefs about child care too often dysfunctional, access to and use of healthcare for infants is inadequate, and early intervention for child disabilities insufficient. It is perhaps not surprising that it is also in these environments that large numbers of child mortality and morbidity are rampant.

CONCLUSIONS

In the Middle Ages, only half of all children lived past age five. Now, child death is relatively rare and the nature of parenting has changed. As standards and expectations for the care and life prospects of children have improved in the last century, developmental risk has become a focal point for research and policy. Thus, parental focus has shifted from sheer quantitative concern with child survival to a qualitative concern with development;

this is a major accomplishment. We also have come to realize that parenting is not solely an individual endeavor, for there is more to child development than the direct impact of parents on their children (Ianni, 1989).

Parents both shape their social surroundings and are shaped by them—an interactive process which can enhance or undermine family functioning. More systematic efforts to study and serve families in context, such as the Moving to Opportunities Demonstration Project, can enrich research and intervention, both preventive and rehabilitative. For many practical purposes, this means examining high-risk neighborhoods as well as high-risk families.

In this chapter, we have explored the sources of supports and stresses for parents that derive from the character of neighborhood and community influences. The research summarized above explored and validated the concept of social impoverishment as a characteristic of high-risk family environments, and as a factor in evaluating support and prevention programs aimed at child victimization. The environmental correlates of child maltreatment and infant mortality provide an empirical basis for screening neighborhoods to identify high- and low-risk areas. The link between neighborhood poverty and child maltreatment continues to be a powerful feature of the problem. Parents and children both suffer when faced with neighborhood poverty, especially when it is coupled with high levels of exposure to community violence. These findings illustrate specific environmental conditions that can influence the consequences of community level variables on childrearing.

Parents can, however, play a significant role in protecting their children from the negative aspects of high-risk communities. Effective parenting behaviors, such as fostering a secure attachment during infancy and providing a warm, supportive relationship during childhood and adolescence are associated with well-being among youth, even in the face of environmental risk. Furthermore, the support provided by parents can be bolstered by strong connections with other adults and families in the community. Finally, macro-level alterations in structural barriers (e.g., poverty, unemployment) through family focused programs and policy changes can ameliorate some of the negative consequences of high-risk communities on parenting.

ACKNOWLEDGMENTS

This chapter was supported in part by the Family Life Development Center at Cornell University, the National Institute of Justice, and the National Consortium on Violence Research. We thank Katrina Davy for helpful comments on an earlier version of this chapter.

REFERENCES

Allen, J. P., & Land, D. (1999). Attachment in adolescence. In J. Cassidy & P. R. Shaver (Eds.), *Handbook of attachment: Theory, research, and clinical applications* (pp. 319–335). New York: Guilford Press.

Amato, P. R. (2000). The consequences of divorce for adults and children. *Journal of Marriage and the Family, 62,* 1269–1287.

Armsden, G. C., & Greenberg, M. T. (1987). The inventory of parent and peer attachment: Individual differences and their relationship to psychological well-being in adolescence. *Journal of Youth and Adolescence, 16*(5), 427–454.

Barclay-McLaughlin, G. (1987). The Center for Successful Child Development, The Ounce of Prevention Fund, Chicago.

Baumrind, D. (1966). Effects of authoritative control on child behavior. *Child Development, 37*(4), 887–907.

Bell, C. C., & Jenkins, E. J. (1991). Traumatic stress and children. *Journal of Health Care for the Poor and Underserved, 2*(1), 175–185.

Bell, C. C., & Jenkins, E. J. (1993). Community violence and children on Chicago's Southside. *Psychiatry, 56,* 46–54.

Beyers, J. M., Bates, J. E., Pettit, G. S., & Dodge, K. A. (2003). Neighborhood structure, parenting processes, and the development of youths' externalizing behaviors: A multilevel analysis. *American Journal of Community Psychology, 31*(1–2), 35–53.

Brody, G. H., Conger, R., Gibbons, F. X., Ge, X., McBride Murry, V., Gerrard, M., & Simons, R. L. (2001). The influence of neighborhood disadvantage, collective socialization, and parenting on African American children's affiliation with deviant peers. *Child Development, 72*(4), 1231–1246.

Bronfenbrenner, U. (1979). *The ecology of human development: Experiments by nature and design.* Cambridge: Harvard University Press.

Bronfenbrenner, U. (1986). Ecology of the family as a context for human development research perspectives. *Developmental Psychology, 22,* 6, 723–742.

Ceballo, R., & McLoyd, V. C. (2002). Social support and parenting in poor, dangerous neighborhoods. *Child Development, 73*(4), 1310–1321.

Center for Successful Child Development (1998, March). *Promising practices.* Retrieved January 10, 2004, from http://www.financeprojectinfo.org/WIN/promising/centerforsuccessfulchilddevelopment.htm

Collins, W. A., Maccoby, E. E., Steinberg, L., Hetherington, E. M., & Bornstein, M. H. (2000). Contemporary research on parenting: The case for nature and nurture. *American Psychologist, 55*(2), 218–232.

Collins, A., & Pancoast, D. (1976). *Natural helping networks.* Washington, DC: National Association of Social Workers.

Danieli, Y. (1985). The treatment and prevention of long-term effects and intergenerational transmission of victimization: A lesson from holocaust survivors and their children. In C. R. Figley (Ed.), *Trauma and its wake* (pp. 295–313). New York: Bruner/Mazel.

Deater-Deckard, K., Dodge, K. A., Bates, J. E., & Pettit, G. S. (1996). Physical discipline among African American and European American mothers: Links to children's externalizing behaviors. *Developmental Psychology, 32*(6), 1065–1072.

Dishion, T. J., & McMahon, R. J. (1998). Parental monitoring and the prevention of child and adolescent problem behavior: A conceptual and empirical formulation. *Clinical Child and Family Psychology Review, 1*(1), 61–75.

Dubrow, N. F., & Garbarino, J. (1989). Living in the war zone: Mothers and young children in public housing development. *Journal of Child Welfare, 68,* 3–20.

Dunifon, R., & Kowaleski-Jones, L. (2002). Who's in the house? Race differences in cohabitation, single parenthood, and child development. *Child Development, 73*(4), 1249–1264.

DuRant, R. H., Cadenhead, C., Pendergrast, R. A., Slavens, G., & Linder, C. W. (1994). Factors associated with the use of violence among urban Black adolescents. *American Journal of Public Health, 84*(4), 612–617.

Egeland, B., & Farber, E. (1984). Infant–mother attachment: Factors related to its development and changes over time. *Child Development, 55,* 753–771.

Elder, G. H. (1974). *Children of the great depression.* Chicago: University of Chicago Press.

Erikson, K. (1976). *Everything in its path: Destruction of community in the Buffalo Creek flood.* New York: Simon & Schuster.

Federal Bureau of Investigation. (n.d.). *Offenses known to law enforcement by city 10,000 and over in population, 2002.* Retrieved February 24, 2003, from http://www.fbi.gov/ucr/02cius.htm

Fletcher, A. C., Darling, N. E., Steinberg, L., & Dornbusch, S. (1995). The company they keep: Relation of adolescents' adjustment and behavior to their friends' perceptions of authoritative parenting in the social network. *Developmental Psychology, 31*(2), 300–310.

Freud, A., & Burlingham, D. (1943). *War and children.* New York: International Universities Press.

Furstenberg, F. F., Cook, T., Eccles, J., Elder, G. H., & Sameroff, A. (1999). *Managing to make it: Urban families and adolescent success.* Chicago: University of Chicago Press.

Garbarino, J. (1995). *Raising children in a socially toxic environment.* San Francisco: Jossey-Bass.

Garbarino, J., & Bedard, C. (2001). *Parents under siege.* New York: Simon & Schuster.

Garbarino, J., & Crouter, A. (1978a). Defining the community context of parent–child relations. *Child Development, 49,* 604–616.

Garbarino, J., & Crouter, A. (1978b). A note on assessing the construct validity of child maltreatment report data. *American Journal of Public Health, 68,* 598–599.

Garbarino, J., Dubrow, N., Kostelny, K., & Pardo, C. (1992). *Children in danger: Coping with the consequences of community violence.* San Francisco: Jossey-Bass.

Garbarino, J., & Kostelny, K. (1992). Child maltreatment as a community problem. *Child Abuse and Neglect, 16*(4), 455–464.

Garbarino, J., & Sherman, D. (1980). High risk neighborhoods and high risk families: The human ecology of child maltreatment. *Child Development, 51,* 188–198.

Gelles, R., & Lancaster, J. (1987). *Child abuse and neglect: Biosocial dimension.* New York: Aldine De Gruyter.

Groves, B. M. (2002). *Children who see too much: Lessons from the Child Witness to Violence Project.* Boston: Beacon.

Harris, J. R. (1998). *The nurture assumption: Why children turn out the way they do.* New York: Simon & Schuster.

Ianni, F. A. (1989). The search for structure and the caring community, *The search for structure: A report on American youth today* (pp. 260–283). New York: Free Press.

Kerr, M., & Stattin, H. (2000). What parents know, how they know it, and several forms of adolescent adjustment: Further support for a reinterpretation of monitoring. *Developmental Psychology, 36*(3), 366–380.

Klebanov, P. K., Brooks-Gunn, J., & Duncan, G. J. (1994). Does neighborhood and family poverty affect mothers' parenting, mental health, and social support? *Journal of Marriage and the Family, 56*(2), 441–455.

Laird, R. D., Pettit, G. S., Dodge, K. A., & Bates, J. E. (2003). Change in parents' monitoring knowledge: Links with parenting, relationship quality, adolescent beliefs, and antisocial behavior. *Social Development, 12*(3), 401–419.

Lehmann, N. (1986). The origins of the underclass. *Atlantic, 257,* 31–61.

Leventhal, T., & Brooks-Gunn, J. (2000). The neighborhoods they live in: The effects of neighborhood residence on child and adolescent outcomes. *Psychological Bulletin, 126*(2), 309–337.

Leventhal, T., & Brooks-Gunn, J. (2003). Moving to Opportunity: What about the kids? In J. Goering & J. Feins (Eds.), *Choosing a better life: Evaluating the moving to opportunity social experiment*. Washington, DC: The Urban Institute Press.

Losel, F., & Bliesener, T. (1990). Resilience in adolescence: A study on the generalizability of protective factors. In K. Hurrelmann & F. Losel (Eds.), *Health hazards in adolescence* (pp. 299–320). New York: Walter de Gruyter.

Mason, C. A., Cauce, A. M., Gonzales, N., Hiraga, Y., & Grove, K. (1994). An ecological model of externalizing behaviors in African-American adolescents: No family is an island. *Journal of Research on Adolescence, 4*(4), 639–655.

Minuchin, S. (1974). *Families and family therapy*. Cambridge, MA: Harvard University Press.

National Clearinghouse on Child Abuse and Neglect Information. (2003). *Child abuse and neglect fatalities: Statistics and interventions*. Retrieved February 24, 2004, from http://nccanch.acf.hhs.gov/pubs/factsheets/fatality.cfm

Orr, L., Feins, J. D., Jacob, R., Beecroft, E., Sanbonmatsu, L., Katz, L. F., Liebman, J. B., & Kling, J. R. (2003). *Moving to Opportunity for fair housing demonstration program: Interim impacts evaluation* (Executive Summary). Washington, DC: U.S. Department of Housing and Urban Development. Retrieved January 10, 2004, from http://www.huduser.org/publications/fairhsg/mtofinal.html

Osofsky, J. (1995). The effect of exposure to violence on young children. *American Psychologist, 50*(9), 782–788.

Osofsky, J. D. (Ed.). (1997). *Children in a violent society*. New York: Guilford Press.

Parents as Teachers National Center. (2003, December 12). Retrieved December 15, 2003, from http://www.patnc.org

Paternoster, R. (1988). Examining three-wave deterrence models: A question of temporal order and specification. *Journal of Criminal Law and Criminology, 79*, 135–179.

Patterson, G. R., DeBaryshe, B. D., & Ramsey, E. (1989). A developmental perspective on antisocial behavior. *American Psychologist, 44*(2), 329–335.

Patterson, G., & Stouthamer-Loeber, M. (1984). The correlation of family management practices and delinquency. *Child Development, 55*, 1299–1307.

Pfannenstiel, J. C., Seitz, V., & Zigler, E. (2002). Promoting school readiness: The role of the Parents as Teachers Program. *NHSA Dialog: A Research-to-Practice Journal for the Early Intervention Field, 6*, 71–86.

Price, R. H., Cioci, M., Penner, W., & Trautlein, B. (1993). Webs of influence: School and community programs that enhance adolescent health and education. *Teachers College Record, 94*, 487–521.

Richters, J. E., & Martinez, P. E. (1993). Violent communities, family choices, and children's chances: An algorithm for improving the odds. *Development and Psychopathology, 5*(4), 609–627.

Rymond-Richmond, W. (2003, November). *Perceptions of safety and danger in a public housing development*. Poster presented at the annual meeting of the American Society of Criminology, Denver, CO.

Sampson, R. J., Morenoff, J. D., & Earls, F. (1999). Beyond social capital: Spatial dynamics of collective efficacy for children. *American Sociological Review, 64*(5), 633–660.

Sampson, R. J., Raudenbush, S. W., & Earls, F. (1997). Neighborhoods and violent crime: A multilevel study of collective efficacy. *Science, 277*(5328), 918–924.

Scales, P. C., Benson, P. L., Leffert, N., & Blyth, D. A. (2000). Contribution of developmental assets to the prediction of thriving among adolescents. *Applied Developmental Science, 4*(1), 27–46.

Scales, P., & Leffert, N. (1999). *Developmental assets: A synthesis of the scientific research on adolescent development*. Minneapolis, MN: Search Institute.

Scheinfeld, D. (1983). Family relationships and school achievement among boys of lower-income urban Black families. *American Journal of Orthopsychiatry, 53*(1), 127–143.

Sedlak, A. J., & Broadhurst, D. D. (1996). *Third national incidence study (NIS-3) of child abuse and neglect.* Washington, DC: U.S. Department of Health and Human Services.

Sickmund, M., Snyder, H. N., & Poe-Yamagata, E. (1997). *Juvenile offenders and victims: 1997 Update on violence.* Washington, DC: Office of Juvenile Justice and Delinquency Prevention.

Shroder, M. (2001). Moving to opportunity: An experiment in social and geographic mobility. In S. M. Wachter & R. L. Penne (Eds.), *Housing policy in the new millennium: Proceedings* (pp. 334–348). Washington, DC: U.S. Department of Housing and Urban Development. Retrieved January 10, 2004, from http://www.huduser.org/intercept.asp?loc=/Publications/pdf/brd/17Shroder.pdf

Snyder, H. N., & Sickmund, M. (1995). *Juvenile offender and victims: A national report.* Washington, DC: Office of Juvenile Justice and Delinquency Prevention.

Snyder, H. N., & Sickmund, M. (1999). *Juvenile offenders and victims: 1999 national report.* Washington, DC: Office of Juvenile Justice and Delinquency Prevention.

Sroufe, L. A. (1989). Relationships, self, and individual adaptation. In A. J. Sameroff & R. N. Emde (Eds.), *Relationship disturbances in early childhood: A developmental approach* (pp. 70–96). New York: Basic Books.

Steinberg, L. (2001). We know some things: Parent–adolescent relationships in retrospect and prospect. *Journal of Research on Adolescence, 11*(1), 1–19.

Steinberg, L., Catalano, R., & Dooley, D. (1981). Economic antecedents of child abuse and neglect. *Child Development, 52,* 975–985.

Stinnett, N., Chesser, B., & DeFrain, J. (1979). *Building family strengths: Blueprints for action.* Lincoln: University of Nebraska Press.

Thornberry, T. P., & Krohn, M. D. (1997). Peers, drug use, and delinquency. In D. M. Stoff, J. Breiling, & J. D. Maser (Eds.), *Handbook of antisocial behavior* (pp. 218–233). New York: John Wiley and Sons.

U.S. Department of Health and Human Services. (2003). *Maltreatment 2001* (Washington, DC: U.S. Government Printing Office, 2003). Retrieved February 24, 2004, from www.acf.hhs.gov/programs/cb/publications/cm01/outcover.htm

U.S. Department of Justice (2002). *Homicide trends in the U.S.: Age trends.* Retrieved February 24, 2004, from http://www.ojp.usdoj.gov/bjs/homicide/teens.htm

Wilson, W. J. (1987). *The truly disadvantaged: The inner city, the underclass, and public policy.* Chicago: The University of Chicago Press.

Wilson, W. J. (1991). Studying inner-city social dislocations: The challenge of public agenda research. *American Sociological Review, 56*(1), 1–14.

Wilson, W. J. (1995). Jobless ghettos and the social outcome of youngsters. In P. Moen, G. H. Elder, & K. Luscher (Eds.), *Examining lives in context: Perspectives on the ecology of human development.* Washington, DC: American Psychological Association.

Wilson, W. J. (1996). *When work disappears: The world of the new urban poor.* New York: Random House.

11

Socioeconomic Status, Ethnicity, and Parenting

Birgit Leyendecker
Ruhr-University Bochum, Germany

Robin L. Harwood
Texas Tech University

Lisa Comparini
Clark University

Alev Yalçınkaya
University of Connecticut

The primary goal in this chapter is to contribute to our understanding of the relationship between SES and parenting across families from differing ethnic backgrounds as well as to differentiate between the effects of socioeconomic status (SES) and the effects of ethnicity on parenting. Paying attention to both SES and ethnicity as dimensions of parenting can help to identify the nature and the extent of variability in normative parenting. Particularly, we want to address issues of: (a) variability in normative parenting styles, and (b) the effects of SES on parenting within and across families from differing ethnic backgrounds. To what extent does SES influence parenting practices and are these effects similar across ethnic groups in the United States? In addition, we want to point out that due to the confound of SES and ethnicity in many studies, some features associated with ethnicity are valid and evident only for parents from a specific socioeconomic strata (e.g., parents living in poverty), yet these characteristics have been associated with the entire ethnic group. This is true both for majority and minority populations. Within the context of parenting and child development, SES matters for two reasons. First, some ethnic groups are more likely than others to experience persistent or temporary poverty and the detrimental effects associated herewith. Aside from lower levels of school achievement, these children are more likely to experience harsh, inconsistent parenting as well as elevated exposure to acute and chronic stressors

(McLoyd, 1998). Second, the parenting styles considered to be most optimal for child development are very sensitive to both SES and ethnicity inasmuch as they are calibrated in Caucasian middle- to upper middle-class families whereas parenting styles practiced in lower SES families as well as in families from other ethnic backgrounds share many features with parenting styles considered to be less optimal (Chao, 1994). We begin the chapter by discussing methodological issues on how to measure and define SES and ethnicity. We then turn to the literature describing SES and parenting as well as ethnicity and parenting. Here, we will take a closer look at the construct of interdependence and independence as broad cultural orientations. We will conclude our chapter with a discussion of the association between optimal and less optimal parenting styles, SES, and ethnic background.

METHODOLOGICAL CONSIDERATIONS: DO SES AND ETHNICITY REPRESENT DISCRETE VARIABLES?

Measuring SES

SES represents a major source of indirect and direct influences on parenting practices and children's development. The social status of parents influences economic resources and consequently the quality of children's (material) lives. For example, neighborhood safety, quality of nutrition, home learning environment, clothing, childcare settings outside the home, access to schools and education, as well as parent–child interactions, parenting styles and the underlying parenting beliefs and long-term socialization goals are all tied to the economic resources available to parents. As a result of these differing experiences, children's academic achievement and cognitive abilities, health status, and socioemotional functioning have been found to vary according to their parents' SES (Duncan & Brooks-Gunn, 1997; McLoyd, 1998). Thus, similar to gender and age, SES represents one of the key sociodemographic marker variables, present on virtually every demographic questionnaire used in developmental psychology. In addition, it is standard to check the results of studies for effects of SES. Although there is little doubt that SES influences parenting practices, there is much doubt and discussion about the appropriate conceptualization of this multi-faceted concept: How do we measure SES and how do we understand the effects of its key components on parenting?

The classical measurements of socioeconomic status are the so-called Hollingshead indexes (Hollingshead, 1975). These scales measure either maternal and paternal occupation and education (four-factor index) or just paternal occupation and education (two-factor index). The composites present a continuous measurement of socioeconomic status, although in empirical research the measures are often collapsed to create groups beyond or above a cut-off point and thus reduced to discrete categories. These discrete categories group people who receive points based on their occupation and education within a certain range into discrete social classes. The classes derived from these or other measures are disadvantageous inasmuch as they obscure individual sources of SES effects, such as mother's or father's education, income, and family structure. In addition, they assume meaningful differences between people who might be only a point apart.

Although the grouping into distinct social classes may be problematic, there is little doubt that SES—just like ethnicity—is a social construct highly relevant to the study of differences in individual's developmental trajectories. Many external factors such as family structure and neighborhood, as well as internal factors such as parenting behavior, parent–child interaction, and school achievement vary with socioeconomic status (Duncan & Magnuson, 2003; Entwisle & Astone, 1994; Hoff, Laursen, & Tardif, 2002; McLoyd, 1998). According to Entwisle and Astone's (1994) measurement of socioeconomic status, we can differentiate between three kinds of capital that parents provide for their children. First, there is the financial capital that allows parents to provide their children with the basic necessities such as food and clothes. Second, there is the human capital which represents the nonmaterial resources. Here, parents' education is of special importance as this is an indicator of the extent to which parents can support children with homework and other school demands, and are likely to encourage higher education. In addition, a higher level of parental education is likely to facilitate communication with teachers. Third, parents have an impact on the social capital which provides a connection between children and the larger world outside their household. Here, the people living in a youngster's household, including the social networks of parents and other household members, are of special importance as they are likely to share these links to the larger community with these youngsters.

Unfortunately, there is no single best stand-in for the effects of SES on parenting; moreover, parenting demands are likely to vary with children's age. Instead, for any consideration of the possible impact of SES on parenting and child development, we need to bear in mind two questions: First, what are the components of SES that are likely to influence parenting at each stage of child development? Second, are these components of SES a stable characteristic of the family or are they likely to fluctuate greatly?

There is evidence that specific aspects of financial, human, and social capital have differing influences on parenting and child development and that the magnitude changes with children's ages. For example, research has documented that for parents of young children, human capital, particularly a mother's participation in formal schooling, is likely to be the single best measurement of SES. In an observational study on parenting behavior of mothers with young infants, Bornstein, Hahn, Suwalsky, and Haynes (2003) examined the effects of SES (Hollingshead four-factor index as well as the Socioeconomic Index of Occupations) on 324 Euro-American mother–infants dyads. Two of their findings are particularly noteworthy in the context of this paper: First, they found mothers' education to be the most robust and thus the single most important individual sociodemographic predictor of their parenting behavior, and second the results of their study indicate that, because maternal education was a unique and consistent predictor of maternal and infant behaviors, various components of the SES indexes are not interchangeable but provide different information on the parenting of young children. The relative importance of mothers' education on their interactions with young children is also supported by an earlier study by Richman, Miller, and LeVine (1992). Although mothers are likely to be the ones who spend the most time with their infants and thus may exert the greatest single influence on an infant's development, the impact of the educational status of the father and of other caregivers is likely to increase with children's age. As children grow older, other parameters such as the social and financial capital are also likely to become more important in the assessment of socioeconomic influences on parenting. Thus, SES composites are not more than the sum of its parts but may be best analyzed separately rather than combined into a single scale (Bornstein et al., 2003). This approach is also strongly advocated by Entwisle and Astone (1994). According to Entwisle and Astone (1994), human capital, specifically parents' education, is the single best measurement of SES. However, this indicator should not be used by itself but only in combination with income and measures of household structure to assess potential social capital: number of birth parents, and whether there is a stepparent or a grandparent in the home. They strongly advise that any analysis of SES should include measures of the financial, human, and social capital separately rather than relying on a composite measure. For example, if we are interested in studying parents' preferences for differing childcare arrangements, the social capital as well as the financial capital are both likely to impact parents' decisions separately and in concert. At a later point in time, parents' education as well as the current and the anticipated financial capital of a family may influence parents' plans and hopes for their children's economic future.

There appears to be, however, a non-linear relationship between parental education and income on parenting and children's socioemotional and cognitive development. For example, a 100% increase in parents' income is more likely to affect children's development in a family living around the poverty line than in an already affluent family. The same is true for education—the difference between dropping out of high school after 10th grade or completing high school is likely to have greater effects on parenting and child development than between having parents with an M.A. versus a

Ph.D. degree. The smaller the numbers of the yearly income or of the years spent in formal education, the greater the likelihood that any variation and change is likely to affect children, inasmuch as development is particularly likely to be impaired by lack of parental resources (Duncan & Magnuson, 2003; McLoyd, 1998). In addition, there is evidence that social capital is particularly critical for families with low financial and human capital, inasmuch as social networks and professional support can serve to buffer the effects of poverty on parenting and child development (Field, Widmayer, Adler, & De Cubas, 1990; Hurrelmann, Klocke, Melzer, & Ravens-Sieberer, 2003).

Although education is likely to remain stable over an adult's life, income and social support may fluctuate greatly and may not be a permanent characteristic of a family (Hauser, 1994). For children living in low SES families, the income of their parents is likely to influence later school attainment (Duncan, Brooks-Gunn, & Smith, 1998). Although parents' education tends to remain stable (or may even increase), financial and social capital are both very volatile. However, there is a general tendency for a family's income to increase as parents grow older, acquire experience, and obtain promotions. Aside from unemployment, decreases and increases in a household's disposable income are not unusual and may fluctuate considerably across a child's childhood. Assessing the monthly or yearly income of a family is a sensitive issue, making it difficult in some cases to obtain accurate data. In addition, these numbers might not represent the actual disposable income because high mortgages, loan payments, property taxes, and medical care may reduce available income considerably. Duncan and Magnuson (2003) suggest that to avoid a somewhat erroneous measure of a household's income, a combination of income measured over several years combined with measurement of wealth and occupation provide a better estimate of the influence of financial capital on parenting and child development. Similar to income, social capital is also subject to change due to fluctuations in the social network due to divorce or relocation of family members or friends.

The fluctuation of the financial and social capital is particularly important when studying parents below or around the threshold of poverty. In 2003, the official U.S. Department of Health and Human Services' definition of poverty was based on a combination of a household's income and the size of a household, e.g., the threshold for two-, three-, and four-person families living in poverty were $12,120, $15,260, and $18,400, respectively, in the 48 contiguous states and Washington, D.C. Duncan and Magnuson (Duncan & Magnuson, 2003; Magnuson & Duncan, 2002) allude to the need to differentiate between persistent poverty and shorter spells of poverty. Persistent poverty has stronger negative association with parenting and child development than shorter spells of poverty. They summarize longitudinal research revealing a considerable fluctuation inasmuch as less than one-half of those who experience poverty remain persistently poor over many years, whereas the majority of poverty spells are less than three years. Duncan et al. (1998) and McLoyd (1998) point out the relationship between poverty and family life cycle. The detrimental impact of poverty on families with young children is much greater than it is when families have older children. This appears to be related to the fact that adequate nutrition has a clearer impact on school achievement in early childhood, and younger parents are likely to have fewer financial resources to buffer themselves from financial strain. In addition, parents living in poverty are less likely than more affluent families to be able to provide their children with an enriched home learning environment (Bradley, et al., 1994). As they grow older, the characteristics of the neighborhood are likely to affect children and their parents' socialization strategies as children increase the time they spend away from home. Parents living in poverty are more likely to live in potentially threatening neighborhoods and to adapt their parenting strategies to these potential dangers (Kusserow, 1999; Magnuson & Duncan, 2002; McLoyd, 1998).

In sum, using discrete categorical variables to analyze SES effects on parenting appears to be problematic, and empirical research should consider the various sources of influence rather than relying solely on a composite measure of SES. Families living below or around the poverty line appear to be particularly vulnerable to even small drops in family income or loss of social support. However, in light of the available literature, we will refer to discrete social classes as well as to individual factors that allow us to unpack SES effects.

Ethnicity and Cultural Communities

One of the problems for research in this domain has been how to define ethnicity. Although often used as a synonym for *minority status*, technically the term means *people*, from the Greek *ethnos*, and thus everyone can be considered to have an ethnic background. From this perspective, it becomes an aspect of culture that corresponds to an individual's national heritage. However, the tendency to equate culture with national heritage runs the risk of perpetuating group stereotypes by treating large, diverse groups of people as all of the same kind. The challenge is to find a way of conceptualizing culture that recognizes group differences without reifying them. For our purposes in this chapter, we elaborate briefly on a perspective articulated by Harwood, Handwerker, Schoelmerich and Leyendecker (2001) which locates culture not in the group but in the contextualized individual; culture is viewed not as an entity equivalent to group membership labels but as a shifting continuum of shared commonality among individuals. In particular, definitions of culture as shared discourse or shared scripts for the understanding of self and other, or as shared norms for social interaction imply a relatively fluid definition of what constitutes a cultural community (Strauss & Quinn, 1997). A parent may simultaneously be a member of multiple groups, each with its own particular "morally enforceable conceptual scheme instantiated in practice" (Shweder, 1996, p. 20).

From this perspective, the boundaries that we draw for ethnic group membership are essentially arbitrary and depend on the particular level of commonality we wish to investigate. We can draw them broadly (e.g., European Americans), or more narrowly (e.g., Italian Americans), or very specifically (Sicilians who immigrated to New York City in the 1920s). In addition, parents with a shared ethnic background may differ among themselves with regard to other variables, such as social class, acculturation, circumstances of arrival in the U.S., and place of origin. For example, it is common to speak broadly of Latinos, but in fact Latinos are a diverse group representing all Spanish-speaking people from Mexico, Central or South America, and the Caribbean; in addition, Latinos differ among themselves with regard to generational status (e.g., whether they are recent immigrants or not), social class, and circumstances of arrival in the U.S. (e.g., whether they obtained citizenship through the annexation of Puerto Rico, or arrived as political refugees from Cuba). Similarly, we use the umbrella term African American for all American-born individuals with origins in Africa. Although we may find some commonalities within these broadly defined groups, a focus on parenting based entirely on ethnic heritage is likely to create a false impression of internal homogeneity, and thus carries the risk of reinforcing stereotypes (Harwood, Leyendecker, Carlson, Asencio, & Miller, 2002; Phinney, 1996). For example, parents of each of the two largest ethnic minority groups in the U.S., Latinos and African Americans, vary considerably among themselves in terms of: (a) country of origin; (b) socioeconomic status; (c) generational status and acculturation; and (d) historical and personal reasons for being in the United States.

A second approach attempts to capture the term *cultural community* from the perspective of the individual parent and his or her multiple, intersecting group memberships. For example, parents in the U.S. typically belong to one or more specific ethnic groups with whom they share a common heritage, and this ethnic group membership is likely to play a role in their parenting beliefs and practices (Lee, 2002). At the same time, they belong to multiple other cultural communities as well, provided for them by biology (e.g., age, gender), by circumstances of birth (e.g., place and family of origin) by choice, or by available opportunities (e.g., education or profession, parental or family status, membership in political or religious communities). Each parent is likely to be a member of both broad and inclusive social groups like ethnicity and religion, and of more specialized social groups like residential or academic communities (see Harwood, et al., 2001; Harwood, et al., 2002). All of these memberships are of more or less importance and contribute to the variation within any identified community. For example, a Muslim mother belonging to the Indian community in the U.S. shares a common heritage with other people with roots in India as well as with other Muslims from all over the world. At the same time, this mother is a member of her own and of her husband's family, she might be a lawyer, an avid supporter of the local soccer team, a mother of teenage children, a college professor, and an enthusiastic bicyclist. Thus, this woman is likely to share practices and discourses relevant to members of her various families, to other mothers, lawyers, college teachers, soccer fans, and her fellow bicyclists. In this way, any identifiable cultural community is comprised of individuals who also participate in multiple other social groups and thereby contribute to the heterogeneity of that group. From this perspective, parents participate in overlapping (and changing) cultural communities. These communities, including the various ethnic groups that are part of these communities, are not entirely distinct or separate but rather are in continuous contact with each other and influence each other (Chao, 2000).

To what extent should the social groups a parent belongs to be viewed as separate factors? Rogoff and Angelillo (2002) argue that too much segmentation into variables is likely to distort the whole picture:

> Instead, research can examine cultural processes in terms of people's participation in practices of their cultural communities—practices that include religious traditions, participation in schooling, languages used for varying purposes, and so on. Such practices, from a participation perspective, are not separate factors treated as attributes of individuals or groups but rather are related aspects of heterogeneous community functioning in which people engage. (p. 216)

Along these lines, Lee (2002) supports and specifies this view by pointing out that it is important to study the variation as well as the commonalities within an ethnic community. With regard to parenting, we can expect to find variation in an ethnic community inasmuch as families differ according to their socioeconomic status as well as to the degree that they participate in various other cultural communities.

In research on parenting practices, however, separate sources of influence have been frequently confounded. For example, much of what we know about parenting in ethnic minority groups is derived from studies on low SES families and is thus not representative of the entire community (Garcia Coll & Pachter, 2002). By contrast, most of our knowledge of what constitutes optimal parenting is derived from studies on middle-class European American families. Since these particular parenting practices and the beliefs and values associated with them are reflected in mainstream institutions, children from ethnic minority families, in particular those from low SES families, are likely to experience a discontinuity between the home culture and societal culture and may be faced with conflicting messages (Greenfield & Suzuki, 1998; Garcia Coll & Pachter, 2002).

In sum, the two errors that are most likely to occur when we look at parenting within an ethnic community is either to treat families of very diverse backgrounds as all of the same kind, or to associate a particular ethnic community with a particular SES-based parenting style. If we want to understand how parenting beliefs and practices are shaped, we need to pay closer attention to the separate effects of parents' ethnic background, their socioeconomic status, and to the matrices of cultural communities in which they participate.

PARENTING AND SES

In order to understand the effects of SES and ethnicity on parenting we need to take a closer look at the parenting practices and parenting styles that are widely accepted to be most optimal. These are not only informed by middle-class samples but by European American samples as well. This raises a question as to what extent the parenting practices and values of European American families are likely to differ from those of parents from other ethnic and socioeconomic backgrounds.

The Four-Fold Scheme—from Authoritarian to Indulgent-Permissive

Parenting styles and practices as well as parental beliefs and socialization goals are areas that have received considerable attention within the last few decades. Both socio-economic status and ethnic background appear to influence parents' socialization goals and parenting styles. Much of the research on parenting styles is connected with Diana Baumrind's (1967) typology of authoritarian, authoritative, and permissive parenting. Maccoby and Martin (1983) further divided the permissive category into indulgent and neglectful parenting, and this fourfold scheme is currently widely accepted (Hoff, et al., 2002; see Maccoby & Martin, 1983, for a historical overview). In addition, Maccoby and Martin further differentiate each of these parenting patterns according to dimensions of parental demandingness and parental responsiveness, even though there is some variation in the degree and the weighting of these components within each of the four categories. Although the authoritarian and the authoritative parenting patterns have been associated most often with SES-related differences, parental indulgence, particularly in the first years of life, has also been associated with ethnic background.

Authoritarian (also labeled authoritarian-autocratic) parents place power-assertive strict limits on the allowable expression of their children's needs and wants. They are parent-centered, high on demandingness and control, and value the maintenance of their authority. They are also low on parental responsiveness, and so do not discuss and do not attempt to reach mutual agreements. Maccoby and Martin (1983) summarize the following characteristics of this parenting pattern: "1. Attempting to shape, control, and evaluate the behavior and attitudes of their children in accordance with an absolute set of standards. 2. Valuing obedience, respect for authority, work, tradition, and preservation of order. 3. Discouraging verbal give-and-take between parent and child" (p. 40).

In contrast, parents who are authoritative or authoritative–reciprocal exhibit a pattern in which they are responsive to their children's needs yet expect their children to be responsive to their demands as well. Children are allowed to express their wishes and desires, to discuss these with their parents, and to reach a mutual agreement. Parents firmly implement rules but are willing to discuss and to amend these rules if necessary. Authoritative parenting is child-centered but in a reciprocal fashion which combines high bidirectional communication with parental demandingness and control. Parents encourage their children's independence and individuality and emphasize the rights of both parents and children. Fairly high levels of mutual involvement, responsiveness, and compliance between parents and children are associated with children's optimal functioning and high self-esteem. However, as Maccoby and Martin (1983) point out, in "making such generalizations we are, of course, glossing over the enormous variations in family styles and in the individual personalities that emerge from the family system" (p. 83).

In comparison to the authoritarian and authoritative patterns, the parenting style labeled indulgent-permissive refers to those who are tolerant and accepting toward children's impulses, moods, and demands, use little punishment, and reduce parental authority to a minimum. These parents are less likely to impose and to enforce strict rules and to make maturity demands, but more likely to allow their children to make their own decisions, e.g. regarding schedules for sleeping or for the amount of TV watching. In contrast to neglectful parents, these parents are described as relatively warm.

Parenting Styles, SES, and Socialization Goals

Much of our thinking about the relationship between socioeconomic status, parenting styles, and childrearing goals has been informed by the work of Kohn and the replication of his findings in various cultures (Hoffman,

1988; Imamoglu, 1988; Kohn, 1969, 1979; Kagitcibasi, 1996). Specifically, Kohn demonstrated that the social context parents live in, particularly their occupational experiences and the life they anticipate for their children as a result of those experiences, influences their parenting goals and subsequently their parenting styles. In particular, parents from low socioeconomic strata were found to value obedience and conformity to societal prescriptions, whereas parents from higher socioeconomic strata were found to value self-confidence and self-direction (see Hoff et al., 2002, for an overview). According to Kohn (1969, 1979), parents' occupation (and in particular the conditions associated with it, such as the degree of self-initiative vs. compliance with authority) is the single major source of influence on parental values and practices, with education being a correlate of occupational success. In addition, the authoritative parenting style, which is considered to be most optimal, is typified by many characteristics generally associated with an independent, individualistic cultural orientation, e.g., bidirectional communication, providing choice, encouragement of discussion, recognition of children's rights on the parents' part, and independence and high self-esteem on the children's part. In contrast, the authoritarian parenting style, which is typically characterized by direct orders, obedience, and a hierarchical family structure, possesses many features generally associated with a interdependent, sociocentric cultural orientation.

Briefly, European American culture is often described as individualistic in that it conceives of the individual as an "independent, self-contained, autonomous entity who (a) comprises a unique configuration of internal attributes . . . and (b) behaves primarily as a consequence of those internal attributes" (Markus & Kitayama, 1991, p. 224). In contrast, many other cultures are described as sociocentric or interdependent in that they emphasize the fundamental connectedness of human beings to one another: "Experiencing interdependence entails seeing oneself as part of an encompassing social relationship and recognizing that one's behavior is determined, contingent on, and, to a large extent organized by what the actor perceives to be the thoughts, feelings, and actions of *others* in the relationship" (Markus & Kitayama, 1991, p. 227).

Unfortunately, specific parallels between an authoritative parenting style and elements of individualism (such as an emphasis on the independent self), and between an authoritarian parenting style and elements of sociocentrism (such as an emphasis on respect for authority), have served to reify the existing association between low-SES and the valuing of conformity. Kusserow (1999) warns about creating an East-West dichotomy within a society, and her findings show that parents from all socioeconomic backgrounds incorporate both individualistic and sociocentric orientations, "but in differing styles and ratios, depending on the local world they in-

habit" (p. 213). Kusserow (1999) took a closer look at the relationship between preferences for independence/individualism and for interdepend-
ence/sociocentrism in three groups of 4-year old European American
children and their parents in Manhattan and Queens. These families represented lower working-class families living in a dangerous environment, as
well as upper working-class and upper middle-class families. Kusserow describes three different styles of individualism that exist alongside sociocentric socialization practices. The low SES parents who live in a dangerous
environment prefer a style of individualism that combines independence
and self-defense in the form of "not relying on anyone else," "not trusting
anyone but yourself." This attempt to toughen up children from early on by
teasing them and by teaching them to speak up and fight back is also described by Miller (1996) in her study of working-class families in South Baltimore. Preparing children for a rough world outside by fostering their independence, self-defense skills, and self-reliance can be combined with the
encouragement of strong moral principles (Kusserow, 1999), as well as with
parents' and teachers' expectations of respect and adherence to strict rules
(Corsaro, 1996). In addition, the controlling behavior of low-SES parents
living in a high-risk inner-city community has been related to positive child
outcomes (Baldwin, Baldwin, & Cole, 1990; Deater-Deckard & Dodge,
1997). Thus, depending on the environment that children are raised in,
parents might teach their children to be emotionally independent and self-
reliant but at the same time they might expect them to follow strict rules.

The upper working-class parents in Kusserow's study were more likely to
emphasize the self-assertive aspects of individualism with the goal of up-
ward mobility. Success was often linked to hard work, self-confidence, tenacity, good grades, and sports (Kusserow, 1999). In contrast to the two
groups of working-class parents, the socialization practices of the upper
middle-class, well educated Manhattan parents were in most respects identical with the ones generally associated both with individualism and with an
authoritative parenting style. These parents, as well as their preschool
teachers, practiced a "soft psychologized individualism, in which self-confidence and assertion of the child's unique feelings were paramount" (Kusserow, 1999, p. 222). Parents pursued the goal of raising children by gently
assisting them to discover their own unique qualities, thoughts and feelings
(Kusserow, 1999). Parenting practices were geared toward the reduction of
the power differential between child and parents by instilling a feeling of
empowerment and control in the child while at the same time maintaining
discipline. Thus, direct commands were avoided. As has been described by
other researchers as well (e.g., Nucci, 1994; Nucci, Killen, & Smetana,
1996), the children were either offered choices or commands which were
phrased as suggestions, even though the children knew how to interpret
them correctly. At the same time, parents and teachers balanced the inde-

pendence of children by teaching them to accommodate to societal constraints, and by enhancing their understanding of socially appropriate behavior and by developing their social skills (see also Kwak, 2003, for a detailed description of this particular aspect of individualism).

In sum, the social context in which parents live and the future they anticipate for their children influence their parenting goals and practices. In addition, very different aspects of independence and interdependence can be found with regard to the context parents live in. A mixture of parental control in combination with fostering independence and self-reliance might thus be suited best to an inner-city environment. By contrast, parents who are well-off and live in a relatively safe environment might prefer to teach their children that the world is their oyster, and at the same time balancing this emphasis on personal needs and the individual self with the need to adhere to societal prescriptions. The study by Kusserow (1999) demonstrates the enormous variation that can be found among parents based simply on socioeconomic status. This heterogeneity and variation would likely increase if minority parents from different SES backgrounds had also been included. These findings caution us against using an overly dichotomous view of individualism and sociocentrism, as both independence and interdependence reflect basic human tendencies and are evident in all socioeconomic strata of a society.

PARENTING AND ETHNICITY

Although, as described above, independence and interdependence are human tendencies likely to be found across all socio-economic strata in a given society, independence and interdependence have also been described as characterizing two deeply different cultural pathways through development. Along these lines, Greenfield, Keller, Fuligni, and Maynard (2003) acknowledge that parental concerns for the child both as an individual and as embedded in social relationships coexist in all cultures. Nonetheless, the patterning of these concerns takes shape differently across different cultural contexts. They thus describe independence and interdependence as broad cultural frameworks which serve to organize larger parenting goals and practices and so influence children's development. They further argue that most research on parenting and child development has been informed by the independent pathway, whereas interdependent pathways have only recently been recognized and are still largely understudied.

Thus, two central aspects of parenting and ethnicity concern the degree of children's autonomy and the types of social relationships. Both aspects vary according to the: (a) instrumental and emotional autonomy granted to a child at a given age combined with the degree and extent of parental control; and (b) the expectations and extent of familial duties and obligations. In the independent framework, instrumental autonomy is practiced from early on, with children sleeping by themselves in their own rooms (Leyendecker, Lamb, Schoelmerich, & Fracasso, 1995; Morelli, Rogoff, Oppenheim, & Goldsmith, 1992) and feeding themselves from an early age (Harwood, Schoelmerich, Ventura-Cook, Schulze, & Wilson, 1996; Harwood, Miller, Carlson, & Leyendecker, 2002; Schulze, Harwood, & Schoelmerich, 2001). However, the children are closely supervised, e.g., by parents, babysitters, or a baby monitor. By encouraging early self-feeding, middle-class Euro-American parents foster the child's sense of control over his or her own body, as well as autonomy and choice in decisions about how much to eat and at what pace (Schulze, Harwood, Schoelmerich, & Leyendecker, 2002). However, parents may also tend to carefully structure their children's day, and to provide and follow a schedule for feeding, sleeping, and napping (Leyendecker et al., 1995). In contrast, early autonomy in feeding, combined with close supervision and the establishment of a schedule, may be of much less importance among parents who emphasize a more interdependent orientation. For example, Central American immigrant parents in the U.S. were found to place little emphasis on schedules for their children (Leyendecker et al., 1995).

With regard to early autonomy, Lebanese-born mothers now living in Australia thought that their 5 to 6 year old children were still babies and should not be given jobs aside from asking them to help mind or amuse their younger siblings (Goodnow, Cashmore, Cotton & Knight, 1984). Similarly, Mexican-born mothers in California did not expect their young children to help with household chores, nor did they coax their children to develop self-care skills or to perform household tasks. "Interdependence in these families means expecting and accepting help when you are very young, then learning to give help as you get older" (Delgado-Gaitan, 1994, p. 69).

This principle has also been described for parenting in Muslim families. According to Khounani (2000), early childhood in Muslim families is characterized by great indulgence towards the child (see Kagitcibasi, 1996, for a description of parent–child relationships in Turkish families). This serves the goals of establishing strong emotional ties from children to their parents and their families. Young children are not expected to follow rules and even their misbehavior is met with great tolerance (Pfluger-Schindlbeck, 1989). This permissive–indulgent parenting style is limited to the first 5 to 7 years, and is likely to be gradually replaced by a parenting style that is much more demanding and authoritarian, and in which children are expected to help their younger siblings or their elders. However, although instrumental independence is taught and valued within an interdependent framework, emotional interdependence remains strong and is less likely to change during childhood and adolescence. Emotional interdependence is strongly related to familial duties and obligations.

Within an independent framework, many parenting practices are geared at fostering emotional independence. This is particularly evident in the custom of letting children sleep by themselves at an early age (e.g., Morelli, et al., 1992; Schulze et al., 2002). At the same time, children are socialized into functioning independently when outside of their parents' proximity and close supervision. Interviews on parents' long-term socialization goals revealed that the preference for autonomy is balanced by a preference for independent regulation of emotions, particularly of self-control when interacting with others (Harwood et al., 2002; Leyendecker, Harwood, Lamb & Schoelmerich, 2002). This preference for an independent regulation of emotions, however, does not mean that parents belonging to an ethnic group with an independent framework strive to detach themselves from their children. Just the opposite is true inasmuch as adolescents still require confidence in their parents' commitment to them. Baltes and Silverberg (1994) point out that even within an independent framework parents still provide the secure psychological base which allows their youngsters' to explore options outside the family. Despite the early emphasis on emotional independence, parenting practices during adolescence are still geared at supporting youngsters' developing sense of self-reliance and individuality. Becoming more autonomous is not facilitated by an increasing separation and detachment from parents but rather by maintaining close relationships with parents and significant others (Kagitcibasi, 2003/submitted paper; Ryan, Deci, & Grolnick, 1995). Greenfield and colleagues (2003) state:

> Even in independence-oriented societies such as the United States, complete autonomy from parents is antithetical to healthy adolescent development. Rather, a complicated balance between what has been called "autonomy and relatedness" or "individuation and connectedness" appears to be most salutary for adolescent adjustment, in that it provides children the opportunity to develop the ability to think and act independently within the context of supportive relationships with parents. (p. 478)

Although striving for a life-long relatedness and an emotional tie with their children is not unique to parents with a interdependent orientation, an important difference appears to be that both the expectations of duty and obligations towards parents as well as to other members of the family are closely associated with the aspect of mutuality. In light of the preference for emotional interdependence, expectations with regard to familial duties and obligations influence both the type of relationships as well as expectations of adherence to family hierarchy. Interdependence works best if the family members remain close and the give-and-take is balanced. This balance, however, does not necessarily happen immediately or between the same persons but has to be viewed over the course of a lifetime and within the entire family network. For example, the individual who is pampered as a young child is later expected to pamper younger siblings and family members and to take care of aging parents. At the same time, however, while growing older, one learns how to respect authority and also how to grow into the role of someone who is treated with respect due to being an older sibling or the oldest male or female in the family. With a reduction in family size and increased financial capital, many of these aspects are likely to change, yet research, for example, on American-born adolescents of Asian or Latin-American descent shows that emotional solidarity and obligation remain especially high. According to Fuligni, Tseng, and Lam (1999) parenting practices in Asian and Latin American families resulted in greater expectations of adolescents regarding their duty to assist, respect, and support their families when compared to their peers with European backgrounds. These feelings of closeness towards their families were consistent across youths' generation, family composition, and socioeconomic backgrounds. Similarly, adolescents from immigrant families with an interdependent cultural orientation, such as Asian and Latin American families, were found to be more willing to accept rather than to fight parental control and to sustain positive family relations in part by delaying their pursuit of autonomy (overviews in Greenfield et al., 2003; Kagitcibasi, 2003; Kwak, 2003).

In sum, parenting styles and practices vary greatly within as well as across ethnic groups. In particular, the types of relationships as well as the adherence to hierarchy varies according to the relative importance of an independent or an interdependent cultural framework. Both frameworks coexist in all ethnic communities and overlap greatly but differ in their emphasis.

SES, ETHNICITY, AND PARENTING VIEWED IN THE CONTEXT OF THE INDEPENDENCE/ INTERDEPENDENCE APPROACH

Finally, we are interested in discussing to what extent the relationship among SES, parenting, and children's outcomes that has been described for parents with an independent orientation applies for parents with an interdependent orientation as well. As stated above, some core features of each of the previously described parenting styles have been related to SES, whereas other core features have been related to the independent or interdependent orientations of specific ethnic or cultural communities. Given that neither ethnicity nor SES are clear-cut discrete variables (even though for research purposes, we often operationalize them as such), the answer is multifaceted. There is evidence that: (a) the effects of SES on parenting styles are similar across families from differing ethnic backgrounds, and (b) some aspects of parenting styles have a different impact on children, depending on ethnic background.

Parallel Effects of SES Regardless of Ethnicity

Directly or indirectly, many studies support the notion that a parenting style should be viewed in light of the socioeconomic strata to which a family belongs, the environment in which they live, as well as their ethnic roots. Parents foster continuity (e.g., with regard to personally and ethnically derived values) and at the same time strive to prepare their children for the perceived future that lies ahead of them. Most of the available studies support Kohn's (1969, 1979) hypothesis that the parents' social context, in particular their education, occupation, and the life they anticipate for their children, influences their parenting goals and their parenting styles, and that these effects largely apply to parents and children from a variety of ethnic backgrounds. In particular, the degree of parental control and power-oriented punishing, as well as the preference for providing explanations or reasons and for encouraging independent thinking, appear to be related to SES across differing countries and ethnicities. Hoffman (1988) for example, who compared parenting practices in differing countries, found mean differences between the countries. Within each country, however, parents with a blue-collar occupation were more likely to stress conformity to rules in their childrearing, whereas more highly educated parents encouraged initiative and independence. Similarly, research in Turkey indicates that punishment-oriented control strategies decrease from lower to higher SES, whereas preference for autonomy and self-reliance increase with SES (Imamoglu, 1988; Kagitcibasi, 1996). The findings of Hill, Bush, and Roosa (2003), who studied Mexican American and European American parents living in the same low-income community, also suggest that experiences of socioeconomic and community factors can be at least as strong as ethnic influences. Kagitcibasi (2003) supports these parallels from another perspective. She points out that ethnic differences often overlap with social class differences, and that what is attributed to ethnicity may in fact be due to lower socioeconomic status.

Several factors might contribute to the difficulty of disentangling the effects of SES from those of ethnicity on parenting. First, while the majority of ethnic minority parents do not live in poverty, the proportion of low SES families is higher in most ethnic minority communities and this is likely to distort the overall picture (Magnuson & Duncan, 2002). In addition, positive and negative racial stereotypes regarding parenting and the cognitive abilities of children from differing ethnic backgrounds (Garcia Coll & Pachter, 2002) may impact both the chances parents see for their children to improve their socioeconomic status and for the quality of support that teachers provide for children from minority backgrounds. Second, many members of ethnic minority communities are likely to be immigrants. Regardless of their previous educational attainment, immigrants who lack English language skills and who do not qualify for high-profile jobs are likely to rely on temporary work arrangements and low wages regardless of their previous educational attainment. In addition, recent immigrants are likely to value education for their children as this is perceived to be important to make advancements in the U.S. (Leyendecker et al., 2002). Yet, due to their lack of experience with the requirements of the American school system, they might encounter difficulties when attempting to support their children's school achievement.

Impact of Parenting Styles on Children's Outcome Depends on Ethnic Background

These parallel effects of SES within families from differing ethnic backgrounds, however, do not capture the entire picture. First, despite the same tendencies, overall differences between ethnic groups should not be ignored. Second, particular attitudes toward personal autonomy and family obligation appear to remain salient in families from differing ethnic groups, regardless of SES or degree of acculturation. For example, Chao (1994) suggests that it is somewhat ethnocentric to regard the authoritative parenting style as the most optimal and the authoritarian as less optimal: "For Asians, parental obedience and some aspects of strictness may be equated with parental control, caring, or involvement. Just as important, for Asians parental control may not always involve 'domination' of children per se, but rather a more organizational type of control for the purpose or goal of keeping the family running smoothly and fostering family harmony" (Chao, 1994, p. 1112). She further points out that, despite some parallel features, the concept of training (guan) should not simply be equated with the concept of authoritarian parenting, inasmuch as the concept of training includes high involvement on the part of the parents, physical closeness as well as parental warmth. Numerous studies indirectly support this view in reporting that emotional closeness with the family, the acceptance of decreasing autonomy with age, and the importance attached to family obligations, all remain high in children and adolescents with roots in ethnic communities who endorse an interdependent framework, regardless of their SES (e.g., Phinney, Ong, & Madden, 2000).

CONCLUSIONS

Parents' childrearing beliefs and practices are influenced by both ethnic background and socioeconomic status; these dual sources of influence need to be considered in our attempts to understand parenting and normative development in all its diverse complexity. Unfortunately, this task is neither simple nor straightforward. First, SES is a multifaceted construct consisting of many components that influence parenting both directly (e.g., the association between a mother's educational level and her vocalizations toward the infant) and indirectly (e.g., the quality of neighborhood or the availability of a variety of toys and books in the home). Thus, depending on our focal group and possible sources of variation, it is necessary to identify those components which are likely to be a relevant indicators of socioeconomic status, and which are likely to influence parenting practices and children's development. When studying lower SES groups, particularly those living at or below the poverty level, small differences in available human, social, or financial capital might have relatively large explanatory power.

Second, the key values of middle-class Euro-American parents have been studied extensively, and central aspects of parenting beliefs and practices prevalent among this group have been associated with socioeconomic status. In particular, many key features of the authoritative parenting style, widely considered to be most optimal for child development, appear linked to both a higher socioeconomic status and an independent framework. For example, more educated European American parents are more likely to provide explanations rather than relying on simple strict orders. However, some socioeconomic effects might be parallel in families from diverse ethnic backgrounds, but others are likely to be dwarfed by the possibly more powerful key cultural values. A recognition of the role of cultural values is necessary to avoid stereotyping normative parenting in minority families.

Third, neither ethnicity nor socioeconomic status can be treated as static index variables. This is particularly true both for first and second generation immigrants who might find it necessary to accept jobs well below their educational attainment and skills due to limited English skills. In addition, although limited education and/or language skills increase the risk that families will live below the poverty line, it is important to recognize that this situation may only be temporary. Similarly, ethnicity is not a clearly defined marker variable but may also be subject to change. Changes may be induced, for example, by shifts within one's own or in other ethnic communities, changes in the composition of the ethnic background of household members, or (in the case of immigrant families) by changes in acculturation. As a result, the increasing diversity (both ethnically and socioeconomically) of the United States as well as of other industrialized countries, forces us to move beyond the safe realm of a developmental psychology based primarily on our knowledge of Euro-American middle-class families. The relations among parenting practices, parenting styles, and children's development are much less clearcut once ethnic, socioeconomic, and acculturative influences are all taken into account. As Miller (1996) points out, going beyond the vantage point of the privileged sector of our society allows us to represent human plurality more fully. In addition, we need to increase our efforts to understand these complex relationships on their own terms beyond comparisons of more and less privileged children or of differing ethnic communities. This is potentially rewarding inasmuch as this allows us to enhance our understanding and appreciation of the diverse complexity of parenting and normative child development.

REFERENCES

Baldwin, A. L., Baldwin, C., & Cole, R. E. (1990). Stress-resistant families and stress-resistant children. In J. Rolf, A. S. Masten, D. Cicchetti, K. H. Nuechterlein, & A. S. Weintraub (Eds.), *Risk and protective factors in the development of psychopathology* (pp. 257–280). Cambridge, UK: Cambridge University Press.

Baltes, M. M., & Silverberg, S. (1994). The dynamics between dependency and autonomy: Illustrations across the life-span. In P. B. Baltes (Ed.), *Life-span development and behavior* (pp. 41–90). New York: Wiley.

Baumrind, D. (1967). Childcare practices anteceding 3 patterns of preschool behavior. *Genetic Psychology Monographs, 75,* 43–88.

Bornstein, M. H., Hahn, C.-S., Suwalsky, J. T. D., & Haynes, O. M. (2003). Socioeconomic status, parenting, and child development: The Hollingshead Four-Factor Index of social status and the Socioeconomic Index of Occupations. In M. H. Bornstein, R. H. Bradley, & A. von Eye (Eds.), *Socioeconomic status, parenting, and child development* (pp. 29–82). Mahwah, NJ: Lawrence Erlbaum Associates.

Bradley, R. H., Whiteside, L., Mundform, D. J., Casey, P. H., Kelleher, K. J., & Pope, S. K. (1994). Early indications of resilience and their relation to experiences in the home environments of low birthweight, premature children living in poverty. *Child Development, 65,* 346–360.

Chao, R. K. (1994). Beyond parental control and authoritarian parenting style: Understanding Chinese parenting through the cultural notion of training. *Child Development, 65,* 1111–1119.

Chao, R. K. (2000). What is the place of culture in describing ethnic diversity in the U.S.? *Cross-Cultural Psychology Bulletin, 34,* 7–13.

Corsaro, W. (1996). Transitions in early childhood. In R. Jessor, A. Colby, & R. Shweder (Eds.), *Ethnography and Human Development. Context and meaning in social inquiry* (pp. 419–457). Chicago: University of Chicago Press.

Deater-Deckard, K., & Dodge, K. A. (1997). Externalizing behavior problems and discipline revisited: Nonlinear effects and variation by culture, context, and gender. *Psychological Inquiry, 8,* 161–175.

Delgado-Gaitan, C. (1994). Socializing young children. In P. M. Greenfield & R. R. Cocking (Eds.), *Cross-cultural roots of minority child development.* Hillsdale, NJ: Lawrence Erlbaum Associates.

Duncan, G. J., & Brooks-Gunn, J. (Eds.). (1997). *Consequences of growing up poor.* New York: Russell Sage.

Duncan, G. J., Brooks-Gunn, J., & Smith, J. (1998). How much does childhood poverty affect the life chances of children? *American Sociological Review, 63,* 406–423.

Duncan, G. J., & Magnuson, K. A. (2003). Off with Hollingshead: Socioeconomic resources, parenting, and child development. In M. H. Bornstein, R. H. Bradley, & A. von Eye (Eds.), *Socioeconomic status, parenting, and child development* (pp. 83–106). Mahwah, NJ: Lawrence Erlbaum Associates.

Entwisle, D. R., & Astone, N. M. (1994). Some practical guidelines for measuring youth's race/ethnicity and socioeconomic status. *Child Development, 65,* 1521–1540.

Field, T. M., Widmayer, S., Adler, S., & De Cubas, M. (1990). Teenage parenting in different cultures, family constellations, and caregiving environments: Effects on infant development. *Infant Mental Health Journal, 11,* 158–174.

Fuligni, A. J., Tseng, V., & Lam, M. (1999). Attitudes toward family obligations among American adolescents with Asian, Latin American, and European family backgrounds. *Child Development, 70,* 1030–1044.

Garcia Coll, C., & Pachter, L. M. (2002). Ethnic and minority parenting. In M. H. Bornstein (Ed.), *Handbook of parenting: Vol. 4. Social conditions and applied parenting* (pp. 1–20). Mahwah, NJ: Lawrence Erlbaum Associates.

Goodnow, J. J., Cashmore, J., Cotton, S., & Knight, R. (1984). Mother's developmental time tables in two cultural groups. *International Journal of Psychology, 19,* 193–205.

Greenfield, P., Keller, H., Fuligni, A. J., & Maynard, A. (2003). Cultural pathways through universal development. *Annual Review of Psychology, 54,* 461–490.

Greenfield, P., & Suzuki, L. K. (1998). Culture and human development: Implications for parenting, education, pediatrics, and mental health. In I. E. Sigel & K. A. Renninger (Eds.), *Handbook of child psychology: Vol. 4. Child psychology in practice* (5th ed., pp. 1059–1109). New York: Wiley.

Harwood, R. L., Handwerker, W. P., Schoelmerich, A., & Leyendecker, B. (2001). Ethnic category labels, parental beliefs, and the contextualized individual: An exploration of the individualism-sociocentrism debate. *Parenting: Science and Practice, 1,* 217–236.

Harwood, R. L., Leyendecker, B., Carlson, V. J., Asencio, M., & Miller, A. M. (2002). Parenting among Latino families in the U.S. In M. H. Bornstein (Ed.), *Handbook of parenting: Vol. 4. Social conditions and applied parenting* (2nd ed., pp. 21–46). Mahwah, NJ: Lawrence Erlbaum Associates.

Harwood, R. L., Miller, A. M., Carlson, V. J., & Leyendecker, B. (2002). Parenting beliefs and practices among middle-class Puerto Rican mother–infant pairs. In J. M. Contreras, K. A. Kerns, & A. M. Neal-Barnett (Eds.), *Latino children and families in the United States* (pp. 133–154). Westport, CT: Praeger Publisher.

Harwood, R. L., Schoelmerich, A., Ventura-Cook, E., Schulze, P. A., & Wilson, S. P. (1996). Culture and class influences on Anglo and Puerto Rican mothers' beliefs regarding long-term socialization goals and child behavior. *Child Development, 67,* 2446–2461.

Hauser, R. M. (1994). Measuring socioeconomic status in studies of child development. *Child Development, 65,* 1541–1545.

Hill, N. E., Bush, K. R., & Roosa, M. W. (2003). Parenting and family socialization strategies and children's mental health: Low-income Mexican-American and Euro-American mothers and children. *Child Development, 74*(1), 189–204.

Hoff, E., Laursen, B., & Tardif, T. (2002). Socioeconomic Status and Parenting. In M. H. Bornstein (Ed.), *Handbook of parenting: Vol. 2. Biology and ecology of parenting* (pp. 231–252). Mahwah, NJ: Lawrence Erlbaum Associates.

Hoffman, L. W. (1988). Cross-cultural differences in childrearing goals. *New Directions for Child Development, 40,* 99–122.

Hollingshead, A. B. (1975). *The four-factor index of social status.* Unpublished manuscript, Yale University, New Haven, CT.

Hurrelmann, K., Klocke, A., Melzer, W., & Ravens-Sieberer, U. (Eds.). (2003). *Jugendgesundheitssurvey. Internationale Vergleichsstudie im Auftrag der Weltgesundheitsorganisation WHO.* Weinheim: Juventa.

Imamoglu, E. O. (1988). An interdependence model of human development. In C. Kagitcibasi (Ed.), *Growth and progress in cross-cultural psychology* (pp. 138–146). Berwyn: Swets North America.

Kagitcibasi, C. (1996). *Family and human development across cultures.* Mahwah, NJ: Lawrence Erlbaum Associates.

Kagitcibasi, C. (2003). Autonomy, embeddedness and adaptability in immigration contexts. *Human Development, 46,* 145–150.

Kagitcibasi, C. (2003). Autonomy and relatedness in cultural context: Implications for self and human development. Manuscript submitted for publication.

Khounani, P. M. (2000). *Binationale Familien in Deutschland und die Erziehung der Kinder: eine Vergleichsuntersuchung zur familären Erziehungssituation in mono- und bikulturellen Familien im Hinblick auf multikulturelle Handlungsfähigkeit.* Frankfurt: Peter Lang.

Kohn, M. L. (1969). *Class and conformity: A study in values.* Homewood, IL: Dorsey Press.

Kohn, M. L. (1979). The effects of social class on parental values and practices. In D. Reiss & H. R. Hoffman (Eds.), *The American family: Dying or developing* (pp. 45–68). New York: Plenum.

Kusserow, A. S. (1999). De-homogenizing American individualism: Socializing hard and soft individualism in Manhattan and Queens. *Ethos, 27*(2), 210–234.

Kwak, K. (2003). Adolescents and their parents: A review of intergenerational family relations for immigrant and non-immigrant families. *Human Development, 46,* 114–136.

Lee, C. D. (2002). Interrogating race and ethnicity as constructs in the examination of cultural processes in developmental research. *Human Development, 45,* 282–290.

Leyendecker, B., Lamb, M. E., Schoelmerich, A., & Fracasso, M. P. (1995). The social world of 8- and 12-month-old infants: Early experiences in two subcultural contexts. *Social Development, 4*(2), 194–208.

Leyendecker, B., Harwood, R. L., Lamb, M. E., & Schoelmerich, A. (2002). External factors versus internal factors: Parental evaluations of desirable and undesirable everyday situations in two diverse cultural groups. *International Journal of Behavioral Development, 26,* 248–258.

Maccoby, E. E., & Martin, J. A. (1983). Socialization in the context of the family: Parent–child interaction. In E. M. Hetherington (Ed.), *Handbook of child psychology: Vol. 4. Socialization, personality, and social development* (pp. 1–101). New York: Wiley.

Magnuson, K. A., & Duncan, G. J. (2002). Parents in poverty. In M. H. Bornstein (Ed.), *Handbook of parenting: Vol. 4. Social conditions and applied parenting* (pp. 95–122). Mahwah, NJ: Lawrence Erlbaum Associates.

Markus, H. R., & Kitayama, S. (1991). Culture and self: Implications for cognition, emotion, and motivation. *Psychological Review, 98,* 224–253.

McLoyd, V. (1998). Socioeconomic disadvantage and child development. *American Psychologist, 53*(2), 185–204.

Miller, P. J. (1996). Instantiating culture through discourse practices. In R. Jessor, A. Colby, & R. A. Shweder (Eds.), *Ethnography and human development. Context and meaning in social inquiry* (pp. 181–204). Chicago: University of Chicago Press.

Morelli, G., Rogoff, B., Oppenheim, D., & Goldsmith, D. (1992). Cultural variation in infants' sleeping arrangements. *Developmental Psychology, 28,* 604–613.

Nucci, L. (1994). Mothers' beliefs regarding the personal domain of children. In J. G. Smetana (Ed.), *Beliefs about parenting: Origins and developmental implications* (Vol. 66, New Directions for Child Development, pp. 81–97). San Francisco: Jossey-Bass.

Nucci, L., Killen, M., & Smetana, J. G. (1996). Autonomy and the personal: Negotiations and social reciprocity in adult–child social exchange. In M. Killen (Ed.), *Children's autonomy, social competence, and interactions with adults and other children: Exploring connections and consequences: Vol. 73. New directions for child development* (pp. 7–24). San Francisco: Jossey-Bass.

Pfluger-Schindlbeck, I. (1989). *"Achte die Älteren, liebe die Jüngeren". Sozialisation türkischer Kinder.* Frankfurt: Athenäum.

Phinney, J. S. (1996). When we talk about American ethnic groups, what do we mean? *American Psychologist, 51,* 918–927.

Phinney, J. S., Ong, A., & Madden, T. (2000). Cultural values and intergenerational value discrepancies in immigrant and non-immigrant families. *Child Development, 71,* 528–539.

Richman, A., Miller, P. M., & LeVine, R. (1992). Cultural and educational variations in maternal responsiveness. *Developmental Psychology, 28,* 81–96.

Rogoff, B., & Angelillo, C. (2002). Investigating the coordinated functioning of multifaceted cultural practices in human development. *Human Development, 45,* 211–225.

Ryan, R. M., Deci, E. L., & Grolnick, W. S. (1995). Autonomy, relatedness, and the self: Their relation to development and psychopathology. In D. Cicchetti & D. J. Cohen (Eds.), *Developmental psychopathology: Vol. 1. Theory and methods* (pp. 618–655). New York: Wiley & Sons.

Schulze, P. A., Harwood, R. L., & Schoelmerich, A. (2001). Feeding practices and expectations among middle-class Anglo and Puerto Rican mothers of 12-month old infants. *Journal of Cross Cultural Psychology, 32,* 397–406.

Schulze, P. A., Harwood, R. L., Schoelmerich, A., & Leyendecker, B. (2002). The cultural structuring of parenting and universal developmental tasks. *Parenting: Science and Practice.*

Shweder, R. A. (1996). True ethnography: The lore, the law and the lure. In R. Jessor, A. Colby, & R. A. Shweder (Eds.), *Ethnography and human development* (pp. 15–52). Chicago: The University of Chicago Press.

Strauss, C., & Quinn, N. (1997). *A cognitive theory of cultural meaning.* New York: Cambridge University Press.

Triandis, H. C. (1995). *Individualism and collectivism.* Boulder, CO: Westview Press.

12

Searches for What Works in Parenting Interventions

Douglas R. Powell
Purdue University

INTRODUCTION

Widespread interest in ecological perspectives on parenting in the 1980s transformed the field of programs aimed at helping parents and significant family caregivers function effectively in their childrearing roles. The century-old idea that the best way to help parents is to disseminate child development information was modified to include a major focus on the social contexts of parenting. Programs experimented with ways to strengthen parents' social networks, community ties, work–family relations, and connections with a range of other systems affecting families as a means of promoting competent parenting.

Ecological perspectives increased the field's sensitivity to population differences at group and individual levels. The long standing idea that a given program model could work with any parent or group of parents gave way to interest in culturally responsive approaches to working with families, matching parents to different types of programs, adapting or developing programs to accommodate particular populations, and methods of individualizing services to parents within their unique circumstances. The rapidity of change in ideas about best ways to help parents was aided by growing interest in extending parenting programs to populations deemed to be in need of special assistance in the parenting role (e.g., low-income parents, adolescent parents). This was a stretch for a field dominated by program content and methods that originated with middle-class European American mothers (Powell, 1988).

Changes in parenting program content, methods, and target populations led to new research questions about factors contributing to program effects. Why is Program A effective? What minimum number of sessions is needed for a program to be beneficial to Population Y? Are paraprofessionals effective providers of parenting programs? Will a program found effective with middle-class European American mothers work equally well with lower-income European Americans or African Americans or Latinas? Researchers broadened a primary focus on program outcomes to embrace questions about "what works" as well as more precise questions about "what works for whom," with concomitant complications in research design (Berlin, O'Neal, & Brooks-Gunn, 1998; Korfmacher, 2001). Treatment and population variables, long degraded in intervention research, moved to center stage.

This chapter examines the status of research on factors contributing to the effectiveness of parenting interventions, a growing focus of parenting intervention investigations since the mid-1980s. It codifies and describes conceptual and methodological approaches to research on what works; reviews selected studies; and identifies needed research directions, including variables that warrant further investigation as potential attributes of effective interventions. The chapter begins with an overview of the parameters of research on what works, followed by a section on methodological strategies and issues, and then provides an overview of conceptual approaches and illustrative studies in three domains of variables: program features, program processes, and population characteristics. It concludes with suggested directions for future research. The chapter draws mostly from studies of preventive interventions targeted to populations at risk due to such factors as low-income, parent characteristic (i.e., adolescent) or child status (i.e., low birth weight).

PARAMETERS OF RESEARCH ON WHAT WORKS

The research shift to identifying critical program features in parenting interventions can be seen as a movement from first-generation studies, focused on program outcomes, to a second generation of research on what works (Guralnick, 1997). The second generation of research began approximately in the mid-1980s, although there was attention to differential program effects prior to this time. Investigators have addressed questions about "what works" and "what works with whom," and occasionally "what works with whom under what conditions," generally as part of a larger study of program outcomes.

The first generation of studies of parenting intervention outcomes yielded a mixed picture of program effects. It is difficult to offer generalizations about results because the field encompasses considerable diversity in program content, method, intensity, population served, and community context (for a recent review, see Cowan, Powell, & Cowan, 1998). In general, results of experimental studies point to modest intervention effects on parents and children that often fall short of the expectations of policymakers and program advocates, leading some scholars to call for a closer look at what actually happens in parenting programs. For example, generally lackluster results from randomized trials of six prominent home visiting programs led one group of analysts to call for research "crafted to primarily help programs improve quality and implementation: for example, to explore which families are most likely to engage in and to benefit from the services . . . and to determine the threshold levels of intensity and duration of services . . ." (Gomby, Culross, & Behrman, 1999, p. 22).

The growing interest in what works in parenting interventions coincides with similar research emphases in related fields, including psychotherapy (Roth & Fonagy, 1996), child care (framed as a quality issue; Lamb, 1998), and education (Slavin, 2002, 2004). For example, a National Research Council (2002) report on education research emphasizes the importance of addressing three types of research questions: description (what is happening?), cause (is there a systematic effect?), and process or mechanism (why or how is it happening?). The federal government has bolstered efforts to use findings from scientifically based research to improve the nation's educational outcomes. As one step to this end, the U.S. Department of Education's Institute of Education Sciences has established a *What Works Clearinghouse* (www.w-w-c.org) to provide educators, policymakers, and the public with high-quality reviews of scientific evidence of the effectiveness of replicable educational interventions, including programs, practices, products or policies. More significantly, the reauthorization of the multi-billion dollar federal Elementary and Secondary Education Act—the No Child Left Behind Act of 2001—actively promotes the use of scientifically based teaching methods. With more than 100 references to the term *scientifically based research*, the No Child Left Behind Act approaches progress in education like advances in the field of medicine, where practice is driven by findings of impartial research rather than folk wisdom or moral philosophy (Traub, 2002).

Calls for increased use of scientific evidence, particularly findings from experimental research, to inform program design and practice decisions have been met with reminders about the difficulty of defining the treatment variable (Olson, 2004) and the complexities of field research, especially the inability of research and broad theory to "incorporate the enormous number or determine the power of the contexts within which human beings find themselves" (Berliner, 2002, p. 19).

Rigorous investigation of questions about what works puts a spotlight on program processes and population characteristics long viewed as static entities in intervention studies (Powell & Sigel, 1991). For certain, "black box experiments are out" (Cook & Payne, 2002, p. 160). Less certain is how to appropriately conceptualize, measure, and analyze program process and population variables, especially in the context of program features and community systems in which families and programs function. The treatment variable is actually an intervention package comprised of many variables (e.g., curriculum, intensity, staffing), usually organized in a complex manner (Campbell, 1986).

First and foremost, investigators of questions about what works need to identify variables and their potential linkages in a coherent model of how a program is expected to make a difference. The model needs to specify how anticipated actions in a parenting program are expected to change parent knowledge or behavior and how, in turn, those changes might lead to specific early, intermediate, and long-term outcomes. This framework can be used as a road map for examining the extent to which a program's theory actually holds (Weiss, 1995). Typically a program's theory of change, also known as a logic model, is implicit. Designers of interventions generally do not articulate in precise terms the assumptions of program strategies (St.Pierre & Layzer, 1998). Moreover, researchers cannot expect program staff to readily provide a short list of variables or a hypothesized model of causal linkages. Although service providers are a valuable and overlooked source of insight into intervention processes (e.g., Kitzman, Cole, Yoos, & Olds, 1997), it appears that program staff often have difficulty articulating the theory or theories upon which their program is based. Researchers who have collaborated with program staff to develop a testable model or theory of change for program evaluation purposes report that early discussions with staff may yield vague terms and ideas, multiple and sometimes competing theories of change for the same program; these "Grand Canyon models" are characterized by a wide gap between the intervention design and desired results (Philliber, 1998, p. 92), and a reluctance to make program assumptions explicit due to political risks of alienating or offending one or more constituencies in a community (Weiss, 1995). Accordingly, the development of a model with program staff may be best approached as an iterative process that moves toward successive refinement of a set of program actions that are both doable and plausibly linked to program goals and anticipated outcomes (Connell & Kubisch, 1998).

As indicated earlier, this chapter examines three domains of variables in searches for what works in parenting interventions: program features; program processes; and population characteristics. Program features include structural (e.g., delivery mode) and staffing (e.g., professional or paraprofessional) arrangements as well as program goals, content, and method of supporting change in parents. Program processes entail the quantity and quality of participation, including the engagement of program content and relationships between participants and program staff. Demographic and mental health (e.g., psychological depression) factors are among the population characteristics in parenting intervention research.

Figure 12.1 depicts the relations most commonly examined among these three categories of variables. Program features have been considered in relation to outcomes (path a) and also have been studied as a context of program processes (path b). Program processes have been examined primarily in relation to outcomes (path c). Population characteristics have been conceptualized as moderators of intervention effects (path d) in some studies and as predictors of program participation (path e) in other studies.

In the next section, I describe methodological approaches and challenges associated with this line of research. In subsequent sections, I describe conceptual approaches and illustrative studies in each of the three categories of variables.

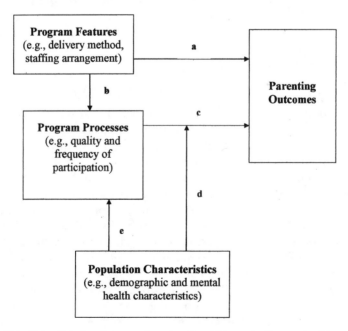

FIG. 12.1. Relations between domains of variables typically examined in research on what works in parenting interventions.

METHODOLOGICAL APPROACHES TO DETERMINING WHAT WORKS

Studies of what works in parenting interventions may be organized into three broad categories of research design:

1. Between-group comparisons of the effects of different programs or planned variation in the delivery of the same program.
2. Within-group comparisons focused on one or more population characteristic and/or natural variation in program participation, usually in relation to program effects.
3. Descriptive research on program implementation, including participant recruitment and retention, staff approaches to program delivery, and participant responses to program content and methods.

Each of these approaches to research has proven to be useful in addressing specific types of questions regarding what works in parenting interventions. Later I describe in general terms how each of these basic research designs has been used in parenting intervention studies, noting some of the methodological challenges commonly encountered. Studies are briefly referenced here as examples of particular methodological challenges or approaches. The results of most of the studies cited below are described in subsequent sections of this chapter.

Between-Group Comparisons. As indicated above, two different types of between-group comparisons have been pursued in research on what works in parenting interventions. One set of studies has examined the relative effectiveness of theoretically distinct programs. For example, Barnard and her colleagues compared the use and effects of two different types of home visiting programs with high-risk mothers: a mental health program that emphasized a therapeutic relationship with the mother, and a information-referral program designed to provide information on infant growth and development (Barnard et al., 1988; see also Booth, Mitchell, Barnard, & Spieker, 1989). Between-group comparisons also may vary the configuration of program services or the frequency and mode of delivery as a test of the effects of program intensity. For example, in the multi-site study of the Early Head Start program, sites were compared on the basis of full versus partial implementation of program services to determine whether there were differential program effects (Love et al., 2002). An experimental study by Luster and his colleagues compared effects on adolescent mothers of weekly home visiting as opposed to less frequent contact via telephone and mail (Luster, Perlstadt, McKinney, Sims, & Juang, 1996).

In the second type of between-group comparison studies, systematic enhancement or adaptation of a particular program, found to be effective in prior investigations, has been examined to determine whether there are better ways to deliver the program. Examples include planned variation in the use of videotapes versus in-person staff to demonstrate effective joint book reading strategies with preschool children (Arnold, Lonigan, Whitehurst, & Epstein, 1994) and in the use of professional nurses versus paraprofessionals to deliver a home visiting program (Olds et al., 2002).

The two types of studies yield different levels of specificity in defining what works. The first set of investigations defines "what" at a program level, whereas the second set of studies targets particular practices or program design features. Results of research involving planned variation in a key attribute of a particular program are especially informative regarding a potentially best practice, examined within the context of a given intervention design and population, because other features of the program are controlled.

Experimental designs offer the most rigorous scientific information on what works in a parenting intervention, and expanded use of randomized experiments is increasingly recommended for establishing causal relations in education and human service programs (Mosteller & Boruch, 2002; National Research Council, 2002; National Research Council and Institute of Medicine, 2000). For example, the four major threats to validity set forth by Donald Campbell (Cook & Campbell, 1979; Shadish, Cook, & Campbell, 2002) are the basis of standards and criteria for selecting research reports to be included in the aforementioned What Works Clearinghouse sponsored by the U.S. Department of Education. The four areas are: construct validity (were the intervention and outcome properly defined?), internal validity (was the intervention the cause of the change in the outcome?), external validity (was the intervention tested on targeted participants and environments?), and statistical conclusion validity (could accurate effect sizes be derived from the study report?; Valentine & Cooper, 2003).

Random assignment of parents to different conditions is not always feasible, leading some researchers to randomly assign settings such as Head Start centers (Webster-Stratton, 1998) or housing projects (Slaughter, 1983) to either intervention or control conditions, or to different types of parenting interventions. Selection bias problems commonly associated with these and other quasi-experimental designs can be partially addressed by matching settings on important variables before randomly assigning to different study conditions. For instance, in two different studies, Webster-Stratton (1998; Webster-Stratton, Reid, & Hammond, 2001) matched Head Start centers on key demographic variables (e.g., ethnicity of children) prior to assigning centers to either a parenting intervention or control condition. This strategy resulted in few significant differences between the characteristics of parents in intervention and control conditions that could be expected by chance (i.e., mothers in the intervention centers had higher depressive symptom scores and a higher likelihood of having a substance abuse history; Baydar, Reid, & Webster-Stratton, 2003). Nonetheless, the best (albeit not always politically or logistically feasible) way to eliminate selection bias is to randomly assign participants to either intervention or control conditions.

Several across-program analyses of outcomes of family-oriented interventions that included parenting components have been conducted recently with an eye toward identifying critical components of program effectiveness. One is a study of the Early Head Start Program in 17 different sites (Love et al., 2002), all of which included a parenting component. The others are meta-analyses, one of 665 studies of 260 family support programs, 98% of which offered parenting education (Layzer, Goodson, Bernstein, & Price, 2001), and a second of 88 preventive interventions aimed at enhancing parental sensitivity and infant attachment (Bakermans-Kranenburg, van IJzendoorn, & Juffer, 2003). Random assignment of families to program or control conditions was used in each of the Early Head Start sites, and randomization was employed in studies of 109 of the interventions included in the family support program analyses. Cross-program comparisons and meta-analyses are inherently limited in the contextual information that can be provided in relation to results. Nonetheless, meta-analyses are particularly useful in helping researchers use all existing data on a topic of programmatic and policy importance (McCartney & Rosenthal, 2000).

Within-Group Comparisons.   Growing interest in the question "For whom is a parenting program most effective?" has led many researchers to investigate the extent to which there are differential effects for subgroups of program participants. In addition to examining a range of demographic and psychological characteristics as moderators of program effects, researchers have investigated differences in the quality and/or quantity of program participation in relation to program outcomes, as noted earlier. The primary interest here is dosage-response relations.

Occasionally, within-group comparisons are investigated in a post hoc search for any intervention effects. For example, in an experimental study of the Mother Child Home Program that found no effects on mothers or children, Scarr and McCartney (1988) looked diligently for interactions between the intervention and a number of child and mother variables "in a fit of post-hoc frustration" (p. 540). These types of exploratory analyses are appropriate when overall results are contrary to the findings of other studies (and perhaps they provide disappointed program stakeholders with assurances that evaluators left no stone unturned). Nonetheless, the post hoc nature of these analyses combined with the usual sample confounds encountered in intervention research (see later) compromise the validity of results. Subgroup differences detected in this manner warrant further investigation in well designed prospective research. Some researchers recommend that analyses of within-group comparisons regarding the magnitude of program effects should use only outcome measures that have demonstrated intervention-control group differences in the main analyses. Interpretation of differential effects by different subgroups is problematic if it is not known whether the intervention is effective overall (Korfmacher, Kitzman, & Olds, 1998).

Within-group comparisons typically employ correlational methods and therefore are unable to establish causality. Strong positive correlations between indices of program participation and program outcomes are difficult to interpret, for instance, especially in the absence of data on preintervention differences that may be related to participation-outcome relations. Are outcomes a function of higher levels of program participation or a participant characteristic that influences both program participation and outcomes? Results of within-group comparisons conducted as part of quasi-experimental studies are especially problematic due to selection bias confounds. True experiments provide the best evidence regarding causal mechanisms in programs (e.g., random assignment to different levels of participation).

Correlational designs are far from useless, however. Appropriately designed correlational studies can be used to formulate hypotheses about causal relation and to inform causal inferences (Thompson, Diamond, McWilliam, Snyder, & Snyder, 2005). Specifically, structural equation modeling has been used productively to compare subgroups of intervention participants. For example, Baydar et al. (2003) investigated whether a parent training program was effective for parents who have elevated levels of mental health risk factors by assessing whether program engagement predicted improvements in parenting skills for all parents, whether mental health risk factors predicted program engagement, and whether mothers with mental health risk factors benefited from a parent training program compared with mothers with mental health risk factors in the control group.

In most intervention studies, sample sizes seriously limit within-group comparisons because homogeneous subgroups often cannot be formed with a sufficient number of participants for adequate statistical power. Even with relatively large sample sizes, it may be impossible to form fully homogeneous subgroups. For example, in an examination of differential intervention effects of the large-scale, multi-site Infant Health and Development Program for subgroups defined by maternal education and ethnicity, the percentage of mothers who had a college degree varied significantly in African American and European American subgroups (20% and 56%, respectively, among those who attended college; Brooks-Gunn, Gross, Kraemer, Spiker, & Shapiro, 1997). Accordingly, within-group comparisons in most intervention studies are exploratory.

Descriptive Studies. Descriptive research on program processes has focused on various aspects of program implementation, including the recruitment of program participants, what actually happens in program settings, changes over time in participation patterns, and staff experiences. Carefully designed and conducted descriptive studies can yield valuable understandings of the nuances of cultural and social class differences in participant responses to program content, and the larger contexts in which parenting interventions are implemented.

Descriptions of program processes cannot determine what works in parenting interventions, but they can help explain why an intervention was or was not effective when conducted in concert with a study of intervention effects. For example, as a companion study to a randomized trial of the Parents as Teachers program (Wagner & Clayton, 1999), Hebbeler and Gerlach-Downie (2002) conducted a longitudinal investigation to explore why the home visiting program was not more effective. Descriptive studies also can be used to identify variables that warrant inclusion in subsequent experimental investigations, and to illuminate complex program processes that need special attention in the design and implementation of parenting interventions. It is helpful for program implementers to know, for example, that descriptive studies generally indicate that personal outreach strategies are far more useful than print and media delivered efforts in recruiting low-income parents to participate in programs (e.g., Wagner, Spiker, Linn, Gerlach-Downie, & Hernandez, 2003).

Qualitative research is well suited to identifying the nuances of interventions (e.g., Erickson & Gutierrez, 2002) and, accordingly, descriptive studies of parenting interventions typically employ qualitative methods, including focus groups, interviews, and observations. Quantitative methods also have been used to describe, for example, stability and change over time in the content of long-term parenting discussion groups (Powell & Eisenstadt, 1988), and patterns of engagement in a home visiting program (Wagner et al., 2003).

I turn now to a delineation and description of illustrative studies in each of three categories of variables: program features, program processes, and population characteristics. The organization of each section follows the paths depicted in Fig. 12.1.

PROGRAM FEATURES

Parenting interventions differ in numerous ways. Program features may be organized into four categories as follows:

There are *structural* features such as: the mode of delivery (e.g., group, home-based); the onset, duration, and frequency of program services;

and whether the parenting intervention is part of a larger program that includes other services (e.g., early childhood education). A related yet separate feature is a program's *staffing* arrangement. Much of the interest in program staffing has centered on the relative merits of using professional versus paraprofessional staff to provide parenting interventions. In many ways, professional versus paraprofessional staffing arrangements are proxy variables for staff qualities thought to be conducive to forming and maintaining interpersonal ties with families that support parental growth and change.

Intervention *goals and content* represent a third set of program features. A key distinction here is whether program goals and content focus primarily on child development, including parental practices in support of child development, or on a broader set of issues that includes child development as well as topics and assistance related to the ecology of individual and family functioning. Another critical difference in program content is the perspective on directors or sources of developmental change in the child. Are the forces regulating developmental change internal to the child (child-focused), external to the child (parent-focused), or a product of the interaction between internal and external forces (parent–child relationship focused)? (Cowan, 1988). A program's perspective on the mechanisms by which parents influence their child's development results in particular sets of messages conveyed to parents about appropriate parenting behaviors and beliefs (Cowan et al., 1998). For instance, programs for parents of preschoolers vary in content when they tell parents that their child's early reading skills (a) will emerge when the child is ready, or (b) are best supported through highly structured and repetitive experiences with print, or (c) are appropriately fostered through frequent parent–child shared book readings in which the child is an active contributor to the story telling and the parent encourages the child to build on and extend her understandings.

Finally, parenting interventions differ in the *pedagogical or clinical strategies* employed to support change in parents. Some programs view the interpersonal relationship between program staff and parents as the primary means for achieving meaningful change in parents. Process (i.e., relationship building) is a central part of the program content. A primary goal of one prominent relationship-based intervention with at-risk mothers, for example, is to provide the mother with "the experience of a stable trustworthy relationship that conveys understanding of her situation" and promotes her sense of self-efficacy (Heinicke, Fineman, Ponce, & Guthrie, 2001, p. 440). In other programs, the staff role is to provide information about child development and parenting practices, sometimes via demonstration (e.g., modeling desired practices in person or via a videotape). Within programs adhering to more of an instructional approach, a finer distinction can be made regarding the use of didactic versus nondidactic teaching methods.

The program features identified above typically are clustered in distinctive patterns. Programs focused on parent–child attachment generally view the relationship between parent and program worker as a therapeutic alliance that is fundamental to changing a mother's approach to significant relationships. Programs focused on parents as teachers of their child tend to employ instructional strategies for disseminating information (Cowan et al., 1998). In general, staff model behaviors that the programs wish to foster in parents' interactions with their child.

Illustrative Studies

Program delivery methods (group- and home-based strategies) and staffing arrangements have been examined in several important studies. Findings are summarized later. The duration and frequency of intervention services also have received significant research attention. Although these structural program features are an inherent element of a good intervention design, the actual frequency and duration of program contact with participants are typically much less than intervention protocols specify. Accordingly, I consider these variables as indicators of program intensity in the section on program processes. The onset of program services has received limited systematic study. Limited attention also has been given to intervention goals and content, and to pedagogical and clinical strategies.

Links to Outcomes (path a).   Discussion groups and home visits are time-honored methods for delivering parenting education and support. Each has rich practice and theoretical traditions that embrace different assumptions about how best to facilitate change in parents, namely the peer learning and support presumed to exist in discussion groups and the individualization to particular circumstances afforded in home visits.

Research comparing the relative effectiveness of these two delivery methods spans several decades. Peer discussion groups produced stronger effects than home visits in an early quasi-experimental study (Slaughter, 1983), and the Layzer et al. (2001) meta-analysis of family support programs found that parent groups produced stronger effects than home visiting. Specifically, the average effect sizes for parent groups as the primary method of delivering parent education were .54 when targeted to children at biological risk and .27 when used with nontargeted populations, compared to average effect sizes for home visiting of .36 when targeted to children at biological risk and .09 when used with nontargeted populations. Further, a cross-program study of Early Head Start found that a combination of center-based and home-based strategies yielded a stronger pattern of impacts than center-based or home-based alone (Love et al., 2002). Perhaps the effectiveness of a program increases when the unique strengths of multiple delivery methods are maximized concurrently or sequentially.

One cannot offer generalizations about the superiority of peer groups or the limited impact of home visits from these types of results alone because program delivery methods are best understood in relation to other program features and, as suggested in the meta-analysis results, population characteristics. A finer grained question needs to be asked: Under what conditions and for whom is a particular program delivery strategy an effective method for achieving positive change in parent and child outcomes?

One cost sensitive program feature is the staffing arrangement. Can paraprofessionals produce positive results in a model home visiting program found to be effective when delivered by professionals? This question was addressed by Olds and his colleagues in a randomized trial of a home visiting program with first-time, low-income mothers in Denver (Olds et al., 2002). They found that, when trained in the Nurse Home Visiting Program model (now known as the Nurse Family Partnership), paraprofessionals produced small effects that rarely achieved statistical or clinical significance, whereas nurses produced significant effects on a wide range of maternal and child outcomes in a population eligible for Medicaid or without private health insurance. For most outcomes on which either paraprofessionals or nurses produced significant effects, the paraprofessionals typically had effects that were about half the size of those produced by nurses. The investigators suggest that perhaps nurses had higher levels of legitimacy than paraprofessionals in the eyes of families who have concerns about complications of pregnancy, labor and delivery, and the care of newborns. Nurses are established authorities on this topic and thus may have more power to engage parents and support adaptive behavior change than paraprofessionals. In a case study of a young mother's experiences in the program, for example, the nurse is viewed by the mother as a trusted authority ("she wouldn't lie") with credible suggestions ("I try to do what the nurse [suggests], because she knows . . ."; Kitzman, Yoos, Cole, Korfmacher, & Hanks, 1997).

As a Context of Program Processes (path b). A study of how nurses and paraprofessionals conducted home visits in the Denver trial described previously illustrates the benefits of examining a program feature (in this case, staffing arrangement) as a context of program processes. Nurses and paraprofessionals were found to implement the program in substantially different ways even though they were provided with a structured and common set of protocols. For example, nurses spent a greater proportion of home visit time focused on personal health and parenting issues whereas paraprofessionals devoted a greater proportion of time to topics related to environmental health and safety. Mothers' ratings of the helping relationship did not differ between nurses and paraprofessionals, however (Korfmacher, O'Brien, Hiatt, & Olds, 1999).

An experimental study of two conceptually different intervention models by Booth and her colleagues also illustrates the value of studying program processes in relation to systematic variation in a program feature (Booth et al., 1989). One model (labeled *Mental Health*) was based on a two-step approach that focused on the mother's interpersonal competence as first step toward optimal parenting and on the mother's parenting knowledge as the second step. Home visitors fostered a therapeutic relationship with the mothers in this model and demonstrated ways of handling family relationships and problems. In the contrasting model (labeled *Information/ Resource*), home visitors provided information on parenting through didactic methods (the second step of the first model). An analysis of program process data revealed that the two models were blurred in implementation. Home visitors (nurses in both models) in the Mental Health condition functioned in ways consistent with the model; 64% of nursing acts were classified as "providing therapy" and 36% were classified as "informing." However, 51% of nursing acts in the Information/Resource condition were classified as "providing therapy" and 49% were classified as "informing." These patterns led the investigators to combine groups in the two conditions for analyses based on individual differences in the amount of two-step treatment provided (e.g., relative frequency of therapy). Program effects varied by mother's social skill, as described in the section on population characteristics.

PROGRAM PROCESSES

Research attention to program processes is generally approached as a question about intervention fidelity: Did parents participate in the program as intended? The lens is defined from the perspective of the program designer, and the usual strategy is to determine the extent to which indicators of participation (e.g., frequency of attendance at group meetings or participation in home visits) match the thresholds deemed necessary for positive program outcomes. A parallel approach in medical and clinical interventions conceptualizes participation as compliance with the treatment regimen (e.g., pill counts, missed appointments; Blackwell, 1998). The inevitable variability in participation found in most programs logically leads to a dose-response perspective on the question of what works in an intervention.

Recently investigators have added depth and breadth to their conceptualizations of interventions as they attempt to unpack program processes. Studies have sought to consider participants' perspectives on their program experiences, partly in recognition of the distinction between program delivery and program receipt; changes over time in patterns of participation; individual differences in patterns of participation; how staff approach their work with parents; and what program staff and parents actually do together (Powell, Okagaki, & Bojczyk, 2004). Many investigators frame this closer examination of life in a parenting program as looking inside the "black box" (e.g., Hebbeler & Gerlach-Downie, 2002). Conceptualizations of program processes that transcend a view of participation as compliance with a program protocol provide an opportunity for researchers to consider parents as active contributors to the intervention process (Eisenstadt & Powell, 1987) and staff as responsive decision makers about the adaptation of program content and resources to specific family circumstances (Kitzman et al., 1997).

Studies of the multidimensionality of interventions have included measures of the quality of participation, generally focused on the relationship between program staff and participants, along with the more common indicators of quantity of participation. The term *engagement* is increasingly used to depict parent interactions with program staff, including the quality and quantity of initial encounters during program recruitment contacts (e.g., Gomby et al., 1999).

Illustrative Studies

Descriptions of Program Processes. Studies of patterns of participation in parenting programs can inform hypotheses about salient aspects of intervention processes. Existing research suggests some dimensions of participation may be independent of others. A multi-site study of the Parents as Teachers program found that parents may consistently participate in home visits but not use program materials and activities in between visits or try recommended practices with their child (Wagner et al., 2003). Similarly, a longitudinal observational study of discussion groups serving low-income mothers found that attendance was not related to the quality of parents' program participation, such as type of verbal contribution to group discussions (Eisenstadt & Powell, 1987). Another descriptive study of parents' responses to a family literacy program found that working-class mothers' positive responses at the program site to the intervention's suggested hands-on literacy activities with their children (e.g., using Playdough to make storybook characters and form letters) were not indicative of their true views of the suggested activities or use of the suggestions at home. In fact, mothers thought the Playdough was dirty and that their houses became untidy as children left books, papers, and other literacy artifacts lying around (Anderson, Fagan, & Cronin, 1998). Together these studies raise questions about the validity of measures of program participation that rely on staff perceptions of parental engagement or response to program ideas, and also suggest that care must be taken in combining data from multiple measures of participation.

Descriptive research can work in tandem with outcome studies to identify possible reasons why a program is or is not effective. Of special interest here are the roles and behavior of staff in helping parents support their child's development. Data on the range of staff actions can yield a useful chronicle of core messages to parents which may or may not match the intentions of program designers, and may or may not be obvious to parents. A qualitative study of the Parents as Teachers Program, conducted to shed light on why the program was not found to be more effective in two randomized trials (Wagner & Clayton, 1999), found that home visitors emphasized their social support role and generally did not discuss parenting behaviors that seemed to be in need of change or improvement, even though program goals emphasized both confidence-building and parenting knowledge and skill improvements. Interestingly, parents viewed the time the home visitor spent interacting with her child as a direct intervention that would enhance the child's development (a "vitamin") whereas the home visitor saw the same interaction as modeling for the parent (Hebbeler & Gerlach-Downie, 2002). These findings echo results of the qualitative study of the Child and Family Resource Program indicating that home visitors spent little time on child development and parenting (Travers, Irwin, & Nauta, 1981). An outcome study found no program impact on child outcomes (Travers, Nauta, & Irwin, 1982). Analyses of other interventions suggest that paraprofessional home visitors may have special difficulty systematically addressing parenting behaviors (Halpern, 1992), especially when parent-clients face issues (e.g., abuse) that are salient in the life history of the paraprofessional (Musick & Barbera-Stein, 1988).

Links to Outcomes (path c). Numerous studies of parenting programs have conceptualized program participation as a matter of dosage, examining differences in program participation frequencies (e.g., Ramey et al., 1992) or level of parent interest in curriculum content (e.g., Belsky, 1986; Korfmacher et al., 1998) in relation to child and/or parent outcomes. There is inconclusive evidence about dosage questions. Many analyses, such as those described below, indicate that higher levels of contact with parents yield stronger results than interventions with lower dosage levels. Yet in contrast to "more is better" patterns of findings, the Bakermans-Kranenburg et al. (2003) meta-analysis of interventions designed to enhance parental sensitivity and infant attachment concluded that "less is more." They found that interventions with fewer than five sessions were as effective as interventions with 5 to 16 sessions, but interventions with more than 16 sessions were less effective than interventions with a smaller number of sessions. A serious limitation of most dosage-response analyses is the absence of experimental study of dosage, as noted later.

The Infant Health and Development Program has been the subject of more dosage analyses than any other intervention to date. Effects of this intervention for low birth weight, premature infants and their parents were examined with concurrent randomized trials involving about 1,000 infants and their families across eight sites (Gross, Spiker, & Haynes, 1997). In the original analyses of program effects, investigators found that intervention effects on the child were related to the degree of family participation in the program as measured by days of child attendance in the child development center, the number of home visits completed, and the number of parent group meetings attended (Ramey, Bryant, Wasik, Sparling, Fendt, & LaVange, 1992). A second set of separate analyses indicated that the rate at which a curriculum emphasizing adult–child interactions was implemented in home visits (i.e., number of activities introduced to a parent in a home visit) and in the child development center added significantly to the prediction of children's IQ scores at 3 years of age (Sparling et al., 1991). A third set of analyses by Liaw, Meisels and Brooks-Gunn (1995) examined the relative contribution of three dimensions of participants' experiences in the intervention: program exposure (i.e., number of contacts in the home and child development center); rate (i.e., number of activities presented per visit to parent in the home or per day to the child at the center); and active experience (i.e., parent's interest in the intervention activities at home and child's mastery of tasks taught at the center). Indices of active experience were stronger predictors of child IQ and quality of home environment scores at age 3 than program exposure or rate of participation. Further, a higher level of active experience on the part of both parent and child was more strongly associated with child IQ and home environment quality than a high level of active experience on the part of the child only or the parent only or neither.

Results of the three analyses of program process–outcome relations summarized previously are consistent in suggesting that "more is better," but they emphasize different answers to the question, "more of what?" The first two analyses focus on the quantity of participation from a program perspective; specifically, variations in the frequency of participation in program components (Ramey et al., 1992) or in the amount of program content delivered (Sparling et al., 1991). The third set of analyses emphasizes the quality and quantity of participation in program components from a participant perspective; specifically, level of active engagement of home visit and child development center components (Liaw et al., 1995).

The attention to quality of program experience in the Liaw et al. (1995) analyses of participation in the Infant Health and Development Program is part of a growing empirical literature that links the quality of program participation to program effects. An early study in this area was conducted by Belsky (1986) in an analysis of the effectiveness of newborn interventions employing the Brazelton Neonatal Behavioral Assessment Scale as a tool for influencing parental behavior (Belsky, 1985; see also Worobey & Brazelton, 1986). The sample population was primarily European American and well educated. Belsky examined within-group variation in the intervention groups upon finding no differences between intervention and control groups regarding parent–infant interaction and marital functioning. The within-group analyses identified short-term positive program effects on mothers and fathers who were highly engaged in the intervention (i.e., intervener ratings of the parent's interest in, involvement with, and enjoyment of the intervention) and who jointly participated in the intervention (vs. the mother participating without the baby's father). Results of other within-group analyses of intervention effects suggest that the quality of parental engagement of the program is linked to program outcomes (e.g., Lieberman, Weston, & Pawl, 1991; Pfannenstiel & Seltzer, 1989; Roggman, Boyce, Cook, & Jump, 2001).

The benefit of measuring multiple dimensions of participation is suggested in the results of an analysis of three dimensions of participation as predictors of outcomes in the Memphis trial of the Nurse Home Visiting Program: length of participation, amount of focus on parenting issues, and the emotional qualities of the relationship between home visitor and program participant (Korfmacher et al., 1998). Results varied by the psychological resourcefulness of the mother. A positive relation between nurses' empathy towards their client–mothers and the mothers' empathy towards their child was found for mothers with higher levels of psychological resources. In contrast, a positive relation between parenting content focus during the home visit and quality of the home environment (an outcome variable) was especially strong for mothers with lower levels of psychological resources. The amount of contact mothers had with their nurse home visitor was predictive of only one outcome—the child's responsiveness to the mother.

In addition to examining dose-response relations, program intensity may be examined as variations in the configuration or types of services offered to families. An experimental study comparing intensive support (weekly home visits) and less intensive support (less frequent contact primarily via phone and mail) to adolescent mothers found that mothers who received the more intensive treatment had higher scores on a measure of the quality of the home environment provided to the infant at 12 months than mothers who received the less intensive intervention (Luster et al., 1996). Results of a 17-site study of the Early Head Start Program indirectly address the question of whether more services offered to families yield stronger program effects. Program sites that fully implemented key elements of the Head Start Performance Standards had a stronger pattern of impacts on children at age 3 years than program sites that did not fully implement all standards (Love et al., 2002).

Most studies of program process–outcome relations acknowledge that unidentified and unmeasured factors may account for systematic relations between frequency of participation and program outcomes (e.g., Ramey et al., 1992). It is common in within-group analyses to statistically control for person and family variables potentially associated with program participation and/or outcomes (e.g., Liaw et al., 1995), but this strategy offers less conclusive information than experimental designs that vary some aspect of program dosage. It appears that only one set of studies, conducted in Jamaica, has systematically varied levels of program frequency, with results indicating that a higher frequency of home visits was associated with positive effects on children's mental functioning (Powell & Grantham-McGregor, 1989). In one of the Jamaican studies, poor neighborhood areas were assigned to one of two different frequencies of home visits with families (twice a month, once a month) or a control condition. In a subsequent study with a different sample, families were randomly assigned to either weekly home visits or a control condition. Data from these two sets of studies could not be combined for analyses because different methods were used to assign families to experimental and control conditions. In the first study, children in the group receiving bimonthly visits showed small but statistically significant increases in scores on the Griffiths Mental Development Scales, and there were no increases among children in families receiving monthly or no visits. In the second study, children in the group receiving weekly home visits showed significant improvements in developmental functioning compared to children of families in the control group.

POPULATION CHARACTERISTICS

The idea of considering differential effects of an intervention by population characteristic holds considerable appeal. The effects of an intervention may depend on a preexisting characteristic of a population. That is, a preexisting characteristic functions as a moderator of program effects. Accordingly, one set of parents (e.g., clinically depressed) may respond poorly to an intervention whereas another set of parents (e.g., not clinically depressed) may derive benefits. Ignoring a key population characteristic in assessing the impact of an intervention runs the risk of concluding that a program has no effects when in reality the intervention may be highly beneficial for one group of parents and actually harmful (e.g., adding stress) to another group of parents (National Research Council and Institute of Medicine, 2000).

A major challenge is to identify the key population characteristic(s). Ideally researchers examine well defined, a priori moderators that previous research suggests are linked to the behavioral or cognitive outcomes targeted by the intervention. Far less satisfactory is a random hunt for subgroup differences in the absence of program effects (National Research Council and Institute of Medicine, 2000) and/or poorly defined moderator variables (e.g., a composite measure with no report of internal reliability).

Illustrative Studies

Some investigators have intentionally considered population differences in sequential intervention trials in order to determine program effects with different populations and communities. For example, Olds and his colleagues conducted randomized trials of the Nurse Home Visitor Program with primarily African American mothers in Memphis, Tennessee and with a diverse population, including a sizable percentage of Latino mothers, in Denver, Colorado after finding positive program effects with primarily European American mothers in the small, semi-rural community of Elmira, New York (Olds et al., 1999). Each trial yielded positive intervention effects, as reported in this chapter, including interactions with population characteristics in Elmira and Memphis trials, as described later. Reid, Webster-Stratton, and Beauchaine (2001) combined data from three cohorts of families who participated in prior studies of the effectiveness of the Incredible Years Parenting Program to compare responses of African American, Asian American, Caucasian, and Hispanic mothers to the program. Results indicated the program was effective with each of these populations.

Demographic factors and the parent's psychological and mental health characteristics have been examined most often as moderators of program effects and/or as predictors of program participation. Below I describe representative studies in these areas.

As Moderators of Program Effects (path d). Within-group analyses of effects of the Infant Health and Development Program demonstrate the usefulness of considering family characteristics as moderators of program effects. Exploratory analyses found that the intervention was more effective for children of mothers with a high school education or less, and the intervention effect on children's IQ scores at 36 months of age (the end of the intervention) was much greater for children from lower-quality homes as measured by the HOME inventory, but this IQ difference declined with age (Bradley, Burchinal, & Casey, 2001). Also, when children were 36 months of age, a significant birth weight by intervention interaction was found among European American mothers with some college, with lighter children less influenced by the intervention than comparable low birth weight children who were heavier. The researchers speculated that there may be a ceiling effect on the amount of improvement that can be expected in low birth weight children who were lighter and reside in relatively enriched environments (Brooks-Gunn et al., 1997). This is one of the few intervention studies to consider a child characteristic as a moderator of program effects.

The finding that the Infant Health and Development Program was more effective with higher-risk families is consistent with results of other intervention researches. In studies of the Nurse Home Visiting Program noted above, treatment differences for child abuse and neglect and emergency room visits were more significant among women who had a lower sense of control over their lives in the Elmira, New York trial (Olds, Henderson, Chamberlin, & Tatelbaum, 1986), and program effects on children's health care encounters for injuries and ingestions were focused on children born to women with few psychological resources in the Memphis, Tennessee trial (Olds, Henderson, Kitzman, Eckenrode, Cole, & Tatelbaum, 1998). Also, the experimental study by Booth et al. (1989) of the Mental Health and Information/Resource intervention models, described previously, found the intervention was more beneficial for mothers who, at the point of program entry, had low social skills. Further, a quasi-experimental study (no randomization) of a home visiting program for mothers of at-risk infants found no main effect of the intervention on infant mental development scores, but a significant interaction effect between intervention and maternal depression. Infants of depressed mothers who received the home visiting intervention achieved significantly higher mental development scores and were twice as likely to be classified as securely attached than infants of depressed mothers who did not receive the home visiting intervention (Lyons-Ruth, Connell, Grunebaum, & Botein, 1990).

As Predictors of Program Participation (path e). Factors associated with parents' decisions to join and stay in a parenting program warrant investigation in light of the high rates of participant attrition and less-than-intended levels of participation experienced by interventions serving high-risk populations. For example, in randomized trials of the Parents as Teachers program with adolescent mothers there was an average attrition rate of 57% by 2 years (Wagner & Clayton, 1999), and mothers completed about half the number of home visits expected by the protocol of the Nurse Home Visiting program (Korfmacher et al., 1998). Population characteristics are prime candidates for predicting who will join and remain in a program. Early research on this topic found that social network and demographic characteristics were significant predictors of length of participation in parenting interventions (Powell, 1984). More recent work indicates that mothers were significantly less likely to actively engage in home visits when living in a county that displayed poor community health (i.e., infant death rate, low birth weight rate) or when isolated from imme-diate family and friendship networks (McGuigan, Katzev, & Pratt, 2003).

In a multi-site study of Hawaii's Healthy Start Program, child and parent risk factors were predictive of prospective participants' willingness to enroll in the paraprofessional home visiting program aimed at improving family functioning, promoting child health and development, and preventing child abuse and neglect. Infant biologic risk greatly increased an at-risk family's willingness to participate in the program. Adolescent mothers who had not completed high school also were more likely to initially agree to participate in the program. Families where the father had multiple risks were more likely to receive more visits (≥ 12 visits) than mothers who were unilaterally violent toward their partner (Duggan et al., 2000).

As Predictors of Program Participation and Moderators of Program Effects (paths d and e). The preexisting population characteristic that moderates program effects also may function as a predictor of program participation patterns, yet few studies have an adequate sample size and/or data on pro-gram participation to examine this possibility. An exception is the work of Baydar and colleagues, who studied the role of mental health factors in Head Start mothers' participation, and the effects of a parent training pro-gram focused on children's social competence and behavior problems (Baydar et al., 2003). In the Baydar et al. analyses, mothers with mental health risk factors (i.e., depression, substance abuse) initially exhibited poorer parenting than mothers without these risk factors, but were en-gaged in and benefited from the intervention at levels that were compara-ble to mothers without these risk factors. The results of this study do not support the persistent concern in the parenting intervention field that par-ents in greatest need of a parenting program may be the least likely to par-ticipate.

NEEDED RESEARCH DIRECTIONS FOR IDENTIFYING CRITICAL INTERVENTION ELEMENTS

This chapter describes conceptual and methodological approaches to de-termining what works in parenting interventions, and reviews selected re-search findings in three domains of variables: program features, program processes, and population characteristics. This second generation of re-search on parenting interventions is beginning to yield some guidance on the design and implementation of parenting interventions. The extant lit-erature is insufficiently robust to specify critical elements of effective inter-ventions, but the studies reviewed in this chapter point to an emerging set of promising candidates.

365

Research Design

Advances in developing a science of parenting interventions require a sequencing of research on a particular intervention where, for example, investigators initially determine whether a theoretically sound program can be implemented as planned and whether the targeted population will actually participate. Descriptive research methods, within-group comparison studies, and quasi-experimental designs have proven to be beneficial for exploring these basic questions. Evidence suggesting that a program or program feature can be implemented and that parents are likely to participate provides an empirical basis for conducting experimental research to determine program effects (National Research Council and Institute of Medicine, 2000).

Thresholds should not be set too high for deciding whether results of initial implementation work warrant an experimental study. Researchers will rarely find problem-free organizational settings to host an intervention, consistently uniform implementation of an intervention, or consensus among program staff on an intervention's theory of change (Cook & Payne, 2002). Moreover, the ecological validity of results of experimental studies conducted under optimal conditions is diminished. With sufficient sample sizes, variability in implementation can be systematically examined as part of outcome research, as was done in the Early Head Start study (Love et al., 2002). Although experimental studies should not be postponed in hopes of finding ideal implementation conditions, it is wasteful to conduct an outcome study without data suggesting a program or program feature has a reasonable chance of being implemented. The intentions of program designers do not readily or necessarily become the actions of program staff or the experiences of program participants.

More broadly, this chapter demonstrates that, individually and collectively, intervention studies need to consider more than one domain of variables. While it appears increasingly common for practitioners to submit that "engagement is everything" to achieve positive program effects (Greenstein, 1998, p. 16), it is important to remember that intervention processes occur in the context of program features and population characteristics that together seem to set the stage for program participation. To study program participation independently of population characteristics, or to examine causal relations between a program feature and participant outcome without regard for program participation experiences, significantly limits our understanding of what works in parenting programs. This requires the use of different research designs and methods while also recognizing that experimental designs yield the best evidence on what works in an intervention. As suggested in this chapter, thoughtful combinations of quantitative and qualitative methods in study designs are particularly informative.

Promising Candidates for Critical Elements
of Effective Parenting Interventions

Because the ultimate goal of research on what works is to identify critical elements of effective interventions, future studies should focus on variables that hold promise of occupying a salient role in the design and implementation of parenting programs. Promising variables and methodological approaches are noted later in each of the three domains of variables considered previously in this chapter. An emerging domain of potential significance also is briefly described.

Program Features. The use of professionals as the primary staff for working with parents is a promising candidate for designation as a critical element of effective interventions. As reviewed in this chapter, results of a randomized trial offer compelling evidence about the merits of using professionals (Olds et al., 2002), and a growing literature, mostly descriptive in nature, points to challenges encountered by paraprofessionals in working with low-income and high-risk populations. We cannot however generalize to all parenting interventions from one study demonstrating the benefits of nurses as staff in prenatal and infancy home visiting programs with low-income, first-time mothers. There may be different outcomes if paraprofessionals were trained and consistently supported in a program model uniquely suited to their backgrounds and abilities (Korfmacher, 2001). Hence, experimental studies on the staffing status question are needed with other types of professionals and with group-based interventions targeted at different types of populations and parenting issues. Further research also is needed on specific practices (e.g., flexible adaptation of program resources) and conditions (e.g., case-loads, staff turnover rates, supervision) that enable staff to function effectively with parents. This information is essential to developing research-based guidance on the supports needed for large-scale adoption of a parenting intervention.

The other program features considered in this chapter—delivery method, curriculum, and pedagogical or clinical approach—are conceptually interesting and programmatically important but there is insufficient research information to determine what works. Data are needed to address existing inferences and assumptions about each of these variables. For example, there are suggestions that a clear and consistent content focus on child development and parenting may yield positive intervention effects on parenting and child outcomes, but currently this idea emanates chiefly from the inferences of intervention results indicating that the absence of a content focus on child development and parenting is associated with no meaningful effects on parent and child outcomes (e.g., Hebbeler & Gerlach-Downie, 2002).

Program features are most appropriately investigated in relation to other elements of an intervention package and, as argued earlier in this chapter, the usefulness of results is significantly increased when studies systematically enhance or adapt a particular element of an intervention found to be effective in prior investigations. The relative dearth of empirical attention to the pedagogical or clinical approach is striking in view of the preponderance of theoretical arguments about the merits of reciprocity (e.g., Dunst & Trivette, 1997), trust (e.g., Heinicke & Ponce, 1999), and caring (e.g., Emde & Robinson, 2000) in relationships between staff and parents, and in view of the considerable amount of time programs presumably devote to selecting and training staff on approaches to working with parents.

Program Processes. Whether the planned program, largely defined by the program features noted above, is actually the delivered and received program deserves more than a perfunctory examination of staff records as an indicator of the fidelity of program implementation. As described earlier in this chapter, researchers increasingly recognize the multidimensionality of parenting interventions, and there is great opportunity and need for future work to improve the measurement of program processes.

More than 30 years ago, a cross-program analysis of parenting education programs identified parents' active participation in the program as a strong predictor of the magnitude of program effects (Goodson & Hess, 1975) and results of more recent research (e.g., Korfmacher et al., 1998) continue to suggest that active engagement of program content is a promising candidate for designation as a critical element of effective parenting interventions. Far less is known about program and parent factors associated with active engagement of program content. Frequent and sustained contact with parents is also commonly cited as an important element of an intervention, but more needs to be understood about how intervention content and method interact with frequency and duration. Is six months of weekly direct feedback on a program participant's observed behavior (via guided discussion of videotaped observations, for example) equivalent to one year of attending biweekly group discussions about child rearing?

Each of these variables especially needs further investigation employing experimental designs. Most of what is known about these variables comes from nonrandomized studies that do not fully accommodate nagging questions about population confounds. Program intensity in particular warrants further research because it is cost sensitive and in need of greater specificity to be helpful to policymakers and program designers. Existing conceptualizations of program intensity described in this chapter offer a range of options. Future studies of "more is better" hypotheses need a clearly defined theoretical framework and careful attention to population characteristics in addition to controls for program features.

As a general direction for future research on program processes, it appears that studies would be well served by measuring multiple indicators of both quantity and quality of program participation, taking care in the development of composite measures of participation because some aspects of participation may be independent of others, and by considering the possibility of change over time in the nature of participation, including parent-staff relationships.

Population Characteristics. The "for whom" questions, and the within-group comparisons typically employed to examine population questions, are the most problematic aspect of research on what works in parenting interventions. There are serious methodological limits on the analysis of population characteristics in intervention research, and investigators need to select and measure population variable(s) carefully. One criterion to use in the selection of population variables is the programmatic implication of possible significant population effects. How might data on how a particular population responds to an intervention, or how a specific preexisting population characteristic moderates intervention effects, help inform improvements in the design and/or delivery of interventions?

Program Context. To date, scant attention has been given to questions about the conditions or circumstances under which positive effects of a parenting intervention are realized. Conditions may be conceptualized at several levels, including the intervention setting (e.g., whether spouse/partner is a joint participant in the intervention), the organizational setting (e.g., characteristics of agencies that effectively implement a parenting program), and the community setting (e.g., quantity and quality of available child and family services). Because a small set of variables can be accommodated in good research designs, it is understandable that study of intervention contexts has been limited.

Intervention context variables are likely to receive greater attention in the future as policymakers and program implementers address the challenges of taking model programs to scale and as early childhood and welfare-to-work interventions include a parenting program as one of many components. What types of agencies are best suited to host a parenting intervention? What types of substantive integrations among parenting intervention and other program components (e.g., early childhood education) are feasible and effective in multiple-component programs? There are provocative indications in recent studies that organizational cultures and capacities are associated with variations in the integrity of program implementation (Kisker, Paulsell, Love, & Raikes, 2002) and with different approaches to basic program tasks such as client assessment and relations with families (Duggan et al., 2000). Perhaps this line of investigation will define the third generation of research on parenting interventions.

REFERENCES

Anderson, J., Fagan, W. T., & Cronin, M. (1998). Insights in implementing family literacy programs. *Literacy and community: Twentieth yearbook of the College Reading Association* (pp. 269–281). Carrollton, GA: College Reading Association.

Arnold, D. H., Lonigan, C. J., Whitehurst, G. J., & Epstein, J. N. (1994). Accelerating language development through picture book reading: Replication and extension to a videotape training format. *Journal of Educational Psychology, 86,* 235–243.

Bakermans-Kranenburg, M. J., van IJzendoorn, M. H., & Juffer, F. (2003). Less is more: Meta-analyses of sensitivity and attachment interventions in early childhood. *Psychological Bulletin, 129,* 195–215.

Barnard, K. E., Magyary, D., Sumner, G., Booth, C. L., Mitchell, S. K., & Spieker, S. (1988). Prevention of parenting alterations for women of low social support. *Psychiatry, 51,* 248–253.

Baydar, N., Reid, M. J., & Webster-Stratton, C. (2003). The role of mental health factors and program engagement in the effectiveness of a preventive parenting program for Head Start mothers. *Child Development, 74,* 1433–1453.

Belsky, J. (1985). Experimenting with the family in the newborn period. *Child Development, 56,* 407–414.

Belsky, J. (1986). A tale of two variances: Between and within. *Child Development, 57,* 1301–1305.

Berlin, L. J., O'Neal, C., & Brooks-Gunn, J. (1998). What makes early intervention programs work: The program, its participant, and their interaction. *Zero to Three, 19,* 4–15.

Berliner, D. C. (2002). Educational research: The hardest science of all. *Educational Researcher, 31,* 18–20.

Blackwell, B. (1998). Compliance. In G. A. Fava & H. Freyberger (Eds.), *Handbook of psychosomatic medicine* (pp. 625–638). Madison, CT: International Universities Press.

Booth, C. L., Mitchell, S. K., Barnard, K. E., & Spieker, S. J. (1989). Development of maternal social skills in multiproblem families: Effects on the mother–child relationship. *Developmental Psychology, 25,* 403–412.

Bradley, R. H., Burchinal, M. R., & Casey, P. H. (2001). Early intervention: The moderating role of the home environment. *Applied Developmental Science, 5,* 2–8.

Brooks-Gunn, J., Gross, R. T., Kraemer, H. C., Spiker, D., & Shapiro, S. (1997). Enhancing the cognitive outcomes of LBW, premature infants: For whom is the intervention most effective? In R. T. Gross, D. Spiker, & C. W. Haynes (Eds.), *Helping low birth weight, premature babies: The Infant Health and Development Program* (pp. 181–189). Stanford, CA: Stanford University Press.

Campbell, D. T. (1986). Relabeling internal and external validity for applied social scientists. In W. M. K. Trochim (Ed.), *Advances in quasi-experimental design and analysis* (pp. 67–77). San Francisco: Jossey-Bass.

Connell, J. P., & Kubisch, A. C. (1998). Applying a theory of change approach to the evaluation of comprehensive community initiatives: Progress, prospects, and problems. In K. Fulbright-Anderson, A. C. Kubisch, & J. P. Connell (Eds.), *New approaches to evaluating community initiatives: Vol. 2. Theory, measurement, and analysis* (pp. 15–44). Washington, DC: The Aspen Institute.

Cook, T. D., & Campbell, D. T. (1979). *Quasi-experimentation: Design and analysis issues for field settings.* Boston: Houghton Mifflin.

Cook, T. D., & Payne, M. R. (2002). Objecting to the objections to using random assignment in educational research. In F. Mosteller & R. Boruch (Eds.), *Evidence matters: Randomized trials in education research* (pp. 150–178). Washington, DC: Brookings Institution Press.

Cowan, P. A. (1988). Developmental psychopathology: A nine-cell map of the territory. In E. Nannis & P. Cowan (Eds.), *Developmental psychopathology and its treatment. New directions for child development* (No. 39, pp. 5–30). San Francisco: Jossey-Bass.

Cowan, P. A., Powell, D. R., & Cowan, C. P. (1998). Parenting interventions: A family systems perspective. In W. Damon, I. E. Sigel, & K. A. Renninger (Eds.), *Handbook of child psychology: Vol. 4. Child psychology in practice* (5th ed., pp. 3–72). New York: John Wiley & Sons.

Duggan, A., Windham, A., McFarlane, E., Fuddy, L., Rohde, C., Buchbinder, S., & Sia, C. (2000). Hawaii's Healthy Start Program of home visiting for at-risk families: Evaluation of family identification, family engagement, and service delivery. *Pediatrics, 105,* 250–259.

Dunst, C. J., & Trivette, C. M. (1997). Early intervention with young at-risk children and their families. In R. Ammerman & M. Hersen (Eds.), *Handbook of prevention and treatment with children and adolescents: Intervention in the real world* (pp. 157–180). New York: John Wiley & Sons.

Eisenstadt, J. W., & Powell, D. R. (1987). Processes of participation in a mother–infant program as modified by stress and impulse control. *Journal of Applied Developmental Psychology, 8,* 17–37.

Emde, R. M., & Robinson, J. (2000). Guiding principles for a theory of early intervention: A developmental-psychoanalytic perspective. In J. P. Shonkoff & S. J. Meisels (Eds.), *Handbook of early childhood intervention* (2nd ed., pp. 160–178). New York: Cambridge University Press.

Erickson, F., & Gutierrez, K. (2002). Culture, rigor, and science in educational research. *Educational Researcher, 31,* 21–24.

Gomby, D. S., Culross, P. L., & Behrman, R. E. (1999). Home visiting: Recent program evaluations—analysis and recommendations. *The Future of Children, 9,* 4–26.

Goodson, B. D., & Hess, R. D. (1975). *Parents as teachers of young children: An evaluative review of contemporary concepts and programs.* Stanford, CA: School of Education, Stanford University.

Greenstein, B. (1998). Engagement is everything. *Zero to Three, 18,* 16.

Gross, D., Spiker, D., & Haynes, C. W. (Eds.). (1997). *Helping low birth weight, premature babies: The Infant Health and Development Program.* Stanford, CA: Stanford University Press.

Guralnick, M. J. (1997). Second-generation research in the field of early intervention. In M. J. Guralnick (Ed.), *The effectiveness of early intervention* (pp. 3–20). Baltimore: Paul H. Brookes Publishing.

Halpern, R. (1992). Issues of program design and implementation. In M. Larner, R. Halpern, & O. Harkavy (Eds.), *Fair start for children: Lessons learned from seven demonstration projects* (pp. 179–197). New Haven, CT: Yale University Press.

Hebbeler, K. M., & Gerlach-Downie, S. G. (2002). Inside the black box of home visiting: A qualitative analysis of why intended outcomes were not achieved. *Early Childhood Research Quarterly, 17,* 28–51.

Heinicke, C. M., Fineman, N. R., Ponce, V. A., & Guthrie, D. (2001). Relation-based intervention with at-risk mothers: Outcome in the second year of life. *Infant Mental Health Journal, 22,* 431–462.

Heinicke, C. M., & Ponce, V. A. (1999). Relation-based early family intervention. In D. Cichetti & S. L. Toth (Eds.), *Rochester symposium on psychopathology: Vol. 9. Developmental approaches to prevention and intervention* (pp. 153–193). New York: University of Rochester Press.

Kisker, E. E., Paulsell, D., Love, J. M., & Raikes, H. (2002). *Pathways to quality and full implementation in Early Head Start Programs.* Princeton, NJ: Mathematica Policy Research.

Kitzman, H. J., Cole, R., Yoos, H. L., & Olds, D. (1997). Challenges experienced by home visitors: A qualitative study of program implementation. *Journal of Community Psychology, 25,* 95–109.

Kitzman, H., Yoos, H. L., Cole, R., Korfmacher, J., & Hanks, C. (1997). Prenatal and early childhood home-visitation program processes: A case illustration. *Journal of Community Psychology*, *25*, 27–45.

Korfmacher, J. (2001). Early childhood interventions: Now what? In H. E. Fitzgerald, K. H. Karraker, & T. Luster (Eds.), *Infant development: Ecological perspectives* (pp. 275–294). New York: Routledge Falmer.

Korfmacher, J., Kitzman, H., & Olds, D. (1998). Intervention processes as predictors of outcomes in a preventive home-visitation program. *Journal of Community Psychology*, *26*, 49–64.

Korfmacher, J., O'Brien, R., Hiatt, S., & Olds, D. (1999). Differences in program implementation between nurses and paraprofessionals providing home visits during pregnancy and infancy: A randomized trial. *American Journal of Public Health*, *89*, 1847–1851.

Lamb, M. E. (1998). Nonparental child care: Context, quality, correlates, and consequences. In W. Damon, I. E. Sigel, & K. A. Renninger (Eds.), *Handbook of child psychology: Vol. 4. Child psychology in practice* (5th ed., pp. 73–133). New York: John Wiley & Sons.

Layzer, J. I., Goodson, B. D., Bernstein, L., & Price, C. (2001). *National evaluation of family support programs. Final report volume A: The meta-analysis.* Cambridge, MA: Abt Associates.

Lieberman, A. F., Weston, D., & Pawl, J. H. (1991). Preventive intervention and outcome with anxiously attached dyads. *Child Development*, *62*, 199–209.

Liaw, F., Meisels, S. J., & Brooks-Gunn, J. (1995). The effects of experience of early intervention on low birth weight, premature children: The Infant Health and Development Program. *Early Childhood Research Quarterly*, *10*, 405–431.

Love, J. M., Kisker, E. E., Ross, C. M., Schochet, P. Z., Brooks-Gunn, J., Paulsell, D., et al. (2002). *Making a difference in the lives of infants and toddlers and their families: The impacts of Early Head Start: Vol. 1. Final technical report.* Princeton, NJ: Mathematica Policy Research.

Luster, T., Perlstadt, H., McKinney, M., Sims, K., & Juang, L. (1996). The effects of a family support program and other factors on the home environments provided by adolescent mothers. *Family Relations*, *45*, 255–264.

Lyons-Ruth, K., Connell, D. B., Grunebaum, H. U., & Botein, S. (1990). Infants at social risk: Maternal depression and family support services as mediators of infant development and security of attachment. *Child Development*, *61*, 85–98.

McCartney, K., & Rosenthal, R. (2000). Effect size, practical importance, and social policy for children. *Child Development*, *71*, 173–180.

McGuigan, W. M., Katzev, A. R., & Pratt, C. C. (2003). Multi-level determinants of mothers' engagement in home visitation services. *Family Relations*, *52*, 271–278.

Mosteller, F., & Boruch, R. (Eds.). (2002). *Evidence matters: Randomized trials in education research.* Washington, DC: Brookings Institution Press.

Musick, J. S., & Barbera-Stein, L. (1988). The role of research in an innovative preventive initiative. In D. R. Powell (Ed.), *Parent education as early childhood intervention: Emerging directions in theory, research, and practice* (pp. 209–227). Norwood, NJ: Ablex.

National Research Council. (2002). *Scientific research in education.* Committee on Scientific Principles for Education Research. Shavelson, R. J. & Towne, L. (Eds.). Center for Education, Division of Behavioral and Social Sciences and Education. Washington, DC: National Academy Press.

National Research Council and Institute of Medicine. (2000). *From neurons to neighborhoods: The science of early childhood development.* Committee on Integrating the Science of Early Childhood Development. J. P. Shonkoff & D. A. Phillips (Eds.). Board on Children, Youth, and Families, Commission on Behavioral and Social Sciences and Education. Washington, DC: National Academy Press.

Olds, D. L., Henderson, C. R., Chamberlin, R., & Tatelbaum, R. (1986). Preventing child abuse and neglect: A randomized trial of nurse home visitation. *Pediatrics*, *78*, 65–78.

Olds, D. L., Henderson, C. R., Kitzman, H. J., Eckenrode, J. J., Cole, R. E., & Tatelbaum, R. C. (1999). Prenatal and infancy home visitation by nurses: Recent findings. *The Future of Children*, *9*, 44–65.

Olds, D. L., Robinson, J., O'Brien, R., Luckey, D. W., Pettitt, L. M., Henderson, C. R., et al. (2002). Home visiting by paraprofessionals and by nurses: A randomized, controlled trial. *Pediatrics, 110,* 486–496.

Olson, D. R. (2004). A triumph of hope over experience in the search for "what works": A response to Slavin. *Educational Researcher, 33,* 24–26.

Pfannenstiel, J. C., & Seltzer, D. A. (1989). New parents as teachers: Evaluation of an early parent education program. *Early Childhood Research Quarterly, 4,* 1–18.

Philliber, S. (1998). The virtue of specificity in theory of change evaluation. In K. Fulbright-Anderson, A. C. Kubisch, & J. P. Connell (Eds.), *New approaches to evaluating community initiatives: Vol. 2. Theory, measurement, and analysis* (pp. 87–99). Washington, DC: The Aspen Institute.

Powell, C., & Grantham-McGregor, S. (1989). Home visiting of varying frequency and child development. *Pediatrics, 84,* 157–164.

Powell, D. R. (1984). Social network and demographic predictors of length of participation in a parent education program. *Journal of Community Psychology, 12,* 13–20.

Powell, D. R. (1988). Emerging directions in parent–child early intervention. In D. R. Powell (Ed.), *Parent education as early childhood intervention: Emerging directions in theory, research and practice* (pp. 1–22). Norwood, NJ: Ablex.

Powell, D. R., & Eisenstadt, J. W. (1988). Informal and formal conversations in parent education groups: An observational study. *Family Relations, 37,* 166–170.

Powell, D., Okagaki, L., & Bojczyk, K. (2004). Evaluating parent participation and outcomes in family literacy programs: Cultural diversity considerations. In B. H. Wasik (Ed.), *Handbook of family literacy* (pp. 551–566). Mahwah, NJ: Lawrence Erlbaum Associates.

Powell, D. R., & Sigel, I. E. (1991). Searches for validity in evaluations of young children and early childhood programs. In B. Spodek & O. Saracho (Eds.), *Yearbook of early childhood education: Vol. 2. Issues in early childhood curriculum* (pp. 190–212). New York: Teachers College Press.

Ramey, C. T., Bryant, D. M., Wasik, B. H., Sparling, J. J., Fendt, K. H., & LaVange, L. M. (1992). Infant Health and Development Program for low birth weight, premature infants: Program elements, family participation, and child intelligence. *Pediatrics, 3,* 454–465.

Reid, M. J., Webster-Stratton, C., & Beauchaine, T. P. (2001). Parent training in Head Start: A comparison of program response among African American, Asian American, Caucasian, and Hispanic mothers. *Prevention Science, 2,* 209–227.

Roggman, L. A., Boyce, L. K., Cook, G. A., & Jump. V. K. (2001). Inside home visits: A collaborative look at process and quality. *Early Childhood Research Quarterly, 16,* 53–71.

Roth, A., & Fonagy, P. (Eds.). (1996). *What works for whom: A critical review of psychotherapy research.* New York: Guilford Press.

Scarr, S., & McCartney, K. (1988). Far from home: An experimental evaluation of the Mother–Child Home Program in Bermuda. *Child Development, 59,* 531–543.

Shadish, W. R., Cook, T. D., & Campbell, D. T. (2002). *Experimental and quasi-experimental designs for generalized causal inference.* Boston: Houghton Mifflin.

Slaughter, D. T. (1983). Early intervention and its effects on maternal and child development. *Monographs of the Society for Research in Child Development, 48*(4, Serial No. 202).

Slavin, R. E. (2002). Evidence-based education policies: Transforming educational practice and research. *Educational Researcher, 31,* 15–21.

Slavin, R. E. (2004). Education research can and must address "what works" questions. *Educational Researcher, 33,* 27–28.

Sparling, J., Lewis, I., Ramey, C. T., Wasik, B. H., Bryant, D. M., & LaVange, L. M. (1991). Partners: A curriculum to help premature, low birthweight infants get off to a good start. *Topics in Early Childhood Special Education, 11,* 36–55.

St.Pierre, R. G., & Layzer, J. I. (1998). Improving the life chances of children in poverty: Assumptions and what we have learned. *Social Policy Report, Society for Research in Child Development, 12,* 1–25.

Thompson, B., Diamond, K., McWilliam, R., Snyder, P., & Snyder, S. (2005). Evaluating the quality of evidence from correlational research for evidence-based practice. *Exceptional Children, 71,* 181–194.

Traub, J. (2002, November 10). Does it work? *The New York Times Education Life,* pp. 4A24–4A27, 4A30–4A31.

Travers, J., Irwin, N., & Nauta, M. (1981). *The culture of a social program: An ethnographic study of the Child and Family Resource Program.* Report prepared for the Administration for Children, Youth and Families. Cambridge, MA: Abt Associates.

Travers, J., Nauta, M., & Irwin, N. (1982). *The effects of a social program: Final report of the Child and Family Resource Program's infant–toddler component.* Cambridge, MA: Abt Associates.

Valentine, J. C., & Cooper, H. (2003). *What works clearinghouse study design and implementation device.* Washington, DC: U.S. Department of Education.

Wagner, M. M., & Clayton, S. L. (1999). The Parents as Teachers Program: Results from two demonstrations. *The Future of Children, 9,* 91–115.

Wagner, M., Spiker, D., Linn, M. I., Gerlach-Downie, S., & Hernandez, F. (2003). Dimensions of parental engagement in home visiting programs: Exploratory study. *Topics in Early Childhood Special Education, 23,* 171–187.

Webster-Stratton, C. (1998). Preventing conduct problems in Head Start children: Strengthening parent competencies. *Journal of Consulting and Clinical Psychology, 66,* 715–730.

Webster-Stratton, C., Reid, M. J., & Hammond, M. (2001). Preventing conduct problems, and promoting social competence: A parent and teacher training partnership in Head Start. *Journal of Clinical Child Psychology, 30,* 283–302.

Weiss, C. H. (1995). Nothing as practical as a good theory: Exploring theory-based evaluation for comprehensive community initiatives for children and families. In J. P. Connell, A. C. Kubisch, L. B. Schorr, & C. H. Weiss (Eds.), *New approaches to evaluating community initiatives: Concepts, methods, and contexts* (pp. 65–92). Washington, DC: The Aspen Institute.

Worobey, J., & Brazelton, T. (1986). Experimenting with the family in the newborn period: A commentary. *Child Development, 57,* 1298–1300.

IV

PARENTAL BEHAVIOR AND CHILDREN'S DEVELOPMENT

13

Research on Parental Socialization of Child Outcomes: Current Controversies and Future Directions

Lynn Okagaki
Purdue University

Tom Luster
Michigan State University

Thirty years ago, Urie Bronfenbrenner (1974) observed that developmental psychology had become the study of "the behavior of children in strange situations with strange adults" (p. 3). In response to this lack of attention to the contexts of development, he proposed "a new theoretical perspective for research in human development" (p. 3) in his now classic book, entitled *The Ecology of Human Development* (1979). This theoretical perspective went beyond the simplistic acknowledgment that context plays a role in human development. Bronfenbrenner described the environment as a set of nested and interacting structures, which countless introductory psychology students would learn as the microsystem, mesosystem, exosystem, and macrosystem, and thereby provided developmental psychologists with a framework for identifying potential influences on human behavior. In subsequent years, Bronfenbrenner continued to refine his theory. In 1986, he observed that "For some years, I harangued my colleagues for avoiding the study of development in real-life settings. No longer able to complain on that score, I have found a new *bête noir*. In place of too much research on development 'out of context,' we now have a surfeit of studies on 'context without development' " (p. 288). To put development back into the model, Bronfenbrenner began writing about development in context as a process–person–context–time model that ultimately came to be called the bioecological model of development (Bronfenbrenner & Ceci, 1994; Bronfenbrenner & Morris, 1998). In the bioecological model, he posited that proximal processes are the activities through which human development occurs—the activities that drive development. Proximal processes are the "progressively more complex reciprocal interaction between an active, evolving biopsychological human organism and the persons, objects, and symbols in its immediate external environment" (Bronfenbrenner & Morris, 1998, p. 996). In this final chapter, we consider parenting practices as potential proximal processes for children's development. We ask the question: Does parenting affect child outcomes?

For generations, people have assumed that parenting matters. For developmental researchers, the question of the causal relation between parenting and child outcomes has traditionally been considered within the context of the nature–nurture debate. From the 1950s through the early 1970s a dominant theme in developmental research was the influence of environmental factors, including parenting on children's development. Criticisms of an unthinking endorsement of environmental effects emerged in the late 1970s, culminating, in Michael Rutter's (2002) words, in "an excessive swing of the pendulum in the opposite directions in terms of a denial of any substantial environmental effects within the normal range" (p. 9).

Where has the debate on parental socialization of child outcomes led researchers? In this chapter, we conclude that parents do influence the socialization of their children, but acknowledge that the evidence for parents' influence is weaker than it should be because of the use of weak research designs. However, socialization researchers do know how to strengthen their research designs so that we can increase knowledge of parents' influence, and this work has already begun. The chapter is primarily intended for students who may not yet be familiar with the debates surrounding parental influence on child outcomes. We begin by discussing why questions arose about the role of parental socialization in children's development in the first place. We then discuss how behavioral genetics research and peer socialization research have challenged the belief that parenting practices act as important proximal processes in children's development and served as an impetus to spur parental socialization researchers to conduct more rigorous research. Finally, we provide illustrative examples of existing research that documents the effects of parental socialization and suggestions for moving socialization research forward in ways that may help clarify whatever contribution parents' socialization makes to children's development.

Why Did Researchers Begin to Question the Role of Parents in Children's Development?

Researchers from various disciplines and with various perspectives agree that parents play an important role in the lives of their children including meeting basic needs for food, clothing, shelter, protection and security (Harris, 1998; O'Connor et al., 2000a; Perry, 2002). Studies of children reared in extreme conditions without an opportunity to form a close relationship with a parent or a small number of parental figures show that these children have more difficulties than other children in the area of social development during childhood and adolescence (Hodges & Tizard, 1989). Children reared in institutions without adequate intellectual stimulation and normal relationships with adults tend to lag behind their peers on indicators of cognitive competence (O'Connor et al., 2000a; Spitz, 1945). Parents also can seriously harm their children by maltreating them physically and emotionally (English, 1998). The relationships that children have with their parents have much to do with whether children are happy or miserable during childhood (Harris, 1998).

If researchers generally agree that parents play an important role in children's lives, what then is the issue? First, across cultural groups, studies suggest that children with markedly different socialization experiences can grow into adults who function competently in their respective cultures (LeVine, 1988). According to LeVine, parents want their child to physically survive, but what parents do to ensure their child's survival depends on their social and physical environment, the challenges they face, and the resources they can access. Parents want their child to gain the skills needed to assume the roles of adult members of society; the types of skills and education the parents might provide their child to accomplish this goal, however, depend on the types of skills needed to work in their society. Finally, LeVine posited that parents want their child to be a good person, and what parents do to accomplish this goal depends very much on the particular context in which they live.

Within a large and diverse society like the United States, there are also marked differences among parents in their parenting practices (Bornstein, 2002; McAdoo, 1993). For the most part, researchers generally agree that there are different approaches to rearing children that are effective for different cultural groups and subgroups, and thus, do not aspire to determine the ideal formula for parenting that would apply to all people, in all places, and at all times. Ideas about "good parenting" or "appropriate care of children" depend on cultural values, cultural beliefs about parenting and children's development, and contextual factors such as the subsistence tasks of men and women and the physical environment where children are reared (Ogbu, 1981). That diverse parenting practices have been associated with similar positive outcomes for children has led some behavioral scientists to question a causal relation between *specific* parenting practices and child outcomes (e.g., Harris, 1998; Rowe, 1994; Scarr, 1992, 1996).

Second, there is considerable controversy among researchers about the extent to which individual differences in parenting practices contribute to individual differences in outcomes such as personality characteristics (Collins, Maccoby, Steinberg, Hetherington, & Bornstein, 2000; Harris, 1995;

Rowe, 1994, 2002; Scarr, 1992). In her memorable presidential address to the Society for Research in Child Development, Sandra Scarr (1992) argued that differences among parenting practices that are within the normal range (i.e., not abusive or neglectful) contribute little to individual differences in the outcomes of children. Other researchers believe that individual differences in parenting are important for understanding individual differences in children on a range of outcomes (e.g., Baumrind, 1993). The difficulty with determining whether, or the degree to which, parenting practices contribute to individual differences in child outcomes lies in the data and the type of studies used to generate the available data.

Critics of socialization research have noted that many researchers have tended to assume that the outcomes of the children can best be explained by the way that they were parented, although other explanations are equally plausible (e.g., Harris, 1998; Scarr, 1992). For the most part, socialization researchers (including the authors of this chapter) have relied on studies using correlational designs to support the thesis that parenting practices affect child outcomes. Indeed, a plethora of studies using correlational designs have shown that differences in parenting practices are associated with individual differences in child outcomes. Of course, one of the basic methodological principles most of us learned in our first research methods course was "correlation does not establish causation." Nonetheless, correlational studies continue to be interpreted as supporting the parental socialization hypothesis.

If the methodological principle did not sufficiently highlight the weakness in the evidence, Bell's (1968) seminal paper, a reinterpretation of the direction of the effects in socialization studies, should have prodded socialization researchers to take a new tack. Subsequent research, including experimental studies, have demonstrated child effects on adult behavior. For example, numerous studies over many years have shown that adults in general, and parents in particular, interpret children's behaviors according to whether they think the child is a boy or a girl (e.g., Condry & Condry, 1976; Rubin, Provenzano, & Luria, 1974). (For more recent examples of child effects on parenting, see Hodapp & Ly, chap. 6, this volume; Karraker & Coleman, chap. 5, this volume).

Furthermore, Scarr (1992) and others (Harris, 1998; Rowe, 1994) have argued that most studies examining the relation between parenting practices and child outcomes are uninterpretable because the studies focus on families in which the parents and children are biologically related. In biologically related families, it is difficult to disentangle the influence of nature and nurture on children's development. For example, aggressive parents are likely to have aggressive children. It is not, however, clear if the aggressive behavior in the children is due to the genes they share with their parents, the modeling of aggressive behavior in the home by the parents (e.g., corporal punishment and marital conflict), or some combination of inherited dispositions and modeled behavior.

Finally, socialization researchers generally overlook the fact that parenting practices, such as those captured by parenting styles measures, are often correlated with parents' IQ (Scarr, 1997). Hence, correlations between parenting styles and children's intelligence or school achievement may reflect, at least in part, the genetic relation between parent and child. For example, in DeBaryshe, Patterson, and Capaldi's (1993) original analysis of their data on parenting and adolescents' antisocial behavior and school achievement, the correlation between parents' achievement (IQ and education) and ineffective disciplinary strategies was −.58; high parental achievement was associated with better disciplinary tactics. The authors' best fit model included direct and indirect (mediated through ineffective discipline, antisocial behavior, and academic engagement) effects of parental achievement on adolescent achievement with a chi-square of 89.45 and a Goodness of Fit Index (GFI) of .94. In Scarr's (1997) re-analysis of the data, however, a more parsimonious model dropping the measures of parenting practices (discipline) and adolescent antisocial behavior and only including parental achievement, academic engagement (as a mediator), and adolescent achievement obtained a chi-square of 18.26 and a GFI of .97. Her point? Little, if anything, was gained by including parenting practices in the model; smarter parents have smarter adolescents.

Thus, the question of whether or not specific parenting practices operate as proximal processes influencing child outcomes grew out of the recognition that (a) diverse approaches to parenting were associated with the normal development of children into fully functioning adults, (b) that the evidence that individual differences in parenting practices were associated with individual differences in child outcomes was weak, and (c) correlational research documenting association between parenting and child outcomes did not substantiate a causal relation. In the following two sections, we briefly review the questions and the data that behavioral genetic researchers and peer socialization researchers have generated that have both challenged and evoked stronger parental socialization research.

Genetic Contributions to Child Outcomes

In the 1980s and early 1990s, findings from behavioral genetics research were cited to raise questions about the extent to which parenting practices contribute to individual differences in personality and cognitive abilities. For example, researchers using studies of twins and adopted siblings concluded that shared environment (experiences that are shared by people who live together) accounts for little if any (0–10%) of the variance in personality outcomes (Dunn & Plomin, 1990; Plomin & Daniels, 1987). In addition, studies of adult identical twins who were reared together or separately indicated that the correlations for personality tended to be around .50 for both types of twins (Bouchard, Lykken, McGue, Segal, & Tellegen, 1990). In other words, identical twins who were reared in the same household tended to be no more alike in terms of the personality characteristics that were measured than identical twins who were reared by different parents.

If identical twins who share 100% of their genes and are reared in the same families are different in terms of personality, behavioral geneticists argued that personality differences among these twins must be attributed to nonshared environmental influences (experiences that are unique to individuals) (Plomin & Daniels, 1987). Unique experiences in a variety of settings could contribute to these differences in personality; differential treatment by parents, siblings, peers, teachers, and other extra-familial adults could contribute to differences in personality, as could chance events such as accidents, illnesses, or fortuitous opportunities (being in the right place at the right time). Some behavioral geneticists concluded that parenting may contribute to individual differences in personality among children but however parenting affects children in the same family, it seems to make them different rather than alike (Dunn & Plomin, 1991; Plomin & Daniels, 1987). Critics of parenting research argued that if parents have different styles of parenting (e.g., authoritative, authoritarian, or permissive) that they use with their children and some parenting styles produce more desirable outcomes in children than others, why are children who are reared by the same parents not more alike in the area of personality (Harris, 1995, 1998)?

Whereas researchers were reporting that monozygotic and dizygotic twin studies indicated that genetic differences among the twins in the samples typically accounted for less than half of the variance in personality outcomes (McCartney, Harris, & Bernieri, 1990), studies of cognitive outcomes generally obtained stronger estimates of heritability effects, and estimates of heritability increased as individuals get older (McCartney, Harris, & Bernieri, 1990; McGue, Bouchard, Iacono, & Lykken, 1993). For example, estimates of heritability in children were around .45 (Neisser et al., 1996). In contrast, McGue and his colleagues (1993) estimated heritability of IQ to be approximately .75 among adults (although Neisser and colleagues, 1996, observed that adults from the lowest socioeconomic groups were under-represented in these samples; hence variation due to contextual factors might be less than what would be found in the entire population). With respect to cognitive abilities, most scientists agreed that genetics plays a significant role in accounting for individual differences in cognitive abilities (Neisser et al., 1996). Indeed, some suggested that further research to determine the heritability of cognitive traits would make little contribution to science (McCartney et al., 1990).

Reviewing the behavioral genetic research and the nature-nurture dialogue through the 1990s in his 2001 presidential address to the Society for Research in Child Development, Michael Rutter (2002) essentially said that we know more at the beginning of the 21st century than we did in the early 1990s, and need to be less simplistic, more accurate, and more current in discussions of the data. For our purposes, his most critical observation was that shared environment is more important than was initially thought to be. For example, Loehlin, Neiderhiser, and Reiss (2003) reporting on data including siblings varying in genetic and environmental similarity found substantial heritability (h^2) effects across their six measures of adolescent adjustment (h^2 ranging from .41 to .86), substantial shared environment effects for autonomy and sociability ($c^2 = .46$ and .32 for autonomy and sociability, respectively), and relatively small effects for e^2 (which includes nonshared environment, gene × environment interaction, and measurement error; e^2 ranging from ranging from .10 to .25). Rutter concluded that reducing measurement error and taking into account continuities over time resulted in "much more of a balance between shared and nonshared effects" (p. 3).

Rutter (2002) re-emphasized that although individual differences are partially a function of genotype, this fact does not rule out environmental effects. In an article written in response to early work on the heritability of intelligence, Bronfenbrenner (1972) observed that when variation in the environmental context is limited, the degree to which context explains variation in child outcomes should also be limited, whereas the degree to which heredity accounts for variance in child outcomes should be greater. Studies of adoptive children may seriously underestimate the influence of parenting because the full range of home environments are not likely to be represented in adoptive families (Stoolmiller, 1999). Adoptive parents are the only parents who have to apply to be parents, and children are only placed in homes where good care is expected based on what is known about the prospective parents. If adoptive homes do not represent the full range of homes that children experience, then drawing conclusions about parental influence from adoption designs is problematic. In addition, families that volunteer to have their twins participate in research studies may not be representative of all families (Stoolmiller, 1999). Thus, the samples used in behavioral genetic studies may contribute to the low estimates of shared environmental influence that have been reported. A recent study by Turkheimer and his colleagues (2003) provides support for this assertion.

From a large national sample of U.S. mothers and their children, 114 monozygotic and 205 dizygotic pairs were identified (Turkheimer, et al., 2003). In typical heritability studies, variation in outcome is distributed across three components—genotype, shared environment, and non-shared environment. However, the socioeconomic diversity of this sample, which included a large proportion of families that were below the poverty level at the time of the study, allowed the researchers to examine the interaction of SES with genotype, shared environment, and non-shared environment. At age 7, children's IQ scores (Wechsler Intelligence Scale for Children) were obtained. Comparing the extent to which the traditional main effects model (i.e., only genotype, shared environment, and non-shared environment) explained variation in IQ scores with an interaction model (i.e., including the main effects and the interactions of each component with SES), the researchers found that the interaction model better accounted for the variation in child outcomes. Specifically, at higher SES levels, shared and non-shared environments account for very little of the variation in IQ scores; however, when SES is low, the opposite is true. To compare their study to typical analyses, the researchers split the sample above and below the median SES. For the higher SES group, 72% of the variation in IQ scores was explained by genotype; shared environment explained only 15%. In contrast, for the low SES group, genotype accounted for only 10% of the variation in IQ scores; whereas, shared environment explained 58%.

Turkheimer and his colleagues (2003) were careful to observe that variation in SES does not simply reflect an environmental difference, but also captures genetic differences between parents. Because the twins in this study lived in the same household, the analyses used in this study cannot tease apart the environmental and genetic aspects of SES. Nonetheless, the study supports the contention that we cannot naively assume that heritability is constant across environmental contexts. Why might environmental factors be more important and genetic factors less important in some contexts than in others? Bronfenbrenner posited that in more advantaged environments heritability effects would be stronger because individuals would be closer to fully actualizing their potential (Bronfenbrenner & Ceci, 1994; Bronfenbrenner & Morris, 1998).

Furthermore, as many have observed, even when heritability is high, there is reason to believe that environment makes a difference (e.g., Bronfenbrenner & Ceci, 1994; Ceci, Rosenblum, de Bruyn, & Lee, 1993). In adoption studies, for example, finding a correlation between biological mother and adoptive child does not mean that the environment did not influence the child. In the French adoption study reported by Schiff and his colleagues (Schiff et al., 1978), children from working class mothers were adopted early into upper-middle-class families and were later compared to their non-adopted half-siblings (i.e., both sets of children had the same biological mothers) and to selected samples of children from the general population. The average IQ score of the adopted children was 110.6, as compared to 94.5, the average IQ score of their non-adopted siblings. Comparisons of school failure rates indicated that the adopted children did much better than their non-adopted siblings and were much like other children from upper-middle-class homes.

For purposes of providing evidence that parenting makes a difference, the French adoption study has an obvious flaw. Being raised in upper-middle-class families meant that the adopted children were exposed to environmental influences other than just the parents that may have contributed to the differences in IQ scores. But consider the classic longitudinal adoption study of Skodak and Skeels (1949). They showed that the correlations between adopted children and their biological mothers, who did not live together for more than a few months, were significant from early childhood through adolescence ($rs = .28$ to $.44$); these correlations provide evidence of genetic influence on intellectual development. IQ tests were not given to the adoptive mothers but their level of education was used as an indicator of their intellectual ability. Correlations between the education level of the adoptive mothers and the IQ scores of the children hovered near zero, suggesting little influence of shared environment. Yet from age 2 through age 13 (the last time the children were tested) their IQ scores tended to be about 20 points higher than the IQ scores of their biological mothers, and their IQ scores tended to be about a standard deviation above the mean for the population. Although the higher IQ scores of the children may not be due solely to the parenting they received from their adoptive parents, the evidence suggests that their adoptive parents helped put them on a positive developmental trajectory in early childhood and the children continued to do well after they entered the world of schools and peer groups in middle childhood and adolescence. The lack of relation between the adoptive mothers' education and children's IQ scores may be due to a restricted range on the maternal education variable; on average the adoptive mothers had high levels of education relative to other people their age who lived in the same area. Thus, in this study, the correlational evidence suggests little or no effect of shared environment on intellectual development, but the higher mean scores of the children suggests a substantial environmental effect; the fact that the higher mean scores were evident when the children were very young and spent most of their time at home is consistent with the view that parenting played a role in these outcomes.

Where does all of this research leave us in terms of understanding the role of parental socialization on child outcomes? First, although genotype has in many cases a substantial influence on development, this does not mean that environmental factors in general and parental socialization in particular do not play an important and significant role in development. Even in studies showing a strong heritability effect, there can be an important environmental effect (Schiff et al., 1978; Skodak & Skeels, 1949). Second, quantitative genetic data on the degree to which siblings are alike does not definitively demonstrate the relative effects of shared and nonshared environments on development (Rutter, 2002). One cannot assume that what happens within a family has the same effect on all members of the family. Moreover, contrary to the initial conclusions of behavioral geneticists, some data now suggest that shared environment is more important than researchers thought.

Peer Influences on Child Outcomes

Many researchers have argued that peers play an important role in development (e.g., Berndt, 1999, 2002; Ladd & Burgess, 2001). Building in part on this research, Judith Rich Harris (1995) proposed the Group Socialization Theory in which she argued that the variance in child outcomes that is not explained by genetic differences among individuals can largely be explained by experiences in peer groups during childhood and adolescence. According to Harris (1995), "children would develop into the same sort of adults if we left them in their homes, their schools, their neighborhoods, and their cultural or subcultural groups, but switched all the parents around" (p. 461).

Harris (1995, 1998) argued that behavior is very context specific. Children learn how to behave inside the home and outside the home, and the expectations regarding appropriate behavior may be quite different in various contexts. Children's behavior inside the home is influenced considerably by their parents, but children learn how to behave outside the home from their peer groups. Outside the home, children associate with a peer group comprised of individuals who tend to be similar to the child on such characteristics as age, gender, ethnicity, attitudes and interests, and they tend to adopt the attitudes and behavior of their peer group.

Children want to fit in with and be accepted by their peers. Harris (1995, 1998, 2000, 2002) asserted that if what children learn at home is not accepted by the peer group, children are likely to adopt the attitudes and behavior of the peer group outside the home. For example, if an immigrant child speaks his parents' language at home and English in the peer group, eventually English will become the preferred language of the child. Likewise, if parents encourage androgynous behavior on the part of their children, and a same-sex peer group has strong rules about behaving in sex-typed ways, children should display sex-typed behavior outside the home. Thus, children are socialized in terms of how to behave outside their home by the peer group they identify with, and what they learn in the peer group continues to influence their behavior into adulthood. Socialization outside the home becomes a part of their adult personality (Harris, 1995, p. 467). With respect to intellectual development, she theorized that children's attitudes toward school and intellectual achievement are shaped by their peers. If a child is a member of a group of children who like school and do well in school, he or she will also like school and do well in school. Children conform to the norms of their peer group.

If the influence of children's peers is as strong as Harris (1995) purported, is there any role for parents to play in Group Socialization Theory? Even though Harris asserted that parenting practices have no influence on individual differences in adulthood, she acknowledged that parents have some influence on their children. For example, children need parents or parental surrogates to meet their most basic survival needs by providing food, clothing, shelter, protection and other necessities. Parents set and enforce the rules for how children behave inside the home influencing what children do when they are at home. If a parent teaches a child skills and attitudes at home that are valued by the peer group, these skills and attitudes can be helpful to the child outside the home. Parents can also influence outcomes that the peer group does not care about one way or another (e.g., political party preference, adult careers, religious beliefs). According to Harris, the relationship between parent and child can influence how happy the child is or how miserable the child is especially in the home context, but these dyadic relationships typically do not have long-term effects on personality or behavior outside the home. Finally, Harris acknowledged that parents can influence the child's peer group composition by determining where the family lives and what schools the children attend and can influence how peers treat their children by the clothes they buy (cool or not cool), the names they give their children (common or unusual names), and things they do to make their children relatively attractive (e.g., braces, acne treatments, hair styling). Nonetheless, the primary social influence on children's development is their peers.

In response to Harris' proposal, several researchers have written critiques of Group Socialization Theory and taken the position that Harris' contention that parents have relatively little influence on their children's long-term development is too extreme (Collins et al., 2000; Vandell, 2000). Those who have been critical of Harris acknowledge that peers exert considerable influence on the behavior of children and adolescents, but they believe that parental practices contribute to individual differences in children's outcomes as well. In the following section, we draw upon these critiques of Group Socialization Theory and other published studies to summarize some key studies that provide evidence that parents play an important role in the development of their children in various domains.

Parental Influences on Child Outcomes

One way to assess the importance of parents is to examine what happens to children when they lack the opportunity for normal parent-child relationships. An example involves children who spent the early months or years in

Romanian orphanages before being adopted into middle-class homes in Canada and Great Britain. These studies show that the longer the children had spent in the orphanages, the greater the likelihood of performing poorly on measures of intellectual ability; in contrast, children who were adopted in the first six months of life appeared to be developing normally (O'Connor et al., 2000a). Duration of deprivation was also associated with the severity of attachment disorder behaviors at age 6 (O'Connor et al., 2000b). Studies of the Romanian children in Canada also showed that those who were adopted later had abnormally high levels of cortisol during normal daily routines (Chisholm, 1998; Chisholm, Carter, Ames, & Morrison, 1995), "indicating that the neuroendrocrine system involved in stress regulation has not developed normally" (Collins et al., 2000, p. 225). Of course, it may be that there were differences between the two groups of children prior to adoption. Children who were chosen early to be adopted may have been, in some way, more personable or brighter, and it was this trait that attracted the adoptive parents to the child and accounts for later differences between children.

An earlier study of institutionalized children was conducted by Barbara Tizard and Jill Hodges (1978; Hodges & Tizard, 1989). The children were placed in the institutions by their parents who felt unable to care for them and spent at least two years being cared for by a large number of caregivers employed at the group homes, who changed frequently because of staff turnover. Those who lived in the institutions for four years, on average, had 50 different caregivers. As a result of a push for deinstitutionalization, most of the children eventually left the group homes. Some of these children were adopted into homes by parents who wanted a child badly enough to take a child out of an institution; others were restored to their natural parents who were often ambivalent about taking them back. At age 8, the children who were adopted or restored were compared with peers in the same classrooms, and ex-institutional children had more problems with teachers and peers than children reared in their families. In addition, children who were restored to their natural parents exhibited more problems than the adopted children, who tended to have better relationships with their adoptive parents. The restored children were much more likely than the adopted children to be referred for counseling, typically by their teachers. In the intellectual realm, both the adopted and restored children had IQ scores in the normal range, but those who were adopted earliest at the highest IQ scores.

Hodges and Tizard (1989) followed up with the children again at age 16. Although ex-institutional children still had some problems in relating to people outside the home, fewer differences were found between the adopted children and their peers than between the restored children and their peers. The restored children tended to exhibit many more problem behaviors than their peers and many more problems than children who had been adopted into supportive homes. The study by Hodges and Tizard is interesting because the children being compared had different experiences early in life (institutional rearing vs. rearing in a family) and later in life (adopted vs. restored). The evidence from both parts of the study suggests that the best outcomes for children are found when they are cared for by supportive parents who really want them. It is also important to point out that because of differences in family income, the peer groups of the adopted and restored children may have also been quite different. Adoptive children may have fewer problems than restored children both because of their adoptive parents and the peers they encounter in more affluent neighborhoods. Both parents and peer groups, in combination with genetic predispositions, may play significant roles in whether or not children develop behavior problems.

Neglected infants are another group of children who do not get enough of what parents are supposed to provide—affection, touch, attention, sensory stimulation, a safe environment, and other basic necessities. Neglected children show a range of problem outcomes in the cognitive, language, social, and emotional domains (Perry, 2002). Evidence reviewed by Perry (2002) shows that severe, global neglect in infancy has a negative effect on brain development. When neglected children were placed in more supportive foster homes, they showed some degree of recovery, but the amount of recovery depended upon the length of time that the children had lived in deprived circumstances. Children who were rescued from their neglectful homes at an earlier age showed greater recovery than those who were older when the neglectful circumstances were identified. Neuroimaging techniques suggest that the experiences in Romanian orphanages also affected the brain development of these children (Chugani et al., 2001). Thus, neglect during infancy seems to fundamentally affect brain development; the prospects for recovery appear to be limited for children who experienced severe neglect for the first two years of their lives.

Animal studies provide experimental evidence of parental influence on their offspring (O'Connor, 2002); unlike humans, rhesus monkeys can be randomly assigned to their parents. In 1987, Suomi published an initial report of a rhesus monkey cross-fostering project in which infant rhesus monkeys were placed within 96 hours of birth either with foster mothers who had displayed low levels of punitive behaviors and high levels of nurturing behaviors with their own offspring or with foster mothers who had displayed moderate levels of punitive behaviors with their own offspring. Half of the infant monkeys were genetically predisposed to be highly reactive; half were genetically predisposed to be relatively calm. In addition, half of the foster mothers within each group were highly reactive monkeys; half were not. During their first 6 months, the infant monkeys were raised by their foster mothers in their home cages and were only separated from the mother once each week for a brief 20-minute testing period. Although the initial report of this research was based on a sample of 12 dyads,[1] analyses of the observations of the dyads during the first 6 months indicated that while the infant monkeys were in their cage with their foster mother, the best predictor of their behavior was whether the foster mother was a punitive or a nurturing mother. At 6 months, the infant monkeys were separated from their foster mothers for brief periods of times. During separations, the best predictor of their behavior was whether or not the infant monkey was in the highly reactive group. At 9 months, the infant monkeys were permanently separated from their foster mother. Preliminary observations suggested that the highly reactive infant monkeys who were placed with nurturing mothers were able to become dominant members of their peer groups, but that highly reactive monkeys reared by highly reactive or punitive mothers may not do as well. These observations are consistent with research on human children that found that children with certain temperamental qualities respond best to certain parenting styles (Kochanska, 1995, 1997).

Suomi (2002) also studied the consequences of growing up without a mother and other adults on rhesus monkeys who were reared with their peers. Peer reared monkeys showed less exploratory behavior than monkeys raised by their mothers; monkeys reared by their mothers use the mother as a secure base for exploration much as securely attached human infants use their mothers. Peer reared monkeys also showed less developed play behavior and tended to be less competent play partners than monkeys reared by their mothers. These less competent peer reared monkeys tended to end up in the bottom of the dominance hierarchies of their social groups. Peer reared male monkeys were found to be more impulsive and aggressive than males reared by their mothers. Peer-reared females were more likely than those reared by their mothers to exhibit neglectful or abusive behavior with their first-born offspring. Females reared in social isolation were even less competent in the parenting role than peer reared females.

Turning to research on human parenting, we consider a particular hypothesis offered by Harris (1995) that dyadic relationships in general have little or no long-term influence on behavior outside of the contexts where the relationships occur. That is, that dyadic relationships, such as parent–child, teacher–pupil, or best friend–best friend, do not have a lasting influence on personality and rarely affect behavior in other contexts unless the peer group also endorses these behaviors; over the long term, behavior and personality are affected by peer groups (three or more people). Vandell (2000) addressed this issue proposing that the multiple dyadic relation-

---

[1]Number of dyads based on personal communication with S. Suomi, November 30, 2004.

ships that children have are important because they meet different developmental needs. Vandell (2000) wrote:

> Parents may serve as a source of love, affection, security, protection, advice, and limit setting. Siblings may offer opportunities related to social understanding, conflict management, and differential status. Friendships offer opportunities for mutual commitment, support, and trust. Whereas teachers and caregivers of young children may offer provisions similar to those of parents, teachers of older children may function as sources of expertise and access to opportunity. A shortcoming of Harris's GS theory is its failure to recognize the importance of these different types of relationships for development, including their possible compensatory or protective functions when other relationships go awry. (p. 705)

Consider the research on self-esteem. If parents have the power to make children feel miserable or valued at home year after year, should we expect these experiences to have no long-term effects on self-esteem or other indicators of psychological well-being? It is difficult to imagine that parents can make children feel insignificant and unlovable at home and that this would not affect how they think about themselves or behave once they step outside the door of the family home. Research by Harter (1988, 1990, 1998) suggests that both accomplishments and relationships with significant others are predictive of self-esteem in childhood and adolescence. Consistent with Cooley's looking-glass self theory (1902), children are sensitive to how significant others view them and incorporate those views into how they think about themselves; the significant others include parents, peers, close friends, and teachers. Harter's work supports the view that self-esteem is influenced by accomplishments in areas of importance to the individual, peer acceptance, and dyadic relationships with parents, close friends, and teachers.

Finally, perhaps the strongest evidence of the effects of parenting comes from intervention studies designed to change parenting practices and to examine the effects of those changes on the children. To date, there have been very few carefully designed intervention studies focusing on parenting behavior and their effects on children (see Powell, chap. 12, this volume). Moreover, most of the studies that have been conducted have focused on children's behavior in the home following intervention and have not observed children's behavior in other contexts. If parenting matters, then we should see effective parenting interventions influence how children behave in the home in addition to their behavior outside the home, such as at school or with peers. We provide here examples of four studies that examine the effects of parenting interventions on child outcomes outside the home. In the first study, Cowan and Cowan (2002) randomly assigned parents with 4-year-old children to an intervention or control group. The intervention group participated in a 16 week couples group led by psychologists, social workers, and marriage and family counselors. The couples groups worked on issues that would help them become more effective parents and marital partners. Half of the couples in the intervention group were assigned to a group that placed a greater emphasis on improving the marital relationship, and the other half were assigned to a group that placed a greater emphasis on improving their parenting skills. The couples who were in the intervention group that emphasized the marital relationship showed improvements in both the marital relationship and in their parenting. Their children had high achievement test scores and were perceived by their teachers as showing less aggressive and acting-out behavior than children in the control group. The couples in the group that emphasized parenting showed improvements in their parenting, and their children showed a decline in shy, withdrawn, depressed behavior from kindergarten to first grade. A follow-up study of the children showed positive effects of the intervention were evident through the end of fourth grade—six years after the intervention program. Importantly, teachers' ratings were based on children's behaviors at school.

In our second example, admittedly, the toddlers are still in the presence of their mothers, but they are playing with an unfamiliar peer to determine if the effects of an earlier parental intervention were sustained approximately three years after the intervention (van den Boom, 1995). Mothers were enrolled in the study shortly after the birth of their first child and were randomly assigned to treatment or control group. When their infant was between 6 and 9 months of age, the mothers in the intervention group received three home visits during which the mothers were taught specific skills to help them understand and be more responsive to their infants' cues. At 42 months, the mother and toddler completed a number of assessments at their home and in a laboratory setting. Among other findings, mothers in the intervention group continued to be more responsive to their child than were mothers in the control group. For the toddler, the assessments included four play periods with an unfamiliar peer in a laboratory playroom. The situation was set up for the toddlers to play together; however, both mothers were present in the room and were able to respond to the children, but not initiate interactions (except to intervene if necessary). Relative to children of mothers in the control group, the toddlers of mothers in the intervention were more cooperative with the unfamiliar peer. At the very least, these data show that different parenting results in specific child behaviors that the child uses when interacting with a peer, and that parental socialization is not limited to child behaviors that are directed to the parent or limited to the context of the home.

The third example is an experimental evaluation of the Dialogic Reading program, an intervention designed to teach parents specific skills for reading with their young child (Whitehurst et al., 1988). In this study, mothers were randomly assigned to intervention or control conditions. Those receiving the one-month home-based intervention were taught to use specific types of questions, to elaborate on their child's responses, and other strategies to actively engage their child in the book reading activity and to increase the child's language development. Not only were the researchers able to confirm that their intervention changed mothers' reading behaviors but were able to detect an effect of the intervention on standardized measures of children's language development. That is, when children were tested by a member of the research team on several standardized measures of language development, children of mothers in the intervention group behaved differently from children of mothers in the control group.

The final example of the effects of a parent intervention program on the behavior of the child comes from David Olds' work on a home visitation parent intervention program (Olds et al., 1998). In the late 1970s, young women who were less than 25 weeks pregnant with no previous live birth, unmarried or from low income homes were randomly assigned to intervention or comparison conditions. The mothers in the comparison conditions received regular prenatal and well child care. Mothers in one intervention group received home visits from nurses during their pregnancy (on average, nine visits); mothers in the second intervention group received home visits from nurses during their pregnancy and through the child's second birthday (on average, 23 visits). During the home visits, nurses provided guidance on health-related behaviors, parenting, and maternal personal development (e.g., family planning, education, jobs). When the offspring were 15, the investigators conducted a follow-up study collecting data on the adolescents. Significant differences were obtained between the adolescents whose mothers were in the intervention groups and adolescents whose mothers were in the comparison condition on a number of variables representing negative and antisocial behavior. For instance, adolescents whose mothers received home visits reported fewer arrests and convictions and fewer violations of probation. These data were corroborated by court records for those adolescents who had not moved away from the county in which the study took place; adolescents whose mothers received home visits through the child's infancy were less likely to have been adjudicated as a person in need of supervision. Differences between treatment and comparison groups were more consistent among adolescents whose mothers were most at risk (both low-SES and unmarried) at the time of intervention.

Does parenting affect children's behavior outside the parent-child relationship? The data from these four intervention studies indicates that it does. Given the importance of this question, however, the data supporting this conclusion is weaker than it ought to be. Fortunately, we do know how to strengthen research designs so that we can increase knowledge of parents' influence. In our final section, we discuss directions we believe would move the field forward.

Future Directions

Obviously we are not unbiased observers in the debate surrounding parental influence on children. We would not be doing a book that focuses on why parents do what they do if we believed that parents were not significant in their children's development. However, as we noted in the beginning of this chapter, we do believe that the evidence of a causal relation between specific parenting practices and children's outcomes is much weaker than it should be. Further we know very little about the conditions under which specific parenting behaviors are likely to affect children's behaviors. Development is likely to depend upon the interplay of genetic factors and a multitude of environmental factors over time (Bronfenbrenner, 2000). The models and methods that we employ to study these processes are probably not nearly as sophisticated or complex as the real life processes that shape individual lives (Turkheimer, 2000). In this final section, we identify a few directions that we believe will help move the field forward.

The first area focuses on genetic studies that may increase our understanding of the conditions under which parenting practices have greater and lesser influence on child outcomes. A fruitful strategy that researchers have already begun to employ is the examination of genotype × environment interactions. For example, in the Dunedin Multidisciplinary Health and Development study, researchers observed a genotype × environment interaction in a cohort of New Zealand children that has been followed from age 3 through young adulthood (Caspi, et al., 2002). The investigators examined the hypothesis that the monoamine oxidase A (MAOA) gene moderates the effect of maltreatment on development of antisocial behavior in males. Prior research has shown that low MAOA enzyme expression has been associated with increased aggression in mice; data on the relation between MAOA expression and aggression in humans, however, have been inconclusive. The analyses indicated a main effect of maltreatment, such that experiencing maltreatment as a child was associated with increased likelihood of antisocial behavior, but no significant effect due to MAOA expression. In addition, a significant genotype × environment interaction was obtained, such that males with low MAOA expression who experienced child maltreatment were more likely to develop antisocial behaviors than their counterparts with high MAOA expression. It seems likely that research on genotype × environment interactions will move the field forward by enabling us to better understand the conditions under which specific parenting practices are more likely to be linked to specific negative or positive outcomes in children.

Molecular genetic approaches to understanding behavior are likely in time to identify genes associated with vulnerability or risk for specific diseases and psychological problems. For example, molecular genetic research techniques have been used to identify single gene disorders, such as fragile X mental retardation (Plomin, 1997). Cautiously optimistic about the advances to our knowledge of human development that will come through molecular genetic research, Rutter (2002) described a number of important findings, such as the identification of the link between the apolipoprotein E4 allele and Alzheimer's disease (Plassman & Breitner, 1996; Rubinsztein, 1995, as cited in Rutter, 2002) and genes that are associated with attention deficit disorder with hyperactivity (Levy & Hay, 2001, as cited by Rutter, 2002). Identifying genes that are associated with specific problems does not solve the problem or cure the disease, but it will provide biological researchers with invaluable insights as to where to look for the causal mechanisms. For those interested in parental socialization, better identification of vulnerability or risk may enable researchers to look at the effects of particular parenting practices on children who may be more sensitive to variation in parenting.

One strategy parental socialization researchers might take is to incorporate behavioral genetic designs into socialization studies. Studies of twins have typically been used by behavioral genetics researchers to determine if genetic differences among individuals contribute to individual differences in phenotypic outcomes such as personality characteristics or IQ scores. However, genetically sensitive research designs are also useful for studying environmental influences on development. An excellent example of such a study is the Environment Risk (E-Risk) Longitudinal Twin Study being conducted in Great Britain. Avshalom Caspi and his colleagues (2004) showed how the influence of parenting on children's antisocial behavior could be studied with this sample in order to avoid some of the shortcomings of earlier research designs. When the children were five years old, the mothers described each of the monozygotic twins. In addition, both the mothers and the children's teachers completed assessments of the children's antisocial behavior at ages 5 and 7. In many cases, mothers expressed much more favorable attitudes about one twin over the other. The twin who was more favorably regarded exhibited fewer behavioral problems at age 7 on ratings by both the mothers and the teachers. Moreover, there was a relation between mothers' expressed emotions and age 7 behavior problems when age 5 behavior problems were controlled. Put another way, changes in twins' antisocial behavior were associated with maternal expressed emotions two years earlier; increases in antisocial behavior were associated with maternal negativity and lack of warmth.

By design, this study addressed a number of concerns raised by critics of socialization research. First, there were two sources of information—mothers and teachers—and data were collected in two settings—home and school. Maternal expressed emotions at home were related to teachers' ratings of behavior in school. Thus the researchers were able to show that what happened inside the home seemed to have an effect on behavior outside the home. Second, they ruled out an alternative hypothesis that the relation between maternal expressed emotion and children's antisocial behavior was purely a child effect (i.e., child antisocial behavior is causing parental negativity). Because data were collected longitudinally, they were able to show that parenting at age 5 was related to child outcomes at age 7, controlling for child outcomes at age 5. Children who were viewed negatively tended to exhibit more problematic behavior two years later. Third, the association between maternal expressed emotion and child behavior problems was not genetically mediated. The twins were genetically identical, and the researchers focused on how maternal behavior contributed to individual differences in the identical twins. The design also avoided another flaw found in between-family designs that study one child per family. The family background characteristics, such as family income and parental education level, were the same for the twins in each family. Thus the relation between maternal expressed emotion and child antisocial behavior cannot be explained by a third variable that differs between families.

In addition, the study addressed a concern raised by many socialization researchers about twin studies reported by behavioral geneticists—namely, the environmental variables are often not measured directly. Many twin studies have suggested that nonshared environment is important for understanding individual differences in an outcome based on partitioning the variance in the outcome into genetic, shared environment, and nonshared environment components; in contrast, this study identified how a specific nonshared environmental experience related to a specific child outcome. It moves beyond simply saying there is something different in the experiences of children from the same family that contributes to individual differences in antisocial behavior.

Other types of studies that will enable our understanding of the effects of parental socialization include research with non-human primates and natural experiments with humans. Animal studies can provide critical evidence regarding the general importance of parenting, per se, because we can randomly assign animal babies to parents. These studies have often been overlooked by socialization researchers. Natural experiments with humans are those instances in which naturally occurring circumstances or institutions (perhaps unintentionally) divide people into treatment and comparison groups in a manner akin to purposeful random assignment. The effects of a parent/primary caregiver condition versus a no parent/primary caregiver condition is demonstrated in the studies of Romanian orphans who experienced severe deprivation early in their lives but were later adopted into families in Great Britain and in Canada and have been compared with children who were adopted in early infancy.

In addition, there is a need for more research using experimental and quasi-experimental designs to test specific and competing hypotheses. Ultimately to determine if specific parenting practices are causally related to specific child outcomes, we will need more experimental studies in which parents are randomly assigned to conditions in which they are taught different parenting skills or information about parenting and both parent behavior and child behavior are observed before and after the intervention. (see Powell, chap. 12, this volume). Researchers need to determine whether an intervention changes specific parenting practices and in turn, whether there is an effect of the intervention on child outcomes that is mediated through the parenting practices. In particular, we need studies that assess the impact of specific parenting practices on measures of child outcomes assessed outside the home.

Furthermore, to facilitate studies of parent interventions, better measures of parenting practices are needed. Global measures of parenting, such as measures of parenting styles, are not likely to be sensitive enough to capture the effects of specific parenting practices on child outcomes. Researchers need to consider measures of parental behavior that are conceptually related to specific child outcomes. For example, in the previously described experimental evaluation of the Dialogic Reading program (Whitehurst et al., 1988), the parenting measures were specific measures of maternal behavior while the mother and child engaged in a book reading activity and included the frequency with which mothers labeled pictures, asked specific types of questions, and elaborated on what the child said. These behaviors, which mothers in the intervention group were taught and subsequently exhibited, are theoretically related to children's language development. To assess the effects of parenting on child outcomes, we need to focus on specific parenting behaviors that are conceptually related to the targeted child outcomes.

Finally, our view of the challenges to parental socialization research from behavioral geneticists and peer socialization theorists is that such challenges have made an important contribution to the literature by highlighting some of the limitations of the parental socialization research. Socialization researchers (including the authors of this chapter) have tended to interpret the results of their study as parental influence on children without ruling out alternative explanations for the findings. Challenges to the rigor and interpretation of our work should push those of us doing research on parenting to adopt and develop more rigorous research designs, including intervention designs, studies of parenting in families in which the children are adopted (i.e., biologically unrelated to the parents), and studies of parenting of more than one child in a family. It is through such effort that the field will move forward.

ACKNOWLEDGMENTS

We very much appreciate the thoughtful and constructive comments we received from Tom Berndt, Karen Diamond, and Marc Bornstein on an earlier version of our chapter.

REFERENCES

Baumrind, D. (1993). The average expectable environment is not good enough: A response to Scarr. *Child Development, 64,* 1299–1317.

Bell, R. Q. (1968). A reinterpretation of the direction of effects in studies of socialization. *Psychological Review, 75,* 81–95.

Berndt, T. J. (1999). Friends' influence on students' adjustment to school. *Educational Psychologist, 34,* 15–28.

Berndt, T. J. (2002). Friendship quality and social development. *Current Directions in Psychological Sciences, 11,* 7–10.

Bornstein, M. H. (Ed.). (2002). *Handbook of parenting: 2nd ed., Vol. 4. Social conditions and applied parenting.* Mahwah, NJ: Lawrence Erlbaum Associates.

Bouchard, T., Lykken, D. T., McGue, M., Segal, N. L., & Tellegen, A. (1990). Sources of human psychological differences: The Minnesota study of twins reared apart. *Science, 250,* 223–228.

Bronfenbrenner, U. (1972). Is 80% of intelligence genetically determined? In U. Bronfenbrenner (Ed.), *Influences on human development* (pp. 118–127). Hinsdale, IL: Dryden Press Inc.

Bronfenbrenner, U. (1974). Developmental research, public policy, and the ecology of childhood. *Child Development, 45,* 1–5.

Bronfenbrenner, U. (1979). *The ecology of human development.* Cambridge, MA: Harvard University Press.

Bronfenbrenner, U. (1986). Recent advances in research on the ecology of human development. In R. K. Silbereisen, K. Eyforth, G. Rudinger (Eds.), *Development as action in context: Problem behavior and normal youth development* (pp. 286–309). New York: Springer-Verlag.

Bronfenbrenner, U. (2000). Ecological systems theory. In A. E. Kazdin (Ed.), *Encyclopedia of psychology* (Vol. 3, pp. 129–133). New York: Oxford University Press.

Bronfenbrenner, U., & Ceci, S. J. (1994). Nature-nurture reconceptualized: A bioecological model. *Psychological Review, 101,* 568–586.

Bronfenbrenner, U., & Morris, P. A. (1998). The ecology of developmental processes. In W. Damon (Editor-in-chief) & R. M. Lerner (Vol. Ed.), *Handbook of child psychology: Vol. I. Theoretical models of human development* (5th ed., pp. 993–1028). New York: John Wiley & Sons, Inc.

Caspi, A., McClay, J., Moffitt, T. E., Mill, J., Martin, J., Craig, I. W., Taylor, A., & Poulton, R. (2002). Role of genotype in the cycle of violence in maltreated children. *Science, 297,* 851–854.

Caspi, A., Moffitt, T. E., Morgan, J., Rutter, M., Taylor, A., Arseneault, L., Tully, L., et al. (2004). Maternal expressed emotion predicts children's antisocial behavior problems: Using monozygotic-twin differences to identify environmental effects on behavioral development. *Developmental Psychology, 40*(2), 149–161.

Ceci, S. J., Rosenblum, T., de Bruyn, E., & Lee, D. Y. (1993). A bio-ecological model of intellectual development: Moving beyond h². In R. J. Sternberg & E. Grigorenko (Eds.), *Intelligence, heredity, and environment* (pp. 303–322). New York: Cambridge University Press.

Chisholm, K. (1998). A three-year follow-up of attachment and indiscriminate friendliness in children adopted from Romanian orphanages. *Child Development, 69*, 1092–1106.

Chisholm, K., Carter, M., Ames, E. W., & Morrison, S. J. (1995). Attachment security and indiscriminately friendly behavior in children adopted from Romanian orphanages. *Development and Psychopathology, 7*, 283–294.

Chugani, H. T., Behen, M. E., Muzik, O., Juhasz, C., Nagy, F., & Chugani, D. C. (2001). Local brain functional activity following early deprivation: A study of post-institutionalized Romanian orphans. *Neuroimage, 14*, 1290–1301.

Collins, W. A., Maccoby, E. E., Steinberg, L., Hetherington, E. M., Bornstein, M. H. (2000). Contemporary research on parenting: The case of nature and nurture. *American Psychologist, 55*, 218–232.

Cooley, C. H. (1902). *Human nature and the social order.* New York: Charles Schribner's Sons.

Condry, J., & Condry, S. (1976). Sex differences: A study of the eye of the beholder. *Child Development, 47*(3), 812–819.

Cowan, P. A., & Cowan, C. P. (2002). What an intervention design reveals about how parents affect their children's academic achievement and behavior problems. In J. G. Borkowski, S. L. Ramey, & M. Bristol-Power (Eds.), *Parenting and the child's world: Influences on academic, intellectual, and social-emotional development* (pp. 75–98). Mahwah, NJ: Lawrence Erlbaum Associates.

DeBaryshe, D. B., Patterson, G. R., & Capaldi, D. M. (1993). A performance model for academic achievement in early adolescent boys. *Developmental Psychology, 29*, 795–804.

Dunn, J., & Plomin, R. (1990). *Separate lives: Why siblings are so different.* New York: Basic Books.

Dunn, J., & Plomin, R. (1991). Why are siblings so different? The significance of differences in sibling experiences within the family. *Family Process, 30*, 271–283.

English, D. (1998). The extent and consequences of child maltreatment. *The Future of Children, 8*(1), 39–51.

Harris, J. R. (1995). Where is the child's environment: A group socialization theory of development. *Psychological Review, 102*, 458–489.

Harris, J. R. (1998). *The nurture assumption.* New York: The Free Press.

Harris, J. R. (2000). Socialization, personality development, and the child's environments: Comment on Vandell (2000). *Developmental Psychology, 36*, 711–723.

Harris, J. R. (2002). Beyond the nurture assumption: Testing hypotheses about the child's environment. In J. G. Borkowski, S. L. Ramey, & M. Bristol-Power (Eds.), *Parenting and the Child's World: Influences on academic, intellectual, and social-emotional development* (pp. 3–20). Mahwah, NJ: Lawrence Erlbaum Associates.

Harter, S. (1988). Developmental processes in the construction of self. In T. D. Yawkey & J. E. Johnson (Eds.), *Integrative processes and socialization: Early to middle childhood* (pp. 45–78). Hillsdale, NJ: Lawrence Erlbaum Associates.

Harter, S. (1990). Causes, correlates and the functional role of global self-worth: A life-span perspective. In R. Sternberg & J. Kolligian (Eds.), *Competence considered* (pp. 67–97). New Haven, CT: Yale University Press.

Harter, S. (1998). The development of self-representations. In W. Damon (Series Ed.) & Nancy Eisenberg (Vol. Ed.), *Handbook of child psychology: Vol. 3. Social, emotional, and personality development* (5th ed., pp. 553–618). New York: Wiley.

Hodges, J., & Tizard, B. (1989). IQ and behavioral adjustment of ex-institutional adolescents. *Journal of Child Psychology and Psychiatry, 30,* 53–75.

Kochanska, G. (1995). Children's temperament, mother's discipline, and the security of attachment: Multiple pathways to emerging internalization. *Child Development, 66,* 597–615.

Kochanska, G. (1997). Multiple pathways to conscience for children with different temperaments: From toddlerhood to age 5. *Developmental Psychology, 33,* 228–240.

Ladd, G. W., & Burgess, K. B. (2001). Do relational risks and protective factors moderate the linkages between childhood aggression and early psychological and school adjustment? *Child Development, 72,* 1579–1601.

LeVine, R. A. (1988). Human parental care: Universal goals, cultural strategies, and individual behavior. In W. Damon (Series Ed.) & R. A. Levine, P. M. Miller, & M. M. West (Vol. Eds.), *New directions for child development: Parental behavior in diverse societies* (Vol. 40, pp. 3–11). San Francisco: Jossey-Bass.

Levy, F., & Hay, D. (2001). *Attention, genes, and ADHD.* Hove, UK: Lawrence Erlbaum Associates.

Loehlin, J. C., Neiderhiser, J. M., & Reiss, D. (2003). The behavior genetics of personality and the NEAD study. *Journal of Research in Personality, 37,* 373–387.

McAdoo, H. P. (Ed.). (1993). *Family ethnicity: Strength in diversity.* Newbury Park, CA: Sage Publications, Inc.

McCartney, K., Harris, M. J., & Bernieri, F. (1990). Growing up and growing apart: A developmental meta-analysis of twin studies. *Psychological Bulletin, 107,* 226–237.

McGue, M., Bouchard, T. J., Jr., Iacono, W. G., & Lykken, D. T. (1993). Behavioral genetics of cognitive ability: A life-span perspective. In R. Plomin & G. E. McClearn (Eds.), *Nature, nurture, and psychology* (pp. 59–76). Washington, DC: American Psychological Association.

Neisser, U., Boodoo, G., Bouchard, T. J., Jr., Boykin, A. W., Brody, N., Ceci, S. J., Halpern, D. F., Loehlin, J. C., Perloff, R., Sternberg, R. J., & Urbina, S. (1996). Intelligence: Knowns and unknowns. *American Psychologist, 51*(2), 77–101.

O'Connor, T. G. (2002). Annotation: The 'effects' of parenting reconsidered: Findings, challenges, and applications. *Journal of Child Psychology and Psychiatry, 43*(5), 555–572.

O'Connor, T. G., Rutter, M., Beckett, C., Keaveney, L., Kreppner, J. M., and the English and Romanian Adoptees Study Team (2000a). The effects of severe privation on cognitive competence: Extension and longitudinal follow-up. *Child Development, 71,* 376–390.

O'Connor, C., Rutter, M., English and Romanian Adoptees Study Team (2000b). Attachment disorder behavior following early severe deprivation: Extension and longitudinal follow-up. *Journal of the American Academy of Child and Adolescent Psychiatry, 39,* 703–712.

Ogbu, J. U. (1981). Origins of human competence: A cultural-ecological perspective. *Child Development, 52,* 413–429.

Olds, D., Henderson, C. R., Jr., Cole, R., Eckenrode, J., Kitzman, H., Luckey, D., Pettitt, L., Sidora, K., Morris, P., & Powers, J. (1998). Long-term effects of nurse home visitation on children's criminal and antisocial behavior: 15-year follow-up of a randomized controlled trial. *Journal of the American Medical Association, 280*(14), 1238–1244.

Perry, B. D. (2002). Childhood experience and the expression of genetic potential: What childhood neglect tells us about nature and nurture. *Brain and Mind, 3,* 79–100.

Plassman, B. L., & Breitner, J. C. S. (1996). Recent advances in the genetics of Alzheimer's disease and vascular dementia with an emphasis on gene-environment interactions. *Journal of the American Geriatric Society, 44,* 1242–1250.

Plomin, R. (1997). Identifying genes for cognitive abilities and disabilities. In R. J. Sternberg & E. Grigorenko (Eds.), *Intelligence, heredity, and environment* (pp. 89–104). New York: Cambridge University Press.

Plomin, R., & Daniels, D. (1987). Why are children in the same family so different from each other? *Behavioral and Brain Sciences, 10,* 1–16.

Rowe, D. (1994). *The limits of family influence: Genes, experiences, and behavior.* New York: Guilford Press.

Rowe, D. (2002). What twin and adoption studies reveal about parenting. In J. G. Borkowski, S. L. Ramey, & M. Bristol-Power (Eds.), *Parenting and the child's world: Influences on academic, intellectual, and social-emotional development* (pp. 21–34). Mahwah, NJ: Lawrence Erlbaum Associates.

Rubin, J. Z., Provenzano, F. J., & Luria, Z. (1974). The eye of the beholder: Parents' views on sex of newborns. *American Journal of Orthopsychiatry, 44,* 47–55.

Rutter, M. (2002). Nature, nurture, and development: From evangelism through science toward policy and practice. *Child Development, 73,* 1–21.

Scarr, S. (1992). Developmental theories for the 1990's: Development and individual differences. *Child Development, 63,* 1–19.

Scarr, S. (1996). How people make their own environments: Implications for parents and policy makers. *Psychology, Public Policy, and Law, 2*(2), 204–228.

Scarr, S. (1997). Behavior-genetic and socialization theories of intelligence: Truce and reconciliation. In R. J. Sternberg & E. Grigorenko (Eds.), *Intelligence, heredity, and environment* (pp. 3–41). New York: Cambridge University Press.

Schiff, M., Duyme, M., Dumaret, A., Stewart, J., Tomkiewicz, S., & Feingold, J. (1978). Intellectual status of working-class children adopted early into upper-middle-class families. *Science, 200*(4349), 1503–1504.

Skodak, M., & Skeels, H. (1949). A final follow-up of one hundred adopted children. *Journal of Genetic Psychology, 75,* 85–125.

Spitz, R. A. (1945). Hospitalism: An inquiry into the genesis of psychiatric conditions in early childhood. In A. Freud et al. (Eds.), *The psychoanalytic study of the child* (Vol. 1, pp. 53–74). New York: International Universities Press.

Stoolmiller, M. (1999). Implications of the restricted range of family environments for estimates of heritability and nonshared environment in behavior-genetic adoption studies. *Psychological Bulletin, 125,* 392–409.

Suomi, S. J. (1987). Genetic and maternal contributions to individual differences in rhesus monkey biobehavioral development. In N. A. Krasnegor, E. M. Blass, M. A. Hofer, & W. P. Smotherman (Eds.), *Perinatal development: A psychological perspective* (pp. 397–419). New York: Academic Press.

Suomi, S. J. (2002). Parents, peers, and the process of socialization. In J. G. Borkowski, S. L. Ramey, & M. Bristol-Power (Eds.), *Parenting and the child's world: Influences on academic, intellectual, and social-emotional development* (pp. 265–279). Mahwah, NJ: Lawrence Erlbaum Associates.

Tizard, B., & Hodges, J. (1978). The effect of early institutional rearing on the development of eight-year-old children. *Journal of Child Psychology and Psychiatry, 19,* 99–118.

Turkheimer, E. (2000). Three laws of behavior genetics and what they mean. *Current Directions in Psychological Science, 9*(5), 160–164.

Turkheimer, E., Haley, A., Waldron, M., D'Onofrio, B., & Gottesman, I. I. (2003). Socioeconomic status modifies heritability of IQ in young children. *Psychological Science, 14*(6), 623–628.

van den Boom, D. C. (1995). Do first-year intervention effects endure? Follow-up during toddlerhood of a sample of Dutch irritable infants. *Child Development, 66,* 1798–1816.

Vandell, D. L. (2000). Parents, peer groups, and other socializing influences. *Developmental Psychology, 36,* 699–710.

Whitehurst, G. J., Falco, F. L., Lonigan, C. J., Fischel, J. E., DeBaryshe, B. D., Valdez-Menchaca, M. C., et al. (1988). Accelerating language development through picture book reading. *Developmental Psychology, 24*(4), 552–559.

About the Authors

Jay Belsky, Ph.D., is Founding Director of the Institute for the Study of Children, Families and Social Issues and Professor of Psychology at Birkbeck College, University of London. He earned his doctorate in Human Development and Family Studies at Cornell University, served on the faculty of Penn State University for 21 years, and was awarded the title of Distinguished Professor. He currently serves as Research Director on the National Evaluation of Sure Start in England. He is an internationally recognized expert in the field of child development and family studies and is the author of more than 200 scientific articles and chapters and the author of several books.

Gary E. Bingham, Ph.D., is an assistant professor in the department of Human Development at Washington State University. He received his Ph.D. from Purdue University with an emphasis in early childhood education and child development. His research focuses on understanding and examining cultural, family, and early education factors that contribute to children's preacademic competence, particularly the development of early literacy skills.

Catherine P. Bradshaw holds a master's degree in Counseling Psychology from the University of Georgia and a doctorate in Developmental Psychology from Cornell University. In 2004, she became an Assistant Professor of Mental Health in the Bloomberg School of Public Health at Johns Hopkins

University. Her research focuses on the development of aggressive and problem behavior during childhood and adolescence. She is particularly interested in the influence of maltreatment and neighborhood violence on problem behavior, as well as community- and school-based prevention and intervention programs for children and families.

Moncrieff Cochran is a Professor of Human Development and Director of the Cornell Early Childhood Program in the College of Human Development at Cornell University, where he conducts research related to the social contexts affecting parent and child development, and develops empowerment-oriented family support and child care programs based on that research. He received his bachelors degree in social relations from Harvard College, and Masters and Ph.D. degrees in education and psychology from the University of Michigan. The content of Dr. Cochran's research and program development work includes child care, early childhood education, home–school relations, the social networks of parents and children, and the empowerment process. In 1990 Dr. Cochran and colleagues published *Extending Families: The Social Networks of Parents and Their Children* (Cambridge University Press), which presents the findings from 10 years of social network research focused on families with young children. His *International Handbook of Child Care Policies and Programs*, reporting on developments in 29 different countries, was published by Greenwood Press in May, 1993. An edited volume, *Empowerment and Family Support*, was published by Cornell Media Services in 1995. The 2nd edition of *Child Care that Works: A Parent's Guide to Finding Quality Child Care*, co-authored with Eva Cochran, was published by Gryphon House in 2000. Dr. Cochran has just completed *Finding Our Way: American Child Care in Global Perspective*, in which he applies lessons learned from his international child care research project to the U.S. child care scene. He is a past member of the Governing Board of the National Association for the Education of Young Children.

Priscilla Coleman, Ph.D. is an Assistant Professor of Human Development and Family Studies at Bowling Green State University in Ohio. Dr. Coleman received her Ph.D. in Life-Span Developmental Psychology from West Virginia University in 1998 and she spent four years as an assistant professor of psychology and education at the University of the South in TN prior to her move to BGSU. Dr. Coleman's recent research has focused on mother–child interaction, attachment, the development of competency beliefs across the transition to parenting, and the psychological outcomes of women who have had an abortion.

Lisa Comparini is Postdoctoral Researcher and Part-time faculty in the Psychology department at Clark University, Worcester, Massachusetts. She received her B.A. at Austin College, and her M.A. and Ph.D. at Clark University. Lisa Comparini was Postdoctoral Fellow at the University of Connecticut's School of Family studies. She is a member of the American Psychological Association, the Society for Research in Child Development, and the American Anthropological Association. Her research interests include child development as a cultural process, language socialization, and the study of parent–child interactions.

Ann C. Crouter is Professor of Human Development and Director of the Center for Work and Family Research at Penn State University. She received her B.A. in Psychology and English at Stanford University and Ph.D. at Cornell University. She arrived at Penn State in 1981. Ann co-organizes, with sociologist Alan Booth, Penn State's National Symposium on the Family, an annual conference and edited book series. She serves on the editorial boards of *Journal of Marriage and the Family, Journal of Research in Adolescence,* and the *International Journal of Behavioral Development,* chairs the Research and Theory Section of the National Council on Family Relations, and serves on the Executive Council of the Society for Research in Adolescence. Her research has focused on the connections between mothers' and fathers' work conditions, daily processes in families (such as parent–child involvement and parental knowledge of children's activities, whereabouts, and companions), and the development of school-aged children and adolescents. She has explored these issues with her collaborator, Susan McHale, in the context of three longitudinal, federally funded research studies focused on gender development and dual-earner families. She currently collaborates on new research to examine similar themes in ethnic minority families, as well as an investigation of the work and family circumstances of low-income, rural parents of young children, part of a program project conducted by researchers at the University of North Carolina and Penn State.

Jessica M. Dennis is a Research Associate in the Department of Psychology at California State University, Los Angeles. Her research interests include social development with a particular focus on changes in family and peer relationships during middle childhood, and adolescence and ethnic and cultural issues.

Frank D. Fincham is Eminent Scholar and Director Florida State University Family Institute. Educated at University of Natal and University of Witwatersrand, he obtained a Rhodes Scholarship to study at Oxford University where he obtained his Ph.D. in psychology. He has since held positions at University of Illinois and University of Wales. A Fellow of the American Psychological Association, British Psychological Society, American Psychological Society, and National Council on Family Relationships, Fincham's research has placed him among the top 25 psychologists in the world in terms of impact (number of citations per published article) and has been recognized by numerous awards, including the President's Award for Distinguished Contributions to Psychological Knowledge (British Psychological Society). His research interests focus on marital relationships, the impact of interparental conflict on children, and forgiveness.

Mary L. Flyr is a Research Associate in the Department of Psychology at the University of California, Riverside. Her research interests include the social development of children from preschool through middle childhood as influenced by family and peers, with particular attention to friendship.

James Garbarino, Ph.D. is Elizabeth Lee Vincent Professor of Human Development at Cornell University. Previously he was President of the Erikson Institute for Advance Study in Child Development. The author of 20 books, his most recent are *And Words Can Hurt Forever: Protecting Adolescents from Bullying, Harassment and Emotional Violence*, 2002 (with Ellen deLara); *Parents Under Seige*, 2001 (with Claire Bedard), and *Lost Boys: Why Our Sons Turn Violent and How We Can Save Them*, 1999. He was the first recipient of the C. Henry Kempe Award in 1985 from the National Conference on Child Abuse and Neglect.

Julie Laser Haddow is an Assistant Professor in the Graduate School of Social Work at the University of Denver. Her research focus is on adolescent resiliency. In particular, she is interested in investigating the influence of both internal and ecological protective and risk factors on resilient outcomes by gender and culture. She recently completed a study of protective and risk factors influencing resilient outcomes in Japanese youth and is currently collecting data on Korean youth.

Julie H. Hall is graduate student in the Department of Clinical Psychology at the University at Buffalo. She received her B.A. from Brown University. She is a student member of the Association for Advancement of Behavior Therapy, the American Psychological Association, and Sigma Xi. Her research interests include the study of marriage and romantic relationships, as well as forgiveness.

Robin L. Harwood got her Ph.D. in 1991 from Yale University. She is currently a Professor in the Department of Human Development and Family Studies at Texas Tech University. She has received several major grants from NIH to study cultural differences in childrearing beliefs and practices, and is the author of numerous journal articles, as well as a book, *Culture and Attachment: Perceptions of the Child in Context*.

Katherine Hildebrandt Karraker is Associate Professor, Director of Graduate Training, and Coordinator of the Life-Span Developmental Psychology

Doctoral Program in the Department of Psychology at West Virginia University. She received her B.A. in Biology from the University of Colorado and her M.A. and Ph.D. n Developmental Psychology from Michigan State University. Her current research interests include parent–infant relationships, infant assessment, parental cognitions (including stereotypes and parenting self-efficacy), stress and coping in infancy, and the effects of maternal sleep deprivation. She is the co-editor of *Life-Span Developmental Psychology: Life-Span Perspectives on Stress and Coping* and *Infant Development: Ecological Perspectives.*

Robert M. Hodapp is a Professor in Peabody College's Department of Special Education and a member of the Kennedy Center for Research on Human Development, both at Vanderbilt University. From 1982 to 1992 he was an Assistant Professor (working with Edward Zigler) at the Yale Child Study Center. From 1992 to 2003, he was at UCLA's Graduate School of Education and Information Studies, before moving to Vanderbilt University in 2003. His research focuses on parent behaviors and emotional reactions to children with genetic conditions such as Down syndrome, Prader-Willi syndrome, and Williams syndrome; and behavioral development of children with each of these genetic mental retardation disorders.

Kathleen Kostelny is Research Associate with the Eikson Institute for Advanced Study in Child Development in Chicago. She serves as an international consultant on issue of children and youth involved in violence and trauma in war zones around the world. She is co-author of *Children in Danger* (1991) and *No Place to Be a Child* (1992).

Melinda Leidy is a graduate student studying Developmental Psychology at the University of California, Riverside. She is studying under Dr. Ross D. Parke. Her research interests include parental influences on children's emotional and social development.

Birgit Leyendecker got her doctoral degree in 1991 from the University of Osnabrueck. She is currently a Research Fellow at the University in Bochum and she is on the faculty of the University of Dortmund. She is author of numerous journal articles. Her research interests include cultural perspectives on child development and parenting; cultural and psychological adaptation of immigrant children and their families, and linking qualitative and quantitative research.

Tom Luster is a Professor in the Department of Family and Child Ecology at Michigan State University. He joined the faculty at MSU in 1985 after completing his doctoral program in the Department of Human Development at Cornell University. His research has focused primarily on three areas: adolescent mothers and their children; risk and resilience; and influences on parental behavior. His latest research includes: a 9-year longitudinal study of adolescent mothers and their children in Flint, Michigan, and a study of the Sudanese refugees known as the "Lost Boys" who lived for most of their lives in refugee camps in Ethiopia and Kenya without contact with their parents.

Tran M. Ly is an NSF Post-Doctoral Fellow at UCLA's Graduate School of Education and Information Studies. Her research interests involve maternal attributions of their children's intellectual performance when children have different genetic syndromes and applications of attribution theory to children with disabilities and their parents. Her dissertation study examined maternal attributions of their children's jigsaw-puzzle performance when children have Prader-Willi syndrome (generally proficient at jigsaw puzzles) versus Williams syndrome (generally weak at jigsaw puzzles).

Susan M. McHale is Professor of Human Development at The Pennsylvania State University. She received her B.A. in Psychology at Bucknell University and her Ph.D. in Developmental Psychology at the University of North Carolina at Chapel Hill, and has been on the faculty at Penn State since 1980. She serves on the editorial boards of *Child Development, Developmental Psychology,* and *Journal of Applied Developmental Science.* Her research focuses on children's and adolescents' family relationships, roles and everyday activities, highlighting gender dynamics in families and the family conditions and experiences that foster similarities and differences between sisters and brothers. Together with her Penn State colleague, Ann C. Crouter, she has studied these issues in the context of the Penn State Family Relationships Project, a longitudinal study of families funded by NICHD. Most recently, her research has extended to examination of the cultural contexts of family gender dynamics and youth development. In two new studies, also funded by NICHD, she and Ann Crouter are working with Penn State colleagues, Drs. Linda M. Burton and Dena P. Swanson and with Dr. Kimberly A. Updegraff at Arizona State University to study family processes and gender development in samples of African American and Mexican American families.

Kristie L. Morris is a graduate student in the Department of Psychology at the University of California, Riverside. Her research interests include children's social and emotional development as affected by familial influences.

Lynn Okagaki is professor of Child Development and Family Studies at Purdue University. She received her bachelor of science degree in applied behavioral sciences from the University of California at Davis and her doctoral degree in developmental psychology from Cornell University. Her research focuses on minority students' school achievement and on parental socialization of children's values. Dr. Okagaki has served as Deputy Director for Science, for the Institute of Education Sciences, at the U.S. Department of Education; associate dean for research for the School of Consumer and Family Sciences at Purdue University; a member of the National Science Foundation's Developmental and Learning Sciences panel, and a member of the National Research Council's Committee on Early Childhood Pedagogy.

Ross D. Parke is Distinguished Professor of Psychology and Director of the Center for Family Studies at the University of California, Riverside. His research interests include the role of the father in children's development, family and peer relationships, and the role of ethnicity in family relationships. He is past editor of *Developmental Psychology* and is currently completing his editorship of the *Journal of Family Psychology*. He has recently served as President of the Society for Research in Child Development.

Douglas R. Powell is a Distinguished Professor in the Department of Child Development and Family Studies at Purdue University. He holds a Ph.D. from Northwestern University and was previously on the faculty at The Merrill-Palmer Institute and Wayne State University, Detroit. Powell has developed and studied parenting interventions for diverse populations, and recently co-developed a parenting education content framework for the federal Even Start Family Literacy Program. He is principal investigator of federally funded studies on professional development in early literacy and on preschool curriculum effects. Powell is former editor of the *Early Childhood Research Quarterly*.

Thomas J. Schofield is currently pursuing his doctoral degree at the University of California, Riverside. His interests center on the family as a resilient, dynamic unit.

Helen Bittmann Sysko, Ph.D. received her Masters of Science in Child Development and doctorate in Counseling Psychology from the University of Pittsburgh. As a clinician, she has worked with children and adults in outpatient community mental health programs in child care centers and urban drug and alcohol treatment facilities. Her research interests include homeless mothers and family reunification intervention.

Joan Vondra, Ph.D., is Professor of Applied Developmental Psychology at the University of Pittsburgh. She earned her doctorate in Human Development and Family Studies at Penn State University. Her research interests include risk and resilience and the role of supportive relationships at home and at school for children from low-income families.

Susan K. Walker is an Assistant Professor of Family Studies at the University of Maryland, College Park and is a state Family Life specialist with Maryland Cooperative Extension. She holds a Ph.D. in Child and Family Studies, and Masters and Bachelors degrees in Nutrition. Her current areas of research include child care provider professional development, and low income rural mothers' use of child care relative to employment and context. For Cooperative Extension, Dr. Walker oversees continuing education for child care professionals and is the evaluator for a five-year youth development project in rural and urban low income areas of the state. Locally, Dr. Walker is an appointed member of the Montgomery County Commission on Child Care. She currently serves as co-chair of the Public Policy subcommittee.

Alev Yalçınkaya is currently affiliated with University of Connecticut, School of Family Studies as a Research Scientist where she recently completed a Postdoctoral Fellowship. She received her B.A. in Psychology and her M.A. in Clinical Psychology at Bosphorus University, Istanbul, Turkey. After moving to the United States she obtained her Ph.D. in Human Development from Boston University where she also worked as a Lecturer. She is currently a member of the Society for Research in Child Development and was a member of the American Psychological Society and Eastern Psychological Association. Her research interests include cross-cultural studies of family and close relationships, including attachment theory and family violence. She also works in the field of childrearing among migrant families, acculturation and ethnic identity development. She is the author of the chapter "Family Violence in Turkey" in the book *International Perspectives on Family Violence and Abuse: A Cognitive Ecological Approach* edited by Kathleen Malley-Morrison.

Author Index

A

Abidin, R., 186, *197*, 221, *227*
Ablow, J., 224, *228*
Adams, M., 117, 121, 122, *137, 142*
Addison, S., 182, *200*
Adelberg, T., 253, *272*
Adler, S., 323, *339*
Ahmeduzzaman, M., 106, *143*
Albersheim, L., 58, *70*
Albus, K., 59, *64*
Albus, K. E., 59, *64*
Alcalay, R., 253, *271*
Aldous, J., 131, *135*
Alexander, K. L., 22, *28*
Allen, J., 112, 113, 134, *136*
Allen, J. P., 166, *171*, 298, *315*
Almeida, D. M., 285, *295*
Almgren, G., 86, *97*
Amato, P., 113, 130, 131, *136, 140,* 210, 221, *227*
Amato, P. A., 129, 130, *136*
Amato, P. R., 299, *315*
Amato, R. R., 130, 131, *136*
Ames, E. W., 388, *399*
Ammons, P., 256, 257, *272*
Anderson, J., 357, *369*

Anderson, K. E., 75, *99,* 154, *171*
Anderson, L., 177, *200*
Anderson, L. L., 177, *197*
Andreas, D., 41, 58, *67,* 162, *174*
Angelillo, C., 326, *341*
Anthony, C., 206, 207, 213, *228*
Antonis, B., 104, *142*
Apfel, N., 80, 82, *101*
Appel, A. E., 213, *227*
Arbuckle, B., 52, *67*
Ardelt, M., 54, *65*
Arias, I., 215, *227*
Arkinson, M. K., 47, *65*
Armsden, G. C., 305, *315*
Arnold, D. H., 349, *369*
Aronson, J., 26, *28*
Arseneault, L., 395, *399*
Asai, M., 9, *33*
Asencio, M., 325, 326, 332, 333, *339*
Asendorpf, J., 18, 19, *32,* 164, *175*
Ashmore, R. D., 26, *30*
Assiter, S., 75, *101*
Astone, N. M., 321, 322, *339*
Atkinson, E., 20, *29*
Atkinson, L., 56, *69,* 187, *201*
Attonucci, J., 107, *143*
Auerbach, C. F., 117, *143*

Avenevoli, S., 162, *174*
Avery, L. S., 47, *65*
Azuma, H., 5, 8, 9, *28*

B

Bacon, M. K., 278, *293*
Bailey, D., 182, *197*
Bailey, W. T., 128, *136*
Baker, B., 180, *197*
Bakermans-Kranenburg, M. J., 51, 56, 57, 70, 350, 358, *369*
Baldwin, A. L., 330, *338*
Baldwin, C., 330, *338*
Baltes, M. M., 333, *338*
Banaji, M. R., 26, *30*
Baradaran, L. P., 52, *67*
Barbara-Stein, L., 358, *371*
Barclay-McLaughlin, G., 311, 313, *315*
Bardone, A. M., 46, 52, *61*
Barnard, K. E., 348, 356, 363, *369*
Barnett, R. C., 127, *136*
Baron, J. N., 280, *293*
Barratt, M. S., 94, *97*, 187, 188, *200*
Barrett, K. C., 9, *29*
Barry, H., 278, *293*
Bartkowski, J. P., 7, 8, *28*, 121, *136*
Baruch, G. K., 127, *136*
Baskiewicz, A., 181, *198*
Bass, B., 222, *229*
Bates, B., 59, *64*
Bates, J., 18, *28*
Bates, J. E., 18, *32, 43*, 52, *64, 68*, 162, *171*, 303, 304, 305, 306, *315, 316*
Bates, K., 162, *171*
Bates, L., 80, 81, 87, 93, 94, *99, 101*
Bates, L. V., 93, *97*
Bathurst, K., 283, *295*
Baucom, D. H., 225, *228*
Baumrind, D., 120, *136*, 152, *171*, 305, *315*, 327, *338*, 380, *398*
Bavolek, S., 90, *97*
Baydar, N., 350, 351, 364, *369*
Bayles, K., 18, *28*
Bayley, H., 180, *198*
Beach, S. R., 45, *61*, 209, 214, *227, 230*
Beal, C. R., 167, *171*
Beaman, J., 40, *69*
Bearss, K., 220, 221, *227*
Beatty, W. W., 106, *141*

Beauchaine, T. P., 362, *372*
Beck, A. T., 186, *197*
Beckett, C., 378, 379, 388, *400*
Beckwith, L., 37, *61*
Bedard, C., 298, 313, *316*
Beecroft, E., 306, 307, 308, *317*
Behen, M. E., 389, *399*
Behrman, R. E., 47, 59, *65*, 345, 357, *370*
Beitel, A., 107, 112, 113, *136*
Bell, C. C., 300, 302, *315*
Bell, K. L., 166, *171*
Bell, R. Q., 149, *171*, 185, 191, 194, *197*, 380, *398*
Belle, D., 239, 259, *271*
Bellugi, U., 185, 190, *197*
Belsky, J., xii, *xiv*, 36, 37, 40, 41, 42, 44, 51, 56, 57, 58, *61, 62, 70, 71*, 74, 75, 80, 81, 82, 83, 84, 85, 86, 88, *97, 99*, 113, 120, 125, *136, 139*, 150, 162, 163, *171, 173, 174, 176*, 205, 208, 210, 213, 215, 216, 217, 220, 222, 223, *227, 230*, 280, *294*, 358, 360, *369*
Bem, D. J., 90, *97*
Benasich, A. A., 17, *28*
Benigni, L., 106, *141*
Bennet, D. S., 18, *28*
Bennett, D. S., 162, *171*
Bensley, L., 95, *101*
Benson, P., 157, *174*
Benson, P. L., 308, *317*
Berglund, P. A., 75, *99*
Berg-Nielsen, T. S., 151, *171*
Berlin, L. J., 45, 56, *63*, 344, *369*
Berliner, D. C., 346, *369*
Bernal, G., 50, *67*
Berndt, T. J., 386, *398*
Bernheimer, L. P., 191, *200*
Bernieri, F., 382, *400*
Bernstein, J., 114, *141*
Bernstein, L., 350, 354, *371*
Bernstein, V. J., 94, *101*, 239, 259, *272*
Bertrand, J. M., 185, 190, *200*
Beyers, J. M., 304, 306, *315*
Bianchi, S. M., 108, *136*, 288, 289, 292, *294*
Bidell, T. R., 150, *171*
Bielby, W. T., 280, *293*
Bierman, K. L., 52, *62*
Bifulco, A., 49, *66*
Birch, H. G., 149, 150, *172, 176*
Bishop, S. J., 89, *99*
Blacher, J., 18, *28*, 180, *197*

Black, J. E., 25, *30*
Black, M. M., 92, *99*
Blackwell, B., 356, *369*
Blasco, P., 182, *197*
Blevins-Knabe, B., 15, *32*
Bliesener, T., 310, *317*
Block, A., 221, *227*
Block, J., 221, *227*
Blue, J., 214, *228*
Blum, J. S., 47, *62*
Blyth, D. A., 308, *317*
Bø, I., 254, *271*
Bogat, G. A., 258, *272*
Bohman, M., 50, *63*
Boissevain, J., 251, *271*
Bojczyk, K., 357, *372*
Boles, A. J., 205, *228*
Bolger, N., 285, 286, *294*
Bolton, F., 84, *97*
Bonney, J. F., 113, 114, *136*
Bontempo, R., 9, *33*
Boodoo, G., 382, *400*
Boomsma, I., 51, 52, *70*
Booth, A., 113, *136*
Booth, C. L., 348, 356, 363, *369*
Borkowski, J., 79, 80, 81, 82, 84, 86, 89, 91, *97*, *101*
Borkowski, J. G., 88, 89, 90, *100*, *101*
Bornstead-Bruns, M., 5, *30*
Bornstein, M. H., 5, 8, 9, *28, 29*, 116, *136*, 147, 151, *171*, 297, *315*, 322, *338*, 379, 387, 388, *398, 399*
Borthwick-Duffy, S., 117, *142*
Boruch, R., 349, *371*
Bosch, J. D., 52, *68*
Bost, K. K., 47, *62*, 242, 255, *271*
Botein, S., 363, *371*
Bott, E., 236, *271*
Bouchard, T., 382, *398*
Bouchard, T. J., Jr., 382, *400*
Bowlby, J., 44, 55, 58, 60, *62*
Bowman, T., 187, *201*
Boyce, L. K., 360, *372*
Boyer, D., 75, 95, *98*
Boykin, A. W., 382, *400*
Boyum, L., 132, *136*
Bradbury, T., 43, *62*
Bradbury, T. N., 209, 210, 214, 225, 226, *227, 230, 231, 232*
Braddock, D., 177, *200*
Bradley, R. H., 324, *338*, 362, *369*
Braithwaite, V. A., 117, *137*

Brassard, J., 236, 237, 238, 252, 259, *271*
Braungart, J. M., 157, *171*
Braungart-Rieker, J., 162, *171*
Braver, S., 117, *142*
Brazelton, T., 360, *373*
Bream, V., 131, *138*
Breitner, J. C. S., 395, *400*
Brewster, K., 76, *98*
Briggs-Gowan, M., 37, *62*
Broadhurst, D. D., 300, *318*
Broderick, J. E., 224, *232*
Brody, G., 40, 43, *62, 67*
Brody, G. H., 22, *28*, 114, *137*, 215, 224, *227*, 304, 306, *315*
Brody, N., 382, *400*
Brodzinsky, D. M., 112, *136*
Bronfenbrenner, U., xi, *xiv, xv*, 3, *28*, 150, 153, 159, *172*, 195, 196, *197*, 205, 206, 224, *227*, 276, 287, *294*, 297, 308, 311, 312, *315*, 377, 378, 383, 384, 394, *398*
Brooks-Gunn, J., 17, *28*, 46, 47, *62, 68*, 78, 80, 81, 82, 85, 91, 93, *98, 100, 101*, 297, 299, 303, 306, *316, 317*, 320, 323, 324, *338*, 344, 348, 350, 351, 354, 359, 361, 363, 365, *369, 371*
Brott, A., 103, 113, 127, 133, 134, 135, *142*
Brown, A., 40, *62*
Brown, B. B., 6, *33*
Brown, G. W., 49, *66*
Brown, J., 26, *28*
Brown, M., 18, *28*
Brown, M. M., 162, *171*
Brownlee, J., 109, *141*
Brunner, J., 221, *227*
Bryant, B., 236, 254, *271*
Bryant, D., 48, *62*
Bryant, D. M., 358, 359, 361, *372*
Buchanan, A., 131, *138*
Buchbinder, S., 364, *369, 370*
Buck, M. J., 3, 4, 25, *31*
Buehler, C., 206, 207, 211, 212, 213, *228, 231*
Bugaighis, M. A., 209, *232*
Bugental, D., 43, *62*
Bugental, D. B., 5, 20, *29*, 214, *228*
Bumpus, M. F., 115, *137*, 287, 291, 293, *294*
Burchinal, M., 48, *62*
Burchinal, M. R., 47, *62*, 242, 255, *271*, 362, *369*
Burgess, B. J., 122, 123, *136*

Burgess, K. B., 386, *400*
Buriel, R., 9, *30,* 116, *142*
Burks, V. S., 52, *64*
Burlingham, D., 302, *316*
Burman, B., 208, 210, 211, 216, *228, 229*
Burns, K., 37, *62*
Burns, W. J., 37, *62*
Burton, L., 75, *98*
Burts, D. C., 4, *31*
Busch-Rossnagel, N. A., 17, *33*
Bush, K. R., 335, *339*
Buss, D. M., 163, *172*
Butler, J., 75, *98*
Byrd, J. E., 284, *295*

C

Cabrera, N., 103, *143*
Cadenhead, C., 303, *316*
Cadoret, R. J., 50, *62*
Cahill, B. M., 187, *197*
Cain, R., 39, *71*
Caldera, Y. M., 161, *174*
Callor, S., 41, 42, 43, *67*
Campbell, D. T., 346, 349, *369, 372*
Campbell, S. B., 51, 58, *61, 62,* 207, *228*
Cannan, T., 168, *173*
Capaldi, D. M., 381, *399*
Cardemil, E. V., 50, *62*
Carels, R. A., 225, *228*
Carlson, E. A., 95, *101*
Carlson, V. J., 325, 326, 332, 333, *339*
Carr, J., 189, *197*
Carroll, R., 166, *175*
Carson, J., 132, *136*
Carter, A., 37, *62*
Carter, M., 388, *399*
Casey, P. H., 324, *338,* 362, *369*
Casey, R. J., 168, *173*
Cashmore, J., 332, *339*
Caspi, A., 38, 53, 54, *62, 63, 65, 66,* 75, 80, 81,
    82, 83, 84, 85, *99,* 394, 395, *398, 399*
Caspi, D., 46, 52, *61*
Cassidy, B., 89, *98*
Cassidy, J., 45, 56, *63,* 217, *233*
Cassidy, S. B., 185, *198*
Castellino, D., 43, *67*
Catalano, R., 298, *318*
Cattell, R. B., 38, *63*
Cauce, A. M., 121, *136,* 304, *317*
Ceballo, R., 263, *271,* 306, 311, *315*

Ceci, S. J., 377, 382, 384, *398, 399, 400*
Cen, G., 5, 7, *29,* 159, *172*
Chamberlin, R., 363, *371*
Champion, L. A., 46, *63*
Chan, S. Q., 9, *30*
Chandler, M., 149, *175*
Chao, R., 124, *136*
Chao, R. K., 5, 6, *29,* 125, *136,* 320, 326,
    336, *338*
Chao, W., 40, *69*
Chapman, R. S., 185, *198*
Charnov, E. L., 107, *140*
Chase-Lansdale, P. L., 91, *101,* 113, *137*
Chavez, F., 37, *65*
Chazan-Cohen, R., 37, *62*
Chen, C., 12, *33*
Chen, F., 90, *98*
Chen, H., 5, 7, *29,* 159, *172*
Chen, X., 5, 7, *29,* 159, 162, 163, *172, 175*
Chen, Z. Y., 12, *29*
Chess, S., 149, 150, 158, 160, *172, 176,* 256,
    271, 272
Chesser, B., 297, *318*
Chethik, L., 37, *62*
Chiang, T., 9, *29*
Chih-Mei, C., 5, 9, *31*
Chilamkurti, C., 53, *67*
Child, I. L., 278, *293*
Child Trends, 73, 74, 78, *98*
Chisholm, K., 388, *399*
Chorost, A. F., 225, *231*
Christal, R. C., 38, *70*
Christensen, A., 210, 213, 216, 220, 224,
    228, 231
Christian, J. L., 45, *68*
Christiansen, S. L., 128, *137*
Chugani, D. C., 389, *399*
Chugani, H. T., 389, *399*
Cicchetti, D., 53, 59, *63, 70*
Cicognani, E., 18, *29*
Cioci, M., 309, *317*
Clark, L., 39, 42, *66, 69, 70*
Clark, L. A., 42, 43, *63,* 162, 165, *172*
Clark, R., 37, *62,* 284, *294, 295*
Clarke, G. N., 50, *63*
Clarke-Stewart, K. A., 105, *137*
Clayton, S. L., 352, 358, 363, *373*
Clements, M., 212, 218, *231*
Clingempeel, G., 222, *229*
Clingempeel, W. G., 166, *173*
Cloninger, C. R., 50, *63*
Cobb, S., 237, 259, *271*

Cochran, M., 236, 238, 239, 240, 241, 243, 244, 249, 252, 254, 267, *271, 272*
Coggins, K., 123, *144*
Cohen, J., 206, *228*
Cohen, M., 56, *70*
Cohen, M. M., 56, *63*
Cohn, J. F., 58, *61*
Coie, J., 75, *100*
Coie, J. D., 52, *63*
Coiro, M. J., 215, *228*
Colbert, K. K., 94, *97*
Cole, R., 346, 355, 357, *370, 371,* 393, *400*
Cole, R. E., 330, *338,* 362, 363, *371*
Coleman, P., 159, *173*
Coleman, P. K., 15, 19, *29,* 164, *172*
Coley, R. L., 113, *137*
Colletta, N., 259, *272*
Collins, A., 298, *315*
Collins, N. L., 47, *63*
Collins, W. A., 3, 4, 25, *30,* 109, *137,* 215, *228,* 297, *315,* 379, 387, 388, *399*
Coltrane, S., 103, 112, 117, 119, 121, 122, *137, 142,* 289, *294*
Comfort, M., 81, 82, 85, *99*
Compas, B. E., 46, *68*
Condry, J., 380, *399*
Condry, S., 380, *399*
Conger, K., 40, 54, *63*
Conger, R., 40, 54, *63, 64, 69,* 114, *137,* 304, 306, *315*
Conger, R. D., 38, 54, *65, 66, 69,* 114, *137,* 207, 225, *228, 230,* 237, *272*
Connell, D. B., 363, *371*
Connell, J. P., 346, *369*
Connors, R., 258, *272*
Conrad, B., 164, *173*
Contrerae, J., 39, *64*
Contreras, J. M., 47, *64*
Cook, G. A., 360, *372*
Cook, T., 297, 302, 303, 304, *316*
Cook, T. D., 346, 349, 365, *369, 370, 372*
Cooksey, E. C., 115, *137*
Cooley, C. H., 391, *399*
Cooper, H., 349, *373*
Cooper, J. E., 117, *137*
Cooper, P. J., 37, *67*
Copeland, J. M., 209, *232*
Coplan, R. J., 20, *29*
Corns, K. M., 58, *69*
Corsaro, W., 330, *338*
Corter, C., 111, 112, *137, 138*
Costa, P. T., 39, *64*

Costigan, C. L., 222, *230*
Cote, L. R., 5, *29*
Cotterell, J., 262, *272*
Cotton, S., 332, *339*
Cowan, C. P., 125, 126, 127, *137,* 205, 212, 213, 216, 222, 223, 224, 225, *228, 231,* 345, 353, *370,* 391, *399*
Cowan, P., 125, 126, 127, *137*
Cowan, P. A., 126, *137,* 205, 212, 213, 216, 222, 223, 224, 225, *228, 231,* 276, *295,* 345, 353, *370,* 391, *399*
Cox, M. J., 47, 58, *62, 64,* 104, *137,* 206, 211, *228, 232,* 242, 255, *271*
Coysh, W. S., 205, *228*
Craig, I. W., 394, *398*
Crichton, L., 161, *176*
Crick, N. C., 52, *64*
Crisafulli, A., 208, 216, *232*
Crittenden, P., 257, 264, *272*
Crittenden, P. M., 51, *64*
Crnic, K., 41, 42, 44, 56, *61,* 120, *139,* 162, 163, *173, 174, 176,* 180, 186, *198, 199,* 213, 220, 222, 227, *230*
Crockenberg, S., 39, *64,* 86, 89, 92, 94, 95, *98,* 237, 238, 239, 256, 264, *272*
Crockenberg, S. B., 162, 165, *172*
Cronin, M., 357, *369*
Cross, C. E., 54, *65*
Cross, P. K., 188, *200*
Cross, T. L., 123, *137*
Cross, W., 248, 249, *272*
Crouter, A., 298, 300, *316*
Crouter, A. C., 10, *29,* 114, 115, *137, 142,* 160, *172,* 275, 276, 281, 282, 286, 287, 289, 290, 291, 293, *294, 296*
Crowell, J., 58, *70*
Cruzcosa, M., 214, *228*
Culp, A., 80, 86, *98, 99*
Culross, P. L., 47, 59, *65,* 345, 357, *370*
Cummings, E. M., 51, *64,* 104, 113, *137,* 206, 207, 214, *228, 229*
Cummings, S., 180, *198*
Curtis-Boles, H., 205, *228*
Cutrona, C., 156, *172*
Cutting, A. L., 148, *172*

D

Daddis, C., 167, *175*
Dadds, M. R., 18, 20, *29,* 224, *229*
Daggett, J., 17, 22, *29*

Daglish, L., 105, *143*
Dahl, A. A., 151, *171*
Dalakas, V., 11, *32*
Daly, K., 110, 112, *137, 138*
Dancy, B., 118, *137*
Danieli, Y., 303, *315*
Daniels, D., 381, 382, *400*
Danso, H., 4, 7, *29*
Darling, N. E., 305, *316*
David, C. G., 46, *66*
Davies, P., 206, 214, *228*
Davies, P. T., 51, *64,* 206, 207, 214, 216, *228, 229*
Davis, K., 256, 257, 272, 292, *294*
Davis-Kean, P. E., 107, 109, 114, 121, *144*
Day, R. D., 130, 131, *140*
Deal, J., 160, *172*
Deal, J. E., 222, *229*
Deater-Deckard, K., 51, *64,* 119, *137,* 148, *172,* 303, *315,* 330, *338*
DeBaryshe, B. D., 14, 17, *29,* 304, *317*
DeBaryshe, D. B., 381, 393, 397, *399, 401*
de Bruyn, E., 384, *399*
Deci, E. L., 333, *341*
De Cubas, M., 323, *339*
DeFrain, J., 297, *318*
DeFries, J. C., 156, 157, *174*
Delgado-Gaitan, C., 268, 272, 332, *338*
DeLongis, A., 285, 286, *294*
Dennis, J., 132, *142*
DePanfilis, D., 47, *64*
DeRubeis, R. J., 51, *69*
DeVito, C., 212, *229*
Diamond, K., 351, *373*
DiBlasio, F. A., 89, 91, 93, 95, *101*
Dickie, J. R., 113, *137*
Dickson, N., 46, 52, *61*
Dickson, W. J., 282, *296*
Dickstein, S., 222, *232*
Diener, M., 39, *64, 65*
Dienhart, A., 112, *138*
Dishion, T. J., 304, 305, *315*
Divecha, D. J., 3, *32,* 155, *174,* 194, *200*
Dix, T., 5, *29,* 43, *64,* 155, *172,* 226, *229*
Dodge, K., 119, *137*
Dodge, K. A., 18, *32,* 43, 52, *64, 68,* 303, 304, 305, 306, *315, 316,* 330, *338*
Doherty, W. E. J., 110, *138*
Dollahite, D. C., 18, *32*
Domenech-Rodriquez, M., 121, *136*
Donahue, M. L., 14, *29*
Donnelly, B., 40, *70*

D'Onofrio, B., 383, 384, *401*
Dooley, D., 298, *318*
Dornbusch, S., 305, *316*
Dornbusch, S. M., 6, *30, 33,* 118, *140*
Down, H. L., 178, *198*
Downey, G., 54, *65*
Dozier, M., 59, *64*
Drotar, D., 181, *198*
Dubow, E., 81, 82, 92, *98, 100*
Dubrow, N., 300, 302, 303, *316*
Dubrow, N. F., 303, *315*
Duggan, A., 364, 369, *370*
Dukewich, T., 81, *97*
Dumaret, A., 384, 385, *401*
Dumas, J. E., 187, 188, *200*
Duncan, G. J., 93, *98,* 299, *316,* 320, 321, 323, 324, 335, *338, 340*
Dunifon, R., 303, 304, *316*
Dunkel-Schetter, C., 47, *63*
Dunn, J., 148, 159, 161, 166, *172, 174,* 381, 382, *399*
Dunn, J. F., 104, *142,* 157, *172*
Dunn, M. G., 37, *64*
Dunn, P. M., 178, *198*
Dunst, C. J., 367, *370*
DuRant, R. H., 303, *316*
Durrett, M. E., 113, *138*
Duyme, M., 384, 385, *401*
Duvesteyn, M. G. C., 59, *70*
Dvir, R., 106, *143*
Dykens, E. M., 178, 181, 185, 186, 189, 190, 194, 196, *198, 199*

E

Eagly, A. H., 26, *30*
Earls, F., 306, 309, *317*
East, P., 75, *98*
Easterbrooks, M. A., 206, 207, 208, 210, 211, 212, 213, 215, *229, 230*
Eaves, L., 50, *69,* 178, *200*
Eaves, L. J., 51, *64*
Eccles, J., 297, 302, 303, 304, *316*
Eckenrode, J., 393, *400*
Eckenrode, J. J., 362, 363, *371*
Edelbrock, C., 51, *65*
Edwards, J., 25, *31*
Egeland, B., 54, 58, *65, 70,* 161, *176,* 303, *316*
Eggebeen, D. J., 128, 129, 130, *138*

Eiden, R. D., 37, 58, *65, 69*
Eisenstadt, J. W., 352, 357, *370, 372*
Elder, G., 40, 54, *63,* 114, *137*
Elder, G. H., 297, 302, 303, 304, 313, *316*
Elder, G. H., Jr., 38, 54, *63, 65, 66, 69,*
    225, *228*
Eley, T. C., 52, *65*
Elins, J. L., 160, *176*
Elkin, I., 47, *66*
Elkins, I. J., 157, *172*
Ellison, C. G., 7, 8, *28, 30*
Elmen, J. D., 281, *296*
Emde, R. M., 367, *370*
Emde, R. N., 206, 212, 215, *229*
Emery, R. E., 207, 212, 215, 217, *228, 229,*
    233
Emory, G., 186, *197*
Engfer, A., 44, *65*
English, D., 379, *399*
Entwisle, D. R., 12, 22, *28, 30,* 321, 322,
    339
Epstein, J. N., 349, *369*
Erel, O., 208, 210, 211, 216, *229*
Erickson, F., 352, *370*
Erickson Warfield, M., 47, *65*
Erikson, E., 127, *138*
Erikson, K., 312, *316*
Erikson, M., 110, *138*
Erikson, M. T., 51, *64*
Erwin, L. J., 247, *273*
Espinosa, M., 37, *61*
Essex, E. L., 182, *198*
Essex, M. J., 162, *174,* 284, *294, 295*
Evans, D. W., 185, *199*
Ey, S., 46, *68*
Eyberg, S., 220, 221, *227*

F

Fabricius, W., 117, *142*
Fagan, J., 114, 121, 133, 134, *138*
Fagan, W. T., 357, *369*
Fagot, B., 163, *172*
Fagot, B. I., 164, 168, *172, 173*
Falco, F. L., 393, 397, *401*
Faleigh, M. J., 6, *30*
Farber, B., 180, *198*
Farber, E., 58, *65,* 303, *316*
Farrington, D., 82, *100*
Fauber, R., 213, *229*

Fauber, R. L., 207, 208, 213, *229*
Fazio, R. H., 26, *30*
Feeney, J. A., 209, *229*
Feinberg, M., 148, *172*
Feinberg, M. E., 221, 223, *229*
Feingold, J., 384, 385, *401*
Feins, J. D., 306, 307, 308, *317*
Feiring, C., 58, *67*
Fendt, K. H., 358, 359, 361, *372*
Ferguson, M., 86, *97*
Festinger, L., 90, *98*
Fidler, D. J., 186, 187, 188, 189, 194, 195,
    198, 199
Field, I., 121, *139*
Field, T. M., 92, *98,* 323, *339*
Fincham, F., 43, *62*
Fincham, F. D., 43, *67,* 207, 209, 210, 212,
    213, 214, 215, 216, 225, 226, *227,*
    229, 230, 231, 232
Fine, D., 75, 95, *98*
Fineman, N. R., 353, *370*
Finucane, B., 178, *198*
Fischel, J. E., 393, 397, *401*
Fischer, C., 240, 241, 242, 243, 244, *272*
Fischer, K. W., 150, *171*
Fish, M., 125, *136*
Fisher, P. A., 59, *64,* 150, 151, 154, 160,
    174
Fiske, S. T., 4, 26, *30*
Fisman, S. N., 187, 188, *200, 201*
Fitzgerald, H., 80, 81, 87, *99*
Fitzgerald, H. E., 37, *70,* 168, *173*
Fleming, A. S., 110, 111, 112, *137, 138*
Fletcher, A. C., 305, *316*
Flor, F. L., 22, *28*
Flouri, E., 131, *138*
Floyd, F. J., 220, 222, 225, *230, 232*
Flyr, M. L., 132, *142*
Fogg, L., 164, *173*
Follmer, A., 48, *62*
Fonagy, P., 345, *372*
Fontaine, R., 52, *64*
Forehand, R., 213, 224, *227, 229*
Foster, C. L., 75, *99*
Foster, E. M., 54, *65*
Fowles, D. C., 163, *172*
Fracasso, M. P., 332, *340*
Fraiberg, S., 47, 53, 59, *65*
Franz, C., 131, *139*
Franz, C. E., 132, *138*
Franzetta, K., 75, *100*
Freeman, S. F. N., 189, *199*

Fremmer-Bombik, E., 58, *70, 71*
Frensch, P. A., 5, 12, 13, 22, *32*
Freud, A., 302, *316*
Freud, S., 180, *198*
Fried, M., 284, *294*
Friedman, D. E., 283, *294*
Friedrich, W., 180, *198*
Friedrich, W. L., 180, *198*
Friedrich, W. N., 180, 186, *198, 199*
Fritz, J., 245, 260, *272*
Frodi, A. M., 106, *140*
Frodi, M., 106, *140*
Frommer, E., 49, *65*
Frone, M. R., 116, *138*
Frosch, C., 220, *230*
Frosch, C. A., 220, 222, *232*
Fuddy, L., 364, 369, *370*
Fuligni, A. J., 331, 333, 334, *339*
Fulker, D. W., 156, *174*
Fung, H., 95, *101*
Furstenberg, F., 78, 80, 81, 82, 85, *98*
Furstenberg, F. F., 129, *138,* 297, 302, 303, 304, *316*

G

Gable, S., 213, 220, 222, *227, 230*
Gable, S. L., 226, *232*
Gadsen, V., 117, 118, 119, *138*
Galambos, N. L., 165, *172*
Galburda, A., 185, 190, *197*
Gallagher, P. L., 185, *200*
Gallimore, R., 191, *200*
Galperin, C., 5, 8, 9, *28*
Galperin, C. Z., 5, 8, 9, *28*
Garbarino, J., 297, 298, 300, 301, 302, 303, 304, 313, *315, 316*
Garcia Coll, C., 326, 327, 335, *339*
Garfinkel, I., 130, *138*
Garfinkel, L., 107, *138*
Garnier, H. E., 191, *200*
Garrett, E., 205, *228*
Garrity-Roukous, F., 37, *62*
Garwood, M. M., 162, *171*
Gaudin, J., 256, 257, *272*
Gaudin, J. M., 47, *65*
Gautier, M., 178, *200*
Gauvain, M., 163, *172*
Ge, X., 40, *64,* 304, 306, *315*
Gelfand, D. M., 156, 161, *173, 176*

Gelles, R., 303, *316*
Gensburg, L. J., 188, *200*
Gerard, J. M., 213, *228*
Gerlach-Downie, S., 352, 357, *373*
Gerlach-Downie, S. G., 352, 357, 358, 366, *370*
Geronimus, A., 77, 78, 83, *98*
Gerrard, M., 304, 306, *315*
Gershoff, E. T., 5, 7, *30*
Gerson, K., 290, *295*
Gervai, J., 57, *66*
Gibbons, F. X., 304, 306, *315*
Gibson, D., 189, *199*
Gibson, N. M., 22, *28*
Gilbreth, J. G., 129, 130, *136*
Gillham, J., 50, *65*
Gilliom, L. A., 222, *230*
Gilliom, M., 51, *62*
Gjerde, P. F., 217, 218, *230*
Glidden, L. M., 178, 187, 196, *197, 199*
Glie, D., 75, 76, *100*
Goerge, R., 84, *98*
Goldberg, W. A., 207, 208, 210, 211, 213, 215, *230,* 282, 283, *295*
Goldman, M., 42, *66*
Goldman-Fraser, J., 14, *31*
Goldsmith, D., 332, 333, *340*
Goldsmith, H., 41, 42, 43, *67*
Goldstein, L., 39, *65*
Gomberg, E. S. L., 37, *71*
Gomby, D. S., 47, 59, *65,* 345, 357, *370*
Gondoli, D., 40, *65*
Gonzales, N., 304, *317*
Gonzales, N. A., 117, *139*
Good, C., 26, *28*
Goodall, G. M., 46, *63*
Goodman, R., 157, *173*
Goodnow, J. J., 3, 4, 9, 13, 15, 18, 22, 25, *30,* 332, *339*
Goodson, B. D., 350, 354, 367, *370, 371*
Goossens, F. A., 37, *66*
Gordis, E. B., 207, 216, 219, 220, 221, 223, *230, 231*
Gordon, E. W., 13, 22, *32*
Gorman, J. C., 5, 17, *30*
Gorman-Smith, D., 117, 118, *138*
Gotlib, I. H., 46, *65*
Gottesman, I. I., 383, 384, *401*
Gottfried, A. E., 283, *295*
Gottfried, A. W., 283, *295*
Gottman, J. M., 104, 113, 131, 133, *138, 142,* 207, 218, 220, 221, *231, 233*

Graham, S., 190, *199*
Grandour, M. J., 161, *176*
Granovetter, M., 239, 272
Grant, K. E., 46, *68*
Grantham-McGregor, S., 361, *372*
Gravestock, F. M., 225, *230*
Gray, F. L., 185, *199*
Greenbaum, C. W., 11, *31*
Greenberg, M., 180, *198*
Greenberg, M. T., 186, *199*, 305, *315*
Greenberger, E., 11, *30*, 115, 127, *138*,
     139, 282, 283, *295*
Greene, A., 80, 81, 82, 84, *100*
Greenfield, P., 327, 331, 333, 334, *339*
Greenstein, B., 365, *370*
Greenwald, A. G., 26, *30*
Grimm-Thomas, K., 115, *139*
Grogger, J., 82, *99*
Grolnick, W. S., 333, *341*
Gross, D., 164, *173*, 359, *370*
Gross, R. T., 351, 363, *369*
Grossman, F. K., 92, *101*, 127, *139*
Grossman, K. E., 58, *71*
Grossmann, K., 58, *70*
Grove, K., 304, *317*
Groves, B. M., 302, *316*
Gruber, E., 6, *31*
Gruber-Baldini, A. L., 280, *295*
Grunebaum, H. U., 363, *371*
Grusec, J. E., 5, 18, 21, *30*, *31*, 156, *173*
Grych, J. H., 207, 211, 212, 213, 214, 216,
     217, *230*
Gunnar, M., 41, 58, *67*, 162, *174*
Gunnarsson, L., 239, 240, 241, 243, 244,
     249, 252, 254, *271*, *272*
Guralnick, M. J., 344, *370*
Gurung, R. A., 46, 47, *69*
Guthrie, D., 353, *370*
Gutierrez, K., 352, *370*

H

Haas, B., 280, *295*
Haas, L., 284, *295*
Hagan, M. S., 222, *229*
Hahn, C.-S., 322, *338*
Haight, W. L., 25, *30*
Haley, A., 383, 384, *401*
Halford, W. K., 225, *230*
Hallahan, D. P., 177, 183, *199*

Halpern, D. F., 382, *400*
Halpern, R., 358, *370*
Hamill, S., 282, 283, *295*
Hamilton, C. E., 58, *65*
Hamilton, S., xi, *xv*
Hammond, M., 212, 213, *233*, 349, *373*
Handal, P., 118, *137*
Handwerker, W. P., 11, *30*, 324, 326, *339*
Hanks, C., 355, *371*
Hanline, M. F., 187, *199*
Hann, D., 86, *99*
Hann, D. A., 79, *100*
Hans, S. L., 94, *101*, 239, 259, 272
Hanson, M., 187, *199*
Hanson, R. F., 53, *66*
Hao, L., 5, *30*
Happaney, K., 5, 20, *29*
Haraven, T., 237, 272
Harding, C., 58, *70*
Hargreaves, W. A., 50, *67*
Harkness, S., 5, *30*
Harold, G. T., 207, *230*
Harris, J. R., xiv, *xv*, 150, *173*, 306, *316*,
     378, 379, 380, 382, 386, 387, 390,
     399
Harris, K. M., 129, *138*
Harris, M. J., 382, *400*
Harris, S., 187, *199*
Harris, T., 49, *66*
Harrison, A. O., 9, *30*
Hart, C. H., 131, 132, *139*
Harter, K., 211, *228*
Harter, S., 391, *399*
Harvey, E., 288, *295*
Harwood, R. L., 5, 10, 11, *30*, *32*, 324, 325,
     326, 332, 333, 336, *339*, *340*, *341*
Hastings, P., 18, 19, *32*, 156, 163, 164, *173*,
     175
Hastings, P. D., 5, 7, 20, 21, *29*, *31*, 159,
     172
Hatch, R. C., 209, *232*
Hatfield, E., 168, *173*
Hauser, R. M., 323, *339*
Hauser, S. T., 166, *171*
Hauser-Cram, P., 47, *65*
Haveman, R., 85, *99*
Hawkins, A., 112, 113, 134, *136*
Hawkins, A. J., 133, 134, *138*
Hawkins, W., 50, *63*
Hay, D., 395, *400*
Hayduk, L. A., 12, *30*
Haynes, C. W., 359, *370*

Haynes, O. M., 5, 8, 9, *28,* 322, *338*
Hazelwood, L., 39, *64*
Head, M. R., 289, 291, *294*
Heath, A. C., 51, *64*
Heath, D. H., 126, 127, *139*
Heath, H. E., 126, 127, *139*
Heavey, C. L., 216, *228*
Hebbeler, K. M., 352, 357, 358, 366, *370*
Heinicke, C. M., 212, *230,* 353, 367, *370*
Heiss, J., 118, *139*
Helms-Erikson, H., 289, 290, 291, 293, *294*
Heming, G., 205, *228*
Hemphill, S. A., 161, *175*
Henderson, C., Jr., 239, 240, 241, 243, 252, 254, *271*
Henderson, C. R., 349, 355, 362, 363, 366, *371, 372*
Henderson, C. R., Jr., 393, *400*
Hernandez, D. J., 275, 287, *295*
Hernandez, F., 352, 357, *373*
Hertzig, M. E., 149, 150, *176*
Herz, E. J., 89, *100*
Herzog, A., 14, *29*
Hesketh, L. J., 185, *198*
Hess, C. R., 92, *99*
Hess, R. D., 5, 9, *31,* 367, *370*
Hesse, E., 49, *66, 67*
Hetherington, E. M., 57, *68,* 148, 159, 163, 166, *172, 173, 174,* 222, *229,* 297, *315,* 379, 387, 388, *399*
Hewitt, J. K., 51, *64*
Hewlett, B. S., 106, 116, *139*
Hiatt, S., 356, *371*
Hickok, G., 185, 190, *197*
Hildebrandt, K. A., 154, 168, *173, 175*
Hill, J., 22, *32,* 46, 47, *68*
Hill, N. E., 335, *339*
Hillenmeier, M., 83, *98*
Hiller, K. A., 10, *32*
Hinde, R., 256, *272*
Hipwell, A. E., 37, *66*
Hiraga, Y., 304, *317*
Ho, D. Y. F., 12, *31*
Hochschild, A., 127, *139*
Hodapp, R. M., 178, 181, 182, 185, 186, 187, 188, 189, 190, 192, 193, 194, 195, 196, *198, 199, 200*
Hodges, J., 379, 388, *400, 401*
Hoeksma, J. B., 162, *176*
Hoff, E., 11, *31,* 321, 327, 329, *339*

Hofferth, S. L., 107, 108, 109, 114, 119, 121, 122, *139, 143, 144*
Hoffman, L. W., 328, 335, *339*
Holden, G. W., 3, 4, 5, 7, 17, 24, 25, *30, 31,* 155, *173,* 213, 227
Hollingshead, A. B., 320, *339*
Hollon, S. D., 51, *69*
Holman, J., 117, *137*
Holroyd, R. M., 186, *199*
Hommerding, K. D., 58, *70*
Hooper, F. H., 106, *143*
Hooven, C., 131, *138*
Hopkins, J., 212, *229*
Hoppes, K., 187, *199*
Hornby, G., 185, 189, *199*
Hossain, T., 121, *139*
Hotz, V. J., 75, 76, 77, 78, *99*
Howard, J., 37, *61*
Howes, P., 216, *230*
Hsieh, K., 223, *227*
Hsu, H., 265, *272*
Hubbs-Tait, L., 86, *99*
Huesmann, R. L., 117, 118, *138*
Hughes, C., 148, *172*
Hughes, J. P., 188, *200*
Hughes, S., 89, *98*
Hunsberger, B., 4, 7, *29*
Hunter, J. E., 53, *67*
Hurlbut, N., 86, *99*
Hurrelmann, K., 323, *339*
Huston, T., 126, *141*
Huston, T. L., 225, *231*
Hwang, C. P., 106, *140*
Hyde, B. L., 118, *139*
Hyde, J., 284, *294*
Hyde, J. S., 284, *295*
Hyman, C., 75, *100*

I

Iacono, W. G., 157, *172,* 382, *400*
Ianni, F. A., 314, *316*
Iannotti, R. J., 206, 207, *229*
Imamoglu, E. O., 329, 335, *339*
Irvin, N., 181, *198*
Irwin, N., 358, *373*
Ishii-Kuntz, M., 124, *139*
Isley, S., 131, *139*
Israelashvilli, R., 41, 42, *67*
Iverson, T. J., 17, *31*

J

Jacklin, C. N., 36, *66*, 166, *174*
Jacob, R., 306, 307, 308, *317*
Jacobs, J. A., 290, *295*
Jacobson, L., 75, *98*
Jacobvitz, D., 51, 54, 56, 57, *65, 67*
Jacoby, T., 214, *233*
Jaffee, S., 75, 80, 81, 82, 83, 84, 85, *99*
Jain, A., 120, *139*, 163, *173*
Jambunathan, S., 4, *31*, 86, *99*
Janiszewski, S., 37, *64*
Jankowiak, W., 124, 125, *139*
Jaycox, L., 50, *65*
Jenkins, E. J., 300, 302, *315*
Jenkins, J. M., 160, 166, 167, *173*
Jennings, K. D., 258, *272*
Jernigan, T., 185, 190, *197*
Joe, J., 6, *31*
John, O. P., 38, *66*
John, R. S., 207, 210, 213, 216, 219, 220, 221, 223, *228, 230, 231*
Johnson, D., 220, *231*
Johnson, J. H., 164, *175*
Johnson, V. K., 217, 218, 224, *228, 231*
Johnston, C., 44, *66*, 161, *174*, 214, *228*
Johnston, F. H., 185, 188, 189, *201*
Jokielek, S. M., 115, *137*
Juang, L., 348, 360, *371*
Juffer, F., 59, *70*, 350, 358, *369*
Juhasz, C., 389, *399*
Jump, V. K., 360, *372*

K

Kaban, B., 107, *143*
Kagitcibasi, C., 329, 332, 333, 334, 335, *340*
Kahn, J. R., 75, *99*
Kaleva, M., 50, *69*
Kalil, A., 79, *99*
Kanter, R. M., 277, *295*
Kapp, S., 267, *272*
Karney, B. R., 210, 214, *231*
Karraker, K. H., 15, 19, *29*, 156, 159, 164, 167, *172, 173, 175*
Kasari, C., 186, 189, *198, 199, 200*
Katz, L., 131, *138*
Katz, L. F., 218, 220, 221, *231*, 306, 307, 308, *317*
Katzev, A. R., 364, *371*

Kauffman, J. M., 177, 183, *199*
Kaufman, J., 53, *66*
Kawaguchi, M. C., 165, *173*
Kawai, H., 124, *143*
Keaveney, L., 378, 379, 388, *400*
Keefe, N., 266, *272*
Keith, B., 114, *144*
Kelleher, K. J., 324, *338*
Keller, H., 331, 333, 334, *339*
Kelley, M. L., 113, 114, *136*
Kemp-Fincham, S. I., 209, *230*
Kengler, K. S., 46, *66*
Kennell, J., 181, *198*
Keogh, B. K., 191, *200*
Keogh, D., 79, 80, 81, 82, 84, 86, 89, 90, 91, *101*
Keough, K., 26, *28*
Kerig, P. K., 213, 216, 218, *231*
Kerr, M., 51, *69*, 289, *295*, 296, 305, *316*
Kessler, R. C., 46, *66*, 75, *99*, 285, 286, *294*
Kestenbaum, R., 41, 58, *67*, 162, *174*
Key, J. P., 80, 81, 87, *99*
Khounani, P. M., 332, *340*
Killen, M., 330, *340*
Killian, C., 132, *142*
Kim, H. K., 45, *66*
Kim, K., 125, *136*
Kim, K. J., 38, *66*
Kim, M., 132, 133, *141, 142*
Kim, S., 40, *62*
Kim-Cohen, J., 53, *66*
King, L., 225, *233*
Kingston, L., 162, *173*
Kinlaw, C. R., 14, *31*
Kirisci, L., 37, *64*
Kirsh, S. J., 56, *63*
Kisker, E. E., 348, 350, 354, 361, 365, 368, *370, 371*
Kitayama, S., 329, *340*
Kitzman, H., 351, 355, 358, 360, 363, 367, *371*, 393, *400*
Kitzman, H. J., 346, 357, 362, 363, *370, 371*
Kitzmann, K. M., 215, 216, 220, *231*
Klaus, M., 181, *198*
Klebanov, P. K., 93, *98*, 299, *316*
Klein, M. H., 284, *294, 295*
Klepinger, D. H., 76, *99*
Kline, M., 276, *295*
Kling, J. R., 306, 307, 308, *317*
Klocke, A., 323, *339*
Kneppers, K., 57, *70*

Knight, G., 117, *139*
Knight, R., 332, *339*
Knoester, C., 128, *138*
Kobak, R., 49, *66*
Kobak, R. R., 45, *63*
Kochanska, G., 17, *31,* 42, 43, *63, 66,* 162, 163, 165, *172,* 390, *400*
Koestner, R., 131, *139*
Kohn, M., 115, *139*
Kohn, M. L., 10, *31, 32,* 277, 278, 279, *295,* 329, 335, *340*
Kohnstamm, G. A., 151, *176*
Komarovsky, M., 275, *295*
Koops, W., 52, *68*
Korenman, S., 77, 78, 83, *98*
Korfmacher, J., 344, 351, 355, 356, 358, 360, 363, 366, 367, *371*
Korn, S., 149, 150, *176*
Kostelny, K., 300, 301, 302, 303, *316*
Kotelchuck, M., 104, *140*
Kouneski, E. F., 110, *138*
Kovacs, M., 75, *99*
Kowal, A., 148, *173*
Kowaleski-Jones, L., 303, 304, *316*
Kraemer, H. C., 351, 363, *369*
Kramer, E., 39, *71*
Kramer, L., 8, 19, *32,* 148, *173*
Krauss, M., 182, *200*
Krauss, M. W., 182, 187, *198, 201*
Kreppner, J. M., 378, 379, 388, *400*
Krieger, H., 110, *138*
Krishnakumar, A., 206, 207, 211, 212, 213, *228, 231*
Krohn, M. D., 304, *318*
Krol, R. M., 75, *99*
Kroll, A. B., 225, *232*
Kromelow, S., 58, *70*
Kropp, F., 11, *32*
Kropp, J., 40, *64*
Krupnick, J. L., 47, *66*
Kubisch, A. C., 346, *369*
Kucera, E., 58, *69*
Kuczynski, L., 17, 18, *30, 31*
Kuersten, R., 225, 226, *231*
Kuersten-Hogan, R., 220, *232*
Kumar, R., 37, *66*
Kunz, J., 79, *99*
Kurdek, L. A., 212, *231*
Kurtz-Costes, B., 14, *31*
Kusserow, A. S., 324, 329, 330, 331, *340*
Kwak, K., 331, 334, *340*

L

Ladd, G. W., 265, 272, 386, *400*
Lagace-Seguin, D. G., 20, *29*
Lahey, B., 40, *64*
Lahti, I., 50, *69*
Laible, D. J., 56, *66*
Laird, R. D., 305, *316*
Lakatos, K., 57, *66*
Lake, M. A., 156, 167, *173*
Lakin, C., 177, *200*
Lakin, K. C., 177, *197*
Lam, M., 334, *339*
Lamb, M. E., 52, *67,* 103, 105, 106, 107, 116, 118, 130, 131, *140, 143,* 332, 333, 336, *340,* 345, *371*
Lamborn, S. D., 6, *33,* 118, *140*
Lancaster, J., 303, *316*
Land, D., 298, *315*
Landry, S. H., 247, *273*
Lang, M. E., 205, *227*
Lang, S., 41, 58, *67,* 162, *174*
Langbehn, D., 50, *62*
Langlois, J. H., 168, *173*
Lansford, J. E., 52, *64,* 212, *233*
Larner, M., 239, 240, 241, 243, 252, 254, *271, 272*
Larrance, D. T., 214, *231*
Larson, R., 109, *140,* 285, 286, *295*
Larson, R. W., 285, *295*
Lasky, K., 50, *69*
Laub, J. H., 47, *66*
Lauretti, A., 219, 220, 225, 226, *231, 232*
Laursen, B., 11, *31,* 321, 327, 329, *339*
LaVange, L. M., 358, 359, 361, *372*
Lawrence, E., 225, *227*
Layzer, J. I., 346, 350, 354, *371, 372*
Leadbeater, B., 78, 80, 85, 93, *99*
Leadbeater, B. J., 89, *99*
Leckman, J. F., 185, *198*
Ledbetter, J. E., 26, *30*
Lee, B. J., 84, *98*
Lee, C. D., 325, 326, *340*
Lee, D. Y., 384, *399*
Lee, S., 9, 12, *33*
Leffert, N., 308, 309, 310, *317*
Lehmann, N., 298, *316*
Leiderman, P. H., 6, *30*
Lejeune, J., 178, *200*
LeMare, L. J., 165, *175*
Leonard, K. E., 37, *65*

Lerman, R., 118, *140*
Lerner, J. V., 92, *99*, 158, *173*
Levant, R. F., 113, 114, *136*
Leve, L. D., 164, *173*
Leventhal, T., 297, 303, 306, *316, 317*
Levin, H., 131, *143,* 149, *175*
Levine, J., 81, 82, 85, *99*
Levine, J. A., 106, 107, 127, *140*
Levine, M., 125, *136*
LeVine, R., 322, *341*
LeVine, R. A., 10, *31,* 379, *400*
Levy, F., 395, *400*
Levy-Shiff, R., 41, 42, *67*
Lewinsohn, P. M., 46, 50, *63, 65*
Lewis, C. E., 207, *231*
Lewis, I., 359, *372*
Lewis, M., 58, *67*
Lewis, M. A., 207, *231*
Lewkowicz, K. S., 106, *143*
Leyendecker, B., 11, *30, 32,* 324, 325, 326, 332, 333, 336, *339, 340, 341*
Li, M., 110, 111, 112, *138*
Liaw, F., 359, 361, *371*
Lichtenstein, P., 52, *65*
Lieberman, A. F., 53, 59, *67,* 360, *371*
Liebman, J. B., 306, 307, 308, *317*
Liker, J. K., 54, *65*
Lindahl, K. M., 212, 216, 218, *231*
Linder, C. W., 303, *316*
Lindsay, L. L., 216, *229*
Linfield, K. J., 209, *230*
Linn, M. I., 352, 357, *373*
Lipovsky, J. A., 53, *66*
Little, C., 37, *62*
Lobato, D., 180, *200*
Lobel, M., 47, *63*
Lochman, J., 75, *100*
Locke, H. J., 209, *231*
Loeber, R., 51, *64*
Loehlin, J. C., 157, *174,* 382, 383, *400*
Lollis, S., 165, *175*
Long, N., 207, 208, 213, *229*
Longfellow, C., 40, *67*
Longo, L. C., 26, *30*
Lonigan, C. J., 349, *369,* 393, 397, *401*
Lopez, I. R., 47, *64*
Lopez, M., 11, *33*
Lorenz, F., 40, 54, *63*
Lorenz, F. O., 38, *66,* 237, *272*
Losel, F., 310, *317*
Losoya, S., 41, 42, 43, *67*

Love, J. M., 348, 350, 354, 361, 365, 368, *370, 371*
Lovejoy, J., 106, *140*
Lowe, R., 225, *230*
Lucca, N., 9, *33*
Luckey, D., 393, *400*
Luckey, D. W., 349, 355, 366, *372*
Luker, K., 75, *99*
Lundberg, S., 76, *99*
Luria, Z., 156, 167, *175,* 380, *401*
Luster, T., xi, xiii, *xv,* 75, 80, 81, 82, 87, 89, 90, 91, 92, 93, 94, 96, 97, *97, 98, 99, 100, 101,* 280, 292, *295,* 348, 360, *371*
Lustina, M. J., 26, *28*
Ly, T. M., 187, 188, 189, 190, 193, *199, 200*
Lykken, D. T., 382, *398, 400*
Lynd, H. M., 275, *295*
Lynd, R. S., 275, *295*
Lyons-Ruth, K., 51, 56, 57, *67,* 363, *371*
Lytton, H., 154, 167, *171, 173*

M

Maarala, M., 50, *69*
MacArthur, D., 186, *199*
Maccoby, E. E., 106, 131, *140, 143,* 149, 166, 167, *174, 175,* 297, *315,* 327, 328, *340,* 379, 387, 388, *399*
MacDonald, K., 105, 132, *140*
Machamer, A. M., 6, *31*
MacKinnon-Lewis, C., 43, 52, *67*
MacPhee, D., 245, 260, *272*
Madden, T., 336, *341*
Maes, H. H., 51, *64*
Magnuson, K. A., 321, 323, 324, 335, *338, 340*
Magnusson, D., 52, *69*
Maguire, M. C., 115, *137,* 287, *294*
Magyary, D., 348, *369*
Main, M., 49, *66, 67*
Maital, S., 5, 8, 9, *28*
Makhijani, M. G., 26, *30*
Malach, R. S., 6, *31*
Malik, N. M., 216, 218, *231*
Malphurs, J. E., 121, *139*
Mammone, N., 156, *173*
Mandara, J., 118, 120, *140*
Manetti, M., 242, 265, *272*
Mangan, T. W., 177, *197*

Mangelsdorf, S., 39, 41, 58, *64, 65, 67,* 162, *174,* 220, *230*
Mangelsdorf, S. C., 220, 222, *232*
Manke, B., 293, *294*
Manlove, J., 73, 75, *100, 101*
Manly, J. T., 59, *70*
Mansbach, I. V., 11, *31*
Mantizicopoulos, P. Y., 15, *32*
Marakovitz, S., 51, *62*
Marcoen, A., 56, *70*
Margolin, G., 207, 210, 213, 216, 219, 220, 221, 223, 224, *228, 230, 231*
Markel, K. S., 116, *138*
Markman, H., 212, 218, *231*
Markman, H. J., 216, *230*
Marks, L. D., 18, *32*
Marks, S. R., 282, *295*
Markus, H. R., 329, *340*
Marshall, L. A., 4, 24, *31*
Marshall, N., 266, *272*
Marsiglio, W., 110, 130, 131, *140*
Martin, J., 394, *398*
Martin, J. A., 327, 328, *340*
Martinez, P. E., 302, *317*
Marx, F., 266, *272*
Masciadrelli, B. P., 108, 109, 112, 114, 126, 128, 130, 131, *142*
Mash, E. J., 161, *174*
Mason, C. A., 304, *317*
Mason, P. L., 118, *140*
Masten, A. S., 163, *174*
Matheson, P., 113, *137*
Maughan, A., 59, *70*
Maughan, B., 46, *68*
Maumary-Gremaud, A., 75, *100*
Maxwell, J. A., 117, *140*
Maxwell, S., 90, *101*
Maynard, A., 331, 333, 334, *339*
McAdoo, H., 81, *100*
McAdoo, H. P., 379, *400*
McAdoo, J. L., 118, 119, *140*
McAllister, R. A., 20, *29*
McAnarney, E. R., 94, *101*
McBride, B. A., 112, 126, *140, 142,* 161, 163, *174*
McBride Murry, V., 304, 306, *315*
McCarthy, J., 40, *64*
McCartney, K., 157, *175,* 266, *272,* 350, *371, 372,* 382, *400*
McClay, J., 394, *398*
McClelland, D., 132, *138*
McCrae, R. R., 39, *64*

McCullough, M., 84, *100*
McDermid, S. M., 126, *141*
McDevitt, S. C., 170, *175*
McDevitt, T. M., 5, 9, *31*
McDowell, D. J., 132, 133, *141, 142*
McElroy, S. W., 75, 76, 77, 78, *99*
McFadyen-Ketchum, S. A., 18, *32,* 43, 52, *68*
McFarlane, E., 364, 369, *370*
McGillicuddy-De Lisi, A. V., 3, 4, 14, 15, 22, *32, 33*
McGroder, S. M., 37, *67*
McGue, M., 157, *172, 174,* 382, *398, 400*
McGuigan, W. M., 364, *371*
McGuire, S., 148, 159, *174*
McHale, J., 220, *230*
McHale, J. P., 219, 220, 221, 225, 226, *231, 232*
McHale, S., 126, *141*
McHale, S. M., 115, *137,* 148, 160, *172, 174,* 275, 287, 289, 290, 291, 293, *294*
McKee, T. R., 132, *139*
McKeering, H., 128, *141*
Mckenry, P. C., 45, *66*
McKinney, M., 348, 360, *371*
McLanahan, S., 107, *138,* 253, *272*
McLanahan, S. S., 47, *68,* 129, 130, *138, 141*
McLoyd, V., 92, *100,* 263, *271,* 319, 320, 323, 324, *340*
McLoyd, V. C., 114, *137,* 306, 311, *315*
McMahon, R., 95, *101*
McMahon, R. J., 304, 305, *315*
McNeilly-Choque, M. K., 131, 132, *139*
McNichol, K., 163, *175*
McWilliam, R., 351, *373*
Meany, M. J., 106, *141*
Measelle, J., 224, *228*
Meens, L. D., 209, *232*
Mehrabian, A., 47, *62*
Meisels, S. J., 359, 361, *371*
Melby, J., 54, *63*
Melhuish, E. C., 37, *66*
Melson, G. F., 265, *272*
Melzer, W., 323, *339*
Menaghan, E. G., 114, 115, *137, 141,* 275, 279, 280, 288, 291, 293, *295, 296*
Mendell, N. R., 45, *68*
Merrick, S., 58, *70*
Mervis, C. B., 185, 190, *200*
Meyer, D., 107, *138*

Meyer, J. M., 51, *64*
Meyers, B. A., 189, *200*
Meyers, C. E., 18, *28*
Meyers, J., 75, *101*
Mezzich, A., 37, *64*
Mill, J., 394, *398*
Miller, A. M., 325, 326, 332, 333, *339*
Miller, B. C., 75, 76, *100*
Miller, D. D., 278, *296*
Miller, J., 10, *32,* 185, *200*
Miller, L. S., 50, *67*
Miller, P. C., 5, 7, 17, *30, 31*
Miller, P. J., 330, 337, *340*
Miller, P. M., 322, *341*
Miller, S. A., 15, *32*
Miller-Heyl, J., 245, 260, *272*
Miller-Johnson, S., 75, *100*
Miller-Loncar, C. L., 247, *273*
Mills, D., 185, 190, *197*
Milner, J. S., 53, *67*
Minton, H. L., 187, *201*
Minuchin, S., 297, *317*
Miranda, J., 50, *67*
Mirandé, A., 121, 122, 123, *141*
Mishel, L., 114, *141*
Mitchell, J. C., 236, 238, 251, *271, 272*
Mitchell, S. K., 348, 356, 363, *369*
Miwa, S., 124, *141*
Mize, J., 132, *141*
Moffitt, T. E., 53, *66,* 75, 80, 81, 82, 83, 84,
    85, *99,* 394, 395, *398, 399*
Moffitt, T. W., 46, 52, *61*
Monshouwer, H. J., 52, *68*
Montemayer, R., 109, *141*
Moore, G., 51, 58, *61, 62*
Moore, K., 80, 81, 82, 84, *100*
Moore, K. A., 75, 76, *100*
Moore, M., 80, 85, *100*
Moran, G., 57, *70*
Morelli, G., 332, 333, *340*
Morenoff, J. D., 306, *317*
Morgan, J., 395, *399*
Morgan, K. M., 94, *97*
Morgan, S., 78, 80, 81, 82, 85, *98*
Morgan, S. B., 186, 187, *200*
Moring, J., 50, *69*
Morison, S. J., 388, *399*
Morris, A. S., 162, *174*
Morris, C. A., 185, 190, *200*
Morris, P., 150, *172,* 393, *400*
Morris, P. A., 377, 378, 384, *398*
Morrison, D., 80, 81, 82, 84, *100*

Morrison, D. R., 75, 76, *100*
Mosley, J., 131, *141*
Mosteller, F., 349, *371*
Mott, F. L., 107, *141*
Moulton, C. E., 20, *29*
Mounts, N. S., 6, *33,* 281, *296*
Mowbray, C. T., 258, *272*
Moyer, J., 47, *66*
Muller, B., 58, *68*
Muller, R. T., 53, *67*
Mulligan, G. M., 131, *135*
Mullins, M. J., 20, *29*
Mulsow, M., 161, *174*
Mundform, D. J., 324, *338*
Mundy, P., 189, *199, 200*
Muñoz, R. F., 50, *67*
Murphy, M., 50, *63*
Murray, C. B., 118, 120, *140*
Murray, L., 37, *67*
Murray, R., 178, *200*
Murry, V., 40, *62*
Musick, J. S., 75, 76, *100,* 358, *371*
Musun-Miller, L., 15, *32*
Muzik, O., 389, *399*

N

Nagel, S. K., 11, *30,* 115, *139*
Nagin, D., 82, *100*
Nagin, D. S., 47, *66*
Nagy, F., 389, *399*
Nauta, M., 358, *373*
Neale, M., 50, *69*
Neale, M. C., 51, *64*
Neiderhiser, J. M., 36, 57, *68,* 157, *176,*
    383, *400*
Neisser, U., 382, *400*
Neitzel, C., 221, 222, *233*
Nelson, D. A., 131, 132, *139*
Nelson, G. M., 214, *227*
Nelson, L. J., 18, 19, *32,* 164, *175*
Nemoda, Z., 57, *66*
New, R., 106, *141*
Newby, K., 51, *62*
Ney, K., 57, *66*
Nguyen, T. V., 54, *65*
Nievar, M. A., 93, 94, *99*
Nihira, K., 18, *28*
Nix, R. L., 18, *32,* 43, 52, *68*
Noh, S., 187, 188, *200, 201*

Noller, P., 209, *229*
Noonan, A., 266, *272*
Norton, R., 209, *232*
Notaro, P. C., 131, *144*
Nucci, L., 330, *340*
Nunez, N. N., 9, *29*

O

Oberklaid, F., 166, *175*
Obiorah, F. C., 209, *232*
O'Brien, M., 17, 22, *29*, 80, *98*, 226, *232*
O'Brien, R., 349, 355, 356, 366, *371, 372*
O'Connell, M., 108, *141*
O'Connor, C., 388, *400*
O'Connor, T. G., 148, 151, 152, 153, 154, 159, 160, 166, 167, 169, 170, *171, 172, 173, 174,* 378, 379, 388, 389, *400*
Ogaki, L., xiii, *xv*
Ogbu, J. U., 10, *32*, 277, 278, *296*, 379, *400*
Ogino, M., 5, 8, 9, *28*
Okagaki, L., 3, 5, 6, 9, 12, 13, 22, *32*, 97, *100,* 155, *174,* 194, *200,* 292, *295,* 357, *372*
Olds, D., 346, 351, 356, 357, 358, 360, 363, 367, *370, 371,* 393, *400*
Olds, D. L., 349, 355, 362, 363, 366, *371, 372*
O'Leary, D. A., 45, *68*
O'Leary, K. D., 45, *61,* 213, 224, *232*
O'Leary, S., 44, *69,* 213, 214, *232, 233*
O'Leary, S. G., 20, 22, *33*
Olsen, C. L., 188, *200*
Olsen, S. F., 131, 132, *139*
Olshanksy, S., 182, *200*
Olson, D. R., 345, *372*
Oltmanns, T. F., 224, *232*
O'Neal, C., 344, *369*
O'Neil, R., 11, *30,* 107, 115, 127, 131, 132, 133, *138, 139, 141, 142,* 282, 283, *295*
Ong, A., 336, *341*
Ontai, L., 47, 59, *69*
Ooms, T., 118, *140*
Oppenheimer, D., 332, 333, *340*
O'Reilly, A. W., 104, 113, *137*
Orobio de Castro, B., 52, *68*
Orr, L., 306, 307, 308, *317*
Orsmond, G. I., 187, 188, *200*

Osborne, L. N., 207, 212, 213, 214, 216, *230, 232*
O'Shea, G., 49, *65*
Osofsky, J., 80, 86, *98, 99,* 300, 302, *317*
Osofsky, J. D., 79, *100*
Ossiander, E., 95, *101*
Otaki, M., 113, *138*
Overstreet, E. J., 267, *272*
Owen, M. T., 58, *64,* 206, *232*
Owens, E. B., 56, *70*

P

Pachter, L. M., 326, 327, 335, *339*
Paff-Bergen, L. A., 209, *232*
Painter, L. M., 5, 8, 9, *28*
Pakenham, K. I., 128, *141*
Paley, B., 104, *137,* 211, *228*
Palkovitz, R., 107, 128, *137, 141*
Pancoast, D., 298, *315*
Panzarine, S., 89, *100*
Papas, M. A., 92, *99*
Papillo, A. R., 75, *100*
Papoušek, H., 9, *32*
Papoušek, M., 9, *32*
Parcel, J. L., 114, *141*
Parcel, T. L., 279, 280, 288, 291, 293, *296*
Pardo, C., 300, 302, 303, *316*
Park, S., 162, *171, 174*
Parke, R. D, 56, *63*
Parke, R. D., 25, *30,* 103, 104, 105, 106, 107, 110, 112, 113, 116, 117, 121, 122, 125, 127, 130, 131, 132, 133, 134, 135, *136, 137, 139, 140, 141, 142*
Pasch, L. A., 225, 226, *232*
Pascual, L., 5, 8, 9, *28*
Patenaude, R., 44, *66*
Paternoster, R., 305, *317*
Patterson, G., 40, *64,* 305, *317*
Patterson, G. R., 51, *68,* 150, 151, 154, 160, *174,* 304, *317,* 381, *399*
Paulsell, D., 348, 350, 354, 361, 365, 368, *370, 371*
Pawl, J., 59, *67*
Pawl, J. H., 59, *67,* 360, *371*
Pawletko, T. M., 148, *174*
Payne, C., 47, *62,* 242, 255, *271*
Payne, C. K., 282, 283, *295*
Payne, M. R., 346, 365, *370*

Pearl, R., 14, *29*
Pedersen, F., 39, *71*
Pedersen, F. A., 113, *142*
Pederson, D., 57, *70*
Peebles, C., 79, *100*
Pendergrast, R. A., 303, *316*
Penner, W., 309, *317*
Perez-Stable, E. J., 50, *67*
Perloff, R., 382, *400*
Perlstadt, H., 348, 360, *371*
Perozynski, L., 8, 19, *32*
Perry, B. D., 378, 389, *400*
Perry-Jenkins, M., 114, 115, *139, 142,* 286, 296
Peters-Martin, P., 166, *174*
Peterson, A. C., 46, *68*
Peterson, E., 85, *99*
Petrill, S. A., 148, *172*
Pettit, G. S., 18, *32,* 43, 52, *64, 68,* 132, *141,* 303, 304, 305, 306, *315, 316*
Pettitt, L., 393, *400*
Pettitt, L. M., 349, 355, 366, *372*
Peyton, V., 17, 22, *29,* 226, *232*
Pezzullo, J. C., 185, *200*
Pfannenstiel, J. C., 311, *317,* 360, *372*
Pfluger-Schindlbeck, I., 332, *341*
Philliber, S., 346, *372*
Phinney, J. S., 325, 336, *341*
Pickens, J., 121, *139*
Pickles, A., 46, 51, *64, 68,* 178, *200*
Pierce, E. W., 51, *62*
Pierce, S., 4, *31*
Pike, A., 148, 159, *172, 174*
Pilkonis, P. A., 47, *66*
Pinderhughes, E., 112, *136*
Pinderhughes, E. E., 18, *32,* 43, 52, *68*
Pine, C. J., 9, *30*
Pitcairn, T. K., 189, *200*
Pittinsky, T. L., 127, *140*
Plassman, B. L., 395, *400*
Pleck, J., 107, *140*
Pleck, J. H., 106, 108, 109, 112, 114, 126, 128, 130, 131, *140, 142*
Plomin, R., 51, 57, *64, 65, 68,* 148, 151, 156, 157, 159, 161, 166, *172, 174, 175,* 381, 382, 395, *399, 400*
Plotnick, R. D., 76, *99*
Poe-Yamagata, E., 300, 302, 306, *318*
Pogarsky, G., 82, *100*
Polansky, N., 256, 257, *272*
Pollack, B., 106, *143*
Pollack, H., 81, 82, 85, *99*

Ponce, V. A., 353, 367, *370*
Pope, S. K., 324, *338*
Porter, C. L., 132, *139*
Poulton, R., 394, *398*
Pouquette, C., 219, *232*
Powell, C., 361, *372*
Powell, D., 357, *372*
Powell, D. R., 344, 345, 346, 352, 353, 357, 363, *370, 372*
Power, T. G., 104, 105, 113, *142*
Powers, J., 117, *142,* 393, *400*
Powers, S. I., 165, *173*
Pratt, C. C., 364, *371*
Pratt, M., 4, 7, *29*
Price, C., 350, 354, *371*
Price, J. M., 52, *64*
Price, R. H., 309, *317*
Price-Bonham, S., 182, *200*
Prior, M., 162, 166, *173, 175*
Prost, J. H., 117, *139*
Prouty, B., 177, *200*
Prouty, R. W., 177, *197*
Provenzano, F. J., 156, 167, *175,* 380, *401*
Pueschel, S. M., 189, *200*
Pueschel, S. R., 185, *200*
Pursley, M., 161, *174*
Putnam, S., 162, *174,* 220, *227*
Putnam, S. P., 161, 163, 167, 168, 170, *175*

Q

Quinn, D. M., 26, *33*
Quinn, N., 325, *341*
Quinton, D., 46, 47, 54, *68,* 94, *100,* 237, 272
Quinton, R. L., 111, *143*

R

Radin, N., 107, 123, *142, 144*
Radin Fox, C. E., 161, *173*
Radke-Yarrow, M., 17, *31,* 37, *68,* 207, *229*
Raikes, H., 368, *370*
Ramey, C. T., 358, 359, 361, *372*
Ramsey, E., 304, *317*
Rane, T. R., 112, *142,* 161, 163, *174*
Rasbash, J., 160, 166, 167, *173*
Rasmussen, J. L., 219, 220, 221, *232*
Rauch-Elnekave, H., 75, *100*

Raudenbush, S. W., 306, 309, *317*
Rauh, H., 58, *68*
Ravens-Sieberer, U., 323, *339*
Raver, C. C., 89, *99*
Raymond-Smith, L., 47, *64*
Ready, R., 42, 43, *63*, 162, 165, *172*
Reichman, N. E., 47, *68*
Reid, M. J., 349, 350, 351, 362, 364, *369, 372, 373*
Reid, W. J., 208, 216, *232*
Reifman, A., 161, *174*
Reis, H. T., 226, *232*
Reis, J. S., 89, *100*
Reiss, D., 36, 57, *68, 159, 174*, 383, *400*
Reivich, K., 50, *65*
Reivich, K. J., 50, *62*
Rende, R., 51, *65*
Repetti, R., 115, *142*, 225, *232*
Repetti, R. L., 114, 115, *142*, 283, 285, 286, *296*
Reynolds, C. A., 51, *64*
Rha, J., 162, *171*
Rhoades, K., 89, *100*, 280, *295*
Rhodes, J., 39, *64*
Ricci, L. A., 187, 188, 189, *199*
Richards, M., 109, *140*, 285, 286, *295*
Richards, M. P. M., 104, *142*
Richards, P., 113, *138*
Richman, A., 322, *341*
Richters, J. E., 302, *317*
Ridge, B., 18, *28*, 162, *171*
Rie, H., 180, *198*
Riksen-Walraven, J. M., 37, *70*, 163, *176*
Riley, D., 239, 240, 241, 243, 252, 254, 261, *271, 272*
Riley, D. A., 268, *272*
Ritter, J. M., 168, *173*
Ritter, P. L., 6, *30*
Rivera, F., 130, 131, *136*
Rivera-Mosquera, E. T., 47, *64*
Roach, M. A., 94, *97*, 187, 188, *200*
Roberts, D. F., 6, *30*
Robins, L. N., 46, *68*
Robinson, B. F., 185, 190, *200*
Robinson, C. C., 131, 132, *139*
Robinson, J., 108, *143*, 349, 355, 366, 367, *370, 372*
Rodgers, J. L., 76, *100*
Roethlisberger, F., 282, *296*
Rogers, K., 75, *101*
Rogers, S. L., 114, *144*
Rogge, R., 225, *227*

Roggman, L. A., 360, *372*
Rogoff, B., 116, *143*, 326, 332, 333, *340, 341*
Rogosch, F. A., 59, *63*, 258, *272*
Rohde, C., 364, 369, *370*
Rohner, R. P., 131, *143*
Romney, D. M., 154, 167, *171, 173*
Roopnarine, J. C., 106, *143*
Roopnarine, J. L., 106, 124, *143*
Roosa, M. W., 335, *339*
Roschelle, A., 245, 246, 247, 248, 251, *272*
Rose, G. M., 11, *32*
Rosenblatt, J., 110, 111, *143*
Rosenblum, T., 384, *399*
Rosenthal, R., 350, *371*
Rosenthal, S., 58, *67*
Ross, C. M., 348, 350, 354, 361, 365, *371*
Rostosky, S. S., 165, *173*
Roth, A., 345, *372*
Rothbart, M. K., 161, 163, 167, 168, 170, *175*
Rothstein, K., 47, *64*
Rovine, M., 113, 125, *136*, 205, 210, 215, 216, *227*
Rowe, D., xiv, *xv*, 41, 42, 43, *67*, 379, 380, *401*
Rowe, D. C., 76, *100*
Rubin, J. Z., 156, 167, *175*, 380, *401*
Rubin, K. H., 5, 7, 18, 19, *29, 32*, 159, 162, 163, 164, 165, *172, 175*
Ruble, D., 43, *64*, 110, *138*
Rueter, M. A., 225, *228*
Rush, A. J., 186, *197*
Ruskin, E. M., 189, *200*
Russell, A., 18, *32*, 105, 109, *137, 143*
Russell, G., 105, 109, *143*
Rutter, M., 46, 47, 49, 50, 51, 54, *63, 64, 68, 69*, 94, *100*, 157, *175*, 178, *200*, 222, *232*, 237, *272*, 378, 379, 383, 386, 388, 395, *399, 400, 401*
Ryan, R. M., 333, *341*
Ryan, S., 75, *100*
Rymond-Richmond, W., 303, *317*

S

Saarento, O., 50, *69*
Saenz, D., 117, *142*
Sagi, A., 106, *143*
St. Pierre, R. G., 346, *372*

Saitzyk, A. R., 225, *232*
Saken, J. W., 58, *69*
Salem, D. A., 131, *144*
Sameroff, A., 149, *175*, 297, 302, 303, 304, *316*
Sampson, R. J., 47, *66*, 306, 309, *317*
Sanbonmatsu, L., 306, 307, 308, *317*
Sandberg, J. F., 107, 108, 109, 114, 121, *143, 144*
Sandefur, G., 129, *141*
Sanders, J. L., 186, 187, *200*
Sanders, M. R., 224, *229*
Sanders, S. G., 75, 76, 77, 78, *99*
Sanson, A., 161, 166, *175*
Sanson, A. V., 161, 163, 167, 168, 170, *175*
Sarason, B. R., 46, 47, *69*
Sarason, I. G., 46, 47, *69*
Sasvari-Szekely, M., 57, *66*
Saunders, B. E., 53, *66*
Saunders, E., 40, *67*
Saunders, W. B., 75, *99*
Sawin, D. B., 168, *173*
Scales, P., 308, 309, 310, *317*
Scales, P. C., 308, *317*
Scaramella, L. V., 164, *173*
Scarr, S., xiv, *xv*, 151, 157, *175*, 350, *372*, 379, 380, 381, *401*
Schaie, K. W., 280, *295*
Scheerenberger, R. C., 178, *201*
Scheinfeld, D., 304, *317*
Scheldt, S., 225, *230*
Schellenbach, C., 90, *101*
Schellenbach, C. J., 88, 89, *100*
Scherman, A., 84, *100*
Schiff, M., 384, 385, *401*
Schmitt, J., 114, *141*
Schneewind, K., 44, *65*
Schneider, B. H., 56, *69*, 242, 265, *272*
Schochet, P. Z., 348, 350, 354, 361, 365, *371*
Schoefs, V., 56, *70*
Schoelmerich, A., 5, 11, *30, 32*, 324, 326, 332, 333, 336, *339, 340, 341*
Schooler, C., 10, *31, 32*, 279, *295*
Schoppe, S. J., 161, 163, *174*, 220, 222, *232*
Schuengel, C., 51, 56, *70*
Schulman, P., 51, *69*
Schulz, P. A., 5, *30*
Schulze, P. A., 11, *32*, 332, 333, *339, 341*
Schumm, W. R., 209, *232*
Schwartz, S., 224, *229*
Schwarz, N., 25, *32*

Scolton, K. L., 56, *63*
Scott, B. S., 187, *201*
Scott, D. A., 22, *32*
Scrimshaw, S., 47, *63*
Sears, R. R., 131, *143*, 149, *175*
Sedlak, A. J., 300, *318*
Seeley, J. R., 46, 50, *63, 65*
Segal, M., 17, *31*
Segal, N. L., 382, *398*
Seginer, R., 12, *33*
Seifer, R., 222, *232*
Seitamaa, M., 50, *69*
Seitz, V., 80, 82, *101*, 311, *317*
Seligman, M. E., 225, *232*
Seligman, M. E. P., 50, 51, *62, 65, 69*
Seltzer, D. A., 360, *372*
Seltzer, J., 107, *138*
Seltzer, M. M., 182, 187, *198, 201*
Sepulveda, S., 59, *64*
Sessa, F. M., 162, *174*
Shadish, W. R., 349, *372*
Shapiro, B., 107, *143*
Shapiro, S., 351, 363, *369*
Sharma, A., 157, *174*
Sharps, P., 89, *100*
Shaw, B. F., 186, *197*
Shaw, D. S., 51, 56, 58, *62, 70*
Sheeber, L. B., 50, *63*, 164, 170, *175*
Shek, D. L. T., 125, *143*
Shek, D. T., 212, *233*
Sheldon, K. M., 225, *233*
Sheldon, S. B., 267, *272*
Shennum, W., 43, *62*
Sherkat, D. E., 8, *30*
Sherman, D., 298, *316*
Shoham, R., 106, *143*
Shoji, J., 124, *143*
Shonkoff, J. P., 47, *65*
Shroder, M., 306, 307, 308, *318*
Shwalb, D. W., 124, *143*
Shweder, R. A., 325, *341*
Sia, C., 364, *369, 370*
Sickmund, M., 300, 302, 306, *318*
Sidora, K., 393, *400*
Siegal, J. M., 207, *231*
Sigel, I. E., 3, 4, 14, 15, 16, 17, 22, *32, 33*, 346, *372*
Sigman, M., 186, 189, *199, 200*
Sigvardsson, S., 50, *63*
Silberg, J., 50, *69*
Silberg, J. L., 51, *64*
Silk, J. S., 162, *174*

Silva, P., 75, 80, 81, 82, 83, 84, 85, *99*
Silva, P. A., 46, 52, *61*
Silverberg, S., 40, *65*, 333, *338*
Silverman, R., 59, *67*
Silverstein, L. B., 117, *143*
Simeonsson, R., 182, *197*
Simmens, D., 47, *66*
Simonof, E., 51, *64*
Simons, R., 40, 54, *63*, *69*
Simons, R. L., 114, *137*, 237, 272, 304, 306, 315
Simpson, K. S., 207, *229*
Sims, K., 348, 360, *371*
Sinclair, R., 220, *231*
Skeels, H., 385, *401*
Skeels, H. M., 49, *69*
Skinner, M. L., 54, *69*
Skodak, M., 49, *69*, 385, *401*
Slater, E., 89, *100*
Slaughter, D. T., 349, 354, *372*
Slavens, G., 303, *316*
Slavin, R. E., 345, *372*
Slep, A., 44, *69*, 213, *232*
Slep, A. M. S., 20, 22, *33*
Slep, A. S., 214, *233*
Small, S., 75, *101*
Small, S. A., 75, *100*
Smart, D., 161, *175*
Smetana, J. G., 167, *175*, 330, *340*
Smith, J., 323, 324, *338*
Smith, K. E., 247, *273*
Smith, P. K., 105, *143*
Smith, R., 85, *101*, 163, *176*
Snarey, J., 126, 127, 128, *143*
Snow, M. E., 166, *174*
Snyder, H. N., 300, 302, 306, *318*
Snyder, J. R., 217, *233*
Snyder, P., 351, *373*
Snyder, S., 351, *373*
Solnit, A., 180, 181, 182, *201*
Sommer, K., 90, *101*
Sorenson, J. L., 50, *67*
Sorri, A., 50, *69*
Sotsky, S. M., 47, *66*
Spagnola, M., 59, *70*
Spangler, G., 58, *71*
Spanier, G. B., 209, *233*
Sparling, J., 359, *372*
Sparling, J. J., 358, 359, 361, *372*
Speechley, M., 187, *201*
Spence, J. T., 9, *33*
Spencer, S. J., 26, *33*

Spieker, S., 348, *369*
Spieker, S. J., 95, *101*, 348, 356, 363, *369*
Spiker, D., 351, 352, 357, 359, 363, *369*, 370, 373
Spitz, R. A., 49, *69*, 379, *401*
Spotts, E. L., 157, *176*
Sprecher, S., 168, *173*
Spritz, B., 56, *61*
Srivastava, S., 38, *66*
Sroufe, L. A., 54, 58, *65*, *70*, 305, *318*
Stagg, V., 258, 272
Stallings, J., 111, *138*
Stang, P. E., 75, *99*
Staples, R., 122, *143*
Stark, M., 180, 181, 182, *201*
Stattin, H., 51, 52, *69*, 289, *295*, *296*, 305, 316
Steele, C. M., 26, *28*, *33*
Steinberg, J., 106, *140*
Steinberg, L., 6, *33*, 118, *140*, 162, *174*, 281, *296*, 297, 298, 304, 305, *315*, *316*, *318*, 379, 387, 388, *399*
Steiner, M., 111, *138*
Stemmler, M., 46, *68*
Stern, M., 154, 156, 167, *175*
Sternberg, R. J., 6, 9, *32*, 382, *400*
Stevenson, H. W., 9, 12, *33*
Stevenson, J., 52, *65*, 157, *173*
Stevenson-Hinde, J., 256, 272
Stevens-Simon, C., 94, *101*
Stewart, J., 106, *141*, 384, 385, *401*
Stewart, M. A., 50, *62*
Stewart, S., 163, *175*
Stewart, S. L., 5, 7, *29*, 159, 162, 165, *172*, 175
Stifter, C., 162, *171*
Stigler, J. W., 12, *33*
Stinnett, N., 297, *318*
Stocker, C. M., 162, *175*, 206, *233*
Stollak, G., 53, *67*
Stone, G., 206, 207, 213, *228*
Stoolmiller, M., 383, *401*
Storey, A. E., 111, *143*
Stouthamer-Loeber, M., 305, *317*
Stovall, K. C., 59, *64*
Strauss, C., 325, *341*
Stright, A. D., 221, 222, *233*
Suess, G., 58, *70*
Sullivan, H. S., 60, *69*
Sullivan, K. T., 214, *231*
Sumner, G., 348, *369*
Sun, L. C., 106, 124, *143*

Sun, Y., 114, *137*
Suomi, S. J., 57, *69*, 106, *142*, 390, *401*
Super, C., 5, *30*
Suwalsky, J., 39, *71*
Suwalsky, J. T. D., 322, *338*
Suzuki, L. K., 327, *339*
Swank, P. R., 247, *273*
Swanson, G. E., 278, *296*
Swearingen, L., 56, *70*

T

Talbot, J., 219, *232*
Tamis-LeMonda, C. S., 5, 8, 9, *28*, 103, *143*
Tamplin, A., 256, *272*
Taraldson, B. J., 161, *176*
Tardif, C., 56, *69*
Tardif, T., 11, *31*, 321, 327, 329, *339*
Tarter, R., 37, *64*
Tatelbaum, R., 363, *371*
Tatelbaum, R. C., 362, 363, *371*
Tayko, N. P., 11, *33*
Taylor, A., 53, *66*, 394, 395, *398*, *399*
Taylor, S. E., 4, 26, *30*
Tein, J., 117, *139*
Tellegen, A., 39, *69*, 382, *398*
Terman, L., 45, *69*
Terry, C., 75, *100*
Terry, E., 73, *101*
Terry-Humen, E., 75, *100*
Teti, D. M., 58, *69*, 156, 161, *173*, *176*
Texidor, M. S., 118, *139*
Thomas, A., 149, 150, 158, 160, *172*, *176*, 256, *271*, *272*
Thomas, A. M., 213, *229*
Thompson, B., 351, *373*
Thompson, E., 131, *141*
Thompson, E. E., 4, 24, *31*
Thompson, L. A., 51, *65*
Thompson, R. A., 47, 56, 58, 59, *66*, *69*
Thornberry, T. P., 304, *318*
Tienari, P., 50, *69*
Tizard, B., 379, 388, *400*, *401*
Tolan, P. H., 117, 118, *138*
Tolson, T. F. J., 241, *272*
Tomkiewicz, S., 384, 385, *401*
Toth, I., 57, *66*
Toth, J. F., 119, 121, 122, *143*
Toth, S. L., 53, 59, *63*, *70*
Touris, M., 58, *70*

Towers, H., 157, *176*
Towles-Schwen, T., 26, *30*
Tracy, E. M., 267, *272*
Traub, J., 345, *373*
Trautlein, B., 309, *317*
Travers, J., 358, *373*
Treboux, D., 58, *70*
Triandis, H. C., 9, *33*, *341*
Trivette, C. M., 367, *370*
Troughton, E., 50, *62*
Troutman, B., 156, *172*
Truett, K. R., 51, *64*
Tseng, V., 124, *136*, 334, *339*
Tsunematsu, N., 187, *201*
Tsunetsugu, K., 124, *143*
Tucker, C. J., 160, *172*
Tuer, M., 212, *229*
Tully, L., 395, *399*
Tupes, E. C., 38, *70*
Turkheimer, E., 383, 384, 394, *401*
Turley, R. N. L., 83, 84, *101*
Turner, P. K., 165, *172*
Turpin, R., 178, *200*
Twentyman, C. T., 214, *231*
Tyler, R., 37, *61*

U

Unger, D., 94, *101*
Updegraff, K., 289, 290, 291, *294*
Upshur, C. C., 47, *65*
Urbina, S., 382, *400*
Uttal, D. H., 12, *29*

V

Valdez, E., 122, *137*
Valdez-Manchaca, M. C., 393, 397, *401*
Valentine, J. C., 349, *373*
Valle, C., 121, *139*
van Bakel, H. J. A., 37, *70*, 163, *176*
Vandell, D. L., 387, 390, 391, *401*
Vandenbelt, M., 80, 81, 87, 93, 94, *97*, *99*, *101*
van den Boom, D. C., 162, *176*, 392, *401*
Van den Oord, E. J., 51, 52, *70*
Vandewater, E. A., 212, *233*
van IJzendoorn, M. H., 51, 56, 57, 59, *70*, 350, 358, *369*

Vargas, M., 17, *33*
Vaughn, B., 58, *70*
Vaughn , B. E., 161, *176*
Veerman, J. W., 52, *68*
Ventura-Cook, E., 332, *339*
Verhuist, F. C., 51, 52, *70*
Verschueren, K., 56, *70*
Vikan, A., 151, *171*
Villareal, M. H., 9, *33*
Vogel, D. A., 156, 167, *173*
Voight, J. D., 94, *101,* 239, 259, 272
Volling, B., 113, *136,* 210, 215, 216, *227*
Volling, B. L., 52, *67,* 160, 163, *176*
von der Lippe, A. L., 11, *33*
Vondra, J., 36, 37, *62, 70*
Vondra, J. I., 56, 58, *70*
Voti, L., 75, *99*
Voydanoff, P., 40, *70*
Vuchinich, S., 217, *233*
Vygotsky, L. S., 150, *176*

W

Wachs, T., 130, *143*
Wachs, T. D., 151, 161, 166, *174, 176*
Wagner, M., 352, 357, *373*
Wagner, M. M., 352, 358, 363, *373*
Wahlberg, K. E., 50, *69*
Wakschlag, L. S., 91, *101*
Walczynski, P. T., 210, *228*
Waldron, M., 383, 384, *401*
Walker, S. K., 268, *272*
Wallace, K. M., 209, *231*
Wallace, L. E., 114, *137*
Wallen, K., 106, *140*
Waller, W. W., 275, *296*
Walsh, C. J., 111, *143*
Walters, E. E., 75, *99*
Wandersman, L. P., 94, *101*
Ward, C., 209, *229*
Ward, H. J., 125, *136*
Ward, M. J., 95, *101*
Wargo, J. B., 52, *62*
Wartner, U. G., 58, *70*
Wasik, B. H., 358, 359, 361, *372*
Waters, E., 58, *70*
Watson, D., 39, *69, 70*
Way, N., 78, 80, 85, 93, *99*
Webster-Stratton, C., 212, 213, *233,* 349, 350, 351, 362, 364, *369, 372, 373*

Wedemeyer, N., 253, *272*
Weed, K., 79, 80, 81, 82, 84, 86, 89, 91, *101*
Weinberger, J., 131, 132, *138, 139*
Weinfeld, N. S., 58, *70*
Weiss, C. H., 346, *373*
Wellman, B., 239, 240, 242, *272*
Welsh, D. P., 165, *173*
Werner, E., 85, *101,* 163, *176*
Weston, D., 360, *371*
Wetherington, E., 285, 286, *294*
Whipple, E. E., 37, *70*
Whitbeck, L., 40, 54, *63*
White, B. L., 107, *143*
White, L., 114, *144*
Whitehurst, G. J., 349, *369,* 393, 397, *401*
Whiteside, L., 324, *338*
Whitman, T., 79, 80, 81, 82, 84, 86, 89, 91, *101*
Whitman, T. L., 88, 89, 90, *100, 101*
Whittaker, A. P., 267, *272*
Widmayer, S., 323, *339*
Wierson, M., 213, *229*
Wijnroks, L., 58, *68*
Wild, M. N., 132, *142*
Williams, A. R., 11, *33*
Williams, E., 123, *144*
Williams, P. D., 11, *33*
Williams, S., 75, *100*
Willis, S. L., 280, *295*
Wilson, B. J., 207, *233*
Wilson, M. N., 9, *30,* 241, *272*
Wilson, S. P., 332, *339*
Wilson, W. J., 298, 299, 300, *318*
Windham, A., 364, *369, 370*
Winn, D. M., 75, *100*
Winokur, G., 50, *62*
Wise, S., 92, *101*
Wishart, J. G., 185, 188, 189, *200, 201*
Witkins, J., 47, *66*
Wodarski, J. S., 47, *65*
Wolf, L. C., 187, 188, *200, 201*
Wolfe, B., 85, *99*
Wong, P. Y., 110, *138*
Wood, J., 115, *142,* 285, 286, *296*
Woodworth, G., 50, *62*
Woodworth, S., 41, 42, 44, *61,* 163, *176*
Worobey, J., 360, *373*
Wothke, W., 164, *173*
Wu, C., 237, *272*
Wyngaarden Krauss, M., 47, *65*
Wynne, L. C., 50, *69*
Wynne-Edwards, K. E., 111, *143*

X, Y

Xu, X., 119, 121, 122, *136, 143*
Yamashiro, G., 86, *97*
Yang, R., 40, *64*
Yardley, J. K., 116, *138*
Yates, W. R., 50, *62*
Yeung, W. J., 107, 109, 114, 121, *144*
Ying, Y., 50, *67*
Yirmiya, N., 189, *199*
Yoerger, K., 51, *68*
Yoos, H. L., 346, 355, 357, *370, 371*
Youngblade, L., 206, 210, 215, 216, *227, 233*
Youngblade, L. M., 51, *71*
Youngblood, L., 113, *136*

Z

Zahn-Walker, C., 206, 207, *229*

Zambarano, R., 43, *64*
Zambarano, R. J., 4, 24, *31*
Zani, B., 18, *29*
Zanolli, K., 17, 22, *29*
Zartler, A. S., 185, *200*
Zaslow, M., 39, *71*
Zeanah, C. H., 53, 59, *67*
Zelkowitz, P., 40, *67, 71*
Zelli, A., 117, 118, *138*
Ziegenhain, U., 58, *68*
Zigler, E., 53, *66*, 311, *317*
Zimet, D. M., 214, *233*
Zimmerman, M. A., 131, *144*
Zimmerman, P., 58, *71*
Zmich, D. E., 220, *230*
Zoccolillo, M., 75, 89, *98, 101*
Zucker, R. A., 37, *70, 71*
Zuravin, S. J., 47, *64,* 89, 91, 93, 95, *101*

Subject Index

A

Academic difficulties, of children born to adolescent mothers, 81–82
Adolescent mothers
  children of
    characteristics of, 91–92
    ecological perspective on, 73–101
    outcomes for, 80–88
    resilient, 86–88
  ecological perspective on, 73–101
  outcomes for, 76–80
  as recurring pattern, 85
  resilient, 85–86
Advice, personal social networks and, 261–264
Affect, in parent–child interactions, 212–213
Affect-specific processes, 44
African American families, complexity of social cognitions in, 23
African Americans
  and early childbearing, 74
  and fathering, 117–120
Age, of child, and parenting, 166–167
Aggression
  origins of, 51–53
  parent–child, 213–214
Agreeableness, and personality, 42
Alan Guttmacher Institute, 73
Alliance of Genetic Support Groups, 184t
American Association on Mental Retardation, 178
The Arc of the United States, 184t
Asians, and fathering, 123–125
Attachment
  interventions for, 58–59
  stability of, 58
Attitudes
  parental, 7–8
    and childrearing behaviors, 17–18
  paternal, maternal and, 112–113
Attributions
  and close relationships, 43–44
  and depression, 50
  marital, and parenting, 214–215
  parental, 9
    and childrearing behaviors, 20–21
Authoritarian parenting, 327–328
Authoritative parenting, 327–328
Availability
  definition of, 106–107
  emotional, 133

B

Beethoven Project, 311
Behavioral phenotypes, 185
Behavior problems
 of children born to adolescent mothers,
  82
 support assets and, 308–310, 309t
Beliefs, parental, 5–6
 and childrearing behaviors, 14–17
Between-group comparisons
 in developmental disability studies,
  181–182
 in intervention research, 348–350
Big Five model of personality, xii, 36–43
Biological generativity, 128

C

Census Bureau, U.S., 116, 118
Center for Successful Child Development,
 311
Centers for Disease Control, 73
Change, theory of, 346
Chiao shun, 6
Child abuse, of children born to adolescent mothers, 84
Child adjustment, coparenting and,
 220–223
Childbearing, early, factors associated with,
 74–76
Child fearfulness, and parental discipline,
 163
Child maltreatment, developmental history
 and, 53–54
Child management (CMT), 224
Child outcomes
 adolescent mothers and, 80–88
 fathering and, processes linking, 132–133
 genetic factors and, 381–386
 maternal personal social networks and,
  264–266
 parental influences on, 387–394
  research directions for, 294–298
 parental socialization and, 375–401
 peer influences on, 386–387
Childrearing. *see* Parenting
Children
 of adolescent mothers
  characteristics of, 91–92

ecological perspective on, 73–101
 outcomes for, 80–88
 resilient, 86–88
characteristics of, xi–xii, 145–201
 historical and theoretical views of,
  149–151
 and parenting, 147–176
with developmental disabilities,
 parenting, 177–201
development of
 father involvement and, 129–133
 marital relationship and, 206–219
 parental behavior and, 375–401
influences on parents, 154–156
 evidence for, 160–168
maternal personal social networks and,
 264–266
Child victimization, community influences
 on, 300–301
Chinese parents
 attitudes of, 7
 beliefs of, 6
Class
 and parental expectations, 10–11
 and personal social networks, 242–249
Clinical strategies, of parenting programs,
 353
Close relationships
 attributions and, 43–44
 quality of, 45–49
  and parenting, 48–49
  personality and, 45–48
CMT. *see* Child management
Communities
 and child victimization and infant mortality, 300–301
 high-risk, 300–301
  challenges of, 301–308
 and parenting, 297–318
 policy on, 312–313
 and support, 308–313
Confucian ethics, and parental expectations, 12
Conscientiousness, and personality, 42–43
Content, of parenting programs, 353
Contextual factors
 and parent–child relationship, xii,
  158–160
 and parenting, 203–373
Continuity, conditions of, 58–60
Coparenting
 intervention research on, 223

as mediator, 221–222
research directions for, 219–223
Corporal punishment
in schools, 311
social cognitions on, complexity of,
24–25
Cri du chat syndrome, 179*t*
Web site on, 184*t*
Cultural communities, definition of,
324–327
Culture
and fathering, research on, deficiencies
in, 116–117
and personal social networks, 244–249
and views of developmental disabilities,
183–184

D

Depression
early childbearing and, 79
origins of, 49–51
Description studies, in intervention research, 352
Developmental assessments, of children
born to adolescent mothers, 80–81
Developmental assets, communities and,
308–310, 309*t*
Developmental disabilities
children with, parenting, 177–201
societal changes regarding, 177–178,
183–184
type of, attention to, 181
Web sites of parent–professional groups
on, 184*t*
Developmental history
and adolescent parenting, 94–96
and adult psychological functioning,
49–53
and parenting, 53–55
role of, 49–55
Developmental stage
and father involvement, 109–110
personal social networks and, 253–254
Difficult temperament, and parenting,
161–164
Disabilities. *see* Developmental disabilities
Discipline, and parent–child interactions,
212–213
Discontinuity, conditions of, 58–60

Domestic violence, and adolescent mothers
and their children, 93
Down syndrome, 178, 179*t*
associated characteristics of, 188–189
and parenting, 185–189
Web sites on, 184*t*
Down syndrome advantage, 186–189
Down syndrome personality, 188–189
Dual-earner families, parenting in, 275–296
Dyadic relationships, influence of, 390–391

E

Early childbearing, factors associated with,
74–76
Educational attainment, early childbearing
and, 76–77
Education for All Handicapped Children
Act, 177
Emotional responses, to stressful environments, 302–304
Emotional support, personal social networks and, 259–261
Emotional transmission, work–family,
285–287
Emotion-based coping, 182
Employment
and father involvement, 114–116
of fathers, effects of, 290–292
of mothers, effects of, 288–290
and parenting, 275–296
Engagement, 365
term, 357
Environment
levels of, relation of, 195–196
mediating influences of, 304–308
neighborhoods and communities, and
parenting, 297–318
stressful, parental responses to, 302–304
Ethnicity
definition of, 324–327
and parenting, 319–341
independence/interdependence approach and, 334–336
Etiology general approach, 192–194
Expectations
of mothers, and fathering, 133–134
parental, 9–13
and childrearing behaviors, 21–22
Extraversion, and personality, 41–42

F

Familism, 121
Family, work influence on, 287–292
Family background, and early childbearing, 75
Family interactions, triadic, 217–219
Fathering
  applied and policy perspectives on, 133–135
  and child outcomes, processes linking, 132–133
  developmental history and, 54
  marital relationships and, 215–217
  variations in
    consequences of, 125–128
    impact of, 130–132
Father involvement, 106–109
  determinants of, 110–133
    biological, 110–112
    cultural, 116–125
    ecological, 114–116
    social, 112–116
Father play style, universality of, 105–106
Fathers
  assumptions on, 103–110
  attitudes of, maternal attitudes and, 112–113
  and children with developmental disabilities, 182–183
  ecological perspectives on, 103–144
  employment and work hours of, 290–292
  roles of, versus mothers, 104–105
Federal Bureau of Investigation, 302
Fragile X syndrome, 178, 179t
  Web site on, 184t

G

Gautreaux Program, 307
Gender
  of child, and parenting, 166–168
  and coparenting, 221
  and effects of marital relationships on parenting, 215–217
Generativity, fathering and, 127–128
Genetic disorders, as behavioral proxies, 191–192
Genetic factors
  and child outcomes, 381–386
  and mental retardation, 178, 179t
  and parent–child influence, 156–158
  research directions for, 394–395
Goals
  parental, 9–13
  of parenting programs, 353
Grand Canyon models, 346
Group Socialization Theory, 386–387

H

Health and Human Services, U.S. Department of, 300
Hispanic Americans
  and early childbearing, 74
  and fathering, 120–122
Hospitalism, 49
Housing and Urban Development (HUD), U.S. Department of, 306

I

Individualism, and parenting, 329
Indulgent parenting, 327–328
Infant mortality
  changes in, 313
  community influences on, 300–301
Informational support, personal social networks and, 261–264
Institute of Education Sciences, U.S. Department of Education, 345
Institute of Medicine, 349, 361–362, 365
Institutionalized children, outcomes with, 387–389
Instrumental support, personal social networks and, 259–261
Interaction, definition of, 106–107
Intervention research, 343–373. see also Parenting programs
  on effects of parenting, 391–393
  on marital relationships and parenting, 223–226
  methodology of, 348–352
  needs in, 364–369
  parameters of, 344–347, 347f

J

Jobs. *see* Employment
Justice, U.S. Department of, 300

L

Latina/os. *see* Hispanic Americans
Life events, personal social networks and, 254–256
Logic model, 346

M

MAOA gene. *see* Monoamine oxidase A gene
Marital conflict
  definition of, 209–210
  and marital satisfaction, 210
  and parenting, 212–214
  research on, 225
  and triadic interaction, 218
Marital power, and triadic interaction, 218–219
Marital quality, issues in, 208–210
Marital relationships
  and child development
    direct effects, 206–207
    indirect effects, 208–219
  coparenting and, 220–223
  and father–child relationships, 113
  fathering and, 126–127
  intervention research on, 223–225
  parenting and, 205–233
    models of association between, 210–211
  research directions for, 219–226
Marital satisfaction
  definition of, 209
  and marital conflict, 210
  and parenting, 211–212
Maternal mourning, 180
Men, development of, fathering and, 125–128
Mental retardation, genetic forms of, 178, 179*t*
Minimum standard of care, maintenance of, 312
Monoamine oxidase A (MAOA) gene, 394

Mothers
  attitudes of, and father involvement, 112–113
  employment and work hours of, 288–290
  marital relationships and, 215–217
  personal social networks of, child-related outcomes of, 264–266
  roles of, versus fathers, 104–105
Moving to Opportunities (MTO) program, 306–308
Murder, of juveniles, community influences on, 300–301

N

National Clearinghouse on Child Abuse and Neglect Information, 300
National Organization of Rare Disorders (NORD), 183, 184*t*
National Research Council, 53, 345, 349, 361–362, 365
Native American parents, beliefs of, 6
Native Americans, and fathering, 122–123
Negative affectivity. *see* Neuroticism
Neglected children, 389
Neglectful parenting, 327
Neighborhoods
  characteristics of, and adolescent mothers and their children, 93
  and parenting, 297–318
Neuroticism, and personality, 38–41
NICHD Early Child Care Research Network, 39, 108, 114, 121
No Child Left Behind Act, 345
Nonresident fathers, contact with children, 129–130
NORD. *see* National Organization of Rare Disorders

O

One-parent families, and personal social networks, 249–251
Openness to experience, and personality, 42

P

Parental behavior
  and children's development, 375–401
  determinants of, xii
  social cognitions and, 3–33
Parental generativity, 128
Parent–child influence
  direction of, 191
  model of, 152–153
Parenthood transition, personal social networks and, 255
Parenting
  by adolescent mothers, 88–96
  advice on, personal social networks and, 261–264
  child characteristics and, 147–176
    historical and theoretical views of, 149–151
    mechanisms connecting, 152–160
  children with developmental disabilities, 177–201
    changing perspectives on, 180–184
  contextual influences on, 203–373
  coparenting and, 220–223
  developmental history and, 53–55
  developmental origins of, 35–71
  in dual-earner families, 275–296
  ecological perspective on, xi–xv
  interventions for, effective, 343–373
  and marital relationship, 205–233
    models of association between, 210–211
  neighborhood and community influences on, 297–318
  personality and, 35–71
    processes linking, 43–45
  personal social networks and, 235–273
    model of, 239–242, 240f
  relationship quality and, 48–49
  socioeconomic status and ethnicity and, 319–341
    independence/interdependence approach and, 334–336
  styles of, 327–328
    ethnicity and, 336
    socioeconomic status and, 328–331
Parenting programs
  features of, 352–356
  impacts of, personal social networks and, 266–269
  population characteristics and, 361–364

processes of, 356–361
Parents
  characteristics of, xii, 1–144
    adolescent, 89–91
  influences on children, 153–154
    questioning in research, 378–381
    research directions for, 394–398
  knowledge of, with children with developmental disabilities, 194–195
  social cognitions of
    complexity of, 23–25
    contextual influences on, 4–14
    and parental behavior, 3–33
    research on, 23–27
  socialization of, and child outcomes, 375–401
Parents as Teachers (PAT) program, 310–311
Pathology-negative perspectives, on developmental disabilities, 180–181
Pedagogical strategies, of parenting programs, 353
Peer influences, and child outcomes, 386–387
Perceptions, parental, 8–9
  and childrearing behaviors, 18–19
Personal identity, personal social networks and, 253
Personality
  Big Five model of, xii, 36–43
  and parenting, 35–71
    processes linking, 43–45
  personal social networks and, 256–258
  and relationship quality, 45–48
Personal social networks
  building process, 251–258, 252f
  definition of, 236–237
  influences on parents, 258–264
  and larger social systems, 242–251, 243f
  of mothers, child-related outcomes of, 264–266
  and parenting, 235–273
    model of, 239–242, 240f
  and program impacts, 266–269
  size of, 258–259
  stability and change over time, 241–242
Phenotypes, behavioral, 185
Physical attractiveness, of child, and parenting, 168
Policy changes
  and community risk factors, 312–313
  and fathering, 133–135

Posttraumatic stress disorder (PTSD), environmental stress and, 302–303
Poverty
   and adolescent mothers and their children, 92–93
   concentration of, parenting and, 298–300
Prader–Willi syndrome, 178, 179t
   and parenting, 185, 189–191
   Web site on, 184t
Prolactin, and paternal behavior, 111–112
Proximal processes, 375–376
Psychological differentiation, 37
Psychological functioning, development in childhood, 55–57
5p- syndrome, 179t
   Web site on, 184t
PTSD. see Posttraumatic stress disorder
Puerto Rican families
   goals and expectations in, 10
   personal social networks of, 247

R

Race, and personal social networks, 244–249
Relationship factors, and parenting, 35–71
Research. see Intervention research
Resilience, of adolescent mothers and their children, 85–88
Responsibility, definition of, 106–107
Restrictive parenting style, high-risk communities and, 303–304

S

Scientifically-based research, 345–346
SES. see Socioeconomic status
Skill development, workplace and, 281–282
Smith–Magenis syndrome, 179t
   Web site on, 184t
Social cognitions
   complexity of, 23–25
   contextual influences on, 4–14
   and parental behavior, 3–33
   research on, 23–27
      methodological developments in, 25–27
Socialization

goals for, socioeconomic status and, 328–331
   parental, and child outcomes, 375–401
Social networks
   personal, and parenting, 235–273
   versus social support, 237–239
Social support, and adolescent mothers and their children, 93–94
Societal generativity, 128
Society, changing views of developmental disabilities, 177–178, 183–184
Socioeconomic status (SES). see also Class
   versus genetic influences on child outcomes, 383–384
   measurement of, issues in, 320–324
   and parental expectations, 10–11
   and parenting, 319–341
      versus ethnicity, 335–337
      independence/interdependence approach and, 334–336
   and parenting styles, 328–331
Special Olympics International, 184t
Spillover effect, 210–211
   processes in, 211
Staffing arrangements, of parenting programs, 353
Stereotype-threat, 26
Stress
   on adolescent parents, contextual sources of, 92–96
   Down syndrome parenting and, 186
   environmental, parental responses to, 302–304
   healthy adaptation to, factors in, 310
   work-related, and parenting, 285–287
Stress-buffering hypothesis, 260–261
Stress-coping perspectives, on developmental disabilities, 180–181
Structural features, of parenting programs, 352–353
Support
   for adolescent parents, contextual sources of, 92–96
   communities and, 308–313
   versus social networks, 237–239
   social networks, and parenting, 235–273

T

Teen mothers. see Adolescent mothers

Temperament
  of child, influence on parenting,
    161–164
    moderators of, 164–166
  definition of, 160–161
Testosterone, and paternal behavior,
    111–112
Triadic family interactions, 217–219

U

University Centers of Excellence, 184

V

Values, parenting, work and, 278–280

W

Williams syndrome, 178, 179t
  and parenting, 185, 189–191
  Web site on, 184t
Within-group comparisons
  in developmental disability studies,
    181–182
  in intervention research, 350–351
Workplace
  and acquisition of parenting values,
    278–280
  characteristics of, and childrearing,
    277–287
  and family, 287–292
  opportunities and constraints for
    parenting, 280–284
  policies of, and parenting, 283–284
  relationships in, and parenting, 282–283
  stress of, and parenting, 285–287